Inside Constitutional Law

ASPEN PUBLISHERS

Inside
Constitutional Law

What Matters and Why

Russell L. Weaver

Professor of Law and
Distinguished University Scholar
University of Louisville

Catherine Hancock

Geoffrey C. Bible and Murray H. Bring
Professor of Constitutional Law
Tulane University

Donald E. Lively

Vice President, Academic Programs
InfiLaw, A Consortium of Independent Law Schools

Steven I. Friedland

Professor of Law
Elon University

Wendy B. Scott

Professor of Law
North Carolina Central University

Law & Business

AUSTIN   BOSTON   CHICAGO   NEW YORK   THE NETHERLANDS

Aspen Publishers
Attn: Permissions Department
76 Ninth Avenue, 7th Floor
New York, NY 10011-5201

To contact Customer Care, e-mail customer.care@aspenpublishers.com,
call 1-800-234-1660, fax 1-800-901-9075, or mail correspondence to:

Aspen Publishers
Attn: Order Department
PO Box 990
Frederick, MD 21705

Printed in the United States of America.

1 2 3 4 5 6 7 8 9 0

ISBN 978-0-7355-6518-0

Library of Congress Cataloging-in-Publication Data

Inside constitutional law : what matters and why / Russell L. Weaver . . . [et al.].
   p. cm.
Includes index.
ISBN 978-0-7355-6518-0 (pbk. : alk. paper) 1. Constitutional law—United States. I.
Weaver, Russell L., 1952-

KF4550.Z9.I545 2009
342.73 — dc22

2008053477

About Wolters Kluwer Law & Business

Wolters Kluwer Law & Business is a leading provider of research information and workflow solutions in key specialty areas. The strengths of the individual brands of Aspen Publishers, CCH, Kluwer Law International and Loislaw are aligned within Wolters Kluwer Law & Business to provide comprehensive, in-depth solutions and expert-authored content for the legal, professional and education markets.

CCH was founded in 1913 and has served more than four generations of business professionals and their clients. The CCH products in the Wolters Kluwer Law & Business group are highly regarded electronic and print resources for legal, securities, antitrust and trade regulation, government contracting, banking, pension, payroll, employment and labor, and healthcare reimbursement and compliance professionals.

Aspen Publishers is a leading information provider for attorneys, business professionals and law students. Written by preeminent authorities, Aspen products offer analytical and practical information in a range of specialty practice areas from securities law and intellectual property to mergers and acquisitions and pension/benefits. Aspen's trusted legal education resources provide professors and students with high-quality, up-to-date and effective resources for successful instruction and study in all areas of the law.

Kluwer Law International supplies the global business community with comprehensive English-language international legal information. Legal practitioners, corporate counsel and business executives around the world rely on the Kluwer Law International journals, loose-leafs, books and electronic products for authoritative information in many areas of international legal practice.

Loislaw is a premier provider of digitized legal content to small law firm practitioners of various specializations. Loislaw provides attorneys with the ability to quickly and efficiently find the necessary legal information they need, when and where they need it, by facilitating access to primary law as well as state-specific law, records, forms and treatises.

Wolters Kluwer Law & Business, a unit of Wolters Kluwer, is headquartered in New York and Riverwoods, Illinois. Wolters Kluwer is a leading multinational publisher and information services company.

Summary of Contents

PART 1 THE FEDERAL GOVERNMENT

PART 2 THE STATES (AND THEIR RELATIONSHIP TO THE FEDERAL GOVERNMENT)

PART 3 INDIVIDUAL RIGHTS

Contents

PART 1 THE FEDERAL GOVERNMENT

PART 2 THE STATES (AND THEIR RELATIONSHIP TO THE FEDERAL GOVERNMENT)

Preface

This book provides an overview of constitutional law and is designed for the reader who desires an introduction to the subject, but who does not wish to read a lengthy treatise.

This book is different from most other study guides because it includes visual aids such as charts, cartoons, and photographs, in addition to presenting the concepts in plain language. Each chapter also contains the following components:

- An **Overview** that briefly summarizes the topics discussed in the chapter.
- A **Connections** section that explains how the topics in that chapter relate to the overall context of constitutional law, and therefore to other topics in the book.
- **FAQs** (Frequently Asked Questions) and **Sidebars** that help explain terminology and offer additional examples.
- **Key terms** in boldface that will help you learn some of the language of constitutional law. As in so many areas of law, learning to speak the language will help you to understand the concepts.

This book has been reviewed by faculty members as well as by law students who have taken constitutional law classes. Why have we asked students to read this book? To make sure that it is understandable and useful to you, which is the ultimate test of its success.

We thank you for buying *Inside Constitutional Law: What Matters and Why*, and we hope that it is valuable for you.

Russell L. Weaver
Catherine Hancock
Donald E. Lively
Steven I. Friedland
Wendy B. Scott

February 2009

Inside Constitutional Law

1

The Federal Government

Judicial Review

1

By their nature, constitutions address fundamental issues of governmental structure and power. Unlike parliamentary democracies, which blend

OVERVIEW

executive and legislative functions, the United States constitutional system is based on the principle of separation of powers, and there is persistent tension among the three branches of government as each branch strives to check and balance (and, at times, to overreach) each other. Judicial review is a vital part of this system of checks and balances. Judicial review establishes the judiciary (defined broadly to include both the United States Supreme Court and the lower federal courts) as the primary interpreter of constitutional doctrine and allows the judiciary (in appropriate cases) to invalidate actions of Congress or the executive branch. Although the power of judicial review is significant, it is not unbounded. There are significant limitations and restraints on the scope of judicial authority.

A. *Marbury* and "the Power to Say What the Law Is"

(1) The *Marbury* Decision

Chief Justice John Marshall's landmark decision in *Marbury v. Madison*[1] is the seminal decision on judicial review. The decision is important because it establishes the proposition that the U.S. Supreme Court can refuse to apply an act of Congress that it believes is unconstitutional.

Marbury arose out of extraordinary circumstances. After the Federalists were defeated in the 1800 elections, but before Thomas Jefferson assumed the presidency of the United States, the Federalists attempted to retain a measure of power by creating new federal judgeships and filling them with Federalist appointees. Under this scheme, William Marbury was confirmed as a magistrate in the District of Columbia, and his commission was signed by President Adams and sealed by the secretary of state. Unfortunately for Marbury, his commission was not delivered before Jefferson assumed office. When a newly inaugurated President Jefferson ordered that all undelivered commissions be withheld, Marbury sought a writ of mandamus to compel Secretary of State James Madison to deliver the commission. He did so through an original action in the U.S. Supreme Court and based his claim on §13 of the Judiciary Act of 1789, which gave the Court the "power to issue writs [of] *mandamus*, in cases warranted by the principles and usages of law, to [any] persons holding office, under the authority of the United States."

In deciding the case, the Court quickly disposed of several important issues. First, the Court decreed that Marbury was entitled to the commission because it became a "vested legal right" when it was signed by the president and sealed by the secretary of state. Second, the Court held that the law should afford Marbury a remedy for the deprivation of his right. Finally, the Court concluded that ordinarily a writ of mandamus (ordering the Executive to deliver the commission) would be an appropriate remedy for the deprivation.

Despite these conclusions, the Court refused to order Madison to deliver the commission. The Court examined the Judiciary Act of 1789, which the Court interpreted as authorizing it to issue writs of mandamus, and expressed concern that the Act might allow the Court to exceed authority granted to it under Article III of the U.S. Constitution, which gives the U.S. Supreme Court original jurisdiction only in "cases affecting ambassadors, other public ministers and consuls, and those in which a state shall be a party." Noting that the case did not involve an ambassador, other public minister, consul, or a state, the Court was troubled by the suggestion that it could exercise *original jurisdiction* over Marbury's case because such authority "appears not to be warranted by the constitution."

The Court then came to the most difficult question: If the Judiciary Act's provision granting it original jurisdiction in cases like Marbury's is unconstitutional, is the Court required to follow the statute, or should the Court declare the act constitutionally infirm? Chief Justice Marshall, in one of the Court's most famous opinions, laid out fundamental principles of judicial review. First, he declared that the Constitution forms the "fundamental and paramount law of the nation, and consequently the theory of every such government must be, that an act of the legislature repugnant to the constitution is void." Second, Chief Justice Marshall emphatically rejected the notion that the judiciary is bound by the legislature's conclusions regarding the legitimacy of a law. In doing so, he made his now famous declaration:

"[it] is emphatically the province and duty of the judicial department to say what the law is. Those who apply the rule to particular cases, must of necessity expound and interpret that rule. If two laws conflict with each other, the courts must decide on the operation of each." Third, he articulated the concept of judicial review: "if a law be in opposition to the constitution: if both the law and the constitution apply to a particular case, so that the court must either decide that case conformably to the law, disregarding the constitution; or conformably to the constitution, disregarding the law: the court must determine which of these conflicting rules governs the case. This is of the very essence of judicial duty." He rejected the notion that judges must "close their eyes on the constitution, and see only the law" because such a notion would "subvert the very foundation of all written constitutions."

After concluding that courts must exercise judicial review, Chief Justice Marshall bolstered his conclusions by referring to the language of the Constitution itself. He argued that various provisions of the Constitution make it clear that the Framers "of the constitution contemplated that instrument as a rule for the government of courts, as well as of the legislature." He noted that the Constitution requires judges to take an oath to support its provisions and noted: "How immoral to impose it on them, if they were to be used as the instruments, and the knowing instruments, for violating what they swear to support!" He concluded with the following exegesis: "[T]he particular phraseology of the constitution of the United States confirms and strengthens the principle, supposed to be essential to all written constitutions, that a law repugnant to the constitution is void, and that courts, as well as other departments, are bound by that instrument."

(2) *Marbury* and Judicial Review

In *Marbury*'s wake, questions have been raised about whether the Framers intended to give the judiciary the power to review the acts of coordinate branches of government and about whether the power of judicial review is a necessary and inevitable aspect of the U.S. constitutional system.[2] These questions have arisen, in part, because some Western countries function without comparable judicial review authority.[3] For example, the United Kingdom does not have a written constitution. Although its courts have exercised the right to review the actions of administrative officials, they have historically refused to exercise judicial review of acts of Parliament. Under such a system, it is up to the government, through Parliament, to decide whether laws are constitutional or unconstitutional. Some question whether this legislative power to interpret the law is good and whether there are effective remedies for "error."[4] Indeed, can there even be "error" in a system of parliamentary supremacy? The ultimate check on the Parliament is the electorate, who, if it is sufficiently unhappy with what Parliament has done, can throw the rascals out. (In light of the British system, questions have been raised regarding the

Sidebar

MARBURY AND THE POLITICAL REALITIES

Chief Justice Marshall's opinion in *Marbury* has been regarded as a masterpiece in many respects. At the time he wrote the opinion, Marshall was confronted by what might charitably be regarded as a hostile audience. Marshall had served as President Adams' Secretary of State, was the official charged with delivering Marbury's commission, and had been nominated and confirmed by the Federalists. Had he rendered a contrary decision (e.g., ordering Madison to deliver Marbury's commission to him) there was a significant possibility that the judicial order might have been ignored or that he might have been impeached. As it was, although Marshall declared the Judiciary Act of 1789 unconstitutional, he did not actually order anyone (particularly Madison and Jefferson) to do anything so there was no risk of noncompliance. However, since Marshall did not actually order anyone to do anything, he later worried about whether he had succeeded in establishing the concept of judicial review.

need for judicial review in this country. *Id.* It is noteworthy that the British courts' historical approach is changing somewhat due to Britain's entry into the European Union and its adoption of the European Charter of Human Rights.)

F   A   Q

Q: One of the most famous parts of the *Marbury* opinion is Chief Justice Marshall's rhetorical flourish: "It is emphatically the province and duty of the judicial department to say what the law is." Is it really correct to say that the judiciary is the "primary interpreter" of the Constitution?

A: Well, not exactly. It's more accurate to say that each branch of government is the "primary interpreter" of the Constitution within its own sphere of influence. President Jefferson offered the example of an individual who is convicted under a statute that he regards as unconstitutional. *See* 8 *The Writings of Thomas Jefferson* 310 (1897). The U.S. Supreme Court affirms the conviction, holding that the statute is constitutional. The defendant-convict asks the president to pardon him. The president agrees that the statute is unconstitutional but is disinclined to grant the pardon if the Supreme Court is regarded as the "primary interpreter" of the Constitution. Under *Marbury*'s logic, the president should grant the pardon because the president takes an oath to support and defend the Constitution. If the president believes that the defendant's conviction is unconstitutional, *Marbury* suggests, the president is morally and legally obligated to grant the pardon notwithstanding the prior judicial decision.

The U.S. Supreme Court building, built in the classical Corinthian architectural style, was begun in 1932 and finished three years later.

Over the last 200 years, the concept of judicial review has been broadly used by the courts to invalidate various actions of federal officials as well as of various state and local officials. As we shall see in later chapters, the Supreme Court has invalidated a variety of laws including those relating to school prayer,[5] the financing of public school education,[6] state-imposed segregated schools,[7] state compulsory school attendance laws,[8] federal regulation of coal production,[9] discrimination against religion,[10] and prohibitions against the possession of guns in school zones.[11]

Example: There are numerous examples of courts exercising judicial review. For example, in *Texas v. Johnson*,[12] the Court struck down a Texas law prohibiting flag desecration. In that case, Johnson burned the flag as a means of protest. The Court concluded that the flag desecration law was inconsistent with the constitutional guarantee of free speech.

In exercising such broad power to invalidate the actions of legislative and executive branch officials, the judiciary not infrequently finds itself in conflict with the executive and legislative branches. In these contexts, the Court's ability to sustain its judgments,

Statue of Chief Justice
John Marshall

and obtain compliance from potentially more powerful coordinate branches, provides much insight into the nature of the U.S. constitutional system. Whereas the president of the United States is the commander-in-chief of the armed forces and therefore has the army, navy, air force, and marines within his or her sphere of authority, the U.S. Supreme Court has a relatively modest staff to enforce its will. Although Congress does not have the armed forces at its disposal, it does have the power of the purse as well as the power to legislate. In addition, Congress is vested with various other powers (for example, the power to ratify treaties and the power to confirm "officers of the United States").

Because of the relative lack of power of the judiciary, the U.S. Supreme Court and the lower federal courts depend on the willingness of the other branches to voluntarily comply with their orders. Indeed, in some instances, the courts are forced to call on other branches of the government, particularly the executive branch, to help enforce their will. The judiciary may also call on state officials to help enforce compliance. However, to obtain and exact compliance, and sometimes support, the Supreme Court must be vested with a modicum of prestige as well as respect for its decisions. If the Court becomes too aggressive or finds itself too far out of step with public opinion, it risks losing the prestige and respect necessary to enforce its decisions.

F   A   Q

Q: Should *Marbury* be construed as suggesting that the judiciary should, or must, independently determine all constitutional questions that come before it?

A: *Marbury* does not *require* the judiciary to independently resolve all legal questions that come before it (or them). In *Chevron v. Natural Resources Defense Council, Inc.*,[13] the Court decreed that a reviewing court should defer to an administrative agency's interpretation of its governing statute in certain situations. In other words, even though the Court may have the power to "say what the law is," *Chevron* held that the courts should be deferential to an agency's interpretation of its governing statute in some contexts. The Court remains involved in the interpretive process, in the sense that it reviews the agency's determination, but it accepts the agency's conclusions if reasonable.

Proponents of judicial review note that federal judges are appointed for life, are protected against diminishment of their salaries, and therefore have the independence to follow their consciences and the law. In other words, because federal judges do not ever face the electorate, they are less subject to the sways and influences of the times or the prevailing political winds and can more rigorously adhere to and enforce the Constitution. Life tenure also allows the justices to fulfill a counter-majoritarian role. If all societal decisions were left to the political process,

CONFIRMATION BATTLES

The U.S. Senate plays a role in the confirmation process by virtue of its power to "confirm" nominees. Over the last 20 or 30 years, there have been bruising confirmation battles over the suitability of particular nominees for appointment to the high court. Some of these battles have focused on a nominee's perceived ideology or political leanings. In other words, the confirmation process has served as a "check" of sorts on the Court's decisions.

THE EXECUTIVE AND LEGISLATIVE BRANCHES VS. THE JUDICIARY

The executive and legislative branches have recourse against the judiciary through the process of making exceptions to the courts' jurisdiction, the issuance of signing statements, impeachment, prosecutorial decisions, briefs and arguments before the courts, and executive constructions of texts. The president can also alter the Court's composition and perhaps its decisions through the appointments power. In the late 1960s, President Nixon perceived the United States Supreme Court as too "pro-defendant" in its criminal procedure decisions. As vacancies occurred on the Court, he appointed judges who he believed would provide what he regarded as a more faithful interpretation of the Constitution on criminal procedure questions. President Nixon's nominations were reinforced by the nominations of later presidents, and the pendulum eventually swung decisively the other way. The Court has since rendered a series of decisions limiting or restricting the rights of criminal defendants. *See, e.g., United States v. Leon*, 468 U.S. 897 (1984); *New York v. Belton*, 453 U.S. 454 (1981). As we shall also see, in the 1930s, there was a constitutional crisis when President Franklin D. Roosevelt clashed with what he regarded as a wayward judiciary.

the majority would almost invariably prevail against the wishes of the minority. The judiciary, insulated as it is from the political process, has the possibility of protecting minorities against the tyranny of the majority.

Nevertheless, life tenure is not without its costs. Some justices serve for very long periods of time that span multiple presidential administrations. Justice Douglas, who was appointed in 1939 and served until 1972, is illustrative. Some commentators fear that, over such a long period of time, justices become out of touch with the electorate as well as with the elected branches of government.

There are obvious limits to the the judiciary's autonomy and its ability to perform a counter-majoritarian function. Although the Court often protects minority groups, it needs the support of elected officials to enforce its judgments. If the Court finds itself too far out of step with public opinion, the Court risks non-compliance or public resistance. In other words, even though federal judges do not have to stand for election, they are not free from the impact of public opinion.

Example: When the Court rendered its decision in *Brown v. Board of Education*, which ended segregation and ordered sweeping changes to existing state systems of public education, there was considerable evidence suggesting that the Court anticipated societal opposition, and deliberately chose a "go slow" approach. In other words, rather than demanding an immediate end to segregation, the Court ordered that desegregation take place with "all deliberate speed." This "all deliberate speed" approach meant that, even though the *Brown* plaintiffs had won their case and had established the unconstitutionality of their local school system, the students remained in the same segregated schools the following academic year. In fact, because of the opposition, the Court did little to enforce its mandate for many years and in fact adopted an "all deliberate speed" approach to desegregation. When the Court finally did move to end segregation, it still encountered significant opposition and ultimately depended on elected officials to enforce its mandate.

B. Judicial Review and the States

Marbury dealt with the limited question of the Court's power to review and refuse to apply a federal legislative enactment. More difficult questions have arisen when courts attempt to impose their interpretations of law (and, more importantly, the U.S. Constitution) on state officials. *Fletcher v. Peck*[14] was the first case in which the Court struck down a state law under the Contract Clause. *Fletcher* was followed by *Martin v. Hunter's Lessee*[15] in which the Court was called on to decide whether it had the power to review a judgment of a Virginia court when federal constitutional issues were involved. The Court answered that question in the affirmative, holding that the Framers contemplated that federal courts would exercise appellate jurisdiction over both federal cases and state cases. The Court cited the language of the Constitution itself—which provides that the Court "shall have *appellate jurisdiction*, both as to law and fact, with such exceptions, and under such regulations, as the congress shall make." The Court construed this language as suggesting that federal cases might arise in the state courts. The Court also relied on the Supremacy Clause for the proposition that state court judges were bound by the U.S. Constitution and the laws of the United States.

Martin also dealt with the question of whether the Supreme Court's authority to review state decisions is consistent with the "spirit of the constitution," and, in particular, the sovereignty of the states. The Court rejected the argument, noting that the Constitution often impinges upon state prerogatives. (For example, Article I, Section 10, imposes various "disabilities and prohibitions" on the states.) In addition, the Court produced various arguments for subjecting state decisions to federal review. First, state judges "are expressly bound to obedience by the letter of the constitution." Second, the Court noted that the right of decision must rest in a court of last resort. Otherwise, judges in various states might render differing interpretations of laws or treaties. Third, the Court emphasized the "importance, and even necessity of *uniformity* of decisions throughout the whole United States, upon all subjects within the purview of the constitution." As a result, the Court concluded that it had the power to review the decisions of the Virginia Court of Appeals, and it reversed that court's judgment.[16]

Following *Martin*, at various points in the country's history, individual states have asserted a right to "interpose" their sovereignty between the power of the federal courts and their own citizens or to "nullify" or disregard federal laws. Perhaps the most dramatic showdown occurred in *Cooper v. Aaron*,[17] a case that arose out of attempts by the Arkansas governor and state legislature to stop desegregation in the Little Rock public schools. Both claimed that they were not bound by the U.S. Supreme Court's decision in *Brown v. Board of Education*,[18] which prohibited the states from imposing segregation in public schools. In reliance on their views, the officials took a number of steps to prevent desegregation,, including amending the state constitution to oppose the Court's desegregation decisions and passing a law relieving children of the obligation to attend racially integrated schools. When local school board officials continued with their desegregation plans, the Governor of Arkansas dispatched units of the Arkansas National Guard to prevent black children from entering previously white schools. Faced with a conflict between state and local officials and *Brown*'s desegregation mandate, school board officials filed a petition to delay desegregation, noting the "extreme public hostility" and suggesting that "the maintenance of a sound educational program at Central High School, with the Negro students in attendance, would be impossible."

In *Cooper*, the Court flatly rejected the notion that Arkansas was not bound by the *Brown* decision, decreeing that the "constitutional rights of children not to be discriminated against" could not be "nullified" by state officials through schemes designed to evade segregation. Relying on the Supremacy Clause, the Court concluded that the Constitution is the "supreme Law of the Land." Since state officials take an oath to support the Constitution, no "state legislator or executive or judicial officer can war against the Constitution without violating his undertaking to support it." Otherwise, "the fiat of a state Governor, and not the Constitution of the United States, would be the supreme law of the land; that the restrictions of the Federal Constitution upon the exercise of state power would be but impotent phrases."

Even though the federal courts have the power to review state court decisions, state courts still retain a measure of independence. Under judicial review power, the federal courts can ensure that state court decisions comply with constitutional minimums.

Example: If the Supreme Court holds that defendants in state criminal cases are entitled to be represented by attorneys, as the Court did in *Gideon v. Wainwright*,[19] the state courts are bound by that decision. Likewise, if the Supreme Court holds that the exclusionary evidence rule applies in state court proceedings, as it did in *Mapp v. Ohio*,[20] the state courts are again bound by that decision. However, there is nothing to prevent state courts from interpreting their own state constitutions to provide individuals with *greater* rights than are provided for under the U.S. Constitution. For example, when the Court created a so-called good-faith exception to the exclusionary evidence rule in *United States v. Leon*,[21] the states were free to decide that their own state constitutions precluded the good-faith exception (as some states did).[22]

Sidebar

THE DISCRETIONARY NATURE OF SUPREME COURT REVIEW

The discretionary nature of the Court's authority is revealed in its case statistics. Over the last couple of centuries, more and more cases have found their way to the Court. In 1853, the Court's docket held 51 cases. By the mid-1990s, the number was 8,000 cases. Despite the dramatic increase, the Court is able to hear only a very small percentage of the cases presented to it. In fact, the number of cases actually heard and decided by the Court on the merits has been declining. In 1986, the Court issued 145 signed opinions; in 1995, it issued only 75. 2 Joan Biskupic & Elder Witt, *Guide to the U.S. Supreme Court* 494 (3d ed. 1996). The reality is that most matters are handled and finally resolved by the lower federal courts or by state courts.

C. Restraints on Judicial Authority

Even if we accept (partially or completely) Chief Justice Marshall's assertion that it is "emphatically the province and duty of the judiciary to say what the law is," there are numerous restraints on federal judicial authority, particularly on the federal courts' authority. Some of these restraints are self-imposed while others are imposed by the Constitution or by other sources. In the remainder of this chapter, we consider the sources and impacts of these various restraints.

(1) Practical Limitations on Judicial Authority

The most important limitation on the Supreme Court's authority is practical rather than theoretical or constitutional: The Court can hear only a limited number of cases each year. As the Constitution establishes and as *Marbury* revealed, the Court's original jurisdiction is limited to cases in which ambassadors or other public ministers or consuls or vice counsels of foreign states are parties; cases between the United States and a state; and cases brought by a state against citizens of another state or aliens. Other cases are heard only by certiorari or by appeal. The overwhelming majority of cases arrive at the Court through certiorari rather than appeal, and the Court views its certiorari jurisdiction as discretionary rather than mandatory. (The only remaining route of "appeal" to the Court is from a three-judge court,[23] and the number of three-judge courts has been significantly curtailed.[24])

As Rule 10 of the Court's rules of procedure make clear, in deciding whether to grant certiorari, the Court makes a discretionary decision. In general, the Court views its job as focusing on important federal questions, on conflicts between the federal circuits, or on conflicts between state courts of last resort. As a result, even if the Court perceives that a lower court has erred, the Court can (and often does) decline to review the case. A petition for a writ of certiorari is rarely granted when the asserted error consists of erroneous factual findings or the misapplication of a properly stated rule of law. Under the so-called Rule of Four, the Court will hear a case only if four justices vote to hear it.

F   A   Q

Q: What is the precedential effect of a denial of certiorari?

A: In theory, since a writ of certiorari is discretionary, a denial has no precedential effect. In theory, the Court's decision to summarily affirm or reverse an appeal, or to dismiss for absence of a federal question, is a decision on the merits. In practice, no one, including and especially the Court itself, attaches much significance to the Court's handling of a summary appeal, especially when the parties were not given the right to file briefs or engage in oral argument, and the case did not result in a full opinion.

(2) Principles of Constitutional Adjudication

In addition to discretionary considerations that limit the Court's jurisdiction, there are also principles of constitutional adjudication that constrain the scope of federal judicial authority. For example, because of the potential problems with judicial review (including the possibility of conflict with coordinate branches of government), the justices usually state that they have a duty to avoid deciding constitutional issues unnecessarily. One way this can be done is by adopting a construction of an ambiguous statute or other law that avoids constitutional difficulties (rather than choosing a construction that presents constitutional concerns).[25] Likewise, if a state court has decided a case on constitutional ground when either a federal or a state ground is available, but also has decided it on "adequate and independent" state grounds, the Court might refuse to hear the case on the ground that the state court could reach the same result on state grounds anyway.[26] As a result, there is no need for the federal courts to resolve the federal constitutional issue, and it can be argued that a federal opinion would involve nothing more than an advisory opinion.

In addition, in some cases, the Court has indicated that federal courts have an obligation to abstain from hearing cases.[27]

(3) Congressional Control over Federal Court Jurisdiction

One restraint on federal judicial authority is provided for in the Constitution itself: Congress's right to control the jurisdiction of the U.S. Supreme Court and the lower federal courts.

(a) The Supreme Court's Appellate Jurisdiction

In addition to giving the Supreme Court original jurisdiction as discussed earlier, Article III of the Constitution also gives the Supreme Court appellate jurisdiction "with such Exceptions, and under such Regulations as the Congress shall make." Given that most cases arrive at the Court by appeal, Congress's control over the Court's appellate jurisdiction represents a potentially significant restraint on the Court's power and prestige. And, the argument has been made at various points in history that Congress should use this authority in certain types of cases. For example, during the 1970s and 1980s, some members of Congress tried to remove the Court's jurisdiction over controversial issues such as school prayer, abortion, the Ten Commandments, and school busing through "jurisdiction stripping" statutes. Even in recent years, there have been suggestions that the Court should be deprived of the authority to hear appeals involving these issues.

Whether so-called jurisdiction stripping statutes would be constitutional is debatable. In perhaps the most famous case of this nature, *Ex Parte McCardle*,[28] the Court upheld Congress's attempt to deprive the Court of jurisdiction. In that case, McCardle was charged with libel for publishing newspaper articles about the post–Civil War military government in Mississippi. After he sought a writ of habeas corpus from a federal court and the writ was denied, McCardle appealed to the U.S. Supreme Court. While the case was pending, Congress passed an act repealing the Court's jurisdiction to hear the case. In upholding the act and dismissing the appeal, the Court emphasized that the Constitution provides the Court with appellate jurisdiction "with such exceptions and under such regulations as Congress shall make." The Court refused to inquire into Congress's motives, emphasizing that "the power to make exceptions to the appellate jurisdiction of this court is given by express words" which must be given effect. "Jurisdiction is power to declare the law, and when it ceases to exist, the only function remaining to the court is that of announcing the fact and dismissing the cause." The Court then dismissed the appeal.

McCardle was qualified by the Court's holding in *Ex parte Yerger*.[29] In *Yerger*, the Court suggested that the repealing act (at issue in *McCardle*) was intended only to prevent cases from going to the Supreme Court by appeal; it was not intended to prevent the Court from exercising certiorari jurisdiction. In other words, it was not Congress's intent to prevent both the U.S. Supreme Court and the lower federal courts from hearing the case.

McCardle was further qualified, if not overruled, by the Court's subsequent decision in *United States v. Klein*.[30] *Klein* involved a law authorizing the U.S. government to seize abandoned or captured property from those who had aided, countenanced, and abetted the Confederacy during the Civil War. Under this law, the United States seized V. F. Wilson's cotton, sold it, and kept the proceeds. However, prior to his death, Wilson took advantage of a presidential proclamation offering a "full pardon" with restoration of all rights to those who agreed to take an oath to support the union and the Constitution of the United States. After Wilson's death, Klein, the administrator of Wilson's estate, sued to recover proceeds from the sale of the cotton, claiming that the pardon had restored Wilson's rights and property. When Klein won in the Court of Claims and the government appealed to the U.S. Supreme Court, Congress passed a statute declaring that a presidential pardon shall not be admissible in the Court of Claims to support a claim for recovery. The statute directed that, to the extent that the Court of Claims has ruled in favor of a claimant based on a presidential pardon, the U.S. Supreme Court "on appeal, shall have no further jurisdiction of the cause, and shall dismiss the same for want of jurisdiction." The statute further provided that acceptance of a pardon for the proceeds from property that had been seized and sold was "conclusive evidence" that the pardoned person had aided the Confederacy.

The Supreme Court ruled the statute unconstitutional. In the Court's view, the statute withheld appellate jurisdiction as a "means to an end. Its great and controlling purpose is to deny to pardons granted by the President the effect which this court had adjudged them to have." Since the Court had already concluded that it was obligated to consider pardons in cases like this, the Court held that Congress's statute was not a legitimate exercise of the authority granted Congress by the Constitution. On the contrary, in the Court's view, Congress was simply trying to make a rule for a particular cause and the Court said allowing it to do so would mean that Congress could prescribe rules of decision for all cases before the judiciary. As a result, the Court concluded that "Congress has inadvertently passed the limit which separates the legislative from the judicial power."

F A Q

Q: Is *McCardle*'s essential holding still valid?

A: There's no easy or clear answer, and commentators disagree. A dissenting Justice Douglas flatly dismissed *McCardle*: "There is serious question whether the *McCardle* case could command a majority view today." *Glidden v. Zdanok*, 370 U.S. 530, 605 n.11 (1962). Former judge and law professor Robert Bork agrees: "*McCardle* is a rather enigmatic precedent. If it stands for the proposition that Congress may take away any category of the Supreme Court's jurisdiction, it obviously is capable of destroying the entire institution of judicial review since *Marbury v. Madison*. So read, there is good reason to doubt *McCardle*'s vitality as a precedent today." *Constitutionality of the President's Busing Proposals* 7 (1972). However, other commentators construe *Klein* more narrowly as suggesting no more than that Congress may not use its jurisdiction stripping authority to dictate substantive outcomes. But see *Boumediene v. Bush*, 127 S. Ct. 1478 (2007).

In a more recent decision, *Plaut v. Spendthrift Farm, Inc.*,[31] the Court also narrowly construed the scope of congressional authority. In that case, petitioners brought a civil action for fraud and deceit in the sale of stock in violation of §10(b) of the Securities Exchange Act of 1934 and Rule 10b-5 of the Securities and Exchange Commission. In prior cases, the Court had held that §10(b) and Rule 10b-5 litigation must be commenced within one year after the discovery of the facts constituting the violation and within three years after the violation. These prior holdings were applied to petitioner's suit and led to dismissal. Subsequently, Congress passed the Federal Deposit Insurance Corporation Improvement Act of 1991, which provided that when an action was commenced prior to a certain date and "would have been timely filed under the limitation period provided by the laws applicable in the jurisdiction, including principles of retroactivity, as such laws existed on June 19, 1991," then it is deemed to be timely. Since petitioners had filed their case prior to June 19, 1991, they moved to reinstate the action previously dismissed with prejudice. The Court held that the legislation was "repugnant to the text, structure and traditions of Article III" because a prior judicial judgment had already resolved the issue. "[By] retroactively commanding the federal courts to reopen final judgments, Congress has violated this fundamental principle [and] effects a clear violation of the separation-of-powers principle." Justice Stevens, joined by Justice Ginsburg, dissented: "A large class of investors reasonably and in good faith thought they possessed rights of action before the surprising announcement of the Lampf rule on June 20, 1991. . . . Congress' decision to extend that rule and procedure to 10b-5 actions dismissed during the brief period between this Court's law-changing decision in *Lampf* and Congress' remedial action is not a sufficient reason to hold the statute unconstitutional."

One can debate the meaning of decisions such as *McCardle*, *Klein*, and *Plaut*. *McCardle* seems to suggest that Congress has broad authority to limit the Supreme Court's appellate jurisdiction while *Klein* and *Plaut* seem to suggest that Congress's authority is more limited, in that Congress cannot prescribe the rule of decision in a particular case or overrule a decided judicial case.

Following decisions like *McCardle* and *Klein*, commentators have debated whether Congress should be allowed to control the Supreme Court's appellate jurisdiction. The argument in favor of the broad congressional authority that *McCardle* voices derives from the Constitution itself, which explicitly authorizes Congress to make exceptions to the Court's appellate jurisdiction. As a result, provided that Congress does not transgress any other provisions of the Constitution, it has the right to make exceptions to the Court's jurisdiction. Others disagree. For example, one law professor has argued that even though Congress has the authority to make "exceptions" to the Supreme Court's jurisdiction, as well as to "regulate" that jurisdiction, Congress cannot "destroy the *essential role* of the Supreme Court in the constitutional plan."[32] A second commentator agreed, arguing that "[i]t is not reasonable to conclude that the Constitution gave Congress the power to destroy [the Supreme Court's] role. Reasonably interpreted the clause means 'With such exceptions and under such regulations as Congress may make,' not inconsistent with the essential functions of the Supreme Court under this Constitution."[33] Others dispute this notion that the Constitution has an "essential" constitutional role.

F   A   Q

Q: If Congress stripped the Court of its review authority over particular issues, wouldn't that alter the jurisprudence in that area of the law?

A: Not necessarily. Many constitutional issues never make it to the Supreme Court today. Indeed, as Congress has gradually eliminated the categories of cases in which the Court must hear an appeal and expanded the scope of the Court's discretionary jurisdiction, nearly all of the Court's appellate docket consists of cases it has chosen to hear. Of the thousands of petitions filed every year, the Court typically hears fewer than 100. Thus, a case that comes up through the state system will probably be heard only by state courts, even if there is a federal question involved. Moreover, even if the Court were denied the right to hear certain types of cases, the Court's existing precedent would remain in effect and, in theory, would be binding on both the lower federal courts and the state courts. However, it's a pretty good guess that, over time, the lower federal courts and the state courts would find ways to distinguish existing precedent.

If the U.S. Supreme Court has an "essential constitutional role," what is it? One commentator has argued that the "supremacy clause of article VI mandates one supreme federal law throughout the land, and Article III establishes the Supreme Court as the constitutional instrument for implementing that clause. [I]ts essential functions under the Constitution are: 1) ultimately to resolve inconsistent or conflicting interpretations of federal law, and particularly of the Constitution, by state and federal courts; 2) to maintain the supremacy of federal law, and particularly the Constitution, when it conflicts with state law or is challenged by state authority."[34] But one can debate whether this is really true. Consider the comments of a dissenting commentator: "[The] courts do not pass on constitutional questions because there is a special function vested in them to enforce the Constitution or police the other agencies of government. They do so rather for the reason that they must decide a litigated case that is otherwise within their jurisdiction and in doing so must give effect to the supreme law of the land."[35]

(b) Control over the Lower Federal Court's Jurisdiction

Congress also has authority over the jurisdiction of the lower federal courts. Under Article III, Section 1, Congress has the power to create the lower federal courts: "The judicial Power of the United States, shall be vested in one supreme Court, and in such inferior Courts as the Congress may from time to time ordain and establish." Since Congress has the power to "ordain and establish" inferior federal courts, it also has the power to abolish them as well as to limit their jurisdiction.[36]

Those who seek to strip the U.S. courts of the power to hear certain types of cases have also tried to strip the lower federal courts of their authority. Over the last 100 years, Congress has considered bills designed to accomplish exactly this result in cases involving such issues as school busing and abortion. However, the overwhelming majority of these bills never make it out of Congress.

F   A   Q

Q: If the federal courts were deprived of the power to hear certain constitutional issues, who would decide them?

A: State court judges would still have the power to hear and decide constitutional issues, even if the lower federal courts were precluded from doing so. These state court judges also take an oath to support and defend the Constitution. As a result, the provisions of the Constitution would still be enforceable. Further, unless Congress also sought to strip the U.S. Supreme Court of all of its review authority, it should still be possible to obtain review (in some manner or fashion such as certiorari) from the Court.

How far can Congress go in stripping the U.S. Supreme Court and the lower federal courts of jurisdiction over an issue? There is no clear answer to this question. One can argue for broad congressional authority in this area. After all, Congress has the right to create the lower federal courts, as well as to abolish them, and therefore arguably has broad authority to control the jurisdiction of the lower federal courts. On the other hand, other commentators argue that congressional authority is limited. For example, one commentator has argued that to "remove or permit the removal from the entire federal judiciary, including the Supreme Court, of the constitutional review of state conduct would be to alter the balance of federal authority fundamentally and dangerously."[37] Another commentator has argued that "[t]he Constitution would not prohibit this sort of comprehensive jurisdiction stripping. The framers considered the state courts to have played a crucial role in the protection of federal constitutional rights, and thus should not viewed as having required federal court jurisdiction over all federal question cases."[38] Finally, Joseph Story, a U.S. Supreme Court justice who served in the early nineteenth century, argued not only that some federal court had to be available to hear every federal question case, but that some federal question cases should be heard *only* by a federal court.[39] The Court has not yet ruled on the constitutionality of these jurisdiction-stripping proposals. In response, it should be noted that the federal courts did not have federal question jurisdiction until the late nineteenth century, and therefore could not exercise review authority.

(4) The Political Question Doctrine

An additional limitation on the scope of judicial authority is provided by the **political question doctrine**. Although commentators have offered different explanations of this doctrine,[40] the traditional view provides that there are instances when the political branches of government (the executive and legislative branches) are more suited to resolving issues than the judiciary. The political question doctrine recognizes this fact and suggests that courts should abstain from hearing these cases, thereby deferring to coordinate branches of government for the decision.

F   A   Q

Q: Does the political question doctrine prevent the courts from hearing or deciding cases simply because the issues raised are controversial or highly politicized?

A: No, not at all. Courts regularly involve themselves in highly controversial and highly political cases. Take, for example, *Brown v. Board of Education*,[41] in which the Court ordered an end to segregated schools, even though the Court anticipated significant (and potentially violent) public opposition. In *Engel v. Vitale*,[42] the Court struck down school prayer and subsequent attempts to amend the Constitution to permit such prayer, to a chorus of protests. In *United States v. Nixon*, 418 U.S. 683 (1974), the Court faced a highly politicized issue when it overruled former president Richard Nixon's claims of executive privilege and ordered him to turn over tapes of his conversations with his subordinates; the disclosed tapes ultimately led to his resignation. Finally, in *Bush v. Gore*, 531 U.S. 98 (2000), the Court intervened in one of the most politicized situations in U.S. history: the question of how to count votes in a contested presidential election.

Political question issues have arisen in a variety of cases, and these cases have produced general rules regarding the resolution of particular types of cases.

Apportionment. The leading political question decision is *Baker v. Carr.*[43] The case arose when Tennessee's legislature refused to apportion legislative districts for more than six decades so that Tennessee's electoral districts became severely mal-apportioned with respect to population. Plaintiffs sued, claiming a violation of equal protection of the laws seeking reapportionment. Despite prior holdings suggesting that reapportionment cases are nonjusticiable political questions, the Court concluded that the Tennessee case was justiciable. The Court held that the political question doctrine is premised on separation of powers concepts and therefore focuses on the relationship between the judiciary and other branches of the federal government. In deciding whether to treat a question as "political," the Court indicated that it would focus on the appropriateness of "attributing finality" to the actions of the political branches of government (Congress and the executive branch), and whether there is "satisfactory criteria for a judicial determination." In addition, the Court would consider whether the issue before it has been "committed by the Constitution to another branch of government, or whether the action of that branch exceeds whatever authority has been committed." In *Baker*, the Court concluded that the political question doctrine did not apply because the case involved only a potential conflict with a state government and did not present a risk of conflict with a coordinate branch of the federal government. Further, there was no "risk embarrassment of our government abroad, or grave disturbance at home." Finally, the Court concluded that "judicially manageable standards" were available under the Equal Protection Clause.

The Guaranty Clause. Baker was preceded by the holding in *Luther v. Borden.*[44] Following the American Revolution, Rhode Island continued to function under a royal charter issued by Charles II in 1663. In the 1840s, Rhode Island citizens called a constitutional convention to draft a state constitution. Although the resulting constitution was ratified by the people of Rhode Island and elections were held, the charter government refused to recognize the constitution or the officials elected under it; it instead declared a state of martial law. When the charter government used force to put down the "rebellion," and "trespassed" by sending soldiers to search Martin Luther's house, Luther sued for trespass. The soldiers defended on the basis that they were acting pursuant to governmental authority, thus presenting the question of whether the charter government or the constitutionally elected government constituted the legitimate authority. In *Luther*, the Court held that the Guaranty Clause (guaranteeing the people a republican form of government) is not a repository of judicially manageable standards that a court may use to identify a state's lawful government. In reaching that decision, the Court noted that a number of factors rendered the question "political," including the fact that other branches of government had been vested with the authority to determine the lawful state government, and the president had unambiguously decided to recognize the charter government as the lawful authority. The Court also emphasized the need for finality and the lack of criteria by which the courts could determine which forms of government was republican. *Baker* departed from the Court's decision in *Luther* in holding that the Equal Protection Clause could be applied in lieu of the Guaranty Clause to claims of malapportionment.

Political Gerrymandering. In *Davis v. Bandemer*,[45] Democrats argued that Indiana's reapportionment scheme unconstitutionally diluted their votes. In that case, the Court rejected claims of nonjusticiability and concluded that the dilution claim was justiciable. As with *Baker*, the Court relied on the Equal Protection Clause in finding justiciability.

Combat Operations. In general, the Court has been unwilling to consider the legality or constitutionality of various combat operations. Although some lower courts have ruled on the constitutionality of individual actions,[46] the Court itself has tended to treat such cases as nonjusticiable. The Court's attitude is undoubtedly due to the fact that control over most foreign policy issues is textually committed to Congress and the president. Article I, Section 8, provides that Congress shall have the power to declare war. Article II, Section 2, provides that the president is the "Commander in Chief of the Army and Navy of the United States, and of the militia of the several States, when called into the actual service of the United States." In general, the Court has left Congress and the president to resolve between themselves the legality of undeclared wars.

Recognition of Foreign Governments. In general, the judiciary has also been unwilling to involve itself in disputes regarding the recognition of foreign governments. Illustrative is the holding in *Goldwater v. Carter*,[47] which involved President Carter's decision to terminate a treaty with Taiwan and recognize instead the People's Republic of China. Members of Congress sought declaratory and injunctive relief challenging the president's decision. They argued that because the Constitution requires Congress to ratify treaties, the Constitution requires Congress to terminate treaties by ratification as well. President Carter disagreed, arguing that the Constitution is silent on the issue of termination, that many aspects of foreign policy are committed to the president's discretion, and therefore that the president has unilateral authority to decide whether to affirm or terminate a treaty. A divided Court refused to hear the case and remanded with directions to dismiss. Justice Rehnquist, joined by three other justices, concurred, concluding that the case was "political" because "it involves the authority of the President in the conduct of our country's foreign relations and the extent to which the Senate or the Congress is authorized to negate the action of the President." Justice Brennan dissented, arguing that "the Constitution commits to the President alone the power to recognize, and withdraw recognition from, foreign regimes. . . . That mandate being clear, our judicial inquiry into the treaty rupture can go no further."

Other Foreign Affairs Questions. As noted, most foreign affairs issues are constitutionally committed to either the president or to Congress, and in any event do not present questions involving judicially manageable standards in an area where it is particularly important to have the government speak with a single voice. Nevertheless, the Court has held that some foreign relations cases are within the scope of judicial cognizance. The Court evaluates each case on its own merits, examining "the particular question posed, in terms of the history of its management by the political branches, of its susceptibility to judicial handling in the light of its nature and posture in the specific case, and of the possible consequences of judicial action."

Example: While the Court will not ordinarily examine whether a treaty has been terminated, it might construe a treaty in the absence of conclusive governmental action. Similarly, questions related to sovereignty over disputed territory is generally regarded as vested in the executive branch. However, once sovereignty issues have been resolved, "courts may examine the resulting status and decide independently whether a statute applies to that area."[48]

Constitutional Amendments. In *Coleman v. Miller*, the Court held that "questions of how long a proposed amendment to the Federal Constitution remained open to ratification, and what effect a prior rejection had on a subsequent ratification, were committed to congressional resolution and involved criteria of decision that necessarily escaped the judicial grasp." The Court noted that it was reluctant to inquire whether an enactment had been passed in compliance with necessary formalities. In doing so, the Court emphasized the importance of giving due "respect . . . to coequal and independent departments" and the "need for finality and certainty," which make the courts reluctant to decide whether an amendment has been passed in compliance with constitutional requisites. However, the Court rejected the idea that "courts will never delve into a legislature's records upon such a quest." For example, if "the enrolled statute lacks an effective date, a court will not hesitate to seek it in the legislative journals in order to preserve the enactment. The political question doctrine, a tool for maintenance of governmental order, will not be so applied as to promote only disorder."

The Seating of Congressional Representatives. In *Powell v. McCormack*,[49] after Adam Clayton Powell Jr. was duly elected to the U.S. House of Representatives, the House refused to seat him because he had allegedly engaged in misconduct. Since Article I, Section 5, of the Constitution provides that "[e]ach House shall be the Judge of the Elections, Returns, and Qualifications of its own Members," the House of Representatives claimed that there was a textually demonstrable commitment of the issue to the House. The Court rejected the argument, concluding that the Constitution precludes the House from excluding "any person, duly elected by his constituents, who meets all the requirements for membership expressly prescribed in the Constitution." In other words, the House can exclude based only on the grounds set forth in Article I, Section 5.

(5) The Case or Controversy Requirement

Article III, Section 2, contains perhaps the most important limitation on the judicial power: the **case or controversy requirement**. That doctrine provides that the federal courts may not hear just any matter, but instead are restricted to hearing "cases" and "controversies." In other words, whether or not the courts can be regarded as the "primary interpreter of the Constitution," they do not have a roving commission to decide constitutional questions. On the contrary, they can decide issues only in the context of a "case" or "controversy" that presents concrete issues in an adverse way. This concreteness and adversity help illuminate the issues and (hopefully) produce better judicial outputs.

The case or controversy limitation has spawned multiple restrictions on the scope of judicial authority including the prohibition against advisory opinions, the ripeness and mootness doctrines, and the standing requirement.

(a) Prohibition Against Advisory Opinions

Another limitation on the scope of judicial authority is the **prohibition against advisory opinions**. In general, the function of the federal courts is not to "advise" the executive or legislative branches, but to decide concrete cases that come before them. This limitation stems directly from Article III, which authorizes the judiciary only to hear "cases" and "controversies" and essentially precludes them from serving as advisors to the executive or legislative branches of government.

The prohibition on advisory opinions is reflected in a 1793 exchange between the Court and Secretary of State Thomas Jefferson. Jefferson solicited input from the U.S. Supreme Court regarding whether it would be willing to help resolve questions of construction in treaties, laws of nations and laws of the land. Chief Justice Jay and his associates refused, noting that "the lines of separation drawn by the Constitution between the three departments of government [afford] strong arguments against the propriety of extrajudicially deciding the questions alluded to."[50] The justices also observed that the Constitution limits the judicial power to the determination of cases and controversies.

Sidebar

STATE COURTS AND ADVISORY OPINIONS

Some state constitutions permit their courts to render advisory opinions, and courts in these states (e.g., Maine) sometimes do render opinions that advise on the constitutionality of a law or on the interpretation of it. Interestingly, some state constitutions *require* their supreme court to give advisory opinions on certain matters.

F   A   Q

Q: Does the prohibition against federal courts rendering advisory opinions mean they can't render declaratory judgments either?

A: Courts have differed in their opinions about whether declaratory judgments should be barred for the same reasons that advisory opinions are barred. In an early case, *Piedmont & Northern Railway Co. v. United States*, 280 U.S. 469 (1930), the Court held that a declaration, without a request for relief, was deemed to involve an advisory opinion. However, in *Steffel v. Thompson*, 415 U.S. 452 (1974), the Court reversed. In that case, a protestor who sought to distribute handbills was told to stop on pain of arrest. Even though the protestor sought only declaratory relief, the Court held that the case was justiciable because petitioner had been warned twice to stop the handbilling and informed that he would be prosecuted if he did not stop. The Court concluded that petitioner was not required to "expose himself to actual arrest or prosecution to be entitled to challenge a statute that he claims deters the exercise of his constitutional rights."

The prohibition is also reflected in the holding in *Muskrat v. United States.*[51] In that case, Congress passed a statute providing for a transfer of Cherokee Indian property from tribal ownership to individual ownership, but also restricted the rights of individuals to alienate the land. A jurisdictional statute authorized plaintiffs to sue the United States and provided for attorneys' fees if plaintiffs prevailed. The Court concluded that the United States had no interest in the litigation because plaintiffs were not asserting any property right against the United States and were not demanding compensation for alleged wrongs. As a result, the Court concluded that any decision would amount to nothing more than an advisory opinion and dismissed the case.

(b) Ripeness

The case or controversy requirement also precludes federal courts from hearing cases that are not **ripe** for consideration — that is, that are brought too early. A case is not ripe if it involves an attempt to prematurely involve a court in an adjudication and threatens to involve the court in abstract disagreements about issues that may never materialize.

Many ripeness cases arise in the administrative context when an administrative agency threatens to take some action against an individual or company or threatens to withhold governmental benefits. In an early decision, *United Public Workers v. Mitchell,*[52] the Court articulated a limited view of ripeness in a case involving the federal Hatch Act, which made it illegal for federal employees to engage in certain political activities. Appellants, who claimed that they wished to engage in prohibited activities, sought injunctive relief preventing enforcement of the act. The Court held that the case was not ripe because plaintiffs had stated their claims in vague terms and had not clearly indicated what they intended to do. Noting that a "hypothetical threat is not enough," the Court refused to "speculate as to the kinds of political activity the appellants desire to engage in or as to the contents of their proposed public statements or the circumstances of their publication." As a result, the Court held that it did not have the power to hear the case. The Court did hear the challenge by the individual employee who had been charged under the act. Justice Douglas dissented, arguing that "what these appellants propose to do is plain enough. If they do what they propose to do, it is clear that they will be discharged from their positions. . . . The threat against them is real not fanciful, immediate not remote."

United Public Workers' more crabbed view of ripeness is not reflected in the Court's later decisions. For example, *Abbott Laboratories v. Gardner,*[53] another administrative case, involved amendments to the Federal Food, Drug, and Cosmetic Act that required manufacturers of prescription drugs to print the "established name" of the drug "prominently and in type at least half as large as that used thereon for any proprietary name or designation for such drug," on labels and other printed material. The "established name" was one designated by the secretary of health, education, and welfare pursuant to the act while the "proprietary name" was a trade name under which the particular drug was marketed. When a group of drug manufacturers challenged the regulations, the Court held that the case was ripe for review. The Court emphasized that the purpose of the ripeness doctrine is to "prevent the courts, through avoidance of premature adjudication, from entangling themselves in abstract disagreements over administrative policies, and also to protect the agencies from judicial interference until an administrative decision has been formalized and its effects felt in a concrete way by the challenging parties." However, in deciding whether a case is ripe, courts consider two factors: "the fitness of the issues for judicial decision and the hardship to the parties of withholding court consideration." The Court concluded that Abbott Laboratories satisfied this test, noting that the issue was a "purely legal one" and that "the impact of the regulations upon the petitioners is sufficiently direct and immediate as to render the issue appropriate for judicial review at this stage." In addition, the regulations placed the drug companies in a dilemma: They could comply with the regulations at great expense or face "serious criminal and civil penalties for the unlawful distribution of 'misbranded' drugs." Moreover, since the prescription drug manufacturers regard customer confidence as vital to their success, it was not reasonable to expect the manufacturers to resist compliance and the possibility of sanctions to challenge the regulations.

S i d e b a r

RIPENESS AND LOYALTY OATHS

One context in which ripeness issues have arisen involves so-called loyalty oaths — oaths swearing allegiance to the state. In *Socialist Labor Party v. Gilligan*, 406 U.S. 583 (1972), an Ohio law restricted the ability of minority party candidates to place themselves on the electoral ballot. After the law was struck down, the Ohio legislature enacted a new law that required candidates to take a loyalty oath. The Socialist Labor Party challenged the new law, claiming that the loyalty oath was unconstitutional. But the evidence revealed that no member of the Socialist Labor Party had ever refused to sign the required oath and had not been denied the right to appear on the ballot. The Court held that the case was not ripe for review: "Problems of prematurity and abstractness may well present 'insuperable obstacles' to the exercise of the Court's jurisdiction, even though that jurisdiction is technically present. . . . Nothing in the record shows that appellants have suffered any injury thus far, and the law's future effect remains wholly speculative."

Abbott Laboratories suggests that the Court is less inclined to apply the ripeness doctrine than in prior cases. Nevertheless, in post-*Abbott* cases, the Court has applied the ripeness doctrine in various contexts. In *Dellums v. Bush*,[54] for example, members of Congress sought to challenge President George H. W. Bush's decision to deploy troops in the Persian Gulf region in anticipation of the first Gulf war. The congressional plaintiffs sued, claiming that military action was imminent and that such action without a congressional declaration "would deprive the congressional plaintiffs of the voice to which they are entitled under the Constitution." After applying the ripeness doctrine, the Court held that the case was not ripe because Congress had not yet declared its intentions on the possible war. The Court concluded that it was reluctant to "encourage small groups or even individual Members of Congress to seek judicial resolution of issues before the normal political process has the opportunity to resolve the conflict." Of course, the holding in *Dellums* may reflect concerns by the Court about involving itself in what is essentially a political question. As discussed earlier in the chapter, the Court generally has refused to rule on the authority of the president to go to war.

Some cases in which the Court has applied the ripeness doctrine involve issues of whether there is a sufficient threat of prosecution to justify judicial intervention. For example, in *Poe v. Ullman*,[55] the Court was confronted by a Connecticut statute that prohibited the use of contraceptive devices and the giving of medical advice regarding the use of such devices. After the plaintiff wife suffered three pregnancies that produced infants with multiple congenital abnormalities who died shortly after birth, doctors informed plaintiffs that the abnormalities were genetic. Plaintiffs (husband and wife) sued, claiming that the possibility of an additional pregnancy placed them under great emotional stress that was damaging their physical and mental health, and claimed that she needed to use birth control to prevent conception. However, the wife claimed that she was unable to obtain contraceptive information because of the Connecticut statute. The Court dismissed the case on ripeness grounds because Connecticut had not enforced its law: "This Court cannot be umpire to debates concerning harmless, empty shadows." Justice Douglas dissented noting that "twice since 1940, Connecticut has reenacted these laws as part of general statutory revisions [so that] the statutes—far from being the accidental left-overs of another era—are the center of a continuing controversy in the State." Justice Harlan also dissented: "I find it difficult to believe that doctors generally—and not just those operating specialized clinics—would continue openly to disseminate advice about contraceptives [in] reliance on the State's supposed unwillingness to prosecute, or to consider that high-minded members of the profession would in consequence of such inaction deem themselves warranted in disrespecting this law so long as it is on the books." Of course, in the Court's later decisions in *Griswold v. Connecticut*,[56] the Court ultimately reviewed and struck down an anti-contraception statute.

(c) Mootness

The **mootness doctrine** also involves a question of timing. Even though a claim may have been ripe at one point, subsequent events may have rendered it moot so that there is no longer a case or controversy. If so, a reviewing court should dismiss the case. By denying judicial intervention, the Court again avoids entangling itself in abstract or hypothetical disagreements.

The mootness doctrine is illustrated by the holding in *DeFunis v. Odegaard*.[57] In that case, DeFunis, who claimed that he had been subjected to reverse discrimination, sought and obtained an injunction requiring the University of Washington School of Law to admit him to its entering class. By the time the case reached the U.S. Supreme Court, DeFunis was in his final term of law school. The Court concluded that the case was moot because DeFunis would receive his diploma regardless of the outcome of the case; the Court therefore was constitutionally precluded from hearing the case. As a result, the "controversy between the parties has thus clearly ceased to be 'definite and concrete' and no longer 'touch[es] the legal relations of parties having adverse legal interests.'" Justice Brennan dissented, arguing that any number of factors might prevent DeFunis from completing the present term, and there is no assurance that the law school would allow him to graduate if he were unable to complete the present term.

There are a number of reasons courts rule that cases are not moot. In cases like *DeFunis*, for example, if the action had been brought as a class action, the case could continue if the controversy was not moot as to a remaining member of the class. Another situation involves a defendant voluntarily ceasing an offending activity. Although at first glance, such an action might appear to render the matter moot, courts have not always ruled that way. In *Los Angeles v. Lyons*,[58] plaintiff sued because two citizens had died when police had used carotid-artery choke holds on them, and he feared that police would use a choke hold on him in the future (as they had done before). While the case was pending, the Board of Police Commissioners imposed a six-month moratorium on the use of carotid-artery choke holds, except under circumstances where deadly force was authorized. Based on the moratorium, the city moved to dismiss plaintiff's case as moot. The Court disagreed, noting that the moratorium was not permanent, could have been lifted at any time, and therefore the moratorium had not "irrevocably eradicated the effects of the alleged violation."

Even when the defendant's cessation is more final, a case may or may not be moot depending on whether it is "absolutely clear" that the conduct will reoccur. In *Laidlaw Environmental Services (Laidlaw), Inc.*,[59] Friends of the Earth (FOE) and Citizens Local Environmental Action Network, Inc. (CLEAN) sued to prevent a hazardous waste incinerator facility and water treatment plant from discharging waste water in excess of the limits established by its permit. The facility argued that the case was moot because it had recently closed the facility. The Court disagreed, noting that a "defendant's voluntary cessation of a challenged practice does not deprive a federal court of its power to determine the legality of the practice." Mootness occurs only if it becomes "absolutely clear that the allegedly wrongful behavior could not reasonably be expected to recur." As a result, the Court regarded the mootness question as a disputed factual matter. Justice Stevens concurred, arguing that the case also involved a claim for prior damages that could not be mooted by a voluntary closure of the facility. Justice Scalia, joined by Justice Thomas, dissented, arguing that the Constitution requires a justiciable case.

The mootness doctrine may not apply if the plaintiff continues to suffer collateral consequences from governmental action. For example, in *Evitts v. Lucey*,[60] the Court held that a challenge to a criminal conviction was not moot, even though the plaintiff (the convicted criminal defendant) had served his jail sentence. The possibility of future consequences from the conviction (for example, the possibility that the conviction could be used to aggravate the sentence for a future conviction under a persistent offender statute) are enough to preclude mootness

In some instances, when a case is "capable of repetition, but evading review," the Court will hear and decide the case notwithstanding the presence of mootness. Illustrative is the holding in *Roe v. Wade*.[61] That case involved a Texas statute that criminalized abortion. Jane Roe, a single unmarried woman who was pregnant, claimed that she wished to terminate her pregnancy by an abortion "performed by a competent, licensed physician, under safe, clinical conditions"; that she was unable to get a "legal" abortion in Texas because her life did not appear to be threatened by the continuation of her pregnancy; and that she could not afford to travel to another jurisdiction "to secure a legal abortion under safe conditions." By the time the case was heard by the Court, Roe was no longer pregnant, and the state moved to dismiss her appeal on mootness grounds. The Court held that the case was not moot, noting that the normal pregnancy period is so short (266 days) that it is unlikely that the judicial process would ever be complete before the pregnancy terminates: "Pregnancy often comes more than once to the same woman, and in the general population, if man is to survive, it will always be with us. Pregnancy provides a classic justification for a conclusion of nonmootness." The Court concluded that the issues are "capable of repetition, yet evading review." As a result, the case remained justiciable.

(d) Standing

The case or controversy requirement also imposes a requirement that the plaintiff have **standing** to bring the case. In other words, the question is whether the plaintiff is suffering sufficient injury to have a meaningful stake in the outcome of the litigation.

Unlike the ripeness and mootness doctrines, both of which focus on whether a suit has been brought in a timely manner (either too early or too late), standing focuses on whether plaintiff has a sufficient interest in the litigation to allow him or her to litigate the issues. In general, the judiciary will not entertain a "generalized grievance against allegedly illegal governmental conduct."[62] Plaintiff must allege facts demonstrating that he or she has been injured and is a proper party to bring the suit.

In a strict constitutional sense, the standing doctrine involves two separate and distinct elements: First, the plaintiff must have suffered an "injury in fact," in the form of an invasion of a legally protected interest, which is both "concrete" and "particularized," and is "actual or imminent, not conjectural or hypothetical." Second, there must be a causal connection between the injury and the defendant's conduct complained so that the plaintiff's injury will be redressed by a favorable decision.[63] In addition, in cases involving allegations of congressionally authorized standing, plaintiffs must show that they fall within the zone of interest sought to be protected by the congressional authorization.

F A Q

Q: Is the standing doctrine any different in the constitutional area than it is in other areas of the law?

A: Yes and no. The idea is basically the same in that the focus is on whether the plaintiff has suffered sufficient injury. However, in traditional tort and contract cases, standing may be easy to ascertain. For example, if A runs into B's car causing significant damage to both B and the car, B has standing to recover for his personal injuries and property damage. However, in constitutional litigation, which often involves litigation against the government, the plaintiff's injury can be more abstract and theoretical. For example, plaintiff, a taxpayer and a citizen, may complain regarding the government's decision to donate surplus property to a private religious college. In such a case, a court might question whether plaintiff is suffering anything more than a hypothetical or speculative injury.

As the Court recognized in *Schlesinger v. Reservists Committee to Stop the War*,[64] in the constitutional context, the standing requirement serves a variety of functions. First, the requirement helps ensure that the plaintiff has a personal stake in the outcome of the case, and therefore is able to "present to a court a complete perspective upon the adverse consequences flowing from the specific set of facts undergirding his grievance." Second, this concreteness helps courts develop rules of law by being able to apply those rules in a specific factual context. Third, a requirement of concrete injury helps ensure that there is a real need to exercise the power of judicial review and allows the court to frame the decree "no broader than required by the precise facts to which the court's ruling would be applied." Finally, the standing doctrine helps to "avoid unnecessary conflicts with coordinate branches of government" that might "create the potential for abuse of the judicial process, distort the role of the Judiciary in its relationship to the Executive and the Legislature and open the Judiciary to an arguable charge of providing 'government by injunction.'"

In addition to the constitutional component, standing cases can also involve a "prudential" component. As we have seen, Article III of the U.S. Constitution limits the judicial authority to cases and controversies. When a plaintiff lacks standing to bring a case, the case or controversy requirement might not be satisfied, and the constitutional basis for judicial intervention is absent. The prudential aspect of standing is more subtle. In some cases, even though a plaintiff may have sufficient standing to satisfy Article III's case or controversy requirement, the level of injury may be sufficiently low so that the Court deems it prudent to deny standing. In other words, as a matter of restraint, the Court refuses to hear the case.

(1) Taxpayer Standing. Standing issues arise in a variety of contexts. In early cases, plaintiffs attempted to base their standing claims on their status as taxpayers, arguing that taxpayers should have an automatic right to enforce the Constitution. However, in *Frothingham v. Mellon*,[65] the Court rejected the idea of **taxpayer standing**. In other words, the Court rejected the idea that taxpayers have standing, as taxpayers, to bring a lawsuit. *Frothingham* involved the federal Maternity Act, which appropriated money from the federal treasury for the purpose of reducing maternal and infant mortality and protecting the health of mothers and infants. Frothingham sued, alleging that the statute "took" her property without due process of law. Essentially, she argued that expenditures under the act would cause Congress to raise taxes, thereby resulting in a "taking" of her property. The Court held that Frothingham's claim (that the appropriations would increase her future taxes) was "speculative," that Frothingham was suffering only in "some indefinite way in common with people generally," and therefore declined to hear the case. In the Court's view, to decide the case would not be deciding a judicial controversy, but rather usurping the authority of "another and coequal department" of the government.

In *Massachusetts v. Mellon*,[66] decided in conjunction with *Frothingham*, the Court held that the Commonwealth of Massachusetts did not have standing to challenge the same act on its own behalf as a federal usurpation of power reserved to the states. Although the act did not impose a direct obligation on the states, Massachusetts contended that it was unconstitutional because it gave states an option to accept Maternity Act monies subject to conditions. The Court also rejected the notion that Massachusetts could bring the suit as on behalf of the citizens of the Commonwealth. Noting that the citizens of Massachusetts are also citizens of the United States, the Court held that it is the United States rather than the state that represents them as "*parens patriae.*"

Even though *Frothingham* held that the plaintiff could not establish standing, the Court has accepted the possibility of taxpayer challenges in some instances. For example, in *Baldwin v. G. A. F. Seelig, Inc.*,[67] the Court held that a taxpayer has standing to challenge a tax that he or she is required to pay. In that case, the Court granted standing to a milk distributor to challenge a direct tax on milk. However, *Baldwin* is distinguishable from *Frothingham* on the basis that the latter involved a challenge to an *expenditure* (the government's decision to spend money under the Maternity Act) rather than to a tax. Although Frothingham expressed a fear that expenditures under the Maternity Act might ultimately raise her tax liability, she was not challenging the federal income taxation system itself. By contrast, in *Baldwin*, plaintiff sought to challenge the validity of the tax itself.

Frothingham also suggested that a municipal taxpayer might have a sufficient interest in the municipality's expenditures to establish standing. However, the Court concluded that a taxpayer's interest in the federal treasury was "very different" because municipal monies are "partly realized from taxation and partly from other sources" as well as because the federal taxpayer's interest "is shared with millions of others, is comparatively minute and indeterminable, and the effect upon future taxation, of any payment out of the funds, so remote, fluctuating and uncertain, that no basis is afforded for an appeal to the preventive powers of a court of equity." The Court went on to note that even though any statute is likely to produce additional taxation, the tax increase is shared among so many taxpayers that the matter is essentially one "of public and not of individual concern." The Court was undoubtedly concerned that if it allowed taxpayer suits to proceed without a demonstration of actual injury, taxpayers might decide to challenge any act or statute that requires the expenditure of public money.

It is important to realize that each case of alleged taxpayer standing or citizen standing must be judged on its own merits. For example, in *Doremus v. Board of Education*,[68] taxpayers and citizens sought to challenge a program of Bible reading in public schools as a violation of the Establishment Clause of the U.S. Constitution. They sought to establish standing, inter alia, based on the fact that the Bible reading would burden them as taxpayers. Finding that the Bible reading was not supported by a special tax and that there was no evidence that plaintiffs' taxes had been increased, the Court held that plaintiffs could not establish standing since there was no "direct dollars-and-cents injury" but rather only a religious difference. Justice Douglas, joined by Justices Reed and Burton, dissented: "There is no group more interested in the operation and management of the public schools than the taxpayers who support them and the parents whose children attend them. Certainly a suit by all the taxpayers to enjoin a practice authorized by the school board would be a suit by vital parties in interest. They would not be able to show, any more than the two present taxpayers have done, that the reading of the Bible adds to the taxes they pay. But if they were right in their contentions on the merits, they would establish that their public schools were being deflected from the educational program for which the taxes were raised. That seems to me to be an adequate interest for the maintenance of this suit. . . ."

Although *Doremus* might seem to doom all suits challenging Establishment Clause violations in the public schools, the circumstances are key. If, for instance, one of the parents' children attended the public schools and was forced to listen to or participate in the Bible readings, that parent and child might be able to establish injury by demonstrating an infringement of their religious beliefs. In addition, in *Everson v. Board of Education*,[69] the Court held that taxpayers could establish standing if they could show that the government was providing direct financial subsidies to parochial schools. The Court concluded that such subsidies could involved a "measurable appropriation or disbursement of school-district funds occasioned solely by the activities complained of."

The Court expanded the concept of taxpayer standing in its later decision in *Flast v. Cohen*.[70] In that case, the Court held that a federal taxpayer could establish standing to challenge a federal expenditure (as opposed to a tax) under Titles I and II of the Elementary and Secondary Education Act of 1965. The statute was enacted to finance instruction in reading, arithmetic, and other subjects in religious schools, and to purchase textbooks and other instructional materials for use in such schools. The *Flast* Court began by questioning the idea that a federal taxpayer does not have standing to challenge an expenditure by the federal government. The Court noted that some large corporate taxpayers have federal tax bills totaling hundreds of millions of dollars. In addition, the Court suggested that its prior concerns — "that taxpayer suits might inundate the courts with litigation challenging federal expenditures" — were unfounded. The Court also rejected its prior holding that "the constitutional scheme of separation of powers, and the deference owed by the federal judiciary to the other two branches of government within that scheme, present an absolute bar to taxpayer suits challenging the validity of federal spending programs." As a result, the *Flast* Court concluded that plaintiff could establish standing if he could show that there is a "logical nexus between the status asserted and the claim sought to be adjudicated" that assures that the plaintiff "is a proper and appropriate party to invoke federal judicial power." For an Establishment Clause challenge, the Court concluded that a taxpayer might be an appropriate plaintiff if he is challenging an exercise of congressional power under the Taxing and Spending Clause (Art. I, §8) and is able to show "that the challenged enactment exceeds specific constitutional limitations imposed upon the exercise of the congressional taxing and spending power and not simply that the enactment is generally beyond the powers delegated to Congress by Art. I, §8." If a taxpayer can satisfy the nexus, then he or she will be "a proper and appropriate party to invoke a federal court's jurisdiction."

Applying the nexus test, the *Flast* Court held that the plaintiffs in that case established standing by challenging a substantial expenditure under Article I, Section 8, and by alleging that the expenditures violated the Establishment and Free Exercise Clauses of the First Amendment. The Court viewed those clauses as providing "a specific constitutional limitation upon the exercise by Congress of the taxing and spending power conferred by Art. I, §8." The Court distinguished the *Frothingham* plaintiff on the basis that Frothingham attacked a federal spending program (which would satisfy the first prong of the nexus requirement), but her attack was not based on an allegation that Congress had "breached a specific limitation upon its taxing and spending power." Instead, Frothingham alleged that her tax liability would be increased because of the Maternity Act and that she would therefore suffer "a deprivation of property without due process of law." The Court concluded that the Due Process Clause did not constitute a specific limitation on the federal spending power. Justice Douglas concurred in the *Flast* decision, noting that "[taxpayers] can be vigilant private attorneys general. Their stake in the outcome of litigation may be de minimis by financial standards, yet very great when measured by a particular constitutional mandate." Justice Harlan dissented, arguing that there was no "allegation that the contested expenditures will in any fashion affect the amount of these taxpayers' own existing or foreseeable tax obligations."

F   A   Q

Q: Has the Court found that other constitutional provisions provide limitations comparable to *Flast*'s holding that the Establishment Clause specifically limits the taxing and spending power conferred by Article I, Section 8?

A: In subsequent cases, the Court has refused to apply the *Flast* test to other clauses of the Constitution. As a result, the Establishment Clause and the Free Exercise Clause are sui generis for purposes of the *Flast* test.

Flast did not control the outcome in *United States v. Richardson.*[71] In that case, a taxpayer challenged the Central Intelligence Agency Act (CIAA), which allowed the government to conceal CIA expenditures from the general public. After unsuccessfully attempting to obtain the expenditure information from various governmental agencies, respondent sued as a citizen and a taxpayer for a detailed statement of CIA expenditures, claiming that Article I, Section 9, Clause 7, of the Constitution ("No Money shall be drawn from the Treasury, but in Consequence of Appropriations made by Law; and a regular Statement and Account of the Receipts and Expenditures of all public Money shall be published from time to time") entitled him to such a statement. The Court held that Richardson could not invoke the *Flast* test because he was not alleging that CIA funds were being spent in violation of a definite constitutional limitations on the taxing and spending power, but rather was alleging only that he was entitled to information about how CIA funds were being spent so that he could "intelligently follow the actions of Congress or the Executive" and "fulfill his obligations as a member of the electorate in voting for candidates seeking national office." The Court concluded that plaintiff's complaint was a general complaint, shared by all members of the public, and therefore did not involve "any particular concrete injury." The Court suggested that plaintiff must seek remedy through the electoral process rather than the courts. Justice Douglas dissented: "The sovereign in this Nation is the people, not the bureaucracy. The statement of accounts of public expenditures goes to the heart of the problem of sovereignty. If taxpayers may not ask that rudimentary question, their sovereignty becomes an empty symbol and a secret bureaucracy is allowed to run our affairs." Justice Stewart, joined by Justice Marshall, also dissented, stating that the Court should find standing when a duty, such as payment of money or providing specific information, runs from the defendant to the plaintiff.

Flast was also distinguished by the holding in *Valley Forge Christian College v. Americans United for Separation of Church and State.*[72] In that case, the General Services Administration declared an army hospital (sitting on a 77-acre tract of land) to be "surplus property" and conveyed it to the Valley Forge Christian College. The purpose of the college was to train laymen and ministers for "Christian service," and the college's faculty was subject to religious restrictions. Under the terms of the conveyance, the college was required to use the property to make "additions to its offerings in the arts and humanities" and to strengthen its psychology and counseling courses to provide services in inner-city areas. Americans United for Separation of Church and State, Inc. ("Americans United"), and four of its employees, challenged the conveyance on Establishment Clause grounds, claiming that the conveyance would deprive them "of the fair and constitutional use of his [or her] tax dollar." The Court held that plaintiffs could not satisfy the *Flast* nexus because they were not challenging a congressional action but were complaining about HEW's decision to transfer federal property, and also were not challenging an expenditure under the Taxing and Spending Clause of Article I, Section 8 (the transfer was made under Congress's power under the Property Clause, Article IV, Section 3). Since *Flast*'s nexus text was inapplicable, the Court applied *Frothingham* and concluded that any effect on plaintiff's tax bill was speculative. Justice Brennan, joined by Justices Marshall and Blackmun, dissented, arguing that the Establishment Clause was enacted "to prevent the use of tax moneys for religious purposes," and that taxpayers are therefore the "direct and intended beneficiary of the prohibition on financial aid to religion" and are the appropriate party to bring suit in federal court. "Moreover, since taxpayer cannot raise the objection at the time they pay their taxes, because there is no injury at that time, challenges should be allowed at the time of the transfer. . . . Whether undertaken pursuant to the Property Clause or the Spending Clause, the breach of the Establishment Clause, and the relationship of the taxpayer to that breach, is precisely the same." Justice Stevens also dissented, arguing that a "taxpayer has a special claim to status as a litigant in a case raising the 'establishment' issue. This [claim] is enough [to] permit us to allow the suit [based on] the interest which the taxpayer and all other citizens have in the church-state issue."

In *Hein v. Freedom from Religion Foundation, Inc.*,[73] the Court's most recent decision, while the Court did not suggest that *Flast* should be limited to its facts, it did suggest that the decision would not apply except in cases challenging congressional appropriations. *Hein* involved an Establishment Clause challenge to President George W. Bush's Faith-Based and Community Initiatives program. That program, which was established by executive order, created Executive Department Centers for Faith-Based and Community Initiatives in several federal agencies and departments. These centers were given the job of ensuring that faith-based community groups were eligible to compete for federal funds without impairing their independence or autonomy, and with eliminating unnecessary bureaucratic, legislative, and regulatory barriers that could impede the ability of faith-based organizations to compete for federal assistance. However, the executive order emphasized that faith-based organizations could "not use direct Federal financial assistance to support any inherently religious activities, such as worship, religious instruction, or proselytization."

"Do you ever have one of those days when everything seems unconstitutional?"

Following establishment of the program, President Bush and former secretary of education Rod Paige gave speeches that used "religious imagery" and praised the efficacy of faith-based programs in the social service context.

In *Hein*, taxpayers sought to challenge expenditures made on behalf of President Bush's and Secretary Paige's conferences and speeches. The Court refused to find taxpayer standing. The Court began by reiterating the idea that a taxpayer could not (as a general rule) show injury from an unconstitutional federal expenditure and expressed doubt that the taxpayers could establish standing by showing that the conferences were paid for with money appropriated by Congress. The Court distinguished *Flast*, noting that the program challenged in that case was funded by a congressional appropriation and was paid out to private schools (including religiously affiliated schools) by congressional mandate. By contrast, in *Hein*, respondents were not attempting to challenge a specific congressional appropriation and did not ask for the invalidation as unconstitutional any legislative enactment or program. In fact, the expenditures were from a general appropriation to the executive branch rather than as the result of any specific congressional action. As a result, the Court concluded that *Flast* did not apply because the "expenditures resulted from executive discretion, not congressional action." The Court concluded that *Flast* was concerned with congressional action, and the Court declined to extend the holding to the executive branch. The Court expressed concern that because "almost all Executive Branch activity is ultimately funded by some congressional appropriation, extending the *Flast* exception to purely executive expenditures would effectively subject every federal action — be it a conference, proclamation or speech — to Establishment Clause challenge by any taxpayer in federal court." The Court was unwilling to go that far. Justice Scalia concurred, but argued that the Court should simply overrule *Flast*, noting that *Flast* "is wholly irreconcilable with the Article III restrictions on federal-court jurisdiction that this Court has repeatedly confirmed are embodied in the doctrine of standing."

(2) Citizen Standing. As with taxpayer standing, plaintiffs have encountered difficulties establishing **citizen standing** — that is, standing based solely on their status as citizens of the United States. In *Frothingham*, in addition to rejecting plaintiff's claim to taxpayer standing, the Court held that Frothingham could not establish citizen standing based on her status as a citizen of the United States. A citizen must still show a cognizable "injury," and Frothingham could show only that she was suffering in "some indefinite way in common with people generally." The Court rendered a similar holding in *Richardson*.

In *Valley Forge*, the Court rejected the argument that plaintiffs could establish citizen standing based on their shared right to a government that "shall make no law respecting the establishment of religion." The Court held that plaintiffs cannot establish standing simply by claiming a right to have a government comply with constitutional mandates. Instead, plaintiffs must identify some "personal injury suffered by them as a consequence of the alleged constitutional error, other than the psychological consequence presumably produced by observation of conduct with which one disagrees." Although the Court recognized that standing could be based on noneconomic injury, the Court doubted that plaintiffs had "alleged an injury of any kind, economic or otherwise."

Likewise, in *Schlesinger v. Reservists Committee to Stop the War*,[74] the Court held that plaintiffs did not have standing to enforce Article I, Section 6, Clause 2, of the U.S. Constitution (the Incompatibility Clause), which prohibited congresspersons from serving as reservists in the U.S. armed forces during their terms of office. At the time of suit, 130 members of Congress were also members of the reserves in its various components (ready, standby, and retired). Plaintiffs argued that congressional reservists were subject to the possibility of undue influence by the executive branch in violation of the concept of the independence of Congress implicit in Article I, and were also subject to possible inconsistent obligations that might cause them to violate their duty to perform faithfully as reservists or as members of Congress. As a result, plaintiffs alleged injury in that citizens and taxpayers were deprived of the opportunity to have reservists and congresspersons who would faithfully discharge their duties. The Court concluded that the case was nonjusticiable because plaintiffs could not establish standing. The Court found the alleged injury to be "abstract," "shared by all citizens," and speculative as whether the claimed nonobservance of the clause would deprive citizens of the faithful discharge of legislative duties, or impinged only the "generalized interest of all citizens in constitutional governance, and that is an abstract injury." The Court flatly rejected the proposition that "all constitutional provisions are enforceable by any citizen simply because citizens are the ultimate beneficiaries of those provisions . . . ." In addition, the Court held that plaintiffs could not establish standing based on their status as taxpayers because they could not satisfy the *Flast* nexus.

Schlesinger produced two dissents. Justice Douglas argued that plaintiffs could establish taxpayer standing by challenging the appropriation acts financing activities of the reservists. He also contended that the "interest of citizens is obvious" since plaintiffs allege "injuries to the ability of the average citizen to make his political advocacy effective. . . . Who other than citizens has a better right to have the Incompatibility Clause enforced? . . . To deny standing to persons who are in fact injured simply because many others are also injured, would mean that the most injurious and widespread Government actions could be questioned by nobody." Justice Marshall also dissented: "Respondents . . . had a right under the First Amendment to attempt to persuade Congressmen to end the war in Vietnam. And respondents have alleged a right, under the Incompatibility Clause, to have their arguments considered by Congressmen not subject to a conflict of interest by virtue of their positions in the Armed Forces Reserves. Respondents' complaint therefore states, in my view, a claim of direct and concrete injury to a judicially cognizable interest."

Consistent with the holdings in *Schlesinger* and *Richardson, Laird v. Tatum*[75] rejected the idea of citizen standing as well. That case involved a challenge to the Department of the Army's decision to surveil "lawful and peaceful civilian political activity" on the basis that it chilled them in the exercise of their First Amendment rights. The Court concluded that standing could not be established merely by a showing that an individual knows that the government is engaged in surveillance. "Carried to its logical end, this approach would have the federal courts as virtually continuing monitors of the wisdom and soundness of Executive action. . . ." Justice Douglas, joined by Justice Marshall, dissented: "The present controversy is not a remote, imaginary conflict. Respondents were targets of the Army's surveillance. . . . This practice directly jeopardized the employment and employment opportunities of persons seeking sensitive positions with the federal government or defense industry.' . . . The Bill of Rights was designed to keep agents of government and official eavesdroppers away from assemblies of people. The aim was to allow men to be free and independent and to assert their rights against government. There can be no influence more paralyzing of that objective than Army surveillance."

The Court's most recent decision on citizen standing is *Lance v. Coffman*.[76] After Colorado was unable to redraw congressional districts following the 2000 census to reflect the addition of a new member of the U.S. House of Representatives, a court redrew the districts. Three years later, the legislature did pass a redistricting plan that effectively overturned the judicial redistricting plan. Colorado citizens sued, claiming that Colorado's Constitution only permits one redistricting per census. The Court concluded that plaintiffs lacked standing, noting that "[t]he only injury plaintiffs allege is that the law—specifically the Elections Clause—has not been followed. This injury is precisely the kind of undifferentiated, generalized grievance about the conduct of government that we have refused to countenance in the past. It is quite different from the sorts of injuries alleged by plaintiffs in voting rights cases where we have found standing."

(3) Congressional Standing. In some instances, legislators have sought to claim standing based on their status as legislators (a/k/a, **legislator standing**), and the question is whether their status as legislators or members of Congress provides an adequate basis for showing injury.

However, legislators do not always have standing to sue. In *Raines v. Byrd*,[77] the Court rejected an attempt by members of Congress to challenge the Line Item Veto Act, which gave the president the authority to "cancel" certain spending and tax benefit measures even though they had been signed into law. The congressmen claimed that they had standing because the line item veto would adversely affect "their constitutionally prescribed lawmaking powers" by allowing the president to rescind a validly enacted appropriation without following prescribed constitutional processes—in particular, passage by both houses of Congress and signed by the president. Even though the Court could have held that legislators had an interest in protecting the integrity of their votes (pros in *Coleman*), the Court held that "individual members of Congress do not have a sufficient 'personal stake' in this dispute and have not alleged a sufficiently concrete injury to have established Article III standing."

F A Q

Q: Does *Raines* doom all claims of legislator standing?

A: No. In *Coleman v. Miller*,[78] the Court held that legislators had standing to challenge a constitutional amendment that they claimed was not properly enacted. The Court concluded that the legislators had a "plain, direct and adequate interest in maintaining the effectiveness of their votes," which was sufficient to give them standing: "[T]he twenty senators whose votes . . . would have been sufficient to defeat the resolution ratifying the proposed constitutional amendment, have an interest in the controversy which, treated by the state court as a basis for entertaining and deciding the federal questions, is sufficient to give the Court jurisdiction to review that decision." Justice Frankfurter dissented: "[T]he claim that the Amendment was dead or that it was not longer open to Kansas to ratify, is not only not an interest which belongs uniquely to these Kansas legislators; it is not even an interest special to Kansas. For it is the common concern of every citizen of the United States. . . ."

(4) Congressionally Authorized Standing. As previously noted, there is both a constitutional aspect and a prudential aspect to standing. The constitutional aspect stems from Article III's case or controversy requirement, and cannot be waived by Congress. As the Court recognized in *Valley Forge Christian College v. Americans United for Separation of Church and State*,[79] neither the Administrative Procedure Act, 5 U.S.C. §702, which authorizes judicial review at the instance of any person who has been "adversely affected or aggrieved by agency action within the meaning of a relevant statute," or any other congressional enactment "can lower the threshold requirements of standing under Art. III." However, the prudential aspect of standing is a limitation that the Court imposes on itself. Under the prudential aspect, even when a case or controversy exists, the Court may refuse to hear a case in deference for a variety of reasons (for example, to give deference to a coordinate branch of government). On the other hand, if Congress has invited the Court to hear a particular type of case, especially a nonconstitutional case, prudential restraints are minimized or disappear.

The leading decision on congressional authorization, especially in nonconstitutional cases, is *Association of Data Processing Service Organizations, Inc. v. Camp*.[80] The decision is important because the Court established a two-part test for evaluating claims of **congressionally authorized standing**: (When Congress seems to have authorized the federal courts to hear a case) plaintiffs must show that they are suffering injury in fact, and they must also show that they fall within the "zone of interest" sought to be protected by the congressional enactment.

Data Processing involved sellers of data processing services that challenged a ruling by the Comptroller of the Currency that allowed national banks to make data processing services available to other banks and to bank customers. Petitioners alleged that competition by national banks might cause them future profit losses, and that at least one national bank was performing or preparing to perform such services for its customers. The Court concluded that plaintiffs were suffering injury in the form of potential pecuniary loss. The Court also found that plaintiffs were "within the zone of interests to be protected or regulated by the statute or constitutional guarantee in question." The Court noted that the Administrative Procedure Act, in particular 5 U.S.C. §702, grants standing to a person "aggrieved by agency action within the meaning of a relevant statute." And the Court noted that there has been a tendency to allow statutes to enlarge the class of people who may protest administrative action. In this case, the Court emphasized that §4 of the Bank Service Corporation Act of 1962, 12 U.S.C. §1864, provided that "[n]o bank service corporation may engage in any activity other than the performance of bank services for banks." The Court found that §4 "arguably brings a competitor within the zone of interests protected by" a statute. Finding that Congress had not prescribed review, the Court held that the association of data processing agencies could establish standing.

(i) THE INJURY-IN-FACT REQUIREMENT. The **injury-in-fact requirement** (which requires plaintiff to show that it suffered a legally cognizable injury) is an essential element of congressionally authorized standing. Courts do not hold that standing exists merely because Congress has invited the courts to hear a particular type of case. For example, in *Lujan v. Defenders of Wildlife*,[81] the Endangered Species Act (ESA) contained a "citizen-suit" provision that stated that "any person may commence a civil suit on his own behalf [to] enjoin any person, including the United States and any other governmental instrumentality or agency . . . who is alleged to be in violation of any provision of this chapter." The trial court held that because the act required interagency consultation, the citizen-suit provision created a "procedural right" so that all "persons" had standing to challenge the secretary's failure to follow consult. The Supreme Court disagreed, noting that plaintiffs could not establish standing because they could not show impairment of a concrete interest and were instead raising only "a generally available grievance about government—claiming only harm to his and every citizen's interest in proper application of the Constitution and laws, and seeking relief that no more directly and tangibly benefits him than it does the public at large." The Court held that it could not allow Congress "to convert the undifferentiated public interest in executive officers' compliance with the law into an 'individual right' vindicable in the courts" without permitting "Congress to transfer from the President to the courts the Chief Executive's most important constitutional duty, to 'take Care that the Laws be faithfully executed.'" Thus, while the Court recognized that Congress could create legal rights, it was unwilling to abandon the requirement that the party seeking review must him- or herself have suffered an injury.

The outer limits of "injury" are revealed by the Court's earlier decision in *United States v. SCRAP*.[82] That suit was brought by Students Challenging Regulatory Agency Procedures (SCRAP), an unincorporated group of five law students, and the Environmental Defense Fund to challenge the Interstate Commerce Commission's failure to suspend a surcharge that SCRAP claimed would discourage the use of "recyclable" materials and promote the use of new raw materials that compete with scrap, thereby adversely affecting the environment. SCRAP also alleged that the rate increase would force plaintiffs to pay more for finished products, and their use of forests and streams would be impaired because of unnecessary destruction of timber and extraction of raw materials, and the accumulation of otherwise recyclable solid and liquid waste materials. The Court held that plaintiffs should be given the opportunity to prove their allegations, noting that the challenged action was applicable to substantially all railroads and thus could have an adverse environmental impact on all the natural resources of the country. "To deny standing to persons who are in fact injured simply because many others are also injured, would mean that the most injurious and widespread Government actions could be questioned by nobody." Justice White, joined by two other justices, dissented in part: "[T]he alleged injuries are so remote, speculative, and insubstantial in fact that they fail to confer standing. . . . Allegations such as these . . . no more qualify these appellees to litigate than allegations of a taxpayer that governmental expenditures will increase his taxes and have an impact on his pocketbook, or allegations that governmental decisions are offensive to reason or morals."

F A Q

Q: How does an association demonstrate injury that would entitle it to bring an action?

A: With an association (or other organization), it may be difficult to show that the association itself is suffering injury. For example, in *Sierra Club v. Morton*, 405 U.S. 727 (1972), the Sierra Club challenged the United States Forest Service's (USFS) decision to build a 20-mile road in the Sierra Nevada Mountains. The Sierra Club claimed standing based on its "special interest in the conservation and the sound maintenance of the national parks, game refuges and forests." While the

Court recognized that "aesthetic and environmental" interests are important enough to confer standing, the Court concluded that the party seeking review must be "among the injured," meaning that, to have standing, an association must show that one of its members actually uses the park and will be subject to the asserted injuries. Justice Blackmun dissented: "I would [allow] an organization such as the Sierra Club, possessed, as it is, of pertinent, bona fide, and well-recognized attributes and purposes in the area of environment, to litigate environmental issues."

Under its more modern precedent, it is unlikely that the Court would reach the same result if a case like *SCRAP* arose today. More illustrative of the Court's modern approach is the holding in *Lujan v. Defenders of Wildlife*.[83] In that case, plaintiffs sought to challenge the secretary of the interior's interpretation of §7 of the Endangered Species Act of 1973 (ESA). The ESA was enacted to protect species of animals against threats to their continuing existence caused by mankind, and Congress instructed the secretary of the interior to promulgate by regulation a list of those species that are either endangered or threatened under enumerated criteria, and to define the critical habitat of these species. Section 7(a)(2) of the act then required that each "Federal agency shall, in consultation with and with the assistance of the Secretary [of the Interior], insure that any action authorized, funded, or carried out by such agency [is] not likely to jeopardize the continued existence of any endangered species or threatened species or result in the destruction or adverse modification of habitat of such species which is determined by the Secretary, after consultation as appropriate with affected States, to be critical." The secretary construed the ESA as applicable only to actions within the United States or on the high seas, and the interpretation was challenged by individuals and environmental organizations concerned about protecting habitat overseas. The Court concluded that the plaintiffs and other environmental organizations that sought to challenge the rule lacked standing because they were unable to show injury (and redressability). While recognizing the "desire to use or observe an animal species, even for purely esthetic purposes, is undeniably a cognizable interest for purpose of standing," the Court held that plaintiffs must show that they are "injured" or "directly affected" apart from their "special interest in the subject." Among the plaintiffs, Joyce Kelly testified that she traveled to Egypt in 1986 and "observed the traditional habitat of the endangered nile crocodile there and intend[s] to do so again," and that she "will suffer harm in fact" as a result of U.S. involvement in Aswan High Dam. A second plaintiff, Amy Skilbred, testified that she traveled to Sri Lanka in 1981 and "observed th[e] habitat" of "endangered species such as the Asian elephant and the leopard," and was concerned about the Mahaweli project. While the Court assumed that certain agency-funded projects might threaten the listed species, the Court found no proof that the damage would produce "imminent" injury to either Kelly or Skilbred. Indeed, the Court concluded that the plaintiffs' statement of intent to return to the affected areas is "simply not enough . . . without any description of concrete plans, or indeed even any specification of when the some day will be."

The Court also rejected plaintiff's arguments that standing should be based on an alleged "ecosystem nexus" or "animal nexus." The ecosystem nexus provided that any person who uses any part of a contiguous ecosystem adversely affected by a funded activity has standing, even if the activity is located a great distance away.

The Court concluded that such allegations were insufficient because "a plaintiff claiming injury from environmental damage must use the area affected by the challenged activity and not an area roughly 'in the vicinity.'" The Court rejected the argument, even though the ESA provided that it was intended in part "to provide a means whereby the ecosystems upon which endangered species and threatened species depend may be conserved," 16 U.S.C. §1531(b). "To say that the Act protects ecosystems is not to say that the Act creates (if it were possible) rights of action in persons who have not been injured in fact, that is, persons who use portions of an ecosystem not perceptibly affected by the unlawful action in question." The animal nexus theory provided that anyone who has an interest in studying or seeing the endangered animals anywhere on the globe has standing; and the vocational nexus approach provided that anyone with a professional interest in such animals can sue. The Court concluded that it is "plausible [to] think that a person who observes or works with animals of a particular species in the very area of the world where that species is threatened by a federal decision is facing such harm, since some animals that might have been the subject of his interest will no longer exist." However, the Court rejected the argument, noting that it involves "pure speculation and fantasy" to "say that anyone who observes or works with an endangered species, anywhere in the world, is appreciably harmed by a single project affecting some portion of that species with which he has no more specific connection."

Also illustrative of the modern, more restrictive approach to standing is the holding in *Los Angeles v. Lyons.*[84] In that case, Lyons brought a civil rights action alleging that the city routinely encouraged police to use choke holds, and that numerous individuals had been injured by this practice. Lyons asked for a court order prohibiting the use of choke holds except to prevent the "immediate use of deadly force." The Court concluded that Lyons could not establish standing, even though he could show that he had been subjected to a choke hold five months earlier. That Lyons may have been illegally choked on a prior occasion "does nothing to establish a real and immediate threat that he would [be] again." The Court suggested that it would be mere conjecture to suppose either that police officers will always act unconstitutionally and inflict harm in encounters with citizens or that Lyons would again be involved in a situation where a choke hold might be used. The Court also refused to apply the "capable of repetition, but evading review" principle (discussed earlier in the section on mootness), noting that Lyons was in fact challenging the policy in a civil suit for damages. Justice Marshall, joined by Justices Blackmun, Brennan, and Stevens, dissented: "It is undisputed that choke holds pose a high and unpredictable risk of serious injury or death. . . . Because Lyons has a claim for damages against the City, and because he cannot prevail on that claim unless he demonstrates that the City's choke hold policy violates the Constitution, his personal stake in the outcome of the controversy adequately assures an adversary presentation of his challenge to the constitutionality of the policy."

Some cases have dealt with the question of whether so-called testers may establish standing to sue. For example, in *Havens Realty Corp. v. Coleman,*[85] plaintiffs claimed that defendants had engaged in "racial steering" at two apartment complexes in violation of §804 of the Fair Housing Act of 1968. The complaint identified three plaintiffs: a black man (Coles) who attempted to rent an apartment from Havens and was falsely told that no apartments were available, and two "tester plaintiffs" (Coleman who was black and Willis who was white) who were employed by an independent organization to determine whether Havens practiced racial steering. Coleman was told more than once that no apartments were available while Willis was told that there were vacancies. All three plaintiffs, who resided in the area, claimed that they had been injured by the discrimination. The two tester plaintiffs alleged that Havens' practices deprived them of the "important social, professional, business and economic, political and aesthetic benefits of interracial associations that arise from living in integrated communities free from discriminatory housing practices." The Court held that the testers could establish standing, even though they were merely testers and did not intend to actually rent or purchase homes. The act made it unlawful for an individual or firm covered by the act "[t]o represent to *any person* because of race, color, religion, sex, or national origin that any dwelling is not available for inspection, sale, or rental when such dwelling is in fact so available." In addition, Congress had given all "persons" a legal right to truthful information about available housing. The Court relied on this statement of congressional intent in concluding that a "tester who has been the object of a misrepresentation made unlawful under §804(d) has suffered injury in precisely the form the statute was intended to guard against, and therefore has standing to maintain a claim for damages under the Act's provisions. That the tester may have approached the real estate agent fully expecting that he would receive false information, and without any intention of buying or renting a home, does not negate the simple fact of injury within the meaning of §804(d)." However, as to the white tester, standing was not found to exist because he was not a victim of a discriminatory misrepresentation. In addition, the Court concluded that the alleged injury (deprivation "of the benefits that result from living in an integrated community") was "indirect," and that plaintiffs must still establish "injury in fact." The Court remanded to allow the plaintiffs to attempt to establish injury, but concluded that it had generally found standing based on the effects of discrimination only within a 'relatively compact neighborhood.' The discrimination was also challenged by HOME, a housing group, which claimed that it "has been frustrated by defendants' racial steering practices in its efforts to assist equal access to housing through counseling and other referral services." The Court concluded that these allegations would be sufficient to establish injury in fact. Such concrete and demonstrable injury to the organization's activities—with the consequent drain on the organization's resources—constitutes far more than simply a setback to the organization's abstract social interests.

(ii) The Zone-of-Interest Test. The **zone of interest test** (which requires plaintiff to show that it fits within the "zone of interest" sought to be protected by the statute) has been applied in a variety of cases. In general, the focus is on whether plaintiff falls within the "zone of interest" sought to be protected by the statute.

Illustrative of the test is the holding in *Federal Election Commission v. Akins.*[86] In *Akins*, the Federal Election Commission (FEC) concluded that the American Israel Public Affairs Committee (AIPAC) was not a "political committee" as defined by the Federal Election Campaign Act of 1971 (FECA) and therefore did not have to make disclosures regarding its membership, contributions, and expenditures under federal election laws. A group of voters challenged the FEC's determination, relying on federal election laws that provided that "[a]ny party aggrieved by an order of the Commission dismissing a complaint filed by such party [may] file a petition" in federal court seeking review of that dismissal. The Court held that voters had standing to challenge the decision. The Court noted that Congress specifically provided in FECA that aggrieved individuals could complain and concluded that plaintiffs fit within the zone of interest protected by the statute because Congress intended "to protect voters such as respondents from suffering the kind of injury here at issue [and] intended to authorize this kind of suit." In addition, they could show injury in that the information sought "would help them (and others to whom they would communicate it) to evaluate candidates for public office, especially candidates who received assistance from AIPAC, and to evaluate the role that AIPAC's financial assistance might play in a specific election." They were also able to show "causation" because the alleged injury was "fairly traceable" to the challenged FEC decision, even though the FEC might still decide against the plaintiffs. "But that fact does not destroy Article III 'causation,' for we cannot know that the FEC would have exercised its prosecutorial discretion in this way."

Individuals who bring *qui tam* actions have been found to be within the zone of interest of a federal statute. In *Vermont Agency of Natural Resources v. United States ex rel. Stevens,*[87] a federal statute authorized *qui tam* actions by private citizens to enforce federal laws. To encourage citizen suits, the statute provided that the citizen shall receive a bounty *out of the United States' recovery* for filing and/or prosecuting a successful action on behalf of the government. The statute gave the private citizen "the right to continue as a party to the action" even when the government itself has assumed "primary responsibility" for prosecuting it, entitled the relator to a hearing before the government's voluntary dismissal of the suit, and prohibited the government from settling the suit over the relator's objection without a judicial determination of "fair[ness], adequa[cy] and reasonable[ness]." The Court concluded that a citizen who brought a *qui tam* action could establish standing: "There is no doubt . . . that as to this portion of the recovery—the bounty he will receive if the suit is successful—a *qui tam* relator has a 'concrete private interest in the outcome of [the] suit.'" "The FCA can reasonably be regarded as effecting a partial assignment of the Government's damages claim. Although we have never expressly recognized 'representational standing' on the part of assignees, we have routinely entertained their suits, and also suits by subrogees, who have been described as 'equitable assign[ees].'"

Likewise, in *Winkelman v. Parma City School District,*[88] the parents of an autistic child were held to be within the zone of interest of the Individuals with Disabilities Education Act (IDEA), when claiming that the child's school was not complying with the IDEA with respect to his education. The Court held that the parents had standing to bring the action on behalf of their child, noting that the statute grants "[a]ny party aggrieved by the findings and decision made [by the hearing officer] . . . the right to bring a civil action with respect to the complaint." The Court emphasized that "the Act does not *sub silentio* or by implication bar parents from seeking to vindicate the rights accorded to them once the time comes to file a civil action. Through its provisions for expansive review and extensive parental involvement, the statute leads to just the opposite result."

(5) Causation. In addition to demonstrating a "concrete and particularized injury" that is "actual or imminent," the Court also requires proof of **causation**. Causation requires that there be a correlation between plaintiff's alleged injury and the challenged governmental action such that a judicial order restraining the action will redress the injury.

In recent decades, the Court has frequently imposed the causation requirement as a significant limitation on the standing doctrine. Illustrative is the holding in *Allen v. Wright.*[89] In that case, the parents of African American children sought to compel the Internal Revenue Service to deny tax-exempt status to racially discriminatory private schools, claiming that the exempt status helped discriminatory schools raise funds and thereby interfered with the ability of plaintiffs' children to be educated in desegregated public schools. The Court denied standing on causation grounds. Even though plaintiffs could demonstrate injury, the Court concluded that the injury was not "fairly traceable" to the tax exemptions. "It is uncertain how many racially discriminatory private schools are in fact receiving tax exemptions, and it is entirely speculative . . . whether withdrawal of a tax exemption from any particular school would lead the school to change its policies. It is just as speculative whether any given parent of a child attending such a private school would decide to transfer the child to public school as a result of any changes in educational or financial policy made by the private school once it was threatened with loss of tax-exempt status." As a result, the Court concluded that the "links in the chain of causation between the challenged Government conduct and the asserted injury are far too weak for the chain as a whole to sustain respondents' standing." Justice Brennan dissented: "Common sense alone would recognize that the elimination of tax-exempt status for racially discriminatory private schools would serve to lessen the impact that those institutions have in defeating efforts to desegregate the public schools." Justice Stevens, joined by Justice Blackmun, also dissented: "If the granting of preferential tax treatment would 'encourage' private segregated schools to conduct their 'charitable' activities, it must follow that the withdrawal of the treatment would 'discourage' them, and hence promote the process of desegregation."[90]

Also illustrative is the holding in *Lujan v. Defenders of Wildlife,*[91] discussed earlier in reference to the concept of injury in fact. In addition to concluding that the plaintiff environmental organizations were unable to demonstrate injury, the Court held that plaintiffs could not satisfy the causation or redressability requirement. Since the agencies funding the projects were not parties to the case, the Court could order relief only against the secretary of the interior in the sense of requiring him to revise agency regulations to require consultation for foreign projects. The Court concluded such an order would not remedy respondents' alleged injury because it was not clear that the funding agencies were bound by the secretary's regulation. The Court also noted that U.S. agencies were providing only a small percentage (less than 10 percent) of the funding for the Mahaweli project, and the Court doubted that the projects would be suspended even if this funding was suspended or withdrawn.

In some instances, a plaintiff seeks to challenge a discriminatory benefits scheme even though plaintiff cannot, by law, receive benefits under that scheme even if the scheme is invalidated. For example, in *Heckler v. Mathews*,[92] a male brought an equal protection challenge to the Social Security Act, which contained a gender-based classification that denied him benefits equal to those received by women. He did so even though the law contained a severability provision that would have prevented plaintiff from obtaining more benefits even if the law was struck down. The Court concluded that even though plaintiff could not receive more benefits, he still had a redressable injury: "[W]e have never suggested that the injuries caused by a constitutionally underinclusive scheme can be remedied only by extending the program's benefits to the excluded class." "[D]iscrimination itself, by perpetuating 'archaic and stereotypic notions' or by stigmatizing members of the disfavored group as 'innately inferior' and therefore as less worthy participants in the political community, can cause serious non-economic injuries to those persons who are personally denied equal treatment solely because of their membership in a disfavored group." The Court concluded that the mandate of equal treatment could be accomplished by withdrawal of benefits from the favored class as well as by extension of benefits to the excluded class.

However, in many cases, the causation requirement proves to be a fatal bar. For example, in *Asarco, Inc. v. Kadish*,[93] an Arizona statute authorized the state land department to lease minerals and school trust lands at a prescribed rate. Individual taxpayers, along with a teacher's association, challenged the statute on the ground that it did not comply with congressionally imposed statutory standards for leasing or selling lands. The Court concluded that none of them could establish standing because they could not show pecuniary injury. The Court concluded that it was "pure speculation" whether, even if more money went to the trust fund, that it would be allocated to education. As a result, the Court concluded that plaintiffs were simply "concerned citizens" bringing "generalized grievances" that are not cognizable in the federal courts. "Although the members of the teachers association might argue that they have a special interest in the quality of education in Arizona, such a special interest does not alone confer federal standing. The argument does not succeed in distinguishing the members in this regard from students, their parents, or various other citizens."

(6) Jus Tertii (Third-Party) Standing. In some instances, third parties have tried to raise the rights and interests of individuals who are not before the court, and courts must decide whether the third parties have standing to assert those rights. This is also referred to as **third-party standing** or **jus tertii**.

In fact, in many instances, there are sound reasons for denying standing in these cases. As a general rule, the individuals themselves (rather than third parties) are the best proponents of their own rights. In addition, when a third party is allowed to litigate, there is always the risk that the holder of the right may not wish for the third party to assert the right or may not wish to assert the right at all. Nevertheless, there are situations where a third party might be the only effective advocate for the right holder. As a result, in deciding whether to recognize third-party standing, courts will often focus on the relationship between the third party and the interests the third party seeks to represent. The goal is to determine whether the third party is likely to be an "effective proponent" of the rights asserted.

S i d e b a r

THE BEER VENDOR AND HIS CUSTOMERS

Craig v. Boren, 429 U.S. 190 (1976), challenged an Oklahoma statute that provided that males between the ages of 18 and 21 could not purchase 3.2 percent beer, but that females could purchase the beer once they had attained the age of 18. The Court held that not only may males bring the lawsuit, but that the suit could also be brought by a beer distributor on the males' behalf. The distributor suffered injury because the law adversely affected it. As a result, "vendors and those in like positions have been uniformly permitted to resist efforts at restricting their operations by acting as advocates of the rights of third parties who seek access to their market or function."

Denial of third-party standing is particularly appropriate when the third party's interests are at odds with the interests of the person whom he or she seeks to represent. For example, in *Gilmore v. Utah*,[94] after Gary Mark Gilmore was convicted of murder and sentenced to death, he waived all of his rights and agreed to submit to execution. When Gilmore's mother sought to establish standing as his "next friend" in order to apply for a stay of execution, the Court found that he had made a knowing and intelligent waiver of his rights and concluded that the mother could not establish standing in face of the son's repudiation. Similarly, in *Elk Grove Unified School District v. Newdow*,[95] the Court rejected a father's attempt to challenge recitation of the Pledge of Allegiance in his daughter's school. The father, an atheist, objected to the Pledge's inclusion of the words "under God," which he viewed as an establishment of religion. When the daughter's mother, the custodial parent, opposed the father's suit, the Court concluded that the father lacked standing to represent his daughter's interest, noting that the interested parties were antagonistic and the father did not have the power to litigate as his daughter's "next friend."

S i d e b a r

ALABAMA'S REGISTRATION STATUTE

In *NAACP v. Alabama*, 357 U.S. 449 (1958) an Alabama statute required foreign corporations to report the names and addresses of their members to Alabama's Attorney General. The NAACP challenged the reporting requirements as a violation of First Amendment speech and assembly rights of itself and its members. In addition, the Court found a nexus between the NAACP and its members because the order threatened to diminish their financial support and membership.

In other cases, the interest of the third party and the right holder are more closely aligned, and the third party's intervention is necessary if the right holder's interests are to be vindicated. For example, in *Hamdi v. Rumsfeld*,[96] following the September 11th attack on the World Trade Center in New York City, Hamdi was detained as an enemy combatant. Although he was a U.S. citizen, detained on U.S. soil, he was denied access to an attorney. His father, as next friend, sought a writ of habeas corpus on his behalf. Although the Court devoted little attention to the issue, it allowed the father to pursue the son's interest. Likewise, in *Singleton v. Wulff*,[97] the Court held that doctors could establish standing to challenge on constitutional grounds a Missouri statute that excluded from Medicaid coverage abortions that are not "medically indicated." The doctors who challenged the law performed nonmedically indicated abortions and alleged that they would suffer financial injury (the loss of payment) if the statute remained in effect. They also sought to assert the rights of their patients. Although the Court recited concerns about third-party representation, it held that the doctors could establish standing. Relying on *Griswold v. Connecticut*,[98] the Court held that a licensed physician could assert the rights of married patients to receive contraceptive advice, and abortion providers could establish standing to represent their patients since a woman cannot safely secure an abortion without a physician, and a poor woman may require state financial assistance. The Court concluded that abortion doctors are "uniquely qualified" to litigate the constitutional claims, and that women seeking abortions might be reluctant to assert their rights for a variety of reasons: They may want to protect the privacy of their decisions, and an individual woman's standing will be lost to mootness relatively quickly. Even though the woman's case might be salvageable under the "capable of repetition, yet evading review" doctrine, the Court concluded that there "seems little loss in terms of effective advocacy from allowing its assertion by a physician."[99]

Third-party standing has also been recognized in cases involving racially restrictive covenants. For example, in *Barrows v. Jackson*,[100] a state statute permitted restrictive covenants that exclude covenanted property from being sold to members of specified minority groups. Plaintiffs, beneficiaries of the covenants, sought damages from those who sold real property in violation of their terms. The Court held that the sellers had standing to assert the rights of the minorities, noting that there "is such a close relationship between the restrictive covenant here and the sanction of a state court which would punish respondent for not going forward with her covenant, and the purpose of the covenant itself, that relaxation of the rule is called for here. It sufficiently appears that mulcting in damages of respondent will be solely for the purpose of giving vitality to the restrictive covenant, that is to say, to punish respondent for not continuing to discriminate against non-Caucasians in the use of her property." Chief Justice Vinson dissented, arguing that the "majority identifies no non-Caucasian who has been injured or could be injured if damages are assessed against respondent for breaching the promise which she willingly and voluntarily made to petitioners, a promise which neither the federal law nor the Constitution proscribes. Indeed, the non-Caucasian occupants of the property involved in this case will continue their occupancy undisturbed, regardless of the outcome of the suit."

SUMMARY

■ Under the concept of judicial review, the courts have the power to review the actions of Congress and executive branch officials and to invalidate those actions if the other branches have exceeded their constitutional authority.

■ Because of their judicial review authority, courts exercise a great deal of power in the U.S. constitutional system, even though they do not have the armed forces at their disposal (as the president does) or have the power of the purse (as Congress does).

■ Even though the courts exercise significant authority under their judicial review authority, the Framers built checks and balances into the constitutional system. In addition to the practical limitations (for example, the fact that the U.S. Supreme Court hears only a limited number of cases per year), there are other very real and substantial restraints on the scope of judicial authority.

■ Congress has the power to control and limit the U.S. Supreme Court's appellate jurisdiction, as well as the authority of the lower federal courts. In addition, under the case or controversy requirement, the scope of federal authority is limited by concepts of ripeness, mootness, standing, and the prohibition against advisory opinions.

CONNECTIONS

Commerce Clause

Judicial review has been frequently invoked in relation to Congress's power under the Commerce Clause. However, as we shall see, the Court was quite deferential to enactments under the Commerce Clause.

Establishment Clause

Judicial review is an important enforcement component under the Establishment Clause of the First Amendment to the U.S. Constitution. However, as cases like *Valley Forge* suggest, some would-be plaintiffs will be unable to establish standing in Establishment Clause cases.

Free Exercise Clause

Frequently, individuals seek to vindicate their free exercise rights through the courts and the process of judicial review.

Intergovernmental Immunities

To the extent that the federal government or state governments argue that they have a right to be free of regulation by the other, one method of raising that issue is through the courts and the process of judicial review.

State Power to Regulate Commerce

Although the federal courts were initially deferential to state and local governments that chose to regulate commerce, in instances when Congress had not exercised its power, later decisions involve a more active and involved judicial review process.

Endnotes

1. 5 U.S. (1 Cranch) 137 (1803).
2. *See, e.g.*, Julius Goebel, 1 *The Oliver Wendell Holmes Devise History of the Supreme Court of the United States — Antecedents and Beginnings to 1801* (1971); Edward S. Corwin, Marbury v. Madison *and the Doctrine of Judicial Review*, 12 Mich. L. Rev. 538, 552 (1914).
3. *See* Russell L. Weaver & Kathe Boehringer, *Implied Rights and the Australian Constitution: A Modified* New York Times, Inc. v. Sullivan *Goes Down Under*, 8 Seton Hall Const. L.J. 101 (1998).
4. *See* Russell L. Weaver & Geoffrey J. G. Bennett, *The N. Ireland Media Ban: Some Reflections on Judicial Review*, 22 Vand. J. Transnatl. L. 1119 (1989).
5. Engel v. Vitale, 370 U.S. 421 (1962).
6. San Antonio Indep. Sch. Dist. v. Rodriguez, 411 U.S. 1 (1973).
7. Brown v. Bd. of Educ., 347 U.S. 483 (1954).
8. Wisconsin v. Yoder, 406 U.S. 205 (1972).
9. Carter v. Carter Coal Co., 298 U.S. 238 (1936).
10. Church of Lukumi Babalu Aye, Inc. v. Hialeah, 508 U.S. 520 (1993).
11. United States v. Lopez, 514 U.S. 549 (1995).
12. 491 U.S. 397 (1989).

13. 467 U.S. 837 (1984).
14. 10 U.S. (6 Cranch) 87 (1810).
15. 14 U.S. (1 Wheat) 304 (1816).
16. *See also* Cohens v. Commonwealth of Va., 19 U.S. (6 Wheat) 264 (1821).
17. 358 U.S. 1 (1958).
18. 347 U.S. 483 (1954).
19. 372 U.S. 335 (1963).
20. 367 U.S. 643 (1961).
21. 468 U.S. 897 (1984).
22. *See, e.g.*, State v. Marsala, 579 A.2d 58 (Conn. 1990); State v. Novembrino, 519 A.2d 820 (N.J. 1987).
23. 28 U.S.C. §1253 (2000).
24. 28 U.S.C. §2281 (2000).
25. *See* Ellis v. Bhd. of Ry., Airline & S.S. Clerks, 466 U.S. 435 (1984).
26. *See* Murdock v. City of Memphis, 87 U.S. (20 Wall.) 590 (1874).
27. *See* R.R. Commn. v. Pullman Co., 312 U.S. 496 (1941).
28. 74 U.S. 506 (1868).
29. 75 U.S. (8 Wall.) 85 (1869).
30. 80 U.S. 128 (1871).
31. 514 U.S. 211 (1995).
32. Henry M. Hart, *The Power of Congress to Limit the Jurisdiction of Federal Courts*, 66 Harv. L. Rev. 1362, 1365 (1953) (emphasis added).
33. Leonard G. Ratner, *Congressional Power over the Appellate Jurisdiction of the Supreme Court*, 109 U. Pa. L. Rev. 157, 157 (1960).
34. *Id.* at 160-161.
35. Herbert Wechsler, *The Courts and the Constitution*, 65 Colum. L. Rev. 1001, 1005-1006 (1965).
36. *See* Yakus v. United States, 321 U.S. 414 (1944); Lockerty v. Phillips, 319 U.S. 182 (1943); Sheldon v. Sill, 49 U.S. (8 How.) 441 (1850).
37. Lawrence Gene Sager, *Foreword: Constitutional Limitations on Congress' Authority to Regulate the Jurisdiction of the Federal Courts*, 95 Harv. L. Rev. 17, 55 (1981).
38. *See* Henry M. Hart, *The Power of Congress to Limit the Jurisdiction of the Federal Courts: An Exercise in Dialectic*, 66 Harv. L. Rev. 1363 (1953).
39. Martin v. Hunter's Lessee 14 U.S. 304 (1816).
40. *See* Alexander Bickel, *The Least Dangerous Branch* 184 (1962); Louis Henkin, *Is There a "Political Question" Doctrine?*, 85 Yale L.J. 597, 622-623 (1976).
41. 349 U.S. 294 (1955).
42. 370 U.S. 421 (1962).
43. 369 U.S. 186 (1962).
44. 48 U.S. (7 How.) 1 (1849).
45. 478 U.S. 109 (1986).
46. *Compare* Holtzman v. Schlesinger, 361 F. Supp. 553 (D.C.N.Y. 1973), *with* Holtzman v. Schlesinger, 484 F.2d 1307 (2d Cir. 1973). *See also* Crockett v. Reagan, 720 F.2d 1355 (D.C. Cir. 1983); DaCasta v. Laird, 471 F.2d 1146 (2d Cir. 1973); Sarnoff v. Connally, 457 F.2d 809 (9th Cir. 1972); Orlando v. Laird, 443 F.2d 1039 (2d Cir. 1971); Campbell v. Clinton, 52 F. Supp. 2d 34 (D.D.C. 1999); Ange v. Bush, 752 F. Supp. 509 (D.D.C. 1990).
47. 444 U.S. 996 (1979).
48. 369 U.S. at 212.
49. 395 U.S. 486 (1969).
50. 3 Correspondence and Public Papers of John Jay 486 (1890).
51. 219 U.S. 346 (1911).
52. 330 U.S. 75 (1947).
53. 387 U.S. 136 (1967).
54. 752 F. Supp. 1141 (D.D.C. 1990).
55. 367 U.S. 497 (1961).
56. 381 U.S. 479 (1965).
57. 416 U.S. 312 (1974).
58. 461 U.S. 95 (1983).
59. 528 U.S. 167 (2000).
60. 469 U.S. 387 (1985).
61. 410 U.S. 113 (1973).
62. *See, e.g.*, Schlesinger v. Reservists Comm. to Stop the War, 418 U.S. 208 (1974).
63. *See* Lujan v. Defenders of Wildlife, 504 U.S. 555 (1992).
64. 418 U.S. 208 (1974).
65. 262 U.S. 447 (1923).
66. *Id.*
67. 294 U.S. 511 (1935).
68. 342 U.S. 429 (1952).

69. 330 U.S. 1 (1947).
70. 392 U.S. 83 (1968).
71. 418 U.S. 166 (1974).
72. 454 U.S. 464 (1982).
73. 127 S. Ct. 2553 (2007).
74. 418 U.S. 208 (1974).
75. 408 U.S. 1 (1972).
76. 127 S. Ct. 1194 (2007).
77. 521 U.S. 811 (1997).
78. 307 U.S. 433 (1939).
79. 454 U.S. 464 (1982).
80. 397 U.S. 150 (1970).
81. 504 U.S. 555 (1992).
82. 412 U.S. 669 (1973).
83. 504 U.S. 555 (1992).
84. 461 U.S. 95 (1983).
85. 455 U.S. 363 (1982).
86. 524 U.S. 11 (1998).
87. 529 U.S. 765 (2000).
88. 127 S. Ct. 1994 (2007).
89. 468 U.S. 737 (1984).
90. *See also* Simon v. E. Ky. Welfare Rights Org., 426 U.S. 26 (1976) (concluding that government policies on the provision of indigent services could not be regarded as the cause of hospital policies on the provision of free services).
91. 504 U.S. 555 (1992).
92. 465 U.S. 728 (1984).
93. 490 U.S. 605 (1989).
94. 429 U.S. 1012 (1976).
95. 542 U.S. 1 (2004).
96. 542 U.S. 507 (2004).
97. 428 U.S. 106 (1976).
98. 381 U.S. 479 (1965).
99. *See* Eisenstadt v. Baird, 405 U.S. 438 (1972) (advocate for the use of contraceptives allowed to assert the rights of those who wish to use contraceptives).
100. 346 U.S. 249 (1953).

National Legislative Power

2

This chapter examines the scope of Congress's legislative power. Although many of the Framers envisioned a Congress of relatively limited and enumerated powers (for example, the spending power, the taxing power, and the Commerce Clause power), the scope of congressional authority has expanded, contracted, and shifted during the last two centuries. In this chapter, we examine how and why the concept of federal legislative power has expanded over time and whether it exceeds the scope contemplated by the Framers of the Constitution.

OVERVIEW

A. Historical Background

As powerful as the U.S. Congress has become over the last two centuries, the Framers did not envision a legislative branch with such sweeping powers. Under the **Articles of Confederation** (the Articles were the initial governing document and preceded the U.S. Constitution), the states were reluctant to vest broad powers in the federal government, so the Articles explicitly precluded the federal government from exercising implied powers and required that "everything granted shall be expressly and minutely described."

The Articles did not provide a sound platform for government. The individual states used their power over commerce to erect such barriers to trade as tariffs and embargos, which made interstate commerce (referring to goods that crossed state lines) difficult. In addition, the Articles created a federal government that did not have sufficient power to provide for foreign affairs and the national defense. By the mid-1780s, the need for change was evident, and a convention was called to amend the Articles of Confederation. That call ultimately led to the **Constitutional Convention** that began in 1787 and produced the present U.S. Constitution.

During the Constitutional Convention, there was much debate regarding the scope of federal power. Alexander Hamilton pushed for a broad definition of federal power, arguing that Congress should be given the "power to pass all laws which [it] shall judge necessary to the common defense and general welfare of the Union." Others argued for a more limited and defined enumeration of federal powers. Framing the debate was the recognition that to the extent that the states granted more power to the federal government, they reduced the scope of their own powers. Even though the states were reluctant to cede too much power to the federal government, a majority of delegates recognized that the new Constitution must create a stronger federal government.

The Framers ultimately agreed to create a federal government of broader authority. However, instead of giving Congress the power to legislate on any matter that it viewed as necessary or appropriate, the Framers created a government of limited **enumerated powers** (the idea that government has only those powers that are enumerated in the Constitution). Article I, Section 8, provides that this section gives Congress "[a]ll legislative powers herein granted. . . ." The concept of limited powers is also reflected in the Tenth Amendment, which provides that "[t]he powers not delegated to the United States by the Constitution, nor prohibited to it by the States, are reserved to the States respectively, or to the people."

Article I, Section 8, provides Congress with a variety of **explicit powers** (powers specifically listed in the Constitution). Included among the 18 paragraphs of enumerated powers are the right to borrow money; to establish uniform rules on naturalization and bankruptcy; to coin money; to provide punishment for counterfeiting, to establish post offices and roads; to regulate commerce among the several states, as well as with foreign nations and Indian tribes; to provide for the protection of scientists and artists through rules governing rights to writings and discoveries; to provide and maintain a navy; to raise and support armies; and to define and punish piracies. Other provisions of the Constitution grant other powers to Congress, including the power to create lower federal courts,[1] to regulate the appellate jurisdiction of the Supreme Court,[2] to define the crime of treason,[3] to stipulate the procedures for providing full faith and credit to the laws and judgments of the states,[4] to admit new states to the Union,[5] and to regulate U.S. territories and properties.[6] In addition, various amendments give Congress the power to abolish slavery,[7] to prohibit discrimination on the basis of race in voting,[8] as well as to do other things.[9]

U.S. Capitol Building

Given the Constitution's plan of enumerated powers, two separate and distinct questions arise in congressional power cases. First, does Congress have the power to pass a given piece of legislation? In other words, does the planned action fit within one of the enumerated powers or the implications that arise from those powers? Second, does the law violate a limitation on that authority (*e.g.*, free speech or equal protection)? By contrast, when a state enacts a law, federal courts do not tend to ask whether the state legislature has the power to enact the law. They do inquire whether the state has transgressed a limitation on its power. In other words, as a general rule, federal courts tend to assume that a state's police powers provide it with the power to pass general legislation.

F   A   Q

Q: Why do we only ask the latter question — whether the enactment violates a limitation — when a state enacts legislation?

A: At the constitutional convention, the Framers decided to create a federal system. Except to the extent that the Constitution conveyed power to the federal government, the states (or the people) retained that power. As a result, it is assumed that the states have the power to pass legislation, and we simply inquire whether they have violated a limitation on that power.

B. The Necessary and Proper Clause

One of the most important enumerated powers is found in Article I, Section 8, paragraph 18. The **Necessary and Proper Clause** provides that Congress shall have the power to "make all Laws which shall be necessary and proper for carrying into Execution the foregoing Powers, and all other Powers vested by this Constitution in the Government of the United States, or in any Department of Officer thereof."

The Necessary and Proper Clause is not a stand-alone power. Rather, it expands the enumerated powers. For example, since Article I, Section 8, explicitly gives Congress the power to "provide and maintain a Navy," paragraph 18 allows Congress to do those things that are "necessary and proper" to the maintenance of a navy.

Sidebar

ASCERTAINING THE FRAMERS' INTENT

Although both Jefferson and Hamilton played key roles in the founding of the country, they disagreed about how to interpret sections of the Constitution. If two such contemporaries could not agree, how then do modern constitutional judges and scholars settle the debate about how to ascertain the Framers' views regarding the meaning and interpretation of the Constitution? Most commentators reject the notion of the "Framers' Intent" on the theory that it is difficult, if not impossible, to ascertain. In searching for that intent, do we consider only the views of those who participated in writing the Constitution, or should we consider the views of those who signed it? Alternatively, or in addition, should we focus on those who participated in the ratification process? Of course, the process of ascertaining intent is hampered by the absence of good records, or votes, regarding the meaning of particular provisions. That is part of the reason that some emphasize contemporary documents such as the *Federalist* papers. The difficulty is that such documents may present only one side. As we see from Jefferson's disagreement with Hamilton regarding the meaning of the Necessary and Proper Clause, even those who were present at the time can disagree regarding the meaning and interpretation of clauses in the U.S. Constitution. Nevertheless, interpreters still draw conclusions regarding the intended meaning of constitutional provisions. This focus on historical intent is necessitated by the fact that constitutional interpretation involves the construction of a historical document. In that task, the justices justifiably focus on interpretive guideposts in the language of the Constitution, as well as in historical evidence.

Federal Reserve Board

There has been much debate regarding the proper interpretation of the Necessary and Proper Clause. Thomas Jefferson, who argued for a strict construction of the clause, believed that it should be interpreted to mean that Congress is authorized to do only those things that are "absolutely necessary" to the enumerated powers. For example, in interpreting the clause authorizing Congress to provide for and maintain a navy, Congress could do only those things that were "absolutely necessary" to the provision and maintenance of a navy. Alexander Hamilton, by contrast, argued for a broader construction that would interpret the clause as giving Congress the authority to do those things that are "helpful" or "convenient" to the enumerated powers. Under Hamilton's interpretation, Congress could do anything that was "helpful" or "convenient" to the provision and maintenance of a navy.

McCulloch v. Maryland[10] is the most important judicial decision on the meaning of the Necessary and Proper Clause. The case arose during the early nineteenth century during a period of economic upheaval. Some believed that the Bank of the United States had contributed to the upheaval by encouraging a speculative boom through the availability of easy credit. As a result, there was a (failed) movement to revoke the bank's charter. The case involved a Maryland statute that taxed the operations of all banks that had not been chartered by the state itself. The Bank of the United States, which had been chartered by Congress and was owned by the federal government, refused to pay the tax, arguing that the state did not have the power to tax an instrumentality of the federal government. In a landmark decision by Chief Justice Marshall, the Court struck down the tax. The Court concluded that Congress had the power to create a bank, even though the Constitution did not explicitly provide for the establishment of a bank.

In a sweeping opinion, Marshall adopted a broad interpretation to constitutional interpretation. In doing so, he emphasized that a constitution cannot detail all powers of government and that the nature of a constitution requires "that only its great outlines should be marked, its important objects designated, and the minor ingredients which compose those objects, be deduced from the nature of the objects themselves." Marshall finished this argument with a flourish: "[W]e must never forget that it is a constitution we are expounding." In other words, because the Constitution sets forth broad principles, it cannot contain the detail of a legal code. Predictably, Marshall rejected a narrow interpretation of the Necessary and Proper Clause. Instead of requiring that a proposed governmental action be "indispensable" to the express powers, he adopted a construction that required that a proposed action be merely "convenient, or useful, or essential" to an enumerated power.

In deciding whether the United States could create a bank, the Court recognized that the Constitution does not explicitly provide for a federal bank. However, the Court emphasized that the Constitution gives the federal government a variety of powers, including the power to lay and collect taxes, to borrow money, to regulate commerce, to declare and conduct a war, and to raise and support armies and navies. The Court held that "a government, intrusted with such ample powers, on the due execution of which the happiness and prosperity of the nation so vitally depends, must also be intrusted with ample means for their execution." In other words, the Court concluded that the means of execution could include the establishment of a bank.

Some argue that even if Article I, Section 8, had not contained a Necessary and Proper Clause, the Court would have been forced to imply one. For example, Madison argued in *Federalist* No. 44: "Had the Constitution been silent on this head, there can be no doubt that all the particular powers requisite as means of executing the general powers would have resulted to the government, by unavoidable implication."

Jefferson's narrow construction of the Necessary and Proper Clause (as requiring that some action be "absolutely necessary" to an explicit power) has some force because if the clause is construed as requiring nothing more than that something be "convenient," it is not clear that the federal government's power has legitimate limits. At one point, Jefferson offered the following example:

> Congress [is] authorized to defend the nation. Ships are necessary for defense; copper is necessary for ships; mines, necessary for copper; a company necessary to work the mines; and who can doubt this reasoning who has ever played at "This is the House that Jack Built."

Sidebar

"[W]E MUST NEVER FORGET THAT IT IS A CONSTITUTION WE ARE EXPOUNDING."

Chief Justice Marshall's sweeping and uplifting language suggests the importance of considering a constitution in context and keeping in mind broad constitutional considerations (*e.g.*, context, as well as pragmatic considerations) in interpreting constitutional language. On the other hand, the statement has not been free of criticism. Justice Frankfurter later argued in a dissenting opinion that "precisely '*because* it is a *constitution* we are expounding,' we ought not to take liberties with it." *National Marine Insurance Co. v. Tidewater Transfer Co.*, 337 U.S. 582, 647 (1949). In addition, Professor Philip Kurland offered the following retort: "[W]henever a judge quotes this passage, you can be sure that the court will be throwing the constitutional text, its history, and its structure to the winds in reaching its conclusion." Philip B. Kurland, *Curia Regis: Some Comments on the Divine Rights of Kings and Courts to Say What the Law Is*, 23 Ariz. L. Rev. 582, 591 (1981).

In later cases, the Court has not always construed the Necessary and Proper Clause so broadly. For example, in *Kansas v. Colorado*,[11] Congress sought to divert water from the Arkansas River to reclaim arid land in Colorado. Although the Constitution does not explicitly empower Congress to divert water or reclaim land, the Constitution does give Congress the power to regulate interstate commerce as well as to regulate navigation. However, the Arkansas River was not navigable in the place where the water diversion occurred, and water was not being diverted to improve navigability. In concluding that Congress had exceeded its authority, the Court emphasized that the "proposition that there are legislative powers affecting the nation as a whole which belong to, although not expressed in the grant of powers, is in direct conflict with the doctrine that this is a government of enumerated powers." In addition, the Court relied on the Tenth Amendment, which the Court viewed as reflecting the Framers' fear that Congress might "attempt to exercise powers which had not been granted." While the Court recognized the government's need to reclaim arid lands, it concluded that "if no such power has been granted, none can be exercised."

While *McCulloch* and *Kansas v. Colorado* accurately represent opposing views of the Necessary and Proper Clause, *McCulloch*'s interpretation has ultimately prevailed. In other words, as Chief Justice Marshall stated in *McCulloch*, "Let the end be legitimate, let it be within the scope of the Constitution, and all means which are appropriate, which are plainly adapted to that end, which are not prohibited, but consistent with the letter and spirit of the Constitution, are constitutional."

C. The Commerce Clause

Article I, Section 8, paragraph 3, contains perhaps the most potent federal power, the **Commerce Clause**: "The Congress shall have Power . . . to regulate Commerce with foreign Nations, and among the several States, and with the Indian Tribes."

The U.S. Constitution differs markedly from the Articles of Confederation in regard to commerce. Under the Articles, the states generally reserved the commerce power to themselves and denied Congress this power. Moreover, although the Articles gave Congress some control over foreign affairs, one provision of the Articles specifically prohibited Congress from entering into treaties limiting the states' power over commerce or their rights to tax imports and exports.

The Articles of Confederation did not provide the foundation for a sound economy. The colonies' trading relationship with England had been ruptured by the Revolution, and the individual states used their powers to protect their own economies at the expense of neighbor states. As a result, there "grew up a conflict of commercial regulations, destructive to the harmony of the States, and fatal to their commercial interests abroad."[12] Many states imposed economic sanctions, including taxes and tariffs, on trade from other states. By 1785-1786, the nation was mired in a recession caused by "a high national debt, increasing trade deficits, and economic infighting."[13]

As the economic situation worsened, many argued that the Articles of Confederation should be amended to give the federal government increased power over commerce. However, not enough states sent delegates to the first meeting. When the delegates finally did meet, they quickly realized that more drastic change was needed, and they called for a subsequent convention to make more sweeping changes. This subsequent convention, which ultimately became known as the Constitutional Convention, began in 1787 and produced our present Constitution and the current version of the Commerce Clause. However, even during the Constitutional Convention, there were some disputes about the scope of federal power and some local jealousies that led to modifications of the constitutional language.[14]

Congress's power over commerce with foreign nations has always been regarded as broad and plenary, and its power over commerce with Indian tribes has been regarded as similarly broad.[15] However, the Framers specifically rejected the idea of granting Congress a general police power, which would have allowed it to pass any legislation appropriate for the health, safety, and welfare of the nation, and opted instead for a system of enumerated powers. As a result, Congress's control over commerce among the several states has been subject to more controversy. Persistent debates have arisen regarding the point at which federal power ends and state power begins. As a result, the courts have been forced to deal with the broad question of whether there are areas of commerce reserved exclusively to the states, as well as whether there are areas where the federal government exercises concurrent authority with the states.

(1) Early Cases

The Constitution does not define the phrase commerce "among the several states." That task was left to the courts — in particular, to the courts in the few cases that arose during the nineteenth century. At the time of the founding, there were relatively clear distinctions between interstate commerce (referring to goods that crossed state lines) as distinguished from manufacturing or agricultural processes, which were regarded as taking place on the local level. Early decisions reflected this distinction, but gradually courts came to realize that the internal commerce of a state could have a substantial effect on interstate commerce.

Unquestionably, the most important decision of that period was *Gibbons v. Ogden*,[16] which offered the Court's first authoritative interpretation of the Commerce Clause. After the New York legislature granted Robert Livingston and Robert Fulton a long-term monopoly to operate steamboats in New York waters, they assigned to Aaron Ogden the exclusive right to run steamships between New York City and Elizabethtown, New Jersey. When Thomas Gibbons was granted a federal license to operate steamboats along a similar route, Ogden sued, claiming that the federal license was invalid. In deciding the case, Chief Justice Marshall discussed the relationship between the states and the federal government, and rejected the notion that the federal government's commerce power should be strictly construed. He concluded that the term *commerce* was not limited to "the interchange of commodities," but instead extended to "intercourse between nations, and parts of nations, in all its branches," and he could not "conceive a system for regulating commerce between nations, which shall exclude all laws concerning navigation, which shall be silent on the admission of the vessels of the one nation into the ports of the other, and be confined to prescribing rules for the conduct of individuals, in the actual employment of buying and selling, or of barter." The commerce power, the court concluded, extends to commerce not only when it is interstate, but wherever it occurs, including within the states.

Gibbons is important because it discusses not only the federal power to regulate commerce but also the states' power to regulate, and the relationship between federal power and state power. In his decision, Marshall conceives the federal power broadly: "This power, like all others vested in Congress, is complete in itself, may be exercised to its utmost extent, and acknowledges no limitations, other than are prescribed in the constitution." But he also recognized that, as to some matters (for example, the power to tax), the federal government and the state governments have concurrent powers. Although the states clearly have the power to pass laws affecting commerce (for example, inspection laws), he viewed this power as affecting a commodity "before it becomes an article of foreign commerce, or of commerce among the States," and he also viewed it as something that "can be most advantageously exercised by the States." In this broad mass, he placed such things as "inspection laws, quarantine laws, health laws of every description, as well as laws for regulating the internal commerce of a State, and those which respect turnpike roads, ferries." In Marshall's view, the Constitution did not vest the federal government with power over such matters. The federal power did not extend to the "purely internal commerce of a State, or to act directly on its system of police." In addition, a state might be free to adopt a measure within the scope of its authority, but as to which Congress has the power to power to regulate, provided that there was no contrary federal legislation.

F   A   Q

Q: In *Gibbons*, Chief Justice Marshall refers to various regulatory issues (*e.g.*, inspection laws, quarantine laws and health laws "of every description") as within the power of the states. Does this mean that the federal government cannot regulate such things?

A: At the time *Gibbons* was decided, the Court (and, indeed, the nation) construed the definition of interstate commerce far more narrowly. For better or for worse, the understanding of commerce has changed considerably over the centuries. As the nature and scope of congressional commerce authority has expanded, under the Court's later decisions, Congress could quite easily assert control over such activities.

Sidebar

THE SUPREMACY CLAUSE

As we shall see when we discuss the negative implications of the Commerce Clause, the Supremacy Clause (used in *Gibbons* to invalidate state action) is ever present in this area of the law. If the Court concludes that congressional legislation is valid and does not offend a limitation on congressional authority, then inconsistent state legislation is invalid. On the other hand, if the federal legislation is invalid (because Congress has exceeded its authority under the Commerce Clause), the state legislation might stand.

As for commerce among the states, Marshall argued for a broad, exclusive view of federal power. Although he was not asked to decide the issue, he posed the question whether the words " 'to regulate' implies in its nature, full power over the thing to be regulated," and he concluded that "it excludes, necessarily, the action of all others that would perform the same operation on the same thing. . . . It produces a uniform whole, which is as much disturbed and deranged by changing what the regulating power designs to leave untouched, as that on which it has operated." Marshall concluded that there "is great force in this argument, and the Court is not satisfied that it has been refuted."

On the facts before it, the *Gibbons* Court found a direct conflict between the New York license and the federal license, and concluded that the Supremacy Clause of the U.S. Constitution required that "the acts of New York must yield to the law of Congress." In other words, not only was the federal license valid, but the New York license was invalid to the extent that it purported to grant exclusivity to the New York license holder.[17]

Gibbons illustrates the importance of the federal commerce power. The decision itself had a significant impact on commerce in New York and the surrounding states.[18] "Shortly after the fourteenth of March, the newspapers of the North carried this item: 'Yesterday the Steamboat *United States*, [entered] New York in triumph, with streamers flying, and a large company of passengers exulting in the decision of the United States Supreme Court against the New York monopoly. She fired a salute which was loudly returned by huzzas from the wharves.' "[19] "A representative Southern paper spoke of 'the immense public advantages that flow[ed] from the decision. The fare in the steamboats that ply between New York and New Haven has been reduced from five to three dollars.' "[20] "Shortly over a year after the decision, the *Niles Register* reported that the number of steamboats plying from New York had increased from six to forty-three."[21] As a result, "[t]he chief importance of the case in the eyes of the public of that day was its effect in shattering the great monopoly against which they had been struggling for fifteen years."[22]

Other nineteenth-century decisions took a similarly expansive view of Congress's commerce power. *The Daniel Ball*[23] involved a steamer that traveled routes wholly within the State of Michigan. The vessel carried merchandise being transported to or from other states and was regulated by a federal safety regulation. In an opinion by Justice Field, the Court concluded that Congress had the power to impose the regulation:

> [W]e are unable to draw any clear and distinct line between the authority of Congress to regulate an agency employed in commerce between the States, when that agency extends through two or more States, and when it is confined in its action entirely within the limits of a single State. If its authority does not extend to an agency in such commerce, when that agency is confined within the limits of a State, its entire authority over interstate commerce may be defeated.

The Court, however, did not always construe the Commerce Clause broadly during the nineteenth century. Nor did it develop definitive standards for evaluating Commerce Clause challenges. *Paul v. Virginia*[24] involved a Virginia statute that discriminated against insurance companies incorporated in other states. The law was challenged as repugnant to the federal commerce power. In an opinion by Justice Field, the Court rejected the challenge concluding that an insurance policy is not "a transaction of commerce," and therefore not within the scope of the federal commerce power. Likewise, in *Kidd v. Pearson*,[25] the Court upheld an Iowa statute that prohibited the manufacture of liquor as applied to an Iowa company that sold all of its product in other states. The Court noted that Congress's power does not extend to "the purely internal domestic commerce of a state, which is carried on between man and man within a state or between different parts of the same state." The Court rejected the proposition that the states were deprived of the authority to regulate the manufacture of domestic products simply because those products may ultimately enter interstate commerce.

(2) Early Twentieth-Century Cases

By the end of the nineteenth century, the economy was in a period of dramatic and rapid transition as it shifted from a largely agrarian society to an industrial one. Industrialization produced profound changes. As railroads and eventually cars came into being, people and goods began to move more freely across state borders. Although many commercial problems may have been local in nature at one time, the mobility of society meant that more problems were becoming national in scope and impact. Because of these changes, Congress began to assume a more active regulatory role, passing the Interstate Commerce Act, the Sherman Antitrust Act, and a host of other legislation, and the Court was forced to confront difficult questions regarding the scope of Congress's power. It did so in several cases decided early in the twentieth century. In the process, the Court developed several important Commerce Clause principles that continue to apply today.

One foundational principle, articulated in *Champion v. Ames*[26] (also known as the *Lottery Case*), is that Congress has broad authority to ban items from interstate commerce. *Champion* involved a challenge to a statute that made it illegal to transport lottery tickets across state lines on the basis that the carrying of lottery tickets from one state to another did not constitute "commerce among the states." The Court concluded that lottery tickets are items of commerce because they provide a prize to the winner and therefore have "real or substantial value." In addition, the Court held that Congress's power included not only the power to regulate commerce, but also the power to prohibit items from commerce, because Congress's power "to regulate commerce among the states is plenary, is complete in itself, and is subject to no limitations except such as may be found in the Constitution." The Court rejected claims that Congress had violated the reserved power of the states under the Tenth Amendment, finding that the power to regulate commerce has "been expressly delegated to Congress." Chief Justice Fuller dissented, arguing that Congress had the power only to prohibit items (for example, diseased animals and infected goods) that are "in themselves injurious to the transaction of interstate commerce," and he argued that lottery tickets cannot "communicate bad principles by contact."

F A Q

Q: So, does the *Lottery Case* give Congress broad authority to ban items from interstate commerce (*e.g.*, machine guns, heroin, diseased animals)?

A: Yes, the *Lottery Case,* and subsequent interpretations of that case, stand for the broad proposition that Congress has discretion to ban items from the channels of interstate commerce.

Early twentieth-century cases also established the proposition that Congress may regulate the internal commerce of a state provided that there is a close and substantial relationship to interstate commerce. In one important case, *Houston, East & West Texas Railway Co. v. United States*,[27] the Court upheld an Interstate Commerce Commission (ICC) decision holding that interstate railroad rates from Shreveport, Louisiana, to named Texas points were unreasonable, and establishing maximum rates for this traffic that were the same as certain intrastate Texas rates. In rendering its decision, the ICC found that the intrastate situation involved "substantially similar conditions and circumstances" as the interstate situation, and that the carriers were giving an unlawful preference to intrastate interests in the form of lower rates. Plaintiffs challenged the order on the basis that the ICC did not have the power to equalize interstate and intrastate rates. The Court disagreed, noting that Congress has the power to enact "all appropriate legislation" for the "protection and advancement" of interstate commerce, and also has the power to adopt measures "to promote its growth and insure its safety" and "to foster, protect, control, and restrain" it. Congress also has the power to control intrastate commerce that has "such a close and substantial relation to interstate traffic that the control is essential or appropriate to the security of that traffic, to the efficiency of the interstate service, and to the maintenance of conditions under which interstate commerce may be conducted upon fair terms and without molestation or hindrance." Although Congress did not have the power to regulate intrastate commerce per se, it did "possess the power to foster and protect interstate commerce, and to take all measures necessary or appropriate to that end, although intrastate transactions of interstate carriers may thereby be controlled." The Court concluded that a carrier's "unjust discrimination" against interstate rates despite substantially similar conditions of traffic constitutes an "evil" that inflicts injury on commerce that Congress has the power to prevent.

Although the *Lottery Case* and *Houston, East & West Texas Railway Co.* both involved expansive interpretations of federal power, not all decisions during this period adopted such a broad view. One of the most famous decisions adopting a restrictive view of federal power was *Hammer v. Dagenhart*.[28] That case involved Congress's attempt to prohibit the interstate shipment of goods produced within the prior 30 days by children under the age of 14, or by children between the ages of 14 and 16 years who have worked more than 8 hours in any day, or more than 6 days in any week, or after the hour of 7:00 P.M., or before the hour of 6:00 A.M. The Court rejected the notion that *Champion* gave Congress plenary authority to prohibit the interstate shipment of goods, concluding that the statute before it did "not regulate transportation among the states," but simply sought "to standardize the ages at which children may be employed in mining and manufacturing within the states." The Court was troubled by the federal law because the goods produced by the child labor were "themselves harmless," and the production by children was over before the goods were shipped. In rejecting the federal law, the Court held that the making of goods is not commerce, and the mere fact that goods "are to be afterwards shipped, or used in interstate commerce, [does not] make their production a part thereof." Instead, the Court regarded "production" as a matter for local regulation and the power to regulate child labor as within the jurisdiction of the states under the Tenth Amendment. "In interpreting the Constitution it must never be forgotten that the nation is made up of states to which are entrusted the powers of local government. And to them and to the people the powers not expressly delegated to the national government are reserved." Justice Holmes dissented, arguing that the "statute confines itself to prohibiting the carriage of certain goods in interstate or foreign commerce." Relying on the *Lottery Case*, he argued that "Congress is given power to regulate such commerce in unqualified terms."

(3) The Constitutional Crisis

In 1929, the stock market crashed. Following the crash, the country settled into a prolonged period of economic depression, and President Franklin D. Roosevelt was elected in 1932 on the promise of a New Deal. The situation facing Roosevelt and the country was grim. In 1931, the year before he was elected, more than 2,000 banks had failed.[29] By the winter of 1932-1933, shortly before FDR assumed office, "one-fourth of the nation's work force was unemployed" and the price of wheat had dropped by "nearly 90 percent."[30] Industrial output had fallen by 60 percent.[31]

FDR took office demanding "action, and action now." One of his first acts was to call an extraordinary session of Congress to begin five days after his inauguration.

During this session, the House passed 11 major bills after only 40 hours of debate. During his first 100 days, Roosevelt managed to push through Congress a host of bills regulating financial markets, creating federal works programs, and regulating prices and wages. Included were the Agricultural Adjustment Act, the Bituminous Coal Act, the Emergency Farm Mortgage Act, the Farm Relief Act, the National Industrial Recovery Act, the Railway Pension Act, and the Truth-in-Securities Act. These acts were hostilely received by the federal courts.

In 1936, the Court decided *Carter v. Carter Coal Co.*,[32] which presented a direct challenge to one New Deal statute, the Bituminous Coal Conservation Act of 1935. That act was designed to stabilize the coal-mining industry and prevent labor strife that might interfere with coal production. The act, which imposed a 15 percent excise tax on the sale of coal from a mine not operated in compliance with the act (which included minimum price provisions), was similar to *Dagenhart* because it imposed labor conditions, including a requirement that employees be given the right to organize and bargain collectively. In striking down the act, the Court found that Congress was trying to regulate the purely internal commerce of a state. The Court found that "two distinct and separate activities" were involved. The Court regarded the "manufacture" of goods as a "purely local" activity and as subject to regulation only by the states. If the manufactured goods are subsequently shipped in interstate commerce, they then become subject to regulation by Congress. However, in the Court's view, the mere fact that manufactured products may ultimately move in interstate commerce does not mean that the manufacture itself involves interstate commerce: "The employment of men, the fixing of their wages, hours of labor, and working conditions, the bargaining in respect of these things — whether carried on separately or collectively — each and all constitute intercourse for the purposes of production, not of trade." While the Court admitted that the production process "has some effect upon interstate commerce," the Court drew a distinction between commerce that has a direct effect on interstate commerce and commerce that has only an indirect effect. If the federal power were deemed to reach commerce that had an indirect effect, then "the federal authority would embrace practically all the activities of the people, and the authority of the state over its domestic concerns would exist only by sufferance of the federal government." The Court viewed the distinction between a direct effect and an indirect effect as turning not on "the magnitude of either the cause or the effect, but entirely upon the manner in which the effect has been brought about." Although the Court did not quarrel with the notion that the evils Congress sought to regulate were important, it held that "the evils are all local evils over which the federal government has no legislative control. . . . The employees are not engaged in or about commerce, but exclusively in producing a commodity. . . . Such effect as they may have upon commerce, however extensive it may be, is secondary and indirect."

Carter involved only one of many setbacks for FDR's New Deal. The Court also struck down the Railroad Retirement Act of 1934,[33] the National Industrial Recovery Act,[34] and the Agricultural Adjustment Act of 1933.[35] In addition to viewing the Commerce Clause restrictively, the Court also struck laws down based on the unlawful delegation doctrine. For example, in *Panama Refining Co. v. Ryan*,[36] the Court struck down Section 9(c) of the National Industrial Recovery Act (NIRA) of 1933 because it did not provide defined standards by which the president was expected to exercise his discretion to prohibit so-called hot oil. In other words, the Court concluded that Congress had improperly delegated its legislative authority. Likewise, in *A. L. A. Schechter Poultry Corp. v. United States*,[37] the Court struck down other sections of the NIRA on unlawful delegation grounds. Even though not all decisions during this period restrictively construed the scope of congressional power,[38] the Court did strike down four major pieces of federal legislation in a two-year time frame, and the federal courts issued hundreds of injunctions against New Deal legislation.

Commerce Clause Interpretation at the Time of *Carter Coal*

Activity	Authority to Regulate
Interstate commerce	Congress (and, to a lesser extent, the states)
Means of production	States
Stream of commerce	Congress (and, to a lesser extent, the states)
Activities that "directly" affect commerce	Congress (and, to a lesser extent, the states)
Activities that "indirectly" affect commerce	States

Decisions like *Panama Refining* and *Schechter*, coupled with the Court's restrictive interpretation of the Commerce Clause in cases like *Carter Coal Co.*, angered President Roosevelt, who viewed the Court as an obstacle to his reform program. At the time, several major pieces of legislation had not been ruled on by the courts, including the National Labor Relations Act, the Social Security Act, and the Public Utility Holding Act. Despite a few decisions upholding New Deal legislation,[39] President Roosevelt had legitimate reasons for concern about whether the Court would strike them down too.

Following his landslide reelection victory in the 1936 elections, President Roosevelt proposed his now infamous Court-packing plan, which would have altered the Court's membership (and, presumably, its decisions) by adding additional members to the Court.[40] The plan provided that when a judge or justice of any federal court reached the age of 70 without retiring, a new member could be appointed by the president. The appointment would be made in the manner prescribed by the Constitution: nomination by the president with confirmation by the Senate.[41] Since 6 justices were age 70 or older, if the plan had passed, the Court's membership would have expanded to a maximum of 15 members, giving Roosevelt the chance to obtain a majority of members sympathetic to his position.

Despite Roosevelt's popularity and the popularity of his New Deal, many opposed the legislation. Everyone agreed that Congress was constitutionally authorized to control the number of Supreme Court justices, as well as that the number of justices had not remained static at nine. While the first Judiciary Act provided for six justices (including the chief justice),[42] later acts provided for as few as five justices[43] or as many as nine.[44] In the mid-1860s, the number of justices was set at six.[45] Nevertheless, many felt that it was inappropriate for FDR to manipulate the Court's membership in an effort to control the Court's decisions.

F   A   Q

Q: If the Court-packing plan had been enacted, how could President Roosevelt have been sure that his new appointees would have changed the course of the Court's jurisprudence on Commerce Clause issues?

A: He couldn't really be sure. One of the great strengths (as well as a potential weakness) of the U.S. Supreme Court and the federal judiciary generally is that the justices are given life tenure as well as guarantees against salary reductions. As a result, when an individual is appointed to the Court, he or she can become quite independent. There are several prominent examples (for example, former Chief Justice Earl Warren) of justices who decided cases differently on the bench than one might have predicted at the time of their appointments. As a result, even if President Roosevelt had been able to make six new appointments to the Court, he had no guarantee that these justices would have decided cases in the manner he preferred. However, with six appointments at his disposal, the odds were good that President Roosevelt could have shifted the balance of the Court (which was split 5-4) in his favor.

Sidebar

OTHER METHODS FOR CONTROLLING THE COURT

In the seven or so decades since the failure of the Court-packing plan, there have been no comparable attempts to pack the Court by altering its size. However, in some instances, presidents have tried to shift the Court's decisions in particular areas of the law through the appointments process. For example, President Nixon attempted to shift, and did shift (with the help of later presidents and their appointments), the Court's criminal procedure jurisprudence through his appointments. Other presidents, desirous of overruling *Roe v. Wade* (the privacy decision that legalized abortion), have been somewhat less successful. In later decisions, the Court has contracted *Roe's* scope and sustained restrictions on abortion, but has not outright overruled that decision.

Interestingly, the Court-packing plan never came to a vote. While the legislation was pending, the Court decided *West Coast Hotel Co. v. Parrish*[46] and *NLRB v. Jones & Laughlin Steel Corp.*[47] *Jones & Laughlin* involved the National Labor Relations Board's holding that a company had engaged in an unfair labor practice by discharging employees in order to interfere with their union organizing activities, and an NLRB order requiring the company to cease and desist from such practices, to offer reinstatement to ten of the employees named, to make good their losses in pay, and to post notices that it would not discharge or discriminate against members or prospective members of the union. The company challenged the order, claiming that federal government did not have the power to regulate production employees and that the National Labor Relations Act invaded the reserved powers of the states under the Tenth Amendment. In rejecting the challenge, the Court noted that the company's Pennsylvania plants drew raw materials from four surrounding states and distributed finished product all over the nation. The Court construed Congress's power as extending to acts "which directly burden or obstruct interstate or foreign commerce, or its free flow," and concluded that Congress's power "is not limited to transactions which can be deemed to be an essential part of a 'flow' of interstate or foreign commerce." Harkening back to its earlier precedent, the Court concluded that Congress has the power to regulate intrastate activities that "have such a close and substantial relation to interstate commerce that their control is essential or appropriate to protect that commerce from burdens and obstructions." While the Court concluded that Congress could not reach intrastate activities that were so "indirect and remote" as to "effectually obliterate the distinction between what is national and what is local and create a completely centralized government," the Court found that the question was one of degree. Moreover, the Court held that the distinction between production and commerce was not determinative, and that the critical question is the extent of the effect on interstate commerce. The Court found that a labor stoppage in the coal industry "would have a most serious effect upon interstate commerce" and the Court considered it "idle to say that the effect would be indirect or remote" because the coal industry was organized on a national scale and its relationship to interstate commerce is a dominant factor in its activities. Justice McReynolds, joined by three other justices, dissented, arguing that the Court had departed from its earlier precedents and that any effect on commerce here was indirect and remote.

> ### Sidebar
>
> **THE SWITCH IN TIME . . .**
>
> Justice Robert's switch in positions has been jokingly referred to as "the switch in time that saved nine."

The Court's change in approach was due to a shift in position by Justice Roberts. While he voted to strike down federal action in *Carter Coal*, in the process affirming the production-commerce distinction, he voted to sustain governmental action in *Jones & Laughlin*, thus rejecting that distinction.

Following *Jones & Laughlin*, support for the Court-packing plan waned. Senator Joseph Robinson developed a modified plan that appeared to have a good chance of passage, but he died suddenly of a heart attack and the plan was voted down.[48]

Franklin Delano Roosevelt

Commerce Clause Interpretation: Post-Constitutional Crisis Cases	
Activity	**Authority to Regulate**
Interstate commerce	Congress (and, to a lesser extent, the states)
Manufacturing	Congress (and perhaps the states)
Activities with an "indirect" effect on interstate commerce	Congress (and perhaps the states)
Commerce that has a "close and substantial" relationship to interstate commerce	Congress (and perhaps the states)

F   A   Q

Q: The prior graph indicates that, in some areas (*e.g.*, manufacturing, activities with an "indirect" effect on interstate commerce, and commerce that has a "close and substantial" relationship to interstate commerce), "Congress (and perhaps the states)" have jurisdiction over these issues. How can *both* the Congress and the states have jurisdiction over an issue?

A: As we shall see, there are instances when Congress has the power to regulate in an area, but congressional power is "dormant" or unexercised. In these situations, the federal courts have sometimes allowed the states to exercise regulatory power. In a later chapter, we will examine the circumstances under which the states may do so.

(4) Post-switch Expansion of Federal Power: A Half-Century of Deference

Jones & Laughlin ushered in a half-century during which the Court upheld essentially every assertion of congressional power under the Commerce Clause, and congressional power (and with it, federal power) expanded dramatically. During this period, Congress could use any of several bases for imposing regulations or restrictions. First, Congress has the power to "regulate the channels of interstate commerce."[49] In addition, Congress could regulate the instrumentalities of interstate commerce.[50] Finally, Congress could regulate intrastate activities that have a "substantial effect" on interstate commerce.[51]

Following the bruising battle over the Court-packing plan, the Court assumed an extraordinarily deferential attitude toward congressional assertions of power under the Commerce Clause. In other words, the Court was inclined to accept and uphold congressional actions. In addition, the Court decisively retreated from the more active judicial review evident in decisions like *Hammer v. Dagenhart* and *Carter Coal*. By and large, the Court tended to apply a "rational basis" standard to congressional enactments under the Commerce Clause.

F   A   Q

Q: What is "rational basis" review?

A: The courts tend to apply different review standards in different types of cases. "Rational basis" review, in theory, provides only a minimal level of review. The legislation must be supported only by a "rational" end, and the means chosen to achieve that end must also be rational. *See Heart of Atlanta Motel, Inc. v. United States*, 379 U.S. 241 (1964). Often, but not always, when rational basis review is applicable, the legislation is upheld. By contrast, the most rigorous level of review is "strict scrutiny," which requires proof that the legislation is supported by a "compelling" or "overriding" governmental interest and that the legislation is narrowly tailored to achieve that objective. Often, but again not always, the Court's decision to apply strict scrutiny standard of review is fatal to the validity of legislation. *See R.A.V. v. City of St. Paul*, 505 U.S. 377 (1992). In later chapters, we will see that the Court also applies other, intermediate, standards of review.[52]

Illustrative of the Court's post-1936 approach is the holding in *United States v. Darby*,[53] which upheld a statute prohibiting the interstate shipment of lumber manufactured by employees whose wages were less than a prescribed minimum or whose weekly hours of labor at that wage were greater than a prescribed maximum. The statute also required employers to maintain records showing the hours worked each day and week by each employee. In other words, the statute was similar to statutes that had been invalidated prior to 1936. In upholding the act, the Court held that since Congress has the power to prescribe rules governing interstate commerce, it also has the power to impose "regulations which aid, foster and protect the commerce" as well as rules which prohibit it. In other words, Congress could indirectly regulate the wages of employees who manufactured lumber. In the Court's view, Congress has the power to regulate intrastate activities which "so affect interstate commerce" as to "make regulation of them appropriate means to the attainment of a legitimate end, the exercise of the granted power of Congress to regulate interstate commerce." In addition, the Court expressed **deference** (a willingness to accept rather than to second-guess) to congressional judgments on the need to regulate manufacture, recognizing that "competition by a small part may affect the whole and that the total effect of the competition of many small producers may be great." Finally, the Court explicitly repudiated *Hammer v. Dagenhart*, noting that it "was a departure from the principles which have prevailed in the interpretation of the commerce clause both before and since the decision." In *Darby*, the Court no longer regarded the Tenth Amendment as an independent limitation on federal power and simply dismissed it as a "truism."

F A Q

Q: What did the *Darby* Court mean by saying that the Tenth Amendment is a "truism"?

A: In prior decisions such as *Hammer* and *Carter Coal*, the Court had regarded the Tenth Amendment as an independent limitation on the scope of Congress's commerce power. In other words, in construing the Constitution, a reviewing court must not only interpret the Commerce Clause (to see whether Congress can reach a particular activity), it must also construe the Tenth Amendment to see whether it precludes the legislation. In saying that the Tenth Amendment is a truism, the *Darby* Court focused only on the congressional enactment. In other words, it attempted to determine whether Congress was able to reach the regulated activity under one of its enumerated powers. If so, then the Tenth Amendment was not offended. Or, as the Court said, the Tenth Amendment is regarded as simply "declaratory of the relationship between the national and state governments as it had been established by the Constitution before the amendment or that its purpose was other than to allay fears that the new national government might seek to exercise powers not granted, and that the states might not be able to exercise fully their reserved powers." Only if Congress is found to have exceeded its authority under the Constitution does the Tenth Amendment potentially come into play. But, in that situation, the Tenth Amendment is unneeded since the Court has already concluded that Congress has exceeded its authority.

In the post-1936 era, the Court adopted increasingly expansive views of the Commerce Clause and of the scope of congressional authority. Perhaps the Court's most expansive interpretation of the Commerce Clause was rendered in *Wickard v. Filburn*,[54] which upheld a marketing penalty imposed under amendments to the Agricultural Adjustment Act of 1938. Under that act, Congress sought to control the volume of wheat in an effort to avoid surpluses, shortages, and fluctuations in prices. To accomplish these objectives, the act authorized the secretary of agriculture to proclaim a national acreage allotment for wheat and to apportion that allotment among states, counties, and individual farms. The case involved the government's attempt to apply the act to a small Ohio farm that produced a small crop of winter wheat, part of which was sold and the remainder of which was used for seeding, home consumption, or livestock feeding. When plaintiff produced wheat in excess of his allotment, he was subjected to a penalty of 49 cents a bushel. Plaintiff challenged the act, claiming that Congress did not have the power to regulate wheat raised on his own farm for home consumption. In a unanimous decision, the Court disagreed, concluding that plaintiff's activities had a "close and substantial relation to interstate traffic" so that "control is essential or appropriate to the security of that traffic, to the efficiency of the interstate service, and to the maintenance of the conditions under which interstate commerce may be conducted upon fair terms and without molestation or hindrance." Noting that homegrown wheat production can affect the overall market, the Court concluded that, while plaintiff's own contribution to the demand for wheat might be regarded as "trivial," Congress could regulate his production because "his contribution, taken together with that of many others similarly situated, is far from trivial." In other words, when plaintiff's activities were considered in the aggregate with others producing wheat for home consumption, the net effect was a significant impact on interstate commerce.

Two years later, in *United States v. South-Eastern Underwriters Assn.*,[55] the Court continued its expansive interpretation of the Commerce Clause by overturning *Paul v. Virginia*, which had held that insurance policies do not constitute commerce within the meaning of the Commerce Clause. In *South-Eastern*, appellees were indicted for violations of the Sherman Act and argued that the Sherman Act could not be applied to them because "the business of fire insurance is not commerce." The Court disagreed:

> [I]t would indeed be difficult now to hold that no activities of any insurance company can ever constitute interstate commerce so as to make it subject to such regulation; — activities which, as part of the conduct of a legitimate and useful commercial enterprise, may embrace integrated operations in many states and involve the transmission of great quantities of money, documents, and communications across dozens of state lines.

F A Q

Q: **If the decisions in *Darby* and *Wickard* are construed broadly, are there any activities that Congress is unable to reach or regulate under its Commerce Clause power?**

A: *Darby* and *Wickard* provide Congress with extremely broad authority to reach and regulate the internal commerce of a state. After all, if Congress can reach homegrown wheat that is used on the farm where it is grown because it is regarded as having a "close and substantial" effect on interstate commerce, it would be difficult to argue that virtually any commercial activity (when considered in the "aggregate") does not have a close and substantial effect on interstate commerce or that there are activities that Congress simply cannot reach.

In the wake of decisions like *Darby* and *Wickard*, the federal government's power over the U.S. economy increased dramatically. The federal government began to assert control over such diverse matters as consumer safety, energy, agriculture, aviation travel, civil rights, drugs, labor, securities, and banking.

Civil Rights Legislation. One area where the breadth of Congress's commerce power has been evident is in the area of civil rights. In earlier decisions, such as the *Civil Rights Cases*,[56] the Court had rebuffed Congress's attempts to premise civil rights legislation on the Fourteenth Amendment. After 1936, the Court has upheld various statutes imposing antidiscrimination provisions. For example, in *Heart of Atlanta Motel, Inc. v. United States*,[57] the Court upheld Title II of the Civil Rights Act of 1964, which prohibited discrimination on the basis of race, color, religion, or national origin in the use of goods, services, facilities, privileges, advantages, and accommodations, as applied to a hotel located in downtown Atlanta near two major interstates. Approximately 75 percent of the hotel's guests came from out of state, and the hotel advertised on in-state billboards and highway signs and in national magazines. The Court held that Congress did not exceed the scope of its Commerce Clause power, noting that racial discrimination places "burdens on interstate commerce" by making it difficult for affected individuals to find transient accommodations. Congress could regulate discrimination in hotels because it may regulate the "local incidents" of commerce, "including local activities in both the States of origin and destination, which might have a substantial and harmful effect upon that commerce."

Heart of Atlanta was not an isolated decision. It was followed and affirmed by *Katzenbach v. McClung*,[58] a case that upheld the Civil Rights Act of 1964 as applied to a family-owned restaurant in Alabama that specialized in barbecued meats and homemade pies. The restaurant catered to a family and white-collar trade, but

Sidebar

THE RELATIONSHIP BETWEEN CIVIL RIGHTS AND COMMERCE

The Civil Rights Act of 1964 and the *Heart of Atlanta* and *Katzenbach* decisions radically transformed the United States. Because of that act, it became possible for African Americans to move freely in interstate commerce and to avail themselves of the instrumentalities of interstate commerce (not only trains and planes, but also hotels, motels, and restaurants) free of discrimination.

offered only a take-out service for blacks. The business employed 36 persons, two-thirds of whom were black, and had seating for more than 200. In upholding the law, the Court emphasized Congress was trying to deal with "the burdens placed on interstate commerce by racial discrimination in restaurants" as evidenced by the fact that blacks spent far less per capita on restaurants in "areas where discrimination is widely practiced." Relying on *Heart of Atlanta*, the Court reaffirmed the notion that Congress's commerce power "extends to those activities intrastate which so affect interstate commerce, or the exertion of the power of Congress over it, as to make regulation of them appropriate means to the attainment of a legitimate end, the effective execution of the granted power to regulate interstate commerce." Applying a rational basis standard, the Court affirmed Congress's conclusion "that racial discrimination in restaurants had a direct and adverse effect on the free flow of interstate commerce."

Federal Criminal Laws. In the post–*Jones & Laughlin* era, Congress has used its Commerce Clause authority to enact an array of federal criminal statutes. Historically, most general criminal legislation (for crimes like murder, robbery, rape, or burglary) was enacted by the states with the federal government enacting more limited federal crimes prohibiting offenses against the United States (for example, filing a false tax return). However, Congress also passed (and the courts upheld) criminal statutes prohibiting activities that crossed state lines (for example, the *Lottery Case* in which Congress prohibited the interstate transportation of lottery tickets), including the Mann Act (which prohibited the interstate transportation of women for immoral purposes), the Dyer Act (which prohibited the interstate transportation of stolen vehicles), and the Lindbergh Act (which prohibited kidnappings related to interstate commerce).

Following *Jones & Lauglin*, Congress began to pass more general criminal legislation with a more attenuated connection to interstate commerce. For example, *Perez v. United States*[59] upheld the Consumer Credit Protection Act, which made it illegal to engage in "extortionate credit transactions," which Congress defined as deals characterized by the use or threat of the use of "violence or other criminal means" in enforcement. When the law was applied to a "loan shark," he claimed that Congress had exceeded its power under the Commerce Clause. Relying on *Darby* and *Wickard*, the Court upheld the law, noting that purely intrastate extortionate transactions "may in the judgment of Congress affect interstate commerce." The evidence showed that extortion was a $350 million per year business, and that

> loan sharks serve as a source of funds to bookmakers, narcotics dealers, and other racketeers; that victims of the racket include all classes, rich and poor, businessmen and laborers; that the victims are often coerced into the commission of criminal acts in order to repay their loans; that through loan sharking the organized underworld has obtained control of legitimate businesses, including securities brokerages and banks which are then exploited; and that "[e]ven where extortionate credit transactions are purely intrastate in character, they nevertheless directly affect interstate and foreign commerce."

Justice Stewart dissented:

> [U]nder the statute before us a man can be convicted without any proof of interstate movement, of the use of the facilities of interstate commerce, or of facts showing that his conduct affected interstate commerce. [T]he Framers of the Constitution never

intended that the National Government might define as a crime and prosecute such wholly local activity through the enactment of federal criminal laws.

Despite the holding in *Perez*, the scope of Congress's authority to pass criminal legislation has been trimmed somewhat in the last decade. We will examine those issues in the next section when we examine the most recent cases.

Environmental and Regulatory Legislation. The Court's expansive interpretation of the Commerce Clause after the 1930s brought with it dramatic growth in the size of the federal government and the scope of its regulatory activities. Over the years, Congress began to legislate in new regulatory areas. *Hodel v. Virginia Surface Mining & Reclamation Association, Inc.*[60] involved the Surface Mining Control and Reclamation Act (SMCRA), a comprehensive statute designed to "establish a nationwide program to protect society and the environment from the adverse effects of surface coal mining operations."[61] In reviewing the SMCRA, the Court held that it would defer to Congress's finding that a regulated activity affects interstate commerce if there is a "rational basis for such a finding," and if the means of regulation chosen by Congress "are reasonably adapted to the end permitted by the Constitution." In upholding the statute, the Court noted that Congress had found that many surface mining operations disturb surface areas, and "adversely affect commerce and the public welfare by destroying or diminishing the utility of land for commercial, industrial, residential, recreational, agricultural, and forestry purposes, by causing erosion and landslides, by contributing to floods, by polluting the water, by destroying fish and wildlife habitats, by impairing natural beauty, by damaging the property of citizens, by creating hazards dangerous to life and property by degrading the quality of life in local communities, and by counteracting governmental programs and efforts to conserve soil, water, and other natural resources." In addition, the Court noted congressional findings to the effect that nationwide standards are needed to prevent the residents of one state from gaining an advantage over those of another state.[62] The Court rejected the argument that the Tenth Amendment precludes Congress from regulating in this area, noting that it had "long ago rejected the suggestion that Congress invades areas reserved to the States by the Tenth Amendment simply because it exercises its authority under the Commerce Clause in a manner that displaces the States' exercise of their police powers."

Development of the Modern Administrative State. The Court's post-1936 decisions also led to a dramatic increase in the size and scope of the federal government, and the development of the modern administrative state. In part, the growth of the federal government was due to changes in the Court's approach to the Commerce Clause that allowed Congress to regulate a wider range of activities (such as civil rights, the environment, and so on). However, it was also due to changes in the Court's approach to delegation. Decisions during the 1930s' constitutional crisis, in particular *Panama Refining* and *Schechter*, limited Congress's authority to delegate power to administrative agencies (the so-called unlawful delegation doctrine). In the post-1930s era, *Panama Refining* and *Schechter* were effectively overruled. As a result, the Court began to sustain increasingly broad assertions of power. For example, in *INS v. Chadha*,[63] the Court recognized that "restrictions on the scope of the power that could be delegated diminished and all but disappeared." Unlike *Panama Refining* and *Schechter*, which demanded that delegations be made pursuant to an "intelligible principle" designed to restrict the delegation, decisions like *Chadha* upheld delegations based on ambiguous formulations including phrases such as "just and reasonable," in the "*public interest*," "public convenience, interest, or necessity," and "unfair methods of competition."

As the unlawful delegation doctrine disappeared, Congress began to delegate more and more power to administrative agencies, and the power of those agencies increased dramatically. As one court observed, "administrative agencies may well have a more far-reaching effect on the daily lives of all citizens than do the combined actions of the executive, legislative and judicial branches."[64] The growth of agency power is reflected in the size of the Code of Federal Regulations, which now includes hundreds of volumes. While the growth of administrative power may have been necessary, and perhaps inevitable, that growth has not been without costs. As Justice Jackson stated, "The rise of administrative bodies probably has been the most significant legal trend of the last century. . . . They have become a veritable fourth branch of the Government, which has deranged our three-branch legal theories. . . ."[65]

(5) Revolution and Retreat?

For half a century, the Court interpreted the Commerce Clause expansively in decisions like *Wickard, Heart of Atlanta, Perez*, and *Hodel*, imposing few limits on Congress's authority.

F   A   Q

Q: Given the Framer's attitudes regarding the scope of federal power and their concept of "enumerated powers," how could the Court go nearly half a century without imposing significant restraints on Congress's Commerce Clause authority?

A: In some respects, the level of deference given by the Court to Congress during this period is remarkable and is probably attributable to the brutal battles leading up to (and involved in) the Court-packing plan. However, as subsequent cases have tried to place limits on the scope of congressional authority, the justices have been sharply divided.

The Court signaled a change in approach when it decided *United States v. Lopez*[66] and struck down the Gun-Free School Zones Act of 1990, which made it a federal offense "for any individual knowingly to possess a firearm at a place that the individual knows, or has reasonable cause to believe, is a school zone." Because the act did not purport to regulate a commercial activity or contain a requirement that the possession be connected in any way to interstate commerce, the Court held that Congress exceeded its power under the Commerce Clause and reasserted the notion that Constitution creates a federal government of enumerated powers.

In some respects, *Lopez* reaffirmed existing precedent in suggesting that Congress could establish jurisdiction over commerce under any of three theories. First, Congress has the power to "regulate the use of the channels of interstate commerce." Second, Congress may "regulate and protect the instrumentalities of interstate commerce, or persons or things in interstate commerce, even though the threat may come only from intrastate activities." Third, Congress can regulate activities that have a "substantial relation to interstate commerce" if they "substantially affect interstate commerce."

In applying these standards, the *Lopez* Court departed from its post-1937 jurisprudence in holding that none of these three bases of jurisdiction applied. The Court readily concluded that Congress was not regulating "the use of the channels of interstate commerce" and was not attempting "to protect an instrumentality of interstate commerce or a thing in interstate commerce." In addition, in a significant departure, the Court doubted that the activities being regulated "substantially affected interstate commerce." Indeed, the Court found that the regulated activity had no connection to " 'commerce' or any sort of economic enterprise, however broadly one might define those terms." In addition, the Court found that the act was "not an essential part of a larger regulation of economic activity, in which the regulatory scheme could be undercut unless the intrastate activity were regulated." Moreover, Congress did not provide findings demonstrating the link to interstate commerce, and the statute was not limited to situation where an impact on interstate commerce could be demonstrated.

Lopez flatly rejected the government's argument that guns in school zones can affect the national economy by increasing insurance costs, limiting the willingness of individuals to travel in areas deemed to be unsafe, and posing a substantial risk to "the educational process by threatening the learning environment," which would result in a less productive citizenry. The Court noted that, if it focused on the government's "costs of crime" and "national productivity" analysis, Congress could justifiably "regulate any activity that it found was related to the economic productivity of individual citizens" (for example, family law, including marriage, divorce, and child custody), and it would be hard to find a limit to federal power even in areas such as criminal law or education, which had historically fallen under the purview of the individual states. Indeed, the Court suggested that it would have a hard time envisioning any activity that Congress could not regulate. To reach that conclusion would require, in the Court's view, the Court to conclude that the Constitution's enumeration of powers was meant to be exclusive and that there would never be a distinction between "what is truly national and what is truly local." The Court was unwilling to do that and struck the law down, concluding that the possession of a gun in a school zone "is in no sense an economic activity," and that there was no indication that the gun in question had moved in interstate commerce or had "any concrete tie to interstate commerce."

Lopez produced a variety of concurrences and dissents. Justice Thomas concurred, arguing for a reassessment of the Court's Commerce Clause jurisprudence, which he believed had "drifted far from the original understanding of the Commerce Clause." He particularly objected to the "substantial effects" test, which he did not believe was consistent with the "text and history of the Commerce Clause." Justice Stevens dissented, arguing that "[guns] are both articles of commerce and articles that can be used to restrain commerce," and that the "market for the possession of handguns by school-age children is, distressingly, substantial." Justice Souter also dissented,

Sidebar

LOPEZ'S SIGNIFICANCE

Lopez was a remarkable decision because it ended 50 years of deference to Congress on Commerce Clause issues and led to a new era in which the Court was willing to hold that Congress had exceeded its power under the Commerce Clause. In subsequent decisions, the Court has struggled to define *Lopez*'s meaning and application.

arguing that the "commercial prospects of an illiterate State or Nation are not rosy." Justice Breyer, joined by Justices Stevens, Souter, and Ginsburg, also dissented, arguing that guns and violence near schools "significantly interferes with the quality of education in those schools," and that "gun-related violence in and around schools is a commercial, as well as a human, problem" since education "has long been inextricably intertwined with the Nation's economy. . . . Increasing global competition also has made primary and secondary education economically more important. . . . Finally, there is evidence that [many] firms base their location decisions upon the presence [of] a work force with a basic education."

Following *Lopez*, the Court did sustain congressional enactments under the Commerce Clause. For example, in *Reno v. Condon*,[67] the Court upheld the Privacy Protection Act, which prohibited state governments from selling information that they receive from driver's license applicants absent consent or an exemption. The Court concluded that the sale of the information constitutes commerce and thus fell within Congress's authority to regulate the channels of interstate commerce. Likewise, in *United States v. Robertson*,[68] the Court upheld the Racketeer Influenced and Corrupt Organizations Act (RICO) as applied to an individual who invested the proceeds of illegal narcotics offenses in an Alaskan gold mine. The Court found a relationship to interstate commerce because the mine's activities were commercial and they crossed state lines.

However, the Court continued its Commerce Clause retreat in *United States v. Morrison*,[69] striking down a portion of the Violence Against Women Act of 1994, which provided a federal civil remedy for the victims of gender-motivated violence as applied to a university student who filed a civil suit for rape. The Court found that the activity was not economic and that there was insufficient evidence that the activity substantially affected interstate commerce. In reaching that conclusion, the Court refused to apply a *Wickard* aggregate effects analysis because the underlying activity was not economic in nature. In addition, the Court rejected evidence suggesting that gender-motivated violence on victims and their families had an economic impact because it deterred "potential victims from traveling interstate, from engaging in employment in interstate business, and from transacting with business, and in places involved in interstate commerce; . . . by diminishing national productivity, increasing medical and other costs, and decreasing the supply of and the demand for interstate products." The Court concluded that to adopt the aggregate effects analysis would be to interpret the Commerce Clause so broadly as "to completely obliterate the Constitution's distinction between national and local authority." The Court worried that Congress might use a contrary decision to justify regulation of "murder or any other type of violence since gender-motivated violence, as a subset of all violent crime, is certain to have lesser economic impacts than the larger class of which it is a part." Indeed, Congress could even regulate "family law and other areas of traditional state regulation since the aggregate effect of marriage, divorce, and childrearing on the national economy is undoubtedly significant." The Court concluded that the Constitution requires a distinction between what is "truly national and what is truly local," noting that the "regulation and punishment of intrastate violence that is not directed at the instrumentalities, channels, or goods involved in interstate commerce has always been the province of the States" within the scope of their police powers. The Court also rejected the argument that Congress could regulate under its Fourteenth Amendment remedial powers because of the absence of state action: "[the Act] is not aimed [at] any State or state actor, but at individuals who have committed criminal acts motivated by gender bias."

Q: Could it be argued that violence against women has a significant commercial impact by discouraging women from spending money or participating freely in society?

A: Absolutely. As we shall see, the *Morrison* dissents take exactly that position. The critical distinction, or so the Court seems to suggest, is that the violence itself does not involve commercial activity.

Like *Lopez, Morrison* also produced an array of concurrences and dissents, which help illustrate the divide on the Court. Justice Souter, joined by Justices Stevens, Ginsburg, and Breyer, dissented, arguing that Congress had complied a "mountain of data" showing "the effects of violence against women on interstate commerce" which included $5 to $10 billion a year in health care, criminal justice, and other social costs in addition to the fact that some women curtail their after dark activities for fear of violence. As a result, they would have found a "substantial adverse effect on interstate commerce, by deterring potential victims from traveling interstate, from engaging in employment in interstate business, and from transacting with business, and in places involved, in interstate commerce[,] by diminishing national productivity, increasing medical and other costs, and decreasing the supply of and the demand for interstate products." The dissenters also argued that the Court's holding was inconsistent with the broad sweep of the Court's Commerce Clause jurisprudence since the 1930s and expressed alarm about whether the "[m]embers of this Court would ever again toy with a return to the days before *NLRB v. Jones & Laughlin Steel Corp.*, which brought the earlier and nearly disastrous experiment to an end."

The Court backed away from *Lopez* and *Morrison*, or at least distinguished them, in its later decision in *Gonzales v. Raich*.[70] That case involved a California statute that authorized the use of marijuana for medicinal purposes. Two women, one of whom grew marijuana at home, and both of whom used marijuana in treating serious medical conditions, sought to challenge the federal Controlled Substances Act's (CSA) provisions that prohibited individuals from possessing, obtaining, or manufacturing cannabis for their personal medical use. The main objectives of the CSA were to conquer drug abuse and to control the legitimate and illegitimate traffic in controlled substances. In enacting the CSA, Congress classified marijuana as a Schedule I drug (Schedule I drugs were highly regulated) because of its high potential for abuse, lack of any accepted medical use, and absence of any accepted safety for use in medically supervised treatment. This classification made it a crime to distribute or possess the drug. In upholding the CSA, the Court reaffirmed the notion that Congress may "regulate purely local activities that are part of an economic 'class of activities' that have a substantial effect on interstate commerce." Once again, the Court invoked *Wickard* and its aggregate effects analysis, as well as rational basis analysis, in concluding that marijuana use has a "substantial effect" on interstate commerce. Using this analysis, the Court found that leaving home-consumed marijuana unregulated would affect price and market conditions. In addition, the Court found that there was a risk that high demand in the interstate market would draw homegrown marijuana into the market. Unlike the holdings in *Lopez* and *Morrison*, the Court was deferential to Congress, concluding that it need determine only that Congress had a "rational basis" for its conclusions. The Court found a rational basis given "the enforcement difficulties that attend distinguishing between marijuana cultivated locally and marijuana grown elsewhere, and concerns about diversion into illicit channels."

In *Gonzales*, the Court distinguished *Lopez* and *Morrison* because the statutes involved in those cases did not involve economic activity, and there was no requirement of a connection to interstate activity "or a predictable impact on future commercial activity." In *Gonzales*, by contrast, the Court found that the regulation of marijuana was "quintessentially economic" because it regulated "the production, distribution, and consumption of commodities for which there is an established, and lucrative, interstate market." Under the Supremacy Clause, Congress was not required to defer to the states' judgment that certain types of marijuana should be exempt from governmental regulation. However, *Gonzales* also produced dissents that suggested that a number of justices were unwilling to find a substantial effect on interstate commerce and arguing that the Court's definition of "economic activity" was "breathtaking."[71]

Sidebar

COMMERCIAL VERSUS NONCOMMERCIAL ACTIVITIES

Morrison illustrates the distinction, suggested earlier, between activities that are more commercial in nature (for example, sale of drivers' license information) and information that is not commercial in nature (for example, violence against women). While Congress's Commerce Clause authority extends to the former, it does not necessarily extend to noncommercial activities.

Despite the holding in *Gonazles* and other recent decisions upholding governmental action (for example, *Reno* and *Robertson*), holdings like *Lopez* and *Morrison* make it clear that the six decades of deference to congressional judgment under the Commerce Clause has come to an end. No longer will the Court automatically, and almost unquestioningly, defer to congressional judgments regarding the interpretation of the Commerce Clause. Additional decisions will be required to determine whether and to what extent the Court will continue its retreat from a deferential approach.

Commerce Clause Interpretation Under *Lopez* and *Morrison*	
Activity	**Authority to Regulate**
Interstate commerce	Congress
Commerce that has a "close and substantial" relationship to interstate commerce	Congress (and perhaps the states)
noncommercial activities	States

BASES FOR CONGRESSIONAL REGULATION OF COMMERCE

Congress may regulate the "channels" of interstate commerce.

Congress may "regulate and protect the instrumentalities of interstate commerce, or persons or things in interstate commerce, even though the threat may come only from intrastate activities."

Congress may regulate commercial activities that have a "substantial relation to interstate commerce" if they "substantially affect interstate commerce."

D. The Taxing Power

Article I, Section 8, also contains the **Taxing Clause**: "The Congress shall have Power To lay and collect Taxes, Duties, Imposes and Excises. . . ." However, the Constitution specifically requires that "direct Taxes shall be apportioned among the several States,"[72] and that all "Duties, Imposts and Excises shall be uniform throughout the United States.[73] In *Pollock v. Farmers' Loan & Trust Co.*,[74] the Court used these sections to conclude that Congress could not impose a federal income tax. Since direct taxes must be imposed in proportion to population, the income tax was invalid because it imposed taxes on the basis of income. *Pollock* was overruled by the Sixteenth Amendment to the Constitution,[75] as well as by the Court's later decision in *New York ex rel Cohn v. Graves.*[76]

Most of the litigation under the Taxing Clause has focused on Congress's power to regulate conduct through the imposition of taxes. "Regulation by taxation" is generally unobjectionable if Congress seeks to tax something that it otherwise has the power to regulate. However, more difficult questions arise if Congress tries to tax activities that it does not have the power to regulate, and it does so in an attempt to regulate.

In *Bailey v. Drexel Furniture Co.*,[77] also known as the *Child Labor Tax Case*, the Court struck down the Child Labor Tax Law. That law involved Congress's attempt to impose by tax the child labor regulations that were struck down in *Hammer v. Dagenhart*, and to do so by imposing a tax penalty on those who did not comply with the regulations. As one might have guessed, employers challenged the law, claiming that it infringed the power of the states under the Tenth Amendment, and that it was essentially a prohibition (rather than a tax) because the tax was so high (one-tenth of the employer's net income for the year). The Court struck down the law, holding that "where the sovereign enacting the law has power to impose both a tax and penalty, the difference between revenue production and mere regulation may be immaterial." However, when the federal government has only the power to tax, and the power of regulation lies in another, a different scenario arises. In the Court's view, a tax is permissible when Congress's primary motive is to raise revenue, and Congress may impose the incidental effect of discouraging certain types of conduct through such a tax. However, Congress exceeds its powers when a tax is not designed to raise money, but it instead becomes a penalty "with the characteristics of regulation and punishment." This is especially true when Congress does not have the power to regulate in an area and cannot use direct regulation to accomplish what it is trying to achieve through taxation. Finally, the Court found that Congress violated the Tenth Amendment because "the so-called tax is a penalty to coerce people of a state to act as Congress wishes them to act in respect of a matter completely the business of the state government under the federal Constitution."

Q: Could Congress have enacted a tax on child labor if the primary goal had been to raise money rather than to regulate by means of a tax?

A: The simple answer is yes. The Court objected to the tax because the primary objective was to regulate child labor rather than to raise money. Had the goal been to raise money, the tax might have been upheld. Under the circumstances, it might have been difficult to convince the Court that Congress was trying to raise the money. Congress's prior attempt to impose the law through regulation (as struck down in *Hammer*) would have raised questions about Congress's motives. Moreover, the amount of the tax was so high that the Court might have struck it down. If the tax were lower, it might not have achieved its objective.

Following the *Child Labor Tax Case*, the Court rendered a similar holding in *United States v. Constantine*.[78] In *Constantine*, the Court struck down a law that imposed a heavy tax on liquor businesses found to be operating in violation of state law. The Court concluded that the law violated the police powers of the states.

However, both *Bailey* and *Constantine* were decided in the 1930s prior to the decision in *Jones & Laughlin* and prior to the Court's development of an expanded view of the Commerce Clause in succeeding decades. Under the Court's later interpretations of that clause, Congress probably did possess the power to impose the child labor restrictions struck down in *Dagenhart* and *Bailey*. In addition, under the Court's later precedent, the Court shifted its interpretation of the Tenth Amendment from an independent limitation on the scope of federal power to a truism. As a result, cases like *Bailey* (in which Congress sought to regulate by tax something that it did not otherwise have the power to regulate) are less likely to arise, and the Court is less likely to find a violation of the Tenth Amendment. Because of these shifts in attitude, the Court's approach to the Taxing Clause began to change as well. The result is that since *Constantine* was decided in 1935, the Court has routinely upheld federal laws imposing taxes.[79]

Example: Illustrative of the Court's modern approach is the holding in *United States v. Sanchez*.[80] In that case, the Court upheld the Marihuana Tax Act against claims that Congress was imposing a penalty rather than a tax. Congress had two primary motives in passing the legislation: raising revenue (while making it difficult for individuals to acquire marijuana for illicit use) and developing an adequate means for publicizing dealings in marijuana in order to tax and control the traffic effectively. The act itself imposed a tax on "every person who imports, manufactures, produces, compounds, sells, deals in, dispenses, prescribes, administers, or gives away marihuana, and requires such persons to register at the time of the payment of the tax with the Collector of the District in which their businesses are located." In particular, the act required that all transfers be recorded on forms issued by the secretary of the treasury and provided for a tax of $1 per ounce on all sales that are registered and taxed, or $100 per ounce on sales that are not registered and on which no tax is paid. The Court upheld the tax "despite the regulatory effect and the close resemblance to a penalty." The Court noted that "a tax does not cease to be valid merely because it regulates, discourages, or even definitely deters the activities taxed," and even though "the revenue obtained is obviously negligible, or the revenue purpose of the tax may be secondary." In addition, the Court concluded that a tax statute does not "necessarily fall because it touches on activities which Congress might not otherwise regulate." Finally, the Court held that this particular tax did not involve a tax on the commission of a crime: "It is . . . the failure of the transferee to pay the tax that gives rise to the liability of the transferor. Since his tax liability does not in effect rest on criminal conduct, the tax can be properly called a civil rather than a criminal sanction."

E. The Power to Spend for the General Welfare

Article I, Section 8, which contains the power to tax and the Commerce Clause, also contains the power to spend for the general welfare. The clause containing the spending power reads as follows: "The Congress shall have Power To lay and collect Taxes, Duties, Imposes and Excises, to pay the Debts and provide for the common Defence and general Welfare of the United States."

From cases like *Dagenhart* and *Bailey*, we know that Congress was initially unable to impose its child labor laws through either its Commerce Clause power or its taxing power. But some have argued that Congress has greater power to control or regulate conduct under its power to spend for the general welfare. For example, James Madison argued that "the grant of power to tax and spend for the general national welfare must be confined to the enumerated legislative fields committed to the Congress." By contrast, Alexander Hamilton suggested that the clause "confers a power separate and distinct from those later enumerated is not restricted in meaning by the grant of them, and Congress consequently has a substantive power to tax and to appropriate, limited only by the requirement that it shall be exercised to provide for the general welfare of the United States." However, Hamilton qualified his view in requiring that the purpose must be "general, and not local."

For a while, the Court adopted a more restrictive interpretation of the spending power. For example, in *United States v. Butler*,[81] a case decided prior to the switch in the Court's Commerce Clause jurisprudence that occurred in the late 1930s, the Court struck down the Agricultural Adjustment Act, which declared an economic emergency because of a disparity in agricultural prices that affected farmers' purchasing power and affected transactions in agricultural commodities. In an effort to deal with this disparity, Congress tried to reduce farm acreage "through agreements with producers or by other voluntary methods," and to provide for rental or benefit payments to be made in exchange for the reduction. To finance the benefits payments, Congress levied processing taxes on various commodities. The Court struck down the act, concluding that the federal government received "delegated powers" and may exercise only those powers "expressly" conferred on it and "reasonably implied" from those granted. The Court found it unnecessary to resolve the differences between the Madisonian and Hamiltonian views of the clause because it held that the act violated the Tenth Amendment. The Court held that Congress's plan to regulate and control agricultural production was "a matter beyond the powers delegated to the federal government." The Court concluded that Congress had no greater authority to purchase compliance than to compel it, even if farmers voluntarily participated. Indeed, the Court concluded that the idea of voluntary participation was illusory because a farmer could not forgo the benefit of the subsidy and remain competitive. As a result, just as Congress lacked the power to impose agricultural regulation of this sort, the Court concluded that Congress could "not indirectly accomplish those ends by taxing and spending to purchase compliance." Justice Stone dissented, arguing that "[the] spending power of Congress is in addition to the legislative power and not subordinate to it. . . . It is a contradiction in terms to say that there is power to spend for the national welfare, while rejecting any power to impose conditions reasonably adapted to the attainment of the end which alone would justify the expenditure."

Butler reflected the Court's more restrictive mid-1930s attitude toward the scope of the Commerce Clause. Modern cases adopt a more expansive interpretation of the Commerce Clause, as well as of the spending power. Illustrative is the holding in *South Dakota v. Dole*,[82] which involved a federal statute that directed the secretary of transportation to withhold a percentage of federal highway funds from any state that allowed individuals under 21 years of age to purchase alcoholic beverages. In that case, the Court rejected *Butler*'s more truncated view of the spending power, noting that Congress has the power "to further broad policy objectives by conditioning receipt of federal moneys upon compliance by the recipient with federal statutory and administrative directives." While the spending power is not "unlimited," in that any spending must be in pursuit of the "general welfare" (although the Court indicated that it would be deferential to Congress on this issue), any conditions imposed on the funds must be unambiguous so that states can knowingly decide whether to accept or reject the conditions, and the spending provision must be related "to the federal interest in particular national projects or programs." In *Dole*, finding these requirements satisfied, the Court upheld the statute, noting that Congress could appropriate money with conditions, even conditions that Congress did not have the power to require, so long as Congress did not try to encourage the states to "engage in activities that would themselves be unconstitutional" (for example, a grant of federal funds conditioned on invidious racial discrimination). Although the Court held out the possibility that it might invalidate financial inducements if they were so coercive as to amount to compulsion, the Court held that Congress had not transgressed the line in this case because of the small percentage (5 percent) of highway funds being withheld. Justice O'Connor dissented, arguing that

> establishment of a minimum drinking age of 21 is not sufficiently related to inter-state highway construction to justify so conditioning funds appropriated for that purpose. . . . When Congress appropriates money to build a highway, it is entitled to insist that the highway be a safe one. But it is not entitled to insist as a condition of the use of highway funds that the State impose or change regulations in other areas of the State's social and economic life because of an attenuated or tangential relationship to highway use or safety.

F   A   Q

Q: *South Dakota v. Dole* seems to give Congress broad authority to "bribe" the states by giving the states incentives to do as Congress wishes. Can Congress really do that?

A: Yes. In a number of instances, Congress has used its spending to bribe or coerce the states into doing what it wants them to do. For example, when Congress wanted to impose a 55 mph speed limit on interstate highways in the 1970s, it chose to do so by requiring the states to adopt the speed limit on pain of losing federal highway funds.

Example: Also illustrative of the modern approach is the holding in *Pennhurst State School & Hospital v. Halderman,*[83] which reaffirmed the idea that a state must knowingly accept a congressional condition. That case involved the Developmentally Disabled Assistance and Bill of Rights Act of 1975, which provided financial assistance to participating states to aid them in creating programs to care for and treat the developmentally disabled. States were free to choose whether to voluntarily comply with the act, but faced a loss of federal funding if they declined. States that chose to participate were subject to the act's "bill of rights" provision, which granted mentally retarded persons a right to "appropriate treatment, services, and habilitation" in "the setting that is least restrictive of . . . personal liberty." The Court rejected the argument that Congress had exceeded its power under the Spending Clause, noting that Congress has the authority to decide the terms on which it will disburse money to the states, and that the states are free to choose whether to accept or reject the federally imposed conditions. In *Pennhurst,* the Court concluded that Pennsylvania "voluntarily and knowingly" accepted the terms that were imposed, but concluded that the act did not require the states to assume the high cost of providing appropriate treatment in the least-restrictive environment to their mentally retarded citizens. As a result, the Court construed the act as encouraging, rather than mandating, that the states provide better services to the developmentally disabled.

Given the shift in approach over the decades, it now seems clear that the *Child Labor Tax Case* is no longer good. In other words, after *Dole,* Congress could probably impose the regulations struck down in the case by giving conditional grants to the states or by threatening to withhold federal funds unless the states restrict child labor.

F. The War Power

Article I also gives Congress a number of powers relating to war and foreign affairs. Included is the power to declare war and to regulate commerce with foreign states. These powers are shared with the president, who also has substantial authority over foreign affairs. For example, under Article II, Section 2, the president is the commander-in-chief of the army and the navy and has the power to appoint ambassadors and consuls. In addition, as noted, the president has the power to make treaties.

In Chapter 3, we examine the scope of presidential power and the intersection between congressional power and executive power, especially with regard to the war power. In this chapter, we focus primarily on congressional powers relating to the treaty power. However, it is important to remember that the Constitution also gives Congress the power to "regulate foreign affairs." For example, in *Perez v. Brownell,*[84] the Court upheld a congressional enactment that mandated a loss of U.S. citizenship for "voting in a political election in a foreign state."

G. The Treaty Power

Although Article II, Section 2, gives the president the power to make treaties, it also provides that a two-thirds vote of the Senate is required for ratification. In this section, we examine the scope of the treaty power and its impact on domestic law.

There has always been some dispute regarding the status of treaties. One question is the relationship between a treaty and the U.S. Constitution. Suppose that Congress ratifies a treaty that conflicts with the terms of the U.S. Constitution. For example, imagine that Congress enters into an international treaty designed to regulate Internet communications. As we shall see in Chapter 10, because of the First Amendment right to freedom of expression, Congress has limited authority to regulate the Internet.[85] As a result, if the treaty conflicts with the First Amendment, may the treaty stand? The accepted wisdom is that Congress's treaty power is subject to the constraints of the Constitution. In the U.S. Supreme Court's decision in *Missouri v. Holland*,[86] which upheld the Migratory Bird Treaty, the Court focused on whether the treaty contravened "any prohibitory words to be found in the Constitution." Likewise, in *Reid v. Covert*,[87] the Court recognized that "no agreement with a foreign nation can confer power on the Congress, or on any other branch of Government, which is free from the restraints of the Constitution." As *Reid* went on to note:

> It would be manifestly contrary to the objectives of those who created the Constitution, as well as those who were responsible for the Bill of Rights — let alone alien to our entire constitutional history and tradition — to construe Article VI as permitting the United States to exercise power under an international agreement without observing constitutional prohibitions. In effect, such construction would permit amendment of that document in a manner not sanctioned by Article V. The prohibitions of the Constitution were designed to apply to all branches of the National Government and they cannot be nullified by the Executive or by the Executive and the Senate combined.

A second question relates to the status of a treaty vis-à-vis a federal statute that has been duly enacted by Congress and signed by the president (or passed over his veto). In *Whitney v. Robertson*,[88] the Court elaborated on the relative status of treaties and statutes, and concluded that a treaty has status equivalent to a statute. *Whitney* involved merchants who imported sugars from San Domingo and claimed that a treaty required that their sugars be admitted on the same basis as similar articles produced in Hawaii. However, after the treaty was signed, Congress passed an inconsistent statute, and the Court held that the later statute controlled:

> A treaty is primarily a contract between two or more independent nations. . . . When the stipulations are not self-executing, they can only be enforced pursuant to legislation to carry them into effect, and such legislation is as much subject to modification and repeal by congress as legislation upon any other subject.

On the other hand, if a treaty is self-executing, in that it requires no legislation to render its provisions effective, the treaty has the "force and effect of a legislative enactment." While Congress may choose to override a treaty's provisions through subsequent legislation, a treaty is regarded as having the status of a statute until that is done. In other words, both a statute and a treaty function as the law of the land, and neither is treated as superior to the other. Although courts will strive to construe statutes and treaties as consistent with each other, the latter in time will control in the event of an irreconcilable inconsistency.

A third question relates to the relative status of treaties and state or local laws. The leading decision is *Missouri v. Holland*.[89] In that case, the Court upheld the Migratory Bird Treaty against a Tenth Amendment challenge. The treaty, between the United States and Great Britain, recognized that many species of birds migrate across the United States and Canada, and that birds have "great value as a source of food and in destroying insects injurious to vegetation." Despite their value, migratory birds were in danger of extermination through lack of adequate protection. The act provided for closed hunting seasons and other protections. Pursuant to the treaty, Congress passed an act prohibiting the killing, capturing, or selling of any of the migratory birds included in the terms of the treaty except as permitted by regulation. In upholding the law, the Court rejected the argument that the Tenth Amendment precluded the United States from entering into the treaty, noting that

> there may be matters of the sharpest exigency for the national well being that an act of Congress could not deal with but that a treaty followed by such an act could, and it is not lightly to be assumed that, in matters requiring national action, "a power which must belong to and somewhere reside in every civilized government" is not to be found.

The Court therefore concluded that this treaty involved "a national interest of very nearly the first magnitude" that "can be protected only by national action in concert with that of another power" because the "subject matter is only transitorily within the State and has no permanent habitat therein."

Example: Illustrative of the supremacy of treaties vis-à-vis state and local laws is the holding in *De Geofroy v. Riggs*.[90] In that case, a U.S. citizen died intestate but owning real property. Although a treaty between the United States and France provided that citizens of one country can inherit property in the other country, local law made it illegal for foreign citizens to own property. Rigg's sister was married to a Frenchman, and her children (who were French) sought to inherit from him. The Court held that the treaty prevailed over local law, noting that "the protection which should be afforded to the citizens of one country owning property in another, and the manner in which that property may be transferred, devised, or inherited, are fitting subjects for such negotiation, and of regulation by mutual stipulations between the two countries." The treaty, "being part of the supreme law of the land," took precedence over Maryland law. As a result, the French heirs were allowed to inherit from Riggs.

H. Congressional Enforcement of Civil Rights

After the Civil War, the power of the federal government was expanded as a result of the ratification of the Thirteenth, Fourteenth, and Fifteenth Amendments, known collectively as the **Reconstruction Amendments**. The Reconstruction Amendments changed the balance of power between the state and federal governments. Prior to the Civil War, states were primarily responsible for protecting the rights of citizens. The Reconstruction Amendments were ratified to support a series of post–Civil War legislation enacted by Congress, namely the Civil Rights Acts of 1866, 1870, and 1871. The Reconstruction Amendments empowered the federal government to grant and protect the citizenship of former slaves.[91] Each amendment contains an enforcement provision to the effect that "Congress shall have the power to enforce, by appropriate legislation, the provisions of this article." However, the legislative debates and congressional record from the deliberations left several interpretive ambiguities and were inconclusive as to the intent of the amendments. In fact, *Slaughterhouse*, the first case to test the scope of post–Civil War federal power had nothing to do with race. Thus, the Supreme Court faced a challenge: interpreting these new constitutional amendments and deciding whether Congress was acting within or beyond the scope of its new authority in enacting legislation to enforce the protection of civil rights.

The early cases examined congressional legislation enacted between 1866-1875 to remove the "badges and incidents of slavery" in public accommodations, transportation, and voting. The Civil Rights Acts of 1866, 1870, 1871, and 1875 survive in various forms today. In the modern cases, the Civil Rights Act of 1964 and most of the Voting Rights Act of 1965 survived judicial review. Recent cases cover such issues as the rights of the disabled and access to court under the Americans with Disabilities Act, religious expression under the Religious Freedom Restoration Act, protection of employment under the Family Medical Leave Act, the prevention of violence against women under the Violence Against Women Act, and the wide array of federal legislation enacted pursuant to the enforcement provisions of the Reconstruction Amendments.

Congressional power to enforce and protect civil rights reflects the ever-changing balance of power between the Supreme Court and Congress, as well as the state and the federal governments. Under the Fourteenth Amendment to the U.S. Constitution, Congress is empowered to enforce by appropriate legislation the command that no state shall deprive any person of "life, liberty, or property, without due process of law" nor deny any person "equal protections of the laws." Just as Congress has broad power to legislate under the Commerce Clause, the Necessary and Proper Clause, and the Taxing and Spending Clauses, Congress also has broad power to legislate under Section 5 of the Fourteenth Amendment, Section 2 of the Thirteenth Amendment, and Section 2 of the Fifteenth Amendment.

(1) Early Developments

The *Civil Rights Cases of 1883*[92] first tested the scope of congressional authority to enforce civil rights. These consolidated cases challenged the constitutionality of the Civil Rights Act of 1875 and raised direct questions regarding Congress's authority to use the Thirteenth and Fourteenth Amendments and the Commerce Clause to enact legislation that prohibited private businesses from discriminating on the basis of race. Four of the cases involved indictments for denying to persons of color the accommodations and privileges of an inn or a theater. The fifth involved an action by a husband and wife based on a railroad conductor's refusal to allow the wife to ride in the ladies' car because she was a person of African descent. In its decision, the Court severely curtailed congressional authority to legislate pursuant to the enforcement provisions of the Thirteenth and Fourteenth Amendments. The resolution of cases continues to revolve around the four major holdings of the case:

■ First, according to the majority, Section 5 of the Fourteenth Amendment did not give Congress affirmative authority, but rather only the remedial power "to enforce the prohibition" against state laws that violate the Equal Protection Clause, as interpreted by judicial decision. Congress does not have plenary power to legislate in areas that the Court determines are not within the domain of national regulation.

■ Second, Section 5 does not give Congress the power to legislate in areas within the domain of state regulation. Congress can provide redress only against the operation of state laws and the actions of state officials that are subversive of the fundamental rights specified in Section 1.

■ Third, the Court limited the scope of the Fourteenth Amendment to "state action." "[U]ntil some State law has been passed, or some State action through its officers or agents has been taken, adverse to the rights of citizens sought to be protected by the Fourteenth Amendment, no legislation of the United States under said amendment, nor any proceeding under such legislation, can be called into activity: for the prohibitions of the amendment are against State laws and acts done under State authority."

■ Finally, the scope of congressional action is limited to the wrong that the Fourteenth Amendment was intended to provide against.

Because the Court found that Congress had exceeded the scope of its authority under the Thirteenth and Fourteenth Amendments, it did not address the issue of whether the Commerce Clause empowered Congress to legislate in the field of civil rights.

After the decision in the *Civil Rights Cases*, Congress enacted no civil rights laws until 1957 when the Civil Rights Act of 1957 became law. It was followed by the Civil Rights Act of 1960. Three years later, on June 19, 1963, the President Kennedy called for civil rights legislation in a message to Congress. Its stated purpose was

> to promote the general welfare by eliminating discrimination based on race, color, religion, or national origin in . . . public accommodations through the exercise by Congress of the powers conferred upon it . . . to enforce the provisions of the fourteenth and fifteenth amendments, to regulate commerce among the several States, and to make laws necessary and proper to execute the powers conferred upon it by the Constitution.

However, it was not until July 2, 1964, on the recommendation of President Johnson following the assassination of President Kennedy, that the Civil Rights Act of 1964 was finally passed.

(2) The Modern Cases

Consistent with the Court's expanded view of federal powers since the 1930s, modern cases have more liberally interpreted the scope of congressional enforcement authority.

(a) The Commerce Clause

Because of the restrictive view of federal power evident in the *Civil Rights Cases*, when Congress began to enact civil rights legislation, it chose not to base its authority solely on Section 5 of the Fourteenth Amendment. Instead, Congress relied on its commerce and spending powers to justify the Civil Rights Act of 1964. Congress's power under the Commerce Clause, and the possible use of that power to pass antidiscrimination legislation, was an issue that was raised but not resolved in the

Civil Rights Cases. In litigation regarding the Civil Rights Act of 1964, Congress's commerce authority was directly presented.

In *Heart of Atlanta Motel v. United States*,[93] previously discussed in relation to the Commerce Clause, the Court upheld the constitutionality of Title II of the Civil Rights Act of 1964. In enacting that statute, Congress found that hotels and restaurants nationwide refused to serve African American patrons, and concluded that the unavailability to African Americans of adequate accommodations "interferes significantly with interstate travel." The government argued that Congress's Commerce Clause power gives it the authority to remove such obstructions and restraints. The legislative history of the act indicated that Congress based the act on Section 5 and the Equal Protection Clause of the Fourteenth Amendment as well as its power to regulate interstate commerce under Article I, Section 8, Clause 3, of the Constitution.

In its decision in the *Heart of Atlanta* case, the Court ruled that the commerce power provided sufficient authority to enact the legislation. However, the Court declined to reconsider the holding in the *Civil Rights Cases* and did not address the question of whether Congress could also enact civil rights legislation pursuant to Section 5 of the Fourteenth Amendment or Section 2 of the Thirteenth Amendment. Instead, the Court concluded that the *Civil Rights Cases* have no relevance where the act explicitly relied on the commerce power to remove impediments to interstate travel resulting from racial discrimination, and where the "record was filled with testimony of obstructions and restraints resulting from the discriminations found to be existing."[94] Moreover, the fact that Congress was legislating against moral wrongs in many areas rendered its enactments no less valid. Congress was not restricted by the fact that the particular obstruction to interstate commerce with which it was dealing was also deemed a moral and social wrong. Finally, the Court reiterated that the power of Congress over interstate commerce is not confined to the regulation of commerce among the states. It extends to those activities intrastate that so affect interstate commerce or the exercise of the power of Congress over it as to make regulation of them appropriate means to the attainment of a legitimate end — the exercise of the granted power of Congress to regulate interstate commerce.[95] The only questions are (1) whether Congress had a rational basis for finding that racial discrimination by motels affected commerce; and (2) if it had such a basis, whether the means it selected to eliminate that evil are reasonable and appropriate.

(b) The Reconstruction Amendments

The *Civil Rights Cases* held that the Reconstruction Amendments (the Thirteenth, Fourteenth, and Fifteenth Amendments) had given Congress only "remedial" authority to pass corrective legislation once the Court pronounced a particular state scheme or practice violated one or more provisions of the Reconstruction Amendments.

During the Warren Court era, the Court took a more expansive view of Congress's lawmaking authority under the enforcement provisions of the amendments. In *Katzenbach v. Morgan*,[96] the State of New York challenged the federal government's authority to enact provisions of the Voting Rights Act of 1965 that prohibited the enforcement of a state law requiring all voters to be able to read and write in English. The state attorney general argued that an exercise of congressional power under Section 5 of the Fourteenth Amendment that prohibits the enforcement of a state law can be sustained only if the judicial branch determines that the state law is prohibited by the provisions of the amendments Congress sought to enforce. Since no judicial finding of a constitutional violation had been made, the state argued that Congress had no legislative authority.

The Court disagreed, reasoning that if the Court adopted New York's argument, it would deprecate both congressional resourcefulness and congressional responsibility for implementing the amendments. "Correctly viewed, Section 5 is a positive grant of legislative power authorizing Congress to exercise its discretion in determining whether and what legislation is needed to secure the guarantees of the Fourteenth Amendment." The Court likened the scope of Section 5 to the Necessary and Proper Clause.

During the Rehnquist era, the Court returned to the more restrictive view of the *Civil Rights Cases,* reemphasizing the limited remedial nature of Congress's power and stressing that Congress was not given the power to determine what constitutes a constitutional violation. The power to interpret the Constitution remains in the judiciary.[97]

(c) The Reserved Power of the States

As broad as the congressional enforcement power might be, it is not unlimited. In particular, Congress exceeds the limits of its power when it legislates to strip the states of their power of self-governance. States have successfully argued that the Tenth Amendment provides constitutional protection against congressional legislation enacted pursuant to Section 5 of the Fourteenth Amendment.

This point is illustrated in cases addressing the constitutionality of certain provisions of the Voting Rights Act. In those cases, the Court relied on a positive grant of authority[98] to Congress to enforce the Fourteenth and Fifteenth Amendments by enacting the Voting Rights Acts of 1965, and held that this authority displaced state and local voting regulations used to discriminate against voters on account of their race.[99] In *Oregon v. Mitchell,* however, the Court declared unconstitutional a 1970 amendment to the Voting Rights Act that lower the voting age to 18 in state and local elections. The majority held that while the federal government is constitutionally empowered to regulate federal elections, the states are free to determine within the limits of the Constitution the qualification for voters in state and local elections, subject to the Reconstruction Amendments' prohibition against racial discrimination. Similarly, in *City of Boerne v. Archbishop of San Antonio & United States,*[100] the Court ruled that a law intended by Congress to protect the free exercise of religious beliefs and practices against state regulation intruded into the traditional prerogatives and general authority of the states to regulate the health and welfare of their citizens.

The holding in the *Civil Rights Cases of 1883* that limited the reach of Congress under Section 5 to "state action" has lost some of its vitality. In the Court's more recent decision in *United States v. Guest,*[101] several members of the Court took the position that Section 5 of the Fourteenth Amendment authorized Congress to make it a crime for white supremacists to conspire to deprive African Americans of their civil rights. While Justice Stewart's majority opinion rested on a finding of state action (defendants had acted in concert with state officials), six justices were prepared to overrule the *Civil Rights Cases.* These justices believed that Section 5 empowered Congress to punish all conspiracies to interfere with the exercise of rights conferred under Section 1, "whether or not state officers or others acting under the color of state law are implicated in the conspiracy."

Nevertheless, in *United States v. Morrison,*[102] the Court again raised the issue of whether Congress could legislate to prohibit private conduct pursuant to Section 5 of the Fourteenth Amendment. A female student sued Virginia Polytechnic Institute and two male football players whom she alleged had raped her while they had been attending the university. She sued under the Violence Against Women Act (VAWA),[103] which provided a federal civil remedy for the victims of gender-motivated violence. The Court referred to the opinions in *United States v. Guest* as "naked dicta" and upheld the *Civil Rights Cases of 1883* prohibition against congressional legislation under Section 5 against private conduct. The section of the VAWA in question was struck down on the grounds that Congress had exceeded its powers under both the Commerce Clause and the Fourteenth Amendment.

Congress is also limited to addressing state action with its Fifteenth Amendment enforcement power. However, in *Jones v. Alfred H. Mayer Co.,*[104] the Supreme Court held that Congress could enforce the provisions of the Thirteenth Amendment against private actors.

Is the scope of congressional action limited to the wrong that the Reconstruction Amendments were intended to prevent? Congress has moved beyond legislating to prohibit race discrimination. Pursuant to its Article 5 powers, Congress has legislated to prohibit sex discrimination, age discrimination, discrimination based on disability, religious practices, and violence against women. Congress can act to enforce the explicit constitutional guarantees of equal protection and due process in Section 1, as well as those incorporated into the Fourteenth Amendment, including the liberties guaranteed by the First Amendment and other provisions of the Bill of Rights.[105] However, Section 5 legislation that reaches beyond the scope of Section 1's guarantees of due process and equal protection must exhibit "congruency and proportionality" between the injury to be prevented or remedied and the means adopted by Congress to that end. In *City of Boerne,*[106] the Court articulated and applied this test because protection of religious freedom is outside the scope of Section 1's actual guarantees. The Court found the evidence of injury by the states' to religious liberties was not congruent with or proportionate to the sweeping legislation embodied in the Religious Freedom Restoration Act.

There is no bright line test for determining when Congress has crossed the line from "enforcing" the substantive provisions of the Reconstruction Amendments to giving substantive meaning to the Constitution. In *Tennessee v. Lane,*[107] the Court stated that "[w]hile the line between measures that remedy or prevent unconstitutional actions and measures that make a substantive change in the governing law is not easy to discern, and Congress must have wide latitude in determining where it lies, the distinction exists and must be observed."[108] The only guidance given by the Court to determine if Congress had crossed the "remedial" line into making "substantive changes" is that there must be "congruence and proportionality" between the injury to be remedied and the means adopted to remedy or prevent the injury.[109]

In *Kimel v. Florida Board of Regents*[110] and *Board of Trustees of the University of Alabama v. Garrett*,[111] the Court applied the congruency and proportionality test and held that the Age Discrimination in Employment Act and Title I of the Americans with Disabilities Act were not appropriate legislation under Section 5 of the Fourteenth Amendment. For that reason, both acts were also deemed an unconstitutional abrogation of the states' sovereign immunity. The dissenting justices rejected the congruency and proportionality test, arguing that Section 5 empowers Congress to "exceed what is necessary to avoid a constitutional violation" to enforce submission to the equal protection and due process guarantes of Section 1. Moreover, they argued against the stringent evidentiary requirements imposed on Congress by the Court. Evidence of general societal discrimination should be coupled with specific instances of discrimination by states in evaluating whether congressional measures to address discrimination are reasonably related to the conduct it seeks to prohibit.

F A Q

Q: How does the Court apply the congruency and proportionality test to determine if legislation is appropriate under Section 5?

A: The test applies when Congress uses its Section 5 power to reach conduct beyond the scope of the actual guarantees of due process and equal protection found in Section 1. To authorize private individuals to recover money damages against the states, there must be a pattern of discrimination by the states that violates the Fourteenth Amendment, and the remedy imposed by Congress must be "congruent and proportional" to the targeted violation. The Court determines if the substantive requirements imposed on the state by the legislation are proportionate or disproportionate to the conduct Congress seeks to end. First, the Court identifies, with some precision, the scope of the constitutional right in issue to determine whether Section 1 places any limitations on the states' treatment of the class of people claiming a constitutional violation. Next, the Court looks at the conduct that Congress considers unconstitutional. Congress must do due diligence and provide a legislative record that identifies, with more than anecdotal evidence, irrational discrimination by the states toward the class. In the Voting Rights cases, the unconstitutional conduct was flagrant, pervasive, widespread, and subject to correction based on the actual guarantees of Section 1.

SUMMARY

- The Framers of the U.S. Constitution intended to create a federal government of limited powers. Although the Framers did not limit Congress to those powers specifically enumerated in the Constitution, the Framers specifically rejected the idea of providing Congress with broad legislative authority.

- In general, for a congressional enactment to be valid, Congress must assert that it acts pursuant to a delegated power as expanded by the Necessary and Proper Clause.

- Congress frequently invokes its Commerce Clause power as the basis for imposing regulation.

- While the scope of the Court's power under the Commerce Clause has waxed and waned over time, it is now construed fairly broadly (despite recent restrictions).

- As a general rule, Congress has the power to "regulate the use of the channels of interstate commerce," may "regulate and protect the instrumentalities of inter-state commerce, or persons or things in interstate commerce, even though the threat may come only from intrastate activities," and can regulate activities that have a "substantial relation to interstate commerce" if they "substantially affect interstate commerce."

- The Constitution delegates various other powers to Congress, including the power to tax, to spend for the general welfare, to declare war, and to ratify treaties.

- Congress's commerce power has been defined broadly enough to allow Congress to pass civil rights legislation.

CONNECTIONS

State Power to Regulate Commerce
As we shall see in Chapter 5, the Commerce Clause has been regarded as contain-ing "negative implications" that limit the authority of the states to regulate com-merce. As the scope of federal power expanded following the constitutional battles of the 1930s, the scope of state power has arguably declined.

Freedom of Speech and Freedom of the Press
Even though the scope of the federal power to regulate commerce has expanded radically, there are still limits on that power. For example, when we discuss free speech, Congress has tried to regulate content on the Internet through its com-merce power, but such regulations have been struck down under the First Amendment.

Equal Protection
The Equal Protection Clause also places limits on the scope of Congress's power by prohibiting discrimination on various grounds.

Endnotes

1. U.S. Const. art. III, §1.
2. U.S. Const. art. III, §2.
3. U.S. Const. art. III, §3.
4. U.S. Const. art. IV, §1.
5. U.S. Const. art. IV, §3, para. 1.
6. U.S. Const. art. IV, §3.
7. U.S. Const. amend. XIII, §5.
8. U.S. Const. amend. XV, §2.
9. U.S. Const. amend. XXIV, §2 (abolish poll taxes); *id.* amend. XVI (levy an income tax).
10. 17 U.S. (4 Wheat) 316 (1819).
11. 206 U.S. 46 (1907).
12. Gibbons v. Ogden, 22 U.S. (9 Wheat) 1 (1824) (Johnson, J., concurring).
13. Daniel A. Farber & Suzanna Sherry, *A History of the American Constitution* 25 (1990).
14. *See, e.g.*, U.S. Const. art. I, §9, cl. 1 (prohibiting Congress from barring the importation of slaves before 1808); U.S. Const. art. I, §9 (prohibiting preferences to individual ports).
15. *See* Cherokee Nation v. Georgia, 30 U.S. (5 Pet.) 1 (1831).
16. 22 U.S. 1 (1824).
17. Chief Justice Marshall was involved in two other major Commerce Clause decisions. *See* Wilson v. Black-Bird Creek Marsh Co., 27 U.S. (2 Pet.) 245 (1829) (upholding a state statute authorizing the building of a dam on a navigable creek); Brown v. Maryland, 25 U.S. (12 Wheat) 419 (1827) (striking down a state statute that imposed a license fee on importers).
18. 2 Charles Warren, *The Supreme Court in United States History* 75 (1922).
19. *Id.*
20. *Id.*
21. *Id.*
22. *Id.*
23. 77 U.S. 557 (1870).
24. 75 U.S. (8 Wall.) 168 (1868).
25. 128 U.S. 1 (1888).
26. 188 U.S. 321 (1903).
27. 234 U.S. 342 (1914).
28. 247 U.S. 251 (1918).
29. *See* Robert S. McElvaine, *The Great Depression* 137 (1984).
30. *Id.*
31. *Id.*
32. 298 U.S. 238 (1936).
33. R.R. Retirement Bd. v. Alton R.R. Co., 295 U.S. 330 (1935).
34. A. L. A. Schechter Poultry Co. v. United States, 295 U.S. 495 (1935).
35. United States v. Butler, 297 U.S. 1 (1936).
36. 293 U.S. 388 (1935).
37. 295 U.S. 495 (1935).
38. *See* Norman v. Baltimore & Ohio Ry. Co., 294 U.S. 240 (1935).
39. *See* Sonzinsky v. United States, 300 U.S. 50 (1937); Ky. Whip & Collar Co. v. Illinois, 299 U.S. 334 (1937).
40. In addition, the plan would have added as many as 50 new federal judges. This was not the only attempt by a president to pack the Court. *See, e.g.*, Sidney Ratner, *Was the Supreme Court Packed by President Grant?*, 50 Pol. Sci. Q. 343 (1935).
41. *See* William E. Leuchtenburg, *The Origins of Franklin D. Roosevelt's "Court Packing" Plan*, 1966 Sup. Ct. Rev. 347, 347-394.
42. Judiciary Act of 1789, §1.
43. Judiciary Act of 1801.
44. Judiciary Act of 1864, §2.
45. Judiciary Act of 1866, §1.
46. 300 U.S. 379 (1937).
47. 301 U.S. 1 (1937).
48. *See* Leuchtenberg, *supra* note 41.
49. *See* United States v. Lopez, 514 U.S. 549, 558 (1995).
50. Shreveport Rate Cases, 234 U.S. 342 (1914).
51. *See* NLRB v. Jones & Laughlin Steel Corp., 301 U.S. 1, 37 (1937).
52. *See* Tinker v. Des Moines Independent Community School District, 393 U.S. 503 (1969).
53. 312 U.S. 100 (1941).
54. 317 U.S. 111 (1942).
55. 322 U.S. 533 (1944).
56. 109 U.S. 3 (1883).

57. 379 U.S. 241 (1964).
58. 379 U.S. 294 (1964).
59. 402 U.S. 146 (1971).
60. 452 U.S. 264 (1981).
61. Among other things, the act required: (a) restoration of land after mining to its prior condition, (b) restoration of land to its approximate original contour, (c) segregation and preservation of top-soil, (d) minimization of disturbance to the hydrologic balance, (e) construction of coal mine waste piles used as dams and embankments, (f) revegetation of mined areas, and (g) spoil disposal.
62. The Court stated that "surface mining and reclamation standards are essential in order to insure that competition in interstate commerce among sellers of coal produced in different States will not be used to undermine the ability of the several States to improve and maintain adequate standards on coal mining operations within their borders."
63. 462 U.S. 919, 985 (1983).
64. Ballerina Pen Co. v. Kunzig, 433 F.2d 1204, 1207-1208 (D.C. Cir. 1970), *cert. denied*, 401 U.S. 950 (1971).
65. FTC v. Ruberoid Co., 343 U.S. 470, 487 (1952) (Jackson, J. dissenting).
66. 514 U.S. 549 (1995).
67. 528 U.S. 141 (2000).
68. 514 U.S. 669 (1995) (per curiam).
69. 529 U.S. 598 (2000).
70. 545 U.S. 1 (2005).
71. Justice O'Connor, joined by Chief Justice Rehnquist and Justice Thomas, dissented, argued that the "Court's definition of economic activity is breathtaking" since the "homegrown cultivation and personal possession and use of marijuana for medicinal purposes has no apparent commercial character" and "was never in the stream of commerce, and neither were the supplies for growing it." Moreover, respondents did not come into possession of the marijuana as a result of a commercial transaction, but instead grew it in their own homes, and she doubted whether the existence of homegrown marijuana for medical purposes "has a substantial effect on inter-state commerce [or] is necessary to an interstate regulatory scheme." Justice Thomas also dissented, arguing that "respondents' local cultivation and consumption of marijuana is not '[c]ommerce . . . among the several States'" because they "neither buy nor sell the marijuana that they consume."
72. U.S. Const. art. I, §2, cl. 3.
73. U.S. Const. art. I, §8, cl. 1.
74. 158 U.S. 601 (1895).
75. U.S. Const. amend. XVI ("The Congress shall have power to lay and collect taxes on incomes, from whatever source derived, without apportionment among the several States, and without regard to any census or enumeration").
76. 300 U.S. 308 (1937).
77. 259 U.S. 20 (1922).
78. 296 U.S. 287 (1935).
79. *See, e.g.*, United States v. Kahriger, 345 U.S. 22 (1953) (tax on firearms); Sonzinsky v. United States, 300 U.S. 506 (1937) (tax on wagering).
80. 340 U.S. 42 (1950).
81. 297 U.S. 1 (1935).
82. 483 U.S. 203 (1987).
83. 451 U.S. 1 (1981).
84. 356 U.S. 44 (1958).
85. *See* Ashcroft v. Free Speech Coalition, 122 U.S. 1389 (2002); Reno v. ACLU, 521 U.S. 844 (1997).
86. 252 U.S. 416 (1920).
87. 354 U.S. 1 (1957).
88. 124 U.S. 190 (1888).
89. 252 U.S. 416 (1920).
90. 133 U.S. 258 (1890).
91. The Slaughterhouse Cases, 83 U.S. (16 Wall) 36 (1873).
92. 109 U.S. 3 (1883).
93. 379 U.S. 241 (1964).
94. That the "intercourse" of which the chief justice spoke included the movement of persons through more states than one was settled as early as 1849. . . . Nor does it make any difference whether the transportation is commercial in character. . . . People of all races travel today more extensively than in 1878 when this Court first passed upon state regulation of racial segregation in commerce. . . .
95. *See* McCulloch v. Maryland, 17 U.S. (4 Wheat) 316 (1819).
96. 384 U.S. 641 (1966).
97. City of Boerne v. Archbishop of San Antonio & United States, 521 U.S. 507 (1997).

98. The positive grant of authority is found in Section 5 of the Fourteenth Amendment and Section 2 of the Thirteenth and Fifteenth Amendments.

99. *See* South Carolina v. Katzenbach, 383 U.S. 301 (1966); Katzenbach v. Morgan, 384 U.S. 641 (1966).

100. 521 U.S. 507 (1997).

101. 383 U.S. 745 (1966).

102. 529 U.S. 598 (2000).

103. 42 U.S.C. §13981 (2000).

104. 392 U.S. 409 (1968).

105. *See also* United States v. Georgia, 546 U.S. 151 (2006).

106. 521 U.S. 507.

107. 541 U.S. 509 (2004).

108. *Id.* at 520-521.

109. The Court used examples of limitations that ensure "congruence and proportionality" from the Voting Rights Act, which includes termination dates, geographic restrictions, and egregious predicates. *Id.* at 533.

110. 528 U.S. 62 (2000) (ADEA).

111. 531 U.S. 356 (2001) (ADA).

Federal Executive Powers

3

In theory, the federal executive powers are limited, cabined by express grants of authority in Article II and restrictions such as the separation of powers doctrine. In practice, federal executive powers in an age of terrorism and globalization seem to be everywhere.

OVERVIEW

The seeming divergence between theory and practice concerning the scope of executive powers is due in part to the broad brush strokes with which the executive's powers are painted in the Constitution. Without an exacting job description, the executive is often guided by his own discretion in carrying out a wide variety of functions, from enforcing the law, to acting as commander-in-chief of the armed forces, to representing the country as its primary foreign diplomat. The scope of federal executive powers often depends on where the courts set the boundaries and on the shifting state of world and domestic affairs.

A. CENTRALIZED POWER IN THE PRESIDENT

1. Express and Inherent Powers
2. Nondelegation of Powers
3. Appointment and Removal Powers
4. Veto Powers

B. PRESIDENTIAL ENFORCEMENT POWERS

C. THE PARDON POWER

D. POWER ABROAD: FOREIGN POLICY; WAR; AND TREATY POWERS

1. Treaties and Executive Agreements
2. War and Terrorism Powers
3. The AUMF
4. The Military Commissions Act of 2006
5. The Early Detention Cases
6. The Modern Detention Cases: Post 9/11

E. EXECUTIVE IMMUNITY AND PRIVILEGE: SHIELDING THE EXECUTIVE FROM JUDICIAL POWER

1. Executive Immunity from Suit
2. Executive Privilege from Disclosure

F. IMPEACHMENT

A. Centralized Power in the President

Significantly, the powers of the executive branch are not distributed among several positions or people, but instead are located entirely within a single person, the president. The Constitution states that "the executive Power shall be vested in a President."

This centralization of power seems counterintuitive to what one would expect of a new country that just broke away from a monarchy. While the fear of a president usurping power in the new United States certainly existed, the country's experience

Sidebar

A PROTOCOL FOR ORGANIZING EXECUTIVE POWERS

Protocols, meaning the maps or framework of a topic, are useful organizing tools. Experts use protocols all of the time, while novices do not. Instead, novices often "fly by the seat of their pants." There are protocols in constitutional law—step-by-step analyses of problems—that help scholars to understand the subject in general and the executive branch in particular. For example, in constitutional law overall, the first step generally is to examine *powers*—first whether they exist and then their boundaries. The second step is to analyze the *limits* on power—whether contained in the body of the Constitution or, more likely, in the amendments.

To understand the executive branch, a similar two-step protocol applies. The first step is to examine what powers exist for the executive and then to review the limits on that power, such as through the separation of powers doctrine or the amendments in the Constitution.

In determining the scope of the executive branch's powers, the first place to look is Article II of the Constitution, which describes the express powers of this branch of the government. The broad outlines of the text of Article II and the Framers' intent do not provide any exacting boundaries, though, particularly when the executive's power is viewed in contrast to the powers of the other branches—the legislature and the judiciary.

Historically, the scope of the executive's powers has ebbed and flowed, often reflected by the state of the times. In times of international conflict, especially when the United States is at war, executive power has seemed to grow. In times of peace, executive power has either recessed or lay dormant (depending on one's perspective).

under the Articles of Confederation in the 1780s apparently was more than enough to show the Framers the benefits of a strong executive. The Articles of Confederation lacked a strong federal government or chief executive and allowed the charter states to act as competitors, rather than as the complementary parts of a larger union. Accordingly, the Constitution ceded significant decision-making power to a chief executive — power to hold the nation together from within and to protect it from adverse forces from the outside.

F   A   Q

Q: Are there executive branches on the state and local levels?

A: Yes. State and local executives generally wield similar enforcement powers, but their powers may be described somewhat differently in state constitutions and local charters than on the federal level. State and local constitutions must not conflict with the federal Constitution, but can go further than the "floors" or "minimums" set by the federal Constitution.

(1) Express and Inherent Powers

The executive's powers have been significantly shaped not only by the express grant of powers in the Constitution, but also by the implied **separation of powers** doctrine. This is the implied constitutional doctrine that views federal powers as divided among the judicial, executive, and legislative branches. This foundational principle helps frame the entire federal government and assists courts in negotiating conflicts between the branches (much like parents negotiating conflicts between siblings). Courts often ask whether an encroachment by one branch on the power of another is constitutionally permissible. While this doctrine resolves interbranch disputes, it also serves to define the scope of each branch's powers.

The separation of powers doctrine provides more than dividers between the branches. The doctrine also governs how the branches share power and work together cooperatively. The sharing principle, based on subdivided complementary responsibilities (for example, one branch pays for the armies, another branch directs the armies), is often described as "checks and balances," since a significant objective of the doctrine is to keep each branch in check to avoid domination by one branch over the others.

The dividing lines between the functions of each branch in the text of the Constitution are often murky. Consequently, the courts act as referees in boundary disputes between the branches, particularly when a branch, such as the executive, claims inherent or implied powers as a justification for acting.

F   A   Q

Q: Where in the Constitution is the "separation of powers" described?

A: The phrase "separation of powers" is not found anywhere in the Constitution. The phrase is attributed to French Enlightenment political philosopher Baron de Montesquieu, who described the doctrine in his book, *The Spirit of Laws* (1748). Yet even though the Constitution does not use this phrase, its description of federal (and often state) powers reflects the Framers' intent to compartmentalize the government into distinct branches with different job descriptions. The idea of separation, however, as suggesting walls between the branches, does not accurately depict what the Constitution is doing. Many powers are shared by two or more branches, such as war powers, which are shared by the executive and legislative branches. A more accurate characterization is "checks and balances," indicating the true intent of the division. A better way to think of separation of powers, then, is as the interdependence of shared powers.

The executive branch has argued over the centuries that it has both implied powers from the positive grants of powers in the Constitution and inherent powers derived from its position as leader of the country. Such powers have been recognized by the courts in limited circumstances.

For example, while there is no clause in Article II equivalent to the Necessary and Proper Clause of Article I, Section 8, which has been used to support implied powers for the Congress, it is widely accepted that the executive branch possesses implied powers as well. As commander-in-chief, for example, the president has the power to commit troops in an armed conflict to protect U.S. citizens, both at home and abroad.

The boundaries of these unstated powers depend on whether the powers in question are domestic or foreign in nature. As a general rule, the president's powers

"I don't think you can distance yourself from the White House on this one. After all, you are the President."

are more circumscribed domestically than abroad. The *Youngstown Sheet & Tube* case brings home this point nicely.

Youngstown Sheet & Tube Co. v. Sawyer,[1] commonly referred to as "the Steel Seizure case" given its most prominent fact, still provides a basic framework for the operation of the separation of powers as it describes the relationship between the legislative and executive branches. *Youngstown* stands for the proposition that the executive generally cannot exercise domestic law-making power, even when the president believes the situation constitutes an emergency.

The facts of *Youngstown Sheet & Tube Co.* are significant. The U.S. steel industry had decided to strike immediately prior to the Korean War. President Truman, claiming the strike would have devastating effects on the making of armaments for the war, threatened to order strikers back to work. The Congress considered enacting legislation supporting President Truman's position, but did not do so. When the steelworkers went out on strike, Truman issued an executive order that effectively propelled the steel operations to recommence. The steelworkers brought suit.

The Supreme Court expedited the hearing in the case. The question before the Court involved the scope of executive power: Did President Truman have the power to issue an executive order that was legislative in nature? Under the circumstances, the Court resoundingly said the answer was no.

Justice Jackson's concurrence has become the lasting legacy of the Steel Seizure case, the opinion that has survived the test of time. Justice Jackson divided up the president's powers into three parts. His trilogy included (1) situations where Congress enacts a law approving the executive's conduct, (2) situations where Congress is silent, and (3) situations where Congress enacts a law disapproving the executive's conduct. Justice Jackson concluded that the president's powers were at their greatest level in category number 1, when Congress had given its approval to the president's actions, and at their lowest point in category number 3, when Congress had disapproved of the president's plan of conduct.

Significantly, Jackson recognized a middle category, category number 2, when Congress is silent about the president's proposed course of conduct. According to Justice Jackson, in this "twilight zone" of silence, the president could step into the breach and wield the unused power.

In its analysis of the Steel Seizure case, the Court observed that Congress had considered President Truman's plan of action through proposed legislation and had rejected the legislation. In the terminology of Justice Jackson's concurrence,

Sidebar

INTERPRETING THE CONSTITUTION WHEN IT IS SILENT ON A TOPIC

While the Constitution is the legal backbone of the U.S. government, it is more of a great outline than a detailed analysis of every problem arising over time in an evolving society. The Constitution is silent on many topics, from the scientific and technological advances not present in the Framers' era, to even those subjects that commonly existed at that time, such as the death penalty. Also, the evolutionary spin of society, from the medical use of marijuana, to instant messaging over the Internet, to the era of private space travel, could not have been contemplated by the Framers.

The courts use various methods to interpret constitutional silence. Because there is no text to interpret, courts attempt to divine what the Framers intended in several ways. Courts look at the Constitution as a whole, the structure of a particular clause or article as well as the context — what was occurring contemporaneously in society at the time the Constitution or an amendment was adopted. If these methods do not supply a sufficiently identifiable meaning, the courts also refer to broader policy — such as utility, competency of the decision maker or the slippery slope — to resolve what a provision means. The courts also defer to the amendment process of Article V, refusing to supply their own interpretation of a provision that may be only tenuously related to the text.

Congress's disapproval moved the situation into Jackson's category number 3, where the president's power was the lowest. Consequently, the president did not have the domestic power to act.

After the Supreme Court's decision, the steelworkers continued their strike. The strike soon ended, however, and the war effort was not irreparably harmed.

The question of whether the executive has inherent powers is the subject of longstanding debate. While the president has incidental powers as chief executive — such as the power to entertain foreign dignitaries and to represent the country in international conferences — these powers arguably emerge from the position of the president as the chief executive of the country as much as from any express grant of power in the Constitution.

In re Neagle[2] is one of the earliest and most significant affirmations that the executive branch possesses some inherent power. Reading almost like a made-for-television drama, the attorney general of the United States assigned a federal marshal to protect a U.S. Supreme Court justice from attack. As feared, an attack was made on the justice, and the marshal did his job by killing the attacker. Because the attorney general did not have the express constitutional authority to assign a protective detail, however, the marshal was arrested and charged with murder. The marshal filed a habeas corpus petition, and the case was heard by the Supreme Court. With the value of the marshal's service perhaps lingering in the backs of their own minds, the Supreme Court justices ruled in favor of the marshal. The Court concluded that unstated "bodyguard" power existed. This power, essentially arising out of the "take care" enforcement powers, included ensuring the safety of government employees.

Many presidents have argued that since the Constitution does not formally reject implied and inherent powers and since the president is the figurative and literal leader of the country, the presidency has a plethora of unstated powers at its disposal. Teddy Roosevelt exemplified those presidents with such a sweeping perspective. He said: "My belief was that it was not only [the president's] right but his duty to do anything that the needs of the Nation demanded unless such action was forbidden by the Constitution or laws."[3] The executive branch of President George W. Bush has to some extent embraced the spirit of this statement, particularly as it relates to fighting enemy combatants and submitting signing statements, which are written objections or clarifications of laws offered contemporaneously by the president as he signed bills into law. (Signing statements are described in further detail below.)

F   A   Q

Q: What is federalism?

A: The term "federalism" indicates there are essentially two sovereigns or governments in the United States: the federal government, and state governments. These dual governments coexist, despite overlapping on occasion. When express or implied conflicts occur between validly enacted federal laws and validly enacted state laws, the federal laws are considered to have supremacy under Article VI, and the state laws must give way.

(2) Nondelegation of Powers

The nondelegation of powers doctrine in effect instructs the branches that they cannot trade or give away their own powers or borrow or usurp the powers of other branches. Essentially, the branches are stuck with their own job descriptions.

This doctrine reached its high-water mark in the earlier part of the 1900s. Since 1935, however, when the Supreme Court struck down two statutes as unconstitutional delegations of power,[4] the nondelegation doctrine has lost much of its steam. Today, it retains its status as a constitutional doctrine, but the branches, especially Congress, have been permitted to shuffle many details of their tasks to other branches to complete.

In general, the Court requires an "intelligible principle" as a predicate to the delegation of powers. *Mistretta v. United States*[5] involved challenges to the sentencing guidelines created by the U.S. Sentencing Commission. The Court found the Commission and its guidelines did not violate the nondelegation doctrine, asserting that so long as Congress provides an "intelligible principle" for the work to be done by a commission or committee, it would be constitutionally permissible. Justice Blackmun noted that in an increasingly complex society, Congress simply could not do it all and instead needed help with the details.

(3) Appointment and Removal Powers

It is perhaps useful to think of appointment and removal powers as parallels to hiring and firing. Unlike private business, the hiring and firing process is more complicated under the Constitution. The Constitution divides government "hires" into two categories — those persons considered an officer of the United States and those who are "inferior officers." The procedure varies for each type of "hire." The president nominates and then appoints officers of the United States, the highest-ranking officials — including ambassadors, federal judges, and the heads of departments such as the secretaries of state and defense — but only after the "advice and consent" (meaning the approval) of the Senate. The appointment of the remaining officers, called "inferior officers" by the Constitution, depends on the Congress. Congress can determine who shall appoint inferior officers, choosing to vest the power entirely in the president, the courts or the heads of departments. As *Buckley v. Valeo*[6] showed, while Congress can create the office, it cannot reserve for itself the authority to appoint the inferior officer.

Buckley involved challenges to the Federal Election Campaign Act of 1971. The Act restructured the Federal Election Commission, allegedly violating the separation of powers. The Supreme Court agreed and struck down the reorganization, finding that Congress effectively took executive power by reserving the appointment of four of the eight members of the commission to Congress alone. The sticking point was the type of powers exercised by the commission. If the commission just investigated and informed, it would function and be treated like other congressional committees. As constructed, however, the commission had enforcement authority, including the power to file a court claim. This type of power belonged to the executive, not the legislature, and the executive character meant that Congress could not retain significant control over it.

F   A   Q

Q: Are interbranch appointments constitutional?

A: Yes. The Appointments Clause states that "the Congress may by Law vest the Appointment of such inferior Officers, as they think proper, in the President alone, in the courts of Law, or in the Heads of Departments." This clause gives Congress the power to determine who appoints an inferior officer. For officers of the United States, the president can nominate the officer, but there also must be Senate approval.

The line between officers of the United States and inferior officers can be a fuzzy one, with little guidance provided for close cases. In *Morrison v. Olson*,[7] Chief Justice Rehnquist attempted to provide some clarity. Congress passed the Ethics in Government Act of 1978, which provided the opportunity to appoint an independent counsel to investigate and prosecute certain high-ranking government officials regarding potential violations of the federal criminal laws. The process by which a special prosecutor would be appointed under the law involved the attorney general requesting a special prosecutor from a court created by the same act. The Court found this interbranch appointment scheme to be constitutional. The Court concluded that because the "hire" was not considered an officer of the United States, but was instead an inferior officer, the appointment could be made by a special court located within the judiciary.

A special appointments issue involves vacancies. If a vacancy exists when the Senate is in recess, the president has the power to fill the vacancy under Article II, Section 2, Clause 3. These recess appointments, as they are known, last only until the end of the Senate's next term. While the appointments last for a limited duration, the recess power has been wielded by numerous presidents with considerable effectiveness. Starting with George Washington, presidents have used this clause to populate the federal judiciary with preferred judges and to fill other governmental vacancies as well, sometimes with controversial candidates. Most officials receiving recess appointments lose their jobs when their terms expire. A lucky few, however, use their time in service as a positive "tryout" and are subsequently affirmed through the regular appointments process. The list of successful appointees includes the former lead counsel for the NAACP and future Supreme Court justice, Thurgood Marshall (appointed to the Second Circuit Court of Appeals).

While the "hiring" or appointments power is outlined in the Constitution, the document is generally silent on whether and how the president can "fire" and remove officers once hired. With respect to Article III judges, who hold their positions for life during "good behavior," the removal process is clear — only impeachment will suffice. For other officials, it long has been assumed that if the president has the power to appoint, the power to remove follows, especially for officers exercising an executive function. This deductive reasoning process, however, is not entirely accurate, and the Supreme Court has drifted toward accepting shared responsibility between the president and Congress for the removal of officers.

The executive's power to remove officials sometimes extends to officials operating at least partially outside of the executive branch. These officials are not "purely executive officers," but can be considered "hybrids." For example, an official in the Federal Trade Commission might have some judicial duties.[8] With hybrid appointees, the president's removal powers are significantly diminished. Attempts to unilaterally fire the official may be impermissible, and Congress may craft job descriptions that include the length of the hybrid officials' terms and the bases for removal. Even if Congress has not specified how a hybrid official can be removed, principles of autonomy and independence from executive interference have created a "keep out executive" approach by the Court, as suggested in *Wiener v. United States.*[9]

Other nuances in the removal power have developed in recent years. For example, if the legislature authorizes "hiring" an officer with an executive function, the legislature cannot wield broad removal power with respect to that officer. In *Bowsher v. Synar,*[10] the Congress passed the Balanced Budget and Emergency Deficit Act of 1985 to try to reduce the federal deficit. The act authorizes the comptroller general to determine the appropriate budget cuts and to relay that information to the president for implementation. The law permitted the removal of the comptroller general based on a number of reasons, including "inefficiency" or "malfeasance," in addition to the more traditional method of removal, impeachment.

In determining the constitutionality of the act's removal scheme, the Supreme Court employed a separation of powers analysis. The Court first determined that the comptroller had an executive or law enforcement function — discretionary authority to make determinations about budget cuts. The Court then found that because of the comptroller's executive nature, the legislature must allow the comptroller to do its job without reserving broad removal authority. Essentially, the legislature cannot make the law and then hold removal power over the office holder charged with executing the law.

However, the Court has upheld some limitations on the president's power to remove inferior officers. *Morrison v. Olson*[11] (discussed above for its appointments ramifications) weighed in on firing decisions as well. In *Morrison*, the Supreme Court upheld a law limiting the president's removal of an independent counsel to good cause. This holding is consistent with the view that even some inferior officers who have only an executive function cannot simply be removed by the president without any interbranch interference whatsoever.

(4) Veto Powers

Pursuant to Article I, Section 7, Clause 3, the president has the power to "disapprove of" properly enacted congressional laws, which has come to mean the power to veto laws presented by Congress. The veto is but one component of the law-making process.

Step number one in the law-making process is the approval of a bill by both houses of Congress, the House of Representatives and the Senate. Step number two is the proper presentment of the bill to the president. Step number three is presidential approval or disapproval of the bill. The president has ten days to disapprove and veto the law. If the president waits the ten days and does nothing, the bill becomes law. Step number four occurs if the president vetoes the bill. If a bill is vetoed, there is still one more opportunity to push the bill into law. Congress can override the veto by repassing the law with a two-thirds majority vote by both the House of Representatives and the Senate.

Historically, Congress attempted to circumvent the ten-day veto time limit by adjourning shortly after approving a bill, thus denying the president the opportunity to return a bill with objections. To create a disincentive for such conduct, the "pocket veto" rule was established. Under this rule, a bill presented to a president during a congressional recess does not become law until signed by the president, even if the normal ten-day limit expires. The pocket veto rule does not apply, though, if only one house of Congress is in recess.

Line-Item Vetoes. The Constitution is silent about whether a president must veto the entire four corners of legislation or whether a veto of a component part, such as the disapproval of one line of a bill, would be permissible. The president's power to veto a "line item" of a bill was authorized by Congress in its Line Item Veto Act of 1997. (As expected, the act was approved by the president and not vetoed.) The act permitted a line-item veto only for certain offending provisions, including the authorization of fixed or discretionary spending and "limited tax benefits."[12]

In *Clinton v. New York*,[13] the Supreme Court struck down the line-item veto provisions of the Line Item Veto Act, finding that the provisions violated the separation of powers doctrine and specific procedures detailed in the Constitution for law making. The Court held that the Presentment Clauses of Article I, Section 7, require the Congress to present bills to the president for approval before the bill becomes a law. The Court found that any unilateral modification of a law by the president — such as a line-item veto — did not comport with the letter of the clause or the Framers' intent regarding the law-making process.

Legislative Vetoes. After recognizing how useful a veto could be, Congress decided to create its own veto mechanism in some laws. The legislative override practice dates back to the 1930s and has been used to permit one of the two houses of Congress to rebut executive application of a law.

The Supreme Court considered and disapproved of this veto practice in *Immigration & Naturalization Service v. Chadha*.[14] *Chadha* held that the veto scheme violated the formal protocols of the Constitution in moving a bill into law. In *Chadha*, Congress enacted a law that permitted one house to effectively override executive action. Congress argued that the one-house override mechanism was not a true legislative act and therefore it should not be subject to veto requirements. The legislative override had been used by Congress after an immigration judge had suspended deportation proceedings for Chadha, an East Indian with a British passport. Shortly thereafter, the Judiciary Subcommittee on Immigration, Citizenship, and International Law offered a resolution to continue the deportation of several individuals, including Chadha. The House of Representatives approved the resolution. Because the action was not considered to be a "legislative act" by the House, it was not sent to the Senate or the president.

The Supreme Court focused on the text of the Constitution in deciding the *Chadha* case. The Presentment Clauses embodied in Article I, Section 7, require both houses of Congress to approve a bill and then to forward the bill for the president's signature prior to it becoming law. This "bicameralism" requirement led the

Supreme Court to conclude that outside of the few instances where the Constitution approved of one house acting alone, such authorization violated the two-house approval rule. Consequently, while the Court called the legislative veto a "convenient shortcut," the Court also found it to be an unconstitutional shortcut.

Presidential Signing Statements. A presidential signing statement is a method by which a president can voice opposition to a law short of vetoing it. The practice has gained considerable currency since the time of President Ronald Reagan. In more recent times, the practice has proliferated. President George W. Bush has become its most ardent practitioner. According to one commentator, President Bush issued more than 500 constitutional challenges to legislation he signed into law during the first six years of his presidency.[15]

The signing statement allows presidents to achieve a variety of goals. By issuing a signing statement about a law the president finds disagreeable, the president can voice displeasure about the law or pertinent parts of it short of exercising a veto. The president also can shape the law by declaring its constitutional boundaries — creating its own "executive" history of sorts.[16] Further, a signing statement may direct how the law will operate, creating advance expectations about the law's implementation and offering greater predictability, much like operating a dam-controlled river. In addition, the signing statement stakes out the president's turf and promotes the idea of a "unitary president," allowing the president to participate in the public debate about what is constitutionally repugnant.

The signing statement often occurs contemporaneously with the approval of a bill by the president. While the use of signing statements has no official constitutional significance, the practice has drawn considerable scholarly and public attention. What effect, if any, should signing statements have? If a president signs a bill into law, is the president constitutionally permitted to adapt the enforcement of the law to the president's point of view? These questions have not been resolved in the courts, but are becoming all too prevalent to ignore.

B. Presidential Enforcement Powers

The Constitution grants the executive the power to enforce and carry out the law. Given the vast quantity, tangle, and scope of federal law in the modern United States, the implementation of law has dictated the rise of the executive bureaucracy. The bureaucracy refers to the many people employed in Washington, D.C. and elsewhere who are tasked with implementing the laws. Significantly, the laws passed by Congress often have latent and overt ambiguity, demanding executive branch interpretation in their implementation. That the executive determines to some extent how to carry out the law is often a

---

Sidebar

HOW CONGRESS'S EXPANSIVE COMMERCE CLAUSE POWER AFFECTS THE EXECUTIVE BRANCH

The Commerce Clause of Article I, Section 8, gives Congress the power to regulate commerce "among . . . the states." This provision has been broadly construed by the judiciary to bestow on Congress the power to design a variety of federal laws, often limited only by whether the regulated activity substantially affects interstate commerce. One illustration of how the broad interpretation of Congress's Commerce Clause powers has impacted the executive branch involves the federal criminal law. In the late 1700s, the number of federal criminal laws could be counted on two hands. In large part fueled by the support of the Commerce Clause, the number today has risen exponentially, into the thousands. These laws require a parallel increase in enforcement by the executive branch, dictating the setting aside of more resources and employees.

cost-effective result, given the executive's experience and expertise in implementing laws. Some interpretations can substantially impact the nature of laws, though, even affecting the laws' substance.

In *Gonzales v. Raich*,[17] the Supreme Court upheld the U.S. attorney general's interpretation of the Controlled Substances Act, even though it meant invalidating a California statute. Specifically, the attorney general issued a rule that essentially interpreted the Act as flatly prohibiting marijuana use, even for alleged medicinal purposes. The California statute had carved out an exception for marijuana consumption, specifically when it was used to relieve the suffering of persons with terminal or severe chronic illness or disease.

The Supreme Court decided the attorney general's rule was a constitutional interpretation of the Controlled Substances Act. The Court reasoned that the act was intended to be a comprehensive regulation, not a partial one that would have allowed some controlled substances to be exempted for medicinal purposes — such as the California law had done. Given that the attorney general's interpretation of the federal act was permissible, the conflict between the federal act and a valid state law led to the state law giving way under the conflict resolution framework of the Supremacy Clause — when valid federal and state laws conflict, the federal law prevails.

One year after its decision in *Gonzales v. Raich*, the Supreme Court took a different view of an interpretation by the attorney general. In *Gonzales v. Oregon*,[18] the Supreme Court struck down the attorney general's interpretation of the Controlled Substances Act as it related to the Oregon Death With Dignity Act. Writing for the Court, Justice Kennedy essentially found that the attorney general's interpretation of the congressional statute went too far. He concluded that the federal law was not intended to prohibit the dispensing of medication for euthanasia purposes under the Oregon law.

The Court explored how much deference the judiciary should give to the executive when the executive interprets ambiguous statutes. Sometimes, substantial deference by the courts is warranted. For example, the Court in *Chevron U.S.A. Inc. v. Natural Resources Defense Council, Inc.*,[19] the seminal case relating to the "deference doctrine," stated that the interpretation must be within the delegated authority to create administrative rules.

While deference is appropriate in many circumstances, the Court found it was not appropriate in *Raich* because the Congress did not delegate the "broad authority" to interpret its law to the executive in the way the executive chose to interpret it. Instead, the areas where the executive was given the authority to interpret the Controlled Substances Act were limited and specific. The Court relied on the federal statute's "text and design" for the permissible scope of statutory interpretation.

F A Q

Q: Why does the Supreme Court give deference to the other branches of government?

A: In resolving cases, the Court recognizes that it acts within the separation of powers doctrine, meaning the Court's job is not to be a "super" legislature or "super" executive officer, second-guessing the wisdom of the decisions made by members of those branches. Instead, the Court's job is simply to review the constitutionality of the other branches' conduct. This role often requires the Court to defer to decisions that might be unwise or unpopular — but are still constitutional. The Court uses the deference doctrine to recognize its limited review role.

C. The Pardon Power

The president is not only charged with the power to enforce the law, but is given the discretion to override the law through the power to grant "Reprieves and Pardons." In a sense, this pardon power is a "super-veto," although not of a law but of a specific criminal charge or conviction.

Because the pardon power is textually committed to the president's discretion and is without standards, pardons are not reviewable by the courts. Instead, the president has the last word on whether to grant such a reprieve from a criminal charge or conviction.

Significantly, there is nothing in the Constitution spelling out when and how the pardon power should be exercised. The Constitution notes only that it covers "Offenses against the United States." The Constitution does specify, however, one type of case the power does not reach, "Cases of Impeachment." This exemption indicates that impeachment cases are left to the coordinate branch of government, the Congress, to resolve. In addition, the pardon power is exclusively criminal and does not extend to civil cases or judgments.

F   A   Q

Q: What are unreviewable presidential actions?

A: Some acts by the executive branch in general and the president in particular are unreviewable in courts. The reasons for this executive immunity from suit are essentially twofold: (1) The separation of powers leaves some acts by the executive branch beyond the checks and balances of the other branches so as not to create a chilling effect over those acts, such as foreign policy decisions; and (2) some presidential acts are based entirely on discretion and have no standards for judicial review, such as decisions to pardon others.

D. Power Abroad: Foreign Policy; War; and Treaty Powers

Like other areas of the Constitution, the powers of the government abroad are shared by the branches of government, generally the legislative and the executive. The theory relating to international action remains the same as the interlocking nature of domestic governmental conduct — it is preferable to have the agreement of two branches before action is taken to deter headstrong and hasty government decision making.

By virtue of the office, the president serves as the primary representative of the United States abroad. This representative function operates on many levels, from the social (entertaining foreign dignitaries), to the political (entering into negotiations with foreign governments), to the military (acting as the commander-in-chief). With the ever-changing international political landscape, the president's powers abroad have grown more complex.

F   A   Q

Q: Given the complexity and extensive nature of the powers of the president abroad, are these powers limited by the Constitution or simply by public opinion?

A: While the answer to this question was unclear in years past, particularly in the mid-1900s, it appears firmly settled today that the Constitution restrains the powers of the president both domestically and internationally. The fact that the Constitution governs, however, does not begin to resolve the many ambiguities that exist in the document and how the document applies to ever-advancing technological and geopolitical issues confronted by the president when functioning as the head of state.

(1) Treaties and Executive Agreements

(a) Treaties

Under the constitutional framework, the president has the power to create foreign policy through treaties with other countries, provided the Senate gives its approval. This power ranges from the mundane details of upcoming summits to nuclear disarmament. Validly enacted treaties take precedence over existing federal law and any conflicting state law. In *Missouri v. Holland*,[20] for example, Justice Holmes determined that the 1918 Migratory Bird Treaty Act between the United States and Great Britain was constitutionally enforceable despite claims to the birds by the State of Missouri.

The treaty power generally does not supersede valid domestic law unless a treaty clearly indicates it will be self-executing, meaning it automatically becomes binding federal law, preempting valid domestic law at the same time. In 2008, the Supreme Court held in *Medellin v. Texas*[21] that a treaty did not displace valid Texas law because it did not clearly intend to be self-executing. The majority opinion, written by Chief Justice Roberts, stated in part: "The President has an array of political and diplomatic means available to enforce international obligations, but unilaterally converting a non-self-executing treaty into a self-executing one is not among them. The responsibility for transforming an international obligation arising from a non-self-executing treaty into domestic law falls to Congress. As this Court has explained, when treaty stipulations are 'not self-executing they can only be enforced pursuant to legislation to carry them into effect.' "[22]

The Chief Justice's analysis in *Medellin* elaborates on the self-executing and non-self-executing treaty distinction, particularly as it relates to the roles of the executive and legislative branches:

> The Constitution vests the President with the authority to "make" a treaty. Art. II, §2. If the Executive determines that a treaty should have domestic effect of its own force, that determination may be implemented "in mak[ing]" the treaty, by ensuring that it contains language plainly providing for domestic enforceability. If the treaty is to be self-executing in this respect, the Senate must consent to the treaty by the requisite two-thirds vote, consistent with all other constitutional restraints.
>
> Once a treaty is ratified without provisions clearly according it domestic effect, however, whether the treaty will ever have such effect is governed by the fundamental constitutional principle that "'[t]he power to make the necessary laws is in Congress; the power to execute in the President.'"[23]

(b) Executive Agreements

In addition to "making" treaties, the president also has the power to enter into agreements with other countries, even without the express ratification of the Senate. These instruments are called executive agreements and are usually justified by implicit congressional approval. The agreements often involve the mundane details of international issues, such as where the heads of state will sit in a meeting, as compared to the broad and important policy issues central to many treaties.

Perhaps the most widely remembered executive agreements were the product of a dark moment in U.S. history, the 1979 Iran hostage crisis. There, Iranian students held Americans captive in the U.S. Embassy in Tehran for 444 days. The release of the hostages, occurring in January 1980 during the presidential transition from Carter to Reagan, involved several executive agreements. In *Dames & Moore v. Regan*,[24] then Justice Rehnquist upheld the executive agreements. After observing that *Youngstown Sheet & Tube Co. v. Sawyer*[25] required presidential action to flow from Congress or the Constitution, Justice Rehnquist concluded the Congress had implicitly approved the use of executive agreements in this type of situation.

(2) War and Terrorism Powers

(a) September 11th

In an era dominated by concerns about terrorism and characterized by the need to fight shadowy networks of individuals operating across national boundaries, outside of the traditional auspices of countries and their uniformed armies, the executive's powers have reached seemingly unprecedented levels. It has been argued that a strong executive branch, capable of acting swiftly and secretly, is necessary to fight the enemy. The limits on the stealth of action and its breadth are still being sorted out, however, as there are many objections lodged against unlimited power for the intelligence community and the executive branch without the usual application of checks and balances.

The war powers are divided between the legislature and the president. The legislature has the sole power to declare war and appropriate money for the armed forces, and the president is the commander-in-chief of the armed forces. Since September 11, 2001, the president has used the commander-in-chief power and the need for expedient action to become the central government figure in fighting terrorist activities. The sweeping power claimed by the president has raised a wide variety of constitutional issues, particularly about the detention, interrogation, and surveillance tactics used.

Article II, Section 2, Clause 1, states that the president is the "Commander-in-Chief of the Army and Navy of the United States." This sweeping declaration offers the president not only a shared role in combating war and foreign aggression, but over time has given the president the upper hand in deploying the armed forces in national security matters.

(b) The War Powers Resolution

The emergence of the executive as the primary decision maker in issues of national security, particularly in its powers over committing troops to armed conflict, led the Congress to reassert its shared constitutional role. In 1973, Congress passed the War Powers Resolution. Over the opposition of President Nixon and his veto, the act attempted to frame the circumstances and length of time the president could commit troops abroad without consulting or seeking the approval of Congress. The president was permitted to deploy troops in certain circumstances, but only if there was a declaration of war, specific statutory authorization, or a national emergency resulting from an attack on the United States, its territories, or its armed forces. If deployment is authorized, the president must still report back to the Congress with the president's rationale and can maintain such an action unilaterally only for a limited amount of time, unless an extension is granted by Congress.

The War Powers Resolution has not been truly tested in the courts, and the act's impact to date has been largely symbolic. Since its adoption, presidents have not appeared to curtail their use of the commander-in-chief powers or bow to congressional participation in combat-related decisions.

It is well established that under the umbrella of the commander-in-chief power, the president has the authority to commit U.S. soldiers to battle. The major constitutional question has been whether such battles constitute wars and, if so, whether the president is limited by Congress's power to declare war. Several significant "wars" in U.S. history have been fought without an actual declaration of war: the Korean War; the Vietnam War; and the invasion of Iraq, to name a few prominent examples. These military actions illustrate that in the modern world, an express declaration of war may be an unnecessary and cumbersome appendage to concerted and effective deployment of the armed forces.

(c) The Detention of Enemy Combatants

The problem of terrorism is a complex one, ranging from the pragmatic issues relating to fighting an unseen enemy associated with an organization and not a country, to the constitutional issues resulting from the surveillance, interrogation, and detention of persons who may be part of or supporters of terrorist groups. After the attacks on the United States on September 11, 2001, a wave of legislation and executive orders occurred with the goal of combating the perpetrators of the attacks, the al Qaeda network, as well as supporters of al Qaeda, such as the Taliban. A new agency was created, the Department of Homeland Security, and a law called the USA PATRIOT Act of 2001 (an acronym standing for "Uniting and Strengthening America by Providing Appropriate Tools Required to Intercept and Obstruct Terrorism Act") was passed.

(3) The AUMF

The Authorization for Use of Military Force (AUMF) was enacted by Congress a week after the September 11th attacks. The act authorized the president to use all "necessary and appropriate force against those nations, organizations or persons" that planned, authorized or committed the attacks or harbored such persons "to prevent any future acts of international terrorism against the United States. . . ." What Congress intended to authorize by this statement has been the subject of much debate, including within the Supreme Court in several of its opinions, as well as in the court of popular opinion.

Pursuant to the AUMF, the president issued an order two months later directing the military to detain any persons who were part of terrorist organizations or who supported those organizations. Many people were captured in Afghanistan and Iraq who were believed to be part of or supporters of terrorist groups. These persons often ended up at the U.S. naval base at Guantanamo Bay, Cuba. While the overwhelming majority of the detainees were foreign nationals, some were U.S. citizens.

Because the response to the terrorist attacks on the United States was novel territory for the country both experientially and constitutionally, the legality of the government's response took time to percolate through the courts. While courts usually defer to the executive and legislative branches with regard to military actions, the Supreme Court has rebuffed the executive's powers in the area of combating terrorism in several major cases. Each time the Court has rebuffed the executive as overreaching, the executive or Congress has generally responded.

For example, after the Supreme Court issued several major decisions, including *Hamdi v. Rumsfeld* and *Hamdan v. Rumsfeld*, both described below, the Congress in September 2006 adopted new legislation to clarify the president's powers. In the Military Commissions Act of 2006, the Congress gave the president broad power to interpret the Geneva Conventions, try enemy combatants by military tribunal, and use hearsay and other typically inadmissible evidence in those tribunal hearings. In addition, the act limited the judicial review of such detentions, prohibiting the habeas corpus petitions that led to some of the Supreme Court decisions.

(4) The Military Commissions Act of 2006

The Military Commissions Act was challenged in the courts and found in 2008 by the Supreme Court to be constitutionally infirm.[26] The 5-4 decision in *Boumediene v. Bush* concluded that foreign nationals detained in the U.S. naval base in Guantanamo Bay retained habeas corpus rights despite a contrary provision in the Military Commissions Act.[27] This "thrust and parry" activity between the courts and the other branches may very well be followed by another reply, but it reveals the significance of the separation of powers and the importance of "checks and balances."

(5) The Early Detention Cases

To best understand *Boumediene* and other recent cases, it is important to review the legal history that precedes it. Pertinent legal rulings can be traced to the Civil War era. In 1862, during the Civil War but prior to a formal declaration of war by Congress, President Lincoln ordered the blockade of southern ports. This order was upheld by the Supreme Court in its decision, *The Prize Cases.*[28] The case was so-named because the United States had captured as "prizes" ships trying to evade the blockade of southern ports. The Court reasoned that the president was acting pursuant to a much earlier act of Congress that gave the president the authority to quell an insurrection or an invasion. The Court noted an actual state of war can exist without a formal declaration of war, and that a civil war can be functionally the same as an invasion by a foreign country.

The other major case of that era, *Ex parte Milligan*,[29] involved the constitutionality of using a military commission to try enemies of the Union. One of these enemies was Lambdin Milligan, who was accused of conspiracy and plotting to aid the confederacy. Milligan was tried by a military commission and sentenced to death in 1864. While the Supreme Court upheld the suspension of habeas corpus used to detain Milligan, the Court found the use of a military commission to be unconstitutional under the circumstances. The Court focused on several facts in reaching its decision—Milligan was not in the military, was not engaged in acts opposing the government when captured, and was a U.S. citizen residing in Indiana, a state where the civilian courts remained open.

Perhaps the most widely used precedent of World War II is *Ex parte Quirin*,[30] involving the invasion of the continental United States by several German agents who were transported to Long Island, New York, and Ponte Vedra Beach, Florida, by German submarine. The eight combatants, one of whom was allegedly a U.S. citizen, were soon captured. The failed saboteurs were tried by military commission under the law of war pursuant to an executive order by President Roosevelt.

The Supreme Court, in an expedited hearing, drew a distinction between lawful and unlawful combatants, saying that lawful combatants are prisoners of war, with certain rights, while unlawful combatants, such as secret spies in plainclothes, are belligerents who are not entitled to the status of prisoners of war. These combatants fell in the unlawful category and were properly brought to trial before military tribunals. Soon after the Supreme Court decision, six of the eight petitioners were executed. (The other two combatants had their death sentences commuted as a result of assisting the United States.)

(6) The Modern Detention Cases: Post 9/11

The modern cases, all decided in the aftermath of September 11th, built on the World War II precedent in deciding the constitutional limits of what the Congress and executive can do in combating terrorists and terrorist activities. The Supreme Court has attempted to answer a variety of questions about enemy combatants, those who participate in terror activities — from what their constitutional rights are to how and by whom these combatants will be tried. Significant legal questions included whether the alleged terrorist was a U.S. citizen and where he was being held, within the United States or abroad.

Hamdi. In *Hamdi v. Rumsfeld*,[31] Yaser Esam Hamdi, a U.S. citizen who was born in Louisiana and grew up in Saudi Arabia, was captured in Afghanistan for allegedly aiding the enemy. He was detained as an "enemy combatant." While being held indefinitely and without charges, Hamdi's father filed a habeas corpus claim on his son's behalf. The Supreme Court was confronted with the question of whether the Constitution provides at least some due process of law to detainees, at least those detainees who are U.S. citizens. Justice O'Connor, in a plurality opinion, explained that the AUMF authorized the detention of enemy combatants, including Hamdi, but did not deal with whether Hamdi had the right to challenge his status as an "enemy combatant." Justice O'Connor concluded that the Constitution protects detainees to the extent that they are permitted to contest their status as enemy combatants. This includes using the writ of habeas corpus, as long as it is not properly suspended, and the ability to "present and rebut facts" about the enemy combatant status, based on due process requirements. In a widely quoted line from her opinion, Justice O'Connor stated, "We have long since made clear that a state of war is not a blank check for the President when it comes to the rights of the Nation's citizens." Several months after the *Hamdi* decision, the government and Hamdi's attorney worked out a deal involving the detainee's release, provided that he leave the U.S., renounce his U.S. citizenship and restrict his travel.

Hamdan. In *Hamdan v. Rumsfeld*,[32] the Supreme Court again had the opportunity to clarify the permissible scope of the executive's power involving enemy combatants, in this case the power to construct military commissions to try the combatants outside that which is authorized by the rules of the Uniform Code of Military Justice and the Geneva Conventions. Salim Ahmed Hamdan, originally from Yemen and not a U.S. citizen, allegedly served al Qaeda as Osama bin Laden's driver. He was captured in Afghanistan in November 2001 and subsequently detained at the U.S. naval base in Guantanamo Bay. Hamdan was charged with conspiracy and designated for trial by special military commission as an enemy combatant. The Supreme Court held that a trial by the special military commission was unconstitutional. The Court found that the rules governing the commission's operation violated both the Uniform Code of Military Justice and the Geneva Conventions. In essence, the Court decided that the president could not try an enemy combatant by a military commission that failed to comply with the military and international community's laws, even with respect to noncitizens.

Padilla. In *Padilla v. Hanft*,[33] Jose Padilla was detained at Chicago's O'Hare Airport as an enemy combatant. He allegedly intended to detonate a "dirty bomb"—an explosive containing nuclear material. Padilla filed a habeas corpus petition to force the government to try him or release him. The government opposed these choices, although after Padilla filed suit in the Supreme Court, the government formally charged him with a crime. Because the government had effectively granted Padilla relief as per his request, the Supreme Court denied his motion for *certiorari.* Justice Kennedy, writing to explain his reasons for voting to deny *certiorari,* wrote that the case would not affect Padilla's custody and therefore should not proceed.

Secret Surveillance. After September 11th, a secret surveillance program was initiated by the executive branch's National Security Agency to identify and stop terrorist activity. The surveillance included obtaining telephone records of people who might be involved in terrorism. The surveillance conducted through the program was not backed by a judicial warrant, even one from the Foreign Intelligence Surveillance Court. This court was created by an act of Congress specifically to handle sensitive international intelligence issues, which would seemingly include secret domestic spying on U.S. citizens or legal aliens to stop domestic terrorism irrespective of its origin.

Pursuant to the law creating the Surveillance Court, if probable cause was shown that the target of the surveillance was an agent of a foreign power or a terrorist, then a warrant would be granted. This standard was problematic for the National Security Agency, however, because its surveillance likely was to determine whether individuals were indeed agents or terrorists.

Whether the president has some power to conduct surveillance without a warrant to combat terrorism remains an open question. The constitutional issues relating to secret surveillance are still being sorted out.

Boumediene. In June 2008, the Supreme Court decided *Boumediene v. Bush*,[34] holding that the detainees at the U.S. naval base in Guantanamo Bay, Cuba, had the constitutional right to assert habeas corpus claims in U.S. federal courts and that the Combatant Status Review Tribunals (CSRT) and other procedures from the Detainee Treatment Act of 2005 did not adequately substitute for a denial of the writ of habeas corpus. In a 5-4 decision written by Justice Kennedy, the Court concluded, "Therefore §7 of the Military Commissions Act of 2006 (MCA), 28 U.S.C.A. §2241(e) (Supp. 2007), operates as an unconstitutional suspension of the writ [of habeas corpus]."[35] The Court conceded there was no direct precedent for determining whether the Constitution applied to foreign nationals being held on foreign soil. Justice Kennedy observed, however, "The detainees . . . are held in a territory that, while technically not part of the United States, is under the complete and total control of our Government."[36] He then concluded that the constitutional privilege of habeas corpus applies to the detainees at the Guantanamo Bay base. The analysis continued, though, because if the writ of habeas corpus was suspended pursuant to the Suspension Clause, that suspension would be acceptable if adequate substitute procedures were erected as a replacement. Justice Kennedy found that the substitute procedures embraced by Section 7 of the Military Commissions Act, relying on the earlier 2005 Detainee Treatment Act, did not suffice, and reinstated the habeas corpus writ privilege to the detainees.

Significantly, the Court did not consider or direct what procedural scheme would suffice in the federal courts for a detainee claiming wrongful detention. Moreover, it was unclear what would happen to the naval base at Guantanamo Bay if many of the 270 remaining detainees were released or transferred. This tension between security and freedom of action undoubtedly will continue unfolding in the enemy combatant context.

E. Executive Immunity and Privilege: Shielding the Executive from Judicial Power

Executive privilege and immunity are unique. Both the privilege and the immunity shield the executive branch from the judicial system. Executive privilege means the freedom from disclosure of information or, conversely, the right to keep secrets. Executive immunity refers to the right not to be sued in court.

(1) Executive Immunity from Suit

There is a limited judicial shield built into the separation of powers that protects the executive branch from lawsuits. The limited shield described as executive immunity from suit can be traced to the seminal case of *Marbury v. Madison*.[37] In *Marbury*, Chief Justice John Marshall took the unusual approach of discussing the merits of the case before dismissing it for lack of jurisdiction. Marshall noted that the lawsuit against James Madison, the secretary of state, an executive officer, was permissible because the suit was based on ministerial, nondiscretionary acts of the executive — delivering William Marbury's commission to become a justice of the peace — and not unreviewable discretionary acts such as foreign policy decisions. Those unreviewable acts of discretion also are committed by the Constitution to one branch without the oversight of the other branches. The recognition in *Marbury* of a partial immunity from suit has turned out to be a mixed blessing for the executive. On the one hand, *Marbury* recognizes a constitutional basis for immunity from judicial power. On the other hand, *Marbury* allows the president to be sued and subjects the president to judicial requests for the disclosure of information. As a practical matter, *Marbury* can be seen as the precedent for cases more than 100 years in the future involving Presidents Nixon and Clinton.

In *Clinton v. Jones*,[38] for example, the Supreme Court considered whether a civil lawsuit against President Clinton arising out of alleged conduct that took place in Arkansas when Clinton was governor could go forward while he was still president or whether the president had immunity from suit. The Court held that the lawsuit could go forward after balancing the interests involved. The Court decided that the drag on the presidency from such a suit would not create significant costs to the operation of the country, particularly when compared to the costs of delaying the lawsuit for several years.

(2) Executive Privilege from Disclosure

United States v. Nixon,[39] the so-called Watergate tapes case, recognized a partial implied executive privilege against the disclosure of information. The case arose from what seemed like an ordinary burglary on June 17, 1972, at the Watergate Hotel in Washington, D.C. The politically motivated burglary led to a cover-up traced to President Richard Nixon. In a trial of the burglars, the district court subpoenaed secret tapes made by the president of his Oval Office discussions. The president refused to relinquish the tapes, citing executive privilege. The Supreme Court found that there was an implied constitutional executive privilege from disclosure, but that the privilege was a qualified one. The court created two categories of presidential communications, those related to national security and foreign policy matters, and all other communications. In the Watergate tapes case, the claim of privilege was not related specifically to national or military security, and the Court held that balancing the president's interest in secrecy against the need for evidence in a criminal trial was the appropriate evaluation. Upon balancing, the Court ruled in favor of the disclosure of the tapes.

The opinion had significant ramifications. Not only did it lead to the release of the tapes, but President Nixon's subsequent resignation could be traced to the Court's decision as well.

More recently, in *Cheney v. United States District Court*,[40] the Supreme Court reaffirmed the basic principles established in *Nixon* concerning the existence of a partial executive constitutional privilege. In *Cheney*, the vice president was sued pursuant to the Federal Advisory Committee Act of 1972. The plaintiffs sought the disclosure of information discussed at meetings of the National Energy Policy Development Group, a private group that the vice president chaired. The plaintiffs made several discovery requests, which were ignored by the vice president.

The Supreme Court remanded for further proceedings, leaving the response to the requests for discovery within the court of appeals' discretion. The Supreme Court noted that separation of powers principles provided the coequal executive branch with protection, even short of the vice president formally invoking executive privilege. The Court distinguished *Nixon* on several grounds, most notably framing the differences between the civil proceedings in the case at bar and the criminal proceedings in *Nixon*. The Court stated that the need for the evidence is not as great in a civil case as compared to a criminal one, that there are fewer natural systemic checks on requests for evidence in civil cases than criminal, and that the particular requests in this civil case were far broader than the one faced by President Nixon.

Significantly, the Court appeared to assume that executive privilege applied to the vice president as well as the president, if not other members of the executive branch. In this regard, the case went beyond the privilege recognized in *Nixon*.

F. Impeachment

Impeachment of the president is the ultimate check on presidential power. This extreme measure is permitted for "the President, Vice President, and all civil officers of the United States," and results only after the "conviction of treason, bribery, or other high crimes and misdemeanors." Article I, Sections 2 and 3. The impeachment process is bifurcated, with the House of Representatives responsible for voting to impeach and the Senate then trying the "case," with a two-thirds majority required for conviction and removal from office.

The impeachment process has been used only twice with presidents — the 17th president, Andrew Johnson, and the 42nd president, Bill Clinton. Both Presidents Johnson and Clinton were impeached by the House of Representatives but acquitted by the Senate. In President Johnson's case, he allegedly violated an act passed by Congress to limit the president's powers, subjecting him to impeachment in 1868. As for President Clinton, the impeachment was the culmination of a special prosecutor's inquiry that uncovered a personal relationship between the president and one of his interns. The impeachment in December 1998 (and subsequent trial) emerged after the president made statements under oath about the relationship.

SUMMARY

■ The executive has express and implied powers, the limits of which are not entirely clear.

■ The executive's powers are greater when the executive acts abroad, rather than domestically.

■ Justice Jackson's concurrence in *Youngstown Sheet & Tube Co.* provides the governing trilogy for when the president can act domestically: (1) when authorized by Congress, the power is at its highest level; (2) when Congress is silent, some power still exists; and (3) when Congress opposes executive action the power is at its lowest level.

■ Constitutional limits exist when an executive appoints or removes some government officers.

■ The president's power over enemy combatants is generally governed by the Constitution, especially for U.S. citizen detainees or noncitizens detained either on U.S. soil or in a place completely controlled by the United States, such as the naval base in Guantanamo Bay, Cuba.

■ The president has both partial immunity from suit and a privilege against disclosure of communications.

■ The president can be removed by impeachment, a process that includes both a vote to impeach by the House of Representatives and a trial and conviction by the Senate.

CONNECTIONS

Judicial Review

Judicial review means the power of the courts to interpret the Constitution in deciding a case. Some actions by the president and the executive officers are solely committed to that branch and are considered political questions, unreviewable by courts. The pardon power is an illustration of an area that is nonjusticiable, beyond review, and the power to act as the commander-in-chief provides another area that is sometimes unreviewable by courts.

Separation of Powers

This is the implied constitutional doctrine that greates judicial oversight of the judicial, executive, and legislative branches, not only for unchecked aggrandizement, but often to ensure the opposite—interdependence. This vision of "checks and balances" underlies the judicially enforced limitations on each branch of government, including the executive.

Congressional War Powers

Under Article I, Congress has the power to declare war. The power has been rarely used, however, given the expediency of conflict and the efficiency of presidential action as compared to congressional approval.

Congress's Power over "Inferior Courts"

Article III of the Constitution provides that Congress may "Ordain and Establish" inferior courts, referring to federal district courts, essentially the trial courts and the federal circuit courts of appeals. How and when Congress may limit the jurisdiction of such courts is a significant question, one that will need further clarification in the area of judicial review of executive actions relating to the fight against terrorism.

Endnotes

1. 343 U.S. 579 (1952).
2. 135 U.S. 1 (1890).
3. Theodore Roosevelt, *Theodore Roosevelt—An Autobiography* (vol. 20 of *The Works of Theodore Roosevelt*, natl. ed.), chap. 10, 347-348 (1926).
4. *See* A. L. A. Schecter Poultry Corp. v. United States, 295 U.S. 495 (1935); Panama Refining Co. v. Ryan, 293 U.S. 388 (1935).
5. 488 U.S. 361 (1989).
6. 424 U.S. 936 (1976).
7. 487 U.S. 654 (1988).
8. *See, e.g.,* Humphrey's Exr. v. United States, 295 U.S. 602 (1935).
9. 357 U.S. 349 (1958).
10. 478 U.S. 714 (1986).
11. 487 U.S. 654 (1988).
12. 2 U.S.C. §691 et seq. (1994 & Supp. II 1997).
13. 524 U.S. 417 (1998).
14. 462 U.S. 919 (1983).
15. *See* Phillip Cooper, *By Order of the President: The Use and Abuse of Direct Presidential Action* (2002) (describing a variety of tools used by presidents to wield power, from executive orders to signing statements).
16. *See, e.g.,* Ameron Inc. v. U.S. Corps of Engrs., 787 F.2d 878 (3d Cir. 1986).
17. 545 U.S. 1 (2005).
18. 546 U.S. 243 (2006).
19. 467 U.S. 837, 842-845 (1984).
20. 252 U.S. 46 (1920).
21. Medellin v. Texas, 128 S. Ct. 1346 (2008).
22. *Id* at 1368, quoting Whitney v. Robertson, 124 U.S. 190, 194 (1888).
23. *Id.* at 1369 (citations omitted).
24. 453 U.S. 654 (1981).
25. 343 U.S. 579 (1952).
26. Boumediene v. Bush, 553 U.S. — (June 12, 2008) (No. 006-1195).

27. *Id.*
28. 67 U.S. (2 Black) 635 (1863).
29. 71 U.S. 2 (1866).
30. 317 U.S. 1 (1942).
31. 524 U.S. 507 (2004).
32. 548 U.S. 557 (2006).
33. 126 S. Ct. 1649 (2006).
34. *Boumediene*, 553 U.S. at—.
35. *Id.* at—.
36. *Id.*
37. 5 U.S. 137 (1803).
38. 520 U.S. 681 (1997).
39. 418 U.S. 683 (1974).
40. 542 U.S. 367 (2004).

2

The States
(and Their Relationship
to the Federal Government)

State Power to Regulate Commerce

4

During the first third of the twentieth century, although Congress had the power to regulate commerce "among" the states, the U.S. Supreme Court

O V E R V I E W

construed the Tenth Amendment as giving the states a reserved power over "purely local" commerce. As a result, most commerce cases involved claims that the federal government was violating the states' reserved power. Following the constitutional crisis of the 1930s, the distinction between "local" commerce and commerce "among" the states substantially eroded. As the Court rendered decisions giving the federal government broader authority under the Commerce Clause, the federal government assumed much greater authority over both interstate and local commerce. Moreover, the Court began to treat the Tenth Amendment as a truism, thereby depriving states of their reserved power over commerce. Even though recent decisions have pared back the scope of federal power somewhat, the federal commerce power remains broad.

Since the 1930s, the federal courts have faced quite different questions regarding the scope of state power. Some cases involve questions about whether federal law preempts state law. In other words, the question is whether the existence of federal regulation (or an attempt by the federal government to regulate in a particular area) precludes state regulation in a given area. The remaining cases involve so-called **dormant power** situations in which the federal government has the power to regulate in an area, but has not done so or has done so incompletely. In dormant situations, the question is whether the Commerce Clause contains negative implications that limit or preclude state regulation. Often, dormant power cases focus on whether the federal government has **exclusive power** over an area, in the sense that only Congress can regulate, or whether it has **concurrent power** with the states. In addition, many cases focus on the role and scope of judicial review.

A. Early Cases

The Constitution provides little guidance on states' regulation of commerce. Article I, Section 8, explicitly gives Congress the power to regulate commerce "among" the several states, but does not say whether the states can also regulate commerce. That issue was left to the courts. In construing the Constitution, a number of early cases focused on whether the federal government's authority over commerce was exclusive or whether the states had concurrent authority. *Gibbons v. Ogden*,[1] one of the earliest cases, adopted an expansive view of federal power and a more limited view of state power. *Gibbons*, yet another landmark decision by Chief Justice Marshall, involved a New York statute that gave Robert Livingston and Robert Fulton the "exclusive" right to navigate steamboats in certain state waters. Livingston and Fulton subsequently assigned the route between New York and New Jersey to Aaron Ogden. When Thomas Gibbons sought to operate ships on the same route under a federal license, Ogden sought injunctive relief on the basis that the federal license was invalid. The U.S. Supreme Court concluded that the federal license was valid and struck down New York's "exclusive" license on Supremacy Clause grounds.

Although *Gibbons* did not resolve the question of whether the state was free to regulate and license navigation in the absence of a conflict between the federal license and the state license, the Court did discuss that issue in dicta. In doing so, the Court recognized that some powers can be simultaneously exercised by both the federal government and state governments, including the "power to lay and collect taxes" (which the Court concluded was "indispensable"). The Court also found that the states had the power to enact inspection laws and other similar regulations because such regulations "act upon the subject before it becomes an article of foreign commerce, or of commerce among the States, and prepare it for that purpose" and "can be most advantageously exercised by the States themselves." Indeed, the Court concluded that Congress was given no "direct general power" over these issues that remained under state regulatory control. However, as to matters within the scope of federal regulatory power, the Court suggested that "the word 'to regulate' implies in its nature, full power over the thing to be regulated," and that an argument can be made that the federal power "excludes, necessarily, the action of all others that would perform the same operation on the same thing." While the Court did not purport to definitely conclude this issue, it did find that there is "great force in this argument [that the federal power is exclusive], and the Court is not satisfied that it has been refuted."

Q: If *Gibbon's* logic (and its suggestion that the federal power to regulate necessarily excludes the states from regulating) were rigorously applied, wouldn't the states today have very little power to regulate commerce given the Court's more expansive attitude toward the scope of the federal commerce?

A: If *Gibbon's* logic were pushed to its logical limits, the states would have very little power to regulate commerce today if the federal power were regarded as "exclusive." Interestingly, one of the powers that the *Gibbons* Court discusses as within the scope of state regulatory authority is the inspection power. Chief Justice Marshall characterizes inspection laws as a state matter and concludes that no "direct general power over these objects is granted to Congress." However, under decisions such as *Wickard* and *Perez* (both discussed in Chapter 2), where the Court increased Congress's reach under the Commerce Clause, it is easy to argue that Congress can impose inspection laws. As a result, if federal power is exclusive rather than concurrent, one can argue that the states now lack power to impose inspection laws. The reality is that, as the scope of federal power has expanded, the Court's willingness to allow the states to regulate matters within the scope of congressional power has expanded as well.

Not all early decisions adopted an expansive view of federal power. For example, *Gibbons* was followed by the holding in *Plumley v. Commonwealth of Massachusetts.*[2] Benjamin Plumley, who was convicted of violating a Massachusetts law prohibiting the sale of adulterated oleomargarine, sought relief through a writ of habeas corpus. The Court denied the writ, holding that Massachusetts law did not violate Congress's commerce power: "If there be any subject over which it would seem the states ought to have plenary control, and the power to legislate[,] it is the protection of the people against fraud and deception in the sale of food products."

In at least one early case, *Cooley v. Board of Wardens,*[3] the Court focused on whether a matter was national or local in deciding whether the states had the power to regulate. That case involved a Pennsylvania law that required ships to use local pilots when they navigate in the Delaware River. Plaintiff, who did not want to use a local pilot, claimed that the law contravened Congress's power to regulate commerce. The case was complicated by the fact that a 1789 federal law seemed to give the states authority to enact local pilot laws. However, since federal laws did not explicitly preclude the states from intervening in this area, the Court focused on whether "the nature of the [federal] power . . . requires that a similar authority should not exist in the states." The Court recognized that commerce is a "vast field" and that some subjects require a "single uniform rule, operating equally on the commerce of the United States in every port," and other subjects require diversity to "meet the local necessities of navigation." In deciding which type of regulation fell into which category, the Court focused on whether the subject is in its "nature national, or admit only of one uniform system, or plan of regulation," and therefore requires "exclusive legislation by Congress."

On the facts of *Cooley*, the Court held that Congress had decided to allow the states to regulate, and that the issue "is local and not national; that it is likely to be the best provided for, not by one system, or plan of regulations, but by as many as the legislative discretion of the several states should deem applicable to the local peculiarities of the ports within their limits." Although the Court found that Congress had legislated on the subject, "its legislation manifests an intention, with a single exception, not to regulate this subject, but to leave its regulation to the several states." As a result, the Court upheld the law. Note that although *Cooley* distinguished between matters that are national and those that are local, the Court did not provide the courts with a precise test for distinguishing between what is national and what is local.

Cooley does suggest that Congress can authorize the states to exercise regulatory authority that they would not have in the absence of congressional authorization. In later cases, particularly *Leisy v. Hardin*,[4] the Court agreed that congressional assent matters.

Example: In *Prudential Insurance Co. v. Benjamin*,[5] the Court upheld a South Carolina tax imposed on foreign insurance companies as a condition of doing business in the state. The Court concluded that a federal law authorized the tax and that Congress "expressly and affirmatively" declared that "continued state regulation and taxation of this business is in the public interest and that the business and all who engage in it 'shall be subject to' the laws of the several states in these respects."

B. Discrimination Against Interstate Commerce

Because of the trade wars that led to the adoption of the U.S. Constitution and that led the Framers to vest the commerce power in the federal government, the Court has always closely scrutinized state and local legislation that involves discrimination against interstate commerce. Statutes that discriminate against or directly regulate interstate commerce are presumptively unconstitutional and survive only if there are no less commerce-restrictive methods of achieving the statute's objectives. In other words, the Commerce Clause embodies a policy of free trade among the states that a state can "countermand only for the most compelling of reasons."

(1) Facial Discrimination

Illustrative of the antidiscrimination principle is the holding in *Baldwin v. G. A. F. Seelig, Inc.*[6] In that case, a milk dealer challenged a New York law that mandated a system of minimum prices to be paid by dealers to producers. Because the dealer purchased its product for less than the minimum price from out-of-state producers, it was denied a license to do business in New York. In striking down the New York law, the Court emphasized that New York did not have the power to regulate the price of milk in nearby states or to prohibit the introduction of "milk of wholesome quality" acquired in other states at lower prices. The Court likened the New York law to the imposition of a customs duty, which the Constitution prohibits: "If New York, in order to promote the economic welfare of her farmers, may guard them against competition with the cheaper prices of Vermont, the door has been opened to rivalries and reprisals that were meant to be averted by subjecting commerce between the states to the power of the nation."

Baldwin rejected New York's argument that the minimum price could be justified under New York's police power and its interest in ensuring a supply of "pure and wholesome milk." New York argued that the quality of milk was jeopardized "when the farmers of the state are unable to earn a living income," and that minimum prices helped ensure that farmers would not be tempted to cut corners in order to make a living. The Court noted that many anti-free trade laws could be justified by similar arguments for protection against competition. The Court held that the Constitution reflects the idea of "national solidarity" in the sense that "the peoples of the several states must sink or swim together, and that in the long run prosperity and salvation are in union and not division." Moreover, while the Court acknowledged that the exclusion of out-of-state milk would enable New York producers to produce higher quality milk, the minimum prices were not needed to ensure that Vermont milk was healthful. If New York was concerned about the wholesomeness of milk, it could regulate the importation of unhealthy products so long it did not try to "neutralize the economic consequences of free trade among the states." However, a state was not free to "place itself in a position of economic isolation" by imposing minimum prices that establish "an economic barrier against competition with the products of another state or the labor of its residents."

F A Q

Q: Not too many legislatures explicitly state their intent to discriminate, do they? So how do reviewing courts determine whether a law involves discrimination against interstate commerce?

A: In general, courts determine whether legislation involves discrimination against interstate commerce by examining the statute's language, as well as its stated objectives and its effects. In *Baldwin*, although New York stated a nondiscriminatory objective (helping to ensure a supply of wholesome milk to consumers), the Court found discrimination in the means chosen (guaranteeing minimum prices). Prior to enactment, out-of-state producers were able to sell, and were in fact selling, at prices below the minimum price. As a result, the net effect of the New York law was to raise the price of out-of-state milk, guarantee New York producers a minimum price, and thereby enhance the competitive position of New York producers.

In a number of cases, the Court has struck down differential licensing requirements on the basis that they discriminate against out-of-state interests. In, for example, *Crutcher v. Kentucky*,[7] the Court invalidated a Kentucky law that required agents of express companies not incorporated in Kentucky to obtain a license before conducting business in the state. To obtain the license, the company was required to prove that it had $150,000 in capital. The Court concluded that the right of "interstate commerce is not a franchise or a privilege granted by the state; it is a right which every citizen of the United States is entitled to exercise under the constitution and laws of the United States."

Example: In *Welton v. Missouri*,[8] the Court struck down a state statute that prohibited the sale of out-of-state goods by peddlers without a license. Although the Court recognized that the state has the power to require licenses for all pursuits and occupations, the Court regarded this licensing requirement as a tax on out-of-state goods: "[T]he commercial power continues until the commodity has ceased to be the subject of discriminating legislation by reason of its foreign character. That power protects it, even after it has entered the State, from any burdens imposed by reason of its foreign origin."

The principle of nondiscrimination also applies to state laws prohibiting the export of state resources. For example, in *Pennsylvania v. West Virginia*,[9] the Court struck down a West Virginia law that prohibited the interstate shipment of natural gas produced in the state unless and until the state's internal needs had been met. The law was passed after a cold winter in which gas supplies were inadequate. In striking down the law, the Court concluded that "we are a single nation — one and the same people." Since the Court regarded natural gas as an article of commerce, and its transmission from one state to another for sale and consumption as interstate commerce, the Court held that a state law "which by its necessary operation prevents, obstructs or burdens such transmission is a regulation of interstate commerce — a prohibited interference." Indeed, the Court noted that if "the states have such power a singular situation might result. Pennsylvania might keep its coal, the Northwest its timber, the mining states their minerals. And why may not the products of the field be brought within the principle?" Justice Holmes dissented: "I see nothing in the commerce clause to prevent a State from giving a preference to its inhabitants in the enjoyment of its natural advantages."

The Court rendered a similar decision in *Hughes v. Oklahoma*,[10] involving an Oklahoma law that made it illegal to "transport or ship minnows for sale outside the state which were seined or procured within the waters of this state." In reviewing the law, the Court held that the party challenging the statute bears the burden of showing discrimination. If it succeeds, the burden shifts to the state to demonstrate "the unavailability of nondiscriminatory alternatives adequate to preserve the local interests at stake." The Court rejected the argument that the law should be upheld as a "conservation measure" because of the state's goal of "maintaining the ecological balance in state waters by avoiding the removal of inordinate numbers of minnows." The Court concluded that the law exceeded the asserted conservation interest: "Far from choosing the least discriminatory alternative, Oklahoma has chosen to 'conserve' its minnows in the way that most overtly discriminates against interstate commerce. The State places no limits on the numbers of minnows that can be taken by licensed minnow dealers; nor does it limit in any way how these minnows may be disposed of within the State. Yet it forbids the transportation of any commercially significant number of natural minnows out of the State for sale." Justice Rehnquist, joined by Chief Justice Burger, dissented, arguing that there was no discrimination "against out-of-state enterprises in favor of local businesses" because neither in-state nor out-of-state interests were allowed to ship minnows out of the state. Moreover, "Oklahoma has not blocked the flow of interstate commerce in minnows at the State's borders. Appellant, or anyone else, may freely export as many minnows as he wishes, so long as the minnows so transported are hatchery minnows and not naturally seined minnows."

As *Hughes* demonstrates, the justices can disagree about whether a facially neutral state law reflects constitutionally suspect discrimination. In general, in finding discrimination, the Court searches for some evidence that the state is trying to advantage local interests to the detriment of interstate interests. For example, in

Kassel v. Consolidated Freightways Corp.,[11] the Court struck down an Iowa statute that prohibited 65-foot trucks on Iowa highways, but allowed the passage of 65-foot mobile homes if they were traveling to or from an Iowa location, and also allowed longer trucks in "border cities" if the other city permitted longer trucks. Although the plurality did not hold that the statute discriminated against interstate commerce, the Court noted: "Iowa's scheme . . . has several exemptions that secure to Iowans many of the benefits of large trucks while shunting to neighboring States many of the costs associated with their use. The origin of the 'border cities exemption' also suggests that Iowa's statute may not have been designed to ban dangerous trucks, but rather to discourage interstate truck traffic." Justice Rehnquist, joined by Chief Justice Burger and Justice Stewart, dissented: "[T]he effort in both the plurality and the concurrence to portray the legislation involved here as protectionist is in error."

F   A   Q

Q: Wouldn't the statute at issue in *Kassel* have been upheld if the statute had not included an exemption for border cities?

A: Perhaps. The border exemption suggested that the state legislature was not as focused on safety considerations. Indeed, if the legislature was really concerned about the fact that longer trucks were dangerous, it might have precluded longer trucks even in border cities. Of course, even if the Court does not conclude that a statute is protectionist, the Court might strike it down if it involves an undue burden on interstate commerce.

One area where the states have been allowed to discriminate against interstate commerce is in imposing quarantine laws designed to prohibit the importation of such things as diseased livestock.[12] In these cases, the Court has characterized quarantine laws as police measures designed to protect the citizenry's health and safety. By contrast, in *Railroad Co. v. Husen*,[13] the Court struck down a Missouri statute banning the importation of Texan, Mexican, or Native American cattle between March 1 and November 1. The Court declined to characterize the law as a valid quarantine measure due to its categorical nature (that is, not banning importation of just diseased cattle, but of all cattle from a certain origin).

Merely because a state attempts to ban harmful "products" does not mean that its quarantine laws or prohibitions will be upheld. For example, in *City of Philadelphia v. New Jersey*,[14] the Court struck down a New Jersey law that prohibited the importation into New Jersey of most "solid or liquid waste which originated or was collected outside the territorial limits of the State." The Court concluded that even the movement of waste is protected under the Commerce Clause, and the Court found that New Jersey was discriminating against it. The Court rejected New Jersey's argument that the discrimination was justified by the fact that New Jersey's existing landfill sites were nearly exhausted and that a prohibition on out-of-state waste would be "of crucial importance in preventing further virgin wetlands or other undeveloped lands from being devoted to landfill purposes." In striking down the legislation, the Court noted that the "evil of protectionism can reside in legislative means as well as legislative ends." While the Court recognized that New Jersey might legitimately be concerned regarding the financial costs of additional landfills, as well as the potential effects on the environment, the Court held that New Jersey may not accomplish its objectives "by discriminating against articles of commerce coming from outside the State unless there is some reason, apart from their origin, to treat them differently." The Court found ample evidence of discrimination: "On its face, [the statute] imposes on out-of-state commercial interests the full burden of conserving the State's remaining landfill space. What is crucial is the attempt by one State to isolate itself from a problem common to many by erecting a barrier against the movement of interstate trade."

The Court rejected New Jersey's claim that its statute was like a quarantine law and was similar to laws that had previously been upheld. The Court distinguished quarantine laws, noting that they "banned the importation of articles such as diseased livestock that required destruction as soon as possible because their very movement risked contagion and other evils." Such laws did not "discriminate against interstate commerce as such, but simply prevented traffic in noxious articles, whatever their origin." The Court concluded that New Jersey's statute was distinguishable because there was no claim that the "very movement of waste into or through New Jersey endangers health, or that waste must be disposed of as soon and as close to its point of generation as possible." Moreover, New Jersey waste is equally harmful, but New Jersey simply prohibits out-of-state waste: "The New Jersey law blocks the importation of waste in an obvious effort to saddle those outside the State with the entire burden of slowing the flow of refuse into New Jersey's remaining landfill sites. That legislative effort is clearly impermissible under the Commerce Clause of the Constitution." Justice Rehnquist, joined by Chief Justice Burger, dissented. "New Jersey should be free under our past precedents to prohibit the importation of solid waste because of the health and safety problems that such waste poses to its citizens. The fact that New Jersey continues to, and indeed must continue to, dispose of its own solid waste does not mean that New Jersey may not prohibit the importation of even more solid waste into the State. I simply see no way to distinguish solid waste, on the record of this case, from germ-infected rags, diseased meat, and other noxious items."

F   A   Q

Q: If New Jersey is legitimately concerned regarding the health effects of garbage and landfills, is there anything it can do to protect its own residents?

A: Yes. While the *City of Philadelphia* case makes clear that New Jersey may not respond to the health problems by prohibiting out-of-state garbage, while at the same time allowing New Jersey garbage to be deposited in state landfills, the state can impose reasonable health, welfare, and safety regulations on all landfills (as well, perhaps, on the transportation of garbage within the state).

(2) Facially Neutral Statutes with Discriminatory Purposes or Effects

Rarely does a legislature explicitly announce its intention to discriminate against interstate commerce. Instead, the legislature usually offers a nondiscriminatory rationale for its actions through a facially neutral statute. For example, in *Baldwin*, in imposing minimum milk prices, the State of New York proclaimed that the "end to be served is the maintenance of a regular and adequate supply of pure and wholesome milk; the supply being put in jeopardy when the farmers of the state are unable to earn a living income." The Court pierced through the state's analysis and concluded that the state's real objective was economic isolation.

In some instances, a state asserts a right to discriminate against interstate commerce in pursuit of a valid health and safety interest. For example, in *Dean Milk Co. v. City of Madison*,[15] a Madison, Wisconsin, ordinance prohibited the sale of milk that had not been processed and bottled at an approved pasteurization plant within a radius of 5 miles from the city's central square. The ordinance also required that milk not be sold in the city without an inspection permit issued by Madison officials, but precluded municipal inspectors from venturing farther than 25 miles from the city center. An Illinois milk distributor, which gathered milk from farms in Illinois and Wisconsin (none of which was within 25 miles of Madison), challenged the law. The distributor was denied a Madison license even though its plants were licensed and inspected by Chicago public health authorities, even though the milk was labeled "Grade A" under the Chicago ordinance, and even though the Chicago ordinance was patterned after the Model Milk Ordinance created by the U.S. Public Health Service. In striking down the ordinance, the Court held that it imposed an undue burden on interstate commerce. Although the Court recognized that the City of Madison had the power to protect the health and safety of its people, the Court held that "reasonable nondiscriminatory alternatives, adequate to conserve legitimate local interests," were available. The Court concluded that, if Madison preferred to rely on its own officials to inspect distant milk sources, it could do so by charging the actual and reasonable cost of such inspection to the out-of-state producers and processors. However, Madison could not simply prohibit out-of-state milk without "placing a discriminatory burden on interstate commerce" and inviting "a multiplication of preferential trade areas destructive of the very purpose of the Commerce Clause." The Court concluded that the regulation "must yield to the principle that 'one state in its dealings with another may not place itself in a position of economic isolation.'"

Example: In *New Energy Co. of Indiana v. Limbach*,[16] the Court struck down an Ohio statute that awarded a tax credit against the Ohio motor vehicle fuel sales tax for each gallon of ethanol sold (as a component of so-called gasohol) by fuel dealers, but only if the ethanol was produced in Ohio or in a state that granted similar tax advantages to ethanol produced in Ohio. Ohio enacted the tax credit to encourage ethanol use because it was produced from corn and had environmental advantages as a replacement for leaded gasoline, but it was more expensive than gasoline. The Court struck down the Ohio credit, noting that the law "on its face appears to violate the cardinal requirement of nondiscrimination." The Court held that a state may not "not use the threat of economic isolation as a weapon to force sister States to enter into even a desirable reciprocity agreement." As "facially discriminatory legislation," the law must be subjected to the "strictest scrutiny." Although "reciprocity requirements are not *per se* unlawful," the Court found that Indiana could not use a threat to Indiana's acceptance by taxing a product made by out-of-state "manufacturers at a rate higher than the same product made by Ohio manufacturers, without . . . justification for the disparity."

In some cases, a state's interest is sufficiently important to justify discrimination against interstate commerce. However, in such cases, the courts closely analyze the asserted interests. For example, in *Maine v. Taylor*,[17] the Court upheld a Maine statute banning the importation of live baitfish. The Court held that the statute satisfied strict scrutiny because the state's asserted purpose (protection of Maine's "unique and ecologically fragile" fisheries) could not be protected by a less burdensome method. The Court concluded that inspection methods, which tested imported baitfish for parasites, could not reliably produce disease-free shipments.

Likewise, in *Exxon Corp. v. Maryland*,[18] the Court upheld a Maryland statute that precluded a producer or refiner of petroleum products from operating a retail service station within the state. Maryland enacted the law based on evidence that gasoline stations operated by producers or refiners received preferential treatment during a prior gasoline shortage. The Court concluded that the law did not favor local producers and refiners since Maryland's entire gasoline supply flowed in interstate commerce, and there were no Maryland producers and refiners. In addition, competition was preserved because there were several major interstate marketers of petroleum that owned and operated their own retail gasoline stations (and which were not precluded from operating retail stations in the state since they did not refine or produce gasoline), and these interstate dealers competed directly with Maryland's independent dealers. "The fact that the burden of a state regulation falls on some interstate companies [for example, refiners] does not, by itself, establish a claim of discrimination against interstate commerce." The Court rejected the argument that the law impermissibly burdened interstate commerce by forcing some interstate companies out of the market because any withdrawing refiners would promptly be replaced by others. The Court also rejected the argument that "because the economic market for petroleum products is nationwide, no State has the power to regulate the retail marketing of gas." Justice Blackmun concurred in part and dissented in part, arguing that the effect of the law "is to protect in-state retail service station dealers from the competition of the out-of-state businesses," and that this "protectionist discrimination is not justified by any legitimate state interest that cannot be vindicated by more evenhanded regulation." He also expressed concern about the fact that the law would require divestiture of property worth more than $10 million, thereby inflicting significant hardship on out-of-state companies.

C. Nondiscriminatory Burdens on Interstate Commerce

Even though a state law does not discriminate against interstate commerce, the law may still affect interstate commerce and therefore may be subject to judicial scrutiny. In general, when statutes regulate local and out-of-state interests evenhandedly with only an indirect effect on interstate commerce, judicial review is less aggressive and focuses on whether the burden on interstate commerce exceeds the anticipated benefits.[19]

(1) The Scope of Judicial Review

In the absence of congressional regulation, some have argued that the federal courts should be deferential to state legislation designed to fill a regulatory gap. If Congress disagrees with the state legislation or finds it offensive, it can pass a law overriding that legislation. The contrary position argues that the courts should actively review state laws and strike down laws that burden interstate commerce.

At one point, the courts were deferential to nondiscriminatory state legislation that affected interstate commerce. Illustrative of the deferential approach is the holding in *South Carolina State Highway Department v. Barnwell Bros.*,[20] in which the Court upheld a South Carolina law that prohibited motor trucks and semi-trailer trucks from using state highways if they exceeded 90 inches in width and weighed more than 20,000 pounds. In upholding the restriction, the Court noted such issues are "matters of local concern, the regulation of which unavoidably involves some regulation of interstate commerce but which, because of their local character and their number and diversity, may never be fully dealt with by Congress." While the Court recognized that the Constitution prohibits the states from discriminating against interstate commerce, as well as from regulating inconsistently with federal statutes or regulations, it held that the states otherwise have discretion to enact regulations designed to promote safety on their highways. If Congress does not agree with what the states have done, it may pass legislation prescribing different rules. However, in the absence of federal legislation, the judicial role is limited and should focus on whether the state legislature "acted within its province, and whether the means of regulation chosen are reasonably adapted to the end sought." In other words, the federal "courts do not sit as Legislatures, either state or national," and a reviewing court is "not called upon to determine what, in its judgment, is the most suitable restriction to be applied of those that are possible, or to choose that one which in its opinion is best adapted to all the diverse interests affected." On the contrary, when "the action of a Legislature is within the scope of its power, fairly debatable questions as to its reasonableness, wisdom, and propriety are not for the determination of courts, but for the legislative body, on which rests the duty and responsibility of decision." Using this deferential approach, the Court concluded that South Carolina's conclusions were rational, and the Court upheld the law.

F A Q

Q: If *Barnwell* provides state legislatures with discretion regarding whether to enact nondiscriminatory legislation affecting interstate commerce, and evaluates such legislation under a rational basis test, what is the "remedy" for state legislation that burdens interstate commerce?

A: Under *Barnwell*, the remedy generally will not be provided by the courts and must instead come from Congress. In other words, those affected by the regulation must petition Congress to enact legislation preempting or overriding the state legislation.

The Court departed from *Barnwell*'s holding in its later decision in *Southern Pacific Co. v. Arizona*[21] and adopted a far less deferential approach to state regulation. *Southern Pacific* involved an Arizona statute that prohibited railroad trains with more than 14 passenger cars or 70 freight cars from passing through Arizona. The Court was undeferential, stating that when "Congress has not acted, this Court, and not the state legislature, is under the commerce clause the final arbiter of the competing demands of state and national interests." While states have some discretion to regulate "matters of local concern," even though those matters affect interstate commerce, they may not "materially restrict the free flow of commerce across state lines, or interfere with it in matters with respect to which uniformity of regulation is of predominant national concern." In the Court's view, the critical question was "whether the relative weights of the state and national interests involved are such as to make inapplicable the rule, generally observed, that the free flow of interstate commerce and its freedom from local restraints in matters requiring uniformity of regulation are interests safeguarded by the commerce clause from state interference."

In striking down the Arizona law, the Court took notice of the fact that trains of 70 cars length or longer (some as long as 160 cars) are the "standard practice" in the United States, and that the Arizona law imposed a "serious burden" on interstate commerce because it "materially impedes the movement [of] trains through that state and interposes a substantial obstruction to the national policy proclaimed by Congress, to promote adequate, economical and efficient railway transportation service." The impact of Arizona's law was that interstate trains had to be broken up and reconstituted as they entered Arizona or had to choose to comply with the Arizona train limit even outside of Arizona so that they were not forced to shorten trains at the Arizona border. Moreover, the Court concluded, after an exhaustive review of the evidence, that Arizona's law could not be justified as a safety regulation because shorter trains were as likely to be involved in accidents as longer trains. As result, the Arizona Train Limit Law, "viewed as a safety measure, affords at most slight and dubious advantage, if any, over unregulated train lengths, because it results in an increase in the number of trains and train operations and the consequent increase in train accidents of a character generally more severe than those due to slack action." Justice Black dissented, arguing that the trial court functioned like a "super-legislature," with a trial lasting five and one-half months, covering 3,000 pages of printed record, and resulting in a 148-page opinion. Justice Douglas also dissented, arguing that "courts should intervene only where the state legislation discriminated against interstate commerce or was out of harmony with laws which Congress had enacted."

In subsequent cases, the Court has followed the *Southern Pacific* approach rather than the *Barnwell* approach. For example, in *Bibb v. Navajo Freight Lines, Inc.*,[22] the Court struck down an Illinois statute that required the use of contoured rear fender mudguards on trucks and trailers operated in the state. The mandated mudflap differed from the mudflap permitted in 45 other states and required in Arkansas. In enacting the law, the Illinois legislature relied on evidence showing that contour flaps promote safety by preventing trucks from throwing debris onto the windshields of drivers of passing cars and following vehicles. Although the Court concluded that a state's safety measures come with a "strong presumption of validity," the Court conducted its own analysis, found that the contoured mudguards had no safety advantages, and determined that the Illinois law was inconsistent with the laws of at least two other states. In addition, the Court found that the law imposed a significant burden on interstate commerce because, if a trailer is to be operated in both Illinois and Arkansas (which have different mudflap rules) "mudguards would have to be interchanged, causing a significant delay" of from two to four hours. Moreover, the contour guard is attached to the trailer by welding and if the trailer is conveying a

Sidebar

JUDICIAL DEFERENCE

The scope of review applied in *Southern Pacific* was undeferential to the state legislature. The trial court took months of testimony, thereby producing a very large transcript, on the safety effects of Arizona's law. It then reached its own conclusions regarding the safety effects and the burden imposed on interstate commerce by the law.

cargo of explosives (e.g., for the U.S. government) it would be "exceedingly dangerous to attempt to weld on a contour mudguard without unloading the trailer." As a result, the Court struck down the law: "This is one of those cases — few in number — where local safety measures that are nondiscriminatory place an unconstitutional burden on interstate commerce. . . . Such a new safety device — out of line with the requirements of the other States — may be so compelling that the innovating State need not be the one to give way. But the present showing — balanced against the clear burden on commerce — is far too inconclusive to make this mudguard meet that test."

In another illustrative case, *Raymond Motor Transportation, Inc. v. Rice*,[23] the Court struck down a Wisconsin statute that prohibited truckers from pulling double trailers or from driving a rig longer than 55 feet in length without a special permit. The Court held that it could not "accept the State's contention that the inquiry under the Commerce Clause is ended without a weighing of the asserted safety purpose against the degree of interference with interstate commerce," and concluded that the law imposed "a substantial burden on the interstate movement of goods" by slowing the movement of goods, forcing truckers to haul doubles across Wisconsin separately, or to incur the delays caused by using single trailers instead of double trailers. In addition, "the regulations prevent[ed] appellants from accepting interline transfers of 65-foot doubles for movement through Wisconsin from carriers that operate only in the 33 States where the doubles are legal." The Court concluded that the law also contained exceptions that involved discrimination against interstate commerce.

(2) Modern Applications of the *Southern Pacific* Test

Modern cases have also used the *Southern Pacific* balancing test rather than the *Barnwell* test, and they have done so in a variety of contexts. In other words, the courts have not been deferential and have tended to conduct their own assessments of the importance of the local safety interests and the burden on interstate commerce.

Of course, even though a court conducts its own review, the result is not necessarily fatal to the local law. Illustrative of the modern approach is the holding in *Minnesota v. Clover Leaf Creamery Co.*,[24] which upheld a Minnesota statute that banned the retail sale of milk in plastic nonreturnable, nonrefillable containers, but permitted sales in other nonreturnable, nonrefillable containers, such as paperboard milk cartons, in an effort to deal with the solid waste management problem of nonreturnables, promote energy conservation, and conserve natural resources. The Court found a rational relationship to the state's objectives and held that the burden on interstate commerce was relatively minor. Under the law, milk could still be shipped into Minnesota, and the Court found a limited burden on interstate commerce because most dairies package their products in more than one type of container anyway. Moreover, the law did not favor Minnesota companies. Although the law produced some advantage for in-state firms that produced pulpwood, out-of-state pulpwood producers were likely to benefit as well (as well as producers of returnable bottles, and paperboard itself), because out-of-state pulpwood producers will presumably absorb some of the business generated by the Act. Even though no Minnesota company produced manufactured plastic resins, the Court found that the burden on the plastics industry was not "clearly excessive" in light of the substantial state interest in promoting conservation of energy and other natural resources and easing solid waste disposal problems. Given the "substantial state purposes," and the nondiscriminatory nature of law, the Court concluded that the law should not be struck down simply because it caused some business "to shift from a predominantly out-of-state industry to a predominantly in-state industry."

F   A   Q

Q: In the *Clover Leaf Creamery* case, should the Court have struck the Minnesota law down because it involved discrimination against out-of-state interests?

A: The Court concluded that the law favored in-state interests in some respects. However, and on balance, the Court found that the favoritism was limited. The state was trying to pursue what the Court perceived as a legitimate state interest.

Under modern precedent, the Court continues to strike down legislation that discriminates against interstate commerce. For example, in *West Lynn Creamery, Inc. v. Healy*,[25] the Court struck down a Massachusetts pricing order that imposed an assessment on all fluid milk sold by dealers to Massachusetts retailers (two-thirds of the milk was produced out of state) and then made payments to Massachusetts producers. The Court concluded that the law unconstitutionally discriminated against interstate commerce by trying to protect Massachusetts dairy farms against ruinously low prices by requiring a monthly payment into the "Massachusetts Dairy Equaliza-tion Fund." The Court regarded the law as the "paradigmatic example of a protective tariff or customs duty, both of which have historically been regarded as attractive because they raise revenue, benefit local producers, and burden out-of-state compe-titors, and artificially encourage in-state production even though the same goods can be produced more cheaply." The Court held that, when "a nondiscriminatory tax is coupled with a subsidy to one of the groups hurt by the tax, a state's political processes can no longer be relied upon to prevent legislative abuse, because one of the in-state interests which would otherwise lobby against the tax has been mollified by the sub-sidy." Justice Scalia, joined by Justice Thomas, concurred: "I [would] allow a State to subsidize its domestic industry so long as it does so from nondiscriminatory taxes that go into the State's general revenue fund." Chief Justice Rehnquist, joined by Justice Blackmun, dissented. "[T]here are still at least two strong interest groups opposed to the milk order—consumers and milk dealers . . . . The wisdom of a messianic insis-tence on a grim sink-or-swim policy of laissez-faire economics would be debatable had Congress chosen to enact it; but Congress has done nothing of the kind."

Likewise, in *Bendix Autolite Corp. v. Midwesco Enterprises, Inc.*,[26] the Court struck down an Ohio law that tolled the statute of limitations in actions for breach of contract or fraud actions for any period that a person or corporation is not "pres-ent" in the state. To be present, a foreign corporation must appoint an agent for service of process, which operates as consent to be sued. The Court found that the burden on interstate commerce outweighed the local interest. The burden was great because the law required a foreign corporation to appoint an agent for service of process in all cases, including those in which there is insufficient connection between the state and the action to otherwise permit the assertion of jurisdiction. While the Court recognized that "serving foreign corporate defendants may be more arduous than serving domestic corporations or foreign corporations with a desig-nated agent for service, and we have held for equal protection purposes that a State rationally may make adjustments for this difference by curtailing limitations protection for absent foreign corporations," the Court noted that Midwesco could have been served through the limitation period under Ohio's long-arm statute. "The Ohio statute of limitations is tolled only for those foreign corporations that do not subject themselves to the general jurisdiction of Ohio courts. In this manner the Ohio statute imposes a greater burden on out-of-state companies than it does on Ohio companies, subjecting the activities of foreign and domestic corporations to inconsistent regulations." Justice Scalia, concurring, articulated a new test under which "a state statute is invalid under the Commerce Clause if, and only if, it accords discriminatory treatment to interstate commerce in a respect not required to achieve a lawful state purpose." In his view, the "Ohio tolling statute is on its face discriminatory because it applies only to out-of-state corporations." That facial discrimination cannot be justified on the basis that "it advances a legitimate local purpose that cannot be adequately served by reasonable nondiscriminatory alternatives." A tolling statute that operated only against persons beyond the reach of Ohio's long-arm statute, or against all persons that could not be found for mail service, would be narrowly tailored to advance the legitimate purpose of preserving claims; but the present statute extends the time for suit even against corporations which (like Midwesco Enterprises) "are fully sueable within Ohio, and readily reachable through the mails."

D. The State as a Market Participant

In some instances, instead of trying to regulate interstate commerce, the states intervene in commercial markets and become market participants. The Court has struggled to determine whether a state should have greater leeway when it is functioning as a market participant rather than as a market regulator.

A seminal market participant decision is the holding in *Reeves, Inc. v. Stake*.[27] That case involved South Dakota's decision to allocate product from a state-owned cement plant to residents to the detriment of nonresidents who had historically purchased almost all of their cement from the plant. The Court upheld the state's action, emphasizing that, as a matter of state sovereignty, each state has the right to act "as guardian and trustee for its people." In addition, like other business owners, states have the right to exercise discretion about with whom they will deal. The Court rejected arguments that South Dakota's action was taken in a protectionist or discriminatory manner, concluding that the action was protectionist "only in the sense that it limits benefits generated by a state program to those who fund the state treasury and whom the State was created to serve." The Court noted that states can limit "the enjoyment of state educational institutions, energy generated by a state-run plant, police and fire protection, and agricultural improvement and business development programs" to citizens because those activities "reflect the essential and patently unobjectionable purpose of state government — to serve the citizens of the State." The Court distinguished its prior holdings in *Baldwin*, *Hughes*, and *Philadelphia v. New Jersey* on the basis that South Dakota's plant involved the "end product of a complex process whereby a costly physical plant and human labor act on raw materials," that South Dakota had not limited access to other raw materials (for example, limestone used to make cement), and that it had not prohibited private companies from establishing similar plants in South Dakota. Justice Powell, joined by Justices Brennan, White, and Stevens, dissented. "[South Dakota's] policy represents precisely the kind of economic protectionism that the Commerce Clause was intended to prevent. . . . If [the] State enters the private market and operates a commercial enterprise for the advantage of its private citizens, it may not evade the constitutional policy against economic Balkanization."

The market participant doctrine has also been applied to government contracts and the hiring of residents. For example, in *White v. Massachusetts Council of Construction Employers, Inc.*,[28] the Court rejected a Commerce Clause challenge to an executive order by Boston's mayor that required construction projects paid for out of city funds to be performed by a workforce of at least 50 percent city residents. Recognizing that "there are some limits on a state or local government's ability to impose restrictions that reach beyond the immediate parties with which the government transacts business," the Court concluded that the city had not transgressed those limits because "[e]veryone affected by the order [was], in a substantial if informal sense, 'working for the city.'" The fact that the employees were "working for the city" was "crucial" to the market-participant analysis.

Simply because the government is functioning as a market participant does not mean that it is without limitation in terms of the restrictions that it may impose on the market. In *South-Central Timber Development, Inc. v. Wunnicke*,[29] the Court struck down an Alaska law that required that timber taken from state lands be processed within the state prior to export. The Court held that *Reeves'* market participant doctrine was inapplicable because Alaska was attempting to impose "downstream conditions" (that is, trying to regulate parties that the state does not deal with directly) in the timber-processing market. Although Alaska, as a state, was free to directly subsidize the timber-processing industry (for example, by giving a purchaser the option of taking advantage of the subsidy by processing timber in the state or forgoing the benefits of the subsidy and exporting unprocessed timber), Alaska could not impose a downstream requirement that the timber be processed in Alaska. The Court distinguished *Reeves*, which it regarded as endorsing "the right of a State to deal with whomever it chooses when it participates in the market," but which did not "sanction the imposition of any terms that the State might desire." Even though Alaska could have processed the natural resource itself or chosen to sell it only to Alaska processors, it could not impose downstream restrictions. The Court rejected the idea that the Alaska was entitled to impose downstream requirements simply because it could achieve the same objective if it chose to participate in the market by processing the timber itself: "Instead of merely choosing its own trading partners, the State is attempting to govern the private, separate economic relationships of its trading partners; that is, it restricts the post-purchase activity of the purchaser, rather than merely the purchasing activity." Justice Rehnquist, joined by Justice O'Connor, dissented. "[Alaska] is merely paying the buyer of the timber indirectly, by means of a reduced price, to hire Alaska residents to process the timber. Under existing precedent, the State could accomplish that same result in any number of ways. . . . It seems to me unduly formalistic to conclude that the one path chosen by the State as best suited to promote its concerns is the path forbidden it by the Commerce Clause."

In *United Haulers Association v. Oneida-Herkimer Solid Waste Management Authority*,[30] a county adopted a "flow control" ordinance that

STATE PROCESSING PLANTS?

The *South-Central Timber* decision obviously prevents the State of Alaska from imposing downstream restrictions on the processing of timber. It does not prevent the state from functioning as a market participant by creating its own processing plants and processing the timber itself. In other words, if Alaska wants to control the processing of timber it must do so itself rather than by imposing downstream conditions.

required all trash haulers to deliver solid waste to a particular waste public processing facility. In upholding the ordinance, the Court distinguished *C & A Carbone, Inc. v. Clarkstown*,[31] which struck down on Commerce Clause grounds a flow control ordinance that required haulers to deliver waste to a particular *private* processing facility. The Court noted that the ordinance in this case required delivery to a state-created public benefit corporation, that trash disposal had "been a traditional government activity for years," and that "laws that favor the government in such areas — but treat every private business, whether in-state or out-of-state, exactly the same — do not discriminate against interstate commerce for purposes of the Commerce Clause." As a result, the Court concluded that any incidental burdens that the ordinance imposes on interstate commerce is outweighed by the benefits they confer on the local residents.

E. Preemption

When the federal government has exercised its power to regulate commerce and there is a conflict or a potential conflict between the federal law and a state law, the federal law may preempt the state law. As *Gibbons* held, if the federal government has regulated a subject within the scope of its authority and a state law conflicts, the state law is invalid by virtue of the Supremacy Clause. As we have seen, even after *Lopez*, the Commerce Clause provides Congress with a great deal of power to regulate economic activity. This power, when combined with the Supremacy Clause, means that if Congress decides to regulate in a given area, conflicting state regulations must give way. Preemption principles help courts determine whether there is a conflict.

Preemption can be either express or implied. In some instances, Congress makes a conscious decision to "preempt" a field and preclude state regulation.[32] It chooses to explicitly preempt state law. However, even in the absence of an explicit preemption, the Court sometimes implies preemption when Congress enacts a "scheme of federal regulation so pervasive as to make reasonable the inference that Congress left no room to supplement it." Preemption may occur "because the Act of Congress may touch a field in which the federal interest is so dominant that the federal system will be assumed to preclude enforcement of state laws on the same subject," or because "the object sought to be obtained by the federal law and the character of obligations imposed by it may reveal the same purpose."[33] In addition, preemption can occur when a state law conflicts with a federal law because "compliance with both federal and state regulations is a physical impossibility," or where state law "stands as an obstacle to the accomplishment and execution of the full purposes and objectives of Congress."[34]

F   A   Q

Q: What types of regulatory schemes involve situations where "the federal interest is so dominant that the federal system will be assumed to preclude enforcement of state laws on the same subject"?

A: Laws regulating aliens and matters relating to foreign affairs fit within the category of situations where the federal interest is so dominant that state laws on the subject are precluded.

Illustrative of the preemption doctrine is the holding in *Hines v. Davidowitz*.[35] In that case, the Court struck down a Pennsylvania law that required all aliens 18 years of age or over to register with the state, pay a $1 annual registration fee, and carry an alien identification card. Following passage of the Pennsylvania law, Congress enacted a federal Alien Registration Act requiring a single registration of aliens 14 years of age and over and requiring detailed information, but not requiring aliens to carry a registration card. In striking down the Pennsylvania law, the Court noted that the purpose of both the federal and state laws was identical (registration of aliens as a distinct group); that the federal law is supreme in the area of immigration, naturalization, and deportation; that state authority in this area is limited; and that the Pennsylvania law stood as an obstacle to accomplishment of Congress's objectives. The Court found that Pennsylvania's law imposed "distinct, unusual and extraordinary burdens and obligations upon aliens" (for example, "subjecting them alone, though perfectly law-abiding, to indiscriminate and repeated interception and interrogation by public officials"), and therefore dealt with the "rights, liberties, and personal freedoms of human beings." In particular, the Court emphasized that Congress had rejected many provisions included in the Pennsylvania law, concluding that "any registration requirement was a departure from our traditional policy of not treating aliens as a thing apart," and providing instead "a single integrated and all-embracing system in order to obtain the information deemed to be desirable in connection with aliens." The purpose of this federal system was to create "one uniform national registration system" and to otherwise leave aliens "free from the possibility of inquisitorial practices and police surveillance that might not only affect our international relations but might also generate the very disloyalty which the law has intended guarding against." Justice Stone dissented, arguing that Congress did not intend to create a single exclusive registration system for aliens. Although the "national government has exclusive control over the admission of aliens into the United States," after entry, "an alien resident within a state, like a citizen, is subject to the police powers of the state and, in the exercise of that power, state legislatures may pass laws applicable exclusively to aliens so long as the distinction taken between aliens and citizens is not shown to be without rational basis."

The Court also found preemption in *Pennsylvania v. Nelson*.[36] That case involved the Smith Act, a federal law that prohibited the knowing advocacy or overthrow of the government of the United States by force and violence. When Pennsylvania subsequently passed the Sedition Act, which proscribed the same conduct against the federal government or the state government, the Court struck down the Pennsylvania law. The Court found that Congress had "occupied the field to the exclusion of parallel state legislation, that the dominant interest of the Federal Government precludes state intervention, and that administration of state Acts would conflict with the operation of the federal plan." Justice Reed, joined by two other justices, dissented: "The federal sedition laws . . . proscribe certain local activity without creating any statutory or administrative regulation. . . . We cannot agree that the federal criminal sanctions against sedition directed at the United States are of such a pervasive character as to indicate an intention to void state action."

The mere fact that the federal government has entered an arena does not necessarily create preemption. The key question is whether the federal government intended to occupy the field. For example, in *Pacific Gas & Electric Co. v. State Energy Resources Conservation & Development Commission*,[37] the Court rejected a preemption claim. Although the federal government had regulated some aspects of nuclear energy under the Atomic Energy Act of 1954 (AEA), California enacted a statute that conditioned the right to build nuclear power plants on evidence that the project included adequate means for storage and disposal of nuclear waste. California's goal was to deal with the problem of "spent fuel," which is radioactive. In upholding the California law, the Court noted that Congress passed the AEA to give the federal government the power to regulate the "radiological safety aspects" involved in the construction and operation of a nuclear plant, but to nevertheless allow the states to retain their traditional authority control over "questions of need, reliability, cost and other related state concerns" related to electrical power plants. The Court was unwilling to assume that the states' "historic police powers" were superseded by the AEA absent a "clear and manifest purpose of Congress." The Court found no clear and manifest purpose, noting that Congress had made a decision to encourage the private sector to develop atomic energy, but gave the Atomic Energy Commission exclusive jurisdiction to license only the transfer, delivery, receipt, acquisition, possession, and use of nuclear materials. Thus, Congress "preserved the dual regulation of nuclear-powered electricity generation: the federal government maintains complete control of the safety and 'nuclear' aspects of energy generation; the states exercise their traditional authority over the need for additional generating capacity, the type of generating facilities to be licensed, land use, rate-making, and the like." Although the Nuclear Regulatory Commission was given exclusive authority over the construction and operation of nuclear power plants, including their safe operation, the Court concluded that California's law was not safety based. The Court held that California could regulate disposal issues because "the nuclear waste problem could become critical leading to unpredictably high costs to contain the problem or, worse, shutdowns in reactors." The Court also concluded that California could consider issues related to the disposal of nuclear waste even though the federal government regulates nuclear waste disposal. The NRC deals with safety issues, not economics, and the California law related to economics. Moreover, the Court found that the California law did not frustrate the federal effort to develop nuclear power.

In some instances, Congress creates a comprehensive federal regulatory scheme but gives the states the ability to "opt out" by creating their own regulatory schemes. Illustrative is the holding in *Gade v. National Solid Wastes Management Association*.[38] That case involved Illinois' Hazardous Waste Crane and Hoisting Equipment Operators Licensing Act and Hazardous Waste Laborers Licensing Act. The goal of these acts was "to promote job safety" and "to protect life, limb and property." The Court held that both acts were preempted by the federal Occupational Safety and Health Act of 1970 (OSH Act), and the regulations promulgated under that act by the Occupational Safety and Health Administration (OSHA). Although Congress authorized the secretary of labor to set mandatory occupational safety and health standards applicable to all businesses affecting interstate commerce, Congress not only reserved certain areas to state regulation (for example, state workers' compensation laws), but it also gave the states the option of preempting federal regulation entirely. However, Illinois chose not to exercise this option. The Court examined "the provisions of the whole law, and . . . its object and policy," and concluded that "nonapproved state regulation of occupational safety and health issues for which a federal standard is in effect is impliedly preempted as in conflict with the full purposes and objectives" of the federal statute. The law allowed a state to create its own plan, but only if the plan is approved by the federal government: The Court also implied preemption from the fact that the secretary was given the power to withdraw her approval of a state plan, finding that

"Congress sought to promote occupational safety and health while at the same time avoiding duplicative, and possibly counterproductive, regulation." Justice Souter, joined by three other justices, dissented, arguing that "in the absence of any clear expression of congressional intent to pre-empt, I can only conclude that, as long as compliance with federally promulgated standards does not render obedience to Illinois' regulations impossible, the enforcement of the state law is not prohibited by the Supremacy Clause."

The mere existence of a detailed federal regulatory scheme does not inevitably lead to the conclusion that a parallel state law is invalid. For example, in *Askew v. American Waterways Operators, Inc.*,[39] the Court upheld Florida's Oil Spill Prevention and Pollution Control Act, which imposed strict liability for any damage incurred by the state or private persons as a result of an oil spill in the state's territorial waters. Several months prior to the enactment of the Florida act, Congress enacted the Water Quality Improvement Act of 1970, which subjected ship owners and terminal facilities to liability without fault up to $14 million and $8 million, respectively, for cleanup costs incurred by the federal government as a result of oil spills. It also authorized the president to promulgate regulations requiring ships and terminal facilities to maintain equipment for the prevention of oil spills. Although the federal law imposed a "pervasive system of federal control over discharges of oil," the Court refused to find preemption, noting that there was "no conflict" between the Florida statute "when it comes to damages to property interests, for the Federal Act reaches only costs of cleaning up." Moreover, "while the Federal Act determines damages measured by the cost to the United States for cleaning up oil spills, the damages specified in the Florida Act relate in part to the cost to the State of Florida in cleaning up the spillage." As a result, the Court regarded the acts as "harmonious parts of an integrated whole. While the Federal Act is concerned only with actual cleanup costs incurred by the Federal Government, the State of Florida is concerned with its own cleanup costs." Hence there need be no collision between the federal act and the Florida act because, as noted, the federal act presupposes a coordinated effort with the states, and any federal limitation of liability runs to "vessels," not to shore "facilities." Moreover, since Congress dealt only with cleanup costs, it left the states free to impose liability in damages for losses suffered both by the states and by private interests.

F. Interstate Privileges and Immunities Clause

Article IV, Section 2, contains the **Interstate Privileges and Immunities Clause**: "The Citizens of each State shall be entitled to all Privileges and Immunities of Citizens in the several States." This clause was designed to ensure that states would not discriminate against the citizens of other states because of their citizenship in those states. Like most constitutional rights, the Privileges and Immunities Clause does not require states to treat nonresidents in exactly the same way that they treat their own citizens and does not impose an absolute ban on discrimination by one state against the citizens of another. The difficulty is to determine what type of distinctions, and which types of discrimination, are permissible.

In *Baldwin v. Fish & Game Commission of Montana*,[40] the Court rejected a privileges and immunities challenge to a Montana law that charged nonresidents $7\frac{1}{2}$ times more to purchase a license to hunt elk if they purchased a combination license (which also allowed hunters to hunt for other things), and 25 times more if they wanted to hunt only elk. The Court noted that elk management is expensive, especially during the winter months, and that Montana had aggressively managed and encouraged its elk population. The Court construed the Privileges and Immunities Clause as prohibiting the states "from imposing unreasonable burdens on citizens of other States in their pursuit of common callings within the State, in the ownership and disposition of privately held property within the State, and in access to the courts of the State." However, the Court noted that states could legitimately make distinctions between citizens and noncitizens in various contexts: "No one would suggest that the Privileges and Immunities Clause requires a State to open its polls to a person who declines to assert that the State is the only one where he claims a right to vote. The same is true as to qualification for an elective office of the State." Indeed, some "distinctions between residents and nonresidents merely reflect the fact that this is a Nation composed of individual States, and are permitted; other distinctions are prohibited because they hinder the formation, the purpose, or the development of a single Union of those States." The key question is whether the "privileges" and "immunities" bear "upon the vitality of the Nation" so that the state must "treat all citizens, resident and nonresident, equally." For example, the "states may not interfere with the 'right of a citizen of one state to pass through, or to reside in any other state, for purposes of trade, agriculture, professional pursuits, or otherwise; to claim the benefit of the writ of habeas corpus; to institute and maintain actions of any kind in the courts of the state; to take, hold and dispose of property, either real or personal.' "

As to the particular issue before it, the Court concluded that the "States may not compel the confinement of the benefits of their resources, even their wildlife, to their own people whenever such hoarding and confinement impedes interstate commerce." The Court held that a state's "interest in its wildlife and other resources must yield when, without reason, it interferes with a nonresident's right to pursue a livelihood in a State other than his own, a right that is protected by the Privileges and Immunities Clause." The Court upheld Montana's distinction between residents and nonresidents finding that it does not "threaten a basic right in a way that offends the Privileges and Immunities Clause." For nonresidents, elk hunting was "merely a recreation and a sport" and not a "means to the nonresident's livelihood." Justice Brennan, joined by Justices White and Marshall, dissented, arguing that the Court should not focus on whether a particular matter is "fundamental." In his view, a state can discriminate against nonresidents only when "(1) the presence or activity of nonresidents is the source or cause of the problem or effect with which the State seeks to deal, and (2) the discrimination practiced against nonresidents bears a substantial relation to the problem they present." He rejected the idea that a higher fee was justified by the fact that "nonresident hunters created a special danger to Montana's elk or to any of its other wildlife species." He also noted that Montana's higher fee for nonresident elk hunters does not reflect an attempt to recoup state expenditures relating to nonresidents.

Q: May states charge out-of-state students higher tuition rates than they charge in-state residents, or are differential charges precluded under the Interstate Privileges and Immunities Clause?

A: Differential tuition systems are permitted. While the Interstate Privileges and Immunities Clause is designed to ensure that the country functions as a nation, differential tuition requirements are simply designed to ensure that out-of-state citizens, who have not contributed to the funding of state universities in the same way that the state's taxpayers have, pay their fair share of the education that they receive.

Despite *Baldwin*'s holding, the Court will not automatically uphold a state's decision to discriminate against nonresidents. Ultimately, each case must be judged on its own merits, and the Court is sensitive to unjustified attempts to discriminate. For example, in *Toomer v. Witsell*,[41] the Court struck down a South Carolina law that imposed a $2,500 per boat fee on nonresident commercial shrimpers while imposing only a $25 fee on residents. The Court noted that nothing "indicates that non-residents use larger boats or different fishing methods than residents, that the cost of enforcing the laws against them is appreciably greater, or that any substantial amount of the State's general funds is devoted to shrimp conservation." The Court specifically rejected South Carolina's "ownership theory," which suggested that states have "power to preserve and regulate the exploitation of an important resource." Thus, while South Carolina could regulate its fisheries (for example, by limiting the type of equipment that could be used or by graduating license fees according to the size of the boats), it could not charge nonresidents additional fees that were unrelated to the "added enforcement burden they may impose or for any conservation expenditures from taxes which only residents pay."

In *Hicklin v. Orbeck*,[42] the Court struck down Alaska's "Local Hire Under State Leases" Act, which required that oil and gas leases and similar agreements contain a provision requiring the employment of qualified Alaska residents in preference to nonresidents. Under the program, Alaskans were given certificates of residence that they could present to their employers. In striking down the law, the Court held that there must be a "reasonable relationship between the danger represented by non-citizens, as a class, and [the] discrimination practiced upon them." The Court found that Alaska was unable to show that nonresidents were "a peculiar source of the evil" that "Alaska Hire was enacted to remedy, namely, Alaska's 'uniquely high unemployment.'" The Court noted that unemployment was not due to an influx of nonresidents, but to the fact that a substantial number of Alaska's jobless residents were Eskimos and Indians who were unemployed due to a lack of education and job training because of their geographical remoteness from job opportunities. The law, which simply granted a flat preference to Alaska residents, did not "bear a substantial relationship" to the "evil" of unemployment because a "highly skilled and educated resident who has never been unemployed is entitled to precisely the same preferential treatment as the unskilled, habitually unemployed Arctic Eskimo enrolled in a job-training program." In addition, the law was not narrowly tailored, a key component of any favorable Privileges and Immunities Clause analysis, because the program extended "to employers who have no connection whatsoever with the State's oil and gas, perform no work on state land, have no contractual relationship with the State, and receive no payment from the State," and extends to activities unconnected with the extraction of Alaska's oil and gas (*e.g.*, refineries and distribution systems). As a result, the Court held that Alaska's ownership of the oil and gas that is the subject matter of Alaska Hire "simply constitutes insufficient justification for the pervasive discrimination against nonresidents that the Act mandates." The Court emphasized that oil and gas is a matter of "profound national importance" and concluded with a rhetorical flourish: The Constitution "was framed upon the theory that the peoples of the several states must sink or swim together, and that in the long run prosperity and salvation are in union and not division."

Likewise, in *Supreme Court of New Hampshire v. Piper*,[43] the Court struck down a New Hampshire law that precluded nonresidents from becoming attorneys as applied to Vermont residents (who had passed the New Hampshire bar and found to be of good moral character) who lived 400 yards from the border. The Court emphasized that the right granted by the Privileges and Immunities Clause extended to the practice of law, which the Court regarded as important to the national economy and therefore a "fundamental right," in part because "[o]ut-of-state lawyers may — and often do — represent persons who raise unpopular federal claims"

S i d e b a r

REGULATING OUT-OF-STATE ATTORNEYS

Even though *Piper* holds that the State of New Hampshire cannot prohibit out-of-state attorneys from becoming members of its bar, the decision does not preclude the states from imposing reasonable restrictions on those attorneys. For example, in an appropriate case, the court might require an out-of-state attorney to retain local counsel.

and provide "the only means available for the vindication of federal rights." Relying on prior precedent, the Court concluded that the New Hampshire law could be sustained only if "(i) there is a substantial reason for the difference in treatment; and (ii) the discrimination practiced against nonresidents bears a substantial relationship to the State's objective." The Court found New Hampshire's numerous asserted justifications inadequate. The Court found no reason to believe that nonresident attorneys would fail "to keep abreast of local rules and procedures" or to maintain ethical standards. Although there is a risk that nonresidents might be unavailable for court proceedings, especially those held on short notice, the Court found that most lawyers who join the New Hampshire bar will live close to the state. Moreover, the courts can require those who do not to retain local counsel to appear in emergency situations. Although nonresidents might be less inclined to do *pro bono* and volunteer work in the state, the state may require "a nonresident bar member, like the resident member, could be required to represent indigents and perhaps to participate in formal legal-aid work." As a result, the Court found that the state did not have a "substantial reason" for prohibiting nonresidents from bar membership and that there was no "close relationship" to the state's reasons for the prohibition. Justice Rehnquist dissented, regarding the practice of law as "fundamentally different" from other professions and finding that "a State has a very strong interest in seeing that its legislators and its judges come from among the constituency of state residents, so that they better understand the local interests to which they will have to respond." Noting that the practice has historically been left exclusively to the states, he would have given states "considerable leeway in analyzing local evils and prescribing appropriate cures," and he would have found that a state "has a substantial interest in creating its own set of laws responsive to its own local interests, and it is reasonable for a State to decide that those people who have been trained to analyze law and policy are better equipped to write those state laws and adjudicate cases arising under them." "A State similarly might determine that because lawyers play an important role in the formulation of state policy through their adversary representation, they should be intimately conversant with the local concerns that should inform such policies." In addition, resident lawyers are more "likely to bring their useful expertise to other important functions that benefit from such expertise and are of interest to state governments—such as trusteeships, or directorships of corporations or charitable organizations, or school board positions, or merely the role of the interested citizen at a town meeting."

SUMMARY

- In this chapter, we have examined the power of the states to regulate interstate commerce. As we have seen, as the scope of federal authority over commerce has expanded over the last century, and fewer and fewer commercial issues can be regarded as solely within the power of the states.

- In most instances, the federal government has at least some power to regulate, and the question is whether state regulation should be permitted notwithstanding the scope of federal authority.

- In cases when the federal government has chosen to regulate a particular area and the state regulation is inconsistent with a valid federal law, the state law is preempted by the federal law.

- When there is no federal regulation, state regulation might be permissible. However, courts routinely strike down legislation when the state has attempted to discriminate against interstate commerce in favor of its own citizens.

- Courts sometimes allow a state to favor its own citizens when the state is acting as a market participant.

- Even when the state is acting neutrally toward interstate commerce, the courts may invalidate state legislation that imposes an undue burden on interstate commerce.

CONNECTIONS

Commerce Clause

There is a direct relationship between the federal commerce power and issues relating to the authority of the states to regulate interstate commerce. As the scope of federal authority has expanded, the scope of state power has arguably diminished.

Substantive Protection of Economic Interests

As we shall see, the Court rarely applies a heightened standard of review to substantive regulations affecting economic interests. In most instances, the Court applies the lowest standard of review, rational basis. Through the negative implications of the Commerce Clause, a regulated entity may have a better chance of challenging an economic regulation.

Equal Protection

Interstate privileges and immunities review bears some relationship to equal protection review. Both types of review focus on discrimination. However, while equal protection focuses on discrimination related to such issues as race, age, sex, and diminished mental conditions, interstate privileges and immunities review focuses on discrimination against citizens of other states as citizens of those states.

Judicial Review

Judicial review is a critical component of this chapter, especially in regard to the dormant Commerce Clause and the Interstate Privileges and Immunities Clause. As the *Southern Pacific* case illustrates, judicial review of state laws that burden interstate commerce can be quite active and involved.

Endnotes

1. 22 U.S. (9 Wheat) 1 (1824).
2. 155 U.S. 461 (1894).
3. 53 U.S. (12 How.) 299 (1851).
4. 135 U.S. 100 (1890).
5. 328 U.S. 408 (1946).
6. 294 U.S. 511 (1935).
7. 141 U.S. 47 (1891).
8. 91 U.S. (1 Otto) 275 (1876).
9. 262 U.S. 553 (1923).
10. 441 U.S. 322 (1979).
11. 450 U.S. 662 (1981).
12. *See, e.g.*, Mintz v. Baldwin, 289 U.S. 346 (1933); Asbell v. Kansas, 209 U.S. 251 (1908).
13. 95 U.S. 465 (1877).
14. 437 U.S. 617 (1978).
15. 340 U.S. 349 (1951).
16. 486 U.S. 289 (1988).
17. 477 U.S. 131 (1986).
18. 437 U.S. 117 (1978).
19. *See, e.g.*, Brown-Forman Distillers Corp. v. N.Y. State Liquor Auth., 476 U.S. 573, 578 (1986).
20. 303 U.S. 177 (1938).
21. 325 U.S. 761 (1945).
22. 359 U.S. 520 (1959).
23. 434 U.S. 429 (1978).
24. 449 U.S. 456 (1981).
25. 512 U.S. 186 (1994).
26. 486 U.S. 888 (1988).
27. 447 U.S. 429 (1980).
28. 460 U.S. 204 (1983).
29. 467 U.S. 82 (1984).
30. 127 S. Ct. 1786 (2007).
31. 511 U.S. 383 (1994).
32. *See* Cipollone v. Liggett Group, Inc., 505 U.S. 504 (1992).

33. Fid. Fed. Sav. & Loan Assn. v. de la Cuesta, 458 U.S. 141 (1982).
34. Hines v. Davidowitz, 312 U.S. 52, 67 (1941).
35. 312 U.S. 52 (1941).
36. 350 U.S. 497 (1956).
37. 461 U.S. 190 (1983).
38. 505 U.S. 88 (1992).
39. 411 U.S. 325 (1973).
40. 436 U.S. 371 (1978).
41. 334 U.S. 385 (1948).
42. 437 U.S. 518 (1978).
43. 470 U.S. 274 (1985).

Intergovernmental Immunities

5

The Constitution creates a system of dual sovereignty that allocates some powers to the federal government and other powers (in fact, the remaining powers) to state governments or to the people. The states are not treated as subdivisions of the federal government but as sovereign governments in their own right. One important principle that supports the integrity and viability of both sovereigns in this constitutional system is the intergovernmental immunities doctrine — the notion that one government (federal or state) has the right to be free from regulation or taxes by the other government.

OVERVIEW

A. STATE POWER TO TAX THE FEDERAL GOVERNMENT

B. FEDERAL POWER TO TAX THE STATES

C. STATE IMMUNITY FROM FEDERAL REGULATION

D. FEDERAL COMMANDEERING OF STATE RESOURCES

A. State Power to Tax the Federal Government

The power to tax raises important and controversial issues because it is an essential element of sovereignty, but it can impose significant burdens on the taxed entity. Questions regarding the power of the states to tax the federal government were resolved very early in U.S. history.

In *McCulloch v. Maryland,*[1] another landmark opinion by Chief Justice Marshall that we examined in Chapter 2 in connection with the Necessary and Proper Clause, the Court held that the states did not have the power to tax the federal government. That case involved a Maryland statute providing that all banks not established under state law choose between paying an annual fee to the state or issuing notes on stamped paper provided (and taxed) only by the state. After holding that the federal government has the power to establish a national bank, the Court struck down the Maryland tax. While the Court recognized that Maryland (like other states) has the power to impose taxes, it held that the state tax could not be imposed on the federal bank. The Court noted that the Constitution and laws of the United States are supreme, and that the "power to create [a national bank] implies a power to preserve [it]" and a power to tax involves a power to destroy. Applying these principles, the Court held that the "states have no power, by taxation or otherwise, to retard, impede, burden, or in any manner control, the operations of the constitutional laws enacted by congress to carry into execution the powers vested in the general government." As a result, the Court struck down the Maryland tax concluding that a state could not tax an entity of the federal government.

In subsequent cases, the Court extended *McCulloch* in holding that the states may not tax federal real estate. Illustrative is the holding in *Van Brocklin v. Anderson,*[2] in which the Court struck down a state tax on federal property. The Court noted that there was a debate about whether a neutral tax that applied to all property and not just to federal property might be sustainable. However, in *Van Brocklin,* the Court held that the tax was invalid because the issue of whether federal land can be taxed "depends upon the will of its owner, the United States, and no state can tax the property of the United States without their consent." If states were allowed to assess and collect taxes from federal lands and sell them for nonpayment, the state's actions would "tend to create a conflict between the officers of the two governments, to deprive the United States of a title lawfully acquired under express acts of congress, and to defeat the exercise of the constitutional power to lay and collect taxes to pay the debts and provide for the common defense and general welfare of the United States." In later cases, the Court upheld the application of state real estate taxes to land owned by private entities that is leased to the federal government.

In a number of cases, the Court has addressed issues relating to the power of the states to tax the salaries of federal employees. One can argue that federal employee salaries ought to be exempt from state taxation because, if taxed, the employees are likely to demand higher salaries to compensate for the taxes. Moreover, as *McCulloch* held, the power to tax is the power to destroy, and the power to tax gives government the power to drive federal employees out of their jobs. However, in *Graves v. New York,*[3] overruling *Dobbins v. Commissioners of Erie County,*[4] the Court upheld a general state income tax as applied to the salaries of federal employees. The Court concluded that there is a logical distinction between taxing the government and taxing the salaries of government employees. So long as the state tax is neutral, in the sense that it is applied to the salaries of all employees (federal, state, or private), then the tax is permissible notwithstanding the possible economic burden of the tax on the federal government. Justice Butler dissented, arguing that "[w]here the power to tax exists, legislatures may exert it to destroy, to discourage, to protect or exclusively for the purpose of raising revenue."

At one time, the Court construed *McCulloch* as prohibiting taxes on individuals and businesses who had contractual relationships with the federal government when the effect of the tax might be to increase the cost to the federal government of performing governmental functions. In later years, however, the Court rejected this precedent.

Examples: Illustrative is *James v. Dravo Contracting Co.*,[5] in which the Court rejected a contractor's claim that it was immune from a state occupation tax (measured by gross receipts) as applied to income received under a contract with the federal government. The Court held that a nondiscriminatory tax is permissible "until Congress declares otherwise." Likewise, in *City of Detroit v. Murray Corp.*,[6] the Court upheld use taxes on machinery and other property used by private companies in conjunction with cost-plus contracts that required the government to reimburse them for state taxes paid by them. The Court held that the "the economic burden on a federal function of a state tax imposed on those who deal with the Federal Government does not render the tax unconstitutional so long as the tax is imposed equally on the other similarly situated constituents of the State."

The states have not, however, been allowed to tax the interest on federal bonds. In *Weston v. City Council of Charleston*,[7] the Court struck down a state tax on federal bonds. The Court held that, "if the tax is imposed, it will be more expensive for the government to borrow money" and could be "ruinous to the federal government." The Court found that no other matter "is of more vital interest to the community than this of borrowing money on the credit of the United States." Justice Thompson dissented: "[T]he tax is not direct upon any means used by the government to carry on its operation. It is only a tax upon property acquired through one of the means employed by the government to carry on its operations. [C]onsidering that the tax in question is a general tax upon the interest of money on loan, I cannot think it any violation of the constitution of the United States, to include therein interest accruing from stock of the United States." In addition, the states have not been allowed to tax federal sales absent Congress's consent. For example, the states cannot tax the sale of liquor sold at U.S. military installations.[8]

Nature of State Tax	Validity
Tax on federal agencies or entities	Invalid
Tax on federal real estate	Invalid
Tax on the income of federal employees	Perhaps valid if nondiscriminatory
Tax on the income of federal contractors	Perhaps valid if nondiscriminatory

B. Federal Power to Tax the States

There has also been a dispute regarding the authority of the federal government to tax the states. In several early cases, the Court held that the federal government had limited power to tax either the states or the salaries of their employees. For example, in *Collector v. Day*,[9] the Court held that the salary of a state judicial officer, in that case a probate judge, was immune from federal income tax. The Court emphasized that the officer was engaged in the performance of a function performed by state governments at the time the Constitution was adopted. However, in the 1930s, in *Helvering v. Gerhardt*,[10] the Court overruled *Day* and held that the salaries of state employees were subject to federal tax. Because the taxes imposed were nondiscriminatory, and thus also applied to the income of those who were privately employed, the Court rejected the argument that the tax would impede the state's ability to hire able persons to perform its essential functions. While the Court recognized that the states might be able to hire employees more cheaply if those employees' salaries were not subject to tax, the Court did not regard that consideration as sufficient to require invalidation of the federal tax. "While a tax on the salary paid key state officers may increase the cost of government, it will no more preclude the States from performing traditional functions than it will prevent private entities from performing their missions."

The more controversial question is whether the federal government can impose a tax directly on the states. Because of the nature of the federal constitutional system, one can argue that the federal government should not have the power to tax state governments or their subordinate entities. Indeed, in *Collector v. Day*,[11] the Court suggested that the federal government could not interfere with traditional state functions. This was consistent with prior decisions that distinguished between "traditional state functions" and "tax revenue-generating activities of the States that are of the same nature as those traditionally engaged in by private persons."

Although some decisions have made a distinction between a state's proprietary functions (when the government is operating a business in a manner similar to an ordinary business) and essential governmental activities (for example, taxing and regulating), later decisions have rejected this distinction and concluded that the federal government might be free to tax both activities. Illustrative is the holding in *Massachusetts v. United States*,[12] in which the Court upheld an annual registration tax on civil aircraft that was applied to a State of Massachusetts helicopter that was used to patrol highways and engage in other police functions. The Court concluded that it would not allow a tax to "impair either the taxing power of the government imposing the tax [or] the appropriate exercise of the functions of the government affected by it." Nevertheless, the Court held that the federal government could impose a nondiscriminatory tax on state entities to help "defray the cost of a federal program by recovering a fair approximation of each beneficiary's share of the cost." While the Court recognized that such taxes might increase the cost of the state activity, the Court doubted that "federal exactions from the States of their fair share of the cost of specific benefits they receive from federal programs offend the constitutional scheme." The Court rejected claims that the federal tax was not related to the state's use of the airways because it involved a flat tax. Instead, the Court found that the tax involved a fair approximation of the state's use of the system and was structured to produce revenues that would not exceed the total cost to the federal government of the benefits to be supplied. Applying these principles, the Court found that the tax was nondiscriminatory (in that it applied to all aircraft and not just state-owned aircraft) and indeed was structured to favor the states who were exempt from the 7-cent-per-gallon fuel tax applied to private noncommercial general aviation. The tax fairly approximated the cost of the benefits civil aircraft receive from the federal activities and was "not excessive in relation to the cost of the Government benefits supplied" because actual revenues fell short of expenses.

F   A   Q

Q: If state governments are not allowed to tax entities of the federal government, then why is the federal government allowed to tax entities of the states?

A: *McCulloch* recognizes that the power to tax is the power to destroy, and that state governments cannot be allowed to exercise this power over entities of the federal government. However, the Court does not provide comparable protections to state entities. The difference can be justified by the Supremacy Clause, which makes the Constitution and laws of the United States supreme and gives the federal government the right to preserve itself against state attacks. Note, however, that the federal government does not have unbridled authority to tax state entities and destroy them. A tax must be calibrated to recover the actual costs of the federal program.

Example: *New York v. United States*,[13] discussed in *Massachusetts v. United States*, upheld a tax on mineral waters sold by a state-owned entity. In upholding the tax, the Court again rejected distinctions based on whether a state government is engaged in "proprietary" as opposed to "governmental" activities, or whether it is simply involved in "historically sanctioned" versus "profit-making" activities. The Court found "no restriction" against including the states in "a tax exacted equally from private persons upon the same subject matter." Justice Douglas dissented: "The fact that local government may enter the domain of private enterprise and operate a project for profit does not put it in the class of private business enterprise for tax purposes. Local government exists to provide for the welfare of its people, not for a limited group of stockholders. If the federal government can place the local governments on its tax collector's list, their capacity to serve the needs of their citizens is at once hampered or curtailed."

The Court has held that the federal government may impose a tax on the interest received by private parties on state and local bonds.[14] In *Willcuts v. Bunn*,[15] the Court held that Congress could exercise discretion regarding whether to tax the interest on state and local bonds as a matter of governmental policy. The Court rejected arguments that the federal tax "should be deemed, as a practical matter, to lay such a burden on the exercise of the State's borrowing power as to make it necessary to deny to the Federal Government

Sidebar

TAXING THE INTEREST ON STATE BONDS

The federal government, as a matter of discretion, has chosen not to tax the interest on most state bonds. Because the bonds are not taxable, this means of raising money is attractive to investors because it increases their net return.

the constitutional authority to impose the tax." The Court concluded that it would not strike down a federal tax under these circumstances unless it clearly appears "that a substantial burden upon the borrowing power of the State would actually be imposed." Moreover, the burden must be "real, not imaginary; substantial, not negligible." The Court held that there was no "warrant for implying a constitutional restriction to defeat the tax."

Just as the states can tax the salaries of federal employees, the federal government is allowed to tax the salaries of state employees. In *Helvering v. Therrell* and *McLoughlin v. Commissioner*,[16] the Court held that application of state income taxes to federal employees did not offend the constitutional scheme.

A more controversial question is whether the federal government may impose a tax on the privilege of exercising corporate franchises granted by a state to public service companies (e.g., a state grants a charter to a local utility company). In *Flint v. Stone Tracy Co.*,[17] the Court answered this question in the affirmative. Even though the states may not tax franchises created by the United States or its agencies or corporations to carry into effect powers conferred upon the federal government in its sovereign capacity, it might have the power to tax corporate franchises. The Court held that the Constitution did not similarly limit Congress's power to tax provided that the taxes are levied for the "public welfare" and are imposed on a uniform basis throughout the United States. The Court rejected the argument that state sovereignty precludes such taxes. The Court concluded that the "true distinction is between the attempted taxation of those operations of the states essential to the execution of its governmental functions, and which the state can only do itself, and those activities which are of a private character." The federal government may not interfere with the states by taxing the agencies of the state. Applying these principles, the Court held that public service corporations were not exempt from taxation.

C. State Immunity from Federal Regulation

Prior to the 1930s, few commentators would have bothered to ask whether state governments were immune from federal regulation. At that time, the Court regarded the Tenth Amendment as a significant independent limitation on congressional power and construed the Commerce Clause more restrictively. As we saw in decisions like *Hammer v. Dagenhart*,[18] the Court struck down restrictions on child labor. During this period, it was highly doubtful that Congress could regulate in such areas as the wages and hours of private sector workers, much less the wages and hours of state workers.

In the post-1937 period, as the Court begin to give great deference to Congress in the exercise of its commerce power, federal assertions of authority expanded dramatically. In *United States v. Darby*,[19] the Court upheld wage and hour restrictions on employees.

Emboldened by these favorable decisions, Congress began to impose more and more restrictions on wages and hours as well as to directly regulate the wages and hours of state employees. In *National League of Cities v. Usery*,[20] the Court held that Congress could not apply the Fair Labor Standards Act (FLSA) to state employees. The FLSA would have required states to pay their employees a minimum hourly wage and overtime for hours worked in excess of 40 hours a week, as well as to keep records to aid in the act's enforcement. The act did make some exceptions for public employment relationships that were without counterpart in the private sector (for example, fire protection and law enforcement personnel). In striking down the act, the Court emphasized that the Constitution assumes the "independent authority of the States" within their spheres. Even though Congress has the power to enact laws applicable to ordinary businesses, it "is quite another to uphold a similar exercise of congressional authority directed [to] the States as States." The Court found that there are attributes of state sovereignty that may not be impaired by Congress. The states' right to determine the wages and hours of governmental employees who are carrying out governmental functions is one of those attributes. Such determinations are "essential" to the states' "separate and independent existence," partially because FLSA might substantially increase employee costs and displace state judgments about how state governments structure and deliver services to citizens. For example, a state might decide that rather than complying with FLSA's wage and hour requirements, it should "employ persons . . . who for some other reason do not possess minimum employment requirements, and pay them less than the federally prescribed minimum wage." In addition, "states may wish to offer part-time or summer employment to teenagers at a figure less than the minimum wage, and if unable to do so may decline to offer such employment at all." The difficulty is that FLSA would preclude states from considering such options and would simply force them to choose between "devoting more revenue to such employment [enough revenue to meet FLSA's wage requirements], or reducing the number of work hours to a level consistent with FLSA's requirements." While the Court recognized that private employers face similar issues under FLSA, the Court regarded states as different because the regulation would "impermissibly interfere with the integral governmental functions of these bodies," and "there would be little left of the States' 'separate and independent existence.'" Justice Brennan, joined by Justices White and Marshall, dissented: "[T]he power over commerce [is] vested in Congress as absolutely as it would be in a single government, having in its constitution the same restrictions on the exercise of the power as are found in the constitution of the United States. The wisdom and the discretion of Congress, their identity with the people, and the influence which their constituents possess at elections, are [the] sole restraints on which they have relied, to secure them from its abuse."

In subsequent cases, the Court struggled to apply *National League of Cities*.[21] Prior decisions had imposed four prerequisites for application of the *Usery* doctrine: the federal statute must regulate the "States as States"; the statute must "address matters that are indisputably 'attribute[s] of state sovereignty'"; state compliance with the federal obligation must "directly impair the States' ability 'to structure integral operations in areas of traditional governmental functions'"; the relation of state and federal interests must not be such that "the nature of the federal interest justifies state submission." However, courts found it difficult to interpret and apply these standards.

Nine years later, in *Garcia v. San Antonio Metropolitan Transit Authority*,[22] the Court overruled *Usery* and held that Congress could apply FLSA to a city-owned bus line. *Garcia* noted that the third *Usury* factor (traditional governmental functions) had proven difficult to apply. While some courts had held that running ambulance services, licensing automobile drivers, operating a municipal airport, performing solid waste disposal, and operating a highway authority were traditional governmental functions, other courts had held that the issuance of industrial development bonds, regulation of intrastate natural gas sales, regulation of traffic on public roads, regulation of air transportation, operation of a telephone system, leasing and sale of natural gas, operation of a mental health facility, and provision of in-house domestic services for the aged and handicapped were not. The Court concluded that it was "difficult, if not impossible, to identify an organizing principle that places each of the cases in the first group on one side of a line and each of the cases in the second group on the other side." The Court noted that some had argued for a historical standard (for example, those things that had historically been treated as a traditional government function should continue to be treated as such in contrast to new functions which should not), but the Court concluded that a historical standard would be difficult to apply. In addition, the Court questioned whether the notion of a "traditional governmental function" would be "faithful to the role of federalism in a democratic society." The Court felt that, within the realm of their discretion, "the States must be equally free to engage in any activity that their citizens choose for the common weal, no matter how unorthodox or unnecessary anyone else [deems] state involvement to be." "The genius of our government provides that, within the sphere of constitutional action, the people — acting not through the courts but through their elected legislative representatives — have the power to determine as conditions demand, what services and functions the public welfare requires."

Justice Powell, joined by Chief Justice Burger and Justices Rehnquist and O'Conner, dissented, arguing that the Court had reduced the Tenth Amendment to "meaningless rhetoric." He also argued that the states' role in the constitutional system "is a matter of constitutional law, not of legislative grace." "[T]he Court's view of federalism appears to relegate the States to precisely the trivial role that opponents of the Constitution feared." Justice O'Connor, joined by Justices Powell and Rehnquist, also dissented, arguing that, because "virtually every state activity, like virtually every activity of a private individual, arguably 'affects' interstate commerce, [t]here is now a real risk that Congress will gradually erase the diffusion of power between State and Nation on which the Framers based their faith in the efficiency and vitality of our Republic."

The critical question after *Garcia* is how the states are to be protected against federal overreaching. Justice O'Connor, dissenting in *Garcia*, argued that the Court seemed quite unwilling to "rein in the scope of federal regulatory authority," and had effectively washed "its hands of all efforts to protect the States." The majority disagreed, arguing that the "principal means chosen by the Framers to ensure the role of the States in the federal system lies in the structure of the Federal Government itself." The Court noted that: "The Framers thus gave the States a role in the selection both of the Executive and the Legislative Branches of the Federal Government. The States were vested with indirect influence over the House of Representatives and the Presidency by their control of electoral qualifications and their role in Presidential elections. They were given more direct influence in the Senate, where each State received equal representation and each Senator was to be selected by the legislature of his State. . . . The political process ensures that laws that unduly burden the States will not be promulgated. In [these] cases the internal safeguards of the political process have performed as intended." However, as Justice O'Connor noted, these protections had not stopped the federal government from impinging on the states.

F   A   Q

Q: After the constitutional battles of the 1930s, in which the Court repeatedly struck down congressional legislation regulating private entities on the basis that those laws invaded the reserved power of the states, has the Court become so deferential that Congress can choose to regulate even the states themselves?

A: Yes, as *Garcia* suggests, the Court is willing to permit Congress to regulate the salaries paid by state governments to their employees. The remedy for congressional excess, it appears, must come from the political process rather than from the courts.

D. Federal Commandeering of State Resources

A similarly difficult question is whether Congress may use its broad regulatory power, including its power to regulate the states, to tell the states which laws to enact. In *New York v. United States*,[23] the Court struck down portions of the Low-Level Radioactive Waste Policy Amendments Act of 1985 because Congress sought to compel the states to use interstate compacts to provide for the disposal of radioactive waste generated within their borders. The act provided three types of incentives to encourage the states to comply with their statutory obligations. First, it imposed surcharges to provide monetary incentives to states, but the incentives were forfeited by states that do not meet the deadline for a disposal plan and that did not take control of radioactive waste within their borders. Second, the act imposed "access incentives" that imposed additional surcharges or denied states access to disposal sites if they fail to meet required deadlines. Finally, the act imposed a "take title" provision that required states that could not provide for the disposal of all such waste generated within such state or compact region to take title to, and possession of, the waste, and be liable for all damages directly or indirectly incurred by such generator or owner as a consequence of the failure of the state to take possession of the waste.

The Court concluded that, in evaluating the states' claims, it must determine whether Congress has exceeded its Article I powers or invaded state sovereignty under the Tenth Amendment. The Court concluded that these two inquiries were "mirror images" of each other in the sense that, if the Constitution gives a power to Congress, the Tenth Amendment is inapplicable. Moreover, "if a power is an attribute of state sovereignty reserved by the Tenth Amendment, it is necessarily a power the Constitution has not conferred on Congress." As in prior cases, the Court regarded the Tenth Amendment as nothing more than a "truism" in the sense "that all is retained which has not been surrendered." The Court held that issues related to the disposal of radioactive waste involve commerce so that Congress has the power to regulate in this area, as well as to preempt state radioactive waste regulation.

Nevertheless, the Court struck down portions of the act. Even though Congress has the authority to impose regulatory requirements on the nation, the Court doubted that the Constitution permits Congress to require the states to govern according to Congress's dictates. Of course, Congress could encourage the states to regulate in its preferred way by providing incentives to the states. For example, Congress may provide federal funds on a conditional basis or offer states the choice of regulating an activity according to federal standards or having their laws pre-empted by federal regulation. Incentive systems are permissible because the states remain free to "regulate in the manner they choose" and "state officials remain accountable to the people." However, the Court concluded that the federal government could not compel the states to regulate according to its dictates. Federal control of state regulatory processes would diminish the accountability of both state and federal officials, and diminish the ability of voters to control governmental officials through the political process. Voters, offended by a state law or regulation, may not realize that it was imposed by the federal government and may impose their disapproval on state officials. Moreover, overall governmental "[a]ccountability is thus diminished when, due to federal coercion, elected state officials cannot regulate in accordance with the views of the local electorate in matters not pre-empted by federal regulation."

Applying these principles to the act, the Court upheld the monetary incentives program even though the incentives involved surcharges that the Court regarded as the equivalent of a tax on interstate commerce. The Court also upheld the monetary incentives as a conditional exercise of Congress's authority under the Spending Clause. Even though the money was kept in a separate account rather than coming from the general treasury, the Court regarded this fact as irrelevant. The Court also held the denial of access provisions as "within the power of Congress to authorize the States to discriminate against interstate commerce," and concluded that Congress may "offer States the choice of regulating that activity according to federal standards or having state law pre-empted by federal regulation."

Despite upholding most of the act, the Court struck down the "take title" provision. The Court believed in that provision that Congress transgressed the line between "encouragement" and "coercion" because it gave states no choice: Either they must regulate according to Congress's will, or they must accept title to waste. As a result, the Court held that the act was unconstitutional because it "commandeers the legislative processes of the States by directly compelling them to enact and enforce a federal regulatory program." The Court emphasized that the states "are not mere political subdivisions of the United States," and that they retain "a residuary and inviolable sovereignty" that is "reserved explicitly to the States by the Tenth Amendment." "Whatever the outer limits of that sovereignty may be, one thing is clear: The Federal Government may not compel the States to enact or administer a federal regulatory program."

F   A   Q

Q: Could Congress have encouraged the states to "take title" to nuclear waste through the exercise of its spending power? In other words, could Congress have "persuaded" the states to take title by offering them financial incentives, or by withholding funds (*e.g.*, federal highway funds) if the states refused to take title?

A: The simple answer is yes. The "take title" provisions at issue in *New York v. United States* were objectionable because the federal government told the states what to do. If Congress chooses to provide financial incentives to the states to persuade them to take title to nuclear waste, it is free to do so. Whether the incentives would be sufficient to persuade the states is another matter. In addition, Congress provided that certain federal funds might be withheld if the states do not take title. However, some justices require that there be linkage between the requested action and the withholding. As a result, if Congress chooses to withhold highway funds to encourage the states to take title to nuclear waste, these justices might find insufficient linkage.

Justice White, joined by Justices Blackmun and Stevens, concurred in part and dissented in part. He argued that Congress could have directly regulated this field and could have preempted state regulation, but it deferred to the states, which wanted to take the lead and which developed the various incentives and penalties. Moreover, since New York accepted the various provisions, including the "take title" provision, he argued that it should be estopped from challenging that provision. Justice Stevens concurred in part and dissented in part, arguing that the federal government "regulates state-operated railroads, state school systems, state prisons, state elections, and a host of other state functions," and argued that Congress may also regulate low-level radioactive wastes. Indeed, had the radioactive waste created a nuisance, he believed that Congress would have had the power to require the states to take remedial action.

Likewise, in *Printz v. United States*,[24] the Court struck down portions of the Brady Handgun Violence Prevention Act, which required state and local law enforcement officers to conduct background checks on prospective handgun purchasers and to perform certain related tasks. Although the local officials (referred to as "CLEOs") were required to make a "reasonable effort to ascertain within 5 business days whether receipt or possession would be in violation of the law," the act did not require the official to take any particular action. In striking down the act, the Court did not regard as controlling historical evidence suggesting that the federal government passed early statutes pressing state courts into service for various purposes. Even though the states had surrendered various powers to the federal government under the Constitution, the Court concluded that they retained "a residuary and inviolable sovereignty" and could not be pressed into service on behalf of the federal government. An important aspect of the *Printz* decision was the recognition that the Framers had rejected the notion of a central government that would "act upon and through the States." In its place, the Framers envisioned a system of independent state governments that were accountable to their own citizens and that created a structural protection for liberty that reduced "the risk of tyranny and abuse from either front." By remaining independent, the states prevented the federal government from becoming too powerful as it might if it could press state and local officials into service at no cost.

The Court also expressed concern regarding the Brady law's consistency with the president's constitutional obligation to take care to ensure "that the Laws be faithfully executed" through officers whom the president appoints. The Brady Act was arguably inconsistent because it transferred administrative responsibilities to state and local officials who were asked to implement the program "without meaningful Presidential control" in the sense of the power to remove. Moreover, the Court expressed concern about governmental accountability: State governments must absorb the financial burden of the federal regulatory program. If the program succeeds, Congress can take credit for solving a problem without being forced to ask for higher federal taxes. Moreover, state officials are faced with the possibility of taking the blame for the burdens and defects of a federal regulatory scheme.

In conclusion, the Court found that the "Federal Government may neither issue directives requiring the States to address particular problems, nor command the States' officers, or those of their political subdivisions, to administer or enforce a federal regulatory program. It matters not whether policymaking is involved, and no case-by-case weighing of the burdens or benefits is necessary; such commands are fundamentally incompatible with our constitutional system of dual sovereignty."

Four justices dissented from the holding. Justice Stevens, joined by Justices Souter, Ginsburg, and Breyer, argued that Congress has the power to regulate hand-guns under the Commerce Clause and that the principal check on federal abuse lies in the political process. "If Congress believes that such a statute will benefit the people of the Nation, and serve the interests of cooperative federalism better than an enlarged federal bureaucracy, we should respect both its policy judgment and its appraisal of its constitutional power." Justice Breyer, joined by Justice Stevens, also dissented, arguing that the Brady Act should not be regarded as overwhelming the state civil service because it requires state officials to use only "reasonable efforts" to enforce the federal law. As a result, they have broad discretion.

However, the "commandeering" principle is not without limits. For example, in *South Carolina v. Baker*,[25] the Court upheld the Tax Equity and Fiscal Responsibility Act of 1982 (TEFRA), which denied federal tax exempt status to state and local bonds that were issued in unregistered[26] forms. The states challenged the act on the basis that the federal government was effectively forcing them to issue bonds only in registered form. The Court disagreed, holding that a state could choose to issue bonds in either format and that states were affected only if they wanted to claim tax exempt status for their bonds. The Court did not regard this requirement as a "constitutional defect" and found no violation of the Tenth Amendment. Justice O'Connor dissented: "I would invalidate Congress' attempt to regulate the sovereign States by threatening to deprive them of this tax immunity, which would increase their dependence on the National Government."

Sidebar

DISTINGUISHING *BAKER* AND *NEW YORK*

Baker is distinguishable from *New York v. United States* because Congress is not requiring the states to regulate in any particular way. On the contrary, it is simply setting forth the criteria under which it will provide tax exempt status to state bonds. Accordingly, if a state chooses to forgo the benefit of tax exemption, it is free to do so.

In another major decision, *Reno v. Condon*,[27] the Court upheld the Driver's Privacy Protection Act of 1994 (DPPA), which limited the ability of state departments of motor vehicles (DMV) to disclose or resell drivers' personal information. The law was passed because state DMVs forced drivers and automobile owners to provide personal information including their names, addresses, telephone numbers, vehicle descriptions, Social Security numbers, medical information, and photographs as a condition of obtaining a driver's license or of registering an automobile, and then the states sold this personal information to individuals and businesses. The DPPA prohib-ited the states from disclosing a driver's personal information without the driver's consent, and imposed civil and criminal penalties for violations. The Court rejected the argument that the DPPA violated the Tenth Amendment to the U.S. Constitution, noting that drivers' information constitutes an article of commerce and therefore is subject to regulation under the Commerce Clause. In addition, the Court refused to apply the holdings in *New York* and *Printz*. The Court concluded that the case was governed by its holding in *South Carolina v. Baker* because Congress did not "require the States in their sovereign capacity to regulate their own citizens," but simply regulated the "States as the owners of data bases." The law did "not require the South Carolina Legislature to enact any laws or regulations, and it does not require state officials to assist in the enforcement of federal statutes regulating private individuals."

SUMMARY

■ *McCulloch's* landmark holding still stands so that the states may not tax entities of the federal government.

■ By contrast, the federal government may tax and regulate entities of the states under certain limited circumstances. In this respect, recent decisions are remarkable because they reveal the extent of the federal commerce power and the limited impact of the Tenth Amendment.

■ The Tenth Amendment still has teeth in limited situations: when the federal government attempts to commandeer local officials to perform federal functions or directs state legislatures to regulate in particular ways.

CONNECTIONS

Federal Commerce Power
Intergovernmental immunities bears a direct relationship to the federal commerce power. To the extent that states have a governmental immunity from regulation (e.g., *New York v. United States*), the attempted federal regulation may be unconstitutional.

Judicial Review
As in most other areas of the law, judicial review permeates this area of the law as well. As we saw in decisions like *McCulloch*, *New York v. United States*, and *Printz*, the courts will become involved to determine whether state or federal regulation violates some aspect of the intergovernmental immunities doctrine.

State Power to Regulate
Intergovernmental immunities, especially when coupled with the Supremacy Clause, provide a direct limitation on the power of the states to regulate.

Federal Taxing Power
The federal government's power to tax is limited by the intergovernmental immunities doctrine.

State Taxing Power

The power of the state to impose taxes is limited by the intergovernmental immunities doctrine.

Supremacy Clause

Under decisions like *McCulloch*, the Supremacy Clause has been used to strike down state taxes on the federal government or entities of the federal government.

Endnotes

1. 17 U.S. (4 Wheat) 316 (1819).
2. 117 U.S. 151 (1886).
3. 306 U.S. 466 (1939).
4. 10 L. Ed. 1022 (1842).
5. 302 U.S. 134 (1937).
6. 355 U.S. 489 (1958).
7. 27 U.S. (2 Pet.) 449 (1829).
8. *See* United States v. State Tax Commn. of Miss., 421 U.S. 599 (1975).
9. 78 U.S. (11 Wall.) 113 (1871).
10. 304 U.S. 405 (1938).
11. 78 U.S. (11 Wall.) 113 (1871).
12. 435 U.S. 444 (1978).
13. 326 U.S. 572 (1946).
14. *See* Willcuts v. Bunn, 282 U.S. 216 (1931); *see also* Group No. 1 Oil Corp. v. Bass, 283 U.S. 279 (1931); Metcalf & Eddy v. Mitchell, 269 U.S. 514 (1926); Pollock v. Farmers' Loan & Trust Co., 157 U.S. 429 (1895).
15. 282 U.S. 216 (1931).
16. 303 U.S. 218 (1938).
17. 220 U.S. 107 (1911).
18. 247 U.S. 251 (1918).
19. 312 U.S. 100 (1941).
20. 426 U.S. 833 (1976).
21. *See* EEOC v. Wyoming, 460 U.S. 226 (1983); Fed. Energy Regulatory Commn. v. Mississippi, 456 U.S. 742 (1982); Hodel v. Va. Surface Min. & Reclamation Assn., 452 U.S. 264 (1981).
22. 469 U.S. 528 (1985).
23. 505 U.S. 144 (1992).
24. 521 U.S. 898 (1997).
25. 485 U.S. 505 (1988).
26. Bonds can be issued as either registered bonds or bearer bonds, and the two types of bonds differ in the way ownership and payments are made. Registered bonds are recorded on a central list, and payments are automatically sent to the registrant. Bearer payments are made on physical delivery of the bond.
27. 528 U.S. 141 (2000).

3

Individual Rights

The U.S. Constitution contains various provisions that protect individuals and individual rights. In this course, we examine various rights, including the First Amendment right to freedom of speech and assembly,[1] the prohibition against establishment of religion,[2] the protection for free exercise of religion,[3] the right to (procedural and substantive) due process,[4] the Takings Clause,[5] the Contract Clause,[6] the right to equal protection,[7] and the right to privacy. In criminal procedure, you will study other individual rights, including, for example, the right to counsel,[8] the prohibition against unreasonable searches and seizures,[9] and the privilege against self-incrimination.[10]

Procedural Due Process

The U.S. Constitution contains two separate procedural due process provisions with identical language. While the Fifth Amendment applies

OVERVIEW

specifically to the federal government (and to the states via the Fourteenth Amendment), the Fourteenth Amendment provision enjoins the states. Both clauses prohibit government from depriving individuals of "life, liberty or property" without due process of law.

This chapter examines the requirements for invocation of the procedural due process clauses. In theory, the clauses apply only when an individual is deprived of life, liberty, or property without due process of law. However, over time, the U.S. Supreme Court has swept in a variety of other governmental deprivations by broadly defining the terms *liberty* and *property*. In the process, the Court has redefined the notion of process through the concept of flexible due process. In other words, not all deprivations require the same level of process. On the contrary, with different types of deprivations, different levels of process might be required.

F   A   Q

Q: What's the difference between *substantive due process* and *procedural due process*?

A: The Due Process Clauses have been interpreted to include both substantive and procedural components. By *procedural due process*, we mean the procedures the state must observe when depriving someone of life, liberty, or property. The substantive aspect of due process involves not just process, but actually provides individuals with substantive rights. For example, the Fourteenth Amendment Due Process Clause has been used to incorporate various rights (for example, the First Amendment rights to freedom of speech, freedom of the press, and the free exercise of religion) and to impose those rights on the states, notwithstanding the fact that the First Amendment explicitly applies only to Congress.

A. Legislative Determinations

In analyzing procedural due process claims, a distinction is made between so-called legislative determinations and adjudicative determinations. As a general rule, when a legislative body such as Congress or a state legislature decides to impose a new law or rule — that is, it makes a **legislative determination** — the citizenry has no right to a hearing other than the processes laid down by the governing constitution for the passage of legislation. For example, if Congress decides to increase the federal income tax rate, Congress can construct its own processes and procedures for passage of the rate increase (subject, of course, to constitutional requirements such as passage by both houses of Congress and signature by the president or a veto override). In other words, Congress may choose whether to hold public hearings and decide who will be allowed to testify if hearings are held. Under such circumstances, parties cannot complain that they were deprived of due process of law if Congress does not grant them a hearing before adopting the rate increase.

Similar principles apply when other governmental agencies take legislative action (as opposed to adjudicative action). When an administrative agency adopts a rule or regulation — that is, when it is functions legislatively — it might constitutionally be able to do so without providing a hearing to those affected by the proposed rule or regulation. On the other hand, the agency may be constitutionally required to grant a hearing when it acts in an adjudicative context (for example, an administrative agency brings an enforcement action to impose sanctions on a regulated entity for violation of a statute or regulation). These principles are illustrated by the holding in *Bi-Metallic Investment Co. v. State Board of Equalization*.[11] In that case, the Court held that the Colorado State Board of Equalization and the Colorado Tax Commission's order increasing the valuation on all taxable property in Denver violated the Fourteenth Amendment Due Process Clause. The Court rejected the argument that those subject to the increase were entitled to due process protections. When "a rule of conduct applies to more than a few people, it is impracticable that everyone should have a direct voice in its adoption." The Court went on to note that the "Constitution does not require all public acts to be done in town meeting or an assembly of the whole" so that "[g]eneral statutes within the state power are passed that affect the person or property of individuals, sometimes to the point of ruin, without giving them a chance to be heard." Under such circumstances, the individual's right of recourse must come through the political process via such means as "the right to vote and the right to choose one's representatives."

Of course, even in legislative contexts, Congress can choose to require agencies to provide an opportunity for input, and sometimes Congress requires agencies to allow comments or it imposes trial-type procedures.[12] However, absent these congressional mandates, an agency might not be constitutionally required to accord regulated entities a hearing or process before adopting new rules or regulations.[13]

Bi-Metallic's rule is qualified by the notion that, once a legislative rule is announced, an individual may have the right to a hearing regarding the rule's application to him or her. In other words, if the governing body adopts a general rate increase (which might not require a hearing), an individual taxpayer affected by the rate increase may be entitled to a hearing on the calculation of his or her individual taxes.

Example: In *Londoner v. City of Denver*,[14] a city council made a legislative decision to require the paving of a street and to impose a tax assessment on nearby landowners on a proportionate basis to cover the cost. While the Court concluded that taxpayer Londoner could not challenge the decision to pave or the decision to assess, he could challenge the calculation of his own taxes. When a legislative body "commits to some subordinate body the duty of determining whether, in what amount, and upon whom it shall be levied, and of making its assessment and apportionment, due process of law requires that, at some stage of the proceedings, before the tax becomes irrevocably fixed, the taxpayer shall have an opportunity to be heard." Plaintiff was entitled to "support his allegations by argument, however brief: and, if need be, by proof, however informal."

> ### Sidebar
>
> **LEGISLATIVE HEARINGS**
>
> As a matter of legislative discretion, legislatures frequently hold hearings before enacting legislation. As part of this process, they may invite interested parties to appear and give comment. However, this right to be heard is a matter of legislative grace rather than constitutional requirement.

Governmental Action	Procedural Due Process Rights
Congress decides to enact a statute	No constitutional right to be heard
Local governmental officials enact a tax	No constitutional right to be heard
Under the taxing ordinance mentioned above, a governmental entity decides how much tax a taxpayer owes	Constitutional right to be heard

F   A   Q

Q: When administrative agencies function legislatively by promulgating regulations, they frequently give affected parties a right to notice of the proposed regulation and an opportunity to comment. Is this right a component of due process?

A: No. In this context, regulated parties do not have a constitutional right to be heard. The notice and comment procedure is statutorily imposed.

B. Adjudicative Determinations

While *Londoner* and *Bi-Metallic* suggest that legislative determinations are generally not subject to due process protections, **adjudicative determinations** might be subject to due process constraints. This section examines the foundational principles governing the application of due process to such determinations.

(1) Foundational Principles

Under both the Fifth Amendment and the Fourteenth Amendment, before the government may subject an individual to imprisonment (deprivation of liberty), a fine (deprivation of property), or capital punishment (deprivation of life), the individual is entitled to due process in the sense of notice and an opportunity to be heard. Likewise, before the state may take an individual's property for public use (for example, a state university forces a nearby landowner to sell his home to the university so that a new dormitory or classroom building can be built), the landowner may be entitled to a hearing and to compensation under the Takings Clause.

There has been considerable litigation regarding the definition and meaning of the terms "life, liberty or property." Early decisions drew a distinction between *rights* and *privileges*. When a right, particularly one implicating life, liberty, or property, was implicated, an individual was entitled to a hearing. On the other hand, when government chose to take away a privilege, it might be able to do so without implicating an individual's due process rights. At one point, the courts defined welfare payments, occupational licenses, and government employment as privileges.[15]

Over time, the courts became increasingly uncomfortable with the right-privilege distinction and began to acknowledge that some "privileges" were extremely important to the individual. As a result, the courts began to qualify or distinguish prior decisions defining the right-privilege distinction. Then, in *Goldberg v. Kelly*,[16] the Court effectively overruled that distinction in holding that welfare recipients were entitled to due process prior to the termination of their benefits. The case involved a dispute about whether welfare benefits should be regarded as "liberty" or "property," or whether they were simply a "gratuity" and therefore outside the protection of the Due Process Clause. In *Goldberg*, the Court held that the Due Process Clause applies to such benefits, concluding that it "may be realistic today to regard welfare entitlements as more like 'property' than a 'gratuity,'" and, in any event, they should be regarded as **entitlements** in the same sense as "subsidies to farmers and businessmen, routes for airlines and channels for television stations; long term contracts for defense, space, and education; social security pensions for individuals." In the Court's view, such entitlements are not regarded as luxuries or gratuities, but are "essentials, fully deserved, and in no sense a form of charity." As a result, due process principles apply. Justice Black dissented in *Goldberg*, arguing that federal entitlement programs have grown dramatically in recent decades, and that it strains "credulity to say that the government's promise of charity to an individual is property . . . when the government denies that the individual is honestly entitled to receive such a payment."

F A Q

Q: How is it possible that an individual has due process rights to a governmental decision to terminate welfare benefits? Are they now regarded as property?

A: Probably not. However, *Goldberg* suggests that they are more like property than a gratuity. It is more likely that the Court's decision to apply procedural due process principles to welfare benefits is correlated to the idea that a "liberty" interest is being deprived.

The Court's subsequent decisions have struggled to determine the limits of the Due Process Clause. If the Clause's injunction against the taking of liberty or property applies to welfare benefits, it conceivably extends to a variety of other governmental benefits. In subsequent decisions, the Court has treated a number of governmental rights and interests as subject to due process constraints when they are removed or terminated. Many of these rights and interests might formerly have been regarded as privileges.

Examples: In *Bell v. Burson*,[17] the Court held that a state could not withdraw a driver's license without providing the license holder with due process. Likewise, in *Morrissey v. Brewer*,[18] the Court held that a parolee's right to remain at liberty could not be revoked absent due process protections. Additionally, the Court concluded that due process applies when government attempts to terminate a professional license,[19] a driver's license, or parental rights.[20]

Sidebar

THE TYPE OF HEARING REQUIRED

Once the Court decided in *Goldberg* that the Due Process Clause applied, it was forced to determine the level of process that was due. The Court did not suggest that a full trial-type hearing must be provided prior to the deprivation of welfare benefits. On the contrary, the Court concluded that the "extent to which procedural due process must be afforded the recipient is influenced by the extent to which he may be 'condemned to suffer grievous loss,' and depends upon whether the recipient's interest in avoiding that loss outweighs the governmental interest in summary adjudication."

Despite the post-*Goldberg* breadth of procedural due process protections, the Court has not imposed due process constraints on every governmental deprivation. For example, in the employment area, the Court has suggested that due process constraints may sometimes apply, but not always. To determine the applicability of the Due Process Clause, one must consider the nature of the employment interest and whether the individual has an expectation of continued employment.

Example: If a professor holds tenure at a university, the employment brings with it an expectation of continued employment absent cause for termination. Under such circumstances, if the university tries to terminate the professor's tenure, it must provide her with a hearing on whether cause exists.

Despite *Roth*'s holding, one cannot say that anyone who holds a position on a year-to-year contract would never be entitled to a hearing related to the decision not to renew. For example, if an individual were dismissed prior to the termination of his contract or the decision not to renew was publicly stated as grounded in incompetence, a court might hold that he is entitled to a hearing on the charges.

By contrast, a contract professor may or may not have an expectation of continued employment, and may or may not have a right to due process when his contract is not renewed. Illustrative is the decision in *Board of Regents v. Roth*.[21] In *Roth*, the professor claimed that he was denied due process when he was not rehired for the next academic year without being given a reason for the nonrenewal and without being given an opportunity to challenge the decision. The Court disagreed. Unlike a tenured professor,[22] Roth was not protected by the Due Process Clause, which protects only "interests encompassed by the Fourteenth Amendment's protection of liberty and property." The Court distinguished *Goldberg* on the basis that a property interest involves "more than an abstract need or desire" and must involve a "legitimate claim of entitlement." Relying on Wisconsin law, which created and defined the terms of Roth's appointment, the Court noted that Roth held only a one-year contract that did not require "cause" for nonrenewal, that "secured absolutely no interest in re-employment for the next year," and therefore did not involve "a property interest sufficient to require the University authorities to give him a hearing when they declined to renew his contract of employment."

Even when an employment contract is involved, each case must be analyzed on its own terms. For example, had Roth been dismissed prior to the termination of his contract,[23] or under circumstances that suggested a "clearly implied promise of continued employment" or that suggested that he was incompetent or in violation of his First Amendment rights,[24] a hearing might have been required. However, a mere failure to renew a term contract did not give rise to due process rights. However, in *Perry v. Sinderman*,[25] the Court held that a contract professor might be entitled to a hearing if the circumstances gave rise to an expectation of continued employment.

One aspect of due process that the Court has struggled to define is the concept of **liberty**. The Due Process Clause has always been construed to apply to certain deprivations of liberty. For example, it applies when an individual is incarcerated[26] or committed to a mental institution.[27] Such deprivations of freedom are regarded as substantial enough that the individual must be given a hearing prior to the deprivation. Moreover, due process may require a full trial-type hearing.

Most courts will hold that an administrative agency violates due process when it fails to follow its own procedural rules.

It is less clear whether, and to what extent, the concept of liberty applies to situations when an individual is not actually confined. For example, in *Paul v. Davis*,[28] an individual claimed that he was denied a liberty interest when the police decided to include him in a shoplifter alert that was distributed to merchants with mug shots of suspected shoplifters. The evidence in that case showed that, while Davis had previously been arrested for shoplifting, the charges were subsequently dismissed (although not by the time the flier was issued). When Davis was confronted by his employer regarding the flier, he sued, claiming that his inclusion in the flier as an "active shoplifter" impermissibly deprived him of a liberty interest because it inhibited him from entering business establishments and seriously impaired his future employment opportunities. While recognizing that government may impose stigma by defamation, the Court doubted that the interest in reputation qualifies as either liberty or property, and therefore was not protected under the Due Process Clause. Justice Brennan, joined by Justice Marshall, dissented, arguing "that a person's interest in his good name and reputation falls within the broad term 'liberty' and clearly require[s] that the government afford procedural protections before infringing that name and reputation by branding a person as a criminal."

Despite the holding in *Paul*, the term *liberty* has been applied to situations that did not involve actual incarceration. For example, in *Goss v. Lopez*,[29] the Court held that a student had a liberty interest in not being expelled from school absent due process. Of course, as we shall see, the individual may not be entitled to much of a hearing for the deprivation of such liberty interests.

One issue that has arisen in subsequent cases is whether the determination of whether an interest qualifies as a liberty or property interest under the Due Process Clause is to be defined by reference to legislative or to judicial standards. In other words, when the legislature creates an interest (for example, welfare benefits), may it stipulate that one who receives those benefits has no due process rights, and must courts accept that stipulation? In *Arnett v. Kennedy*,[30] the Court upheld a statute that provided that a discharged employee was entitled to a full trial-type hearing following dismissal, but was precluded from receiving a pretermination hearing (although the statute also provided for backpay if the employee was reinstated). A plurality of the Court held that the statute that created the job also imposed conditions on the process that was due, and that the employee must take the "bitter with the sweet." In other words, the employee was not entitled to a pretermination hearing. However, in *Cleveland Board of Education v. Loudermill*,[31] the Court overturned *Arnett* and rejected the "bitter with the sweet" analysis. The Court held that "the Due Process Clause provides that certain substantive rights — life, liberty, and property — cannot be deprived except pursuant to constitutionally adequate procedures." Although the legislature may choose not to confer a "property interest in [public] employment, it may not constitutionally authorize the deprivation of such an interest, once conferred, without appropriate procedural safeguards."

(2) Procedural Requirements

Once a court concludes that due process principles apply, it must then determine the level of process that is due. Historically (in other words, prior to *Goldberg*), for deprivations of life, liberty, or property, the individual was entitled to a full trial-type hearing. As a result, if the government sought to incarcerate an individual for committing a crime or to take her life for committing murder, nothing less than a trial-type hearing would do (absent a decision to plead guilty) that included the right to present witnesses, to cross-examine opposing witnesses, and to be represented by counsel. In addition, courts required that the hearing be "on the record" in the sense that a transcript was prepared. These requirements could be dispensed with only when the facts were not in dispute.[32] The difficulty was that *Goldberg* expanded the range of interests protected by the Due Process Clause, bringing within the scope of that clause an increasing array of governmental activities, and raised questions regarding the nature of the hearing required for a deprivation of these newly protected interests. For example, if due process rights apply to welfare benefits, must government provide the full panoply of trial-type rights to the deprivation of such benefits (or other benefits such as the deprivation of an important interest such as a driver's license)?

In *Goldberg*, the Court provided a partial answer to this question, holding that while welfare recipients were not entitled to a full trial-type hearing, they were entitled to a fair hearing that need not include a "complete record and a comprehensive opinion." In reaching this result, the Court noted that welfare agencies and welfare recipients have an "interest in relatively speedy resolution of questions of eligibility," but that they are "used to dealing with one another informally" in the context of heavy and "burdensome caseloads." Weighing these conflicting considerations, the Court required only "minimum procedural safeguards, adapted to the particular characteristics of welfare recipients, and to the limited nature of the controversies to be resolved." In other words, welfare recipients were entitled to an "opportunity to be heard" at a "meaningful time and in a meaningful manner," and were to be given timely and adequate notice of the reasons for the termination, and an opportunity to "defend by confronting any adverse witnesses and by presenting [their] own arguments and evidence orally." The Court did not require that recipients be given the opportunity to submit a written brief, especially since many welfare recipients may lack the "educational attainment" necessary to make an effective written presentation. In addition, if the agency's decision is based on factual conclusions, the agency must allow welfare recipients to retain attorneys if they so choose (although it need not provide attorneys). Finally, the agency's decision must rest on legal rules, rely on evidence adduced at the hearing, and state the reasons for the ultimate conclusion as well as the evidence relied on (though the agency need not state a full opinion or even formal findings of fact and conclusions of law).

In *Goldberg*, the Court went on to hold that a pretermination hearing was required prior to the cut-off of welfare benefits. In reaching this conclusion, the Court emphasized the importance of welfare to the individual: "For qualified recipients, welfare provides the means to obtain essential food, clothing, housing, and medical care. Thus the crucial factor in this context . . . is that termination of aid pending resolution of a controversy over eligibility may deprive an eligible recipient of the very means by which to live while he waits. Since he lacks independent resources, his situation becomes immediately desperate." The Court rejected the government's argument that it was entitled to terminate benefits without a hearing on the theory that most terminations are upheld and that the agency would have difficulty recovering benefits that were paid in the interim: "the interest of the eligible recipient in uninterrupted receipt of public assistance, coupled with the State's interest that his payments not be erroneously terminated, clearly outweighs the State's competing concern to prevent any increase in its fiscal and administrative burdens."

Interest	Process Rights
Capital punishment	Full trial
Incarceration	Full trial
Fine (imposed as penalty)	Full trial
Deprivation of welfare benefits	Fair hearing

F   A   Q

Q: When an indigent criminal defendant is charged with a crime that may carry the penalty of imprisonment, defendant is entitled to have counsel appointed and paid for by the state. Does an indigent in a welfare termination proceeding have a similar right to state provided counsel?

A: No. While the Court has recognized that an indigent has the right to be heard in a welfare termination proceeding, it has refused to hold that indigents have the right to state provided and paid-for counsel.

After *Goldberg*, questions arose about the level of process that would be required in other contexts. In subsequent decisions, the Court concluded that it would not require full trial-type hearings for all deprivations protected by the Due Process Clause. In the Court's decision in *Mathews v. Eldridge*,[33] the Court suggested that the type of hearing that would be required would depend on the circumstances. In other words, the Court would apply **flexible due process** principles based on the context. The Court would not require that a full evidentiary hearing be given every time that government affects some type of property or liberty interest. On the contrary, each case would be evaluated based on its own merits. In a given case, the Court would require only such procedural protections "as the particular situation demands" considering the nature of the governmental and private interests that are affected.

In addition to articulating the concept of flexible due process, *Mathews* laid out a three-part test for determining the level of process that is due: "First, the private interest that will be affected by the official action; second, the risk of an erroneous deprivation of such interest through the procedures used, and the probable value, if any, of additional or substitute procedural safeguards; and finally, the Government's interest, including the function involved and the fiscal and administrative burdens that the additional or substitute procedural requirement would entail."

Goss v. Lopez[34] illustrates the flexible due process test. *Goss* involved high school students who claimed that they had been deprived of their right to an education when they were suspended from school for "disruptive or disobedient conduct" (*e.g.*, a demonstration in the auditorium that disrupted a class and an attack on a police officer) during a period of student unrest. The alleged misconduct was committed in the presence of the school administrator who ordered the suspensions. Even though the Court concluded that the right to an education is protected under the Due Process Clause, and that the students were entitled to "fundamentally fair procedures," the Court held that school administrators were not required to use trial-type procedures in making the suspensions. Instead, the Court weighed the students' interest (in protecting against improper suspension and a possible adverse effect on reputation) against the school's interest in prompt action, and held that the students must be given "some kind of notice and afforded some kind of hearing," but that the due process requirement should not be allowed to interfere with the educational process.

The hearing required in the *Goss* context is not, necessarily, a full trial-type hearing. On the contrary, the Court suggested that, when there is a need for immediate action, the school administrator might be required to do nothing more than provide the student "oral or written notice of the charges against him and, if he denies them, an explanation of the evidence the authorities have and an opportunity to present his side of the story." The Court concluded that administrators can satisfy the requirements of due process if they provide students with "rudimentary precautions," including informing the student of what he is accused of doing, including the basis of the accusation, and provided that the administrator provides the student with a hearing prior to removal (if possible, under the circumstances). However, the Court concluded that the hearing can be informal and can occur almost immediately. In other words, the Court refused to impose trial-type procedures because of the potential diversion of resources and administrative costs.

Applying these principles, the *Goss* Court concluded that, when the disciplinarian has observed the wrongful conduct, the requirements of due process are satisfied by an informal give and take between the disciplinarian and the student. Once the give and take occurs, the disciplinarian can decide whether more formal procedures are both necessary and appropriate. However, the Court suggested that longer suspensions (for example, longer than ten days or for the remainder of the term) may require more formal procedures. In *Goss*, since none of the students were given even an informal hearing, either before or after the suspensions, the Court refused to uphold the disciplinary suspensions.

The decision in *Goss* has not been beyond criticism. In the post-*Goldberg* era, some commentators have decried the increasing tendency to judicialize every relation between citizens and governmental officials. For example, in *Goss*, Justice Powell (joined by Chief Justice Burger and Justices Blackmun and Rehnquist) dissented, arguing that a suspension of not more than ten days does not assume constitutional dimensions. He argued that one "of the more disturbing aspects of today's decision is its indiscriminate reliance upon the judiciary, and the adversary process, as the means of resolving many of the most routine problems arising in the classroom."

Of course, under the *Mathews* flexible due process approach, not all educational decisions will require the same due process approach. In a disciplinary context like *Goss*, due process constraints require a hearing, albeit an informal one. In other contexts, the hearing might take another form. Illustrative is the holding in *Board of Curators of the University of Missouri v. Horowitz.*[35] *Horowitz* involved a medical student who was dismissed because of poor academic performance. Horowitz was initially placed on probation after concerns (academic, attendance, and hygiene related) were raised regarding her clinical performance during a pediatrics rotation. Subsequently, Horowitz was allowed to take a series of oral and practical examinations while working with seven practicing physicians who concluded that her performance was "low-satisfactory." While she was not given a trial-type hearing prior to the dismissal, the university did follow an academic review process that involved a Council on Evaluation, which received input from various faculty at the school. The council's recommendations were reviewed by the Coordinating Committee, a body composed of faculty members, and ultimately were approved by the dean. However, Horowitz was not allowed to appear before either the council or the committee.

In upholding the dismissal, the *Horowitz* Court distinguished between a disciplinary suspension, as in *Goss*, and an academic decision, and suggested that "far less stringent procedural requirements" are required for an academic dismissal. The Court noted that a "school is an academic institution, not a courtroom or administrative hearing room," and that courts have been reluctant to attach trial-type procedures to academic decisions: "Such a judgment is by its nature more subjective and evaluative than the typical factual questions presented in the average disciplinary decision. Like the decision of an individual professor as to the proper grade for a student in his course, the determination whether to dismiss a student for academic reasons requires an expert evaluation of cumulative information and is not readily adapted to the procedural tools of judicial or administrative decisionmaking."

In *Horowitz*, the Court concluded that a trial-type hearing would be inappropriate in this context because the "educational process is not by nature adversary," and judicial presence would "risk deterioration of many beneficial aspects of the faculty-student relationship." While the Court emphasized that it would be on guard against the possibility of arbitrariness or capriciousness, it found neither in this case. While the Court recognized that Horowitz had been deprived of a liberty interest, it concluded that she had received all of the due process that she was due. The school had fully informed respondent of the faculty's dissatisfaction with her clinical progress and the danger that this posed to timely graduation and continued enrollment. In addition, the decision to dismiss was "careful and deliberate" with procedures deemed sufficient under the Due Process Clause.

Whether a student is entitled to a trial-type hearing may depend on the nature of the issues. Suspension and expulsion issues can arise in a variety of contexts. For example, when a student receives consistently failing grades and is ultimately dismissed from school, courts will be disinclined to grant a trial-type hearing. The issues are not susceptible to judicial resolution. On the other hand, if a student is charged with plagiarism, the issues may be more susceptible to judicial resolution. Depending on the nature of the allegations, the student may have the right to a trial-type hearing on the issue of whether there actually was plagiarism. In some instances, the school's disciplinary rules may provide for a trial-type hearing.

A recurring question in due process cases is whether an individual is entitled to a pretermination hearing or whether the hearing can be provided post-termination. As previously noted, *Goldberg* required a hearing prior to the termination of welfare benefits. However, post-*Goldberg* cases rarely require a full pretermination hearing. In *Loudermill*, the Court held that a public employee was entitled to a pretermination hearing, but the Court required only an informal opportunity for give and take. Likewise, in *Mathews*, the Court upheld a limited process that again did not involve a full adversary hearing. The process involved an administrative review of Eldridge's medical reports followed by a letter setting forth the agency's tentative decision that his disability had ceased and an opportunity to obtain and submit additional information pertaining to his condition. After considering Eldridge's submission, the agency terminated his benefits but gave him the right to seek reconsideration within six months. While recognizing that disability benefits are an interest deserving of protection under the Due Process Clause, the Court held that a pretermination hearing was not required, noting that the initial decision to terminate Eldridge's benefits was made by a team consisting of a physician and an agency official, and was based on a questionnaire and other medical information provided by his treating doctors. Moreover, Eldridge was given the right to a hearing before an administrative law judge and a right of appeal to the SSA Appeals Council. Given the nature of the interests affected, the Court held that Eldridge had been provided with adequate process, even though he had not been accorded a pretermination hearing. If Eldridge prevailed, he would receive retroactive benefits. As a result, the interest in a pretermination hearing was simply the interest in an uninterrupted flow of benefits pending final resolution. The Court viewed disability benefits as different from welfare benefits in regard to pretermination hearings because "welfare assistance is given to persons on the very margin of subsistence" who do not have the means to survive while they wait for final resolution. By contrast, disability benefits are granted without regard to whether a recipient has other means of support, and therefore an erroneous deprivation of Social Security benefits is not potentially as severe as an erroneous deprivation of welfare benefits. Even though it may take a long time to resolve the disability claim (sometimes more than a year), the Court concluded that the disabled worker's need is likely to be lower than that of a welfare recipient, and the worker can always seek welfare assistance in the interim. Further, because disability decisions are "frequently based on unbiased medical reports by physicians who have examined the recipient," questions of veracity and credibility are less likely to be present, and the Court concluded that there was a lesser need for an evidentiary hearing. Finally, the Court emphasized that pretermination hearings would require increased cost for additional hearings, as well as the potential loss of benefits paid to individuals who were undeserving. As a result, the Court concluded that the "additional safeguard to the individual affected by the administrative action and to society in terms of increased assurance that the action is just, may be outweighed by the cost of providing benefits to the undeserving."

SUMMARY

■ For many years, the Due Process Clause provided hearings only for those deprived of life, liberty, or property. A distinction was drawn between a right and a privilege.

- With the landmark decision in *Goldberg v. Kelly*, the Court began to realign what had formerly been regarded as privileges to entitlements and to require hearings associated with terminations.

- In subsequent cases, the Court developed the concept of flexible due process to govern these extensions of the entitlements concept. Although a full hearing might be required in some cases, some processes might satisfy due process standards even though something less than a full hearing was required.

CONNECTIONS

Commerce Clause

When Congress enacts legislation under the Commerce Clause, it is not required to provide the public with notice and an opportunity to be heard. However, in some cases, Congress chooses to hold hearings to inform its legislative judgment and may give interested individuals notice of those hearings and an opportunity to be heard.

Takings Clause

Under the Takings Clause, the government is allowed to take private property for public use, but only if it provides just compensation. Under that clause, an individual will ordinarily be entitled to a trial-type hearing to determine the amount of compensation to be paid.

Presidential Power

In a number of instances in which the president decides to take action, he is not required to provide the citizenry with notice of his intentions or an opportunity to be heard. For example, if the president decides to commit federal troops to a war zone, he may have an obligation to consult with Congress or seek a declaration of war, but may have no obligation to hold hearings. However, if presidential subordinates act adjudicatively or subject to a statute requiring a hearing, a hearing may be required.

Endnotes

1. U.S. Const., amend. I.
2. *Id.*
3. *Id.*
4. U.S. Const., amends. I & XIV.
5. U.S. Const., amend. V.
6. U.S. Const., art. I, §10, cl. 1 ("No State shall . . . pass any . . . law impairing the Obligation of Contracts").
7. U.S. Const., amend. XIV.
8. U.S. Const., amend. VI.

9. U.S. Const., amend. IV.
10. U.S. Const., amend. V.
11. 239 U.S. 441 (1915).
12. *See* Administrative Procedure Act, 5 U.S.C. §§553, 554, 556 & 557.
13. *See* William F. Funk, Sidney A. Shapiro & Russell L. Weaver, *Administrative Practice and Procedure: Problems and Cases* 48-185 (3d ed. 2006).
14. 210 U.S. 373 (1908).
15. *See* McAuliffe v. Mayor, 29 N.E. 517 (Mass. 1892).
16. 397 U.S. 254 (1970).
17. 402 U.S. 535 (1971).
18. 408 U.S. 471 (1972).
19. *See* In re Ruffalo, 390 U.S. 544 (1968).
20. *See* Santosky v. Kramer, 455 U.S. 745 (1982).
21. 408 U.S. 564 (1972).
22. *See* Slochower v. Bd. of Educ., 350 U.S. 551 (1956).
23. *See* Wieman v. Updegraff, 344 U.S. 183 (1952).
24. *See* Perry v. Sindermann, 408 U.S. 593 (1972).
25. 408 U.S. 593 (1972).
26. *See* Mullaney v. Wilbur, 421 U.S. 684 (1975).
27. *See* O'Connor v. Donaldson, 422 U.S. 563 (1975).
28. 424 U.S. 693 (1976).
29. 419 U.S. 565 (1975).
30. 416 U.S. 134 (1974).
31. 470 U.S. 532 (1985).
32. *See* Codd v. Velger, 429 U.S. 624 (1977).
33. 424 U.S. 319 (1976).
34. 419 U.S. 565 (1975).
35. 435 U.S. 78 (1978).

Substantive Protection of Economic Rights

7

OVERVIEW

Controversy regarding the judiciary's authority to review the substance (and substantive wisdom) of legislation has existed for most of the country's judicial history. For the first century of this nation's existence, the U.S. Supreme Court was reluctant to interfere with or overturn legislative judgments. However, by the beginning of the twentieth century, the Court's attitude had changed, and it embraced the concept of substantive due process. The Court began to examine the ends served by legislation and the means used to accomplish those ends to determine whether they were reasonable or rational. During the ensuing decades, the Court evolved its modern approach to the role of judicial review.

Evident in the substantive due process cases is the debate regarding the role of the judiciary and its relationship to the legislative branches (federal and state) of government. Also evident are debates about whether certain types of interests (such as freedom of speech) can or should receive greater protection than other types of interests (such as economic interests). Over the decades, the Court has adopted and applied different levels of review to different types of interests.

A. Substantive Due Process: *Lochner* to *Nebbia*

Whether economic interests warrant protection as a matter of constitutional right or liberty involves a long-running controversy over the role of the judiciary and its relationship to the elected branches of government. The outlines of the debate were evident early in our constitutional history in the decision in *Calder v. Bull*.[1] In *Calder*, two justices disagreed regarding the authority of the judiciary to invoke natural law in deciding cases. Whereas Justice Chase argued fervently in favor of the authority of judges to invoke natural law,[2] Justice Iredell argued just as fervently that courts should not invoke natural law in deciding cases. He believed that the justices must rely on specific constitutional provisions to invalidate acts of the legislative and executive branches.

By and large, during the early years of the country's existence, the Court rarely overturned governmental actions of any sort. In the Court's landmark decision in *Marbury v. Madison*, the Court purported to overturn portions of the Judiciary Act of 1789. Then, in the 1850s, the Court invalidated a second act.[3] But otherwise during the early years, the Court was disinclined to review the wisdom of legislation.

The Court was even less inclined to invalidate state legislation. The Fourteenth Amendment to the U.S. Constitution, which was used to incorporate the Bill of Rights and to apply most of its provisions to the states, was not ratified until 1868, and it was not actually applied to the states until much later.[4] During the period before the Bill of Rights applied to the states,[5] most constitutionally imposed restrictions on the actions of state officials came from other provisions of the Constitution.[6] Review came, if at all, through the Contract Clause. Interpretation of the Commerce Clause, depending on prevailing doctrine, also expanded or restricted a state's power to regulate economic activity.

The emergence of substantive due process to develop and account for economic rights and liberties was previewed in *Dred Scott v. Sandford*[7] when the Court attempted to resolve the slavery issue on constitutional grounds. As Chief Justice Roger B. Taney put it, "the right of property in a slave is distinctly and expressly affirmed in the Constitution." And, federal legislation depriving a citizen of "his property in[ ] a particular Territory . . . could hardly be dignified with the name due process of law."

Notwithstanding the eventual repudiation of *Dred Scott* by war, constitutional amendment, and later judicial review, economic rights theory gained increasing currency as the latter half of the nineteenth century progressed. In the *Slaughterhouse Cases*,[8] the Court's seminal interpretation of the Fourteenth Amendment, Justice Field argued that "the right to acquire and possess property of every kind" was a matter that "of right belong[s] to the citizens of all free governments." Justice Field's argument, joined by three other dissenting justices, pertained to the Privileges and Immunities Clause of the Fourteenth Amendment. His broad interpretation of the incidents of federal citizenship did not command a majority of the *Slaughterhouse* Court, and the Privileges and Immunities Clause largely has been of limited consequence since.

Economic rights theory, which the Court repudiated in the privileges and immunities context, broke through slightly more than two decades later as an animating source for the Due Process Clause. In *Allgeyer v. Louisiana*,[9] the Court embraced the Due Process Clause broadly saying it is the basis for: "the right of the citizen to be free in the enjoyment of all his faculties; to be free to use them in all lawful ways; to live and work where he will; to earn his livelihood by any lawful calling; to pursue any livelihood or avocation; and for that purpose to enter into all contracts which may be proper, necessary and essential to his carrying out to a successful conclusion the purposes above mentioned."

Allgeyer heralded an era of judicially identified and developed rights and liberties that engendered controversy not only with respect to the Court's decisions but also its standards of review and role in the context of representative governance. Debate over the Court's performance and function has persisted long after economic rights doctrine was abandoned in the late 1930s. Among other things, it is a reference point for modern dialogue regarding the Due Process Clause as a source of fundamental albeit unenumerated rights and liberties.

It is well established that states possess police powers that predated and were acknowledged by the Constitution. To the extent a nexus exists to the commerce power or some other enumerated basis, the federal government also may enact laws that account for the health, welfare, safety, and morals of society. These "police power" regulations (or "health and welfare regulations") can take many different forms. For example, a legislature might limit the number of hours that employees can work or mandate minimum compensation. Alternatively, a legislature might place conditions on the ability of out-of-state companies to do business within the state or choose to prohibit certain types of businesses (for example, brothels).

Such regulations might be challenged on any number of constitutional grounds including the Contract Clause, the protection for liberty contained in the Fourteenth Amendment, the Equal Protection Clause, and sometimes the Privileges and Immunities Clause. For example, in *Allgeyer*, a state law prohibited foreign insurance companies from doing business in the state without a license and without retaining an agent authorized to conduct business on its behalf. The Court struck down the law:

> [W]e think the statute is a violation of the fourteenth amendment of the federal constitution, in that it deprives the defendants of their liberty without due process of law. . . . The "liberty" mentioned in that amendment means, not only the right of the citizen to be free from the mere physical restraint of his person, as by incarceration, but the term is deemed to embrace the right of the citizen to be free in the enjoyment of all his faculties; to be free to use them in all lawful ways; to live and work where he will; to earn his livelihood by any lawful calling; to pursue any livelihood or avocation; and for that purpose to enter into all contracts which may be proper, necessary, and essential to his carrying out to a successful conclusion the purposes above mentioned.

Substantive due process cases necessarily raise questions regarding the scope of judicial review, especially regarding whether the judiciary should be deferential to legislative judgments or should engage in a more independent review process. Early substantive due process review, which focused largely on economic rights and liberties, proceeded on the premise that the judiciary should evaluate both legislative means and ends. This practice was challenged by critics then and now who viewed it as an "antidemocratic" function that transformed the Court into a super-legislature.

Ordinarily, in reviewing the validity of legislation under the Due Process Clause, the Court invokes means-ends analysis. Under such analysis, a reviewing court examines the end that the legislature is seeking to accomplish and the means by which the legislature seeks to accomplish it. Means-ends analysis remains important today, and we will examine how it applies in various contexts. However, as we shall see, at various points, the Court has reviewed the means and ends of legislation more closely than at other times.

The high point of substantive due process review, as applied to economic regulation, is evident in the Court's 1905 decision in *Lochner v. New York*.[10] In *Lochner*, the Court struck down a New York law that prohibited bakers from working more than 60 hours in a single week. In what is regarded as a classic example of substantive due process, in the sense of the Court substituting its judgment for that of the legislature, the Court struck the law down as an infringement of the bakers' right to contract. The Court rejected the notion that the law could be sustained as a "fair, reasonable, and appropriate exercise of the police power of the state." On the contrary, the Court concluded that the legislature had "no reasonable ground for interfering with the liberty of person or the right of free contract, by determining the hours of labor, in the occupation of a baker." "Clean and wholesome bread does not depend upon whether the baker works but ten hours per day or only sixty hours a week," and there is "no reasonable foundation for holding this to be necessary or appropriate as a health law to safeguard the public health, or the health of the individuals who are following the trade of a baker." As a result, the Court regarded statutes of this nature as "mere meddlesome interferences with the rights of the individual, and they are not saved from condemnation by the claim that they are passed in the exercise of the police power and upon the subject of the health of the individual whose rights are interfered with, unless there be some fair ground, reasonable in and of itself, to say that there is material danger to the public health, or to the health of the employees, if the hours of labor are not curtailed."

F   A   Q

Q: How could the *Lochner* Court have concluded that there is no rational relationship between the number of hours people work and their health?

A: The Court certainly could have been deferential to the legislature and found a rational relationship between health and work hour restrictions. After all, New York was not attempting to tightly restrict the number of hours that someone could work. The limit imposed by New York's law was 60 hours per week, and the Court has held that workers have a constitutional right to work more hours than that number. The lesson of *Lochner* is that the Court took the right to contract much more seriously at that time and was less willing to allow the government to interfere with that right. The Court had much more of a laissez-faire philosophy regarding government's relationship with the individual.

Following *Lochner*, the Court used that decision to strike down legislation in several other cases.[11] However, by the mid-1930s, the Court's approach to substantive due process was beginning to change as applied to economic regulations. *Nebbia v. New York*[12] involved a New York law that established a milk control board with the power to establish minimum and maximum retail prices for milk as applied to Nebbia, who sold below the stated price. With a nod to the Contract Clause ("Under our form of government the use of property and the making of contracts are normally matters of private and not of public concern"), the Court recognized that contract rights are not absolute and can be regulated to further the common interest. Instead of the searching scrutiny involved in *Lochner*, the Court asked only whether the end to be accomplished was "unreasonable, arbitrary, or capricious" and whether the means used to achieve that objective bore "a real and substantial relation to the object sought to be attained." Noting that the "law of supply and demand was insufficient to correct maladjustments detrimental to the community," the Court upheld the law, concluding that the order "appears not to be unreasonable or arbitrary, or without relation to the purpose to prevent ruthless competition from destroying the wholesale price structure on which the farmer depends for his livelihood, and the community for an assured supply of milk." The Court's more deferential approach was reflected in its conclusion: "With the wisdom of the policy adopted, with the adequacy or practicability of the law enacted to forward it, the

Sidebar

MEANS-ENDS ANALYSIS

The *Nebbia* Court focused on means-ends analysis, an approach that is still used today. When using a means-end analysis, the Court asks, "What is the end or objective that the legislature is seeking to accomplish, and what are the means that it is using to accomplish that objective?" Of course, in addition to means-ends analysis, one needs to be cognizant of the standard of review being applied. If the Court is applying a high standard of review (for example, strict scrutiny), the governmental enactment is more likely to be struck down. On the other hand, if the Court is applying a rational basis test, the Court is more likely to sustain the enactment.

courts are both incompetent and unauthorized to deal. [T]he Legislature is primarily the judge of the necessity of such an enactment, [every] possible presumption is in favor of its validity, [and] though the court may hold views inconsistent with the wisdom of the law, it may not be annulled unless palpably in excess of legislative power."

By the 1930s, following the constitutional crisis (see the discussion of President Roosevelt's so-called Court-packing plan in Chapter 2), Lochnerian analysis disappeared along with the Court's more restrictive interpretation of the Commerce Clause. Besides *Nebbia*, the Court also decided *West Coast Hotel Co. v. Parrish*.[13] That case involved a constitutional challenge to a State of Washington law stipulating minimum wages for women and minors. In an opinion by Justice Hughes, the Court upheld the law and rejected a Contract Clause claim, noting that the "exploitation of a class of workers who are in an unequal position with respect to bargaining power and are thus relatively defenseless against the denial of a living wage is not only detrimental to their health and well being, but casts a direct burden for their support upon the community." The Court went on to note that "[w]e may take judicial notice of the unparalleled demands for relief which arose during the recent period of depression and still continue to an alarming extent despite the degree of economic recovery which has been achieved."

In *Williamson v. Lee Optical*,[14] the Court upheld an Oklahoma law that made it illegal for anyone except a licensed optometrist or ophthalmologist to fit lenses to a face or to duplicate or replace into frames lenses or other optical appliances, except on written prescriptive authority of an Oklahoma licensed ophthalmologist or optometrist. In other words, the law precluded an optician from fitting old glasses into new frames or supplying a lens, whether it be a new lens or one to duplicate a lost or broken lens, without a prescription. In an opinion by Justice Douglas, the Court articulated a deferential approach and upheld the law: "The Oklahoma law may exact a needless, wasteful requirement in many cases. But it is for the legislature, not the courts, to balance the advantages and disadvantages of the new requirement." In addition, the Court flatly rejected Lochnerian analysis: "The day is gone when this

Court uses the Due Process Clause of the Fourteenth Amendment to strike down state laws, regulatory of business and industrial conditions, because they may be unwise, improvident, or out of harmony with a particular school of thought. We emphasize again what Chief Justice Waite said in *Munn v. State of Illinois*, 94 U.S. 113, 'For protection against abuses by legislatures the people must resort to the polls, not to the courts.'"

Deference to Legislature!

By 1938, the Court had adopted a very deferential approach to economic regulation. In *United States v. Carolene Products Co.*,[15] the Court held that economic legislation should be upheld if "any state of facts either known or which could reasonably be assumed affords support for it." Concluding that it is debatable whether commerce in filled milk "should be left unregulated, or in some measure restricted, or wholly prohibited," the Court concluded that "as that decision was for Congress, neither the finding of a court arrived at by weighing the evidence, nor the verdict of a jury can be substituted for it." However, the Court distinguished between economic rights and other rights, suggesting that it might apply a more rigorous review standard to some constitutional rights, "such as those of the first ten Amendments, which are deemed equally specific when held to be embraced within the Fourteenth."[16]

In subsequent cases, the Court has reaffirmed these principles and suggested that it would distinguish between economic regulation and legislation affecting such matters as the right to vote, restraints on the dissemination of information, interferences with political organization, prohibitions on peaceable assembly, or restrictions on religious or racial minorities. Issues relating to the right to vote, as well as to assemble or disseminate information, can distort the political process and prevent citizens from communicating with each other. By contrast, discrete and insular minorities, by virtue of their minority status, are unable to vindicate their rights and interests through the political process.

F   A   Q

Q: *Carolene Products* distinguished between laws affecting economic rights and laws affecting rights within a "specific prohibition of the Constitution" and suggested that there may be a "narrower scope for operation of the presumption of constitutionality when a specific prohibition is involved." Did *Lochner* rely on a "specific prohibition" of the Constitution in striking down New York's law?

A: Yes, *Lochner* relied on the Contract Clause. However, in modern decisions, the Court has been less willing than in *Lochner* to use the Contract Clause to strike down general economic legislation involving, say, the number of hours a baker can work. Nevertheless, the Court has placed much greater emphasis on prohibitions like the First Amendment right to freedom of speech.

B. The Takings Clause

The Fifth Amendment Takings Clause prohibits the government from taking private property for "public use" without providing "just compensation." A taking for purposes of this clause may be a function of acquisition or regulation that limits land use.

Two major issues arise under this clause. First, some litigants question whether their property is being taken for a public use (as opposed to a private use) and therefore argue that the taking is impermissible. Second, at times, there are disputes about whether there is a taking at all.

(1) The Requirement of a "Public Use"

Whether a taking is for a public use is an issue that has generally been resolved in favor of the government. Examples of this tendency are plentiful. In *Hawaii Housing Authority v. Midkiff*,[17] the State of Hawaii condemned a fee title to real estate, thereby taking it from lessors and transferring it to the lessees with compensation. The Court sustained the law because its goal was to reduce the concentration of land ownership in Hawaii, and the Court found a public use in the purpose of eliminating the "social and economic evils of a land oligopoly."

In *Berman v. Parker*,[18] the Court upheld a Washington, D.C., redevelopment plan that targeted a blighted part of the district. Although some of the condemned land was to be used for explicitly public uses (for example, streets, schools, and other public facilities), the rest would be sold to private parties for redevelopment. A department store owner challenged the condemnation of its property, noting that his property was not blighted and claiming that the goal of creating a "better balanced, more attractive community" was not a "valid public use." The Court disagreed, noting that the redevelopment plan was designed to serve the public good and that the plan must include the entire area to achieve its objectives.

In yet another case, *Ruckelshaus v. Monsanto Co.*,[19] the Court upheld the Federal Insecticide, Fungicide, and Rodenticide Act under which the Environmental Protection Agency could consider data and trade secrets submitted by a prior pesticide applicant in evaluating a subsequent application provided that the second applicant was required to pay just compensation. The Court held that Congress could readily conclude that "the cost of time-consuming research eliminated a significant barrier to entry in the pesticide market and thereby enhanced competition."

Kelo v. City of New London[20] is the Court's most recent public use decision. Like *Berman*, that case involved a redevelopment plan designed to create jobs, increase tax revenue, make the city more attractive, create leisure and recreational opportunities, and revitalize an economically distressed part of a city, which was to be achieved through the power of purchase and eminent domain. The plan, which included a waterfront conference hotel, restaurants, shopping areas, marinas, new housing, and research and development office space, was challenged by a woman whose property was condemned, even though it was not blighted or in poor condition. She claimed that her property was not being taken for public use.

Although *Kelo* rejected the challenge, it restated the fundamental proposition that the government may not take property solely for the purpose of transferring it to another private party, whether or not the government is willing to pay just compensation for the property. But since the New London development plan focused on "redevelopment," the Court found a public use, even though the entire piece of property would not be opened up to the general public. The Court also suggested that it normally gives deference to legislative judgments on takings issues, quoting *Berman* for the proposition that "[w]e do not sit to determine whether a particular housing project is or is not desirable. . . . It is within the power of the legislature to determine that the community should be beautiful as well as healthy, spacious as well as clean, well-balanced as well as carefully patrolled." Although the redevelopment project in New London did not involve blighted property, the Court deferred to the conclusion that the area was "sufficiently distressed to justify a program of economic rejuvenation" that will create "appreciable benefits to the community, including — but by no means limited to — new jobs and increased tax revenue." The Court suggested that it might not permit the state to transfer land from one person to another simply because the second citizen would put the property to a more productive use. However, since that issue was not before the Court, the Court did not address or resolve it. On the facts before it, the Court found a public use that satisfies "the public use requirement of the Fifth Amendment."

Kelo involved a couple of important dissents that illustrate divisions on the Court regarding government's right to take property. Justice O'Connor, joined by three other justices, argued that private property can be condemned and transferred to another private party only when the "precondemnation use of the targeted property inflict[s] affirmative harm on society — in *Berman* through blight resulting from extreme poverty and in *Midkiff* through oligopoly resulting from extreme wealth." Finding no comparable situation here, she would have invalidated the taking because the "beneficiaries are likely to be those citizens with disproportionate influence and power in the political process, including large corporations and development firms." Justice Thomas also dissented, arguing that a public use must necessarily entail a situation in which the government "actually uses or gives the public a legal right to use the property." He agreed with Justice O'Connor that a broader interpretation of the clause might allow "those citizens with disproportionate influence and power in the political process, including large corporations and development firms," to victimize the weak.

F   A   Q

Q: So government can condemn and take someone's private property, even though that property is not blighted and does not itself need "renewal"?

A: *Kelo* produced a storm of public reaction because it allowed the government to condemn nonblighted property when the government would prefer to see that property redeveloped for a different use. Critics of the decision suggested that people should be free to retain their nonblighted property notwithstanding the government's desire to redevelop it.

(2) The Definition of a "Taking"

The other major issue in takings cases is whether government actions have actually "taken" property in the constitutional sense. In theory, the definition of a taking is relatively straightforward. A taking clearly occurs when the government condemns a person's property and assumes title to it, as well as when the government occupies the property for its own purposes despite the fact that the occupation may be temporary.[21] For example, suppose the government wants to build a road through a plaintiff's property and decides to take the property for that reason. Under such circumstances, the government is allowed to take the property, but is required to pay for it.

The difficulty is that some takings involve something less than a complete condemnation of the property. As the Court stated in *Pennsylvania Coal Co. v. Mahon*,[22] a taking occurs "when the state makes a 'direct appropriation' of property, or the functional equivalent of a '*practical ouster* of [the owner's] possession.'" Under this test, in *Loretto v. Teleprompter Manhattan CATV Corp.*,[23] the Court held that a taking occurred when the government required landlords to permit the installation of cable lines in their buildings to provide cable television access for apartment tenants. In *United States v. Causby*,[24] the Court held that flights over the claimant's land constituted a taking because the government essentially appropriated the claimant's land as a flight path and destroyed the present use of the land as a chicken farm.

However, many taking cases do not involve a literal taking in the sense of an acquisition, but instead concern land use or zoning restrictions that are imposed for the greater public good. These cases involve the question of whether the government may regulate property use without paying the property owner for the diminished value of the property. Or, to put it another way, may the government make a regulatory taking? In *Goldblatt v. Hempstead*,[25] the Court held that no taking occurred when a city safety ordinance banned excavations below the water table because the taking was designed to effectuate a "substantial public purpose" (protection of surrounding properties), did not have an unduly harsh impact on the value of the property (even though the regulation effectively terminated claimant's sand and gravel mining business that had been in operation for 40 years), and did not prevent other reasonable uses of the property. However, not all regulatory actions are free of the requirement of compensation. *Pennsylvania Coal Co. v. Mahon*[26] is the "leading case for the proposition that a state statute that substantially furthers important public policies may so frustrate distinct investment-backed expectations as to amount to a 'taking.'" In that case, the claimant sold the surface rights to particular parcels of property, but reserved the right to remove the coal underneath the land. When Pennsylvania passed a law that prohibited the mining of coal that caused the subsidence of any house not owned by the owner of the underlying coal, and thereby made it commercially impracticable to mine the coal, the Court concluded that the law effectively destroyed the "rights claimant had reserved from the owners of the surface land" and therefore involved a taking that required compensation.

The Court, however, has recognized that in some cases government may have the right to regulate, or even to order the destruction of property, without paying compensation. For example, in *Miller v. Schoene*,[27] the Court held that a state statute providing for the destruction of cedar trees infected with blight did not constitute a taking and therefore required no compensation. The blight was an infectious fungoid organism capable of destroying the fruit and foliage of apple trees, and apple production was a major industry in Virginia. Although cedar trees were indigenous to Virginia and had some value as lumber, the cedar industry was small compared to the apple industry. Plaintiff sued when the state entomologist ordered that plaintiff's blighted cedar trees be cut down. In rejecting the idea that there was a taking, the Court held that "the state does not exceed its constitutional powers by deciding upon the destruction of one class of property in order to save another which, in the judgment of the legislature, is of greater value to the public."

F   A   Q

Q: How is it possible for the government to take one person's property and destroy it, without paying compensation?

A: The government has always exercised the power to destroy harmful things, and in *Miller* it is possible to justify destruction of the cedar trees because they suffered from blight. However, the *Miller* decision is extraordinary because it suggests that government can save one thing because it is more valuable than another, without the decision constituting a taking that requires compensation.

Likewise, in *Block v. Hirsh*,[28] the Court upheld a Washington, D.C., rent control law against a takings challenge. The law limited the amount that landlords could charge tenants. The Court concluded a "public exigency" could justify restricting property rights in land to a certain extent without compensation. The Court noted that D.C. property was monopolized in the hands of a few individuals, that housing is a necessary, and that the public interest justified "some degree of public control." The Court rejected the idea that the law went "too far," so that compensation was required, noting that the law provided landlords with reasonable rents. In determining whether rents were reasonable, the Court considered "the sudden influx of people of Washington caused by the needs of Government and the war, and thus of a right usually incident to fortunately situated property," as well as the fact that it was unjust "to pursue such profits from a national misfortune." The Court viewed the rent control law as going no farther than "the restriction put upon the rights of the owner of money by the more debatable usury laws."

In later decisions, the Court has construed the concept of a taking fairly broadly. For example, in *United States v. General Motors Corp.*,[29] the Court indicated that the concept of property should be broadly defined: Property refers to the entire "group of rights inhering in the citizen's relation to the physical thing, as the right to possess, use and dispose of it. . . . The constitutional provision is addressed to every sort of interest the citizen may possess."

Sidebar

WAGE AND PRICE RESTRICTIONS

Just as the Court upheld rent control restrictions in *Block*, the Court has also upheld wage and price restrictions in other cases. These sorts of restrictions are considered to be "regulation" as opposed to a "taking," and therefore are subject to limited judicial oversight.

In *Phillips v. Washington Legal Foundation*,[30] the Court was confronted by a challenge to the District of Columbia's Interest on Lawyers Trust Account (IOLTA) program. Under this program, the interest generated on client funds held by attorneys in connection with their practices were paid into foundations that financed legal services for low-income individuals. The Court held that the interest was the property of the client.

In *Penn Central Transportation Co. v. City of New York*,[31] which upheld a law designed to protect historic landmarks, the Court attempted to provide guidance regarding the scope of permissible regulatory takings. Under the law, the City did not "take" an historic landmark, but did prohibit modifications without governmental approval. When the law was applied to prevent the owners of the Grand Central Terminal from constructing a multistory office tower over the station, the owners sued, claiming that their property had been taken without compensation because the government had deprived them of the air rights above the terminal. In determining whether there was a taking, the Court considered various factors, including the economic impact of the regulation on the claimant; the extent to which the regulation interfered with distinct investment-backed expectations; and the character of the governmental action, with a "physical invasion" more likely to be considered a taking than an "interference [that] arises from some public program adjusting the benefits and burdens of economic life to promote the common good." But the Court also recognized that government could not function if it were required to pay compensation every time it made a change in its general regulatory law, and the Court held that government could promote "the health, safety, morals, or general welfare" by prohibiting particular uses of land, even though those regulations destroy or adversely affect recognized real property interests. The Court offered the example of local zoning laws, which are permissible even though they may prohibit "the most beneficial use of the property."

In deciding that no taking occurred, the Court focused "on the character of the action and on the nature and extent of the interference with rights in the parcel as a whole." The mere fact that the landmarks law diminished the value of plaintiff's property did not amount to a taking unless the owners of the terminal had been singled out to bear a public burden. Even though the law in general had a more severe impact on some landowners than on others, the Court concluded that this fact alone did not effect a taking because legislation designed to promote the general welfare frequently burdens some landowners more than others, and the New York law applied to buildings in 31 historic districts and more than 400 individual landmarks, some of which were proximate to the Grand Central Terminal. Since the law benefited all "New York citizens and all structures, both economically and by improving the quality of life in the city as a whole," the Court concluded that the owners of Penn Central had benefited from the law as well. The Court also rejected the argument that the interference with appellants' property was of such a magnitude that "there must be an exercise of eminent domain and compensation to sustain [it]." The Court noted that the law did not interfere with the "present uses of the Terminal" and therefore allowed the owners of Penn Central to earn a profit and a reasonable return on their investment.

Even with regard to the alleged taking of airspace, the Court noted that there was not a complete taking. Plaintiffs were not barred from using the airspace, but were precluded only from doing so without approval, and a smaller or modified structure might be approved. Second, even if the right to build above or modify this structure were denied, appellants were given the possibility of transferring their building rights to other parcels within the city. Even though the Court concluded that these transfer rights might not have qualified as just compensation for a taking, the Court concluded that they could be considered in evaluating the impact of the landmarks law and in deciding whether there was a taking.

Despite the holding, there was considerable disagreement on the Court regarding government's right to regulate property without paying compensation. Since some of these views remain viable on the Court today, it is worthwhile to examine them. For example, Justice Rehnquist, joined by Chief Justice Burger and Justice Stevens, offered a vigorous dissent. He argued that while the typical zoning restriction limits an owner's ability to use real property and thereby affects the property's value, the impact is diminished by the fact that overall property values are increased by virtue of the zoning restrictions. The Court viewed New York's landmarks law differently because it singled out "a relatively few individual buildings, all separated from one another," so that the cost to an individual landowner may be substantial (several million dollars for the owners of Penn Central), but there are no reciprocal benefits. Moreover, the New York law placed a property owner "under an affirmative duty to *preserve* his property *as a landmark* at his own expense." Moreover, while adjoining landowners could use their air rights, the owners of Penn Central could not. He concluded with the argument that the "Fifth Amendment's guarantee that private property shall not be taken for a public use without just compensation was designed to bar Government from forcing some people alone to bear public burdens which, in all fairness and justice, should be borne by the public as a whole."

F   A   Q

Q: When a regulatory requirement has as big an impact as the landmarks law did in *Penn Central*, shouldn't the government be required to pay compensation?

A: The difficulty is that much of what government does involves regulation. If government was forced to pay compensation every time it tried to regulate, it would be impossible for government to function. Of course, *Penn Central* raises difficult questions about whether compensation should be required if governmental regulation goes "too far."

After the *Penn Central* decision, questions remained about the government's authority to regulate land use. At some point, would a regulation be deemed to have gone "too far" so that compensation would be required? The Court provided a partial answer to this question in *Lucas v. South Carolina Coastal Council*.[32] In that case, South Carolina's Beachfront Management Act effectively prohibited Lucas from building any permanent habitable structures on parcels that he purchased for nearly $1 million with the intent of constructing single family buildings. The Court held that a taking occurs when governmental regulation physically invades private property or when the "regulation denies all economically beneficial or productive use of land." While the Court recognized that government must have the right to regulate without paying compensation, even if the regulation impairs property values, takings that deprive landowners of all economically beneficial uses "carry with them a heightened risk that private property is being pressed into some form of public service under the guise of mitigating serious public harm."

In evaluating whether a property owner had been deprived of all economically beneficial uses, courts should consider a variety of factors, including "the degree of harm to public lands and resources, or adjacent private property, posed by the claimant's proposed activities, the social value of the claimant's activities and their suitability to the locality in question, and the relative ease with which the alleged harm can be avoided through measures taken by the claimant and the government (or adjacent private landowners) alike." In general, if a use has been permitted for a long time, and especially if it is engaged in by similarly situated landowners, it must generally be considered permissible absent changed circumstances. Moreover, the Court concluded that South Carolina could not prevail merely by showing that "the uses Lucas desires are inconsistent with the public interest." It must, instead, prove that Lucas's activity was enjoinable in a common law action for public nuisance. Although the Court left the matter for resolution by the lower courts, it expressed doubt about whether "common-law principles would have prevented the erection of any habitable or productive improvements on petitioner's land."

The *Lucas* Court qualified its holding by suggesting that a taking does not occur, even when all economically beneficial uses are prohibited, if the regulation is one that could have been imposed anyway, for example under nuisance laws. In that case, no compensation is required. The Court offered the example of a lakebed owner who could be denied a permit to fill in the lake on the ground that nearby landowners would suffer flooding. Likewise, the owner of a nuclear generating plant could be ordered to cease operations if the plant lay on an earthquake fault.

Sidebar

FINDING A DENIAL OF "ALL ECONOMICALLY BENEFICIAL USES"

Of course, *Lucas* provides only limited protection to landowners because the governmental regulation must deprive the landowner of "all economically beneficial uses." That degree of taking will rarely be present.

Lucas produced a number of concurrences and dissents that illustrate the confining divide on the Court regarding the scope of government's regulatory power. Justice Kennedy concurred, arguing that the finding of no value must be considered in "reference to the owner's reasonable, investment-backed expectations," and he would find a taking here because South Carolina's act was not passed until nearby properties had been improved, thereby "throwing the whole burden of the regulation on the remaining lots." Justice Blackmun dissented, arguing that Lucas's lots had frequently been flooded over the prior 40 years and that building on such land would cause serious harm. He concluded that the "Court consistently has upheld regulations imposed to arrest a significant threat to the common welfare." Justice Stevens also dissented, arguing that the Court's new rule is "wholly arbitrary" because a "landowner whose property is diminished in value 95% recovers nothing, while an owner whose property is diminished 100% recovers the land's full value." Moreover, he objected to the fact that the Court's decision "effectively freezes the State's common law, denying the legislature much of its traditional power to revise the law governing the rights and uses of property." He would have upheld the South Carolina law because it established a statewide policy rather than focusing on a particular tract of land.

The Court distinguished *Lucas* in *Tahoe-Sierra Preservation Council v. Tahoe Regional Planning Agency*,[33] in upholding a moratorium on land development during the creation of a master land use plan. Even though the moratorium arguably imposed a denial of all economically beneficial uses during the period of the moratorium, and even though the moratorium lasted for a considerable period of time, the Court upheld it. The case arose when Lake Tahoe was found to be deteriorating due to rapid development. California and Nevada entered into the Tahoe Regional Planning Compact, which set goals for the protection and preservation of the lake and created the Tahoe Regional Planning Agency (TRPA). To give itself time to develop a plan, TRPA imposed an 8-month moratorium on development and followed it with a 32-month moratorium, which was challenged as a taking because it denied a property owner all viable economic use of her property during the moratorium. The Court upheld the moratorium, noting that land use regulations almost inevitably affect property values, but to require compensation for such regulations would "transform government regulation into a luxury few governments could afford." The Court suggested that a temporary denial of use might not constitute a taking under *Lucas* because property "cannot be rendered valueless by a temporary prohibition on economic use, because the property will recover value as soon as the prohibition is lifted." In addition, the Court was reluctant to find that the "normal delays in obtaining building permits, changes in zoning ordinances, variances, and the like," as well as with "orders temporarily prohibiting access to crime scenes, businesses that violate health codes, fire-damaged buildings," constitute takings because of the risk of rendering "routine government processes prohibitively expensive or encourag[ing] hasty decisionmaking." Moreover, the Court emphasized that moratoria are widely used by land use planners to preserve the status quo while formulating a comprehensive development plan. The Court was reluctant to treat such moratoria as takings because its feared imposing high costs on regulatory deliberations that "may force officials to rush through the planning process or to abandon the practice altogether." Finally, the Court noted that a moratorium involves less risk that individual landowners will be "singled out" to bear a special burden that should be shared by the public as a whole, and that landowners will benefit from the planning process and that land values will continue to rise during that process because of the promise of a coordinated development plan. The Court found that a moratorium of this length (32 months) was not "constitutionally unacceptable."

Despite the holding, a number of justices would have required compensation even for a moratorium. Chief Justice Rehnquist, joined by Justices Scalia and Thomas, dissented, noting that this "temporary" prohibition lasted nearly six years and suggested that governments might label any prohibition as "temporary" to avoid being forced to pay compensation. Justice Thomas, joined by Justice Scalia, also dissented: "[I] would hold that regulations prohibiting all productive uses of property are subject to *Lucas' per se* rule, regardless of whether the property so burdened retains theoretical useful life and value if, and when, the 'temporary' moratorium is lifted. [S]uch potential future value bears on the amount of compensation due and has nothing to do with [whether] there was a taking in the first place."

F   A   Q

Q: Would a moratorium be permissible if it were indefinitely imposed with no suggestion that the government was engaged in a long-range planning process?

A: Presumably, the Court would be less likely to uphold a moratorium that did not involve compensation under these circumstances. In *Tahoe-Sierra Preservation Council*, the Court emphasized that government can impose a moratorium as a "tool" in the planning process, but the Court also emphasized that the moratorium was imposed for a limited period of time. Even though the *Tahoe-Sierra Preservation* order lasted for several years, it is not clear that the Court would uphold such an order if no planning process were announced or contemplated, and the moratorium was imposed without any end in sight.

One type of regulatory taking that has generated significant litigation is when government imposes restrictions as part of its permitting process. For example, in *Nollan v. California Coastal Commission*,[34] the Court found a taking when California's Coastal Commission approved an application to demolish a small old oceanfront home and build a new one on a condition that the owners create a public easement across their oceanfront property. The Commission imposed the condition because the new home would block ocean views. The Commission concluded that it could properly require the Nollans to offset that burden by providing additional lateral access to the public beaches in the form of an easement across their property. The Court concluded that the easement requirement constituted a taking without just compensation. Had California simply required the Nollans to make an easement across their beachfront available to the public on a permanent basis to increase public access to the beach, rather than conditioning their permit to rebuild their house on their agreeing to do so, the Court would not have found a taking. Although a land use regulation does not involve a taking if it "substantially advance[s] legitimate state interests" and does not "den[y] an owner economically viable use of his land," the Court found that the Commission's asserted purposes (protecting the public's ability to see the beach, assisting the public in overcoming the "psychological barrier" to using the beach created by a developed shorefront, and preventing congestion on the public beaches) were valid, but that the condition must be related to those objectives. But the Court concluded that the condition imposed was unrelated to the purpose of the restriction and therefore required compensation.

Likewise, in *Dolan v. Tigard*,[35] the Court struck down a requirement that plaintiff dedicate portions of her property for a public greenway and pedestrian/bicycle pathway as a condition of obtaining a building permit. The permit would have allowed Dolan to double the size of her store and pave her gravel parking lot. Under the city's land development plan, property that bordered Fanno Creek (as plaintiff's did) was to be used only for "greenways" to minimize flooding. The city granted Dolan's request on condition that she dedicate portions of her property for a public greenway. Although the Court held that the city was entitled to engage in land use planning, notwithstanding a potential adverse impact on property values, the Court noted that ordinarily land use regulations classify an entire area of the city (rather than an individual parcel of property) and simply limit the use of that property (as opposed to requiring

S i d e b a r

NOLLAN, LUCAS, AND FORCED EASEMENTS

The *Nollan* decision provides an important restriction on governmental power. Even though decisions like *Penn Central* seem to provide the government with broad power to impose regulatory restrictions without paying compensation, *Lucas* and *Nollan* suggest that governmental power is not without limits. *Lucas* holds that the government cannot deprive a landowner of all economically beneficial uses. *Nollan* prevents government from forcing the landowner to provide an easement, as a condition for a regulatory approval, when the condition is unrelated to the regulatory need or concern.

a property owner to deed land to the government). Applying the "unconstitutional conditions" doctrine, the Court held that the city could not require the landowner to relinquish the constitutional right to receive just compensation "in exchange for a discretionary benefit conferred by the government where the benefit sought has little or no relationship to the property." The Court failed to find an "essential nexus" between the "legitimate state interest" and the permit condition. While the prevention of flooding was a legitimate purpose, and there was a nexus between preventing flooding along Fanno Creek and limiting development in the floodplain, the required conditions were not sufficiently related to those purposes. "[It] is difficult to see why recreational visitors trampling along petitioner's floodplain easement are sufficiently related to the city's legitimate interest in reducing flooding problems along Fanno Creek."

With respect to the pedestrian/bicycle pathway, the Court noted that dedications "for streets, sidewalks, and other public ways are generally reasonable exactions to avoid excessive congestion from a proposed property use. But . . . the city has not met its burden of demonstrating that the additional number of vehicle and bicycle trips generated by petitioner's development reasonably relate to the city's requirement for a dedication of the pedestrian/bicycle pathway easement." Justice Stevens, joined by Justices Blackmun and Ginsburg, dissented: "Everyone agrees that the bike path 'could' offset some of the increased traffic flow that the larger store will generate. . . . Even if Dolan should accept the city's conditions in exchange for the benefit that she seeks, it would not necessarily follow that she had been denied 'just compensation' since it would be appropriate to consider the receipt of that benefit in any calculation of 'just compensation.' [W]e should not presume that the discretionary benefit the city has offered is less valuable than the property interests that Dolan can retain or surrender at her option."

C. The Contract Clause

As noted at the outset of this chapter, contractual interests and expectations have implicated more than one constitutional provision. The emergence of liberty of contract, as a fundamental right driven by judicial construction rather than textual specificity, was a defining aspect of the *Lochner* era of substantive due process review. Prior to this controversial and eventually abandoned application of the Fourteenth Amendment, constitutional protection of contractual interests was grounded in the Contract Clause. As set forth by Article I, Section 10, this clause prohibits the state from enacting any "Law impairing the Obligation of Contracts." This provision specifically applies to existing contracts.

The reasons that led to the adoption of that clause, and of the other prohibitions of Section 10 of Article 1, are fairly clear. Following the Revolution, there was widespread distress, and debtors sought legislative relief from their debts, some of which involved the defeat of existing contractual obligations. Indeed, there was sufficient legislative interference to undermine the "confidence essential to prosperous trade" and threaten the "utter destruction of credit."[36] "The sober people of America" were convinced that some "thorough reform" was needed, which would "inspire a general prudence and industry, and give a regular course to the business of society."[37]

The Contract Clause represented a seminal constitutional restraint on state police power. Although states may not bargain away their police power, the Contract Clause has imposed a reasonableness requirement on its exercise. Case law has varied with respect to the intensity of reasonableness as a standard of review.

With the Fourteenth Amendment as a primary incident of Reconstruction, the growing significance of the commerce power over the course of the twentieth century, and preemption principles under the Supremacy Clause, the Court acquired more powerful tools for evaluating the constitutionality of action pursuant to state police power. Varied as these constitutional reference points may be, each in its own way implicates and engenders an ongoing debate over whether the judiciary's role should be greater or lesser in reviewing outputs of the political branches of government.

Early use of the Contract Clause yielded results that were consistent with the Marshall Court's vision and facilitation of nation building. In *Fletcher v. Peck*,[38] the Court overturned the Georgia legislature's rescission of a land grant that had been tainted by bribery and fraud. When the law was challenged by persons who acquired land in the aftermarket and claimed they were purchasers in due course, the Court relied on the Contract Clause and principles of natural law in overturning the rescission.[39] Modern interpretation of the Contract Clause is less expansive and ambitious but not without potential force, particularly with respect to a state's power to modify public contracts and private expectations. However, the Court has upheld state prohibitions on the sale of beer[40] or lottery tickets,[41] even though both activities were previously valid.

The modern approach to the meaning of the Contract Clause is reflected in *Home Building & Loan Association v. Blaisdell*.[42] In that case, the Court upheld Minnesota's Mortgage Moratorium Law, which gave Minnesota courts the power to impose moratoria on mortgage foreclosures provided that the mortgagor paid the reasonable rental value of the property. Noting that the obligations of the Contract Clause are not absolute, the Court emphasized the importance of contractual enforcement mechanisms, but concluded that the focus should be on "whether the legislation is addressed to a legitimate end and the measures taken are reasonable and appropriate to that end." A restriction would not be permissible if it involved "the repudiation of debts or the destruction of contracts or the denial of means to enforce them." But the Court emphasized that Minnesota was only providing temporary relief in an effort "to protect the vital interests of the community" during a period of economic distress. The Court held that not only was the objective legitimate, but the relief provided was appropriate to the emergency. "[T]he integrity of the mortgage indebtedness is not impaired; interest continues to run; the validity of the sale and the right of a mortgagee-purchaser to title or to obtain a deficiency judgment, if the mortgagor fails to redeem within the extended period, are maintained; and the conditions of redemption, if redemption there be, stand as they were under the prior law." Although the mortgagor can keep possession of the property during the moratorium, he was required to pay the rental value of the premises as determined by a judge. The Court also noted that the mortgagees were primarily corporations, rather than small investors, whose principal interest was in the "reasonable protection of their investment security." The Court felt that this interest was reasonably protected. In addition, the relief was temporary. Justice Sutherland dissented, arguing that "the contract impairment clause denies to the several states the power to mitigate hard consequences resulting to debtors from financial or economic exigencies by an impairment of the obligation of contracts of indebtedness. . . . A statute which materially delays enforcement of the mortgagee's contractual right of ownership and possession does not modify the remedy merely; it destroys, for the period of delay, all remedy so far as the enforcement of that right is concerned."

Even though *Blaisdell* reflected a broad interpretation of governmental authority to alter contractual obligations, the Court has recognized that there are limits to the scope of legislative authority. In *Allied Structural Steel Co. v. Spannaus*,[43] for example, the Court struck down a state's attempt to regulate a company's pension obligations. Prior to the passage of Minnesota's Private Pension Benefits Protection Act, Allied Structural Steel Co. created a pension plan for its salaried employees and made annual contributions to the fund. Although the contributions were not revocable, the plan did not require the company to make specific contributions or impose any sanction for failing to adequately fund the plan. An employee who did not die, quit, or get fired prior to meeting the plan requirements would receive a fixed pension at age 65 if the company remained in business and elected to continue the pension plan in its existing form. The act provided that a private employer with 100 or more employees (and at least one Minnesota resident) who provided a qualified pension plan was subject to a "pension funding charge" if he either terminated the plan or closed a Minnesota office. The charge was assessed if the pension funds were not sufficient to cover full pensions for all employees who had worked at least ten years. The state sought to apply the charge to Allied when it closed its plant and there were unvested employees. In concluding that the Contract Clause prohibited the charge, the Court focused on whether the PPBPA "operated as a substantial impairment of a contractual relationship," and the Court indicated that it would undertake "a careful examination of the nature and purpose of the state legislation" when a severe impairment is involved. The Court was troubled by the act because Allied set aside the amount required each year for its plan, as required by the plan and by the federal tax laws, and it did not expect that employee's rights would "vest" except in accordance with the plan. Allied "relied heavily, and reasonably, on this legitimate contractual expectation in calculating its annual contributions to the pension fund," and the act had a "severe impact" because it altered a "basic term of the pension contract" and required a substantial infusion of cash ($185,000) on the closing of Allied's offices that was a completely unexpected liability. The Court found that this "severe disruption of contractual expectations was necessary to meet an important general social problem" akin to the "broad and desperate emergency economic conditions of the early 1930's." Justice Brennan, joined by Justices White and Marshall, dissented, arguing that the act did not abrogate a contract right, but instead, "like all positive social legislation, [imposed] new, additional obligations on a particular class of persons." "While such laws may be conceptualized as 'enlarging' the obligation of a contract when they add to the burdens that had previously been imposed by a private agreement, such laws cannot be prohibited by the Clause because they do not dilute or nullify a duty a person had previously obligated himself to perform."

However, not all contractual impairments are invalid. In general, the Court will balance the severity of the impairment against the governmental interest. For example, in *Exxon Corp. v. Eagerton*,[44] the Court upheld a state law that prohibited oil and gas producers from passing severance taxes paid on the product to customers. The law was applied to contracts entered into before the act that contained contractual obligations requiring reimbursement for severance taxes. The Court held that the Contract Clause is not violated simply because a statute restricts, or even bars, the performance of duties created by contracts entered into prior to its enactment. The Court emphasized the "broad societal interest" in protecting consumers from excessive prices and concluded that the anti-pass-through law was distinguishable from the law struck down in *Spannaus*. Although the Court concluded that preemption principles precluded the state from applying the act to interstate gas sales, the Court upheld "the pass-through prohibition and the royalty-owner exemption against appellants' challenges under the Contract Clause and the Equal Protection Clause."

In *Block v. Hirsh*,[45] discussed earlier in regard to the Takings Clause, the Court upheld a Washington, D.C., rent control law despite claims that tenants were allowed to remain in possession at the same rent that they had been paying, thereby interfering with the landlord's right "to do what he will with his own and to make what contracts he pleases." In upholding the law, the Court noted that it was a temporary measure, designed to deal with a passing emergency, and landlords were assured of a "reasonable rent" considering the large influx of potential tenants into the market and the government's desire to prevent "unjust profits." Justice McKenna dissented, arguing that contractual obligations are "impregnable. . . . 'No doctrine, involving more pernicious consequences, was ever invented by the wit of man than that any of its provisions can be suspended during any of the great exigencies of government.' . . . Contracts and the obligation of contracts are the basis of life and of all its business. . . . [I]f one contract can be disregarded in the public interest every contract can be. . . ."

The scope of government's power to alter the terms of contracts is also reflected in *Energy Reserves Group v. Kansas Power & Light Co.*[46] In that case, following federal deregulation of energy prices, Kansas passed a law capping the price of natural gas and applied it to preexisting contracts that provided for price increases in the event of deregulation. The Court rejected a Contract Clause challenge indicating that a "substantial impairment" must be supported by a "significant and legitimate public purpose behind the regulation, such as the remedying of a broad and general social or economic problem." In concluding that there was no substantial impairment, the Court emphasized that plaintiff was functioning in a regulated environment, did not expect to make unregulated profits at the time it entered into the contracts, and that price regulation was foreseeable because the contracts provided that they were subject to present and future state and federal law. In any event, the Court concluded that the law was supported by "significant and legitimate state interests" because "higher gas prices have caused and will cause hardship among those who use gas heat but must exist on limited fixed incomes." As to the means for achieving those interests, the Court was deferential to the Kansas legislature's judgment, noting that "natural gas subject to indefinite price escalator clauses poses the danger of rapidly increasing prices in Kansas," and Kansas simply limits the application of such clauses.

SUMMARY

- *Lochner v. New York* is the classic example of "substantive due process" in the negative sense in that the Supreme Court substituted its judgment for a legislature's judgment regarding the wisdom of legislation.

- After the mid-1930s, the approach to substantive due process began to change as courts stopped second-guessing legislative judgments in the economic area.

- In general, courts engage in substantive review (as opposed to procedural review) only in cases involving fundamental rights such as freedom of speech.

■ Courts continue to apply heightened review in some instances under the Takings Clause. Nevertheless, the Court has tended to be deferential to executive and legislative branch officials on the question of whether a taking is for a "public purpose."

■ Courts have broad discretion to take private property for public purposes such as urban renewal, and even to convey that property to private individuals, provided that government pays just compensation.

■ By contrast, if the government chooses to regulate private property rather than take it, courts are reluctant to find a taking unless the government has deprived the landowner of all economically beneficial use of the property.

■ The Contracts Clause limits the power of government to regulate in the economic area. That clause prohibits the impairment of existing contracts rather than future contracts.

■ The Contracts Clause does not prohibit all impairments of contracts. Only when impairments go too far (*e.g.*, changing a company's pension obligations after the fact) are they prohibited.

CONNECTIONS

Judicial Review

Judicial review is an important ingredient in substantive due process cases. This chapter notes the shift from heightened review to a lesser standard in cases of economic regulation, and then examines judicial review of local legislation under the Takings Clause and the Contracts Clause.

Police Powers

Chapter 4 discusses how the states have traditionally retained the police power to regulate for the health, safety, and welfare of society. In this chapter, we see that governments attempt to impose various types of regulations, many of them imposed under the police power.

Free Speech

In this chapter, we see that the Court draws a distinction between a state's decision to impose economic regulation and its imposition of regulations affecting enumerated rights such as free speech. *Carolene Products* suggests that the courts should apply a higher level of scrutiny in the latter situation. We shall see this heightened standard of review in Chapter 10 on free speech.

Endnotes

1. 3 U.S. (3 Dall.) 386 (1798).
2. Justice Chase argued that "[a]n act of the Legislature (for I cannot call it a law) contrary to the great first principles of the social compact, cannot be considered a rightful exercise of legislative authority."
3. *See* Dred Scott v. Sandford, 60 U.S. (19 How.) 393 (1856).
4. *See* Barron v. Mayor & City Council of Baltimore, 32 U.S. (7 Pet.) 243 (1833) (summarizing and discussing whether the United States Bill of Rights can be applied to state governments).
5. *See* Hague v. C.I.O., 307 U.S. 496 (1939); Duncan v. Louisiana, 391 U.S. 145 (1968).
6. *See, e.g.,* U.S. Const., art. I, §10.
7. 60 U.S. (19 How.) 393 (1857).
8. 83 U.S. (16 Wall.) 36 (1873).
9. 165 U.S. 578 (1897).
10. 198 U.S. 45 (1905).
11. *See, e.g.,* Coppage v. Kansas, 236 U.S. 1 (1915) (striking down state law that made it illegal for an employer to require employees not to join a union); Adair v. United States, 208 U.S. 161 (1908).
12. 291 U.S. 502 (1934).
13. 300 U.S. 379 (1937).
14. 348 U.S. 483 (1955).
15. 304 U.S. 144 (1938).
16. *See* Lovell v. Griffin, 303 U.S. 444 (1938); Stromberg v. California, 283 U.S. 359 (1931).
17. 467 U.S. 229 (1984).
18. 348 U.S. 26 (1954).
19. 467 U.S. 986 (1984).
20. 545 U.S. 469 (2005).
21. *See* United States v. Gen. Motors Corp., 323 U.S. 373 (1945).
22. 260 U.S. 393 (1922).
23. 458 U.S. 419 (1982).
24. 328 U.S. 256 (1946).
25. 369 U.S. 590 (1962).
26. 260 U.S. 393 (1922).
27. 276 U.S. 272 (1928).
28. 256 U.S. 135 (1921).
29. 323 U.S. 373 (1945).
30. 524 U.S. 156 (1998).
31. 438 U.S. 104 (1978).
32. 505 U.S. 1103 (1992).
33. 535 U.S. 302 (2002).
34. 483 U.S. 825 (1987).
35. 512 U.S. 374 (1994).
36. Home Bldg. & Loan Assn. v. Blaisdell, 290 U.S. 398, 427 (1934).
37. *Id.,* quoting The Federalist No. 44 (James Madison).
38. 10 U.S. (6 Cranch) 87 (1810).
39. *See also* Dartmouth Coll. v. Woodward, 17 U.S. (4 Wheat) 518 (1819) (striking down New Hampshire's effort to alter the college's charter so as to change the composition of the board; violated the existing charter that gave the board the right to fill vacancies).
40. *See* Beer Co. v. Massachusetts, 97 U.S. 25 (1878).
41. *See* Stone v. Mississippi, 101 U.S. 814 (1880).
42. 290 U.S. 398 (1934).
43. 438 U.S. 234 (1978).
44. 462 U.S. 176 (1983).
45. 256 U.S. 135 (1921).
46. 459 U.S. 400 (1983).

Substantive Due Process: Fundamental Rights

Rights grounded in the Due Process Clause are inferred and not specifically enumerated by the Constitution. They derive instead from judicial

O V E R V I E W

interpretation of the liberty provision of the Due Process Clause. For this reason, they serve as flash points in the debate over fundamental rights development and the corresponding role of the judiciary. Whether a right or liberty is fundamental turns on whether it is "implicit in the concept of ordered liberty" or "rooted in the Nation's traditions and history." The evolution of these standards, however, has not stemmed arguments that substantive due process review undermines the process of representative governance. Court decisions involving substantive due process rights form the basis for two other important debates: (1) whether or in what way the rights expressed in the Bill of Rights apply to the states, and (2) how to formulate a right of privacy when such a right is not expressly stated in the Constitution. It is these two debates that this chapter addresses.

A. Incorporation

In addition to being a source of procedural and substantive fairness, the Fourteenth Amendment's Due Process Clause also is the means by which provisions of the Bill of Rights have been applied to the states, a concept known as **incorporation**. The Bill of Rights, as originally conceptualized, operated only against the federal government. This understanding was confirmed in *Barron v. City Council of Baltimore*,[1] when the Court rejected the argument that the Fifth Amendment prohibition against takings extended to state government. As the Court put it, "the Constitution was ordained and established by the people of the United States [for] their own government, and not for the government of the individual [states]."[2] Although the opinion had a dismissive tone, numerous courts had viewed the Bill of Rights as binding on the states. The outcome represents an instance in which Chief Justice Marshall departed from the nationalistic orientation that otherwise defined his legacy. It was a position that eventually was turned around by the ratification of the Fourteenth Amendment and eventual interpretations of its meaning.

The Fourteenth Amendment established a new federal role in the creation and allocation of civil rights. The Court's first interpretation of this amendment responded, among other things, to the argument that the Bill of Rights applied to the states through the Privileges and Immunities Clause. The Court in the *Slaughterhouse Cases*[3] foreclosed the Privileges and Immunities Clause as a means of incorporation, but not the incorporation process itself. Critics maintain that this virtual negation of the Privileges and Immunities Clause twisted the meaning of the Fourteenth Amendment, insofar as its architects viewed the clause as the platform for incorporation. When the Court eventually embraced incorporation, it turned to another provision of the Fourteenth Amendment — the Due Process Clause. The liberty component of the Due Process Clause initially was used not as a pass-through mechanism for the Bill of Rights but as an independent source of fundamental rights and liberties. Many of these judicially identified rights and liberties paralleled provisions of the Bill of Rights, but others, such as liberty of contract, did not. Either way, the rights and liberties discerned through this process represented the Court's interpretation of liberty rather than an extension of the Bill of Rights to the states.

Sidebar

UNINCORPORATED PROVISIONS

Provisions of the Bill of Rights that clearly have failed the incorporation test are the Second Amendment guarantee of the right to bear arms, the Fifth Amendment grand jury clause, and the Seventh Amendment guarantee of a jury trial in civil cases. The Third Amendment, which prohibits quartering of soldiers in private homes, has not been reviewed.

The shift from amplifying the meaning of liberty in the Due Process Clause to using it as a transfer agent was presaged by *United States v. Carolene Products Co.*[4] The Court in this case put an end to economic rights doctrine and indicated that it would reserve heightened review for instances "when legislation appears to be within a specific provision of the Constitution, such as the first ten amendments, which are deemed equally specific when held to be embraced within the Fourteenth."[5] The Court thus indicated that the Fourteenth Amendment was not an independent source of rights or liberties but a means by which provisions of the Bill of Rights might be incorporated. The notion that rights and liberties did not flow directly from the Fourteenth Amendment was undone by subsequent jurisprudence.

How and to what extent incorporation should take place emerged as the basis for more immediate debate. In *Palko v. Connecticut*,[6] the Court rejected the argument that the Double Jeopardy Clause was incorporated through the Fourteenth Amendment. It also established an analytical framework that precluded the possibility of wholesale incorporation of the Bill of Rights. The necessary inquiry in this, as the Court saw it, was whether the guarantee of double jeopardy accounted for an interest that was "of the very essence of a scheme of ordered liberty," and its denial would violate a "principle of justice so rooted in the traditions and conscience of our people as to be ranked as fundamental."[7]

Competing perspectives on incorporation were set forth in *Adamson v. California*,[8] when the Court held that the Fourteenth Amendment did not incorporate the right against self-incrimination. Justice Black, a leading proponent of total incorporation, maintained that the Fourteenth Amendment's Framers intended to displace prior law and make the entire Bill of Rights applicable to the states. Justice Frankfurter contended that if the Framers had intended to incorporate the Bill of Rights, they would have done so in less ambiguous terms. Frankfurter also was uneasy with selective incorporation because it required the judiciary to make essentially subjective determinations.

F   A   Q

Q: What's the difference between selective incorporation and total incorporation?

A: Selective incorporation requires the Court to determine individually whether a particular provision of the Bill of Rights should be incorporated through the Fourteenth Amendment. The Court historically has made this determination by assessing whether the federal guarantee is "implicit in the concept of ordered liberty" or "so rooted in the traditions and conscience of our people as to be ranked as fundamental." Total incorporation would incorporate all provisions of the Bill of Rights and make them applicable to the states on a wholesale basis.

The incorporation controversy is largely of historical significance. Most provisions of the Bill of Rights, including those at issue in *Palko* and *Adamson*, have been incorporated through the process of selective incorporation.

B. The Right of Privacy

(1) Seminal Developments

The Constitution by its specific terms does not set forth a general right of privacy. The Court has observed, however, that a "right of personal privacy, or a guarantee of certain areas or zones of privacy does exist under the Constitution" and traces back "perhaps as far as" late-nineteenth-century case law.[9] In this regard, it has referenced *Union Pacific Railway Co. v. Botsford*, which announced that "[n]o right is held more sacred, or is more carefully guarded, by the common law, than the right of every individual to the possession and control of his own person, free from all restraint or interference of others, unless by clear and unquestionable authority of law." As well said by Judge Cooley, "The right to one's person may be said to be a right of complete immunity: to be let alone."[10] The *Botsford* decision was rendered one year after Samuel D. Warren and Louis D. Brandeis authored an influential law review article that proposed a right to privacy as a tort concept and characterized it as "the right to be let alone."[11] Although grounded in the common law, this right over the course of the twentieth century evolved into a constitutional principle.

An important precursor of the right was established in *Meyer v. Nebraska*,[12] when the Court invalidated a state law mandating the use of English for instruction in public and private schools. As the Court put it, the liberty provision of the Due Process Clause included

> not merely freedom from bodily restraint but also the right of the individual to contract, to engage in any of the common occupations of life, to acquire useful knowledge, to marry, establish a home and bring up children, to worship God according to the dictates of his own conscience, and generally to enjoy those privileges long recognized at common law as essential to the orderly pursuit of happiness by free men.[13]

The *Meyer* decision was reinforced by the Court's ruling in *Pierce v. Society of Sisters*,[14] which struck down a state law requiring parents to send their children to public schools.

F   A   Q

Q: What's the relevance of cases like *Meyer* and *Pierce* in light of indications by the Court in *United States v. Carolene Products Co.* that it generally would defer to legislative judgment?

A: Although these decisions were rendered prior to *Carolene Products*, the Court's contemporary substantive due process decisions cite them as foundations of the right of privacy.

Justice Brandeis, in *Olmstead v. United States*,[15] further developed the foundation for privacy as a fundamental right. In an opinion dissenting from the Court's holding that wiretapping did not constitute an unreasonable search and seizure under the Fourth Amendment, he described "the right to be let alone" as "the most comprehensive of rights and the right most valued by civilized men."[16] The majority decision in *Olmstead*, and Fourth Amendment case law for several decades thereafter, correlated privacy to notions of place. At least for purposes of searches and seizures, a reasonable expectation of privacy ultimately became grounded in the notion that the Fourth Amendment "protects people, not places."

Despite the indication in *Carolene Products* that searching review would be reserved for instances when enumerated rights and liberties were abridged or discrete and insular minorities were burdened, the Court's decision in *Skinner v. Oklahoma*[17] suggested otherwise. At issue in this case was a state law that mandated sterilization for habitual felons. Although having determined in *Buck v. Bell*[18] that compulsory sterilization was not a constitutional concern, the Court invalidated the Oklahoma enactment on grounds it burdened fundamental interests in marriage and procreation.

The *Skinner* ruling was based on the Equal Protection Clause rather than the Due Process Clause. Two decades later, in *Ferguson v. Skrupa*, the Court appeared to indicate that substantive due process review was a dead concept. Writing for the Court, Justice Black observed that the Court had "returned to the original constitutional proposition that courts do not substitute their social and economic beliefs for the judgment of legislative bodies, who are elected to pass laws."[19] The next decade of case law concerning the right to privacy, however, prefaced the Court's revitalization of substantive due process review.

F   A   Q

Q: Does use of the Equal Protection Clause in cases like *Skinner* address the concerns of critics who object to substantive due process analysis?

A: For detractors, the problem is the same regardless of whether the Due Process Clause or Equal Protection Clause is employed. The concern of critics is with the judiciary's identification and development of rights and liberties that are not specifically enumerated by the Constitution. Their objections do not abate simply because the basis for the unenumerated right or liberty shifts from one provision to the other.

(2) Reproductive Freedom

A general constitutional right of privacy was articulated for the first time in *Griswold v. Connecticut*.[20] At issue in this case was a state law that prohibited distribution of contraceptives or counseling their use. In striking down the enactment, the Court cited not to a specific constitutional provision. Rather, it maintained that several provisions of the Bill of Rights converged to create a constitutionally protected zone of privacy. The resulting penumbras emanated from the First Amendment right of association, the Third Amendment guarantee forbidding government from quartering soldiers in private homes, the Fourth Amendment protection against unreasonable searches and seizures, the Fifth Amendment safeguard against

Estelle Griswold, the executive director of Planned Parenthood of Connecticut, and a physician who worked with Planned Parenthood were arrested for providing birth control counseling to a married couple. They eventually prevailed when the Supreme Court struck down the 1879 state law that was the basis for their conviction.

self-incrimination, and the Ninth Amendment, which reserves for the people rights that are not specifically enumerated by the Constitution. Taken together, these guarantees established a right of privacy "surrounding the marriage relationship."[21]

The Court in *Griswold* offered assurances that it was not reverting to the type of intensive review that it repudiated in *Carolene Products*. Justice Douglas maintained that the Court did not function as a "super-legislature" that assessed the wisdom of social and economic policies. Justice Black maintained that effected just such a reversion. As he put it,

> I do not believe that we are granted power by the Due Process Clause or any other constitutional provision or provisions to measure constitutionality by our belief that legislation is arbitrary, capricious or unreasonable, or accomplishes no justifiable purpose, or is offensive to our own notions of "civilized standards of conduct." Such an appraisal of the wisdom of legislation is an attribute of the power to make laws, not of the power to interpret them.

Sidebar

THE CONTROVERSY REGARDING THE NINTH AMENDMENT

In his concurrence in *Griswold*, Justice Goldberg asserted that the Ninth Amendment provides a textual basis for rights and liberties, including the right of privacy, that were not enumerated by the first eight amendments to the Constitution. This premise is consistent with the founding notion that the Bill of Rights was a nonexclusive recitation of fundamental rights and liberties. For Goldberg, the solution was objective criteria to guide the judiciary's analysis. Toward this end, he suggested that courts focus on discerning what is rooted in the nation's "traditions and conscience." This formula does not satisfy critics, who see the same potential for judicial subjectivism that exists pursuant to due process analysis. As Justice Black put it, there is no assurance either way that judges "will not consider 'their personal and private notions.'"
Writing off the Ninth Amendment because of concerns regarding subjectivity, however, creates other problems — not the least of which is that it essentially denies the provision any meaning.

Justices Harlan and Goldberg concurred in the result but would have based it respectively on the Due Process Clause and Ninth Amendment.

Justice Black dissented on grounds that the government action was not prohibited by a specific constitutional prohibition. Insofar as the Court struck down the law without a clear constitutional basis, Black maintained that it assumed the role of a super-legislature. From his perspective, penumbras were a thin disguise for what he viewed as an essentially antidemocratic role. Although agreeing that privacy was a desirable concept, he maintained that the Court must respect that the Constitution does not provide for it. Black observed that "[f]or myself it would be most irksome to be ruled by a bevy of Platonic Guardians, even if I knew how to choose them, which I assuredly do not."

In *Eisenstadt v. Baird*,[22] the Court used the Equal Protection Clause to extend the freedom to use contraceptives to unmarried persons. In *Carey v. Population Services International*,[23] it struck down a state law permitting only pharmacists to sell nonprescription contraceptives and prohibiting their sale to persons under the age of 16. The Court characterized *Griswold* as "teaching . . . that the Constitution protects individual decisions in matters of childbearing from unjustified intrusion by the State."

(3) Abortion

The Court, in *Roe v. Wade*,[24] established that the right of privacy comprehended "a woman's decision whether or not to terminate her pregnancy."[25] It also abandoned the penumbra premise and grounded the right squarely in the Due Process Clause of the Fourteenth Amendment. At issue in *Roe v. Wade* was a Texas law prohibiting abortion unless the mother's life was endangered. The state justified the restriction on grounds that a fetus is a person, whose life is protected by the Due Process Clause of the Fourteenth Amendment. Justice Black-mun, writing for the majority, acknowledged that a fetus may be a life in some religions or under some moral codes but refused to embrace the premise in a constitutional sense.

Although concluding that "the right of personal privacy includes the abortion decision," the Court observed that the "right is not unqualified and must be considered against important state interests in regulation."[26] It thus acknowledged that states had legitimate interests in protecting a woman's health and the potential for life. Regulation had to serve a compelling governmental interest, however, and be narrowly tailored to achieve its objective.

> ### Sidebar
>
> **ABORTION REGULATION AT THE FOUNDING**
>
> Regulation of abortion was not common when the Constitution was framed but had become widespread by the middle of the nineteenth century. At the time *Roe v. Wade* was decided, most states outlawed abortion or permitted it under special circumstances such as when the mother's life was in danger, the pregnancy was the result of rape or incest, or the baby would have birth defects.

The Court established a trimester framework for balancing the state's and woman's concerns and adjusted them depending on the stage of pregnancy. Because abortion is less risky to the mother than childbirth during the first three months of pregnancy, a state may not prohibit abortion during this time and may regulate only to protect the mother's health. Examples of permissible regulation in the first trimester include licensing requirements for facilities where abortions are performed and for personnel who perform abortions. The Court indicated that, for the course of the second trimester, a woman's freedom should be largely unrestricted. Based on its understanding that viability commenced with the third trimester, the Court determined that the state's interest in prohibiting abortion was compelling at that point.

The decision quickly became a lightning rod for criticism that the Court was commandeering an issue that should be resolved by the political process. Detractors maintained that the Court had reverted to a discredited mode of judicial review reminiscent of economic rights doctrine. The Court differentiated its role on grounds it was advancing not a favored ideology but discerning what was "implicit in the concept of ordered liberty."[27]

Justice Rehnquist in dissent noted that because most states banned abortion, the nation's traditions and history provided no support for the liberty. Because he found no constitutional right or liberty at stake, Rehnquist maintained that the only legitimate question was whether the regulation had a rational relationship to a legitimate state objective. Justice White likewise asserted that abortion was not within the Constitution's ambit of concern. He thus contended that the issue should be resolved by the people and their elected representatives.

The decision in *Roe v. Wade* stands as one of the most controversial rulings in the Court's history. A central theme of criticism is that the Court cut the right from its own cloth rather than from constitutional fabric. Despite arguments that the Court

ROE'S LEGITIMACY

A primary legacy of *Roe v. Wade* is the persistence of challenges to its legitimacy. Critics include those who favor a woman's freedom of choice pursuant to the legislative process. John Hart Ely has maintained that "[t]he problem with *Roe* is not so much that it bungles the question it sets itself, but rather that it sets itself a question the Constitution has not made the Constitution's business. . . . It is [a bad decision] because it is bad constitutional law, or rather because it is *not* constitutional law and gives almost no sense of an obligation to try to be." John Hart Ely, *Democracy and Distrust: A Theory of Judicial Review* (1980). A competing perspective is offered by Sylvia Law, who has contended that no Supreme Court decision has been more tangibly important to women. Sylvia A. Law, *Rethinking Sex and the Constitution*, 132 U. Pa. L. Rev. 955 (1984).

stretched and warped the Constitution to achieve a desired result, the decision has continued to operate as a barrier against regulations that would unduly limit a woman's freedom to obtain an abortion. The aftermath of *Roe v. Wade*, however, has been characterized by persistent challenges aimed at undoing it.

Through the late 1980s, and although divided, the Court held fast to *Roe v. Wade* and struck down laws that it perceived as a significant burden on a woman's liberty to elect an abortion. In *Doe v. Bolton*,[28] the Court invalidated provisions of a state law that required abortions to be performed in a hospital approved by a specific accrediting agency, to be authorized by a hospital committee, and done only after examination by two other physicians. Critical to the Court's analysis was the fact that these restrictions applied to no other surgical procedure but abortion.

The Court, in *Planned Parenthood v. Danforth*,[29] struck down requirements for spousal consent and parental consent for unmarried women under the age of 18. The basis for this holding was that the state did not have power to regulate during the first trimester and thus could not delegate authority to a third person. Because the woman "is the more directly and immediately affected by the pregnancy," the Court found that "the balance weighs in her favor."[30] Given age and maturity factors, the Court also noted that some minor children might not be able to provide effective consent.

Following up on this point, the Court in *Planned Parenthood v. Ashcroft*,[31] upheld a parental consent or notification requirement provided that the minor could bypass it through a judicial procedure. When the parental bypass option is exercised, it is a court's responsibility to determine that the minor is sufficiently mature to make the decision herself or that an abortion is in her best interest.

Consistent with its record of striking down laws that it perceived as significant roadblocks to a woman's freedom to choose an abortion, the Court in *Akron v. Akron Center for Reproductive Health*[32] invalidated a state law requiring physicians to provide information concerning the medical risks and morality of abortion, imposing a 24-hour waiting period, and requiring abortions after the first trimester to be performed in hospitals. These restrictions, as the Court saw them, imposed on the woman "a heavy and unnecessary burden."

A law mandating the disclosure of referring and performing physicians and the patient, and compelling the use of post-viability abortion procedures that maximized the possibility of fetal survival, was struck down in *Thornburgh v. American College of Obstetricians & Gynecologists*.[33] The Court concluded that these conditions were too likely to deter a woman from exercising her freedom to choose an abortion.

One of the most significant challenges to *Roe v. Wade* arose in *Webster v. Reproductive Health Services*,[34] when the federal government formally weighed in on the side of anti-abortion forces. The Department of Justice, in an amicus curiae brief, asserted that the Court's abortion jurisprudence adopted "an unworkable framework" that tied permissible regulation to trimesters and usurped the role of the political process in balancing social, ethical, and scientific factors. At issue in this case was a Missouri law that prohibited abortion in state-funded hospitals and required fetal viability testing after 20 weeks. The enactment included a preamble that repudiated *Roe v. Wade* and set forth findings that life begins at conception and the unborn have constitutionally protected interests in life and liberty. Although acknowledging that the preamble made "a value judgment favoring childbirth over abortion,"[35] the Court observed that the state was not precluded from expressing this preference. The Court found that the provision imposed no substantive restrictions on abortions and thus was of no constitutional significance.

Citing to case law that upheld restrictions on public funding, the Court approved the prohibition of abortions in public hospitals. A decade earlier, the Court had determined in *Harris v. McRae*[36] and *Maher v. Roe*,[37] that neither federal nor state government respectively was obligated to fund abortion for an indigent woman. The rationale for these outcomes was that the obstacle to obtaining an abortion was not government but the woman's financial condition. With respect to viability testing, Chief Justice Rehnquist concluded that the procedure properly reflected and accounted for advances in medical technology. This outcome effectively unraveled the strict trimester model insofar as viability was pushed back to an earlier stage of pregnancy. The Court, however, refused to dump *Roe v. Wade* altogether. In a concurring opinion, Justice O'Connor agreed that the Missouri law did not present the right case for overruling *Roe v. Wade*. She had no problem with viability testing or a revised starting point for viability.

Justice Scalia, in a concurring opinion, maintained that the Court was ignoring the main issue. He argued that the Court simply should overrule *Roe v. Wade* on grounds it was erroneously decided. Justice Blackmun expressed concern that the Court had relaxed the standard for reviewing abortion regulation by asking not whether the reason for it was compelling but whether it was legitimate. From his perspective, the cost of additional medical testing constituted an undue burden. For Blackmun, the decision cast a pall on *Roe v. Wade's* future. As he put it, "[f]or today, at least, the law of abortion stands undisturbed. For today, the women of this Nation still retain the liberty to control their destinies. But the signs are evident and very ominous, and a chill wind blows."[38] The Court's ruling left *Roe v. Wade* modified but still intact. It also ensured that future challenges lay ahead.

This photograph shows activists from both sides of the abortion controversy demonstrating outside the Supreme Court.

Used with permission of LifeNews.com.

Three years after the *Webster* decision, the Court in *Planned Parenthood of Southeastern Pennsylvania v. Casey*[39] reviewed a state enactment that imposed several restrictions on the availability of abortion. At issue was a law that (1) required abortion providers to give women information identifying the physical and psychological risks of abortion, (2) prohibited abortion pending a 24-hour waiting period, (3) required minors to obtain the consent of a parent or judge, (4) required a married women to notify her spouse, and (5) obligated physicians to file reports showing compliance with the law for every abortion they performed. Each provision of the law, other than the reporting requirement, included an exception in the event of a medical emergency. A trial court had struck down the regulatory scheme on grounds that it violated a woman's freedom to end her pregnancy. The court of appeals reversed much of the lower court's ruling, finding only that the spousal notification provision was unconstitutional.

Although no majority position coalesced, Justices Sandra Day O'Connor, Anthony Kennedy, and David Souter authored an influential plurality opinion. This opinion reaffirmed the vitality of *Roe v. Wade* but upheld most provisions of the state law. As the plurality described it, the central meaning of *Roe v. Wade* was that the state cannot deny an abortion prior to fetal viability. The three justices concluded, however, that the trimester framework was too "rigid." In this regard, they noted that state interests had been slighted and laws had been struck down even though they did not meaningfully impair a woman's freedom to terminate her pregnancy. The plurality proposed that abortion regulations thus should be assessed on the basis of whether they "unduly burden" a woman's freedom prior to viability. The plurality found that the spousal notification requirement constituted an undue burden because it redistributed the power of choice from the woman to a third party. The risk for women with abusive spouses was particularly unacceptable, insofar as some might forgo an abortion to avoid harm to themselves or to their children.

The plurality found no other provision of the law to be unduly burdensome. Disclosure of the physical and psychological risks of abortion was viewed as an appropriate means of ensuring an informed decision by the woman. Without evidence indicating that the 24-hour waiting period would interfere unreasonably with a woman's freedom to chose, and although it might increase the cost of an abortion, the plurality was satisfied that the waiting period also advanced the objective of informed judgment. Precedent supported the parental consent requirement, provided there was a judicial bypass option. Reporting requirements, to the extent they are based on value to medical research and maternal well-being, also presented no undue burden.

Replying to critics who maintained that the Court should exit the abortion controversy, the plurality maintained that the greater harm would be to retreat in response to political pressure. To reaffirm the central meaning of *Roe v. Wade*, it thus drew on the doctrine of **stare decisis** ("to stand by things decided"). Although critics saw the Court itself as the source of the abortion controversy, the plurality determined that the interests of certainty and predictability favored continuation of the judiciary's role.

Justice Stevens did not disagree with the standard of review but maintained that the plurality understated the magnitude of burden imposed by the Pennsylvania law. He was especially concerned that the information and waiting requirements were subtle means of influencing a woman to change her mind. Although pleased that the Court had embraced *Roe v. Wade*'s basic meaning, Justice Blackmun expressed concern with what he perceived as a relaxed standard of review. Blackmun singled out the reporting requirement as particularly burdensome, insofar as it might deter physicians from performing abortions due to concern that they might be harassed or subject to personal harm.

Chief Justice Rehnquist and Justice Scalia in dissent argued that *Roe v. Wade* should be overturned. Rehnquist maintained that the plurality missed the point of stare decisis. As he saw it, the Court's reputation would be enhanced rather than lessened by a forthright acknowledgment of error. Consistent with his original dissent in *Roe v. Wade*, Rehnquist restated his concern that deep public divisions on abortion demonstrated a lack of consensus necessary to define a fundamental right. He favored a standard of review that allowed states to regulate abortion on the basis of any reasonable justification. Pursuant to this criterion, Rehnquist would have upheld all provisions of the Pennsylvania law. Even if the wisdom of the policy might be arguable, Rehnquist maintained that the Court's role was not to debate politics but to interpret the Fourteenth Amendment. In this regard, he stressed that the Fourteenth Amendment does not announce a general right of privacy.

Justice Scalia asserted that the Constitution establishes no barrier to laws prohibiting abortion. The question of whether to permit or restrict it, from his perspective, should be resolved by the process of representative governance. Like Rehnquist, Scalia criticized the Court's use of stare decisis. From Scalia's perspective, *Roe v. Wade* was decided erroneously because it failed to resolve the life status of the fetus and establish a settled principle. In circumstances where a court realizes that a case was wrongly decided, he contended that stare decisis should not apply. The legacy of challenges to *Roe v. Wade*, in Scalia's view, further evidenced the law's unsettled nature. Like other decisions in the aftermath of *Roe v. Wade*, the ruling in *Planned Parenthood of Southeastern Pennsylvania v. Casey* did not end the controversy over abortion or the Court's role in it. The "central meaning" of *Roe v. Wade*, which the plurality reaffirmed, is that fetal viability determines whether the mother's or state's interest is dominant. Instead of reliance on a fixed trimester regimen, the plurality's model balanced competing state and personal interests by focusing on whether a regulation is "unduly burdensome."

The undue burden test advanced by a plurality in *Casey* has gained continuing traction with the Court. In *Mazurek v. Armstrong*,[40] the Court reviewed a state law limiting performance of abortions to licensed physicians. The enactment was upheld on grounds that it did not impose a substantial obstacle to obtaining an abortion.

Criticism of the undue burden standard focuses largely on its ad hoc nature. Detractors maintain that it reduces analysis to an exercise in value selection and judgment. From their perspective, the undue burden test replicates the evils of Lochnerism and correlates outputs to the unpredictable perspectives of individual justices. Although differences were evident with respect to what constituted an undue burden, a majority of the Court in *Stenberg v. Carhart*[41] determined that a state law prohibiting partial birth abortions created substantial obstacles to a woman's freedom.

The Court revisited the issue of partial birth abortions several years later in *Gonzales v. Carhart*.[42] This case concerned the Partial Birth Abortion Act of 2007, which Congress enacted following the decision in *Stenberg v. Carhart*. Like the state law in that case, the federal enactment banned the procedure known as intact dilation and evacuation. The vast majority of abortions are performed during the first trimester using a vacuum procedure. Abortion in later term pregnancies typically requires a surgical process. The most common is a method that requires anesthesia, dilation of the cervix, and extraction of the fetus in pieces. A less frequently used method removes the fetus intact. This procedure, used when the physician is concerned with bleeding, infection, or injury, requires partial delivery of the fetus and crushing of the skull to facilitate removal.

Lower courts had found the law unconstitutional on grounds it was too vague and did not provide exceptions for instances in which the mother's health was at risk. Historically, the Court had required restrictions on abortion to provide exceptions under such circumstances. Congress in this instance had made findings that the procedure is never medically necessary to protect the mother's health. The Court, in *Gonzales v. Carhart,* noted that there was medical disagreement regarding whether the prohibition ever would impose a risk to the mother's health. Writing for the majority, Justice Kennedy concluded that medical uncertainty did not foreclose the exercise of legislative power in this or any other context. Speaking in general but important framing terms, it noted that government may use its authority "to show its profound respect for the life within the woman."[43] Stressing the law's potential to "devalue human life,"[44] the Court in a 5-4 vote upheld the law.

The enactment largely paralleled the state law that the Court had struck down in *Stenberg v. Carhart.* The Court identified what it viewed as a material distinction, however, insofar as the federal law provided specific guidance and allowable procedures and was limited to instances in which the banned procedure was "deliberately and intentionally" performed.

In a dissenting opinion, Justice Ginsburg characterized the decision as "alarming." As she noted, it represented the first time since *Roe v. Wade* that the Court upheld a prohibition minus an exception for protecting the mother's health. On this point, Ginsburg cited the testimony of experts who had identified the safety advantages of intact dilation and evaluation for women with certain medical conditions. From her perspective, the majority's departure from precedent requiring a health exception and disregard of lower court findings were "bewildering."

Viewing the decision in its entirety, Justice Ginsburg maintained that it only could be understood as an effort to chip away at a right that had been affirmed repeatedly. As she saw it, the Court's decision reflected "hostility" toward the underlying right secured by *Roe* and *Casey.*

Ginsburg also noted recent changes in the Court's composition as a factor bearing on the outcome. This observation referred to the resignation of Justice O'Connor, a key architect of the *Casey* framework, and appointment of Justice Alito as her successor.

The long-term effect of this personnel change remains uncertain. Justices Thomas and Justice Scalia joined the majority opinion but wrote separately to make the point that, from their perspective, the Court's abortion jurisprudence had no constitutional basis. The most recent appointees, Chief Justice Roberts and Justice Alito, subscribed to the majority opinion. Even if they are generally hostile toward the Court's abortion jurisprudence, some observers believe their votes in this case indicated a preference for doctrinal change that is incremental rather than wholesale. Justice Kennedy, although having dissenting in *Stenberg v. Carhart,* joined in reaffirming *Roe*'s central meaning in *Casey.*

(4) Marriage and Family Life

An individual's right to "marry, establish a home and bring up children"[45] predates the right of privacy. The Court, in the words of Justice Powell, "has long recognized that freedom of personal choice in matters of marriage and family life is one of the liberties protected by the Due Process Clause of the Fourteenth Amendment."[46] Modern case law accounts for these interests as incidents of the right of privacy. In *Village of Belle Terre v. Boraas*,[47] the Court determined that this liberty did not preclude zoning laws that limited occupancy of single-family dwellings to persons related by blood. A few years later, in *Moore v. City of East Cleveland*,[48] a plurality of justices struck down a law that prohibited extended families from living together in the same home. Writing for the plurality, Justice Powell found that the ordinance "slic[ed] deeply into the family itself." It referenced case law dating back a half century for the proposition that there is "a private realm of family life which the state cannot enter."[49]

To the extent that government intrudes into this domain, the plurality maintained that traditional deference toward the legislature is inapt. Rather, it must take a careful look at the importance of the government interest and the extent to which it is advanced by the challenged regulation. The inquiry into whether the government's interest was important indicated a standard of review that was heightened, but not strict. The plurality acknowledged that the city had a legitimate interest in managing traffic and parking congestion, avoiding financial burdens on the school system, and preventing overcrowding. It found the ordinance served these interests only marginally. Because these risks could be presented by nuclear as well as extended families, the Court determined that the regulation had only a tenuous connection to alleviating the problem identified by the city. It thus found the regulation invalid.

The plurality observed that "[s]ubstantive due process has at times been a treacherous field for this Court."[50] Citing to "the history of the *Lochner* era," it acknowledged that "there is reason for concern lest the only limits to such judicial intervention become the predilections of those who happen at the time to be Members of this Court." The plurality interpreted this history, however, as counsel for "caution and restraint" and not "abandonment." Pursuant to this premise, it maintained that guidance for due process review should come from "respect for the teachings of history [and] solid recognition of the basic values that underlie our society." In this regard, the plurality determined "that the Constitution protects the sanctity of the family precisely because the institution of the family is deeply rooted in this Nation's history and tradition."

Justice Brennan, in a concurring opinion joined by Justice Marshall, stressed the importance of the extended family as a means for reckoning with economic and emotional hardship. He noted it is "a means of survival for large numbers of the poor and deprived minorities of our society."[51] Brennan saw the ordinance as a function of "cultural myopia" that reflected a preference for the nuclear family model found in much of white suburbia and "a depressing insensitivity toward the economic and emotional needs of a very large part of our society."[52] Justice Stevens concurred on grounds that the ordinance constituted a taking without due process or just compensation.

Justice Stewart, joined by Justice Rehnquist, dissented on grounds the interest in sharing living space was not "implicit in the concept of ordered liberty" and stretched "the limited substantive contours of the Due Process Clause beyond recognition."[53]

Justice White agreed with Justices Stewart and Rehnquist that the interest of extended families in living together did not rise to the level of a constitutionally protected liberty. His dissent stressed that the "Court is the most vulnerable and comes nearest to illegitimacy when it deals with judge-made constitutional law having little or no cognizable roots in the language or even the design of the Constitution."[54] White maintained that the Court should be "extremely reluctant" to use the

Due Process Clause to invalidate laws enacted by states or cities to promote their welfare. Such review, from his perspective, exceeded the judiciary's constitutional authority and invaded legislative turf. White also criticized inquiry into the nation's deeply rooted traditions as a basis for determining fundamental rights. These traditions were debatable, from his perspective, and which of them merited constitutional protection was even more debatable.

Marriage, as previously noted, is a relationship that the Court has long recognized and protected on a constitutional basis. The right to marry was one of several grounds that the Court referenced, in *Loving v. Virginia*,[55] to strike down anti-miscegenation laws. In *Zablocki v. Redhail*,[56] the Court reviewed a state law that prohibited marriage by residents who were not meeting their child support obligations and failed to show that their children would not become "public charges." The Court determined the right of privacy includes the right to marry. Especially because the right of privacy comprehended other aspects of family life, the Court observed that it would make no sense to deny protection to their foundation.

The *Zablocki* Court used a strict scrutiny standard because the law directly impaired the right to marry. Pursuant to this criterion, the Court found that the state had other means for securing compliance that were less burdensome to the right. If a regulation did not interfere significantly with the decision to marry, the Court indicated that it merely would assess whether the law was reasonable.

Justice Rehnquist dissented on grounds there was no fundamental right at stake. Consistent with this premise, he maintained that the Court wrongly employed a heightened standard of review. As he saw it, the state needed only to demonstrate a constitutionally permissible objective. Rehnquist thus maintained that the law constituted a legitimate exercise of the state's power to regulate family life and ensure the support of minor children.

F   A   Q

Q: Why doesn't the right to marry include polygamy?

A: Like any other right or liberty, the right to marry is not absolute. In *Reynolds v. United States*, 98 U.S. 145 (1878), the Court upheld a federal law prohibiting polygamy. This decision rejected a claim that the enactment violated the Free Exercise Clause of the First Amendment. The *Reynolds* decision did not directly implicate a right to marry. Justice Scalia, in a dissent from the majority opinion in *Lawrence v. Texas*, 539 U.S. 558 (2003), suggested that the Court's broad definition of liberty in that case potentially disables states from prohibiting polygamy.

The dissenting justices in *City of East Cleveland v. Moore* and *Zablocki v. Redhail* objected to a judicial function that, from their perspective, undermined the political process. This same concern was the basis for a decision, in *Michael H. v. Gerald D.*,[57] that narrowed due process protection of parental rights. At issue in this case was whether a natural father could be denied visitation rights with a daughter who was conceived in an extramarital affair. The father contended that biological fatherhood and a parental relationship established a liberty interest protected by the Due Process Clause. The Court disagreed. In an opinion joined for the most part by three of his colleagues, Justice Scalia maintained that the liberty interest hinged not on the factors cited by the father "but upon the historic respect — indeed, sanctity would not be too strong a term — traditionally accorded to the relationships that develop within the unitary family." The interest of the adulterous natural father in this case, as the plurality saw it, was "not the stuff" from which fundamental rights are made. The plurality also was concerned that protecting the adulterous natural father would deny protection to the marital father. In this regard, it noted that the natural father's parental interest was in competition with the marital father's interest in preserving the integrity of a traditional family. It maintained that the choice between these two "freedoms" was more appropriately made by the people than by the Court.

A notable aspect of Justice Scalia's opinion was his argument that the inquiry into whether a right or liberty is fundamental should "refer to the most specific level at which a relevant tradition can be identified."[58] Defining the liberty interest at a high level of specificity correspondingly diminishes the likelihood that the interest will be denominated fundamental. Although the general concept of parental rights may be understood as rooted in the nation's traditions, societal support predictably would diminish for this proposition when extended to parents of children who were conceived in an adulterous relationship.

By framing the liberty interest with more detail and precision, Scalia advanced a model of review that would limit the judiciary's role in identifying rights that are not textually enumerated. Justices O'Connor and Kennedy, who otherwise joined Scalia, parted ways with him on this point. Both indicated that there may be instances in which the interest at stake should be defined in general rather than specific terms. They thus refused to embrace "the most specific level" standard as a wholesale constraint in defining tradition.

Although agreeing with and thus providing majority support for the judgment, Justice Stevens maintained that there might be circumstances in which the natural parent's interest should prevail. In this regard, he noted that the state should provide a process for determining what constitutes the best interest of the child.

Justice Brennan, in a dissenting opinion joined by Justices Marshall and Blackmun, criticized the plurality for employing a "misguided" standard of review. In Brennan's view, the appropriate inquiry was not whether the nation's history and traditions protected an interest but whether they regarded it as important. He pointed out that the Court would not have protected the use of contraceptives in *Griswold* if its focus had been on the interest unmodified by its importance. Brennan maintained that, by asking whether an interest historically and traditionally was protected, rather than regarded as important, the plurality reduced the role of the Due Process Clause to the point that it merely confirmed the importance of interests that most states already protect.

Justice White also dissented on grounds that a biological father who seizes the opportunity for a relationship with his child and provides support should have a protected liberty interest. The plurality opinion reflected concern with the risk that substantive due process review presents to the political process. Brennan's dissent set forth the counterpoint that due process review is essential to ensure that the Constitution does not become "a stagnant, archaic, hidebound document steeped in the prejudices and superstitions of a time long past."[59]

The boundaries of parental liberty were further delineated in *Troxel v. Granville*,[60] when the Court struck down a state law that gave grandparents rights to visit the children of a sole surviving parent. Writing for a four-justice plurality, Justice

O'Connor affirmed a fundamental right of parents to make decisions concerning care, custody, and control of their children. Minus evidence that a parent is not providing adequate care, the plurality indicated that the state typically has no basis to inject itself into the private realm of the family. Insofar as a "fit parent's" decision was subject to judicial review, as in this case, the plurality maintained that there must be some "special weight" assigned to the parent's determination. Justices Thomas (in a concurring opinion) and Scalia (in a dissenting opinion) raised concern with the Court's enforcement of a right that is not enumerated by the Constitution.

(5) Sexual Orientation

The right of privacy cases in many instances reflect tension between respect for personal autonomy and state interests in managing social and moral interests. Even as the Court has persisted in developing the right of privacy and its multiple incidents, it has expressed an awareness of the need for caution in overriding the political process. The Court, in *Whalen v. Roe*,[61] determined that it cannot find a law unconstitutional merely because it has an impact on personal liberty or privacy and finds it unnecessary in whole or in part. The Court at times has demonstrated not just reserve but resistance to expanding the dimensions of the right of privacy. This disposition was exemplified in *Bowers v. Hardwick*,[62] when the Court rejected what it characterized as a proposed "constitutional right of homosexuals to engage in acts of sodomy."

The case concerned an arrest and prosecution of two men who engaged in oral sex in the bedroom of their house. (Prior to trial, the prosecution dropped charges. Consequently, there was no criminal conviction. The case thus was framed as a challenge to the criminal statute.) In the marital context, the Court had identified bedrooms as "sacred precincts."[63] The state law at issue prohibited oral or anal sex between any persons regardless of gender. The defendants argued that the sex was consensual, within the context of a private association, and thus within the protected realm of the right of privacy. Although the law on its face did not differentiate between homosexual and heterosexual sodomy, the Court focused its attention on the same-sex aspect.

The Court, in an opinion authored by Justice White, characterized the issue as "whether the Federal Constitution confers a fundamental right upon homosexuals to engage in sodomy" and thus invalidates state laws that historically have declared it illegal.[64] The Court referenced a line of privacy decisions that comprehend child rearing and education, family relationships, procreation, marriage, contraception, and abortion. None of these rights, from the Court's perspective, "bears any resemblance to the claimed constitutional right of homosexuals to engage in acts of sodomy."[65]

The Court's decision was grounded in a strong statement on behalf of judicial restraint. It thus stressed the importance of ensuring that development of "rights not readily identifiable in the Constitution's text involves much more than the imposition of the Justices' own choice of values." To determine whether a right was fundamental, the Court stated that it was necessary to determine whether the interest was "implicit in the concept of ordered liberty, such that neither liberty nor justice would exist if [they] were sacrificed" or "deeply rooted in this Nation's history and traditions."

In the Court's view, a right to engage in acts of consensual homosexual sodomy met neither criterion. To the contrary, it found that anti-sodomy provisions have "ancient roots." The Court noted that every state prohibited sodomy from the time the Constitution was framed and ratified through the mid-twentieth century. Nearly half of the states, moreover, still banned it at the time the action under review was brought. Viewing history and tradition in this light, the Court dismissed the claim of a right to engage in such conduct as "facetious" at best. The decision in *Bowers v. Hardwick* reflected the Court's unease with using its authority to use the Due Process Clause as a source of rights.

Chief Justice Burger authored a concurring opinion that repudiated the right of privacy case even more bluntly. Building on the Court's observation that proscriptions against sodomy "have ancient roots," Burger characterized the condemnation of homosexuality as anchored "in Judeo-Christian moral and ethical standards" and condemned by both Roman and English law. Recognizing a right of homosexual sodomy, from Burger's perspective, would "cast aside millennia of moral teaching."[66]

Forceful as the majority and concurring opinions were, the Court was narrowly divided in its thinking and outcome. Justice Blackmun, joined by three of his colleagues, questioned the Court's grasp of the issue. Blackmun asserted that the Court had mischaracterized the issue. The question, as he saw it, was not about "a fundamental right to engage in homosexual sodomy." Rather, it was "about 'the most comprehensive of rights and the right most valued by civilized men,' namely, 'the right to be let alone.' "[67]

By framing the issue in terms of homosexual sodomy, as Blackmun viewed it, the Court blinded itself to the fundamental interest that all persons have in controlling and managing their intimate associations. Even if sodomy had been condemned "for hundreds of years, if not thousands" of years, Blackmun maintained that neither long history nor intensity of conviction could shield a law from meaningful judicial review. Citing to *West Virginia Board of Education v. Barnette*,[68] which concerned a student's freedom not to salute the flag, Blackmun noted that "freedom to differ is not limited to things that do not matter much. That would be a mere shadow of freedom."[69] Consistent with this premise, Blackmun maintained that the Court should be particularly sensitive to those personal choices that "upset the majority."

In *Lawrence v. Texas*,[70] the Court revisited the underlying premise of *Bowers v. Hardwick*. This case concerned the conviction of two adult men under a state law that criminalized same-sex intimate conduct, specifically prohibiting "deviate sexual intercourse, namely anal sex, with a member of the same sex."[71] The conduct, which was the basis for the conviction, was consensual and occurred in a private residence. The Court found no legitimate governmental interest, absent physical or mental harm, in prohibiting private sexual activity between consenting adults. The Court noted the strong liberty interest in the privacy of the home, but then noted that "there are other spheres of our lives and existence, outside the home, where the State should not be a dominant presence. Freedom extends beyond spatial bounds. Liberty presumes an autonomy of self that includes freedom of thought, belief, expression, and

Sidebar

SEXUAL ORIENTATION AND EQUAL PROTECTION

The Court left open the question of whether discrimination on the basis of sexual orientation might constitute an equal protection violation. In *Romer v. Evans*, 517 U.S. 620 (1996), it struck down a Colorado constitutional amendment prohibiting the state and municipalities from extending the protection of antidiscrimination laws to homosexuals. From the Court's perspective, the law was so unrelated to a legitimate state interest that it could be understood only as a reflection of "animus" toward homosexuals. The Court did not indicate whether sexual orientation provided the basis for a heightened standard of review.

certain intimate contact." The issue, as the Court saw it, thus concerned personal liberty in both a "spatial and more transcendent dimension."

The majority's portrayal of a broad liberty interest echoed and embraced the tone and direction of Justice Stevens's dissenting opinion in *Bowers v. Hardwick*. With respect to the holding in *Bowers v. Hardwick* itself, the Court determined that it had misunderstood the nature and extent of the liberty claim.

The Court's turnaround from its decision in *Bowers v. Hardwick* did not entail recognition of a fundamental right. To the contrary, in finding that there was no "legitimate state interest," the Court employed the terminology of rational basis review. The decision thus appears to fit into the narrow category of decisions that employ a rational basis test in an assertive rather than deferential manner.

F   A   Q

Q: Are grooming and dress within the scope of personal autonomy that is protected by the right of privacy?

A: The argument for such a right was captured by Justice Marshall's dissenting opinion in *Kelley v. Johnson*, 425 U.S. 238, 253 (1976). He maintained that "the right in one's personal appearance is inextricably bound up with the historically recognized right of 'every individual to the possession and control of his own person.'" The Court in this case rejected a challenge to a police department's grooming regulations. In so doing, it noted that grooming and dress codes for law enforcement personnel are subject to a presumption of legislative validity.

The Court repudiated not only the result but the underlying reasoning of *Bowers v. Hardwick*. Contrary to the Court's earlier findings, it noted that prohibitions against same-sex relations were more recent and limited. Nearly half of the states that had anti-sodomy laws when *Bowers* was decided had repealed them. Several more did not enforce them against consenting adults whose actions were in private. Even if homosexuality is morally objectionable to some, the Court reasoned that the state could not impose these values as a matter of criminal law.

The Court cited *Planned Parenthood of Southeastern Pennsylvania v. Casey* for the proposition that "[a]t the heart of liberty is the right to define one's own concept of existence, of meaning, of the universe, and of the mystery of human life."[72] It further observed that personal autonomy in a relationship was the same regardless of sexual orientation. The Court further found that the *Bowers* ruling denied this right and, because it was incorrectly decided, should be overruled. It distinguished the outcome from a case that might concern a minor, coercion, public activity, or prostitution. In closing, the Court observed that the meaning of constitutional liberty is not locked into any time in history and may be invoked by persons from "every generation" in their "search for greater freedom."

Justice O'Connor concurred in the judgment but disagreed with the majority's overruling of *Bowers*. She would have found the law unconstitutional under the Equal Protection Clause. As she saw it, moral disapproval by itself was not a legitimate basis for discriminating among groups of persons. Because the state criminalized "deviate sexual intercourse" in the context of same-sex relationships, but not opposite-sex relationships, Justice O'Connor maintained that the law could not stand. By relying on the Equal Protection Clause, she would have provided space for the state to enact an anti-sodomy law that applied both to heterosexual and homosexual relationships.

In a dissenting opinion joined by Chief Justice Rehnquist and Justice Thomas, Justice Scalia challenged the majority's opinion as essentially hypocritical, driven by irrelevant considerations, and the product of a "law-professor culture, that has largely signed on to the homosexual agenda."[73] With respect to the first point, Justice Scalia noted the Court's "sententious response" a decade before when *Roe v. Wade* was under attack. Scalia's reference was to the Court's observation, in *Planned Parenthood of Southeastern Pennsylvania v. Casey*, that "[l]iberty finds no refuge in the jurisprudence of doubt."[74] With the Court having deferred to precedent in *Casey*, but departed from it in overruling *Bowers*, Justice Scalia perceived an outcome that was merely a "result-oriented expedient."

Scalia also criticized the Court for departing from the norms that establish fundamental rights only on the basis of what is "deeply rooted in this Nation's history and tradition." Without the power to enact legislation based upon moral choices, state laws against a range of behavior including incest, prostitution, bestiality, and obscenity could be called into doubt. Justice Scalia thus viewed the overruling of *Bowers* as a potential source of "massive disruption of the current social order."

The Court's determination that there was "no rational basis for the law" struck Scalia as being "most out of accord." The basis for prohibiting sex crimes, he noted, was societal belief that certain sexual behavior was "immoral and unacceptable." To find that the state has no legitimate interest that justifies intrusion into personal and private lives, as Justice Scalia saw it, would "decree the end of all morals legislation." Against this backdrop, he perceived the majority's opinion as the extension of an "agenda promoted by some homosexual activists directed at eliminating the moral opprobrium that has traditionally attached to homosexual conduct."[75] Justice Scalia also accused the Court of "tak[ing] sides in the culture war, departing from its role of assuring, as neutral observer, that the democratic rules of engagement are observed."[76]

Central to Justice Scalia's reasoning was the notion that some people view homosexuality as "immoral and destructive" and as a "lifestyle" rather than "immutable characteristic." Consistent with this premise, he contended that the issue of homosexuality and its incidents should be resolved by "normal democratic means," which gives every person the opportunity to influence his or her fellow citizens. It is another matter, Scalia observed, when matters move beyond attempts at persuasion to imposing one's views without a democratic majority.

In closing, Scalia observed that the Court's opinion had far-reaching consequences that were inevitable. Of particular concern to him was the Court's statement that "persons in a homosexual relationship may seek autonomy for . . . purposes" that include "marriage."[77] This observation, from Justice Scalia's perspective, undid constitutional principle that

Sidebar

THE STANDARD OF REVIEW

One significant loose end in the Court's decision relates to the standard of review. Typically, when accounting for fundamental rights, the Court engages in strict scrutiny. In *Lawrence*, the Court used its lowest standard of review in finding that the law had no rational basis. The invalidation of a law in this manner places *Lawrence* in a small universe of equal protection outcomes. It also sends mixed signals. One possibility is that the rational basis standard of review has a level of rigor that typically is on reserve. If so, there is a need for a transparent explanation with regarding when and why the higher intensity version should be actualized. Another possibility is that there are instances in which a law is entirely and utterly irrational. This explanation would be challenged to the extent it is to identify a law without at least some arguable justification.

enables states to prohibit same-sex marriage. The Court had indicated that it did not address this question. Scalia was not comforted, however, by a decision that to him suggested a disconnect between principle or logic and outcome.

Justice Thomas found the law "silly" and, if a member of the legislature, would have voted to repeal it. He found, however, no constitutional provision that established a "general right of privacy" and thus no basis for invalidating it.

(6) Right to Refuse Medical Treatment

The issue of whether a person can decline unwanted medical care predates contemporary concepts of the right of privacy. In *Jacobson v. Massachusetts*,[78] the Court determined that the government's interest in disease prevention outweighed an individual's freedom to refuse a smallpox vaccination. This decision thus found a mandatory vaccination law to be a proper exercise of the state's police power in protecting the public health.

A decision to refuse medical treatment as a chosen means of ending life places personal autonomy in conflict with societal values and laws that disfavor suicide and criminalize its facilitation. In *Cruzan v. Director, Missouri Department of Health*,[79] the Court considered whether the right to refuse medical treatment was an aspect of the right of privacy. This case concerned a woman who had suffered severe brain damage in an automobile accident and was on long-term life support. Given her vegetative state, which medical experts maintained was permanent, the parents sought a court order directing the hospital to remove their daughter from life support. Withdrawal of life support, they argued, was consistent with their daughter's wishes. The Missouri Supreme Court determined that, absent "clear and convincing evidence" of the daughter's intent, the parents had insufficient authority to obtain the court order and in effect make the decision for her.

The U.S. Supreme Court upheld the decision. It assumed for purposes of the case that a competent person possesses a constitutional liberty interest in declining unwanted medical treatment. The Court further observed, however, that "[a]n incompetent person is not able to make an informed and voluntary choice to exercise a hypothetical right to refuse treatment or any other right." Under such circumstances, the right "must be exercised for her, if at all, by some sort of surrogate."

Under Missouri law, a third party could make a decision to end life support provided there was "clear and convincing evidence" that it reflected the incompetent person's wishes. For the Court, the key question was whether the right to refuse medical treatment outweighed the state's interest in a rigorous evidentiary safeguard. In making this assessment, the Court found that the Missouri law reflected a valid interest in protecting and preserving human life. It noted that a state need not be neutral when a physically able adult makes a voluntary and informed position to starve to death. Because a choice between life and death is deeply personal and the consequences are final, the Court concluded that the state had a legitimate concern with the decision's integrity. Among the risks that the Court identified was the possibility that a third party may not be dedicated to the best interests of the incompetent person. Family membership by itself, as the Court noted, does not guarantee that the interest of close family members and the patient will be identical. The Court also found a higher standard of review warranted to minimize the fatal risk of a bad court decision.

Justice Scalia agreed with the outcome but, in a concurring opinion, objected to reliance on the Due Process Clause. He would have preferred that an unambiguous statement that the courts had no role in the matter. Scalia maintained "that the point at which life becomes worthless . . . [is] neither set forth in the Constitution nor known to the nine Justices of this Court any better than they are known to nine people picked at random from the Kansas City telephone directory."[80] He would have left resolution of the matter to the political process.

Justice Brennan authored a dissenting opinion that was joined by Justices Marshall and Blackmun. Brennan commenced by noting medical technology's ability to create "a twilight zone of suspended animation" where death and life coexist. He maintained that the petitioner, pursuant to her express will, had a fundamental right to be free of artificial life support—and this interest was not outweighed by the state's interest. In Brennan's view, the state had no valid interest in a life removed from the person's interest in living that outweighed his or her decision with respect to medical treatment. The state regulatory interest, in Brennan's view, extended no further than ensuring and protecting the integrity of her will. The key inquiry for Brennan was whether an incompetent person would want to live in a persistent vegetative state or refuse medical treatment. Brennan argued that, instead of imposing a "clear and convincing evidence" requirement, the state should respect the choice of the person to whom the decision most likely would have been delegated.

In a separate concurrence, Justice Stevens also disagreed with the enhanced evidentiary standard. From his perspective, the conflict between life and liberty was artificial and a result of both the state's and Court's willingness to "abstract" the petitioner's "life" from her "person." Insofar as the state declared a policy in favor of life in the abstract and used a specific life to symbolize its objectives, he maintained that its responsibility for protecting life was "desecrate[d]."

In *Washington v. Glucksberg*,[81] the Court upheld a state law that prohibited assisted suicide. Noting traditional prohibitions against suicide, and the fact that the act was a crime in most states, the Court found no support for assisted suicide in the nation's history and tradition. The Court in *Glucksberg* spoke to the concept and risks of due process in a manner that built on Justice Scalia's concerns in *Michael H. v. Gerald D*. It thus observed that substantive due process secures fundamental rights and liberties that "are *objectively*, 'deeply rooted in this Nation's history and tradition.' "[82] The Court also maintained that a fundamental right must be "carefully described" using the nation's "history, traditions, and practices" as reference points.[83] Noting that it had recognized in *Cruzan* not a right to die but to refuse life-saving medical treatment, the Court rejected the premise that due process safeguards are "any and all important, intimate, and personal decisions."[84] It found that the state had a valid interest in protecting human life, particularly those in a vulnerable state, and the integrity and ethics of the medical profession. Because the law was reasonably related to important and legitimate state interests, the Court found no basis for a constitutional violation.

Justice O'Connor, joined by Justices Breyer and Ginsburg in a concurring opinion, noted that the majority did not address whether patients suffering from pain might have a constitutional interest in relief that include the hastening of death. Justice Souter observed that legislative competence was superior to the judiciary's "at this time." These reservations suggest the possibility that significant issues in this area of the law still lie ahead.

In *Vacco v. Quill,* the Court rejected an equal protection challenge to a state law prohibiting physician-assisted suicide. In so doing, it determined that there was no fundamental right at stake. The Court also found that the state made a legitimate differentiation between permitting persons to decline unwanted medical treatment and enabling assisted suicide. In this regard, the Court noted that refusal of medical treatment results in death from the underlying disease. The cause of death by means of assisted suicide, however, is not the disease but the chosen modality for ending life. Also differentiating the process from the right to refuse unwanted medical treatment is the facilitator's intent to end life.

F   A   Q

Q: Is there a clear formula for determining what constitutes a fundamental right pursuant to the Due Process Clause?

A: To determine whether a right is fundamental, the Court assesses whether it is "implicit in the concept of ordered liberty" or "deeply rooted in this Nation's history and tradition." Critics maintain these criteria do not eliminate the risk of subjective decision making. A counterpoint to this concern was articulated by Justice Harlan in an opinion dissenting from the Court's refusal to review a state's prohibition of contraceptives. In *Poe v. Ullman*, 367 U.S. 497 (1961), Harlan noted:

> Due process has not been reduced to any formula; its content cannot be determined by reference to any code. The best that can be said is that through the course of this Court's decisions it has represented the balance which our Nation, built upon postulates of respect for the liberty of the individual, has struck between that liberty and the demands of organized society. If the supplying of content to this Constitutional concept has of necessity been a rational process, it certainly has not been one where judges have felt free to roam where unguided speculation might take them. The balance of which I speak is the balance struck by this country, having regard to what history teaches are the traditions from which it developed as well as the traditions from which it broke. That tradition is a living thing. A decision of this Court which radically departs from it would not long survive, while a decision which builds on what has survived is likely to be sound. No formula could serve as a substitute, in this area, for judgment and restraint.[85]

The sourcing of fundamental but textually unenumerated rights is not restricted to the Due Process Clause. The Court, for instance, has recognized interstate travel and voting as rights that are fundamental. These guarantees, although not textually enumerated, have been inferred from the structure of the Constitution and representative nature of the political process it creates. These rights, as discussed in the next chapter, typically are analyzed within the context of the equal protection guarantee.

SUMMARY

■ Modern substantive due process review has been and continues to be a source of significant controversy with respect to the judiciary's function. Insofar as courts identify rights or liberties and denominate them as fundamental, critics maintain that the judicial process usurps legislative power and becomes antidemocratic.

■ Although modern substantive due process review prioritizes a different set of values than its antecedent, critics note that this variance is inconsequential. From their perspective, it is the process of identifying and protecting rights not enumerated by the Constitution that is terminally wrong.

■ Whether substantive due process review accounts for liberty of contract or the right of privacy, detractors maintain that judicial management of unenumerated rights and liberties is reducible to an exercise in natural law.

■ Constitutionalization of the right of privacy is a primary incident of modern substantive due process review. It is a multifaceted right that, as evolved over the latter part of the twentieth century, has addressed and accounted for procreation, abortion, marriage, sexual orientation, family, and death.

■ Exponents of modern substantive due process review have differentiated it from the early model on grounds that the interests protected are more profound and, in some instances, impact concerns that require special solicitude. They acknowledge that legislatures have more competence to assess general social and economic matters and generally are entitled to a deferential standard of review.

■ Modern fundamental rights analysis reflects sensitivity to the negative legacy of economic rights doctrine. Standards of review are grounded in principles designed to manage the risk of subjectivism in determining what is fundamental. Identification of a fundamental right thus hinges on whether an interest is adjudged "implicit in the concept of ordered liberty" or "rooted in the Nation's traditions and history."

■ The continuing controversy over fundamental rights development indicates that these criteria have not been entirely successful in quelling a debate that is nearly as old as the republic itself.

CONNECTIONS

Economic Rights

The protection of economic rights was a central aspect of early substantive due process review. Liberty of contract was a primary example of an unenumerated right that the Court referenced in displacing a wide range of social and economic policies enacted by legislatures during the early twentieth century.

Fourth Amendment

This guarantee establishes that "[t]he right of the people to be secure in their persons, houses, papers, and effects, against unreasonable searches and seizures, shall not be violated." It also establishes conditions for the issuance of warrants. This enumeration safeguards persons against government processes for gathering evidence that are unduly invasive. The general right of privacy established pursuant to the Fourteenth Amendment is concerned primarily with personal autonomy.

Police Power

This power refers to a state's authority to regulate matters of local concern, including health, safety, and morality. This power antedates the Constitution and is reaffirmed by the Tenth Amendment. Substantive due process review pursuant to the Fourteenth Amendment typically assesses the constitutionality of an enactment, such as a restriction on abortion, that is based on the police power.

Procedural Due Process

This guarantee of the Fourteenth Amendment's Due Process Clause ensures that government cannot deprive a person of life, liberty, or property without a fair procedure. Procedural due process operates against adjudicative process, such as courts, to ensure fairness. Elementary requirements of procedural due process are notice and a hearing.

Stare Decisis

This principle binds courts to precedent, even if a different outcome might be reached if the issue was being heard for the first time. The policy accounts for interests of certainty and predictability. It may be departed from when a court determines that the original ruling was decided wrongly, as some justices have urged with respect to *Roe v. Wade.*

Endnotes

1. 32 U.S. 242 (1833).
2. *Id.* at 247.
3. 83 U.S. 26 (1873).
4. 304 U.S. 144, 154 n.4 (1938).
5. *Id.* at 154 n.4.
6. 302 U.S. 319 (1937).
7. *Id.* at 325.
8. 332 U.S. 46 (1947).
9. Roe v. Wade, 410 U.S. 113, 152 (1973).
10. Union P. Ry. Co. v. Botsford, 141 U.S. 250, 251 (1891).
11. Samuel D. Warren & Louis D. Brandeis, *The Right to Privacy*, 4 Harv. L. Rev. 193 (1890).
12. 262 U.S. 390 (1923).
13. *Id.* at 399.
14. 268 U.S. 510 (1925).
15. 277 U.S. 438 (1928) (Brandeis, J., dissenting).
16. *Id.* at 478.
17. 316 U.S. 535 (1942).
18. 274 U.S. 200 (1927).
19. Ferguson v. Skrupa, 372 U.S. 726, 730 (1963).
20. 381 U.S. 479 (1965).
21. *Id.* at 486 (majority opinion).

22. 405 U.S. 438 (1972).
23. 431 U.S. 678 (1977).
24. 410 U.S. 113 (1973).
25. *Id.* at 153.
26. *Id.* at 154.
27. *Id.*
28. 410 U.S. 179 (1973).
29. 428 U.S. 52 (1976).
30. *Id.* at 71.
31. 462 U.S. 476 (1983).
32. 462 U.S. 416 (1983).
33. 476 U.S. 747 (1986).
34. 492 U.S. 490 (1989).
35. *Id.* at 506.
36. 448 U.S. 297 (1980).
37. 432 U.S. 464 (1977).
38. *Webster*, 492 U.S. at 560 (Blackmun, J., concurring in part and dissenting in part).
39. 505 U.S. 833 (1992).
40. 520 U.S. 968 (1997).
41. 530 U.S. 914 (2000).
42. 127 S. Ct. 1610 (2007).
43. *Id.* at 1633.
44. *Id.*
45. Meyer v. Nebraska, 262 U.S. 390, 399 (1923).
46. Moore v. City of East Cleveland, 431 U.S. 494, 499 (1977), quoting Cleveland Bd. of Educ. v. LaFleur, 414 U.S. 632 (1974).
47. 416 U.S. 1 (1974).
48. 431 U.S. 494 (1977).
49. *Id.* at 499.
50. *Id.* at 502.
51. *Id.* at 508 (Brennan, J., concurring).
52. *Id.* at 507-508.
53. *Id.* at 537 (Stewart, J., dissenting).
54. *Id.* at 544.
55. 388 U.S. 1 (1967).
56. 434 U.S. 374 (1978).
57. 491 U.S. 110 (1989).
58. *Id.* at 127 n.6.
59. *Id.* at 141.
60. 530 U.S. 57 (2000).
61. 429 U.S. 589 (1977).
62. 478 U.S. 186 (1986).
63. 381 U.S. at 485.
64. Bowers v. Hardwick, 478 U.S. at 190.
65. *Id.* at 190-191.
66. *Id.* at 197 (Burger, C.J., concurring).
67. *Id.* at 199 (Blackmun, J., dissenting).
68. 319 U.S. 694 (1943).
69. 478 U.S. at 211 (Blackmun, J., dissenting).
70. 539 U.S. 558 (2003).
71. *Id.* at 563.
72. *Id.* at 574 (quoting Planned Parenthood of S.E. Pa. v. Casey, 505 U.S. 833, 851 (1992).
73. *Lawrence*, 539 U.S. at 602 (Scalia, J., dissenting).
74. *Id.* at 586.
75. *Id.* at 602.
76. *Id.*
77. *Id.* at 604.
78. 197 U.S. 211 (1905).
79. 497 U.S. 261 (1990).
80. *Id.* at 293 (Scalia, J., concurring).
81. 521 U.S. 702 (1997).
82. *Id.* at 719 (emphasis supplied).
83. *Id.* at 727.
84. *Id.*
85. Poe v. Ullman, 367 U.S. 497, 542 (1961) (Harlan, J., dissenting).

Equal Protection

9

The equal protection guarantee has been a tool of significant societal change. The provision's hallmark achievement has been its undoing of

official segregation. For most of its history, however, the Equal Protection Clause has been relatively toothless and has been interpreted in a manner that often accommodated rather than precluded official segregation and discrimination. Equal protection outcomes are a function of standards of review which mostly are deferential. Review of general economic and social classifications is governed by the rational basis test. Heightened standards of review operate when classifications differentiate on the basis of race, gender, alienage, non-marital children or selectively deny a fundamental right. The intensity of a particular standard of review is evidenced by its key terms. In assessing the significance of a state's reason for classifying (discriminating), for instance, the Court will ask whether it is reasonable (for rational basis review), important (for intermediate scrutiny), or compelling (for strict scrutiny).

Equal protection is not synonymous with equality in a general sense. Rather, it is a term of art that speaks to specific types of discrimination. Most laws, by their nature, differentiate. The equal protection guarantee is implicated when government discriminates invidiously. There are two categories of invidious discrimination: when government discriminates on the basis of a particular group status, as specified previously, and when government selectively deprives any individual of a fundamental right. In the fundamental rights context, equal protection and due process analysis parallel each other. A significant difference exists, however, with respect to the nature of an equal protection and a due process violation. Unlike the Due Process Clause, which precludes government action altogether, the Equal Protection Clause merely requires a recalibration of the law's sweep.

A. HISTORICAL ORIGINS

B. ECONOMIC (AND OTHER CONSTITUTIONALLY INSIGNIFICANT) CLASSIFICATIONS

C. RACIAL CLASSIFICATIONS

1. Race and the Nation's Founding
2. Separate but Equal
3. Desegregation
4. The Discriminatory Purpose Requirement
5. Affirmative Action

D. GENDER CLASSIFICATIONS

1. Formal versus Substantive Equality
2. Levels of Scrutiny

E. ALIENAGE CLASSIFICATIONS

F. CLASSIFICATIONS OF UNMARRIED PARENTS AND THEIR CHILDREN

G. CLASSIFICATIONS OF PERSONS WITH MENTAL DISABILITIES

H. CLASSIFICATIONS BASED ON SEXUAL ORIENTATION

I. THE FUNDAMENTAL RIGHTS STRAND OF EQUAL PROTECTION

1. Freedom of Speech
2. Access to the Justice System
3. Right to Interstate Travel
4. Voting
5. Education

A. Historical Origins

The Equal Protection Clause of the Fourteenth Amendment post-dates the original framing and ratification of the Constitution. It is a primary output of the reconstruction process that eventually reunited the North and South after the Civil War. Although foreign to the Constitution in the nation's seminal decades, equality concepts were present in the republic's precursor documents and early history. The Declaration of Independence, for instance, stated that "all men are created equal." Despite this declaration, laws, policies, and conventions that limited the distribution of rights, liberties, and immunities on the basis of group status pervaded the republic's early history in both the North and the South. Consistent with this reality, Chief Justice Taney, in *Dred Scott v. Sandford*,[1] maintained that it was "too clear for dispute, that the enslaved African race were not intended to be included" within the Declaration's ambit.

F   A   Q

Q: Prior to the Fourteenth Amendment, how were civil rights and equality interests established and protected?

A: Civil rights and equality interests, to the extent they were accounted for, were within the province of the states. The Fourteenth Amendment made federal citizenship the basis for state citizenship (instead of having federal citizenship derive from state citizenship). This inversion of traditional understanding established a basis for the federal government to assume a primary role in developing and distributing civil rights. This function was executed through an enabling provision of the Fourteenth Amendment, which authorized Congress to "enforce this article by appropriate legislation."

The equal protection guarantee has a legacy of mixed relevance and varying utility. It represents a limited rather than general constitutional interest in equality. By its terms, the Equal Protection Clause provides that no state shall "deny to any person within its jurisdiction the equal protection of the laws."[2] In its first reading of the Fourteenth Amendment, the Supreme Court in the *Slaughter-House Cases*[3] cast the Equal Protection Clause in narrow terms. It noted that "[t]he existence of laws in the States where the newly emancipated negroes resided, which discriminated with gross injustice and hardship against them as a class, was the evil to be remedied by" the guarantee.

Members of Congress generally agreed that the Fourteenth Amendment at minimum was "designed to embody or incorporate the Civil Rights Act."[4] Within this framework, the equal protection guarantee responded to the "gross injustice and hardship" of the Black Codes.[5] Against this backdrop, the *Slaughter-House* Court expressed a disbelief that "any action of a State not directed by way of discrimination against the negroes as a class, or on account of their race, will ever be held to come within the purview of this provision."[6]

The Court's initial understanding of the Equal Protection Clause as a race-specific guarantee was reaffirmed in *Bradwell v. Illinois*.[7] This case concerned a state law that denied women the opportunity to practice law. The Court's determination that gender-based discrimination did not implicate the Fourteenth

Sidebar

THE BLACK CODES

The state laws referenced by the *Slaughter-House* Court were the Black Codes that southern states adopted after the Thirteenth Amendment abolished slavery. The codes represented a comprehensive scheme of racial management. They perpetuated disadvantage by defining racial status, prohibiting intermarriage, creating dual systems of criminal justice, and restricting employment, travel, residence, and assembly. The codes reduced the Thirteenth Amendment to a formalism and prompted Congress to pass the Civil Rights Act of 1866, the nation's first civil rights law. It prohibited "discrimination in civil rights or immunities" and extended to persons of every race "the same rights to make and enforce contracts, to sue, be parties, and give evidence, to inherit, purchase, lease, sell, hold and convey real and personal property, and to full and equal benefit of all laws and proceedings for the security of persons and property, [and] be subject to like punishment." Cong. Globe, 39th Cong., 1st Sess. 474 (1866).

Amendment remained the law of the land for a century thereafter. During this time, the equal protection's utility was constrained not just with respect to nonracial discriminations but to racial discrimination itself. The disfavored nature of the Equal

Protection Clause was captured effectively by Justice Holmes's description of it in *Buck v. Bell* as "the usual last resort of constitutional arguments."[8]

Except for the equal protection guarantee's vitalization in the mid-twentieth century, when it was the basis for striking down segregation and other forms of discrimination, the Equal Protection Clause has had limited reach and impact. Modern equal protection review, minus discrimination that classifies on the basis of race, gender, alienage, or the non-marital status of a child's parents (or that selectively denies a fundamental right), mostly is consistent with standards articulated a century ago. As the Court put it in *Lindsley v. Natural Carbonic Gas Co.*, "if any state of facts reasonably can be conceived that would sustain the classification, the existence of that state of facts at the time the law was enacted must be assumed."[9] Consistent with this deferential standard, classifications that have a reasonable basis generally do not violate equal protection "merely because [they] are not made with mathematical nicety or because in practice [they] result in some inequality." The Court nonetheless occasionally has struck down laws pursuant to this **"rational basis" standard of review**. Examples include the invalidation of a state constitutional amendment prohibiting legislation against discrimination on the basis of sexual orientation[10] and a municipality's denial of a special use permit for a group home for mentally disabled children.[11] Critics have suggested in these instances that the Court has obscured its use of a more rigorous inquiry than the standard of review permits.

Sidebar

EQUAL PROTECTION STANDARDS OF REVIEW

Standards of review for equal protection claims are similar to those used in the due process context. Equal protection jurisprudence has been shaped by the same concerns that, in *United States v. Carolene Products Co.*, 304 U.S. 144 (1938), caused the Court to curb use of the Due Process Clause for substantive purposes. Specifically, the Court determined that it would engage in searching review only when a specific provision of the Bill of Rights was implicated or a burden was imposed on a group that was excluded formally from the political process. The latter concern established a template for more active review under the Equal Protection Clause. It led eventually to the determination, in *Korematsu v. United States*, 323 U.S. 214 (1944), that racial classifications must be strictly scrutinized.

Legislation, by its nature, classifies and differentiates in the distribution of burdens and benefits. In theory, the equal protection guarantee's ambit could be extended to the point that the legislative process's capacity to enact laws was disabled. This concern underlies the Court's caution in framing modern standards of review. As the Court noted in *Washington v. Davis*, an unbounded equal protection guarantee has the potential to invalidate "a whole range of tax, welfare, public service, regulatory, and licensing statutes."[12] Consistent with the centrifugal tendencies of any principle once established, moreover, "[t]he notion of equal protection as it spreads out tends to lift all to the level of the most favored."[13]

Marking the equal protection guarantee's boundaries has been a primary interpretative challenge of the Court. In this regard, the Court has determined that some classifications on the basis of group status count for equal protection purposes and others do not. Modern equal protection jurisprudence establishes that purposeful classification on the basis of race commands the highest standard of scrutiny. Classifications based on gender, alienage, or the non-marital status of a child's parents trigger **heightened scrutiny** but not necessarily **strict scrutiny**. Classifications that selectively deny a fundamental right, regardless of group status, also are reviewed in a more rigorous manner. Classifications on any other basis are subject to rational basis review.

B. Economic (and Other Constitutionally Insignificant) Classifications

A leading example of rational basis review, for general social or economic classifications, is the Court's decision in *Railway Express Agency v. New York*.[14] The Court in this case reviewed a city ordinance that prohibited display advertising on motor vehicles except those that were owner operated. The law was justified as a traffic safety measure. It was challenged on grounds that the enactment's means and the ends were at odds with equal protection. Deferring to legislative judgment, the Court noted that "local authorities may well have concluded that those who advertised their own wares on their trucks do not present the same traffic problem in view of the nature or extent of the advertising which they use. It would take a degree of omniscience which we lack to say that such is not the case." As the Court saw it, the classification did not represent the type of discrimination that concerned the equal protection guarantee. Notwithstanding that there may have been advertising displays even more distracting to motorists, such as those in Times Square, the state was not required to choose between eliminating all hazards or none at all.

F A Q

Q: Why didn't the Court strike down the law in *Railway Express Agency* on First Amendment grounds?

A: If the *Railway Express Agency* case were to be decided today, freedom of speech would be the basis for a strong constitutional challenge. Commercial speech at the time, however, was not protected by the First Amendment. Not until *Virginia State Board of Pharmacy v. Virginia Citizens Consumer Council*, 425 U.S. 748, 763 (1976), did the Court unequivocally find that commercial speech was constitutionally protected expression. Pursuant to this determination, an ordinance that discriminated among mobile advertisers might be challenged not only on First Amendment grounds but as the selective denial of a fundamental right.

Justice Jackson, in a concurring opinion, drew some important distinctions between the Due Process Clause and Equal Protection Clause. He would have imposed a heavy burden on anyone who challenged a law under the Due Process Clause because a successful claim disabled government action on a wholesale basis. A successful equal protection claim, however, merely obligated government to broaden the sweep of its regulation. Justice Jackson viewed the Equal Protection Clause as a key safeguard against arbitrary or unreasonable government action. Such risk, from his perspective, was best managed by a constitutional principle that "impose[d] upon a minority [what] must be imposed generally."

Jackson further warned that "nothing opens the door to arbitrary action so effectively as to allow those officials to pick and choose only a few to whom they will apply legislation and thus to escape the political retribution that might be visited upon them if larger numbers were affected." Whether advertising is displayed on an owner-operated or for-hire basis, the risk to traffic safety is the same. Jackson's sense of a growing trend toward for-hire advertising is what caused him to concur rather than dissent.

How to strike the balance between managing the risk of arbitrary government action and tying its hands has been a primary challenge for the Court in developing appropriate standards of review. As they have developed, and minus a suspect classification or selective deprivation of a fundamental right, pertinent standards of review accommodate the power of interest groups to broker and secure economic advantage through the legislative process. The law unsuccessfully challenged in the *Railway Express Agency* case singled out a particular group for purposes of managing the traffic safety problem. This experience raises the possibility that legislatures can disadvantage discrete groups without concern for political accountability, at least to the extent the group impacted is relatively powerless.

Jackson noted that "claims of denial of equal protection are frequently asserted, [but] they are rarely sustained." This pattern reflects the Court's use of the rational basis of standard review for ordinary social and economic classifications (those that are not suspect or do not deny a fundamental right on a selective basis). Consistent with this orientation, the Court has upheld laws mandating retirement from public employment at a specified age.[15] This deferential mode also was evidenced in *United States Railroad Retirement Board v. Fritz*,[16] when the Court rejected discrimination claims with respect to a benefits plan.

Justice Blackmun has described the Court's efforts to define the exact nature of the equal protection guarantee as "at times . . . almost metaphysical." In a plurality opinion joined by three other justices, in *Logan v. Zimmerman Brush Co.*,[17] Blackmun also maintained that rational basis review is not "toothless." As the plurality put it, a regulatory rationale "must be something more than the exercise of a strained imagination; while the connection between means and ends need not be precise, it, at the least, must have some objective basis." There is some case law that aligns with this premise. The use of rational basis review, to strike down a county tax assessment system[18] and a city ordinance that prohibited a home for the mentally disabled,[19] indicates that the standard is not without potential rigor. Minus a suspect classification or fundamental right, however, the dominant line of equal protection jurisprudence reflects significant deference toward the legislature.

The *Railway Express Agency* Court's allowance of piecemeal legislation highlights two key equal protection concepts: **overinclusiveness** and **underinclusiveness**. The burden of the law prohibiting display advertising on a for-hire basis arguably was underinclusive because it allowed mobile commercial signage that was no less distracting to motorists. The allowance of owner-operated signage arguably constituted a benefit that was overinclusive, insofar as it presented an identical risk to traffic safety. The burden arguably was overinclusive insofar as for-hire advertising was no less distracting than other modes. The benefit arguably was underinclusive to the extent owner-operated signage presented a comparable risk to traffic safety.

C. Racial Classifications

(1) Race and the Nation's Founding

The Constitutional Convention in 1787 represented an effort to reorganize the nation, which had languished under the Articles of Confederation, into a viable economic union. A particularly thorny issue for the delegates was slavery. James Madison, in his Convention notes, observed that "the great division of interests in the

United States . . . did not lie between the large [and] small states; it lay, between the Northern [and] Southern states."[20]

With a viable political and economic union being the Framers' overarching priority, and opponents of slavery being less fervent than its champions, slavery made its way into the new union. This result reflected a principle of formal federal neutrality, which made slavery a matter of self-determination by each state. The Constitution, as originally framed, spoke to slavery in several ways. Proportionate representation in the House of Representatives and factoring of direct taxes, for example, was based on a population count that recognized a slave as three-fifths of a person. Congress was barred from regulating American participation in the international slave trade until 1808. A fugitive slave clause became the basis for federal laws enabling slave owners to recapture runaway slaves without any legal process.

F   A   Q

Q: Was the Constitution as originally framed and ratified a pro-slavery document?

A: The Constitution contained several provisions that spoke to slavery but anticipated that the federal government would be neutral. For practical purposes, this position was difficult to maintain. Congress prohibited American participation in the international slave trade on the first day of the year that it was constitutionally permitted to take such action. The fugitive slave clause, for instance, became the basis for federal legislation that enabled slave owners to recapture runaway slaves without due process. Although the Constitution anticipated federal neutrality, the national government invariably became implicated in the policy aspects of slavery.

Management of the slavery controversy at the Constitutional Convention merely forestalled an ultimate reckoning with the issue. Any expectation that slave and nonslave states could coexist within a single union proved unrealistic, as the consequences of territorial expansion and implications of fugitive slave legislation manifested themselves. Slavery was the pivotal issue in the creation of each new territory and state. Through the first half of the nineteenth century, Congress attempted repeatedly to broker lasting compromises.

None of these efforts achieved a lasting solution. Continuing westward expansion increased, and mutually escalating fears that the other side would gain an upper hand, hardened positions to a point that dialogue became increasingly futile.

The Supreme Court's decisions generally were accommodating and increasingly highlighted the principle of federal neutrality as applied led to pro-slavery outcomes. In *Prigg v. Pennsylvania*,[21] the Court invalidated an anti-kidnapping law on grounds

This portrait of Dred Scott was painted from the only known photograph of him and presented by a group of African American citizens to the Missouri Historical Society in 1882.

it conflicted with federal law allowing slave owners to recapture runaway slaves. This decision had unsettling consequences both for the North and the South. The invalidation of state anti-kidnapping laws sensitized the North to its engagement in slavery. The Court's emphasis on the federal government's exclusive interest in the subject matter, however, signaled to the South the potential for slavery to become a matter of national rather than state resolution.

By the 1850s, the political process had become gridlocked. Against this backdrop, the Supreme Court stepped forward with a decision that was anticipated by many as a final resolution of the slavery controversy. In *Dred Scott v. Sandford*,[22] the Court determined that no person of African descent (slave or otherwise) could be a citizen of the United States or was entitled to rights under the federal constitution. This finding was grounded in the premise that African Americans were "beings of an inferior order . . . and so far inferior, that they had no rights which the white man was bound to respect; and that the negro might justly and lawfully be reduced to slavery." In addition to finding that Congress had no power to regulate slavery in the territories, Chief Justice Roger B. Taney advanced the premise that slave owners' rights were grounded in the Constitution. He thus referenced original constitutional provisions (for example, restrictions on ending American participation in the international slave trade and the fugitive slave clause) as evidence that "the right of property in a slave is distinctly and expressly affirmed in the Constitution."

The *Dred Scott* decision evolved the principle of federal neutrality into a premise that the national constitution enshrined the institution. Although offered as a final resolution of the slavery issue, the decision became another way station toward the union's inevitable breakdown. President Lincoln ignored the ruling and, midway through the Civil War, issued the Emancipation Proclamation. Congress repealed fugitive slave legislation in 1862, and the Thirteenth Amendment[23] formally repudiated the *Dred Scott* decision by prohibiting slavery.

Congress began the process of reconstructing the union by establishing a constitutional bulwark against slavery. The Thirteenth Amendment provides that "[n]either slavery nor involuntary servitude, except as a punishment for a crime whereof the party shall have been duly convicted, shall exist within the United States, or any place subject to its jurisdiction." Former slave states responded to the Thirteenth Amendment with the Black Codes, which established a comprehensive set of race-based burdens on opportunity, residence, travel, assembly, voting, and other activities.

The Civil Rights Act of 1866 extended to "inhabitants of every race . . . the same rights to make and enforce contracts, to sue, be parties, and give evidence, to inherit, purchase, lease, sell, hold and convey real and personal property, and to full and equal benefit of all laws and proceedings for the security of persons and property."[24] The goals of the Civil Rights Act of 1866 were secured further by the Fourteenth Amendment. The Court's first review of the amendment arose in a setting that did not implicate race. The primary focus of the

Sidebar

THE RESPONSE TO *DRED SCOTT*

Reaction to the *Dred Scott* decision was profoundly negative in the North. Defiance was evidenced by a state court ruling that freed two persons convicted in federal court for aiding runaway slaves. In *Ableman v. Booth*, 62 U.S. 506 (1859), Chief Justice Taney stressed the importance of federal immunity to conflicting state policy and urged respect for precedent. Opposition to the *Dred Scott* decision, however, generally was not grounded in premises of racial equality. Racial segregation and discrimination were common aspects of the northern cultural landscape. Even when declaring slaves emancipated, President Lincoln observed that "when you cease to be slaves, you are far removed from being placed on an equality with the white man. . . . I cannot alter it if I could. It is a fact." C. Vann Woodward, *The Burden of Southern History* 81 (1960).

Court's decision in the *Slaughter-House Cases*[25] was on the Privileges and Immunities Clause, which the Court cast in terms that narrowed the significance of federal citizenship. With respect to the Equal Protection Clause, the Court doubted whether its concern ever would extend beyond "negroes." It is so clearly a provision for that race and that emergency, that a strong case would be necessary for its application to any other.

The Court's first racially significant assessment of the Fourteenth Amendment's substantive terms came in *Strauder v. West Virginia*.[26] In this case, the Court overturned a state law excluding African Americans from juries. It described the Fourteenth Amendment as establishing a "right to exemption from unfriendly legislation against them distinctively, as colored — exemption from legal discriminations, implying inferiority in civil society, lessening the security of their enjoyment of the rights which others enjoy, and discriminations which are steps toward reducing them to the condition of a subject race." With respect to the Equal Protection Clause itself, the Court found that it "declar[ed] that the law in the States shall be the same for the black as for the white; that all persons, whether colored or white, shall stand equal before the laws of the States."

The *Strauder* decision represented the first instance of a racially discriminatory law being struck down as unconstitutional. Its potential force was quickly diminished, however, as the Court moved toward an understanding of equal protection that accommodated separation and burdens on the basis of group status. This evolution was previewed by the Court's ruling in the *Civil Rights Cases*,[27] which invalidated the Civil Rights Act of 1875 and its prohibition of discrimination in certain public accommodations. The ruling indicated concern with the potential for a federal "code of municipal law" that regulated private rights. It also reflected a sense that it was time for former slaves to assume "the rank of mere citizen, and cease[ ] to be the special favorite of the laws."

(2) Separate but Equal

The *Civil Rights Cases* decision was a precursor to constitutional doctrine that countenanced official segregation on the basis of race. Jim Crow laws that began to emerge in the late 1880s were designed to separate the races, protect racial integrity, preserve white supremacy, and minimize cross-racial interaction. This system of racial management actually was invented in the North, where legislatures enacted and courts upheld prescriptive racial segregation in education and other settings.[28] In *Plessy v. Ferguson*,[29] the Court referenced this reality in determining that official segregation was a permissible exercise of a state's police power.

The *Plessy* decision concerned a state law mandating "equal but separate accommodations for the white and colored races" on passenger trains. Consistent with the terms of *Strauder v. West Virginia*, the Court asserted that the Fourteenth

Sidebar

THE FOURTEENTH AMENDMENT'S IMPACT

The Fourteenth Amendment on paper represented a significant redistribution of power over civil rights. Early judicial interpretations indicated a reluctance to acknowledge the full sweep of this change. In *United States v. Cruikshank*, 92 U.S. 542 (1876), the Court invalidated a federal law that made interference with a person's civil rights a criminal offense. The enactment was the basis for prosecutions following a racial massacre in Louisiana that culminated a racially grounded political dispute. The decision reflected the Court's sense that the states, notwithstanding the Fourteenth Amendment, retained responsibility for their traditional concerns.

Amendment was intended to establish "the absolute equality of the two races before the law." It further determined, however, that the amendment did not "abolish distinction based upon color, or . . . enforce social, as distinguished from political inequality, or a commingling of the two races upon terms unsatisfactory to either." The Court viewed official segregation as a reasonable exercise of the state's police power because it accounted for a public good. In this regard, it found that the process did not oppress a certain class but rather reflected established customs or traditions.

One challenge for the *Plessy* Court was to reconcile its holding with the understanding in *Strauder* that the Fourteenth Amendment prohibits discrimination that implies inferiority. On this point, the Court observed that official segregation did not imply racial inferiority, and any interpretation to the contrary was "not by reason of anything found in the act, but solely because the colored race chooses to put that construction on it." From the Court's perspective, no racial group could be "constitutionally inferior" to another so long as "civil and political rights are equal." This statement was conditioned by the observation, however, that insofar as "one race is inferior to the other socially, the Constitution of the United States cannot put them on the same plane."

The characterization of official segregation as a social management scheme rather than one that implicated civil or political rights was the descriptive key for bypassing constitutional concern. Justice Harlan, in a dissenting opinion, criticized the Court for denying segregation's true nature. As he saw it, prescriptive separation on the basis of race rested on the premise that blacks were inferior, and he viewed segregation as inconsistent with a Constitution that prohibited any "superior, dominant, ruling class of citizens." Disagreeing with the majority's depiction of segregation as a reasonable exercise of police power, Harlan maintained that "[t]he sure guarantee of the peace and security of each race is the clear, distinct, unconditional recognition by our governments, national and State, of every right that inheres in civil freedom, and of the equality before the law of all citizens of the United States without regard to race."

Sidebar

CONTRASTING APPROACHES TO REVIEW

The Court's deference toward the legislative process with respect to segregation contrasted with its vigorous review of laws that limited economic liberty. One year after its decision in *Plessy v. Ferguson*, the Court in *Allgeyer v. Louisiana*, 165 U.S. 757, 592-593 (1897), construed the Due Process Clause as a guarantee that a person may use "all his faculties . . . [and is] free to use them in all lawful ways." Although race was the primary driver of the Fourteenth Amendment, the Court vitalized the provision in a manner that emphasized nonracial concerns.

Harlan predicted that the *Plessy* decision ultimately would prove to be "as pernicious as the decision made . . . in the *Dred Scott* case." Unlike the *Dred Scott* decision, which civil war and reconstruction undid in a decade, the *Plessy* legacy endured through the middle of the twentieth century. During this time, *prescriptive segregation* became a dominant system of racial management, particularly in the South where it defined opportunity and advantage comprehensively on the basis of group status. Like slavery, this system of racial management also drove policy and practice where systems collided at the national level. A primary example was the segregation of the military through the mid-twentieth century.

The **separate but equal doctrine** presented itself in theory on the basis of symmetry and neutrality, insofar as it accounted for racial tradition but commanded equality of condition. In actual practice, and at least through the mid-1930s, separation was a priority and equality was a secondary and even dispensable consideration. In *Cumming v. Richmond County Board of Education*,[30] the Court upheld the closure of an African American high school. The school board justified its decision on grounds that financial resources were limited. The Court upheld the board's action, despite the racially unequal outcome, on grounds that shutting down the all-white school would burden one set of students without benefiting the other.

Consistent with this outcome, public spending on education in the South was characterized by significant disparities. In 1915, South Carolina funding of white schools was ten times greater than it was for schools attended by African Americans. By 1954, when funding was being increased in an effort to stave off desegregation, southern states expended an average of $165 per white student and $115 per African American student.

Constitutional challenges to segregation through the early decades of the twentieth century generally made no headway. Standards of review were deferential toward the legislature. Even when a constitutional wrong might be identified, the Court was reluctant to provide relief.

Example: In *Giles v. Harris*,[31] a case concerning the categorical deprivation of the right to vote, the Court concluded that it would be "pointless" to provide relief against the state. Correction of such a "great political wrong," the Court observed, must come from "the legislative and political department of the government of the United States." The emptiness of this pronouncement was manifested by the racial animus evidenced by these "departments." Although the *Giles* case raised a Fifteenth Amendment claim, the analysis is relevant to the Fourteenth Amendment insofar as it evidenced a sense of institutional powerlessness to "to deal with the people of the State in a body."

The Court, in *Berea College v. Kentucky*,[32] extended the segregation principle into a mandate that prohibited voluntary integration in higher education. In *McCabe v. Atchison, Topeka & Santa Fe Railway Co.*,[33] the Court determined that railroads must provide separate accommodations regardless of demand or usage. The Court, in *Buchanan v. Warley*,[34] struck down a city ordinance that specified the racial composition of blocks in residential neighborhoods. The law was invalidated not on grounds that segregation was unconstitutional but because it interfered with property rights in violation of due process of law.

A primary incident of formal segregation was a detailed system of racial management that governed relationships and interaction on the basis of group status.

Segregation in public schools was revisited in *Gong Lum v. Rice*,[35] when a student of Chinese descent challenged her placement in a "colored" school. The Court found no basis for differentiating the outcome "where the issue is between white peoples and the peoples of the yellow race." A key factor in the eventual dismantling of official segregation was the National Association for the Advancement of Colored People's (NAACP) emergence as a litigation force. The NAACP, in the 1930s, launched a desegregation strategy that successfully attacked the profound inequalities in education. Its early successes included a ruling, in *Missouri ex rel. Gaines v. Canada*,[36] that a state must create a racially separate law school for nonwhites or admit them to its only public law school.

The potential for wholesale doctrinal change was signaled by the Court's observation, in *United States v. Carolene Products Co.*, that "prejudice against discrete and insular minorities may be a special condition, which tends seriously to curtail the operation of th[e] political processes ordinarily relied upon to protect minorities, and which may call for a correspondingly more searching inquiry."[37] In the *Carolene Products Co.* decision, the Court demonstrated its readiness to scrutinize more closely laws that imposed disadvantages on groups excluded from the political process. The Court followed through with a more rigorous standard of review in *Korematsu v. United States.*[38] The *Korematsu* case concerned the federal government's relocation of persons of Japanese descent from the West Coast during World War II. Although the Court deferred to the action on national security grounds, the Court established the basis for taking a harder look at the constitutionality of racial classifications. As the Court put it, "all legal restrictions which curtail the civil rights of a single racial group are immediately suspect [and] courts must subject them to the most rigid scrutiny."

Sidebar

THE ATTACK ON "SEPARATE BUT EQUAL"

Beginning in the 1930s, public education became the focal point for more rigorous assessment of the separate but equal doctrine. The eventual defeat of segregation is traceable to the litigation strategy of the National Association for the Advancement of Colored People (NAACP). The NAACP initially concentrated on graduate and professional schools, pursuant to the sense that pushing for desegregation in those areas would generate less resistance than seeking change in the public and secondary education context. A consequent focus on manifest inequalities at this level, such as the total absence of professional education for African Americans in some states, resulted in a series of successes. States operating single-race graduate and professional schools typically were given the choice of establishing similar institutions for nonwhites or allowing nonwhites to matriculate at the established institutions and thus desegregating the institutions. *E.g., Missouri ex rel. Gaines v. Canada*, 305 U.S. 337 (1938); *Pearson v. Murray*, 182 A. 590 (Md. 1936).

The *Korematsu* decision evolved standards of review beyond the reasonableness criterion of *Plessy* to the modern model of strict scrutiny. From the *Korematsu* ruling to the invalidation of segregated public education in *Brown v. Board of Education*,[39] funding of minority schools in segregated systems increased. This investment represented an effort to rescue segregation from the growing challenge of the NAACP's desegregation strategy. By midcentury, the Court had expanded its focus beyond financing to factors such as institutional prestige, faculty qualifications, extracurricular activities, alumni influence, facilities, and linkage to professional opportunities. Even when equality of funding could be demonstrated, the Court took note of inequality with respect to these types of intangibles. In *Sweatt v. Painter*,[40] the Court was convinced that segregated legal education would remain unequal even if tangible differences were equalized. It thus ordered desegregation of the University of Texas School of Law. It reached a similar result, in *McLaurin v. Oklahoma State Regents for Higher Education*,[41] when it held that restrictions on an African American student's classroom, library, and cafeteria seating options were impermissible.

(3) Desegregation

The *Sweatt* and *McLaurin* decisions effectively dismantled segregation at the specific institutions where it was challenged. Key to the comprehensive defeat of segregation was a change in the Supreme Court's leadership and a reassessment of the Fourteenth Amendment's history. When *Brown v. Board of Education* first was argued in 1952, the Court deferred a decision pending presentations by both sides on what the amendment's history indicated. With the emergence of Earl Warren as the successor to Chief Justice Vinson, the Court set a dramatic new course reflected in its conclusion that racial segregation in public education inherently was unequal.

As the NAACP's record of success grew, states gave more attention to the equalization aspect of the separate but equal doctrine. Increases in funding of minority schools was a hallmark of segregation's final years. Last-minute efforts to shore up the separate but equal doctrine failed, however, when the Court revisited *Brown* and heard rearguments. Under the leadership of Chief Justice Vinson, the Court had asked lawyers for both sides to consult history and focus their arguments the following term on what the Fourteenth Amendment's framers intended. Much relevant history actually supported segregation. The same Congress that framed the Fourteenth Amendment provided for segregation of District of Columbia schools. The amendment also was ratified by states that maintained segregated public schools. After hearing both sides, however, the Court concluded that original intent was indeterminate.

The *Brown* litigation consisted of four cases from Delaware, Kansas, South Carolina, and Virginia. Each represented the final phase of the NAACP's strategy, which had evolved beyond challenging segregation on equalization grounds to contesting it as conceptually deficient. Notwithstanding historical indications that segregation was consistent with the framers' and ratifiers' view of the Fourteenth Amendment, the Court refused "to turn the clock back to 1868 when the Amendment was adopted, or even to 1896 when *Plessy v. Ferguson* was adopted."

In this regard, it noted that public education had become such a significant function of local government and so key to personal development and success that it must be assessed from a contemporary perspective. Referencing psychological data, the Court found that segregation has "a detrimental effect upon the colored children . . . [and] is usually interpreted as denoting the inferiority of the negro group." Finding "that in the field of public education, the doctrine of 'separate but equal' has no place," the Court concluded that "[s]eparate educational facilities are inherently unequal." Because the equal protection guarantee, by its terms, does not apply to the federal government, the Court turned to the Fifth Amendment's Due Process Clause as the basis for declaring segregated schools unconstitutional in the District of Columbia. In *Bolling v. Sharpe*,[42] the Court effectively glossed the equal protection guarantee onto the Due Process Clause. Noting that both provisions emanate from the "American ideal of fairness," it characterized the equal protection guarantee as "a more explicit safeguard of prohibited unfairness" that essentially was incorporated into the Due Process Clause. The Court also concluded that school segregation had no reasonable relationship to a legitimate government objective and thus constituted an arbitrary deprivation of liberty under the Due Process Clause.

Affirm. Action - page 240 (handwritten)

Thurgood Marshall, a chief architect of the NAACP strategy to defeat official segregation, is pictured on the Supreme Court steps with two other lawyers (James M. Nabrit and George E. C. Hayes) who played key roles in the litigation of *Brown v. Board of Education.*

Knowing that it was imposing a mandate of profound change on states where segregation was deeply rooted, and to minimize the potential for pushback, the Court deferred the matter of remedies until the next term and invited input from both sides. In *Brown v. Board of Education II*,[43] it announced that racial segregation in public schools must be eliminated with "all deliberate speed." This standard reflected an effort to secure local buy-in. Toward this end, the Court charged federal district courts with the responsibility of determining whether compliance effort were in good faith. The Court anticipated that the lower courts would use their traditional equitable powers to fashion relief. It counted on "a prompt and reasonable start toward full compliance" and put the burden on the states to demonstrate the need for addition time to dismantle segregated schools.

The "all deliberate speed" standard was framed pursuant to input that the Court had solicited from the parties and those states that would be most impacted by the desegregation mandate. Participation in the construction of remedial terms, however, did not defuse resistance to their effective implementation. Lower courts, which the Court had designated as the primary authors of relief, generally interpreted *Brown* in undemanding ways. Typifying immediate reaction to the desegregation mandate was the South Carolina district court's response on remand. In *Briggs v. Elliott*, the district court in a per curiam opinion concluded that "[t]he Constitution [does] not require integration. It merely forbids discrimination. It does not forbid such segregation as occurs as the result of voluntary action. It merely forbids the use of governmental power to enforce segregation."[44] As the South Carolina court saw it, the state only had to abandon prescriptive segregation (rather than achieve racially unitary schools) to satisfy the *Brown* mandate. Notwithstanding its hope that the desegregation process would be managed effectively by the lower courts, the Supreme Court's engagement in the process was prolonged. Especially through the 1960s, the Court repeatedly was called on to reaffirm the point that desegregation required affirmative and effective action to eliminate the reality and legacy of racial segregation.

Early desegregation plans often were shams, subterfuges, or inactions that effectively maintained segregation as a function of custom rather than official dictate. The first major test of the *Brown* principle arose in *Cooper v. Aaron*,[45] when the state resisted desegregation of a high school in Little Rock, Arkansas. Heightening the sense of stakes and conflict was the governor's dispatch of the National Guard to prevent African American students from entering the city's all-white high school. President Eisenhower responded by sending federal troops to enforce desegregation. These events, and the intensity of the public reaction, caused the school board to seek a delay in the implementation of its plan.

The Court unanimously rejected the school board's request. Citing to *Marbury v. Madison*, the Court reaffirmed its power "to say what the law is" and characterized the desegregation mandate as binding on the states. A key message of this decision was that the desegregation process could not be slowed by violence and disorder, and law and order was not "to be preserved by depriving the Negro children of their constitutional rights."

Despite *Cooper v. Aaron*'s strong message, early desegregation plans typically were calibrated to have minimal impact. The first decade of the *Brown* era was characterized by limited progress toward desegregation. Congressional enactment of the Civil Rights Act of 1964 harnessed the political process to what until then was a largely judicial enterprise. Authorization

Sidebar

EFFORTS TO DELAY AND EVADE

Political responses to the desegregation mandate in numerous instances attempted to undermine or negate it. The Arkansas legislature, for instance, denounced the desegregation decision as unconstitutional. Some states resorted to preemptive tactics in an effort to deter desegregation lawsuits. As the primary driver of desegregation litigation, the NAACP was targeted by state laws designed to cripple its influence. The State of Alabama passed a law requiring the NAACP to disclose its membership list. *NAACP ex. rel. Alabama v. Patterson*, 357 U.S. 449 (1958). The State of Virginia applied an anti-solicitation rule to the NAACP, so that any lawyer bringing a desegregation lawsuit assumed the risk of disbarment. *NAACP v. Button*, 371 U.S. 415 (1963). Although the Court ruled against the states in both of these cases, the enactments reflected the generally hostile climate in which the desegregation mandate operated.

of the attorney general to bring desegregation actions, and the conditioning of federal funding on compliance with *Brown*, were particularly instrumental in driving progress. Responding to the record of underachievement that characterized the first decade of *Brown*, the Court eventually announced that "[t]he time for mere 'deliberate speed' has run out."[46] It thus retooled the standard for compliance from "all deliberate speed" to a demand that school boards come forward with a desegregation "plan that promises realistically to work, and promises realistically to work *now*." The "affirmative duty" of segregated schools was "to take whatever steps might be necessary to convert to a unitary system in which racial discrimination would be eliminated root and branch."

F   A   Q

Q: What is a racially unitary school?

A: Racially unitary status is achieved when all vestiges of racial discrimination have been eliminated. Attainment of this condition, pursuant to *Green v. County School Board of New Kent County, Virginia*, was the basis for achieving compliance with the desegregation mandate.

As the 1970s unfolded, the Court increasingly narrowed the boundaries of the desegregation mandate. In *Swann v. Charlotte-Mecklenburg Board of Education*,[47] the Court revisited the federal judiciary's role in the desegregation process. Relying on its traditional equitable powers, the Court observed that its authority was broad enough to order pupil assignments on the basis of race. It noted in particular that busing of students, which had become a central point of controversy, was permissible so long as "time or distance of travel is [not] so great as to either risk the health of the children or significantly impinge on the educational process." With respect to faculty assignments, the Court approved fixed ratios as a starting point for achieving racial balance.

The *Swann* decision defined the federal judiciary's remedial power in broad terms, and the *Swann* Court made it clear that the duty to desegregate was not limitless or endless. It observed that once a dual school system had been dismantled, minus evidence of official action causing resegregation, the desegregation duties were complete. Viewed in the context of subsequent case law, the *Swann* ruling became the wellspring for a series of principles that narrowed the boundaries of the desegregation mandate.

The first of these limiting principles, set forth in *Keyes v. School District No. 1*,[48] conditioned desegregation on proof of segregative intent. The distinction between *de jure segregation* and *de facto segregation* was particularly significant as challenges to school segregation spread to northern and western cities. In these environments, desegregation typically was a function of community demographics rather than legal prescription.

Critics have argued that the distinction between de jure and de facto segregation is artificial. In this regard, they reference government's role in enforcing restrictive racial covenants, locating public housing, and red-lining neighborhoods through federal home loan policies.

Q: What is de jure segregation, and why is it significant?

A: De jure segregation exists when government purposefully or intentionally separates on the basis of race. It is this factor of official motive that makes segregation constitutionally actionable.

A second significant boundary of the desegregation mandate was etched in *Milliken v. Bradley*,[49] which reversed a lower court decision ordering the interdistrict busing of students. At issue was the incorporation of suburban school districts into a plan designed to desegregate Detroit public schools. The record established that the school board had induced segregation by policies for optional attendance zones, transportation of students, and school siting. "White flight" had resulted in a predominately African American student population to the point that meaningful integration was impossible without suburban participation in the remediation process. After rejecting the trial court's findings that the state had played a significant role in purposely segregating the city's schools, the Court stated that the scope of the remedy could not exceed the ambit of the constitutional violation. Interdistrict remedies thus could be used only if the intentional actions of one district contributed significantly to segregation in the other district. Given the demographic realities of urban communities and relatively short history of suburbs, and consequent unlikelihood of cross-district manipulation or impact, the desegregation in many settings became characterized by an impact that was more formal than functional. The Court, in *Milliken v. Bradley II*,[50] reaffirmed its finding of a constitutional violation. The remedy it upheld for intentional segregation was not a plan for racial diversification or balance, which had been foreclosed by its earlier decision, but state funding of compensatory and remedial education programs.

In *Pasadena City Board of Education v. Spangler*,[51] the Court circled back to the limiting premise introduced in *Swann*. It thus restated that the duty to desegregate ended once racially unitary status was achieved. Any further duty to desegregate hinged on proof of official intent to segregate. Racial disparities owing to what the Court described as "quite normal pattern[s] of human migration" thus did not implicate the Constitution.

Q: What are the key principles that determine whether there is a duty to desegregate?

A: The duty to desegregate is conditioned on a finding of de jure segregation, the scope of the remedy may not exceed the scope of the violation, and there is no duty to desegregate if resegregation is not linked to an official intent to segregate.

Justice Marshall, who had been a primary architect of the challenge to segregation, became an increasingly strident critic of the Court's direction. Dissenting from the invalidation of cross-district busing in *Milliken v. Bradley*, he maintained that the Court provided "no remedy at all ... guaranteeing that Negro children ... will receive the same separate and inherently unequal education in the future as they have been unconstitutionally afforded in the past."[52] Marshall found the Court's accommodation of "white flight" especially objectionable. Insofar as states had created segregated school systems, he maintained that they were "responsible for the fact that many whites will react to the dismantling of that segregated system by attempting to flee to the suburbs."

The trilogy of limiting principles enunciated in *Keyes, Milliken,* and *Spangler* previewed growing reservations by some justices about the utility of desegregation and the ability of courts to fashion meaningful and lasting change. Justice Powell, in *Columbus Board of Education v. Penick*, observed that, "in city after city," desegregation merely was a prelude to "resegregation, stimulated by resentment against judicial coercion."[53] He also adverted to "familiar segregated housing patterns ... caused by social, economic, and demographic forces for which no school board is responsible." Justice Rehnquist noted that "[e]ven if the Constitution required it, and it were possible for federal courts to do it, no equitable decree can fashion an 'Emerald City' where all races, ethnic groups, and persons of various income levels live side by side."[54]

By the 1990s, case law began to stress an interest in disengaging the federal courts from the desegregation process and reverting control to local school officials. The terms of compliance, which had been framed as eliminating the vestiges of segregation "root and branch," were relaxed and retooled in *Dowell v. Oklahoma City Board of Education*. The Court found that, insofar as a school board had complied with a desegregation order in good faith, it should be terminated when vestiges of past discrimination had been eliminated "to the extent practicable."[55] Although courts retained wide-ranging authority to remedy segregation, the *Dowell* Court stressed that the long-term goal is to restore control over schools to local authorities.

F   A   Q

Q: How does the standard in *Dowell* modify desegregation duties from what were established in the 1960s?

A: The Court, in *Green v. County School Board of New Kent County, Virginia*, announced that the *vestiges of racial discrimination* must be eliminated "*root and branch.*" In *Dowell*, this requirement was downsized so that these vestiges must be undone "to the extent practicable."

In *Freeman v. Pitts*,[56] the Court determined that control can be reverted to local authorities on an incremental basis. This case concerned a school system in Georgia that had been placed under the supervision and control of a federal court. The district court eventually found that the school system had achieved unitary status in some but not all respects. The Court determined that withdrawal of judicial supervision and control may be on an incremental or partial basis. Factors relevant to termination include whether full compliance has been achieved, judicial control is necessary to achieve compliance, and the school system has demonstrated good-faith efforts to comply. It noted that a transition phase, which provides for relinquishing responsibility gradually, may provide an orderly means for returning school districts to the control of local authorities.

The Court, in *Missouri v. Jenkins*,[57] applied the standards for judicial withdrawal developed in *Freeman v. Pitts*. At issue was a court order requiring the state to fund magnet programs and teacher salary increases in Kansas City schools. These enhancements were designed to make the city schools more attractive to white suburban students. The order was based on student achievement levels that were below national norms. The Court determined that these scores were irrelevant to whether the school system had achieved unitary status, and the question of judicial control should be settled pursuant to the standards set forth in *Freeman*. The Court determined that the lower court had exceeded its authority by adopting an interdistrict remedy for an intradistrict violation.

As demographic trends continued to erode many of the diversity gains incident to desegregation, and consistent with a sense that student diversity has inherent value, some school systems adopted plans to achieve or maintain racially balanced student bodies. The Court, in *Parents Involved in Community Schools v. Seattle School District No. 1*,[58] assessed two of these plans (in Seattle and Louisville respectively). The result was a decision that narrowly circumscribed the use of race as a factor in determining where students attend school. The case split the Court into two factions (four justices each), one that advocated absolute color-blindness and the second that viewed this position as compromising the "promise" of *Brown*.

Noting that racial classifications are subject to "strict scrutiny," the Court observed that government is required to show that race-based distributions of burdens or benefits are narrowly tailored to achieve a compelling government interest. It acknowledged that remedying the effects of past intentional discrimination is a compelling interest, but found no evidence of wrongdoing in these cases. In one instance, the city never had been segregated by law or subject to a desegregation order. The other school district had been subject to a desegregation decree, but it had been dissolved.

The Court distinguished the prohibition of race in primary and secondary school from higher education, where it may be a nonexclusive factor in the admission process. Minus any evidence that school officials districts had considered other methods to attain their goals, the Court determined that they had failed to meet the narrow tailoring requirement of "serious, good faith consideration of workable race-neutral alternatives."

The *Parents Involved in Community Schools* decision in significant part mirrors the Court's affirmative action jurisprudence discussed later in this chapter. Chief Justice Roberts, joined by Justices Scalia, Thomas, and Alito, advocated the principle of comprehensive color-blindness. In his concurring opinion, Justice Kennedy noted that diversity is a compelling educational goal that a school district may account for—provided no individual is burdened or rewarded because of race. Coupled with the position of the four dissenters, Kennedy's argument left open the possibility that race may be factored to some extent.

Justice Breyer, in a lengthy dissenting opinion joined by Justices Stevens, Souter, and Ginsburg, faulted the Court for departing from its legacy of requiring and encouraging efforts to achieve racially integrated education. Breyer noted that the Court traditionally had embraced the proposition that communities could adopt desegregation plans even when not required to do so. He criticized the plurality for, in his view, distorting precedent, misapplying principles, disregarding context, and creating obstacles that would impede efforts to address growing resegregation of public schools.

The rulings did not preclude the use of income and other social factors to achieve a diverse student-body composition. Nor did they address segregation or integration maintenance plans grounded in state constitutions.

(4) The Discriminatory Purpose Requirement

By the 1970s, the type of state-prescribed segregation that the Court had condemned in *Brown v. Board of Education* "largely had been eliminated."[59] Case law quickly extended the desegregation principle to other public venues, such as parks and beaches. The Equal Protection Clause also operated against laws that, although not overtly differentiating on the basis of race, were grounded in racist ideology.

Example: In *McLaughlin v. Florida*,[60] the Court struck down a law that criminalized interracial cohabitation by persons of opposite sexes. This decision overturned a ruling, in *Pace v. Alabama*,[61] prohibiting cross-racial adultery or fornication.

The Court's invalidation of a law prohibiting interracial marriage, in *Loving v. Virginia*,[62] repudiated the notion that restrictions on all racial groups for racial purposes could survive constitutional challenge. Anti-miscegenation laws, even if racially neutral on their face, reflected the value system underlying racial discrimination. The Court in *Loving* not only found that the law constituted invidious racial discrimination, but it also determined that the enactment abridged the "freedom to marry" and thus constituted a due process violation.

The dismantling of formal racial classifications did not account for all sources of racial disadvantage. A residual issue, given the nation's legacy of racial discrimination, was whether an equal protection claim could be established on the basis of disparate effect alone. The Court, in *Keyes v. School District No. 1*, had indicated that official purpose to segregate was a prerequisite for establishing a constitutional violation. In *Washington v.* Davis,[63] the Court determined that an equal protection violation hinged on proof of **discriminatory purpose**.

This case concerned a test used to screen applicants for positions with the Washington, D.C., police department. White candidates performed significantly better on the examination than African American candidates. Despite the disparity, the Court determined that statistical evidence by itself did not establish a prima facie case. Minus proof of a discriminatory purpose, the Court was concerned that otherwise racially neutral laws might be susceptible to constitutional challenge. In this regard, the Court noted the risk to "a whole range of tax, welfare, public service, regulatory, and licensing statutes that may be more burdensome to the poor and to the average black than to the more affluent white."

The Court, in *Arlington Heights v. Metropolitan Housing Development Corp.*,[64] identified some circumstantial factors that might support a finding of discriminatory intent. The case concerned a zoning ordinance that effectively precluded development of racially integrated and low-income housing. In finding no constitutional violation, the Court reaffirmed that an equal protection claim cannot stand minus proof of discriminatory purpose. Relevant circumstantial evidence, for purposes of showing discriminatory intent, include statistical disparities, patterns or effects that are inexplicable except on grounds of race, legislative history, and departures from normal procedures.

The Court, in *McCleskey v. Kemp*,[65] upheld Georgia's capital punishment law despite a showing of racially disparate impact. The backdrop for the case included the state's legacy of a dual system of criminal justice. In a dissenting opinion, Justice Brennan pointed out that defense lawyers invariably (and pursuant to their ethical obligations) would factor race into the advice they gave clients with respect to accepting or rejecting a plea agreement. The Court was unmoved by statistical disparities that, in its words, "appear[ ] to correlate to race."

In the jury selection process, as the Court determined in *Batson v. Kentucky*,[66] discriminatory purpose is established on a prima facie basis when the defendant shows peremptory challenges were used to exclude persons on the basis of race. Irregularly shaped voting districts may be the basis for inferring racial discrimination. In *Shaw v. Reno*,[67] the Court found that an oddly configured congressional district could be understood only as a function of racial motivation. Although the lower court discerned no constitutional violation on remand, the Court in *Shaw v. Hunt*[68] concluded that the plan was not tailored narrowly enough to achieve the compelling interest in remedying past discrimination.

Motive-based inquiry in the equal protection context has elicited criticism to the effect that intent is too difficult to prove when not manifest on the face of the law. The challenge of proving intent pursuant to circumstantial indications was perceived as so great in the First Amendment context that the Court dispensed with it. In *United States v. O'Brien*,[69] the Court observed that legislative motive is an elusive factor. It also observed that, at least for First Amendment purposes, "the stakes are sufficiently high for us to eschew guesswork."

(5) Affirmative Action

Affirmative action is a term that, in the equal protection context, characterizes a formal system of managing opportunity on the basis of group status or experience. Processes for distributing opportunity on the basis of race relate back to the nation's founding. Slavery laws in the South and official discrimination and segregation in the North prior to the Civil War exemplified the use of government power to secure group advantage. Official segregation through the middle of the twentieth century perpetuated this regimen. The desegregation process altered the traditional priorities of racial management. It also established a model of remediation and diversification that was transported to contexts such as higher education, employment, and public contracting. As they evolved, these applications have been challenged on grounds they violate the Equal Protection Clause. A key bottom line of affirmative action case law is that all racial classifications are suspect and will be strictly scrutinized regardless of their purpose.

(a) Remedial Classifications

Early affirmative action cases typically concerned racial preferences that were intended to compensate for generalized past discrimination. In *Regents of the University of California v. Bakke*,[70] the Court reviewed a public university's medical school admissions program that set aside 16 of 100 seats for minority applicants. Four justices refused to address the constitutional issue but found a violation of Title VI of the Civil Rights Act of 1964. Four other justices determined that the program violated neither Title VI nor the equal protection guarantee. Justice Powell found that the program as structured violated the equal protection guarantee and Title VI. He observed, however, that race could be a factor in the admission process provided it was not an exclusive consideration.

F A Q

Q: In *Bakke*, why did only five justices reach the equal protection issue?

A: There is an established principle that the Court does not reach a constitutional claim if it can be resolved on statutory grounds. The four justices who found a Title VI violation resolved the controversy on a statutory basis and did not assess the merits of the equal protection claim.

Justice Powell's opinion introduced principles that, although not immediately embraced by a majority, influenced the eventual coursing of affirmative action decisions. Key points that ultimately captured majority support were that racial preferences should be strictly scrutinized and could not be justified on the basis of societal discrimination. The university identified four key points in support of its preferential admissions policy, which included (1) ensuring that the school enrolled a minimum number of minority students, (2) eliminating discrimination, (3) improving health care in disadvantaged communities, and (4) maintaining a diverse student body.

Powell asserted that an admission process with fixed racial goals was facially invalid. Although acknowledging that remedying past discrimination represented a valid interest, he maintained that such action required specific legislative or judicial findings of wrongdoing by the institution itself. He viewed the goal of improved health care in disadvantaged

Sidebar

DEFUNIS

When first presented with the issue of racially preferential admissions, the Court declined the opportunity to review it. In *DeFunis v. Odegaard*, 416 U.S. 312 (1974), it dismissed as moot a claim that the University of Washington School of Law's minority set-aside program was unconstitutional.

Powll
diversity
interest

communities as a function of misplaced assumptions with respect to the career aspirations of minority graduates. The one compelling interest he identified was diversification of the student body. In this regard, he noted that "students with a particular background—whether it be ethnic, geographic, culturally advantaged or disadvantaged—may bring to a professional school of medicine experiences, out-looks, and ideas that enrich training of its student body and better equip its graduates to render with understanding their vital service to humanity."

Justice Brennan, joined by three other justices, advocated an **intermediate standard of review** that differentiated the law's good intentions from traditionally invidious racial classifications. His proposed standard of review reflected the sense that white persons historically had not been excluded from or underrepresented in political processes, so their interests were unlikely to be overlooked. Justice Blackmun, also dissenting, reasoned that "to get beyond racism, we must first take account of race." He argued that affirmative action policies would not be required over the long run and projected that they could be phased out "within a decade at the most."

A decade later, affirmative action continued to operate in a variety of settings, and the Court's decisions remained fragmented in their reasoning and mixed in their results. In *Fullilove v. Klutznick*,[71] the Court upheld a federal set-aside program for minority contractors in public works projects. In an opinion authored by Chief Justice Burger, a three-justice plurality referenced Congress's power to enforce the Fourteenth Amendment as a key consideration.

The Court moved closer to a majority position on affirmative action in *Wygant v. Jackson Board of Education.*[72] This case concerned a collectively bargained layoff plan that protected recently hired minorities in the event of job cutbacks. Writing for a four-justice plurality, Justice Powell maintained that societal discrimination by itself was "too amorphous a basis for imposing a racially classified remedy." The plurality identified strict scrutiny as the appropriate standard of review.

In *United States v. Paradise*,[73] the Court ordered a race-conscious response to an identifiable instance of discrimination. At issue was a court order setting aside 50 percent of promotions to the rank of corporal for qualified African American state troopers in Alabama. Justice Brennan, in a plurality opinion, expressed the sense that the order would survive even strict scrutiny.

A majority position on affirmative action finally coalesced in *Richmond v. J. A. Croson Co.*[74] when the Court embraced strict scrutiny. At issue in *Croson* was a municipal government's set-aside of 30 percent of construction contracts for minority business enterprises. The program paralleled the same federal set-aside plan that the Court had upheld in *Fullilove v. Klutznick*. It was grounded in congressional findings of nationwide discrimination in the construction indus-try and a local study showing that African Americans, who constituted 50 percent of the city's population, received less than 1 percent of municipal building contracts.

Justice O'Connor, writing for a four-justice plurality, asserted that racial clas-sifications regardless of their nature should be strictly scrutinized. In her view, remedial classifications presented risks that included stigmatic harm, reinforce-ment of stereotypes, and perpetuation of maintenance of race as a factor that "will always be relevant in American life." Without "searching inquiry," O'Connor maintained there was no way to determine if a classification was grounded in a benign purpose or impermissible prejudice or stereotype. The value of strict scrutiny, from her perspective, was as a tool to "smoke out" illegitimate uses of race. It also enabled courts to assess whether regulatory methods closely fit regulatory objectives.

F   A   Q

Q: Is there a difference between the strict scrutiny that the Court used to review and strike down segregation and the strict scrutiny it employs for purposes of assessing affirmative action?

A: Strict scrutiny, as the Court used it in the desegregation cases, has been described as "strict in theory, but fatal in fact." This characterization is consistent with the Court's record of consistently striking down laws that officially segregated on the basis of race. Although concluding that racial classifications should be strictly scrutinized regardless of whom they burden or benefit, the Court has determined that there are instances in which affirmative action serves a compelling government interest. Instances in which traditional racial classifications could have a reasonable basis, much less a compelling justification, are difficult to imagine. One such instance was suggested by Justice Stewart, who, in *Lee v. Washington*, 390 U.S. 333 (1968), indicated that segregation might be justified as a means of managing racial violence in a prison.

The O'Connor plurality's determination that the set-aside policy violated the Equal Protection Clause was echoed in even stronger terms by Justice Scalia, who provided the fifth vote in support of a strict scrutiny standard of review. Justice Scalia, in his concurring opinion, proposed a more rigorous model of strict scrutiny. From his perspective, race could be taken into account only "when necessary to eliminate the[ ] maintenance of a system of unlawful racial classification."

In a dissenting opinion joined by Justices Brennan and Blackmun, Justice Marshall characterized the decision as "a deliberate and giant step backward." Referencing congressional and local studies on which the program was based, he maintained that the evidence was "a far cry from the reliance on the generalized 'societal discrimination' which the majority decries." Marshall advocated a standard of review that focused on whether government's objectives were substantially related to remedying the effects of past discrimination and narrowly tailored toward this purpose. This model reflected his sense that analytical criteria should hinge on whether a classification was designed to burden or benefit traditionally disadvantaged minorities.

F   A   Q

Q: What are the key differences between a *strict scrutiny* and an *intermediate standard* of review?

A: Strict scrutiny assesses whether the government regulatory interest is "compelling" and the regulatory means are "narrowly tailored" toward the regulatory objective. An intermediate standard of review considers whether the regulatory interest is "important" and the regulatory means are "substantially related" to the regulatory objective. Both standards denote modalities of review that are more rigorous than the highly deferential rational basis test, which is used when the challenged government action does not implicate a constitutional interest. Although their operative terminology is less than precise, strict and intermediate standards of review imply a differentiation with respect to their level of intensity. It thus follows that laws are at a higher constitutional risk when reviewed pursuant to a strict or intermediate standard of review rather than a rational basis test. The risk is even greater when the review is based on strict rather than intermediate scrutiny.

The *Croson* decision left open the question of whether, consistent with the outcome in *Fullilove v. Klutznick* and in deference to Congress's enforcement power under the Fourteenth Amendment, a different standard might govern federal affirmative action programs. In *Metro Broadcasting, Inc. v. Federal Communications Commission*,[75] the Court employed an intermediate standard of review for purposes of evaluating racial preferences in the broadcast licensing process.

F   A   Q

Q: What was the rationale for employing different constitutional standards in reviewing federal and state governments with respect to affirmative action policies?

A: The primary rationale for greater deference to Congress was that the Constitution assigned it specific powers to enact legislation. Particularly relevant are its enumerated powers to enforce the reconstruction amendments, the Necessary and Proper Clause, and its authority to regulate commerce among the several states. The Court unequivocally abandoned this basis for distinction in *Adarand Constructors, Inc. v. Pena.*

Five years later, in *Adarand Constructors, Inc. v. Pena*,[76] the Court eliminated the dual standard and concluded that federal affirmative action programs should be reviewed pursuant to the same strict scrutiny criteria applied to state programs. At issue in this case was a bonus plan for contractors who subcontracted with socially and economically disadvantaged persons. Consistent with the rule set forth in *Croson*, government must demonstrate a compelling reason for the program, which must be tailored narrowly to achieve its purpose. The relevant governmental unit also must identify some instance of past racial discrimination, for which it is responsible, as a basis for taking race-conscious remedial action.

(b) Diversity as a Compelling Interest

Justice Powell, in his stand-alone opinion in *Regents of the University of California v. Bakke,* endorsed the use of race as a nonexclusive factor in a university medical school's admission process. In *Grutter v. Bollinger,*[77] a majority embraced the premise that a diverse student body constitutes a compelling interest. At issue in *Grutter* was the University of Michigan Law School's admission policy, which was structured to ensure a "critical mass" of students from designated historically disadvantaged groups (African Americans, Hispanics, and Native Americans). **Diversity** was not defined exclusively in racial and ethnic terms but was identified as a value that enriched the educational experience. This interest extends beyond the classroom experience insofar as it facilitates a student's readiness for an increasingly multicultural life experience. The critical mass factor was important, from the school's perspective, because it improved minority student engagement. Although critical mass did

not translate into a specific numeric, the admission process consciously took race into account. If it did not, and admission decisions were based solely on traditional academic quality indicators (GPAs and LSAT scores), substantial minority enrollment could not be achieved.

The Court determined that, at least in the context of higher education, student body diversity was a compelling state interest. It agreed that the benefits of diversity are substantial and include "cross-racial understanding" and dispelling of stereotypes. Citing to the value that U.S. businesses and the military places on multicultural competence, the Court noted that the "benefits are not theoretical but real." Good faith on the part of the university with respect to its purpose was presumed absent evidence to the contrary. The Court also determined that the law school did not trade in impermissible stereotypes and, to the contrary, was committed to diminishing their force.

In assessing whether the policy was narrowly tailored, the Court reaffirmed that quotas are an impermissible methodology. Unlike a quota, the factoring of race or ethnicity as a "plus" did not insulate an applicant from comparison with other candidates for admission. A key bottom line thus is that race or ethnicity may be used as a positive factor, provided each candidate is individually evaluated without regard to race. From the Court's perspective, the program reflected not a quota system but a "highly individualized, holistic review of each applicant's file, giving serious consideration to all the ways an applicant might contribute to a diverse educational environment."

Despite upholding the admissions program, the Court observed that a central goal of the Fourteenth Amendment is to eliminate "all governmentally imposed discrimination based on race." Consistent with this premise, the Court stated that "race-conscious admissions policies must be limited in time." It also announced an expectation "that 25 years from now, the use of racial preferences will no longer be necessary to further the interest approved today."

Chief Justice Rehnquist, in a dissenting opinion joined by Justices Scalia, Kennedy, and Thomas, characterized the "critical mass" concept as a "veil" that covered "a naked effort to achieve racial balancing." He maintained that the majority had not employed strict scrutiny because it had not insisted on a showing that the admission policy was necessary to achieve a compelling interest. Referencing admission data over a period of several years, Rehnquist asserted that the numbers were consistent with a fixed quota system.

Justices Scalia and Thomas, who joined each other in respective dissenting opinions, and Justice Kennedy in a separate dissent also maintained that the school was using a quota system. Kennedy argued that no system of numerical goals could satisfy the narrowly tailored requirement of strict scrutiny. Justices Scalia and Thomas maintained that the process represented a quota system and thus failed the narrowly tailored standard.

The Court also reviewed the University of Michigan's undergraduate admission policy, which awarded 20 extra points to admission scores for applicants from designated minority groups. Chief Justice Rehnquist, writing for the majority in *Gratz v. Bollinger*,[78] indicated that diversity in education could be a compelling interest. The Court found, however, that the university's admission policy was not tailored narrowly enough. Unlike the university's law school admissions program, the undergraduate process did not consider each student individually. The incremental boost in scores resulted in virtually automatic admission for minorities who met minimum standards. Nonminorities did not receive individual consideration until after most admission decisions had been made and did not secure automatic admission on a basis comparable to designated minorities.

Although acknowledging that individualized consideration of applicants may be impossible for a large university, the Court found this problem irrelevant to the program's constitutionality. Accordingly, the Court determined that the award of extra points for minority status fell short of the narrowly tailored requirement.

Justice O'Connor concurred in the opinion and judgment on grounds the school's assignment of significant numbers of points amounted to a quota or set-aside of seats for minorities. Justice Kennedy concurred with her. Justice Thomas concurred in the opinion and stressed that racial classifications in higher education are constitutionally impermissible.

Justice Ginsburg, joined in whole by Justice Souter and in part by Justice Breyer, dissented. With Justice Souter, she maintained that a diverse student body was a narrowly tailored remedy for undoing the effects of racial discrimination. Justice Breyer joined a part of her opinion that supported government efforts to eliminate the legacy of a racial caste system.

D. Gender Classifications

The Supreme Court's approach to **gender-based classifications** has changed over the decades.[79] For more than a century, the Court applied minimal scrutiny to classifications based on gender. During this period, the Court gave great deference to law makers to legislate in a manner consistent with the prevailing social norms that women took care of home and family, while men worked. Thus, laws that disadvantaged women in the workplace and gave men control of the home were rarely disturbed.[80]

At the turn of the twentieth century, progressive jurists challenged the **liberty of contract theory** of *Lochner* by defending state laws protecting women in the workplace. At that time, the Court took judicial notice of the prevailing beliefs "that woman's physical structure and the performance of maternal functions place her at a disadvantage in the struggle for subsistence. . . . Though limitations upon personal and contractual rights may be removed by legislation, there is that in her disposition which will operate against a full assertion of those rights."[81]

These differences, especially biological differences, between men and women were used to justify upholding protectionist legislation, even though protectionism limited the ability of women to obtain the more lucrative positions in the workplace.

As a result of notions such as these, state and federal laws gradually became laden with gross, stereotyped distinctions between the sexes that were not based on actual relevant differences. For example, women were prohibited from holding office, serving on juries, voting, or bringing suit in their own names. In addition, married women traditionally were denied the legal capacity to hold or convey property or to serve as legal guardians of their own children.[82]

Illustrative is the holding in *Holt v. Florida*,[83] in which the Court, as late as 1961, characterized women as "the center of home and family life," and upheld a statute that exempted women from jury duty. The Court reasoned that women should be allowed to decide whether jury duty would be consistent with their "special responsibilities." In cases after *Holt*, legislative and judicial attitudes toward sex discrimination began to change.

Sidebar

THE WEAKER SEX

Nineteenth-century courts used a variety of authorities to justify their decisions to maintain existing gender classifications. In *Bradwell v. Illinois*, 16 Wall. 130 (1873), for instance, the Court cited divine and natural authorities: "Man is, or should be, women's protector and defender. The natural and proper timidity and delicacy which belongs to the female sex evidently unfits it for many of the occupations of civil life. The constitution of the family organization, which is founded in the divine ordinance, as well as in the nature of things, indicates the domestic sphere as that which properly belongs to the domain and functions of womanhood. The harmony, not to say identity, of interests and views which belong, or should belong, to the family institution is repugnant to the idea of a woman adopting a distinct and independent career from that of her husband."

(1) Formal versus Substantive Equality

Legislatures choose either to realign their substantive laws in a gender-neutral fashion or to adopt procedures for identifying those instances where the sex-centered generalization actually comports with fact. A distinction is usually made between formal equality and substantive equality.

Formal equality is a principle of equal treatment: Individuals who are alike should be treated alike rather than being treated differently based on assumptions and stereotypes about sex, race, ethnicity, sexual orientation, or other impermissible characteristics.[84] Under principles of formal equality, women and men are viewed as "similarly situated" for most purposes and therefore treated as equal. For instance, Congress enacted the Title VII and Equal Pay Act of 1963 as remedial legislation intended to restructure wage scales and end the exclusion of women from salaries and jobs typically held by men. The act was premised on the gender-neutral principle that the Equal Protection and Due Process Clauses require that men and women be treated the same in the workplace under the law. The Equal Rights Amendment to the Constitution, which fell 3 votes short of the 38 needed to gain ratification, would have provided a constitutional mandate for formal equality.[85] Moreover, despite the failure of the amendment, the Court has premised most of its gender discrimination decisions on notions of formal equality.[86]

Sidebar

REHNQUIST DISCRIMINATION AGAINST MEN?

Applying the principle of formal equality produced questionable results. In *Craig v. Boren*, 429 U.S. 190 (1976), a dissenting Justice Rehnquist observed that "[i]t is true that a number of our opinions contain broadly phrased dicta implying that the same test should be applied to all classifications based on sex, whether affecting females or males. . . . However, before today, no decision of this Court has applied an elevated level of scrutiny to invalidate a statutory discrimination harmful to males."

On the other hand, the Court has also recognized that the government can consider relevant differences between men and women, as long as they do so to advance important governmental interests. However, determining what differences should be taken into account and in what ways is not always easy.[87]

Substantive equality is a principle that concerns the effect or outcome of a law. It underlies affirmative action and other government actions intended to remedy the effects of past discrimination in the workplace and family.[88] Substantive equality theory also focuses on biological differences between men and women in cases dealing with parental leave and job security for women who become pregnant. For example, Congress enacted the Pregnancy Disability Act to make discrimination on the basis of pregnancy a form of sex discrimination.[89] Other proponents of substantive equality look beyond biological differences and try to "change social expectations and practices that steer women into low wage jobs, encourage their dependence on men and perpetuate their disproportionate share of caretaking responsibilities."[90] Moreover, as some recognize, to "fail to acknowledge even our most basic biological differences . . . risk making the guarantee of equal protection superficial. . . . Mechanistic classifications of all our differences as stereotypes would operate to obscure those misconceptions and prejudices that are real. . . . The difference between men and women in the birth process is a real one, and the principle of equal protection does not forbid Congress to address the problem at hand in a manner specific to each gender."[91]

Cases upholding the use of gender-based classifications rest on the Court's perception of the laudatory purposes of those laws as remedying disadvantageous conditions historically suffered by women in economic and military life.[92] Thus, in *Califano v. Webster*,[93] the Court upheld a congressional statute that provided higher Social Security benefits for women than for men. The majority reasoned that "women . . . as such have been unfairly hindered from earning as much as men," but did not require proof that each woman so benefited had suffered discrimination or that each disadvantaged man had not; it was sufficient that even under the former congressional scheme "women *on the average* received lower retirement benefits than men" (emphasis supplied).

In *Rostker v. Goldberg*,[94] the Court deferred to Congress and upheld as constitutional the requirement that men but not women must register for the draft. The Court reasoned that "[s]ince women are excluded from combat, . . . the exemption of women from the draft was not only sufficiently but also closely related to Congress' purpose" of raising an army through the "registration and draft." Again, in *Nguyen v. INS*[95] the Court deferred to Congress and upheld a statute that treated women more favorably than men for purposes of deciding the citizenship of a child born to a citizen/noncitizen unwed couple.

F A Q

Q: What differences between men and women matter when it comes to determining whether a person is being denied equal protection on account of sex?

A: In general, courts consider biological differences between men and women relevant when dealing with issues of childbirth, workplace safety, medical benefits, military service, and participation in sports. In determining whether the asserted biological distinction is real, courts apply intermediate scrutiny. In other words, to sustain the restriction, the government must persuade the court that an important governmental interest is served (for example, protecting health and safety or national security) by laws treating men and women differently.

(2) Levels of Scrutiny

In *United States v. Carolene Products*,[96] the Supreme Court suggested that laws that adversely affect "discrete and insular minorities," or infringe fundamental rights, should be subject to more searching scrutiny than laws that affect social and economic arrangements. What is now known as strict scrutiny applies to laws employing racial classifications. In the 1970s, the Court began to apply heightened scrutiny to legislative classifications based on gender. While initially, the Court applied the traditional rational basis test to gender classifications,[97] it went on to apply the same strict scrutiny to laws based on race and sex discrimination. Eventually a majority settled on, and continues to apply, intermediate scrutiny.

Rational Basis Review. Early cases tended to apply rational basis review to gender classifications. In *Reed v. Reed*,[98] the Court considered a state law governing the appointment of an administrator over an intestate estate that provided, "[o]f several persons claiming and equally entitled . . . to administer, males must be preferred to females, and relatives of the whole to those of the half blood." The question presented by this case was whether a difference in the sex of competing applicants for letters of administration bears a rational relationship to a state objective that is sought to be advanced by the operation of the statute. The Court applied rational basis review and struck the law down as an unconstitutional violation of the Fourteenth Amendment. The Court reiterated that it had consistently recognized that the Fourteenth Amendment does not deny to states the power to treat different classes of persons in different ways. The Equal Protection Clause does, however, deny to states the power to legislate that different treatment be accorded to persons placed by a statute into different classes on the basis of criteria wholly unrelated to the objective of that statute. A classification "must be reasonable, not arbitrary, and must rest upon some ground of difference having a fair and substantial relation to the object of the legislation, so that all persons similarly circumstanced shall be treated alike."

A common justification offered by government actors, especially the military, for using gender classifications has been the "administrative convenience" defense. The Court in *Reed* acknowledged that the objective of reducing the workload on probate courts by eliminating one class of contests had some legitimacy. In some instances, for example in *Reed*, it is argued that a mandatory preference for male applicants is in itself reasonable since "men [are] as a rule more conversant with business affairs than . . . women." Indeed, in that case, appellee maintained that "it is a matter of common knowledge, that women still are not engaged in politics, the professions, business or industry to the extent that men are." The Idaho Supreme Court, in upholding the constitutionality of this statute, suggested that the Idaho legislature might reasonably have "concluded that in general men are better qualified to act as an administrator than are women."

In *Reed*, the crucial question was whether the state law advanced that objective in a manner consistent with the command of the Equal Protection Clause. Despite applying only a rational basis standard of review, the Court held that the state law did not advance the objective: "To give a mandatory preference to members of either sex over members of the other, merely to accomplish the elimination of hearings on the merits, is to make the very kind of arbitrary legislative choice forbidden by the Equal Protection Clause of the Fourteenth Amendment; and whatever may be said as to the positive values of avoiding intra-family controversy, the choice in this context may not lawfully be mandated solely on the basis of sex. . . . By providing dissimilar treatment for men and women who are thus similarly situated, the challenged section violates the Equal Protection Clause." *Reed* also exemplifies the formal equality approach.

Strict Scrutiny. Two years later, in *Fontiero v. Richardson*,[99] a plurality of the Supreme Court employed strict scrutiny in a challenge to sex discrimination under the Fifth Amendment.[100] *Fontiero* involved a suit by a married female air force officer and her husband against the secretary of defense seeking declaratory and injunctive relief against enforcement of federal statutes governing quarters' allowance and medical benefits for members of the uniformed services. Such benefits were automatically granted to the wife of a male member of the uniformed services, but a female member had to demonstrate that her husband was in fact dependent on his wife for more than half of his support. Thus, the statute discriminated in two ways: Procedurally, the burden is imposed on a female member to prove her spouse dependent while no such burden is imposed on males. Second, as a substantive matter, a male member who did not provide more than half of his wife's support received the housing and medical benefits, while a similarly situated female member did not.

The government argued that its system was reasonably because it was administratively convenient to require only women to demonstrate their spouse's dependency since women comprised only about 1 percent of all members of the uniformed services. "Although the legislative history of these statutes sheds virtually no light on the purposes underlying the differential treatment accorded male and female members, a majority of the three-judge District Court surmised that Congress might reasonably have concluded that, since the husband in our society is generally the 'breadwinner' in the family—and the wife typically the 'dependent' partner—'it would be more economical to require married female members claiming husbands to prove actual dependency than to extend the presumption of dependency to such members.' Indeed, given the fact that approximately 99% of all members of the uniformed services are male, the District Court speculated that such differential treatment might conceivably lead to a 'considerable saving of administrative expense and manpower.'"

The Fontieros contended that classifications based on sex—like classifications based on race, alienage, and national origin—are inherently suspect and must therefore be subjected to close judicial scrutiny. The Court defines a **suspect class** as a group that is a discrete and an insular minority with immutable characteristics that has suffered historical discrimination, exclusion from the political process, and legal burdens that bear no relationship to an individual's ability to perform or contribute to society.[101] While the justices unanimously agreed that the air force system of conferring benefits was unconstitutional, only a plurality adopted strict scrutiny as the standard of review. A plurality of the Court found at least implicit support for such an approach in *Reed* and reasoned that a departure from traditional rational basis analysis with respect to sex-based classifications was clearly justified. These four justices, led by Justice Brennan, reasoned that classifications based on sex, like race, alienage, and national origin, are "inherently suspect" and should be subject to "close judicial scrutiny." Justice Rehnquist concurred in the judgment, but dissented on the issue of applying strict scrutiny. He reasoned that "[i]t is unnecessary for the Court in this case to characterize sex as a suspect classification, with all of the far-reaching implications of such a holding. [*Reed*] abundantly supports our decision today, [and] did not add sex to the narrowly limited group of classifications which are inherently suspect. In my view, we can and should decide this case on the authority of *Reed* and reserve for the future any expansion of its rationale."

Finally, in *Craig v. Boren*[102] a majority of the Court agreed that something more than rational basis but less than strict scrutiny should be applied to sex-based classifications under the Fourteenth Amendment. In *Craig*, male plaintiffs challenged an Oklahoma statute that allowed women to purchase beer at 18 years of age, while men had to be 21 to purchase the same product. Citing a number of cases that relied on the requirement of heightened scrutiny after *Fontiero*, Justice Brennan wrote that "[t]o withstand constitutional challenge, previous cases establish that classifications by gender must serve *important governmental objectives and must be substantially related to achievement of these objectives*" (emphasis added). Without equating gender classifications, for all purposes, to classifications based on race or national origin, the

> **Sidebar**
>
> **THE "ADMINISTRATIVE CONVENIENCE" DEFENSE**
>
> A common justification offered by government actors, especially the military, for using gender classifications has been the "administrative convenience" defense. In most cases, the Court has rejected this defense whether applying rational basis as in *Reed* or heightened scrutiny as in *Fontiero*.

> **Sidebar**
>
> **A "DISCRETE AND INSULAR" MINORITY?**
>
> Some have argued that men do not constitute a "discrete and insular" minority, but a "large and diverse" majority. *See Fontiero v. Richardson (dissent).*

Court carefully inspects official actions that deny opportunities to women or men.[103] Thus, the Court formally adopted what is now called intermediate scrutiny.

Sidebar

DEFINING INTERMEDIATE SCRUTINY

To overcome the presumption of unconstitutionality that operates when the government's action adversely impacts a suspect or quasi-suspect class, intermediate scrutiny requires the government to prove that

A. the sex-based classification serves an important governmental objective, and
B. the means chosen are substantially related to achieving the objective.

In support of the statute, the State of Oklahoma argued that the statute served the purpose of enhancing traffic safety. The Court found this to be an important governmental objective. However, the statute used gender for "administrative convenience." The Court had already on numerous occasions found that the use of gender for administrative convenience was based on "an inaccurate proxy for 'archaic and overbroad' generalizations about the financial position of women, and increasingly outdated misconceptions concerning the role of females in the home rather than in the 'marketplace and world of ideas.'"[104] In this case, the "archaic and overbroad" generalization was about males. In other words, the Court rejected the state's claimed connection between maleness and unsafe driving under the influence, without specific empirical proof of such a connection. Therefore, although the state objective of improving traffic safety was permissible, the means chosen were not substantially related to the objective.

After *Craig v. Boren*, a majority of the Court continued to employ intermediate scrutiny to evaluate claims of unconstitutional gender-based discrimination.[105] Several justices who concurred in the decision to declare the law unconstitutional disagreed with Justice Brennan's endorsement of the new intermediate scrutiny standard.[106] However, the majority opinion in *United States v. Virginia*[107] engendered even sharper debate between Justice Ginsburg, who authored the opinion and served as counsel in such cases as *Fontiero* prior to joining the bench, and Justices Rehnquist and Scalia over the articulation and application of the intermediate scrutiny test.

United States v. Virginia addressed the issue of whether the Virginia Military Institute (VMI) could continue as a single-sex male school. VMI was a state-supported military college with a long and illustrious history. Founded in 1839, VMI prided itself on what it described as its unique "adversative" method of education, which emphasized physical hardship, mental stress, lack of privacy, and exacting regulation of behavior. First-year cadets, called "rats," had to endure seven months of harsh and demeaning treatment by upperclassmen in a boot-camp atmosphere (the "rat line"). The goal of the system was to mold character and produce leaders, and indeed many of VMI's alumni, bonded through adversity, had gone on to prominent positions in both military and civilian life.[108]

The Court held that parties who seek to defend gender-based government action must demonstrate "an exceedingly persuasive justification" for that action. The burden of justification is demanding and rests entirely on the state. The Court's "skeptical scrutiny of official action" is required in response to "volumes of history" of such actions denying rights or opportunities based on sex.[109] The state must show at least that the challenged classification serves important governmental objectives and that the discriminatory means employed are substantially related to the achievement of those objectives. The justification must be genuine, not hypothesized or invented post hoc in response to litigation. And it must not rely on overbroad generalizations about the different talents, capacities, or preferences of males and females.[110]

Justice Rehnquist dissented over the use of the phrase "exceedingly persuasive justification" as a way of explaining the requirement of the intermediate scrutiny test. The Chief Justice wrote, "It is unfortunate that the Court . . . introduces an element of uncertainty respecting the appropriate test. . . . While terms like 'important governmental objective' and 'substantially related' are hardly models of precision, they have more content and specificity than does the phrase 'exceedingly persuasive justification.'"

Justice Scalia also dissented, devoting most of his analysis "to evaluating the Court's opinion on the basis of our current equal protection jurisprudence, which regards this Court as free to evaluate everything under the sun by applying one of three tests: 'rational basis' scrutiny, intermediate scrutiny, or strict scrutiny. These tests are no more scientific than their names suggest, and a further element of randomness is added by the fact that it is largely up to [the Court] which test will be applied in each case." Scalia had "no problem with a system of abstract tests such as rational basis, intermediate, and strict scrutiny. . . . [But] 'when a practice not expressly prohibited by the text of the Bill of Rights bears the endorsement of a long tradition of open, widespread, and unchallenged use that dates back to the beginning of the Republic, we have no proper basis for striking it down.'"

Like Chief Justice Rehnquist, Scalia criticizes the "'exceedingly persuasive justification' phrase" as "amorphous" and "not the standard elaboration of intermediate scrutiny." Scalia insisted that "[i]ntermediate scrutiny has never required a least-restrictive-means analysis" as does the strict scrutiny test, "but only a 'substantial relation' between the classification and the state interests that it serves. . . . The reasoning in our other intermediate-scrutiny cases has similarly required only a substantial relation between end and means, not a perfect fit."

F   A   Q

Q: Why didn't *United States v. Virginia* doom all single-sex schools?

A: The Court did not say that single-sex schools are always unconstitutional. As long as the state can offer an "exceedingly persuasive justification" for such schools and establishes a "substantial relationship" between the justification for single-sex education and the means chosen, a single-sex school can survive intermediate scrutiny. Single-sex schools that are based on stereotypes (men do not make good nurses, women do not make good soldiers) will not pass scrutiny. The state must base its justifications on real differences that are relevant to achieving a better education.

Justice O'Connor joined the majority in crafting the reformulation of the intermediate scrutiny test in *United States v. Virginia*. However, in *Nguyen v. INS*,[111]

Justice O'Connor complained that even though the majority claimed to evaluate the government's action with heightened scrutiny, "the manner in which it explains and applies this standard is a stranger to our precedent." The fact that the Court gives more deference to Congress's decision to discriminate based on gender in cases involving the military and matters of national security like immigration may help to explain what O'Connor characterizes as "a stranger to our precedent."

E. Alienage Classifications

The Supreme Court's modern precedents recognize that the Equal Protection Clause applies to noncitizens, known as "aliens," and that **alienage classifications** in state laws must withstand strict judicial scrutiny. Such scrutiny requires a law to "advance a compelling state interest by the least restrictive means available."[112] However, there are some categories of cases in which a more deferential standard of scrutiny is employed. For example, when a state law excludes aliens from civil service jobs that fit the criteria for the "political function exception," such a law is exempt from strict scrutiny and may be validated under the rational basis standard of review. A similarly deferential standard is used to evaluate federal laws that restrict the rights of aliens when those laws are enacted pursuant to the congressional power to regulate immigration and naturalization. By contrast, the Court has used the intermediate scrutiny standard when evaluating a state law that restricts the rights of aliens who are not lawful U.S. residents, namely "illegal aliens."

Strict scrutiny is used for laws that classify persons based on their national origins, as well as for alienage classifications. Unlike an alienage classification, which simply treats citizens differently from noncitizens, a classification based on national origin treats citizens differently according to their ancestors' country of origin. Some laws employ both types of classifications. Moreover, an alienage classification, though origin-neutral on its face, may be motivated by legislative hostility toward aliens who share a particular national origin.

The Court did not exercise meaningful scrutiny of classifications based on alienage or national origin until the decade before *Brown v. Board of Education*,[113] and the Court took the first significant step toward protecting the economic rights of aliens in *Takahashi v. Fish & Game Commission*.[114] At the time, if a person of Japanese ancestry was not born in the United States, then that person would never be eligible to become a naturalized citizen; instead, such a person was stuck with the status of "permanent resident alien" for life. In the years before 1943, any person in California could obtain a commercial fishing license, irrespective of alien status or eligibility for citizenship. However, in 1943, the California statute at issue in *Takahashi* was enacted to prohibit the issuance of a commercial fishing license to any "alien Japanese," and then it was amended in 1945 to apply to those "ineligible for citizenship," so as to achieve the same result. The 1943 enactment of the law occurred soon after the forced relocation of West Coast citizens and noncitizens of Japanese ancestry to wartime internment camps in 1942.

Based on this suggestive legislative history, the plaintiff in *Takahashi*, a permanent resident alien of Japanese ancestry, who lost his fishing license when he returned to California from an internment camp, challenged the alienage classification in the 1945 law as a violation of equal protection. The *Takahashi* Court noted the plaintiff's argument that the law was motivated by "racial antagonism" in violation of *Korematsu*'s declaration that such legislative hostility can never justify a legal restriction that curtails the civil rights of any one racial group. But the Court found it unnecessary to address this argument. Instead, the Court invalidated the statute on the grounds that the nature of the state's governmental interests could not satisfy the demands of equal protection doctrine, as interpreted in novel ways in *Takahashi*.

The *Takahashi* Court recognized that the California licensing statute operated to exclude particular aliens from one type of employment, namely commercial fishing. Initially, the state justified this exclusionary law by arguing that if the federal naturalization laws could use "race and color" classifications to restrict the rights of aliens, then a state should be entitled to regulate aliens within its borders using the same classifications. The Court squarely rejected this argument based on reasoning that was rooted in Supremacy Clause concerns. Congress is constitutionally vested with the exclusive power to govern the admission, naturalization, and residence of aliens. In making the legislative policy decision to admit aliens of Japanese ancestry, Congress implicitly recognized that such admitted aliens should enjoy the right to "entrance and abode" in any state. Such a right, in turn, necessarily includes the right to obtain employment to make a living, and since the California law impaired this right of abode, the *Takahashi* Court determined that the law conflicted with federal immigration policy. Under the Supremacy Clause, a state legislature cannot usurp the power of Congress, and the Court interpreted the federal immigration policy as requiring the judicial enforcement of the rights of aliens to obtain employment.

One question remained for the *Takahashi* Court, which was how to reconcile the invalidation of the state law with earlier precedents in which the Court had endorsed the argument that state laws could impose discriminatory burdens on aliens when a state legislature determined that these laws were "were necessary to protect special interests either of the state or of its citizens." More specifically, a state legislature could determine that a "special public interest" required that particular state resources or assets should be preserved from depletion, and that the enactment of alien exclusion laws was necessary to diminish the demand for those state resources or assets. The Court's uncritical deference to these legislative judgments was exhibited in precedents decided over many decades, which upheld state laws that barred aliens from access to certain occupations, to land ownership, and to the use of natural resources such as fish and game. This is why the state in *Takahashi* argued, as a fall-back position, that the purpose of prohibiting the issuance of fishing licenses to aliens was to preserve the coastal fishing stocks from depletion.

But surprisingly, the *Takahashi* Court rejected the public interest argument and thereby cast doubt on the continuing validity of the precedents endorsing it as a justification for alien exclusion laws. Again, the *Takahashi* Court turned to the concept of the right of abode for aliens and found this concept embodied in equal protection law. In the Court's words, the policy of the Fourteenth Amendment and federal civil rights laws is to protect the right of all persons "lawfully in this country" to "abide in any state" on "an equality of legal privileges with all citizens under non-discriminatory laws." When compared with that constitutional policy, the state's "purported ownership interest" in the preservation coastal fishing stocks was inadequate to justify the state's prevention of "lawfully admitted aliens within its borders" from earning a living from fishing in the same way as other state inhabitants. Therefore, the California law violated equal protection because the Court now viewed the state's interest as being too weak to justify discrimination based on alien status alone.

In modern terms, the *Takahashi* Court's expansion of the equal protection rights of aliens could be described as a shift from a rational basis philosophy to a closer scrutiny perspective. In essence, the state argued that the Court should defer to the state legislature's regulation of economic rights without requiring proof that the denial of such rights to aliens was necessary to preserve state resources or was the most effective way to achieve this goal. But suddenly, the Court refused to defer to a state legislative judgment that the economic interests of alien residents who could never be citizens should be sacrificed for the "greater good" of citizen residents and of alien residents who were eligible for naturalization. The state argued in *Takahashi* that permanent resident aliens had no "community interest" in the "state-owned" coastal fish, but the *Takahashi* Court treated all residents as having such community interests. In 1948 the Court chose not to describe the state's "no-community-interest" argument as a thinly veiled form of invidious discrimination, motivated by what the Court would later call "illegitimate notions of racial inferiority or simple racial politics."[115] Nor was the Court ready to repudiate all its "public interest" precedents that sanctioned the state legislative power to protect citizens from economic competition from aliens by establishing monopolies for the state "insiders" whose "community interests" outranked those of alien "outsiders." This reluctance helps to explain why state attorneys general continued to defend alien exclusion laws using "public interest" arguments in later years, thereby ignoring the implicit message of the *Takahashi* Court that these arguments were inherently antithetical to the policies of equal protection.

When the Court revisited the issue of alienage classifications in 1971, the equal protection landscape provided a new framework for the analysis of the alien exclusion statute in *Graham v. Richardson*,[116] which addressed the question whether a state could deny welfare benefits to aliens who become indigent after admission to the United States. The Court viewed the state resource of welfare funds in *Graham* as being analogous to the resource of coastal fishing stocks in *Takahashi*; similarly, the welfare funds in *Graham* provided indigent aliens with de facto salary substitutes for private sector jobs lost because of disability or illness, just as the fishing license in *Takahashi* provided aliens with access to private sector jobs. The *Graham* Court borrowed *Takahashi*'s reasoning and attached it to the framework of strict scrutiny established in the post-*Brown* racial classification cases. The Court endorsed two propositions in applying this framework: (1) aliens are a "discrete and insular minority" who deserve heightened judicial solicitude for the protection of their rights; (2) alienage classifications are subject to "close" or "strict" judicial scrutiny because they are inherently suspect.[117]

The only state interest proffered in defense of the two state laws at issue in *Graham* was the "special public interest" in preserving the limited resources of state welfare benefit funds for the use of indigent citizens or for the use of indigent aliens with a long history of state residence. The evidence showed that the percentage of aliens denied benefits under one of the state laws constituted .01 percent of the pool of people who received benefits. The effect of the alien exclusion laws was to deny financial support to people who became ill or disabled and therefore unable to work, possibly after many years of working and paying taxes; the lack of benefits left people without money for food, clothing, and shelter.

The *Graham* Court relied on four strands of reasoning in invalidating the state statutes because of the inadequacy of the state interest in "favoring citizens over aliens" in the distribution of state welfare funds. First, *Takahashi* rejected an outdated public interest argument involving natural resources instead of money; moreover, like the license-exclusion law in *Takahashi*, the welfare-exclusion laws denied the right to "entrance or abode" to aliens in the state, recognized in *Takahashi* as an equal protection right.[118] Second, a state's interest in preserving the fiscal integrity of any program may not be accomplished through the use of invidious classifications. Third, no meaningful distinctions existed between needy citizens and needy aliens, or between needy aliens with long or short state residencies, for purposes of equal protection analysis, because all such persons contributed equally to the state tax revenues that provide the source for welfare benefits. Fourth, these statutes exhibited the same flaw as the *Takahashi* statute because they implicitly expressed the state's unconstitutional assertion "of a right to deny entrance and abode" to aliens who become indigent after admission. By deterring aliens from entering the country and from settling or remaining in a state, such state laws encroach on overriding federal immigration policy, which confers on admitted aliens the entitlement of the full and equal benefit of all state laws.

F   A   Q

Q: What is the "special public interest" doctrine, and is it considered valid?

A: The Court used this doctrine before 1948 to validate state laws prohibiting aliens from owning property, obtaining licenses to pursue occupations, and gaining access to the use of natural resources. The Court retreated from the doctrine because it embodied an extreme type of deference to state legislative decisions to favor citizens at the expense of aliens, which decisions might be based solely on racial antagonism or racial politics. Initially, the Court shelved the doctrine and recognized the equal protection right of aliens to "abode" in any state. The Court later adopted strict scrutiny for alienage classifications, based on the recognition that aliens need the protection of the heightened judicial solicitude provided for a discrete and insular minority.

Thus, the *Graham* opinion affirmed *Takahashi*'s reasoning while applying it to a different context to reach the same outcome. The *Graham* opinion also filled in gaps left in the *Takahashi* opinion, which neither defined the potential scope of the equal protection right of abode, nor explained why alien residents have the same "community interest" in state resources as citizen residents. In *Graham*, the Court explained that indigent aliens deserved the same access to state welfare benefits as indigent citizens because aliens share the obligations of citizens to support the state and national communities through paying taxes and serving in the armed forces. Moreover, both aliens and citizens "may live within a state for many years, work in the state and contribute to the economic growth of the state." Given these equal contributions, equal access to community tax-revenue-funded programs must be required by equal protection law.

Notably, however, the full trappings of the modern strict scrutiny concept did not appear in the *Graham* opinion. No mention is made of the requirement of a compelling state interest or the need for a state law to be narrowly tailored so as to advance that compelling interest by the least restrictive means available. In later alienage cases in the 1970s, the Court described its strict scrutiny standard as requiring that a state law must advance a "substantial" state interest, achieved by means that are "necessary and precisely drawn."[119] By 1984, the Court's alienage analysis referred to the need for a compelling interest, rather than a substantial interest, and included reference to the least restrictive means requirement; this amended version of the strict scrutiny formula matches the modern counterpart used for racial classifications.[120] In examining the bulk of the Court's alienage opinions that date from the 1970s, it is helpful to recognize that the many invalidated statutes presumably would be viewed as even more clearly unconstitutional under the modern strict scrutiny formula.

The post-*Graham* strict scrutiny cases illustrate two kinds of state failures to satisfy the requirements of equal protection. The first kind of failure occurred in cases where the Court dismissed the proffered state interest as insubstantial, and the Court's analysis in these cases resembles the analysis of *Takahashi* and *Graham*. For example, the state law in *Nyquist v. Mauclet*[121] provided that resident aliens were not eligible to apply for state-funded college scholarships. The state's proffered interest in enhancing the education of the electorate was rejected as too insubstantial to survive strict scrutiny, given the insignificant impact that state awards to resident aliens would have on the total pool of awards. A second kind of failure occurred in cases where the Court determined that, in effect, there was no adequate nexus between the state's interest and the characteristic of alien status, even if the state's interest might be substantial; therefore, the statute could not satisfy the narrow tailoring requirement. For example, in *Application of Griffiths*,[122] a state law barred aliens from the practice of law, based on the state interests in requiring attorneys to be loyal to courts and to clients. While acknowledging the substantial nature of this interest, the Court found that the state could not establish the necessary link between citizenship status and the powers and responsibilities of attorneys. Given the fact that the work of most lawyers neither involves matters of state policy nor provides "meaningful opportunities adversely to affect the interest of the United States," the Court found it implausible that alien lawyers might have a conflict of loyalties and choose to ignore their "responsibilities to the courts or even [to] clients in favor of the interest of a foreign power."

A handful of post-*Graham* precedents address the exclusion of aliens from state civil service jobs. In two cases, such exclusions have been invalidated under strict scrutiny, whereas in three cases, the particular jobs met the criteria for the political function exception, and therefore the exclusions were validated. The inherently rational relationship between the political function criteria and a citizenship requirement is viewed by the Court as sufficient to satisfy the concerns of equal protection. The theory supporting this exception to strict scrutiny is that the state has the "historical power to exclude aliens from participation in its democratic political institutions," and therefore the state should have the same power of exclusion with regard to jobs with "important policy responsibilities" that "can often more immediately affect the lives of citizens" than their votes. The Court characterizes a public function job as one that "goes to the heart of representative government," namely "important nonelective executive, legislative, and judicial positions," held by "officers who participate directly in the formulation, execution, or review of broad public policy." Such a job must involve "discretionary decisionmaking, or execution of policy, which substantially affects members of the political community."[123]

Moreover, any state law delineating the specific jobs for which citizenship is required must not be substantially overinclusive or underinclusive to avoid weakening the state's claim that the exclusion of aliens "serves legitimate political ends."[124] For example, in *Sugarman v. Dougal*,[125] the Court was not willing to assume that all civil service positions should qualify automatically for exemption from strict scrutiny. Therefore, the Court invalidated a state law that barred aliens from all competitive civil service jobs, holding that the statute was not narrowly tailored as required by strict scrutiny. Although the Court recognized that the state had a substantial interest in ensuring the loyalty of policymaking employees, no nexus existed between this interest and the categorical exclusion of aliens from such jobs as clerk typist and office worker.

The three civil service categories for which the Court has approved alien exclusions include the jobs of state police officers, public schoolteachers, and peace officers.[126] In explaining why the political function exception fits each of these jobs, the Court later emphasized that each job requires the civil servant to exercise discretionary power routinely, to perform a basic government function, and to occupy a position of direct authority over others.[127] As a counterexample, the Court rejected the applicability of the **political function doctrine** to state law that barred aliens from the position of notary public because the duties of this position were essentially clerical and resembled those of other common occupations in the private sector. The Court then invalidated the law using strict scrutiny; the state could not demonstrate the required link between a citizenship requirement and the state interests because no evidence showed that aliens were incapable of becoming familiar with state law or unlikely to be available as witnesses.[128]

F   A   Q

Q: What types of state alienage classifications have been invalidated under the strict scrutiny standard?

A: The Supreme Court has invalidated restrictions on the right of aliens to obtain licenses to practice law or civil engineering, to serve as notary publics, to be employed in competitive state civil service jobs that are unrelated to a political function, and to obtain state welfare benefits and financial aid for college or graduate education.

During the years following *Graham*'s adoption of strict scrutiny as the equal protection standard for challenges to state alienage classifications, the Court encountered the need to reaffirm the complementary *Graham* and *Takahashi* holdings under the Supremacy Clause. In *DeCanas v. Bica*,[129] the Court explained that *Takahashi* and *Graham* stand for the broad principle that "state regulation not congressionally sanctioned that discriminates against aliens lawfully admitted to the country is impermissible if it imposes additional burdens not contemplated by Congress." In *Toll v. Moreno*,[130] the Court invalidated a state law that disqualified some aliens with state domiciles from qualifying for in-state tuition, reasoning that Congress would view such a discriminatory burden as impermissible because federal law allowed such aliens to qualify for state domiciles and provided them with tax exemption incentives to work in this country. By contrast, the state law in *DeCanas* did not conflict with federal immigration policy because it simply penalized employers for hiring people with the status of "illegal aliens" under federal immigration law. The mere fact that aliens are the subject of a state statute does not make that law an impermissible attempt by the state to regulate immigration under *Takahashi* and *Graham*.

The Court does not apply strict scrutiny to the alienage classifications established by federal legislative or executive authorities because they are a "routine and normally legitimate part" of the federal business of regulating immigration, naturalization, and foreign policy.[131] An overriding interest deriving from federal lawmaking authority in these fields can justify a citizenship requirement "even when an identical requirement may not be enforced by a State."[132] For example, when President Ford issued an executive order excluding aliens from competitive federal civil service jobs, the federal courts upheld the order because the interest in creating an incentive for aliens to become naturalized citizens was sufficient to justify the restriction,[133] even though *Sugarman* invalidated a state law that excluded aliens from all state civil service jobs. Likewise, the Court upheld a law that granted federal medical insurance benefits to a small class of permanent resident aliens and denied benefits to most aliens,[134] even though *Graham* invalidated a state law that excluded aliens from welfare benefits.

The class of illegal aliens is not a suspect class entitled to strict scrutiny of alienage classifications, but in *Plyler v. Doe*,[135] the Court invalidated a law that excluded illegal child aliens from public schools. The *Plyler* Court noted that illegal aliens are "persons" entitled to equal protection rights of some kind, and that when a classification imposes a discriminatory burden on illegal child aliens, it penalizes these children for conduct over which they have no control, namely the conduct of their parents who establish an unlawful residence in this country. Given the enduring nature of the disability and stigma of illiteracy, and the essential role of education for success in life, the Court refused to uphold the child exclusion law under the rational basis standard, and instead required the state to satisfy an intermediate scrutiny standard by showing how the exclusion law furthered a substantial state interest. Such a showing could not be made because the state law did not mirror a federal policy,[136] and because the state's evidence did not show that the law would mitigate a significant burden on the state's economy, improve the quality of education, or reduce the likelihood that children would fail to put their education to use within the state. The *Plyler* dissenters advocated the validation of the state law under the rational basis standard, and the equal protection right in *Plyler* has not been expanded in subsequent decisions.

F. Classifications of Unmarried Parents and Their Children

The Supreme Court first extended the equal protection guarantee to the classes of unmarried parents and their children in 1968, in an era when children were described as being born out of wedlock or as **illegitimate**. Twenty years later, the Court ultimately endorsed the use of an intermediate scrutiny standard in *Clark v. Jeter*[137] for evaluating laws restricting the rights of these children and their parents. One state interest offered to justify these laws in the earliest cases was the policy of discouraging childbirth outside of marriage; this interest could be described as grounded in the moral condemnation of such conduct or in the state's right to enforce the legal formalities of marriage. The Court quickly labeled this interest as the expression of a bias that created an "invidious" classification in violation of equal protection; the Court also condemned the state's willingness to punish nonmarital children for a birth status beyond their control. The second, more longstanding state interest was the need to avoid proof problems in ascertaining the paternity of children; this interest was significant enough in the decades before *Clark* to persuade the Court to validate some laws that burdened nonmarital children with special proof-of-paternity requirements not imposed on children of married parents. However, as the *Clark* Court recognized, by 1988 it was possible for DNA testing to exclude over 99 percent of "those who might be accused of paternity."

The timing of this scientific advance creates a quandary for the retrospective interpretation of the Court's precedents relating to the rights of unmarried parents and their children, because most of these precedents were decided during the era before DNA testing became commonplace. In that era, the state interest in avoiding proof-of-paternity problems carried considerably more weight with the Court that it would in the modern era. The Court's pre-*Clark* precedents relied on a demanding version of rational basis review, and the holdings that invalidated classifications based on birth status remain good law; a modern application of intermediate scrutiny presumably would reach the same results based on even more critical assessments of the invalidated laws. However, the pre-*Clark* precedents that upheld the rationality of some classifications have been cast into doubt, not only because *Clark* requires the statutes in these cases to be reevaluated using intermediate scrutiny, but also because these old precedents invariably relied on the now less-substantial state interest in avoiding proof-of-paternity problems. These perspectives should be kept in mind when assessing the likely current precedential value of all of the Court's pre-*Clark* precedents.

In several cases before *Clark*, the Court considered the validity of laws restricting the rights of **nonmarital children** to obtain court orders of support from their parents, typically from their fathers.[138] The most extreme restriction was a law that completely barred these children from seeking such orders, while allowing children born to married parents to obtain these orders. In *Gomez v. Perez*,[139] the Court invalidated this law as invidious discrimination and reasoned that the state's interest in avoiding proof-of-paternity problems could not be weighty enough to justify the complete denial of the substantial benefit of rights accorded to children generally. The *Gomez* holding is a typical example of the Court's response before *Clark* to state legislative decisions to deny rights entirely to nonmarital children. For example, in *Trimble v. Gordon*,[140] the Court invalidated a law completely excluding nonmarital children from sharing in their father's intestate estate, reasoning that the state could find more narrowly tailored strategies to reach a "middle ground" solution to the proof-of-paternity problem.

Similarly, in *Weber v. Aetna Casualty & Surety Co.*,[141] the Court invalidated a law that deprived "unacknowledged" nonmarital children of eligibility for worker's compensation benefits, and subsequent decisions followed *Weber*'s reasoning in invalidating similar eligibility bars to state welfare benefits and federal disability insurance benefits.[142] Each of these holdings relied on even earlier authorities that invalidated laws that completely denied nonmarital children the right to recover for the wrongful death of a parent and vice versa. Although the avoidance of proof-of-paternity problems did not figure in the latter decisions, these earliest cases established the understanding that the pre-*Clark* scrutiny standard of rational basis would be more demanding than the deferential version and would require state legislatures to attempt to satisfy the need for proofs of paternity with statutory measures that did not entirely nullify the rights of nonmarital children and their parents.

The more difficult problem repeatedly confronted by the Court in the pre-*Clark* era was what to do with a restrictive statute that established a less-than-complete denial of rights. This was the kind of problem that was raised in *Clark*. The endorsement of the intermediate scrutiny standard in *Clark* did not necessarily make this kind of problem easier to solve, but it framed the issue in *Clark* as follows: Is a six-year time limit on support suits by nonmarital children substantially related to an important governmental objective, namely the avoidance of proof-of-paternity problems? The *Clark* Court invalidated this time limit because the type of narrow tailoring required by intermediate scrutiny, embodied in the concept of a "substantial relationship" between the statutory means for the advancement of a state interest, could not be satisfied. Given the alternative solution of relying on DNA testing to eliminate fraudulent support claims, the outdated time-limit requirement lost its substantial relationship to the achievement of the state's objective. The *Clark* Court reasoned further that the lack of the required substantial relationship was evidenced by the state's failure to require time limits for other kinds of suits raising paternity issues and by statutory loopholes that authorized the filing of some support suits after the six-year time limit expired. Thus, the *Clark* opinion illustrated how a classification restricting the rights of nonmarital children may be invalidated because of simultaneously overinclusive and underinclusive tailoring.

Using *Clark* as a template for the application of the intermediate scrutiny standard to laws restricting rights on the basis of proof-of-paternity problems, it appears that three decisions have been cast into doubt by *Clark*, although their likely outcomes under the intermediate scrutiny standard may be debated. In *Parham v. Hughes*,[143] the Court upheld a law that prohibited an unmarried father from bringing a suit for the wrongful death of a child whom he had not legitimated in life. To avoid proof-of-paternity problems, the law required an unmarried father to file a petition for a court order of legitimation during a time when evidence would be available from both mother and child to support or contest the issue of paternity. Four dissenters in *Parham* argued that the Court should endorse intermediate scrutiny and invalidate the law, reasoning that the state could have no important interest in protecting tortfeasors from litigating the issue of paternity in suits involving the deaths of unlegitimated children. Instead of allowing the state to impose "blanket discrimination against unmarried fathers," the *Parham* dissenters would have required the state to address paternity concerns by simply assigning the burden of proving paternity to any parent bringing a wrongful death action. In the era of DNA testing, the *Parham* Court's greater deference to the state's solution for resolving paternity issues is outdated and seems unlikely to prevail in a similar case.

Similarly, in *Labine v. Vincent*[144] and *Lalli v. Lalli*,[145] the Court upheld the validity of laws conditioning intestate succession rights on specific proofs of paternity, such as a father's notarized acknowledgment of the "desire to legitimate" a child in *Labine* or a court order of filiation obtained during the father's lifetime in *Lalli*. Four dissenters in each case argued that the laws should be invalidated because the state interest in verifying paternity could be achieved by the acceptance of less onerous proofs.

A final example of a debatable decision is *Mathews v. Lucas*,[146] where the weight given to the government interest in administrative convenience now seems excessive. This impression undermines the Court's validation of the Social Security Act's barriers for nonmarital children seeking surviving-child-insurance benefits. The act allowed children of married parents with particular proofs of paternity to obtain such benefits, but denied benefits to all nonmarital children who could not show that their deceased father supported them at the time of his death, even if they could prove that he had supported them for many years before death. While the *Mathews* majority allowed such disparate treatment of similarly situated offspring to survive rational basis review before *Clark*, the *Mathews* dissenters viewed "the blanket and conclusive exclusion" of nonmarital children as "odious" and would have invalidated the contested provision of the act because it allocated benefits on grounds "which have only the most tenuous connection" to the "supposedly controlling factor" of a child's dependency on a deceased father.

Even in the pre-*Clark* era, however, the Court protected the constitutional rights of unmarried fathers to retain custody of their children in *Stanley v. Illinois*[147] and *Caban v. Mohammed*.[148] In *Stanley*, the Court relied on due process as well as equal protection to invalidate a law that deprived an unmarried father automatically of child custody when the mother died, while allowing an unmarried mother or married parents to be deprived of custody only after a fitness hearing in which proof of child neglect was established. In *Caban*, the Court relied on equal protection to invalidate a law on grounds of gender discrimination because it denied unmarried fathers the right to block an adoption, while providing that right to unmarried mothers.

When classifications relating to unmarried parents and their children are made in federal statutes that regulate immigration or naturalization, the Court does not use intermediate scrutiny, and its decisions reflect the same deference toward government interests that is reflected in the decisions involving federal alienage classifications.[149]

F   A   Q

Q: What rights cannot be denied to the children of unmarried parents, or to those parents, under equal protection precedents?

A: Children of unmarried parents cannot be barred from bringing suit for the wrongful death of a parent or from bringing suit for support from a father.

Nonmarital children who are dependent on a parent cannot be declared ineligible for worker's compensation benefits, welfare benefits, or disability benefits. Unmarried parents cannot be barred from bringing suit for the wrongful death of a child, and an unmarried father cannot be deprived of custody of his child without proof of neglect and a fitness hearing that are accorded to married parents. An unmarried father has the right to refuse to consent to the adoption of his child.

G. Classifications of Persons with Mental Disabilities

In 1985 the Supreme Court decided that classifications concerning the treatment of **persons with mental disabilities** should be evaluated according to a rational basis standard in *City of Cleburne v. Cleburne Living Center*.[150] The Court acknowledged the history of legal and social discrimination against this group, but determined that "in the vast majority of situations," modern laws do not create a burden based on mental disability unless it is "relevant to an interest" that the government should have "the authority to implement." Thus, such laws are not analogous to classifications based on race, national origin, or alienage, which are "seldom relevant to the achievement of any legitimate government interest." Nor are such laws analogous to classifications based on gender or "legitimacy" of birth status, which often reflect outmoded stereotypes or prejudice. The Court also observed that if strict or intermediate scrutiny were required for classifications related to mental disability, then the same scrutiny would have to be adopted for other groups with immutable disabilities and a history of discrimination, such as the mentally ill, the physically disabled, the aged, and the infirm. To avoid that floodgates problem, the Court preferred to use the rational basis standard.

The *City of Cleburne* Court emphasized several other factors supporting the use of the rational basis standard. First, the Court noted that judges might be ill equipped to make substantive policy judgments required for heightened scrutiny of legislative decisions requiring the assistance of experts in the field of mental disability. Second, given the proliferation of modern civil rights laws that provide some protections for mentally disabled people, the Court expressed doubts that continuing legislative prejudice exists to justify strict scrutiny of mental disability classifications. Third, the Court observed that modern public support for protective legislation suggests that mentally disabled people are no longer politically powerless as a group because their interests have attracted the attention of law makers. Finally, the Court concluded that the rational basis standard would provide sufficient protection for the rights

PRIOR INVIDIOUS DISCRIMINATION

Justice Marshall's opinion for three justices in *City of Cleburne* noted that during the late nineteenth century and the early decades of the twentieth century, mentally disabled people were subjected to discrimination in legal regimes that resembled Jim Crow laws. They were segregated by law in large custodial institutions. Sterilization laws were enacted in 29 states as part of the eugenics movement, for the purpose of denying mentally disabled people the right to marry and to have children. Mentally disabled children were excluded from public schools, and adults were deemed "unfit for citizenship." As recently as 1979, most state laws barred mentally disabled people from voting.

of mentally disabled people by requiring courts to invalidate any law that can serve no possible purpose other than the desire to discriminate against them.

The city ordinance at issue in *City of Cleburne* required group homes for mentally disabled people to obtain a special use permit, while it did not require permits for any other homes or facilities inhabited by groups that did not include mentally disabled people, such as apartment houses, boarding houses, dormitories, hospitals, nursing homes, and private clubs. In examining the record to determine the city council's justifications for denying a use permit to the plaintiff, the Court relied on two reasons for its conclusion that the denial of the permit constituted an invidious classification that could serve no possible purpose other than discrimination based on prejudice against mentally disabled people. First, the city argued that two permissible interests supported the permit denial, namely the potential hostility of adjacent property owners and the potential harassment of disabled group home residents by neighbors. The Court rejected these interests as illegitimate because the law "cannot give effect to private bias." Second, the Court recognized that even though the city relied on many other reasons to justify the denial of the permit, each of these reasons applied equally to other facilities that did not house the mentally retarded. Yet none of these reasons were considered important enough by the city to justify similar permit restrictions on those facilities. These reasons included concerns based on the site of the home, the legal responsibility for actions by residents of the home, the size and number of people in the home, the need to lessen congestion in the streets, the danger of fire hazards, the serenity of the neighborhood, and potential dangers to other residents in the home. Therefore, the Court concluded that the city's denial of the permit was based on none of the alleged reasons but on prejudice and invidious discrimination against mentally disabled people. By contrast, three justices in *City of Cleburne* advocated a more demanding scrutiny standard, arguing that the city should be required to show that the interests underlying the permit requirement were "substantial enough" to overcome the suspicion that the law rested on "impermissible assumptions or outmoded and perhaps invidious stereotypes."

In *Heller v. Doe*,[151] the Court divided over the meaning of the rational basis test, with a majority upholding the rationality of a classification that distinguished between mentally disabled and mentally ill persons, and four dissenters finding no persuasive differences between the two classes that could justify different treatment. The law in *Heller* required a finding beyond a reasonable doubt that a person suffered from the type of mental illness that justified commitment, but required only clear and convincing evidence for the commitment of mentally disabled people. The law also allowed family members and guardians of mentally disabled people to participate as parties, but protected mentally ill people from the participation of such

Sidebar

MODERN LEGISLATIVE PROTECTIONS

The *City of Cleburne* Court relied on a variety of modern legislative protections for the mentally disabled in concluding that such persons should not be treated as a "quasi-suspect class." The Rehabilitation Act of 1973 bans discrimination against mentally disabled persons in federally funded programs. The Developmental Disabilities Assistance and Bill of Rights Act protects their right to "appropriate treatment, services, and habilitation" in a setting that is "least restrictive" of their personal liberty. The Education of the Handicapped Act requires states to ensure that mentally disabled children enjoy an education that is integrated with other children "to the maximum extent appropriate" and to ensure that an "individualized educational program" must be tailored to the needs of each mentally disabled child. Some states recognize the right of mentally disabled persons to live in the least restrictive setting appropriate, including a group home, and some states prohibit zoning that excludes the mentally disabled.

individuals. The *Heller* Court based its conclusion of rationality on the state's need for information about family history in cases involving mentally disabled persons, and on the need for a protective higher proof standard for mentally ill people because of the greater difficulties involved in proving mental illness and the more invasive treatments that could result from commitment. The *Heller* dissenters concluded that the less favorable treatment of mentally disabled people was based on stereotypical and outmoded legislative judgments about them.

H. Classifications Based on Sexual Orientation

Sexual orientation refers to a person's sexual identity as homosexual, heterosexual, bisexual or transgendered. Sex or gender-based discrimination references discriminatory treatment of a male or female based on gender. Although the Supreme Court applies intermediate scrutiny to claims of gender discrimination, it continues to apply rational basis in cases of sexual-orientation-based discrimination.

Romer v. Evans[152] challenged the constitutionality under the Equal Protection Clause of a state referendum, passed by a majority of citizens in Colorado, that repealed all state and local laws prohibiting discrimination against gays, lesbians, and bisexuals. The majority of the Supreme Court applied rational basis and held that the referendum offended the Equal Protection Clause. *Romer* is one of those rare cases in which the Court struck down a state law under rational basis.[153] Although the Court would not classify sexual orientation as a "suspect class," it was less deferential to the legislative judgment than is typical when rational basis is applied.

In *Lawrence v. Texas*,[154] the Court once again declined to apply heightened scrutiny to determine if sodomy laws violated the fundamental right to privacy. However, the Court applied "a more searching form of rational basis" to overrule *Bowers v. Hardwick*.[155] "The issue is whether the majority may use the power of the State to enforce these views on the whole society through operation of the criminal law. 'Our obligation is to define the liberty of all, not to mandate our own moral code.'" Kennedy concludes that the analysis in Steven's dissent in *Bowers* should have been controlling: Due process "liberty" includes protection of choices concerning intimacy in sexual relationships of married and unmarried persons. The Court found that consensual same-sex relationships are within the "realm of personal liberty which the government may not enter." Justice O'Connor concurred, arguing that she would have decided the issue on equal protection grounds because heterosexual sodomy was not prosecuted while homosexual sodomy was.

Since the Court has declined to categorize sexual orientation as a suspect class, a variety of approaches have been taken to provide heightened protection against discrimination. First, a number of states have general laws protecting gay, lesbian and transgendered citizens from harassment and employment discrimination.[156] Second, a few lower federal and state supreme courts have applied heightened scrutiny in cases dealing with the constitutionality of same-sex marriage.[157] Finally, some courts and commentators analogize discrimination based on sexual orientation with gender-based discrimination.[158]

Litigation to resolve discrimination based on sexual orientation has become increasingly important. In particular, the issue of whether same-sex marriage is protected under due process and equal protection remains unresolved by the Supreme Court. In general, marriage is a local matter, unless as in *Loving v. Virginia*,[159] the law violates the equal protection or due process rights of members of a suspect class.

The majority of states continue to define marriage as between a man and a woman. However, the high courts in California, Connecticut, Hawaii, Massachusetts, New Jersey, and Vermont struck down marriage laws that excluded same-sex couples as a violation of the states' constitutions.[160] Congress, in response to developments at the state level, passed the Defense of Marriage Act, which authorizes states to deny full faith and credit to same-sex marriages performed in states and countries that permit them. However, some states that do not sanction same-sex marriage have given full faith and credit recognition to marriages performed in states that do.[161]

I. The Fundamental Rights Strand of Equal Protection

Discrimination on the basis of group status alone does not implicate the equal protection guarantee, unless the victim is within the narrow range of categories that the Court has identified as being within the provision's ambit of concern. A classification without such an impact may be constitutionally significant nonetheless if it qualifies enjoyment of a **fundamental right** on a selective basis. Denial of a fundamental right on a discriminatory basis thus creates the basis for a heightened standard of review, regardless of the group burdened.

A useful benchmark for grasping the fundamental rights track of equal protection case law is modern substantive due process review. The same debate over the role of the judiciary, in identifying and developing rights and liberties not specified by constitutional text, operates in the equal protection context. In both instances, the judiciary has been criticized on grounds its development of fundamental rights usurps legislative authority and represents an antidemocratic function.

In determining whether due process or equal protection analysis governs the deprivation of a fundamental right or liberty, it is important to focus on the impact of the violation. Government action that operates in a broad spectrum manner and thus denies a right or liberty to all persons is reviewable under the Due Process Clause. Equal protection interests are implicated only when government channels burden (or benefit) to a particular subset of persons. The right of privacy cases, which pertain to abortion, marriage, procreation, sexual orientation, and termination of life, have both due process and equal protection dimensions. The following sections focus on rights and liberties that are not textually enumerated or derived but derived from premises other than the Due Process Clause.

F   A   Q

Q: What difference does it make whether the Due Process Clause or Equal Protection Clause is the basis for a finding that a law violates a fundamental right?

A: The Due Process Clause prohibits government action altogether insofar as it burdens a fundamental right (and there is no compelling justification for the abridgment and narrowly tailored fit between means and ends). The equal protection guarantee denies government the power to regulate only to the extent that it classifies impermissibly. The law thus may be permissible to the extent it can be structured in a manner that avoids over- or underinclusiveness.

(1) Freedom of Speech

When government discriminates on the basis of content or viewpoint, its action implicates both equal protection and First Amendment concerns. The Court in *Police Department of Chicago v. Mosley*[162] observed that, pursuant to the equal protection guarantee, "government may not grant the use of a forum to people whose views it finds acceptable, but deny use to those wishing to express less favored or more controversial views. And it may not select which issues are worth discussing or debating in public facilities." In striking down the ordinance, the Court noted that "[t]here is an 'equality of status in the field of ideas,' and government must afford all points of view an equal opportunity to be heard." This view of equal opportunity for expression is a fundamental predicate for First Amendment jurisprudence relating to public forum management. The basic principle is that when a forum is opened to assembly or speaking, individuals may not be excluded on the basis of content or viewpoint. This premise and related concepts are discussed further in Chapter 10.

(2) Access to the Justice System

Limitations on **access to the criminal justice system** may implicate the equal protection guarantee. The Sixth Amendment provides a person accused of a crime "the Assistance of Counsel for his defense." Equal protection jurisprudence as it relates to this right reflects an understanding, as enunciated by Justice Black in *Griffin v. Illinois*, that "[there] can be no equal justice where the kind of trial a man gets depends on the amount of money he has."[163]

Through the Equal Protection Clause, the **right to counsel** was extended to the appellate process. In *Douglas v. California*,[164] the Court determined that the state must appoint counsel to indigent appellants who were pursuing a first appeal as a matter of right. The right was extended to discretionary appeals in *Ross v. Moffitt*.[165] Unless the state provided counsel to indigent appellants, the *Douglas* Court believed that the state maintained "an unconstitutional line between rich and poor." This outcome represented a departure from general constitutional principles that typically do not require government to subsidize the exercise of a right or liberty.[166]

In *Bearden v. Georgia*,[167] the Court explained the differing nature of inquiries pursuant to the Due Process and Equal Protection Clauses. Due process analysis, as the *Bearden* Court explained, focuses on the fairness of the relationship between the defendant and criminal justice process. Equal protection review centers on whether the defendant invidiously has been denied an important benefit afforded other classes of defendants. At issue in *Bearden* was whether a court could revoke probation, absent findings that the defendant had failed to pay or to make restitution. As the Court saw it, the question of whether indigence could be a factor in the outcome was similar to whether it was "fundamentally unfair or arbitrary" to revoke probation for inability to pay. Either way, resolution of the issue required "a careful inquiry" into such factors as " 'the nature of the individual interest affected, the extent to which it is affected, the rationality of the connection between legislative means and purpose, [and] the existence of alternative means for effectuating the purpose.' "[168] Minus findings of an inability to pay or inadequacy of alternative punishment, the Court determined that the revocation of probation was inconsistent with the demands of fundamental fairness.

(3) Right to Interstate Travel

Residence-based eligibility requirements have been a primary source of equal protection case law concerning the **right to travel**. These cases do not turn on the state's legitimate interest in establishing bona fide residence. Such requirements consistently have been upheld on grounds they reflect reasonable government interests and are reviewed pursuant to a rational basis standard. The standard of review intensifies, however, when eligibility for a benefit or right hinges on residence for a designated length of time. When the benefit constitutes a basic necessity of life, an extended delay in qualifying for it may be construed as a burden on the right to interstate travel.

F   A   Q

Q: What are the basis and nature of the right to interstate travel?

A: The Constitution, as previously noted, does not indicate specifically a right to interstate travel. It is difficult to imagine a viable political and economic union, however, without the right to travel freely across state lines. The right to travel thus has been established as a logical incident of the nation's structure. In *Saenz v. Roe*, 526 U.S. 489 (1999), the Court noted that the right to travel has three separate and distinct components. It "protects the right of a citizen of one State to enter and to leave another State, the right to be treated as a welcome visitor rather than an unfriendly alien when temporarily present in the second State, and for those travelers who elect to become permanent residents, the right to be treated like other citizens of that State."

The seminal equal protection decision on the subject is *Shapiro v. Thompson*.[169] This case concerned a state law that imposed a one-year residence requirement on eligibility for welfare benefits. The state maintained that the eligibility standard was necessary to protect the fiscal integrity of its public assistance programs. The Court found that the waiting period unduly burdened the right to interstate travel. Although noting that the state's concern with fiscal integrity was valid, it determined that deterrence of interstate migration was an unconstitutional purpose. It rejected any differentiation between long-term and short-term residents pursuant to their disparate tax contributions.

The Court in *Shapiro v. Thompson* applied a strict scrutiny standard of review. In *Memorial Hospital v. Maricopa County*,[170] it used the same standard to strike down a one-year residence requirement to establish eligibility for nonemergency medical care at county expense. As in *Shapiro*, the Court determined that the restriction burdened the right to interstate travel. The Court noted that residency requirements and waiting periods are not per se unconstitutional. Deployment of strict scrutiny, however, hinges on whether welfare benefits, medical care, or some other necessity of life is at stake. A one-year residency requirement to file for divorce thus was upheld as reasonable in *Sosna v. Iowa*.[171] So too, in *Vlandis v. Kline*,[172] was a one-year residency requirement to qualify for in-state tuition at a public university.

The Court in *Zobel v. Williams*[173] invalidated an Alaska program that distributed royalties from oil production to citizens on the basis of length of residence in the state. This result was achieved pursuant to a rational basis standard of review, which the Court identified as the normative criterion. The state advanced three justifications for the dividend program that included (1) a financial incentive to establish and maintain residence in Alaska, (2) encouragement of prudent management of the fund, and (3) apportionment of benefits on the basis of contributions made by residents over the years. The Court found no rational relationship between a financial incentive or prudent management of the fund and distinctions on the basis of residence. Rewards tied to past contributions, as the Court saw it, "could open the door to state apportionment of other rights, benefits, and services according to length of residency. It would permit the states to divide citizens into expanding numbers of permanent classes. Such a result would be clearly impermissible." The Court thus saw "no valid state interests which are rationally served by the distinction it makes between citizens" and found the dividend distribution plan at odds with the equal protection guarantee.

Allocation of benefits to veterans on the basis of their time or length of residence has triggered differing levels of review. In *Hooper v. Bernallilo County Assessor*,[174] the Court invalidated a tax exemption awarded to Vietnam veterans who resided in the state prior to a designated date. The state justified the law as a means of recognizing its citizens' military contributions. The Court, however, found no reasonable relationship between the state's interest and the classification of its residents.

Unlike the rational basis standard of review used in *Hooper*, a plurality in *Attorney General of New York v. Soto Lopez*[175] used strict scrutiny to strike down a hiring preference for veterans who lived in the state when they joined the military. The plurality viewed the benefits as being important enough, and deprivation of them permanent enough, that a more rigorous level of review was justified. The state's interest in recognizing military contributions could have been achieved more appropriately, from the Court's perspective, by extending the preference to all veterans living in the state.

Q: What is the key trigger for strict scrutiny in the right to travel cases?

A: Strict scrutiny appears to be reserved for those instances in which the state establishes a residence requirement that significantly qualifies access to a necessity of life.

(4) Voting

The Constitution creates a republican form of government but does not by specific terms establish a general **right to vote**. The Court has observed that "the right to vote in federal elections is conferred by Art. I, sec. 2, of the Constitution, but the right to vote in state elections is nowhere expressly mentioned."[176] It nonetheless has characterized voting, in the context of state elections, as "a fundamental matter in a free and democratic society, [e]specially since the right to exercise the franchise in a free and unimpaired manner is preservative of other basic civil and political rights." The importance of the franchise is further evidenced by the number of constitutional amendments concerned with protecting it. The Fifteenth Amendment prohibits denial of the right to vote "on account of race, color, or previous condition of servitude." The Nineteenth Amendment prohibits abridgment of the right to vote "on account of sex." The Twenty-fourth Amendment prohibits poll taxes. The Twenty-sixth Amendment extends the right to vote to citizens who are 18 years or older.

Voting was declared a fundamental right in *Baker v. Carr*[177] when the Court struck down a state legislative apportionment scheme on grounds it violated the premise of "one man, one vote." This principle of equal calibration became the benchmark for reviewing laws that were challenged on grounds they denied or diluted the right to vote.

(a) Denial of the Right to Vote

Although the states have authority to establish the basic terms of voting, qualifications unrelated to age, citizenship, or residence will "be carefully and meticulously scrutinized."[178] This standard of review may extend to residence requirements, as evidenced by the Court's invalidation of a one-year state and three-month county waiting period for local, state, and congressional elections.[179]

Poll taxes and voter eligibility requirements for special purpose government districts are primary examples of devices or rules that may deny the opportunity to participate in the political process. The Twenty-fourth Amendment prohibited poll taxes. The Court's output with respect to voter requirements for special purpose district elections has been mixed, both with respect to standards of review and results.

Poll Taxes. In *Harper v. Virginia State Board of Elections*,[180] the Court found no basis for making wealth a qualification for voting. As Justice Douglas put it for the Court, "[w]ealth, like race, creed, or color, is not germane to the power to participate intelligently in the electoral process. Lines drawn on the basis of wealth or property, like those of race, are traditionally disfavored. To introduce wealth or payment of a fee as a measure of a voter's qualifications is to introduce a capricious or irrelevant factor. The degree of the discrimination is irrelevant. In this context—that is, as a condition of obtaining a ballot—the requirement of fee paying causes an 'invidious' discrimination."

Land Ownership. Special restrictions on eligibility for school board elections also have been the basis for "a close and exacting examination." In *Kramer v. Union Free School District*,[181] the Court reviewed a state law that narrowed eligibility for voting in school board elections to otherwise qualified voters who owned or leased property in the district or who had children enrolled in the district's schools. The eligibility requirements were designed to limit electoral participation to resident citizens who had a primary interest in decisions affecting schools. The Court determined that this objective was not promoted with "satisfactory precision." To the contrary, it excluded some who had a distinct and direct interest in school affairs and included others who had a remote and indirect concern with them.

For districts that have a special purpose, eligibility requirements may be a function of how narrow the scope of governmental authority is. Case law suggests that districts with a narrower purpose may have the ability to establish more detailed voter eligibility standards. In *Salyer Land Co. v. Tulare Lake Basin Water Storage District*,[182] the Court upheld a law limiting participation in water storage district elections to land owners. Absentee land owners thus could vote, but district residents who did not own land were excluded from the electoral process. The result reflected the Court's sense that the water storage district was not a " 'normal government' authority" and "its actions disproportionately affect landowners." It also was achieved pursuant to rational basis review rather than the strict scrutiny standard used in *Kramer*. The different standards of review appear to correlate with a sense that, as a district's ambit of concern narrows, there is more room needed to establish requirements that ensure an "interested" electorate. Barring a special interest election, as the Court noted in *Hill v. Stone*,[183] classifications restricting the right to vote are impermissible unless the state demonstrates they account for a compelling state interest.

(b) Dilution of the Right to Vote

The right to vote may be abridged not only by deprivation but by means of dilution. Votes may be diluted by apportionment processes, restrictions on ballot access that may narrow the range of voter options, and processes for recording and counting votes. Districting processes for political representation generally are governed by the principle of one-person, one-vote. Allowable deviations from the norm and standards of review vary depending on whether federal, state, or local representation is implicated. With respect to ballot access, the focus is on the degree of burden imposed by the restriction.

Apportionment. The basis for determining representation in the political process is an issue that has been a source of contention since the nation's founding. Next to slavery, representation in the national government probably was the most divisive issue at the Constitutional Convention. The Framers resolved the controversy by establishing a bicameral legislature that correlated representation in the House to state population and gave every state the same number of senators. Most states have adopted a bicameral model for their legislative process. The dual sovereign relationship between the federal and state government, however, is not replicated at the state level. Counties and districts are subsets or units of state government, rather than independent sovereigns. Minus a true parallel to the federal system, as reflected in *Reynolds v. Sims*,[184] the Court has concluded that representation in state legislatures must follow a rule of proportionality that translates generally into one-person, one-vote.

In *Reynolds*, the Court invalidated a system of electoral districts that had substantial variations in the proportionality of representation. Pursuant to the districting plan, 25 percent of the population could elect a majority of the state senate and house. As the Court saw it, "the effect of state legislative districting schemes which give the same number of representatives to unequal numbers of constituents" diluted the right to vote. The Court described "the basic principle of representative government" to be that "the weight of a citizen's vote cannot be made to depend on where he lives." It characterized population as "the starting point for consideration and the controlling criterion for judgment in legislative apportionment controversies." In this regard, it found that "[t]he Equal Protection Clause demands no less than substantially equal state legislative representation for all citizens, of all places as well as of all races." Because the state apportionment schemes were not correlated to population, the Court found them constitutionally invalid. More specifically, it held "that the Equal Protection Clause requires both houses of a state legislature to be apportioned on a population basis."

The Court noted the "practical impossibility" of establishing districts that had precise equality of residents, citizens, or voters. Against this backdrop, it required "an honest and good faith effort to construct districts, in both houses of its legislature, as nearly of equal population as is practicable." In this regard, it noted that "neither history alone, nor economic or other sorts of group interests, are permissible factors in attempting to justify disparities from population-based representation." The Court also foresaw the potential for demographic change and indicated that the equal protection guarantee was no barrier to periodic redistricting. In this regard it required a "reasonably conceived plan for periodic readjustment of legislative representation. Decennial reapportionment [would] clearly meet the minimal requirements for maintaining a reasonably current scheme of legislative representation." Less frequent reapportionment, the Court observed, would be constitutionally suspect.

Political Gerrymandering. The principle of one-person, one-vote has had a significant impact on how state legislative districts are drawn. The *Reynolds* decision itself responded to apportionment models that, although demographically outdated, had become entrenched. Equal weighting of votes may be difficult to achieve with mathematical precision. The one-person, one-vote principle also operates in conjunction with other legitimate apportionment factors. As the Court noted in *Karcher v. Daggett*,[185] these concerns may include "making districts compact, respecting municipal boundaries, preserving the cores of private districts, and avoiding contests between incumbent Representatives." Against this backdrop, legislative districting for state purposes has a higher margin for deviation than does congressional districting. State apportionment may factor traditional political boundaries, but it must reflect a good-faith effort to achieve equality of representation. Because congressional districts do not correlate to traditional state subdivisions, deviation from the equality principle should be minimal. In the *Karcher* case, a 0.7 percent deviation was found impermissible.

For state legislative districting processes, which may consider traditional political boundaries, there is more tolerance for deviation. A 16.4 percent deviation thus was allowed in Virginia and an 89 percent underrepresentation factor permitted in Wyoming.[186] The allowable deviation in the first instance was coupled with the observation that there are no "specialized calipers" that enable courts or legislatures to determine "what range of percentage deviations are permissible, and what are not." In the Wyoming case, the deviation largely owed to assignment of a legislative seat to the state's least populated county.

Multimember districts may represent a subtle mechanism for diluting the right to vote. Systems of at-large representation on city councils, for instance, historically have operated to diminish the influence of minority voters. At-large voting schemes that discriminate on the basis of race, as noted in *Rogers v. Lodge*,[187] violate the equal protection guarantee. To prevail on a claim of discrimination, as in other equal protection contexts, it is necessary to prove discriminatory purpose.[188]

Inherent in a political process driven by competing self-interests is the motivation to tilt the playing field for partisan purposes. The opportunity to achieve this result is presented by the processes of reapportionment that the *Reynolds* Court mandated on at least a decennial basis. In *Davis v. Bandemer*,[189] a four-justice plurality in an opinion by Justice White found that challengers must prove intentional discrimination against an identifiable group and discriminatory effect. The fact that Democrats won a smaller percentage of elections than their percentage of votes, however, did not establish intentional discrimination. This determination was made pursuant to review of an apportionment plan that gave Democrats 43 percent of seats despite receiving 52 percent of the statewide vote. The plurality observed that intentional discrimination could be established only when the apportionment plan consistently "degrades" a voter's or a group of voters' influence in the political process taken as a whole.

A four-justice plurality in *Vieth v. Jubelirer*[190] maintained that a claim of political gerrymandering is nonjusticiable. This conclusion reflected the sense that the Court could not develop an adequate standard of review and the political process is the appropriate source of remedy for such matters.

The Court in *League of United Latin American Citizens v. Perry*[191] affirmed that political gerrymandering cases or controversies are justiciable under the equal protection guarantee. It also noted that disagreement persists with respect to the appropriate standard of review. Writing for himself, Justice Kennedy determined that mid-decennial reapportionment was not a per se equal protection violation. He was joined by Justices Souter and Ginsburg in support of the proposition that the challengers presented no impermissible use of political classifications. Justice Stevens, joined by Justice Breyer, asserted that a partisan efforts to minimize the voting strength of racial or political elements of the voting population did not constitute "a legitimate government purpose." Justice Breyer perceived an equal protection violation on the basis of the accelerated reapportionment and departure from traditional districting criteria. Justices Scalia and Thomas maintained that political gerrymandering cases do not present a justiciable case or controversy.

Racial Gerrymandering. Political gerrymandering cases establish that a mere failure of proportionality in state districting does not establish an equal protection violation.

Rather, there must be purposeful discrimination and a demonstrable discriminatory effect on the targeted group. Considerations such as compactness, contiguity, and respect for political subdivisions and communities with common interests have been recognized bases for deviation from otherwise strict proportionality. Bloc voting on the basis of race is a common electoral phenomenon. Districting plans that overtly accounted for this factor presented an analytical choice for the Court. They could be assessed pursuant to the political gerrymandering decisions, in which case race simply would be another factor among many competing interests. Or, race-conscious policies could be analyzed as an affirmative action modality that triggered strict scrutiny.

In *Shaw v. Reno*,[192] the Court opted for strict scrutiny. This case concerned the creation of a congressional district in North Carolina that was predominantly African American but irregularly configured. The state maintained that its apportionment plan had been enacted to achieve compliance with the Voting Rights Act of 1965. The Court found that the layout of the district was so odd, however, that there could have been no motivation for it but race. Pursuant to this finding, it remanded the case to the lower court.

The Court in *Shaw v. Hunt*[193] determined that race was the predominant factor in configuring the congressional district, and the plan could not withstand strict scrutiny. Because it was not designed to remedy past discrimination, the plan was not supported by a compelling state interest. Although compliance with the Voting Rights Act of 1965 may represent a compelling state interest, the Court found that the plan exceeded the law's mandate and thus was not narrowly tailored.

In *Hunt v. Cromartie*,[194] the Court reversed a summary judgment that was granted pursuant to a claim that the redrawn congressional district still was motivated by racial factors. In addition to noting competing evidence of political motivations, the Court stressed "the sensitive nature of redistricting" and the need to presume that legislation was enacted in "good faith."

In *Miller v. Johnson*,[195] the Court strictly scrutinized a Georgia redistricting plan that created three predominantly African American districts. Although the districts were not unusually configured, the Justice Department had insisted on majority-minority districts to eradicate the effects of past discrimination. The Court acknowledged a compelling state interest in remedying past discrimination. Although compliance with the Voting Rights Act of 1965 may be an imperative, the Court indicated that it will strike down plans that reflect or facilitate racial stereotyping.

When legislative efforts to construct a new districting plan broke down, a federal court devised a scheme that included one majority-minority district. This plan was found to be consistent with traditional districting principles and was upheld in *Abrams v. Johnson*.[196] Insofar as race is a consideration in redistricting, strict scrutiny depends on whether it is a predominant factor. This point was reaffirmed in *Bush v. Vera*[197] when the Court struck down a congressional districting plan that had three majority-minority districts. Although race was not the exclusive factor, it was the predominant consideration, and thus the plan was subject to strict scrutiny. For such a redistricting plan to survive, it must be a narrowly tailored remedy that responds to specific instances of discrimination. Compliance with the Voting Rights Act of 1965 may constitute a compelling interest, but legislators must be careful not to exceed the scope of the enactment's requirements.

Vote Recording and Counting. Election officials provide voters with instructions on how to execute their ballots properly. The quality of this guidance may vary from one district or state to another. Differences also exist with respect to voting equipment and the methodology for counting votes. The relative efficacy and reliability of the voting process itself thus may bear on whether the right to vote is denied or diluted.

The Court, in *Bush v. Gore*,[198] cited data indicating that approximately 2 percent of votes cast in presidential elections are not counted. This phenomenon owes to voter error or defects in counting technology. At issue in *Bush v. Gore* was the manual recount of votes in three Florida counties cast in the 2000 presidential election. The Florida Supreme Court had ordered the recount of ballots that appeared to have been punched, but were not entirely perforated, to discern the "intent of the voter." The state court provided no guidance for the process, and each county established different standards for the recount. The Court described the interest in discerning voter intent as "unobjectionable as an abstract proposition." Minus a uniform standard, however, the recount process undermined the equal weight accorded to each vote. A total of seven justices agreed that the original counting problem warranted a remedy. A majority refused to permit further recount procedures because of an impending deadline for the state to choose its electors.

(c) Access to the Ballot

Standards of review for determining ballot access depend on the degree of burden that a requirement or process imposes. Regulations that seriously impede access to the ballot will be evaluated more carefully than those perceived as imposing minimal burdens. In *American Party of Texas v. White*,[199] the Court upheld a provision requiring parties receiving less than 2 percent of the gubernatorial vote in the prior election to obtain signatures of at least 1 percent of those who voted. This prescription, from the Court's perspective, was not excessively burdensome. A law requiring candidates to pay a filing fee, totaling 2 percent of the annual salary of the office sought, was found to violate the equal protection guarantee. In *Lubin v. Panish*,[200] the Court found that the regulation unduly burdened the ability of indigent candidates to secure a position on the ballot. In addition to diluting the right to vote, restrictions on ballot access also may implicate the right of association.

(5) Education

An understanding that the **right to education** is a fundamental right relates back to the early twentieth century. In *Pierce v. Society of Sisters*,[201] the Court struck down a state law requiring parents to send their children to public schools. The holding was accompanied by the observation that the statute "unreasonably interferes with the liberty of parents and guardians to direct the upbringing and education of their children." The importance of education was the basis for the Court's decision that officially segregated public schools were unconstitutional.

Case law concerning educational opportunity has implicated not only race but also broader social, philosophical, and economic concerns. These factors converged in *San Antonio Independent School District v. Rodriguez*,[202] a case concerning the state's reliance on local property taxes to finance public education. Given variations in wealth and the consequent value of property and differences in resources from district to district, the system was characterized by substantial funding disparities.

The Court acknowledged that education constitutes an important interest, but maintained that it was not a fundamental right. Although the funding scheme differentiated on the basis of wealth, the Court found that it did not create a suspect classification. Minus either of the triggers for strict scrutiny, the Court assessed the state's funding plan pursuant to the rational basis test. The Court concluded that, barring deprivation of an education altogether, or the teaching of minimal skills necessary for effective citizenship, a reasonable relationship existed between the funding model and state's interest in facilitating local control of schooling.

The *Rodriguez* decision demonstrated the Court's reluctance to use the Equal Protection Clause as a means for redistributing wealth. The majority opinion, authored by Justice Powell, nonetheless left open the possibility of a different result in the event that the state denied educational opportunity altogether.

This reservation prefaced the Court's determination, in *Plyler v. Doe*,[203] that a state's deprivation of public education to the children of illegal aliens violated the Equal Protection Clause. Professing consistency with *Rodriguez*, the Court noted that neither a fundamental right nor suspect classification was at issue. It characterized children of illegal aliens as "a permanent caste" and "discrete class," however, who were "not accountable for their disabling status." The Court also found that the state "impose[d] a lifetime hardship" upon them. Using terminology associated with an intermediate scrutiny rather than a rational basis standard of review, the Court concluded that the classification was not supported by "a substantial state interest."

The *Plyler* decision was anomalous in two regards. First, it departed from the Court's reluctance to use the Equal Protection Clause for redistributing social or economic opportunity. Second, although applying the rational basis test in form, the Court independently reviewed the logic and utility of the state's methods. This mode of analysis flowed from the premise that education, although not a fundamental right, is more than "some governmental 'benefit' indistinguishable from other forms of social welfare legislation."

Subsequent case law offers no sign that the Court has altered its position that education is not a fundamental right. The *Plyler* scenario actually fits into a category of state action (that is, deprivation of an education altogether) that the Court in *Rodriguez* identified as potentially unreasonable. An indication that the *Rodriguez* ruling is the relevant benchmark was provided, in *Kadermas v. Dickinson Public Schools*,[204] when the Court upheld a state law that allowed school districts to charge a school bus transportation fee. Although indigent children could not afford the cost, the Court restated that education was not a fundamental right and employed a traditional rational basis standard of review. Education thus appears to be bundled with interests like shelter and welfare that, although recognized as important, alone are not constitutionally significant.

SUMMARY

- Since its framing and ratification as part of the Fourteenth Amendment, the scope of the Equal Protection Clause has expanded beyond its initial concern with race. Its ambit nonetheless has been narrow, insofar as the only classifications that count are race, gender, alienage, nonmarital children, and those that selectively deny a constitutional right or liberty.

- For classifications that do not fit within this range of concern, the traditional standard of review is highly deferential and requires a plaintiff to prove that a classification is not rationally related to advancing a legitimate government interest.

- Even for those groups or interests that are within the equal protection guarantee's scope of interest, review until the latter part of the twentieth century was less than rigorous.

- Strict scrutiny emerged as a standard of review that, as used by the courts, struck down official regimes of racial segregation and discrimination and eventually any race-conscious program, even if conceptualized to remedy past societal discrimination.

- Heightened scrutiny for other protected statuses (gender, alienage, and nonmarital children), although not necessarily strict, reflects the sense that classifications on these grounds tend to be invidious and thus must be examined more carefully.

- The propensity for judicial restraint in other contexts, however, reflects an understanding that classification of persons or interests is a primary incident of law making.

CONNECTIONS

Commercial Speech

Historically, commercial expression fell outside of the First Amendment's protective ambit. Selective prohibition of a right to advertise, prior to the Court's recognition of commercial speech as protected expression, thus was reviewable primarily on equal protection grounds. Even then, minus a suspect classification or implication of some other fundamental right, the regulation would be reviewed pursuant to the rational basis test.

Power of Judicial Review

The Court's power "to say what the law is" originally was announced in *Marbury v. Madison.* As it encountered resistance to the desegregation mandate, the Court found it necessary to reaffirm this principle. Whether its desegregation orders would have the effective force of law ultimately was dependent on support from the political branches. Key developments in this regard included President Eisenhower's decision to send federal troops to enforce desegregation in Little Rock, Arkansas, and enactment of the Civil Rights Act of 1964.

Right to Counsel

The right to counsel is secured by the Sixth Amendment and has been incorporated through the Fourteenth Amendment. The Court has used the Equal Protection Clause to provide access to counsel for defendants who otherwise could not afford it at key stages of the criminal justice process.

Substantive Due Process

Development of fundamental rights, which are not enumerated by the Constitution, originated with the judiciary's interpretation of the Due Process Clause. Modern substantive due process cases often are viewed through an equal protection lens. The consequence of a due process violation is that government regulation of the interest is foreclosed. An equal protection offense does not preclude regulation, but requires only that government avoid using certain classifications. From an impact standpoint, therefore, equal protection review may be considered less invasive of government authority than due process review.

Endnotes

1. 60 U.S. 393 (1857).
2. U.S. Const., amend. XIV.
3. 83 U.S. 36 (1873).
4. Howard J. Graham, *Everyman's Constitution* 291 n.73 (1968).
5. Charles Fairman, 7 *History of the Supreme Court of the United States, Reconstruction and Reunion*, pt. 1, at 134 (1987).
6. Slaughter-House Cases, 83 U.S. at 81.
7. 83 U.S. 130 (1873).
8. 274 U.S. 200, 208 (1927).
9. 220 U.S. 61 (1911).
10. Romer v. Evans, 517 U.S. 620 (1996).
11. City of Cleburne v. Cleburne Living Center, 473 U.S. 432 (1985).
12. 426 U.S. 229, 248 (1976).
13. Fairman, *supra* note 5, at 134.
14. 336 U.S. 106 (1947).
15. Vance v. Bradley, 440 U.S. 93 (1979) (mandatory retirement from foreign service at age 60); Mass. Bd. of Retirement v. Murgia, 427 U.S. 307 (1976) (mandatory retirement from public employment at age 50).
16. 449 U.S. 166 (1980).
17. 455 U.S. 422 (1982).
18. Allegheny Pittsburgh Coal Co. v. County Commn., 488 U.S. 336 (1989).
19. City of Cleburne v. Cleburne Living Center, 473 U.S. 432 (1985).
20. 1 M. Farrand, The Records of the Federal Convention of 1787, at 486 (1937).
21. 41 U.S. 539 (1842).
22. 60 U.S. 393 (1857).
23. U.S. Const., amend. XIII.
24. Cong. Globe, 39th Cong., 1st Sess. 474 (1866).
25. 83 U.S. 36 (1873).
26. 100 U.S. 303 (1879).
27. 109 U.S. 3 (1883).
28. *E.g.*, State v. McCann, 21 Ohio St. 198 (1872); Roberts v. City of Boston, 59 Mass. 198 (1850).
29. 163 U.S. 537 (1896).
30. 175 U.S. 528 (1899).
31. 189 U.S. 475 (1903).

32. 211 U.S. 45 (1903).
33. 235 U.S. 151 (1908).
34. 245 U.S. 60 (1917).
35. 275 U.S. 78 (1927).
36. 305 U.S. 337 (1938).
37. 304 U.S. 144, 154 n.4 (1938).
38. 323 U.S. 214 (1944).
39. 347 U.S.483 (1954).
40. 339 U.S. 629 (1950).
41. 339 U.S. 637 (1950).
42. 347 U.S. 497 (1954).
43. 349 U.S. 294 (1955).
44. 132 F. Supp. 776 (E.D.S.C. 1955).
45. 358 U.S. 1 (1958).
46. Green v. County Sch. Bd., 391 U.S. 430, 438 (1969).
47. 402 U.S. 1 (1971).
48. 413 U.S. 189 (1973).
49. 418 U.S. 717 (1974).
50. 433 U.S. 257 (1977).
51. 427 U.S. 424 (1976).
52. Milliken v. Bradley, 418 U.S. at 782 (Marshall, J., dissenting).
53. Columbus Bd. of Educ. v. Penick, 443 U.S. 449, 483 (1979) (Powell, J., dissenting).
54. Cleveland Bd. of Educ. v. Reed, 445 U.S. 935, 938 (1980) (Rehnquist, J., dissenting from denial of certiorari).
55. Bd. of Educ. of Oklahoma City Schs. v. Dowell, 498 U.S. 237 (1991).
56. 503 U.S. 467 (1992).
57. 495 U.S. 33 (1990).
58. 127 S. Ct. 2738 (2007).
59. Columbus Bd. of Educ. v. Penick, 443 U.S. 449, 481 (1979) (Powell, J., dissenting).
60. 379 U.S. 184 (1964).
61. 106 U.S. 583 (1883).
62. 388 U.S. 1 (1967).
63. 426 U.S. 229 (1976).
64. 429 U.S. 252 (1977).
65. 481 U.S. 279 (1987).
66. 476 U.S. 79 (1986).
67. 509 U.S. 630 (1993).
68. 517 U.S. 899 (1996).
69. 391 U.S. 367 (1968).
70. 438 U.S. 265 (1978).
71. 448 U.S. 448 (1980).
72. 476 U.S. 267 (1986).
73. 480 U.S. 149 (1987).
74. 488 U.S. 469 (1989).
75. 497 U.S. 547 (1990).
76. 515 U.S. 200 (1995).
77. 539 U.S. 306 (2003).
78. 539 U.S. 244 (2003).
79. For a detailed discussion of the major Supreme Court decisions, see *Supreme Court Decisions and Women's Rights: Milestones to Equality*, Clare Cushman, ed., http://www.supremecourthistory.org.
80. Bradwell v. Illinois, 83 U.S. (16 Wall.) 130 (1873) (rejecting a woman's claimed right to practice law on the grounds that women do not have the same "privileges and immunities" common law or constitutional claim as men "to engage in any lawful employment"); *see also* Minor v. Happersett, 88 U.S. 162 (1875) (upholding a state law that denied women the right to vote).
81. Muller v. Oregon, 208 U.S. 41 (1908) (upholding state law that prohibited women from working more than 10 hours in a laundry); *see also* Goeseart v. Cleary, 335 U.S. 464 (1948) (barring a woman from working as a bartender unless she is the wife or daughter of the male bar owner).
82. Fontiero v. Richardson, 411 U.S. 677, 685 (1973).
83. 368 U.S. 57 (1961).
84. Katherine T. Bartlett & Deborah L. Rhode, *Gender and the Law: Theory, Doctrine, and Commentary* 1 (4th ed. 2006).
85. The amendment read, "Equality of rights under the law shall not be denied or abridged by the United States or by any state on account of sex."
86. *See, e.g.*, UAW v. Johnson Controls, Inc., 499 U.S. 187 (1991); Califano v. Goldfarb, 430 U.S. 199 (1977); Weinberger v. Wiesenfeld, 430 U.S. 313 (1975); Reed v. Reed, 404 U.S. 71 (1971).

87. Bartlett & Rhode, *supra* note 84, at 151.
88. Johnson v. Transp. Agency, 480 U.S. 616 (1987).
89. The Pregnancy Disability Act overruled Geduldig v. Aiello, 417 U.S. 484 (1974), after the Court, using formal equality theory, reasoned that discrimination on the basis of pregnancy was discrimination between pregnant and nonpregnant persons, not between women and men.
90. Bartlett & Rhode, *supra* note 84, at 151.
91. Nguyen v. INS, 533 U.S. 53 (2001).
92. *See, e.g.*, Schlesinger v. Ballard, 419 U.S. 498, 508 (1975); Kahn v. Shevin, 416 U.S. 351, 353-354 (1974).
93. 430 U.S. 313 (1977) (per curiam).
94. 453 U.S. 57 (1981).
95. 533 U.S. 53 (2001) (upholding a statute that required unmarried men but not women to establish paternity for child born to U.S. and non-U.S. citizens).
96. 304 U.S. 144 (1938).
97. Ry. Express Agency v. New York, 336 U.S. 106 (1949).
98. 404 U.S. 71 (1971).
99. 411 U.S. 677 (1973).
100. The Fourteenth Amendment does not apply to the federal government. However, the Supreme Court has recognized an equal protection component in the Fifth Amendment's Due Process Clause. In *Fontiero*, the Court stated that while the Fifth Amendment contains no Equal Protection Clause, it does forbid discrimination that is "so unjustifiable as to be violative of due process." Shapiro v. Thompson, 394 U.S. 618, 641-642 (1969); Schneider v. Rusk, 377 U.S. 163, 168 (1964); Bolling v. Sharpe, 347 U.S. 497 (1954).
101. "There can be no doubt that our Nation has had a long and unfortunate history of sex discrimination. Traditionally, such discrimination was rationalized by an attitude of 'romantic paternalism' which, in practical effect, put women, not on a pedestal, but in a cage. Indeed, this paternalistic attitude became so firmly rooted in our national consciousness that, 100 years ago, a distinguished Member of this Court was able to proclaim: 'The paramount destiny and mission of woman are to fulfill the noble and benign offices of wife and mother. This is the law of the Creator.' Bradwell v. State of Illinois, 16 Wall. 130, 141, 21 L. Ed. 2d 442 (1873) (Bradley, J., concurring). [T]he position of women in America has improved markedly in recent decades. Nevertheless, it can hardly be doubted that . . . women still face pervasive, although at times more subtle, discrimination in our educational institutions, in the job market and, perhaps most conspicuously, in the political arena. Moreover, since sex, like race and national origin, is an immutable characteristic determined solely by the accident of birth, the imposition of special disabilities upon the members of a particular sex because of their sex would seem to violate 'the basic concept of our system that legal burdens should bear some relationship to individual responsibility. . . .' And what differentiates sex from such non-suspect statuses as intelligence or physical disability, and aligns it with the recognized suspect criteria, is that the sex characteristic frequently bears no relation to ability to perform or contribute to society. As a result, statutory distinctions between the sexes often have the effect of invidiously relegating the entire class of females to inferior legal status without regard to the actual capabilities of its individual members." *Fontiero*, 411 U.S. at 686-687.
102. 429 U.S. 190 (1976).
103. United States v. Virginia, 518 U.S. 515, 532 (1996).
104. Craig v. Boren, 429 U.S. at 199.
105. *See* Heckler v. Mathews, 465 U.S. 728, 744 (1984); Miss. Univ. for Women v. Hogan, 458 U.S. 718, 724 (1982); Personnel Admin. of Mass. v. Feeney, 442 U.S. 256, 273 (1979); Caban v. Mohammed, 441 U.S. 380, 388 (1979); Orr v. Orr, 440 U.S. 268, 279 (1979); Califano v. Webster, 430 U.S. 313, 316-317 (1977); Califano v. Goldfarb, 430 U.S. 199 (1977).
106. Justice Stevens wrote, "There is only one equal protection clause. . . . Whatever criticism may be leveled at a judicial opinion implying that there are at least three such standards applies with the same force to a double standard." Justice Powell, also concurring, said, "I do have reservations as to some of the discussion concerning the appropriate standard for equal protection analysis. . . ."
107. 518 U.S. 515 (1996).
108. For a detailed discussion, see *The Supreme Court Historical Society*, http://www.supremecourthistory.org.
109. *See, e.g.*, Kirchberg v. Feenstra, 450 U.S. 455 (1981) (affirming invalidity of Louisiana law that made husband "head and master" of property jointly owned with his wife and giving him unilateral authority to dispose of property without the wife's consent); Stanton v. Stanton, 421 U.S. 7 (1975) (invalidating Utah requirement that parents support boys until age 21, girls only until age 18).
110. Wengler v. Druggists Mut. Ins. Co., 446 U.S. 142 (1980); Califano v. Goldfarb, 430 U.S. 199, 223-224 (1977) (Stevens, J., concurring in judgment); Weinberger v. Wiesenfeld, 420 U.S. 636 (1975).
111. 533 U.S. 53 (2001).

112. Bernal v. Fainter, 467 U.S. 216, 219 (1984).
113. 347 U.S. 483 (1954).
114. 334 U.S. 410 (1948).
115. City of Richmond v. J. A. Croson Co., 488 U.S. 469, 493 (1989).
116. 403 U.S. 365 (1971).
117. *Id.* at 372 (citing United States v. Carolene Products, 304 U.S. 144, 152-153 n.4 (1938)).
118. *Id.* at 378 (citing Truax v. Reich, 239 U.S. 33, 42 (1915)).
119. *See, e.g.,* Nyquist v. Mauclet, 432 U.S. 1 (1977).
120. Bernal v. Fainter, 467 U.S. 216, 219 (1984).
121. Nyquist v. Mauclet, 432 U.S. 1 (1977).
122. 413 U.S. 717 (1973).
123. Foley v. Connelie, 435 U.S. 291 (1978).
124. Cabell v. Chavez-Solido, 454 U.S. 432, 440 (1982).
125. 413 U.S. 634 (1973).
126. *Cabell,* 454 U.S. at 440-441; Ambach v. Norwick, 441 U.S. 68, 81, 86 (1979); *Foley,* 435 U.S. at 296.
127. Bernal v. Fainter, 467 U.S. 216, 220, 221 (1984).
128. *Id.* at 226-227.
129. 424 U.S. 351, 358 n.6 (1976).
130. 458 U.S. 1 (1982).
131. Mathews v. Diaz, 426 U.S. 67, 85 (1976).
132. Hampton v. Mow Sun Wong, 426 U.S. 88, 101 (1976).
133. Mow Sun Wong v. Campbell, 626 F.2d 739, 744-745 (9th Cir. 1980).
134. *Mathews,* 426 U.S. at 84-87.
135. 457 U.S. 202 (1982).
136. 457 U.S. at 225 (citing DeCanas v. Bica, 424 U.S. 351 (1976)).
137. 456 U.S. 456 (1988).
138. *See* Pickett v. Brown, 462 U.S. 1, 9 (1983); Mills v. Habluetzel, 456 U.S. 91, 99-100 (1982).
139. 409 U.S. 535 (1973).
140. 430 U.S. 762 (1977).
141. 406 U.S. 164 (1972).
142. Jiminez v. Weinberger, 417 U.S. 628 (1974); N.J. Welfare Rights Org. v. Cahill, 411 U.S. 619 (1973).
143. 441 U.S. 347 (1979).
144. 401 U.S. 532 (1971).
145. 439 U.S. 259 (1978).
146. 427 U.S. 495 (1976).
147. 405 U.S. 645 (1972).
148. 441 U.S. 380 (1979).
149. *See, e.g.,* Nguyen v. INS, 533 U.S. 53 (2001); Miller v. Albright, 523 U.S. 420 (1998).
150. 473 U.S. 432 (1985).
151. 509 U.S. 312 (1993).
152. 517 U.S. 620 (1996).
153. *See also* City of Cleburne v. Cleburne Living Center, 473 U.S. 432 (1985).
154. 539 U.S. 558 (2003).
155. 478 U.S. 186 (1986).
156. http://lambdalegal.org/our-work/states/, last visited October 22, 2008.
157. *See, e.g.,* Goodridge v. Dep't of Pub. Health, 798 N.E.2d 941 (Mass. 2003), 440 Mass. 309 (2003); Watkins v. U.S. Army, 875 F.2d 699 (9th Cir. 1989).
158. Baehr v. Lewin, 852 P.2d 44 (Haw. 1993), 74 Haw. 645 (1993) (concluding that denying same-sex marriage is gender discrimination); *but see* DeSantis v. Pacific Telephone & Telegraph Co., 608 F.2d 327 (9th Cir. 1979) (discrimination against gay and lesbian employees does not constitute sex discrimination under Title VII).
159. 388 U.S. 1 (1967).
160. Kerrigan v. Comm'r of Pub. Health, 2008 Conn. LEXIS 385; 2008 WL 4530885; *In re* Marriage Cases, 183 P.3d 384 (Cal. 2008), 43 Cal. 4th 757 (2008); Lewis v. Harris, 908 A.2d 196 (N.J. 2006), 188 N.J. 415 (2006); Goodridge v. Dep't of Pub. Health, 798 N.E.2d 941 (Mass. 2003), 440 Mass. 309 (2003); Baker v. State, 744 A.2d 864 (Vt. 1999), 170 Vt. 194 (1999); Baehr v. Lewin, 852 P.2d 44 (Haw. 1993), 74 Haw. 645 (1993) (overruled by state constitutional amendment).
161. Godfrey v. Spano, 33 Family Law Reporter 1219 (N.Y. Sup. Ct. 2007).
162. 408 U.S. 92 (1972).
163. Griffin v. Illinois, 351 U.S. 12 (1956).
164. 368 U.S. 815 (1963).
165. 417 U.S. 600 (1974).
166. *E.g.,* Harris v. McRae, 448 U.S. 297 (1980) (no government duty to subsidize a woman's abortion).
167. 461 U.S. 660 (1983).

168. *Id.* at 666-667, quoting Williams v. Illinois, 399 U.S. 235, 260 (1970) (Harlan, J., concurring).
169. 394 U.S. 618 (1969).
170. 415 U.S. 250 (1974).
171. 419 U.S. 393 (1975).
172. 412 U.S. 441 (1973).
173. 457 U.S. 55 (1982).
174. 472 U.S. 612 (1985).
175. 476 U.S. 898 (1986).
176. Harper v. Va. Bd. of Elections, 383 U.S. 663, 665 (1966).
177. 369 U.S. 186 (1962).
178. *Harper*, 383 U.S. 663.
179. Dunn v. Blumstein, 405 U.S. 330 (1972).
180. 383 U.S. 663 (1966).
181. 395 U.S. 621 (1969).
182. 410 U.S. 719 (1973).
183. 421 U.S. 289 (1975).
184. 377 U.S. 533 (1964).
185. 462 U.S. 725 (1983).
186. *See* Mahan v. Howell, 410 U.S. 315 (1973).
187. 458 U.S. 613 (1982).
188. City of Mobile v. Bolden, 446 U.S. 55 (1980).
189. 478 U.S. 109 (1986).
190. 541 U.S. 267 (2004).
191. 548 U.S. 399 (2006).
192. 509 U.S. 630 (1993).
193. 517 U.S. 899 (1996).
194. 526 U.S. 541 (1999).
195. 515 U.S. 900 (1995).
196. 521 U.S. 74 (1997).
197. 517 U.S. 292 (1996).
198. 531 U.S. 98 (2000).
199. 415 U.S. 767 (1974).
200. 415 U.S. 709 (1974).
201. 268 U.S. 510 (1925).
202. 411 U.S. 1 (1973).
203. 457 U.S. 202 (1982).
204. 487 U.S. 450 (1988).

Freedom of Expression

Two of the most important provisions of the Bill of Rights are those protecting the right to expression and the right to assembly. This chap-

OVERVIEW

ter explores the history of the First Amendment, as well as its limits. As we shall see, although the First Amendment is phrased in broad and unconditional terms, neither the right to free speech nor the right to assemble receives unqualified protection under the U.S. Constitution. The rights are subject to numerous exceptions, qualifications, and limitations.

A. **THE HISTORY OF EXPRESSIVE FREEDOM**

B. **SPEECH ADVOCATING VIOLENT OR ILLEGAL ACTION**

C. **CONTENT-BASED REGULATION OF SPEECH**

4. Telecommunication
5. The Internet

A. The History of Expressive Freedom

Expressive freedom (the idea that individuals should be entitled to express themselves through their words or their actions) was given a prominent position in the First Amendment to the U.S. Constitution, a reflection of its importance. Prior to the late seventeenth century, the concept of free expression was not widely accepted. Beginning in the thirteenth century, England used the crime of seditious libel to prosecute those who criticized government. The crime was premised on the notion that the head of state could do no wrong and thus could not be criticized. Moreover, under the traditional formulation of the crime, truth was not a defense. On the contrary, truth was regarded as an aggravating factor on the theory that truthful criticism was more likely to be harmful to the government.

With Johannes Gutenberg's invention of the printing press in the late fifteenth century, it became possible to publish and disseminate information much more easily. While this invention made it easier for the government to distribute its commands, it also made it easier for the people to communicate more easily with each other. In an attempt to control the press's impact, the English government imposed licensing requirements that required submission of proposed publications to governmental censors. Publication was prohibited absent the Crown's approval and license. These prepublication reviews were inevitably accompanied by censorship.

Eventually, new philosophies began to challenge government's right to control publication and expression. In the seventeenth century, John Locke proposed natural law limits on the scope of governmental authority. He argued that a government's legitimacy depends on the consent of the governed. Locke's theory viewed expressive freedom as a basis for discovering truth and provided the basis for what eventually became the American system of representative governance. John Milton argued that expressive liberty is the most important freedom, and he advocated the notion that the truth could best be found through the free competition of ideas. He argued that "the liberty to know, to utter, and to argue freely according to conscience, [is] above all liberties. . . . Though all the winds of doctrine were let loose to play upon the earth, so Truth be in the field, we do injuriously by licensing and prohibiting to misdoubt her strength. Let her and falsehood grapple; whoever knew Truth put to the worse in free and open encounter."[1] Milton's writings led to the formulation of the "**marketplace of ideas**" theory. As Justice Holmes would later summarize the theory, "the ultimate good is better reached by free trade in ideas and . . . the best test of truth is the power of thought to get itself accepted in the marketplace of ideas."[2]

F A Q

Q: Was Holmes correct in saying that the "marketplace of ideas" will inevitably lead to the discovery of the truth?

A: The simple answer is no. Holmes's statement represents an ideal, but there is no guarantee that a "free trade in ideas" will lead to truth or to correct conclusions. Indeed, our society generally has no arbiter of truth in political debate other than through elections and the ability of people to have their ideas accepted by others as part of the political process or the collective wisdom.

In the English colonies, in what became the United States, freedom of expression was not initially taken for granted. Although many colonists fled Europe in an effort to escape persecution, they were not always tolerant of those who disagreed with them. Even though licensing restrictions were generally abandoned by the late seventeenth century, the crime of seditious libel was imposed in the colonies. Taxation of printers in the eighteenth century was a particular source of aggrievement in the American colonies.

However, the colonists were not always tolerant of restrictions on expressive freedom. In 1735, John Peter Zenger, a printer, published articles that criticized the royal governor of New York and created pressure for change. After a grand jury refused to indict Zenger on seditious libel charges, the governor arranged to have Zenger arrested and prosecuted for the crime. Under the law, the government was not required to prove truth and was instead obligated to prove only the publication of critical articles. Contrary to the law and the facts, the jury returned a verdict in Zenger's favor. The Zenger trial eventually became a rallying point for expressive freedom.

During the drive for independence from England, colonial newspapers vigorously debated the desirability of independence, as well as the issues of the time. But the colonists were not uniformly tolerant of speech and sometimes vandalized or intimidated pro-British newspapers. In other words, they did not accept the Holmesian idea that First Amendment protects not only "free thought for those who agree with us, but freedom for the thought that we hate."[3]

Sidebar

THE PRESENT STATUS OF THE CRIME OF SEDITIOUS LIBEL

The crime of seditious libel is considered dead today. Like prior restraints on speech, it is regarded as inconsistent with the First Amendment's guarantee of freedom of speech.

Despite the history of speech repression in England and the colonies, the U.S. Constitution did not include any specification of rights and liberties, and in particular did not provide protections for expressive freedom. This absence led to an intense reaction that threatened to derail the ratification process. To obtain ratification, it was agreed that the First Congress would adopt a Bill of Rights that would include protections for expressive freedom. The First Amendment provided that "Congress shall make no law . . . abridging the freedom of speech, or of the press."[4] Although the First Amendment did not initially apply to the states, almost the entire Bill of Rights was eventually incorporated into the Fourteenth Amendment and applied to the states.

Because there was such widespread support for the notion of expressive freedom, it is difficult to know the precise intent of those who framed and ratified the First Amendment. Regardless of the Framers' intent, there are strong philosophical justifications for protecting speech. John Stuart Mill argued for the "marketplace of ideas" theory:

> First, if any opinion is compelled to silence, that opinion for aught we can certainly know, be true. To deny this is to assume our own infallibility. Secondly, though this silenced

opinion be in error, it may and very commonly does, contain a portion of the truth, and since the generally prevailing opinion of any subject is rarely or never the whole truth, it is only by the collision of adverse opinion that the remainder of the truth had any chance being supplied. Thirdly, even if the received opinion be not only true but the whole truth; unless it is suffered to be, and actually is vigorously amid earnestly contested, it will, by most of those who receive it, be held in the manner of a prejudice, with little comprehension or feeling of its natural grounds. And not only this, but fourthly, the meaning of the doctrine itself will be in danger of being lost or enfeebled.[5]

Mill's observations represent a classic libertarian perspective on expressive freedom as a means for discovering truth. By and large, the Court has embraced the First Amendment in terms framed by Mill and viewed it as an instrument of "enlightened public decision-making in a democracy."[6] However, other justifications for protecting expressive freedom have been offered, including the idea that liberty of expression advances personal knowledge and facilitates self-development,[7] has inherent value for purposes of promoting participatory decision making[8] (the idea that the people will deliberate and vote on their representatives as well as various ballot measures) and checking the potential for official abuse,[9] and provides a social safety value (a way to let off steam through speech rather than through violence).[10]

The Court's decisions suggest that it places the highest value on the goal of ensuring an informed electorate, including speech relating to government and debate regarding the wisdom of governmental actions. In addition, the Court has referred to freedom of speech as the "indispensable condition" for other basic rights and liberties, and it is therefore accorded a "preferred position" in the constitutional hierarchy.[11] However, the Court has generally been unwilling to prioritize the First Amendment over other constitutional provisions when conflicts arise.

Regardless of its importance, and even though the First Amendment is phrased in broad and absolute terms, the Court has refused to treat the First Amendment as an absolute command. Justice Black, a staunch advocate of the absolutist position, consistently maintained that "the First Amendment's unequivocal command that there shall be no abridgment of the rights of free speech . . . , shows the men who drafted the Bill of Rights did all the 'balancing' that was to be done."[12] Justice Harlan rejected the absolutist position, arguing that the language of the First Amendment should not be read literally. Ultimately, the Court too rejected the absolutist position.

F A Q

Q: Does Justice Harlan's position suggest that free speech rights receive more limited protections — equivalent to the level of protection provided in the post-*Lochner* era to governmental regulation of economic matters?

A: No. The Court typically evaluates economic regulations under a "rational basis" test, but the Court typically applies a higher standard of review when government regulation affects free speech interests. The level of review depends on the category of speech being regulated.

Although commentators have developed various theories regarding the meaning of the First Amendment, the true meaning of the First Amendment has been developed through judicial decisions applying that Amendment.

B. Speech Advocating Violent or Illegal Action

During the nation's early years, ideological conflicts between the Federalists and Jeffersonians led to passage of the Sedition Act, which made it a crime to "write, print, utter, or publish . . . any false, scandalous and malicious writing or writings against the government of the United States, or either house of the Congress of the United States, or the President of the United States, with intent to defame the said government, or either house of the said Congress, or the said President, or to bring them, or either of them, into contempt or disrepute, or to excite against them or either of them, the hatred of the good people of the United States, or to stir up sedition within the United States." The government used the act to punish its critics in the manner of seditious libel, except that truth was treated as a defense.

The Sedition Act evidences how fidelity to freedom of speech is more readily achieved in form than in fact. Congress eventually repealed the act and ordered repayment of all fines levied under it. The accepted wisdom now recognizes that the Sedition Act was an aberration and that its provisions were inconsistent with, and contrary to, the dictates of the First Amendment. In the Court's later decision in *New York Times Co. v. Sullivan*,[13] the Court noted that "[a]lthough the Sedition Act was never tested in this Court, the attack upon its validity has carried the day in the court of history. Fines levied in this prosecution were repaid by Act of Congress on the ground that it was unconstitutional. President Jefferson pardoned those who had been convicted and sentenced under the Act, stating: 'I . . . consider, that law to be a nullity, as absolute and as palpable as if Congress had ordered us to fall down and worship a golden image.'"

Over the course of the nineteenth century, expressive freedom received only limited protection. Prior to the Civil War, slavery states routinely banned the literature of abolitionists. Moreover, efforts to unionize were restricted by hostile legislation.

Judicial efforts to define the First Amendment began in earnest during World War I. In the earliest free speech cases, antiwar protesters who challenged American participation in World War I or urged resistance to the draft were prosecuted under the federal Espionage Act of 1917, which prohibited interference with military recruiting and enlistment. These prosecutions corresponded to the rise of Bolshevism in Russia and the perceived security risk precipitated by the so-called Red Scare. The act, punishable by up to 20 years in prison, was aggressively enforced. Even Eugene Debs, a presidential candidate who received nearly a million votes, was convicted and sentenced to ten years in prison for his antiwar sentiments. In addition to the Espionage Act, Congress passed the Sedition Act of 1918, and many states passed criminal syndicalism laws. These laws provided the basis for prosecuting individuals who advocated communism or espoused anarchic or revolutionary doctrine.

Case law during wartime and its aftermath commenced a half-century journey toward doctrine that eventually struck a settled balance between legitimate societal interests in thwarting subversion and providing the breathing room necessary for political dissent. The key issue, in the cases concerning advocacy of violence or unlawful action, is not whether government may forbid speech that incites illegal conduct, but when it may intervene. Undoubtedly, government has a strong interest in self-preservation, but it also has an obligation to avoid action that abridges freedom of speech and of the press.

The first major free speech case was a lower court decision. In *Masses Publishing Co. v. Patten*,[14] a federal district court enjoined a postmaster from excluding a revolutionary journal. Judge Learned Hand argued the Espionage Act prohibited only speech that "counsel[ed] the violation of law" and did not extend to expression that merely "arouse[d] a seditious disposition." Otherwise, government could suppress any expression critical of the government. Notwithstanding the importance of the distinction, Judge Hand was reversed by the court of appeals, even though his ideas would ultimately prevail in the U.S. Supreme Court.

Two years later, the Supreme Court decided several cases in which it first introduced the clear and present danger test in applying the Espionage Act. The cases arose during the rise of Bolshevism during the so-called Red Scare during which there were fears that communism would sweep the world. During this period, governmental officials worked aggressively to identify and prosecute individuals who advocated or promoted subversive action.

In the first case, *Schenck v. United States*,[15] the Court upheld the conviction of protesters who disseminated leaflets urging draft-eligible men to resist military service. In *Schenck*, writing for a unanimous Court, Justice Holmes defined the issue as "whether the words are used in such circumstances and are of such a nature as to create a clear and present danger that they will bring about the substantive degree of evils the Congress has a right to prevent."

F   A   Q

Q: In *Schenck*, was there evidence suggesting that the protestors actually induced any draft-eligible men to resist induction into the armed forces?

A: In fact, there was no evidence that the leaflets had a deleterious impact on the government's ability to conduct the draft or that the leaflets precipitated a "clear and present" danger of draft resistance. Nonetheless, the Court sustained the convictions, focusing on the intent of those who distributed the leaflets.

Schenck established that the First Amendment was not an indefeasible bar to regulating expression. As Justice Holmes observed, "[t]he most stringent protection of free speech would not protect a man in falsely shouting fire in a theater and causing a panic." The Court noted the relevance of context, specifically that the outcome might have been different had the case arose during peacetime. This observation is consistent with the Court's general tendency to defer toward the political branches when national security is a significant factor. The clear and present danger test, as articulated in *Schenck*, indicated that the harm must be both identifiable and close at hand. The standard did not insist on any likelihood that the harm would actually occur.

In two companion cases, *Frohwerk v. United States*[16] and *Debs v. United States*,[17] the Court upheld convictions of antiwar protesters under the Espionage Act. Instead of applying clear and present danger principles, the Court focused on the speech and its "natural tendency and reasonably probable effect." The focus on bad tendency was the basis, in *Abrams v. United States*,[18] for upholding the Espionage Act convictions of several self-styled "rebels," "revolutionaries," and "anarchists." In *Abrams*, Justice Holmes rendered his now famous dissenting opinion, which established the basis for modern illegal advocacy principles. Speech should not be punished, Justice Holmes argued, unless it "so imminently threaten[s] immediate interference with the lawful and pressing purpose of the law that an immediate check is required to save the country." Holmes's dissent also introduced the "marketplace of idea" metaphor, stating that "the ultimate good is better reached by free trade in ideas and that the best test of truth is the power of thought to get itself accepted in the competition of the market." Although Holmes's view did not prevail in *Abrams*, it eventually persuaded the Court and became the dominant view.

Despite Holmes's dissent, some later cases purported to apply the "bad tendency" test, which suggested that speech could be restricted if it had a "bad tendency" to produce disruption. For example, in *Gitlow v. New York*,[19] the Court upheld the convictions of individuals who printed and distributed a manifesto advocating class struggle and mass political strikes. The prosecutions were brought under the state's criminal anarchy statute, which prohibited advocacy of violent insurrection. *Gitlow* held that when the legislature had specifically identified the type of speech to be prohibited, there was no room for judicial inquiry. It thus consigned clear and present danger analysis to instances when the state prohibited an activity but made no reference to any expression that might be punishable. Although *Gitlow* perpetuated the bad tendency test, the decision is also notable for incorporating the freedom of speech and press clauses into the Fourteenth Amendment.

F   A   Q

Q: The bad tendency test seems very open-ended. Does it give government too much authority to suppress speech?

A: Yes. The test is so broad that it gives government a great deal of discretion. Note how the *Gitlow* decision states that since the government had specifically identified the speech to be prohibited, there is little room for judicial inquiry.

In *Whitney v. California*,[20] the Court also applied bad tendency principles in affirming the conviction of an individual who helped organize a Marxist-oriented group in violation of a state criminal syndicalism statute. The statute prohibited the advocacy, teaching, or aiding and abetting the commission of a crime, sabotage, unlawful force and violence, or unlawful methods of terrorism as a means of effecting economic or political change. Defendant was a member of the Communist Labor

Party who signed a resolution at an organizing convention noting "the value of political action as a means of spreading communist propaganda" and stressing the value of political power as a means of facilitating the liberation of workers. Although the organization supported violent methods of change, the defendant maintained that she advocated reform through the established political process and was unaware of group's illegal aims. She nonetheless was prosecuted on the basis of her participation in the organizing convention and role with a group that engaged in unlawful activity.

Whitney is primarily important because of Justice Brandeis's concurrence, joined by Justice Holmes, that provided the basis for the Court's modern approach to subversive advocacy. Brandeis began by challenging *Gitlow*'s conclusion that judicial review is precluded when the legislature has prohibited a specified form of expression and argued that defendant's conduct did not present a clear and present danger of serious harm. Then, drawing on history, Brandeis argued that the nation's founders valued liberty both as a means and an end, and believed the "freedom to think as you will and to speak as you think are means indispensable to the discovery and spread of political truth." He also argued that "fear breeds repression; repression breeds hate; that the path of safety lies in the opportunity to discuss freely supposed grievances and proposed remedies; and that the fitting remedy for evil counsels is good ones." Based on these ideas, he argued that, under the Court's view of the clear and present danger standard, mere advocacy of illegal action provided inadequate justification for denying free speech "where the advocacy falls short of *incitement* and there is nothing to indicate that the advocacy would be immediately acted upon. No danger flowing from speech can be deemed clear and present unless the incidence of evil apprehended is so imminent that it may befall before there is opportunity for full discussion."

Justices Brandeis and Holmes saw their concurrence employed in two cases decided during the 1930s and 1940s. In *DeJonge v. Oregon*,[21] the Court recognized that freedom of speech, press, and assembly could not be abridged minus "incite[ment] to violence and crime." Likewise, in *Herndon v. Lowrey*,[22] the Court reversed the conviction of a Communist Party organizer for inciting insurrection in violation of state law by attempting to recruit party members and by possessing party literature. In striking the law down on vagueness grounds, the Court held that expression could not be punished merely because of its dangerous tendency that involved "pure speculation as to future thoughts and trends" and thus essentially was standardless. The Court thus held that the conviction could not stand without "a reasonable apprehension of danger to organized government."

Although the holdings in *DeJonge* and *Herndon* were not consistently applied in later cases, the Court eventually moved toward heightened review of enumerated rights. In *United States v. Carolene Products Co.*,[23] although the Court announced the end of substantive due process review as applied to economic rights, the Court indicated that it would be less deferential toward regulation that implicated "a specific prohibition of the Constitution, such

Sidebar

COMPETING MODELS OF REVIEW

The Brandeis-Holmes model of analysis competed against a standard that allowed government to squelch expression at the first sign of possible risk. As the Court put it in *Gitlow*, "A single revolutionary spark may kindle a fire that, smouldering for a time, may burst into a sweeping and destructive conflagration." *Gitlow v. New York*, 268 U.S. 652, 669 (1925). Consistent with this perspective, government was not required to defer action until "revolutionary utterances lead to actual disturbances . . . [or] destruction." This orientation, somewhat more slowly than surely, eventually gave way to doctrine that reflected the perspective of Brandeis and Holmes.

as those of the first ten amendments." This rhetoric became reality in the Court's subsequent decision in *Bridges v. California*,[24] in which the Court determined that a contempt citation could be upheld only if the speech would effect an "extremely serious" substantive evil and imminence factor was "extremely high."

However, the Court backtracked somewhat in the aftermath of the Cold War and the development of McCarthyism following World War II. In this context, the Court returned to the bad tendency test in reviewing convictions under the Smith Act for conspiring to organize the Communist Party. In *Dennis v. United States*,[25] a plurality of the Court applied the clear and present danger test, but focused on "whether the gravity of the 'evil,' discounted by its improbability, justifies such invasion of free speech as is necessary to avoid the danger." This formulation was deferential, and the plurality found a substantial interest in preventing violent insurrection so that the government need not "wait until the *putsch* is about to be executed, the plans have been laid and the signal is awaited" before acting. Under the plurality's approach, the government could intervene even if the prospect for evil was remote rather than probable. Given the gravity of the evil (violent insurrection), government could abridge speech even if the danger was not imminent. Justice Black dissented, arguing that the plurality's version of the clear and present danger test reduced judicial review to an inquiry into whether abridgment of speech was "reasonable" and subjected individual rights to popular "pressures, passions, and fears."

F   A   Q

Q: Did the fact that many of the early subversive advocacy cases involved Communists affect the outcome of the decisions?

A: Undoubtedly. As some have argued, it is easy to talk about the importance of free speech in times of peace and tranquility. The real test of a society's commitment to speech arises in times of war or other emergencies when law makers, and judges, are concerned regarding external threats.

Sidebar

DENNIS AND THE SEEDS OF CHANGE

Although viewed as inconsistent with more speech-protective principles, the *Dennis* decision planted the seeds of more fortified free speech doctrine. Justice Douglas, in his dissenting opinion, urged a distinction between the teaching of abstract doctrine and the actual incitement of illegal action. Although agreeing that speech was not absolutely protected, he argued that it should be protected until it "fan[ned] such destructive flames that it must be halted in the interests of the safety of the Republic." Post-*Dennis* case law eventually incorporated a requirement of "imminence."

In the following years, additional cases arose involving prosecutions for membership in the Communist Party. For example, in *Yates v. United States*,[26] several Communist Party officials were convicted under the Smith Act for advocating and teaching the necessity of violent overthrow of the government, and organizing the Communist Party with the intent of causing violent overthrow of the government. The Court overturned the convictions, concluding that *Dennis* had not "obliterated the traditional dividing line between advocacy of abstract doctrine and advocacy of action." It thus distinguished *Dennis* as a case concerning "a conspiracy to advocate presently the taking of forcible action in the future." Thus, the Court was willing to uphold a conviction if it was reasonable to believe that the action would occur when conditions were ripe.

In the Court's next major decision, *Scales v. United States*,[27] the Court upheld Smith Act convictions of individuals based on their membership in the Communist Party and their knowledge of its illegal aims and of its advocacy of violent overthrow of the government whenever "circumstances would permit." The Court distinguished individuals who might be convicted based merely on association and sympathies, and concluded that present advocacy of future violence, rather than immediate action, must be shown to convict.

Modern cases drew more heavily on the Brandeis-Holmes model of analysis. But, even then, the Court did not move swiftly to adopt that model. For example, in *Noto v. United States*,[28] the Court concluded that advocacy of actual action was punishable regardless of whether it was imminent or remote. However, in *Bond v. Floyd*,[29] the Court reviewed the Georgia legislature's refusal to swear in and seat an elected representative based on his criticism of the Vietnam War and the draft, which house members viewed as advocating resistance to military service. In ruling in favor of the representative and against the legislature, the Court refused to view the antiwar statements as an incitement. Likewise, in *Watts v. United States*,[30] the Court reviewed a conviction under a federal law prohibiting threats against the president's life. The defendant had been convicted for making a statement, during an antiwar protest, that the first person he would aim his rifle at if drafted would be the president. The Court considered the context of the statement and determined that it was an instance of "political hyperbole" rather than an actual threat or incitement. Important too was the fact that the speech posed no imminent danger to the president. Consideration of this factor represented an important step toward a more speech-protective model of review.

Brandenburg v. Ohio[31] represents the Court's modern approach to subversive advocacy, and it embraced but expanded on the Brandeis-Holmes approach. The case involved several Ku Klux Klan members who were prosecuted under the state's criminal syndicalism law for a rally that involved a cross burning. The speech that triggered their prosecution related to the group's intention to march on Washington, D.C., and included a statement that, if the political process "continues to suppress the white, Caucasian race, it's possible that there might have to be some revengeance [*sic*] taken."

For practical purposes, the state law was indistinguishable from the statute providing the basis for conviction in *Whitney v. California*. In *Brandenburg*, however, the Court described *Whitney* as a "thoroughly discredited" decision and formally overruled it. In so doing, the Court conclusively disassociated itself from the bad tendency test. The standard of review set forth in *Brandenburg* provides that government may not abridge advocacy of illegal action unless it "is directed to inciting or producing imminent lawless action and is likely to incite or produce such action." This standard reflected the distinction between abstract discussions regarding the desirability or morality of using force or violence as an instrument of social change, and the actual incitement of such consequences. It broadened the First Amendment's reach even further, however, by distinguishing between imminent and remote consequences and requiring a showing of imminence.

The *Brandenburg* opinions reflects the "marketplace of ideas" theory and suggests that governmental suppression of speech is inappropriate so long as time exists for the "marketplace of ideas" to respond to speech with dangerous tendencies. In other words, reasoned discourse is to be preferred to suppression, and suppression is permissible only when speech is intended to incite an immediate violent response and is likely to produce that response.

Justices Black and Douglas, concurring, worried that the *Brandenburg* formulation might be distorted during peak periods of national insecurity since it involves balancing and therefore is subject to judicial manipulation. Indeed, as Justice Douglas noted, "Every idea is an incitement."

F A Q

Q: How far does the *Brandenburg* test extend? Does it suggest, for example, that two bank robbers cannot be convicted of conspiracy to rob banks if they discuss the possibility of robbing banks and agree to do so, but do not plan to do so imminently?

A: Probably not. While the Court has not specifically addressed the issue, it would probably find a way to distinguish political speech like that at issue in *Brandenburg* from two criminals who agree to rob a bank. Nevertheless, the precise dividing line between such "criminal solicitation" and "subversive advocacy" remains unclear.

Sidebar

BRANDENBURG AND THE DENNIS REFERENCE

Although viewed generally as an improvement on prior case law, the *Brandenburg* decision includes a peculiar reference to *Dennis* as precedent for discrediting *Whitney*. This notation is puzzling because the *Dennis* plurality applied an analytical regimen associated with *Whitney* and other decisions that focused on bad tendencies.

Post-*Brandenburg* decisions have generally been consistent with both the letter and spirit of that decision. For example, in *Hess v. Indiana*,[32] the Court overturned a disorderly conduct conviction that arose from threats of illegal action during an antiwar demonstration when defendant yelled out "we'll take the fucking street later." Since defendant's statement was not targeted at any particular person, it could not have produced an imminent lawless response. Moreover, given the ambiguity, the Court was unwilling to construe the statement as an incitement. As a result, *Hess* might be construed as suggesting that courts must focus not solely on the speaker's intent, but on whether objectively the speech could be understood as inciting such results.

Although *Brandenburg* has brought doctrinal stability to this area of the law, it is important to realize that terms like *incitement, imminence,* and *likelihood* are inherently ambiguous. Thus, in periods of crisis, they can be construed more narrowly. As a result, even had the *Brandenburg* test been in effect during the 1920s and 1950s, when the nation was feeling greater insecurity, cases like *Gitlow, Whitney,* and *Dennis* might have been resolved the same way. During periods of insecurity, fears are elevated and risks that otherwise may seem distant or improbable can be exaggerated. As a result, since *Brandenburg* does not absolutely protect speech, context will always be relevant and can perpetuate a different outcome than might be achieved in a less volatile atmosphere.

C. Content-Based Regulation of Speech

As a general rule, the Court has consistently recognized that the First Amendment denies government the "power to restrict expression because of the message, ideas, its subject matter or its content."[33] Despite this broad statement, the Court has upheld content regulation by holding that some categories of speech are unprotected because of their content. For example, in *Chaplinsky v. New Hampshire*,[34] the Court recognized that the right to free speech is not absolute and that there are "certain well-defined and narrowly limited classes of speech, the prevention and punishment of which have never been thought to raise any Constitutional problem." The Court included within these categories the lewd and obscene, the profane, the libelous, and insulting or "fighting words." It should be noted, however, that government may not engage in viewpoint discrimination, even when unprotected categories of speech are involved. For example, even though the government may prohibit fighting words, it may not prohibit fighting words relating only to race, religion, and gender.[35]

F   A   Q

Q: If the First Amendment prohibits government from regulating based on content, why has the Court created so many exceptions in *Chaplinsky*?

A: In fact, when political speech is involved, the Court is particularly vigilant about prohibiting content-based and viewpoint-based restrictions on speech. As a result, if government tried to stamp out particular views that it disagreed with (for example, opposition to affirmative action), the governmental restriction would likely be struck down. However, as *Chaplinsky* suggests, the Court has carved out particular categories of speech (for example, obscenity) that it treats as low-value speech.

(1) Fighting Words

One category of speech that has been denied protection under the First Amendment is that of so-called fighting words. *Chaplinsky* involved a Jehovah's Witness who gave a speech and distributed literature on the streets of Rochester, New Hampshire, on a Saturday afternoon. In the speech, he denounced religion as a "racket." When members of the crowd complained, the police informed them that Chaplinsky was acting lawfully, but also informed Chaplinsky that the crowd was getting restless. When the crowd caused a disturbance, the police escorted Chaplinsky toward the police station, but did not tell him that he was under arrest. On the way to the station, they encountered the city marshall, who was hurrying to the scene after he had been informed that Chaplinsky's remarks had precipitated a riot. When Chaplinsky saw the marshall, he stated, "You are a God damned racketeer" and "a damned Fascist and the whole government of Rochester are Fascists or agents of Fascists." Chaplinsky was found guilty of violating a New Hampshire law that prohibited anyone from addressing "any offensive, derisive or annoying word to any other person who is lawfully in any street or other public place" and also prohibited anyone from calling such person by any "offensive or derisive name."

In affirming Chaplinsky's conviction, the Court defined fighting words as those words "which by their very utterance inflict injury or tend to incite an immediate breach of the peace." In the Court's view, such "utterances are no essential part of any exposition of ideas, and are of such slight social value as a step to truth that any benefit that may be derived from them is clearly outweighed by the social interest in order and morality. 'Resort to epithets or personal abuse is not in any proper sense communication of information or opinion safeguarded by the Constitution, and its punishment as a criminal act would raise no question under that instrument.'"

F   A   Q

Q: Why wasn't Chaplinsky's speech considered political speech and therefore afforded the high level of protection accorded to such speech?

A: Chaplinsky's comments probably did involve political speech since he was commenting on the city's political officials. Ordinarily, then, they would have been entitled to a high level of protection. However, because the comments were rendered in the context of fighting words, the Court concluded that they were not protected. In other words, it was speech likely to provoke an imminent breach of the peace. Because of the governmental interest in preventing such breaches, the Court treats fighting words as low-value speech.

Sidebar

VAGUENESS AND OVERBREADTH DOCTRINES AS APPLIED TO FIGHTING WORDS

Although *Chaplinsky* held that fighting words are not protected under the First Amendment, the Court frequently reverses fighting words convictions on vagueness and overbreadth grounds. For example, in *Gooding v. Wilson*, 405 U.S. 518 (1972), defendant was convicted under a Georgia law that provided that "[a]ny person who shall, without provocation, use to or of another, and in his presence . . . opprobrious words or abusive language, tending to cause a breach of the peace . . . shall be guilty of a misdemeanor." The evidence showed that he stated to a police officer: "White son of a bitch, I'll kill you." "You son of a bitch, I'll choke you to death.'" He also stated: "You son of a bitch, if you ever put your hands on me again, I'll cut you all to pieces." The Court concluded that the terms "opprobrious" and "abusive" were impermissibly imprecise. Likewise, in *City of Houston v. Hill*, 482 U.S. 451 (1987), the Court struck down a Houston ordinance as unconstitutionally overbroad.

Of course, following *Chaplinsky*, the Court was left with the problem of how to define the term *fighting words*. The *Chaplinsky* Court concluded that the term included such words "as have a direct tendency to cause acts of violence by the person to whom, individually, the remark is addressed." "The test is what men of common intelligence would understand would be words likely to cause an average addressee to fight." The Court ultimately upheld the New Hampshire law because it did no more than "prohibit the face-to-face words plainly likely to cause a breach of the peace by the addressee, words whose speaking constitute a breach of the peace by the speaker—including 'classical fighting words,' words in current use less 'classical' but equally likely to cause violence, and other disorderly words, including profanity, obscenity and threats."

(2) Defamation

The tort of defamation provides compensation for reputational injury that is caused by written or spoken falsehoods (libel and slander, respectively). Under British colonial law, truth was an aggravating rather than ameliorating factor with respect to defamation. In the United States, until the middle of the twentieth century, the courts treated defamation as unprotected. Indeed, under *Chaplinsky*, libelous speech was listed as one of the categories of unprotected speech.

In addition, in *Beauharnais v. Illinois*,[36] the Court upheld a conviction under a group libel statute that criminalized any publication that portrayed a racial or religious group as showing "depravity, criminality, unchastity, or lack of virtue" or that brought "contempt, derision, [or] obloquy" on that group, or produced a "breach of the peace or of riots." Beauharnais's leaflets advocated resistance to racial integration and exhorted white persons to preserve their racial identity and avoid "forced mongrelization." By a 5-4 vote, the Court held that Beauharnais's expression was not constitutionally protected. From the majority's perspective, group libel was not protected because it facilitated the denigration of individual dignity. Although the *Beauharnais* decision has never been explicitly overruled, subsequent decisions and the Court's attitude toward hate speech control indicate that it has little, if any, vitality.

F   A   Q

Q: Didn't *Beauharnais* involve protected political speech in the sense that the petitioner was focused on communicating with public officials?

A: Yes. *Beauharnais* illustrates the proposition that even if we have clearly defined legal principles, the Court does not always apply them. Few commentators would regard the decision as good law today.

The Court's next major case decision was rendered in *New York Times Co. v. Sullivan*[37] and reversed a state court damage judgment in favor of the police commissioner of Montgomery, Alabama. The case arose from an editorial advertisement published in the *New York Times* that criticized police handling of civil rights demonstrations in Montgomery and other locations and referenced the efforts of "southern violators" who responded to nonviolent protests with intimidation and violence. The advertisement contained some inaccuracies that were fairly minor. For example, even though the police commissioner was not specifically named in the advertisement, he argued that the article implied that his office had condoned improper conduct. A jury found in the commissioner's favor and awarded him one-half $500,000 in damages based on state law that enabled the jury to presume damages without a demonstrated showing of loss.

In *Sullivan*, the Court held that large defamation judgments were potentially inconsistent with the national commitment to speech. Indeed, the immediate impact of the trial court judgment was to cause the *New York Times* to stop circulating its newspaper in Alabama. Under these circumstances, the potential for defamation awards to chill political discourses was evident, and the potential impact of defamation liability was similar to the chilling effect of seditious libel laws. Indeed, when the action for defamation was being used as a political tool, traditional defamation defenses such as truth were found to provide inadequate protection to the defamation defendant. Plaintiffs could seize on minor and inconsequential inaccuracies to construct a defamation case. Moreover, while a newspaper might have been negligent in publishing the inaccuracies without independently checking the facts, the cost and consequences of the potential liability was clearly disproportionate to the error. *Sullivan* reflected a sensitivity to these realities and sought to create more of a balance with the goal of creating more breathing space for First Amendment interests.

In an effort to protect speech, the Court articulated a new and higher standard for defamation actions by public officials. In doing so, the Court emphasized that public officials occupy a position at the center of government activity and policy, and that their decisions are subject to monitoring by the electorate. In addition, public officials are immune from liability for defamatory statements they make in the course of their official duties.[38] It followed that critics of public officials should have expanded freedom of criticism. As a result, the Court held that a public official cannot recover for defamation unless he or she proves, by clear and convincing evidence, that the statement was made with "actual malice." The term *actual malice* is a term of art that is not synonymous with mean-spiritedness or ill will. Rather, it relates to the state of mind that produced the defamatory statement and can be lost only if plaintiff can show that defendant acted with "knowledge that [the statement] was false or . . . [with] reckless disregard of whether it was false or malicious." At least for public officials, therefore, defamation cannot be established on the basis of strict liability or negligence. Indications of reckless disregard, however, are a defendant's "high degree of awareness of probable falsity" or "entertain[ing] serious doubts as to the truth of his publication." When a person has the opportunity to check the truthfulness of information, but doesn't do so, she technically may not have the requisite state of mind for actual malice. Such a declined opportunity, however, may prevent her from claiming protection under the actual malice standard.

F   A   Q

Q: If the *New York Times* actual malice standard makes it extremely difficult for public officials to recover for defamation, as it seems to do, how do they vindicate their reputations?

A: The practical effect of the actual malice standard is that governmental officials are essentially precluded from recovering for defamation. Few politicians ever sue, and it is virtually unheard of for a politician to obtain a recovery. Even when trial courts award defamation judgments, they are usually overturned on appeal. As a result, politicians have very few remedies at their disposal. They can respond to allegations through the media, but the public often discounts such denials.

In subsequent cases, the Court struggled to determine the meaning of the term *public official*. A public official has been defined as a person empowered with significant responsibility and discretion in managing public affairs.[39] Candidates for public office,[40] and former officeholders to the extent comments relate to performance of official duties,[41] are included in the concept.

The boundaries of constitutionally protected defamation soon expanded beyond public officials to include persons who, although not holding public office, nonetheless had a significant public presence. In *Curtis Publishing Co. v. Butts*,[42] the Court extended the actual malice standard to public figures. The increased protection for defamatory speech thus reflected an understanding that, like public officials, public figures are "intimately involved in the resolution of important public questions or, by reason of their fame, shape events in areas of concern to society at large."

Sidebar

NO "EDITORIAL PRIVILEGE"

Actual malice is a constitutional question and thus will be reviewed independently by an appeals court. *Bose Corporation v. Consumers Union*, 466 U.S. 485 (1984). For a plaintiff to determine whether actual malice exists, he or she must be able to probe the editorial process. In recognition of this need, the Court has rejected arguments for an editorial privilege against discovery. *Herbert v. Lando*, 441 U.S. 553 (1979).

F   A   Q

Q: Why did *Sullivan* focus on the status of the person defamed (for example, public official or public figure) rather than on whether the subject of the communication relates to a matter of public interest?

A: There is no clear answer. In *Rosenbloom v. Metromedia, Inc.*, 403 U.S. 29 (1971), a plurality of three justices determined that the actual malice standard should extend to defamatory statements concerning matters of general or public interest. This plurality view failed to command a majority of justices then or over the long run. The actual malice standard has remained fixed over the past few decades on the public status of the defamed individual. However, considerations of public interest have crept into the differential standards applied to different types of individuals (for example, public official or figure versus private individual in a matter of purely private interest). Of course, if the Court had opted for a public interest standard, it would have been faced with the potentially difficult task of defining the term "public interest."

As the Warren Court increasingly transitioned into the Burger Court, a majority coalesced against shifting the focus of actual malice from persons to issues. In *Gertz v. Robert Welch, Inc.*,[43] the Court reviewed the defamation claim of an attorney who had represented a family in a wrongful death action against a police officer. A magazine had described the lawyer as a "Communist fronter" and his efforts were part of a "Communist campaign against the police" and "frame-up" of the particular officer. In addition to his role as an attorney, and thus an officer of the court, the plaintiff served on various government boards and commissions. The Court rejected the notion that Gertz was a public official or public figure, and held that private individuals should not be subjected to the actual malice standard. Unlike public officials or figures, they do not invite public attention or warrant an assumption that they voluntarily have exposed themselves to a higher risk of reputational harm. Nor do they command access to the media and possess an ability to undo or mitigate reputational injury. Based upon these premises, the Court concluded that it should be easier for a private individual to recover for defamation. So long as a state does not impose strict liability, therefore, it may establish a standard for recovery that is less than actual malice. Minus a uniform standard for defamation actions by private individuals, criteria vary among the states. Some have adopted the actual malice standard, while others use a negligence or public interest criterion.

In addition to delimiting the reach of the actual malice standard, the *Gertz* Court provided some definition of the term "public figure" and the availability of damages in a defamation action. Public figures are persons who "have assumed roles of especial prominence in the affairs of society." They come in two main varieties. The first category consists of those individuals who "occupy positions of such pervasive power and influence that they are deemed public figures for all purposes."[44] The second category comprises persons who "have thrust themselves to the forefront of particular public controversies in order to influence the resolution of the issues involved." The common denominator of a public figure, fitting either one of these classifications, is that he or she invites attention or comment. The Court acknowledged, at least hypothetically, the possibility of an "involuntary public figure" who achieves this status unwillingly. It noted, however, that such a person would be rare.

Applying these standards to Gertz, the Court found that he did not have widespread fame in the community and thus did not fit into the first category of public figures. To the extent Gertz took on a relatively high profile case, however, the argument could be made that he thrust himself into the controversy with an intent (and even obligation) to influence the outcome. The Court, however, refused to draw trial lawyers into the actual malice web.

Subsequent case law has narrowed the concept of a public figure. In *Time, Inc. v. Firestone*,[45] the Court determined that a well-known socialite was not a public figure. This finding was made in the context of a divorce proceeding that, because of the lurid testimony it generated, drew extensive public attention. At the trial's conclusion, a national news magazine published a brief report that the husband was granted a divorce on the basis of his wife's adultery and extreme cruelty. The characterization of adultery as a basis for the divorce decree technically was inaccurate.

Two factors were critical to the outcome in *Firestone* and hence material to understanding the concept of a public figure. First, the plaintiff's prominent stature in elite social circles was not sufficient to make her a public figure. Nor had she

Sidebar

DEFAMATION STANDARDS AND INFORMED SELF-GOVERNANCE

Gertz halted the Court's expansion of the actual malice standard; allowed states to set the standard of fault in cases that did not concern public officials or public figures, provided they did not impose strict liability; and limited recovery to actual damages when liability is established on the basis of negligence. Presumed and punitive damages remained possible for instances when actual malice was established. The decision made it clear that the actual malice standard does not extend to private persons, at least in the instance of a media defendant. The stopping point for the actual malice standard may defy the logic of standards designed to facilitate informed self-governance. They nonetheless comport with the nature and process of balancing competing interests. In this context, it is predictable that a point will be reached at which one concern must give way to another. Private individuals typically have less access to the media than public officials or public figures, so are less able to secure remedies for reputational damage through self-help. They also do not thrust themselves into public controversies. These considerations helped convince the Court that the status of the plaintiff, rather than the content of the speech, provided the basis for a logical dividing line between constitutionally protected and unprotected defamation.

voluntarily injected herself into a public controversy for purposes of influencing its outcome. This determination was made even though the plaintiff had conducted news conferences, retained a public relations expert to present her story to the public, and maintained a clipping service. Second, the Court found that a divorce proceeding was not the type of controversy that rose to the level of public concern. Although the public might have an interest in such matters, and a divorce trial implicated the process of governance, the impact of such proceedings on the public are relatively remote. In such circumstances, the Court views the stakes as too trivial to merit First Amendment protection. It effectively limited public figure status, therefore, to contexts in which serious issues of public policy clearly are present.

F   A   Q

Q: In light of the *Firestone* holding, does the public figure distinction have any vitality? After all, she was socially prominent and even retained a news service to keep track of her press clippings. Why was she not treated as a public figure?

A: The answer is not entirely clear. Under the circumstances, one could have made a strong argument that Mrs. Firestone was a public figure. The Court seemed to treat her as a private individual because she had no choice but to use the court system to obtain her divorce. Also, the matters involved were completely unrelated to the political process.

Examples: The public figure configuration was detailed further in *Proxmire v. Hutchinson*[46] and *Wolston v. Reader's Digest Association, Inc.*[47] In *Proxmire*, the Court reviewed a U.S. senator's comments characterizing a researcher's federally subsidized research as worthless and a waste of taxpayer money. The senator's comments were well publicized, but these by themselves could not be the basis for making the plaintiff a public figure. Because the plaintiff possessed neither pervasive fame or notoriety nor had pursued the limelight, the Court reversed a lower court finding that he was a public figure.

Wolston concerned publication of a book identifying the plaintiff as a Soviet agent. Although having been subpoenaed in the somewhat distant past to testify in an investigation and held in contempt for failing to comply,

Sidebar

SHYING AWAY FROM THE PUBLIC INTEREST STANDARD

Perhaps the Court decided to shy away from *Rosenbloom*'s public interest standard for fear that it might become ensnared in making ad hoc judgments regarding whether an issue falls within the ambit of the "public interest." Whether a statement relates to a matter of public concern also is relevant in other defamation contexts. In *Philadelphia Newspapers, Inc. v. Hepps*, 475 U.S. 767 (1986), the Court determined that a private plaintiff suing a media defendant need not prove actual falsehood if the statement does not touch a matter of public concern.

he denied any Soviet relationship. As in *Proxmire*, the Court found that the plaintiff had not sought public attention. Mere involvement in a criminal matter did not provide a sufficient basis for achieving public figure status. Coupled with *Firestone* and *Proxmire*, the *Wolston* decision evidenced reticence toward defining the concept of limited public figures expansively or animating the notion of an involuntary public figure.

The *Gertz* Court adopted a similar framework for purposes of framing the scope and availability of damages. The Court announced, in a case concerning a media defendant, that presumed or punitive damages must be conditioned on a showing of actual malice. Minus such proof, a plaintiff's compensation is limited to "actual damages." These include "out-of-pocket loss" and "impairment of reputation and standing in the community, personal humiliation, and mental anguish and suffering."[48] This standard thus factors into actual damages at least some of the considerations that traditionally have been referenced in connection with presumed damages.

The Court provided further clarification in *Dun & Bradstreet, Inc. v. Greenmoss Builders, Inc.*[49] That case involved a credit reporting agency's dissemination of an inaccurate credit report. Instead of focusing on the status of the defendant for purposes of damages, parallel to considering the nature of the defendant for the question of liability, a plurality looked to whether the defamatory statement related to a matter of public interest. Pursuant to this standard, the actual malice standard governs presumed or punitive damages only when the defamation implicates a matter of public concern. The analytical framework rejected in *Gertz* for purposes of determining the reach of actual malice, therefore, was embraced in *Dun & Bradstreet* for a similar albeit more limited purpose.

In *Dun & Bradstreet*, members of the Court also raised questions regarding the actual malice standard. Justice White, who embraced the standard in *Sullivan*, had become convinced that the Court had struck an "improvident balance" with respect to freedom of speech and reputational interests. From his standpoint, the actual malice standard "countenances two evils: first, the stream of information about public officials is polluted and often remains polluted by false information; and second, the reputation and professional life of the defeated plaintiff may be destroyed by falsehoods that might have been avoided with a reasonable effort to investigate the facts." Despite criticism by Justice White and others, the actual malice standard as defined by *Sullivan* and *Gertz* remains intact.

Sidebar

ENFORCEABILITY OF NON-U.S. DEFAMATION JUDGMENTS

It is much easier to recover for defamation in many foreign countries, thereby making it possible for plaintiffs to circumvent the *Sullivan* decision by seeking recovery in those countries. However, the efficacy of a foreign judgment is limited by the fact that such judgments are not enforceable in U.S. courts unless they were rendered under standards consistent with the First Amendment to the U.S. Constitution (the *Sullivan* decision and its progeny). *See Sarl Louis Feraud Intl. v. Viewfinder, Inc.*, 406 F. Supp. 2d 274 (S.D.N.Y. 2005).

F A Q

Q: Under the First Amendment, can there be a "false idea"?

A: In *Gertz*, the Court flatly stated that "there is no such thing as a false idea" under the First Amendment. It further noted that society depends on the "marketplace of ideas" rather than the judicial process to correct opinions that may be pernicious. This premise reflects John Stuart Mill's theory of expressive freedom, which assigns utility to false ideas for purposes of keeping minds active, achieving informed judgment, and strengthening the processes of autonomous judgment. The Court in *Gertz* also suggested the possibility that unlike false statements of fact, opinions were beyond the pale of defamation law. The Court largely repudiated this distinction in *Milkovich v. Lorain Journal*, 497 U.S. 1 (1990), when it refused to find a privilege for expressions of opinion. Insofar as opinions can be understood to relate or imply falsehood, they are as actionable as a statement of fact. Although this ruling may be perceived as unfriendly toward First Amendment interests, defendants may argue that a particular fact should not be inferred from a given opinion. They also retain the common law privilege of fair comment.

(3) Intentional Infliction of Emotional Distress

The tort of intentional infliction of emotional distress also has the potential to dampen speech and prevent public discussion of issues. As a result, in *Hustler Magazine v. Falwell*,[50] the Court held that the Constitution significantly restricts recovery in intentional infliction cases. The case involved the Reverend Jerry Falwell, "a nationally known minister who [was] active as a commentator on politics and public affairs." *Hustler Magazine* ran a parody of actual Campari Liqueur advertisements that involved interviews with celebrities about their "first times." Although the actual ads focused on the "first time" the celebrities drank Campari, the ads were tied to sexual first encounters. The Falwell parody depicted a fictitious "interview" with Falwell in which he stated that his "first time" involved "a drunken incestuous rendezvous with his mother in an outhouse." The ad portrayed Falwell and his mother as drunk and immoral, and suggested that Falwell was a hypocrite who preached only while drunk. The ad contained a disclaimer, "ad parody — not to be taken seriously," that was set forth in small print at the bottom of the page, and the magazine's table of contents listed the ad as "Fiction; Ad and Personality Parody." Since the disclaimer prevented Falwell from showing the material misstatement of fact required to bring a defamation action, he sued *Hustler* for intentional infliction of mental distress and obtained a judgment of $100,000 in compensatory damages and $50,000 in punitive damages. Before the U.S. Supreme Court, Falwell argued that the ad parody was patently offensive and intended to inflict emotional injury, and therefore should be denied First Amendment protection.

In denying Falwell's claim, the Court emphasized that someone who intentionally inflicts emotional distress on another is not entitled to "much solicitude," and that virtually all jurisdictions have imposed liability when the infliction is "sufficiently 'outrageous.'" Nevertheless, the Court held that *Hustler*'s parody was entitled to First Amendment protection. Otherwise, the imposition of liability could inhibit speech "if the speaker must run the risk that it will be proved in court that he spoke out of hatred." In addition, the Court recognized that even hateful utterances can "contribute to the free interchange of ideas and the ascertainment of truth" when honestly believed. The Court was particularly concerned that if Falwell's "patently offensive" standard was adopted, political cartoonists and satirists might be subject to liability because the "appeal of the political cartoon or caricature is often based on exploitation of unfortunate physical traits or politically embarrassing events — an exploitation often calculated to injure the feelings of the subject of the portrayal." Moreover, the "art of the cartoonist is often not reasoned or evenhanded, but slashing and one-sided." Indeed, some of the most effective political speech has involved political satire, including Thomas Nast's portrayals of William M. "Boss" Tweed and his corrupt associates in New York City's "Tweed Ring." Earlier cartoons also portrayed George Washington as an ass. As a result, the Court concluded that our "political discourse would have been considerably poorer" without satire.

In an attempt to distinguish his case from traditional political cartoons, Falwell argued that the *Hustler* parody was "outrageous." Although the Court viewed *Hustler*'s parody as "a distant cousin of" political cartoons, the Court doubted whether it could draw a "principled standard" separating the *Hustler* parody from traditional political cartoons. The Court specifically rejected the "outrageousness" standard because of its "inherent subjectiveness" and because of concerns that this standard would "allow a jury to impose liability on the basis of the jurors' tastes or views, or perhaps on the basis of their dislike of a particular expression." Nevertheless, the Court reaffirmed the idea that "speech that is vulgar, offensive, and shocking is not entitled to absolute constitutional protection under all circumstances" and that "a State could lawfully punish an individual for the use of insulting fighting words — those which by their very utterance inflict injury or tend to incite an immediate breach of the peace." But the Court held that Falwell was required to satisfy the *New York Times* actual malice standard in order to recover. In other words, he (like public figures and public officials in defamation actions) could recover intentional infliction of emotional distress only if he could show that the publication contained a false statement of fact that was made with "actual malice" (that is, "with knowledge that the statement was false or with reckless disregard as to whether or not it was true"). The Court concluded that the actual malice standard was necessary to provide "adequate 'breathing space' to the freedoms protected by the First Amendment." The Court readily concluded that Falwell was a public figure and could not satisfy the actual malice standard.

There are other equally outrageous forms of satire that have been accorded constitutional protection. For example, *Dworkin v. Hustler Magazine, Inc.,*[51] involved another *Hustler* parody, this time of a feminist advocate (Andrea Dworkin) who had drafted an (unconstitutional) ordinance prohibiting pornography. When *Hustler* published a series of sexual parodies involving Dworkin, she sued, claiming that *Hustler* should be denied First Amendment protection except for when it is engaged in what she referred to as "high-minded discourse." Since she regarded *Hustler*'s ads as base, she sought recovery. The Ninth Circuit disagreed, concluding that First Amendment protections are not limited to "high-minded discourse."

(4) Privacy

The tort of invasion of privacy can also have constitutional dimensions and implications. For example, the Fifth and Fourteenth Amendments have been construed as protecting the right to make personal choices in certain settings, and the Fourth Amendment protects individuals against unreasonable searches and seizures. In addition, Samuel Warren and Justice Brandeis described the "right to be let alone," which is not specifically enumerated in the Constitution, as "the most comprehensive of rights and the right most valued by civilized men."[52] Warren and Brandeis were disturbed by what they regarded as growing media curiosity that probed into "the sacred precincts of private and domestic," editorial practices that overstepped the boundaries of decency and propriety, and unauthorized circulation of private portraits. Virtually every state has adopted privacy torts that provide for compensation when personal, embarrassing, or intimate information is revealed.

But can liability be imposed when the information is truthful? While the Court has generally been reluctant to impose liability on truthful communications, it has not definitively resolved this issue. For example, in *Cox Broadcasting Corp. v. Cohn*,[53] the Court refused to uphold a damages claim premised on a state law prohibiting publication of a rape victim's name. Noting that the victim's identity had been obtained legally from a public record, the Court concluded that liability could not be imposed. Likewise, in *Landmark Communications, Inc. v. Virginia*,[54] the Court concluded that liability could not be imposed based on a newspaper report regarding a confidential judicial disciplinary proceeding because the information not only was truthful but lawfully obtained. In *Smith v. Daily Mail Publishing Co.*,[55] although the Court refused to establish an absolute privilege for disclosure of truthful private information, it established that liability for publishing accurate information on an issue of "public significance" (a child murderer's name) could not be established minus "a state interest of the highest order."

Of particular significance is the Court's holding in *The Florida Star v. B.J.F.*[56] The case was similar to *Cohn* in that a newspaper published a rape victim's name in violation of state law. However, the paper had inadvertently received the victim's name from law enforcement officials and mistakenly published the name in violation of its own policy prohibiting the publication of the name of sex offense victims. After the article was published, the victim allegedly received threatening phone calls from the perpetrator of the crime. Even though the newspaper negligently violated its own policy, the Court noted that the information had been lawfully obtained, and that a state court could not impose liability on privacy grounds absent a demonstration of state interest of the highest order and implementation that was narrowly tailored. Because the law did not distinguish between inadvertent or intentional publication, the Court found that the narrowly tailored requirement was not satisfied.

As *Cohn* and *Florida Star* suggest, the Court has been reluctant to impose liability when arguably private information was obtained in a lawful matter and involves matters of public interest. Although some balancing of interests occurs, it generally does not extend to such situations. Indeed, even when information has been obtained illegally, the Court has been reluctant to impose liability. For example, in *Bartnicki v. Vopper*,[57] the Court refused to sustain liability when a cellular telephone conversation was illegally intercepted and replayed on a radio show. The conversation involved a teacher's union president's threats regarding physical harm to management during a discussion with his chief negotiator. While the Court recognized that privacy is an important interest and that fear of public disclosure of private communications might chill private speech, the Court found that these concerns were outweighed by the conversation's newsworthiness. Given that the subject matter related to a matter of public interest, the Court found the statutes invalid as applied to defendants who were not involved in the illegal interception. The Court did not decide whether a similar publication would have been sustainable had it involved disclosure of trade secrets, domestic gossip, or other matters of purely private concern.

The Court has also imposed constitutional limitations on recovery in "false light" privacy actions. Like defamation cases, false light claims

Sidebar

ACTUAL MALICE AND PRIVATE INDIVIDUALS

In *Cantrell v. Forest City Publishing Co.*, 419 U.S. 245 (1974), the Court applied the actual malice standard to a case involving a newspaper's mischaracterization of a family's living conditions. Although the Court concluded that the standard was satisfied in that case, it suggested that the standard might not be applied when plaintiff is a private individual.

involve false statements or suggestions that cause injury. However, unlike defamation cases, the false light information does not necessarily cause reputational injury. The most important false light case is *Time, Inc. v. Hill*,[58] which arose when a magazine misrepresented a family's hostage experience. In deciding the case, the Court overrode state law by imposing the *New York Times* actual malice standard to false light privacy cases. In other words, absent proof that defendant published the false light information with knowledge of falsehood or reckless disregard of the truth, plaintiff could not recover.

A constitutional overlay has also been imposed on the right of privacy that protects an individual's economic interest in the use of name, image, or talent. The plaintiffs in this branch of the tort are commonly athletes, entertainers, and performers. For example, in *Zacchini v. Scripps-Howard Broadcasting Co.*,[59] the Court sustained a recovery to protect an entertainer's right to publicity. That case involved a television station's broadcast of a human cannonball entertainer's performance. In protecting the entertainer's interest, the Court emphasized the entertainer's right to profit from his talents, as well as society's interest in facilitating and rewarding an entertainer for his creative energy. Although the Court recognized the importance of news gathering to the media, the Court concluded that the media could be required to account to plaintiff without incurring a significant burden. If the public desired access to the performance, they could obtain it for the required admission price. On the other hand, if the entertainer were not compensated, he would be deprived of the incentive to produce the performance, and the public might be deprived of the opportunity to view it.

(5) Obscenity

Even though the Court has provided constitutional protection to many different types of speech, it has routinely held that obscenity is unprotected. The Court has gone so far as to suggest that obscenity plays "no essential part of any exposition of ideas, and [has] slight social value as a step to the truth."[60] In *Roth v. United States*,[61] the Court held that obscenity is "utterly without redeeming social importance." Because obscenity is unprotected, the Court is more willing to permit governmental regulation and generally subjects that regulation to a minimal level of review. Note, however, that *Roth* and other decisions suggest only that *obscenity* plays "no essential part of any exposition of ideas, and [has] slight social value as a step to the truth." As the *Falwell* case makes clear, just because a publication portrays sexuality does not mean that it conveys no ideas. There is an essential difference between material that portrays sexuality and material that is obscene.

The primary problem with obscenity is definitional. Merely because speech involves sex or sexual issues does not mean that it is obscene. In a number of cases, the Court has struggled to define the concept of obscenity. In an early decision, *Roth v. United States*,[62] the Court acknowledged that *sex* and *obscenity* are not synonymous terms and suggested that obscenity "deals with sex in a manner appealing to the *prurient interest.*" However, the Court indicated that obscene publications would have to be evaluated on a case-by-case basis with an inquiry that focused on whether "the average person, applying contemporary community standards, [would find that] the dominant theme of the material taken as a whole appeals to prurient interest." Because the standard focused on "contemporary community standards," it precluded a finding of obscenity based on a particularly sensitive group's response to sexually explicit publication. Likewise, because the standard required consideration of the work "as a whole," it prevented material from being deemed obscene based on an isolated passage.

The *Roth* decision did not produce workable jurisprudential standards. Indeed, through the 1960s and the early 1970s, the Court struggled to establish a viable definition of obscenity as applied to the broad range of circumstances that arise in obscenity cases. The futility of the task was underscored by Justice Potter Stewart's observation that the Court was engaged in a process of "trying to define the undefinable."[63] Although Justice Stewart could not define obscenity, he maintained that "I know it when I see it." In subsequent decisions, the Court held that, because application of obscenity statutes might implicate constitutional rights, the Court must independently assess whether material in fact was obscene in a given case. Of course, without a clear definition of obscenity, the Court was forced to deal with each case on an individual basis. Decisions often involved the inconsistent standards of individual justices. In *Mishkin v. New York*, 383 U.S. 502 (1966), the Court held that the obscenity standard could vary depending on a publisher's or distributor's target audience, which could focus on groups outside the sexual mainstream. Likewise, *Ginsberg v. New York*, 390 U.S. 629 (1968), upheld the conviction of a defendant who sold a sexually explicit magazine to a minor on the basis that the definition of obscenity could vary with the age of the audience.

Post-*Roth* cases illustrated the difficulties with the Court's approach. In *A Book Named "John Cleland's Memoirs of a Woman of Pleasure" v. Attorney General of Massachusetts*,[64] the Court reversed an obscenity conviction for distribution of a book (*Fanny Hill*) that some regarded as a classic. In doing so, a three-justice plurality refined the *Roth* test into a three-part standard. First, the material must appeal to the prurient interest. Second, it must be found offensive pursuant to contemporary community standards. Third, it must be utterly lacking in redeeming social value. This final factor proved critical. Even if material satisfied the other two prongs, it could not be deemed obscene if the work has *some* redeeming social value. However, the Court qualified the test in *Ginzburg v. United States*,[65] by holding that an inquiry into a sexually explicit magazine's social value might not be necessary if the distributors consciously attempted to pander to the prurient interest.

F   A   Q

Q: How often does it occur that a publication is "utterly without redeeming social value"?

A: Not very often. The Court was ultimately forced to alter this third prong of the *Memoirs* case because virtually everything has "some" value. The Court ultimately evolved to a "serious" value standard.

Finally, in *Miller v. California*,[66] the Court refined *Roth* to create an analytical structure for juries to consider in evaluating allegations of obscenity. Under *Miller*, while the Court recognized the dangers "inherent" in regulating any form of expression and noted that laws regulating obscenity must be "carefully limited," the Court articulated an altered three-part test that focused on "(1) whether the average person applying contemporary community standards would find that the work, taken as a whole, appeals to the prurient interest, (2) whether it depicts or describes, in a patently offensive way, sexual conduct specifically defined by the applicable state law, and (c) whether the work taken as a whole, lacks serious literary, artistic, political, or scientific value." The Court held that local standards should be applied.

Miller was significant because the new test commanded a majority of the Court. Prior to *Miller*, it was unclear whether a court should consider national or local standards in deciding whether a publication appeals to the prurient interest. In *Miller*, the Court rejected the requirement of a national standard, although a trial court could opt to use one.[67] In addition, if a trial court chooses to apply a community standard, it need not provide a geographical reference, instead leaving the determination to the jurors. Of course, under such an approach, the definition of obscenity could vary based on the jury's class, culture, and neighborhood. The Court also has determined that a state cannot define through legislation the community standards that apply in determining prurient interest or patent offensiveness.[68]

Sidebar

VAGUENESS, OVERBREADTH, AND OBSCENITY

Given the difficulties encountered by the Court in defining obscenity, the Court has sometimes invoked overbreadth and vagueness principles to strike down obscenity convictions. In *Miller*, the Court held that obscenity prosecutions must be limited to materials that "depict, or describe patently offensive 'hard core' sexual conduct specifically defined by the regulating state law, as written or construed." The specificity requirement is satisfied by a statute that reaches "[p]atently offensive representations or descriptions of ultimate sexual acts, normal or perverted, actual or simulated" and "[p]atently offensive representations or descriptions of masturbation, excretory functions, and lewd exhibition of genitals." However, the Court indicated that its suggested terminology should be regarded as "examples" of acts that could be prohibited rather than an "exhaustive" listing.

While *Miller* created the possibility that a local jury's standards could be out of the mainstream, the Court ameliorated this problem by holding in *Jenkins v. Georgia*[69] that appellate courts must independently review constitutional claims in obscenity cases. Although the Court reaffirmed the notion that questions of pruriency and patent offensiveness are jury questions, jury findings cannot be sustained unless the publication involves "patently offensive 'hard core' sexual conduct." As a result, even if a jury concludes that a publication is inconsistent with contemporary community standards, the Court can review and reverse for constitutional deficiencies.

An important aspect of the *Miller* decisions was its alteration of the "utterly lacks social value" portion of the standard to whether there is an absence of "serious" literary, artistic, political, or scientific value. Of course, this shift makes it easier to find that a publication is obscene. Unlike the prurient interest and patent offensiveness standards, courts need not use "contemporary community standards" to assess whether material lacks the required social value. In *Pope v. Illinois*,[70] the Court held that the focus should be on whether a "reasonable person" would find the material so lacking.

Even if obscenity is outside constitutional protection, it may be entitled to protection in limited contexts. In *Stanley v. Georgia*,[71] the Court invalidated a homeowner's conviction for possession of obscene material in his own home as inconsistent with his right to privacy. The Court held that the homeowner's privacy rights outweighed the state's interest in controlling the dissemination of obscenity in the context of his own home.

F   A   Q

Q: If *Stanley* provides individuals with a constitutional right to possess pornography in the privacy of their own homes, does it also create a correlative right to sell, purchase, or view obscenity?

A: The Court has answered this in the negative. In *Paris Adult Theatre I v. Slaton*,[72] Justice Brennan argued for an extension of *Stanley's* logic to adult movie theaters that posted content warnings and refused admission to children. The majority in *Paris Adult Theatre I* disagreed. The Court reaffirmed the notion that obscenity is outside the bounds of First Amendment protection, focusing not only on the risk of exposure to unconsenting adults and minors, but also on other considerations such as the quality of life and neighborhoods, the tone of urban commerce, and public safety. Although none of the harms could be demonstrated conclusively or empirically, the Court applied only rational basis review.

(6) Near Obscene Speech

The Court has also developed special rules governing near obscene speech and the secondary effects of that speech. In a number of cases, the Court has held that government may create zoning laws that restrict the location of adult entertainment enterprises because of the secondary effects of those enterprises. For example, in *City of Renton v. Playtime Theatres, Inc.*,[73] the Court upheld a local ordinance that regulated the placement of adult businesses. The law prohibited adult movie theaters from operating within 1,000 feet of any residential zone, church, park, or school, with the net effect that 94 percent of the community's land could not be used for that purpose. While the Court recognized that the law was content based, the Court concluded that the city's "'predominate' intent" was to regulate and control the secondary effects of crime and neighborhood decline. Under these circumstances, the Court declined to apply a content-based standard of review and instead focused on whether the regulation "serve[s] a substantial governmental interest [unrelated to speech] and allows for reasonable alternative channels of communication." The Court concluded that the secondary effects of adult movie theaters represented a substantial interest and that the reasonable alternative channels of communication criterion was satisfied.

Sidebar

ADULT ENTERPRISES AND FUNDAMENTAL VALUES

The *Playtime Theatres* decision is consistent with the result in *Young v. American Mini-theatres, Inc.*, 427 U.S. 50 (1976). That case involved a Detroit zoning ordinance that prohibited the location of adult enterprises close to certain other properties and uses, including churches and schools. Both holdings were influenced by the content of the speech, which the Court viewed as imposing adverse social and economic consequences. As the Court recognized, "[F]ew of us would send our sons and daughters off to war to preserve the citizen's right to see [sexually explicit expression] in the theaters of our choice."

Secondary interests analysis was also invoked in *City of Erie v. Pap's A.M.*[74] In that case, the Court upheld a city ordinance prohibiting knowing or intentional nudity because of the governmental interest in neighborhood quality and crime abatement. A four-justice plurality concluded that these secondary effects justified the restriction.

Of course, "secondary effects" creates the risk that governmental officials will articulate facially valid reasons for regulating content, but have the ulterior motive of prohibiting the content. In *Renton*, the Court held that the government must show a link between concentrated adult theaters and a substantial and independent government interest, but held that the government may rely on any evidence that it "reasonably believe[s] to be relevant."[75] The Court qualified this analysis in *City of Los Angeles v. Alameda Books, Inc.*,[76] a case upholding density limits on adult establishments. Noting that a municipality cannot rely on "shoddy data or reasoning," the Court concluded that secondary effects regulation "must fairly support" the rationale for the law. Justice Kennedy, concurring, expressed concern that the characterization of content neutrality is a "fiction" that is "more confusing than helpful." He argued that even though these laws are content based, the Court should not apply strict scrutiny because of the unique nature of zoning laws and the lesser chance that such laws will be used as an instrumentality of content discrimination.

F A Q

Q: Does the Court distinguish between permit requirements that relate to the location of adult businesses rather than to the content of adult movies?

A: Yes. In *City of Littleton v. Z.J. Gifts D-4, L.L.C.*, 541 U.S. 774 (2004), the Court upheld a permit requirement in this context. The courts may provide after-the-fact review of permitting decisions.

(7) Offensive Speech

The government's power to regulate offensive speech is considerably more limited. Perhaps the most famous offensive speech case is *Cohen v. California*,[77] which held that Cohen could not be convicted for wearing an offensive phrase on the back of his jacket. The case involved California Penal Code §415, which prohibited "maliciously and willfully disturb[ing] the peace or quiet of any neighborhood or person [by] offensive conduct." Cohen was punished by 30 days' imprisonment for wearing a jacket bearing the words "Fuck the Draft" in the Los Angeles County Courthouse while women and children were present. Although his goal was to protest the Vietnam War and the draft, he was not violent and did not provoke a violent response.

In overturning Cohen's conviction, the Court held that the words on his jacket involved "pure speech" rather than "conduct," and that the conviction was based on the "offensiveness" of the words and the content of the message. Since the state could not show that Cohen intended to "incite disobedience to or disruption of the draft," the Court concluded that he could not be punished for his choice of words. Even though he used the "F" word, the Court concluded that the reference was not obscene because it was not erotic and was not intended to be erotic.

In addition, the words could not be construed as fighting words because they did not involve "personally abusive epithets" likely to provoke a violent reaction. While Cohen's words could have been invoked in a "personally provocative fashion," the Court concluded that no direct personal insult was involved in this case. The Court rejected the idea that Cohen's jacket provoked a hostile crowd reaction.

Although Cohen could have made his point in less objectionable language, the Court concluded that the courts could not dictate the content or form of public discourse: "To many, the immediate consequence of this freedom may often appear to be only verbal tumult, discord, and even offensive utterance. These are, however, within established limits, in truth necessary side effects of the broader enduring values which the process of open debate permits us to achieve. That the air may at times seem filled with verbal cacophony is, in this sense not a sign of weakness but of strength. . . . Surely the State has no right to cleanse public debate to the point where it is grammatically palatable to the most squeamish among us." As the Court noted, while Cohen's expression might be regarded as "more distasteful than most others of its genre," it is "nevertheless often true that one man's vulgarity is another's lyric." Indeed, "distasteful" language may be chosen because of its emotional impact on the listener: "much linguistic expression serves a dual communicative function: it conveys not only ideas capable of relatively precise, detached explication, but otherwise inexpressible emotions as well. In fact, words are often chosen as much for their emotive as their cognitive force." Accordingly, the Court held that it could not control the form of words without running the risk of suppressing ideas, noting that it is "because governmental officials cannot make principled distinctions in this area that the Constitution leaves matters of taste and style so largely to the individual."

F   A   Q

Q: Why does the state not have the right to protect the public against Cohen's decision to subject unwilling members of the public against his vulgar language?

A: While the state may prohibit a speaker from intruding into the privacy of another person's home, the Court found that individuals are often "captives" outside of their homes, where they can be subject to objectionable speech. Such speech can be prohibited only if it invades "substantial privacy interests" in an "essentially intolerable manner." The Court viewed a courthouse as different from a home and noted that those offended by Cohen's jacket could simply avert their eyes.

Many offensive speech cases are resolved on vagueness or overbreadth grounds. In *Cohen*, the Court noted that the statute sought to "preserve an appropriately decorous atmosphere in the courthouse where Cohen was arrested," and the Court concluded that the statute failed to put Cohen on notice that his conduct was not permissible: "No fair reading of the phrase 'offensive conduct' can be said sufficiently to inform the ordinary person that distinctions between certain locations are thereby created." Interestingly enough, although Cohen removed his jacket and stood with it folded over his arm in the courthouse, a policeman nonetheless asked the judge to hold Cohen in contempt of court. When the judge refused, the officer arrested Cohen as he left the courtroom. Other illustrations of the vagueness doctrine include the holdings in *Gooding v. Wilson*,[78] *Lewis v. City of New Orleans*,[79] and *Hess v. Indiana*.[80] All three cases involved graphic and offensive depictions: Gooding said to a policeman, "You son of a bitch. I'll choke you to death"; Lewis said, "You gaddamn motherfucking police"; and Hess said, "We'll take the fucking streets later."

Despite *Cohen*'s holding, there are situations when offensive speech is subject to governmental restriction. For example, in *FCC v. Pacifica Foundation*,[81] the Court upheld the FCC's decision to ban offensive broadcasts to late-night hours when children would be less likely to be listening. The case involved a broadcaster's decision to air George Carlin's monologue "Filthy Words," which contained a variety of curse words. Carlin's monologue used "the words you couldn't say on the public, ah, airwaves, um, the ones you definitely wouldn't say, ever," and then repeated them over and over again. The radio station aired the monologue as part of a program on contemporary attitudes toward speech. In its order, the Commission characterized the monologue as "patently offensive," though not necessarily obscene, and expressed the opinion that it is subject to regulation. The Court upheld the order because of the special attributes of broadcast technology, which receives "the most limited First Amendment protection" because of its "uniquely pervasive presence" and its ability to confront "the citizen, not only in public, but also in the privacy of the home, where the individual's right to be left alone plainly outweighs the First Amendment rights of an intruder." Because "the broadcast audience is constantly tuning in and out, prior warnings cannot completely protect the listener or viewer from unexpected program content," and such programs are "uniquely accessible to children." The Court emphasized that the FCC did not try to ban the speech altogether, but simply to channel it to late-night hours when children were less likely to be listening.

The Court also upheld limitations on offensive speech in *National Endowment for the Arts v. Finley*.[82] That case involved a congressional requirement that the National Endowment for the Arts consider "general standards of decency and respect for the diverse beliefs and values of the American public" in making art awards. The Court upheld the restriction, noting that the statute required the NEA merely to take "decency and respect" into consideration, and therefore there was no assurance that provision would be used to engage in "invidious viewpoint discrimination."

However, in *Erznoznik v. City of Jacksonville*,[83] the Court sustained a facial challenge to a local ordinance that prohibited the showing of films containing nudity by a drive-in movie theater when its screen was visible from a public street. Although the films were not "obscene" under *Miller v. California*, the state argued that it could protect its citizens against unwilling exposure to materials that may be offensive. The Court rejected the argument, noting that "we are inescapably captive audiences for many purposes." Even if speech offends "our political and moral sensibilities," the Court held that "the Constitution does not permit government to decide which types of otherwise protected speech are sufficiently offensive to require protection for the unwilling listener or viewer." On the contrary, the unwilling viewer is required to avert his eyes, and the Court found that the screen of a drive-in theater is not "so obtrusive as to make it impossible for an unwilling individual to avoid exposure to it."

The Court also found that the ordinance was excessively broad because it extended beyond explicit nudity to sweep in depictions of uncovered buttocks or breasts, irrespective of context or pervasiveness. As a result, the law would prohibit depictions of a "baby's buttocks, the nude body of a war victim, or scenes from a culture in which nudity is indigenous. The ordinance also might prohibit newsreel scenes of the opening of an art exhibit." The Court also rejected the state's attempt to justify the ordinance as a "traffic regulation" on the theory that nudity on a drive-in movie screen might distract passing motorists. The Court found that the law was underinclusive because a variety of other movie scenes could be equally distracting to passing motorists. Chief Justice Burger, joined by Justice Rehnquist, dissenting, argued that a motion picture screen is "highly intrusive and distracting" and that the state has a legitimate interest in regulating displays of nudity.

(8) Child Pornography

Another category of unprotected speech is child pornography. In the 1970s, many states began passing laws that prohibited not only "obscene" but nonobscene depictions of child sexuality. The U.S. Supreme Court confronted the constitutionality of these laws in *New York v. Ferber*,[84] a case that involved a New York criminal statute prohibiting persons from knowingly distributing depictions of sexual performances by children under the age of 16. At the time, the federal government and 47 states had passed similar laws, and 35 states had enacted laws banning the distribution of child pornography whether or not it was obscene under *Ferber*. The New York law defined "sexual performance" as "any performance or part thereof which includes sexual conduct by a child less than sixteen years of age." "Sexual conduct" was defined as "actual or simulated sexual intercourse, deviate sexual intercourse, sexual bestiality, masturbation, sado-masochistic abuse, or lewd exhibition of the genitals." A performance was defined as "any play, motion picture, photograph or dance" or "any other visual representation exhibited before an audience." "Promote" was defined as conduct designed to "procure, manufacture, issue, sell, give, provide, lend, mail, deliver, transfer, transmute, publish, distribute, circulate, disseminate, present, exhibit or advertise, or to offer or agree to do the same." Article 263.10 banned the knowing dissemination of obscene material. Ferber was charged under the New York law for distributing films depicting young boys masturbating.

In upholding the law, the Court concluded that the state possesses broader authority to ban the portrayal of children engaged in sexual acts or lewd exhibitions of genitalia without regard to the *Miller* obscenity test. Although the states were free to apply *Miller* to depictions of child pornography, the Court found that the states have a "particular and more compelling interest" in prosecuting those who sexually exploit children. The Court offered several justifications for giving states greater leeway to ban child pornography. First, the Court held that New York had a "compelling" interest in "safeguarding the physical and psychological well-being" of minors, and the Court was deferential to the legislature regarding its conclusion that suppression of child pornography was necessary to achieve this objective. Second, the Court held that the distribution of photographs and films depicting sexual activity by juveniles was intrinsically related to the sexual abuse of children because it created a permanent record of a child's participation and the harm is reinforced by circulation. Moreover, the Court concluded that the most effective means of "drying up the market" for child pornography was to impose severe criminal penalties on those who sell, advertise, or promote it. Third, the Court found that the advertising and selling of child pornography provided an "economic motive" for the production of such materials. Fourth, the Court emphasized that the speech value of child pornography was "exceedingly modest, if not de minimis," and the Court expressed doubt about whether "visual depictions of children performing sexual acts or lewdly exhibiting their genitals would often constitute an important and necessary part of a literary performance or scientific or educational work." Fifth, even though the child pornography restrictions were content-related, the Court held that New York's law was so closely related to the welfare of children that "the balance of competing interests" was "clearly struck" so that these materials could be denied First Amendment protection.

F   A   Q

Q: If the Court regards child pornography as of de minimis social value, is there nonetheless a risk that child pornography laws will chill individuals who might engage in protected speech that is close to the line?

A: Yes. Anticipating this problem, the Court held that the statute must adequately define the prohibited conduct, but concluded that the New York law in *Ferber* satisfied that requirement because New York limited the offense to works that visually depict sexual conduct by children below a specified age. In addition, the statute must particularly describe the sexual conduct being prohibited.

Ferber was followed by the holding in *Osborne v. Ohio*.[85] That case involved an Ohio law that made it illegal to possess child pornography as applied to a man who possessed four photographs of nude adolescents in sexually explicit positions in his own home. The Ohio Supreme Court read §2907.323(A)(3) as applying only to depictions of nudity involving a lewd exhibition or graphic focus on a minor's genitals. In an opinion by Justice White, the Court upheld the law, distinguishing its prior holding in *Stanley v. Georgia*[86] in which the Court struck down a Georgia law prohibiting the private possession of obscene material in the privacy of one's own home. *Osborne* reaffirmed *Ferber*'s conclusion that the "value of permitting child pornography" is "'exceedingly modest, if not de minimis,'" and held that "the interests underlying child pornography prohibitions" are far more important than the interests involved in *Stanley*. In *Stanley*, Georgia was concerned that pornography might "poison the minds of its viewers," and the Court held that Georgia did not have the right to control "a person's private thoughts." In *Osborne*, the Court found that the state was trying to destroy the "market for the exploitative use of children," and it was "surely reasonable for the State to conclude that it will decrease the production of child pornography if it penalizes those who possess and view the product, thereby decreasing demand." The Court concluded that Ohio could try to "stamp out this vice at all levels in the distribution chain." Moreover, relying on *Ferber*, the Court noted that child pornography "permanently record[s] the victim's abuse" and "causes the child victims continuing harm by haunting the children in years to come," so that a ban on possession and viewing encourages the possessors of these materials to destroy them. Moreover, the Court found that the state could encourage destruction of such materials because pedophiles might use child pornography to seduce other children into sexual activity. Justice Brennan, joined by Justices Marshall and Stevens, dissented, arguing that the states have other means to combat such abuse including enacting laws prohibiting the creation, sale, and distribution of child pornography and obscenity involving minors. As a result, he would have applied *Stanley*'s holding to child pornography.

Ferber and *Osborne* were qualified by the Court's holding in *Ashcroft v. The Free Speech Coalition*,[87] a case dealing with the question of whether the state could prohibit "virtual" child pornography. The Child Pornography Prevention Act of 1996 extended child pornography prohibitions to "virtual child pornography," which the act defined as "any visual depiction, including any photograph, film, video, picture, or computer or computer-generated image or picture [that] is, or appears to be, of a minor engaging in sexually explicit conduct." In enacting the law, Congress recognized that it was possible to use computer images to create what appear to be realistic images of children engaged in sexual activity, and Congress sought to prohibit those images whether or not they are created using real children. Another provision of the law prohibited a more common and lower-tech means of creating virtual images, known as "computer morphing," in which innocent pictures of real children are altered to make it appear that they are engaged in sexual activity. The Free Speech Coalition, a trade association, challenged the CPPA on the basis that no children were exploited in the production of virtual child pornography. The Coalition did not challenge the "computer morphing" provisions.

In an opinion by Justice Kennedy, the Court struck down the law. Although the Court recognized that the age of participants could be relevant to a determination of obscenity under *Miller*, the Court noted that the CPPA did not prohibit obscenity and could be applied even to depictions with "redeeming social value." In addition, the Court rejected the argument that virtual child pornography should be treated as unprotected speech. Part of the problem was that the CPPA prohibited a broad range of pictures, including pictures in psychology manuals depicting the problem of child sexual abuse, as well as images that were not "patently offensive," that did not "contravene community standards," and that had "serious literary, artistic, political, or scientific value." As a result, the Court found that the statute proscribed "the visual depiction of an idea — that of teenagers engaging in sexual activity." The Court was troubled by the law because it prohibited depictions of "children" who were above the age of consent for sexual relations, as well as for marriage, as well as because youth sexuality has been a theme of art and literature "throughout the ages." The Court referenced classics (for example, *Romeo and Juliet*, in which one of the lovers was only 13 years old), as well as recent prominent movies (for example, *Traffic*), that depicted child sexuality. In refusing to extend *Ferber* to virtual pornography, the Court viewed *Ferber* as applying to instances of child sexual abuse that could be prohibited without regard to their social value, and the CPPA did not involve speech that recorded a crime or created victims by its production.

F   A   Q

Q: Should society be able to prohibit virtual child pornography because of the risk that it might encourage or incite pedophiles and therefore lead to the actual abuse of children?

A: In *Ashcroft*, the Court regarded the causal link between virtual child pornography and actual abuse as "contingent and indirect" because the harm did not flow from the speech itself (or its production), but from some "unquantified potential for subsequent criminal acts." Even though pedophiles could use virtual child pornography to seduce children, the Court noted that many "innocent" things can be abused — including cartoons, video games, and candy — but such items cannot be prohibited merely "because they can be misused." The Court concluded that government should respond to this problem by punishing adults who provide unsuitable materials to children and by enforcing criminal penalties for unlawful solicitation. The Court also found inadequate the argument that virtual child pornography "whets the appetites of pedophiles and encourages them to engage in illegal conduct." Relying on *Brandenburg v. Ohio*, 395 U.S. 444 (1969), the Court held that the "mere tendency of speech to encourage unlawful acts is not a sufficient reason for banning it." The Court found that there was "no attempt, incitement, solicitation, or conspiracy" and that there was "no more than a remote connection between speech that might encourage thoughts or impulses and any resulting child abuse."

An additional issue in the case was whether virtual child pornography could be prohibited to help eliminate the market for pornography that uses real children. Part of the problem was that virtual images were arguably indistinguishable from real ones, but were part of the same market for real ones. As a result, the government argued it could prohibit virtual images to stop the trafficking in works involving the exploitation of real children. The Court rejecting the argument, concluding that pornographers would be more likely to use virtual images than real ones if there were no criminal penalties for using virtual pictures. The government also argued that the existence of virtual child pornography might make it difficult to prosecute those who produce pornography using real children because advancing technology might make it difficult to determine whether a particular picture was made using real children or by using computer imaging. The Court concluded that the government could not suppress lawful speech as the means of suppressing unlawful speech.

Ashcroft produced various concurrences and dissents that suggest the scope of divisions on the Court. Justice Thomas concurred, but noted that technology may evolve to the point that those who possess and distribute pornographic images of real children can "escape conviction by claiming that the images are computer-generated, thereby raising a reasonable doubt as to their guilt," and argued that government may well

Sidebar

THE PROBLEM OF ADVANCING TECHNOLOGY

Ashcroft did not necessarily preclude the state from regulating virtual child pornography if technology advances to the point where it is impossible to distinguish virtual child pornography from actual child pornography.

have a compelling interest in prohibiting virtual child pornography if that happens. Justice O'Connor, joined by Chief Justice Rehnquist and Justice Scalia, concurred in part and dissented in part, arguing that the statute should be upheld to the extent it is construed as applying only to images that are "virtually indistinguishable from actual children." Chief Justice Rehnquist, joined in part by Justice Scalia, dissented, arguing that Congress has a compelling interest in enforcing prohibitions against actual child pornography, and that the prohibition of virtual images is justified by the fact that "rapidly advancing technology" might soon make it virtually impossible to enforce prohibitions against actual images. While he agreed that "[s]erious First Amendment concerns would arise were the Government ever to prosecute someone for simple distribution or possession of a film with literary or artistic value," he concluded that the act "need not be construed to reach such materials."

(9) Pornography as Discrimination Against Women

Given that the Court has not treated the First Amendment as providing absolute protections for speech, some have argued that nonobscene pornography can be prohibited because of the negative images it sends to society regarding women.[88] As a result, in 1983, the City of Indianapolis adopted a model ordinance that prohibited pornography on the theory that it is a practice that discriminates against women. The ordinance defined prohibited pictures or representations that involved

> the graphic sexually explicit subordination of women, whether in pictures or in words, that also includes one or more of the following: (1) Women are presented as sexual objects who enjoy pain or humiliation; or (2) Women are presented as sexual objects who experience sexual pleasure in being raped; or (3) Women are presented as sexual objects tied up or cut up or mutilated or bruised or physically hurt, or as dismembered or truncated or fragmented or severed into body parts; or (4) Women are presented as being penetrated by objects or animals; or (5) Women are presented in scenarios of degradation, injury, abasement, torture, shown as filthy or inferior, bleeding, bruised, or hurt in a context that makes these conditions sexual; or (6) Women are presented as sexual objects for domination, conquest, violation, exploitation, possession, or use, or through postures or positions of servility or submission or display.

The statute provided that the "use of men, children, or transsexuals in the place of women in paragraphs (1) through (6) above shall also constitute pornography under this section." The ordinance applied to obscene pornography, as defined by *Miller*, as well as to nonobscene pornography that did not satisfy the *Miller* test.

Even though the ordinance applied even to sexual depictions that had serious "literary, artistic, political, or scientific value," Indianapolis attempted to defend on the basis that "pornography influences attitudes" and that "the statute [was] a way to alter the socialization of men and women rather than to vindicate community standards of offensiveness." A drafter of the statute argued, "if a woman is subjected, why should it matter that the work has other value?"[89] It was also argued that the ordinance would "play an important role in reducing the tendency of men to view women as sexual objects, a tendency that leads to both unacceptable attitudes and discrimination in the workplace and violence away from it."

In *American Booksellers Association, Inc. v. Hudnut*,[90] in an opinion by Judge Easterbrook, the Ninth Circuit struck down the law because it involved "content discrimination" against speech. Easterbrook noted that speech that refers to women in the "approved way" (for example, in positions of equality) is permissible, but speech that portrays women in a "disapproved way" (for example, as submissive in matters sexual or as enjoying humiliation) is prohibited without regard to "how significant the literary, artistic, or political qualities of the work taken as a whole." Judge Easterbrook concluded that the state "may not ordain preferred viewpoints" and may not "declare one perspective right and silence opponents." "If there is any fixed star in our constitutional constellation, it is that no official, high or petty, can prescribe what shall be orthodox in politics, nationalism, religion, or other matters of opinion or force citizens to confess by word or act their faith therein."

Judge Easterbrook also rejected the argument that nonobscene pornography could be prohibited on the basis that "pornography affects thoughts" in that men "who see women depicted as subordinate are more likely to treat them so." While he recognized that people "often act in accordance with the images and patterns they find around them," he concluded that "this simply demonstrates the power of pornography as speech." "Racial bigotry, anti-Semitism, violence on television, reporters' biases — these and many more influence the culture and shape our socialization. None is directly answerable by more speech, unless that speech too finds its place in the popular culture." However, he concluded that "all is protected as speech, however insidious. Any other answer leaves the government in control of all of the institutions of culture, the great censor and director of which thoughts are good for us."

Defenders of the ordinance argued that some pornographers depict "sexual torture, penetration of women by red-hot irons and the like." In addition, they noted that some pornographers use fraud, trickery, or force to compel women to perform. But Judge Easterbrook rejected these arguments as a permissible basis for regulation, noting that the state is free to prohibit such conduct and that it can do so without prohibiting the ideas conveyed by the pornographers.

Indianapolis also argued that the "marketplace of ideas" metaphor was inapplicable to this type of speech because it is "unanswerable." However, Judge Easterbrook rejected this argument, noting that "the Constitution does not make the dominance of truth a necessary condition of freedom of speech. To say that it does would be to confuse an outcome of free speech with a necessary condition for the application of the amendment." He rejected the argument that government has the power to declare "truth." "If the government may declare the truth, why wait for the failure of speech? Under the First Amendment, however, there is no such thing as a false idea so the government may not restrict speech on the ground that in a free exchange truth is not yet dominant."

In *Hudnut*, Judge Easterbrook rejected the argument that pornography is "low-value" speech. He noted that, even with lower-value speech, the government is not allowed to choose

Sidebar

THE DESIRABILITY OF REGULATING SOFT PORNOGRAPHY

In *Hudnut*'s wake, Professor Nadine Strossen argued that regardless of their constitutionality, prohibitions on soft pornography are undesirable. Nadine Strossen, *A Feminist Critique of "the" Feminist Critique of Pornography*, 79 Va. L. Rev. 1099 (1993). She questioned whether such provisions could be effective and argued that censorship schemes are likely to push pornography underground where it may have more impact. She also questioned the alleged causal link between "exposure to 'pornography' and misogynistic discrimination or violence." Moreover, she argued that the "speculative benefits" of censorship are outweighed by the "demonstrable costs" of censorship on women's rights. She noted that such censorship has historically been used to "stifle women's sexuality, women's expression, and women's full and equal participation in our society." As a result, women have a strong interest in preserving free expression and should use that expression to turn society against pornography.

among viewpoints. Moreover, he questioned whether pornography qualifies as low-value speech since Indianapolis chose to prohibit this speech because it "influences social relations and politics on a grand scale, that it controls attitudes at home and in the legislature." He found that this "precludes a characterization of the speech as low value." Indeed, he noted that free speech has generally "been on balance an ally of those seeking change. Governments that want stasis start by restricting speech. Culture is a powerful force of continuity; Indianapolis paints pornography as part of the culture of power. Change in any complex system ultimately depends on the ability of outsiders to challenge accepted views and the reigning institutions. Without a strong guarantee of freedom of speech, there is no effective right to challenge what is." Judge Easterbrook did hold that the state could impose liability on a pornographer if it were shown that a woman suffered physical attack and she could show that the attack was "directly caused by specific pornography." Of course, the constitutionality of such a provision would depend on how it was interpreted and applied.

(10) Hate Speech

While the label *hate speech* is very imprecise, the term refers to expression that targets individuals or groups by reason of their race, ethnicity, sex, or sexual preference. Some prefer to refer to this speech as "discriminatory speech." No label is completely satisfactory.

Beauharnais v. Illinois[91] was one of the U.S. Supreme Court's earliest discussions of the issue. That case involved an Illinois criminal statute that provided: "It shall be unlawful for any person, firm or corporation to manufacture, sell, or offer for sale, advertise or publish, present or exhibit in any public place in this state any lithograph, moving picture, play, drama or sketch, which publication or exhibition portrays depravity, criminality, unchastity, or lack of virtue of a class of citizens, of any race, color, creed or religion which said publication or exhibition exposes the citizens of any race, color, creed or religion to contempt, derision, or obloquy or which is productive of breach of the peace or riots." Petitioner was convicted under the law and fined $200 for distributing leaflets setting forth a petition calling on the mayor and city council of Chicago "to halt the further encroachment, harassment and invasion of white people, their property, neighborhoods and persons, by the Negro. . . ." The leaflet also called on "One million self respecting white people in Chicago to unite," adding that if "persuasion and the need to prevent the white race from becoming mongrelized by the Negro will not unite us, then the aggressions [rapes,] robberies, knives, guns and marijuana of the Negro, surely will." The leaflet concluded with an application for membership in the White Circle League of America, Inc. In an opinion by Justice Frankfurter, the Court upheld the conviction, noting that every jurisdiction punishes libels directed at individuals. Justice Frankfurter found that it is "libelous falsely to charge another with being a rapist, robber, carrier of knives and guns, and user of marijuana." He viewed this analysis as extending to allegations made against groups. In doing so, Justice Frankfurter applied a rational basis standard and concluded that the State of Illinois had a valid basis for the regulation: "wilful purveyors of falsehood concerning racial and religious groups promote strife and tend powerfully to obstruct the manifold adjustments required for free, ordered life in a metropolitan, polyglot community," and "it would be out of bounds for the judiciary to deny the legislature a choice of policy, provided it is not unrelated to the problem and not forbidden by some explicit limitation on the State's power."

Beauharnais produced a host of dissents, some of which reflect the modern approach to hate speech. Justice Black argued that defendant was making a "genuine effort" to petition his representatives and therefore suggested that the petition had speech value. In addition, he questioned whether the petition should be regarded as libel since it was directed at a group rather than an individual. Justice Douglas also dissented with a similar argument: "[Today] a white man stands convicted for protesting in unseemly language against our decisions invalidating restrictive covenants. Tomorrow a Negro will be hailed before a court for denouncing lynch law in heated terms." Justice Jackson also dissented, noting that: "Punishment of printed words, based on their *tendency* either to cause breach of the peace or injury to persons or groups, in my opinion, is justifiable only if the prosecution survives the 'clear and present danger' test. Its application is important in this case because it takes account of the particular form, time, place, and manner of communication in question." Justice Reed dissented, arguing that the words *virtue*, *derision*, and *obloquy* were unconstitutionally vague.

F   A   Q

Q: Is *Beauharnais* still good law?

A: *Beauharnais*'s holding has been subject to much criticism and is no longer regarded as good law or sound precedent. But the case was never formally overruled. The Court's later decision in *R.A.V. v. City of St. Paul* is much more reflective of the Court's current attitude.

R.A.V. v. City of St. Paul[92] reveals the Court's current approach to hate speech and reflects a lesser willingness to uphold hate speech regulation. In that case, R.A.V., a minor, allegedly burned a crudely made cross in the yard of a black family. Although R.A.V.'s action might have violated various criminal laws, he was charged, inter alia, with violating St. Paul's Bias-Motivated Crime Ordinance, which provided: "Whoever places on public or private property a symbol, object, appellation, characterization or graffiti, including, but not limited to, a burning cross or Nazi swastika, which one knows or has reasonable grounds to know arouses anger, alarm or resentment in others on the basis of race, color, creed, religion or gender commits disorderly conduct and shall be guilty of a misdemeanor." The Minnesota Supreme Court construed the law as applying only to fighting words.

In overturning the conviction, the Court observed that content-based and viewpoint-based restrictions on speech are generally invalid and have been upheld only "in a few limited areas, which are 'of such slight social value as a step to truth that any benefit that may be derived from them is clearly outweighed by the social interest in order and morality.'" These categories of speech include child pornography and fighting words, and they can be restricted based on content as long as they do not discriminate on the basis of viewpoint as well. "[B]urning a flag in violation of an ordinance against outdoor fires could be punishable, whereas burning a flag in violation of an ordinance against dishonoring the flag is not." In other words, government may not regulate speech based on hostility — or favoritism — toward the underlying message. Under this analysis, the Court held that the Minnesota ordinance was facially unconstitutional. The Court found proscribable content discrimination because, although the ordinance was directed at fighting words, a speaker's words could contain "invective, no matter how vicious or severe," unless "they are addressed to one of the specified disfavored topics." The Court held that the First Amendment did not permit "St. Paul to impose special prohibitions on those speakers who express views on disfavored subjects." The Court also held that the ordinance went "beyond mere content discrimination, to actual viewpoint discrimination." The Court noted that speakers were free to use fighting words "*in favor* of racial, color, etc., tolerance and equality, but could not be used by those speakers' opponents." The Court concluded that "St. Paul has no such authority to license one side of a debate to fight freestyle, while requiring the other to follow Marquis of Queensberry rules."

The opinion also rejected the notion that R.A.V.'s speech could be regulated because of its "secondary effects." The city argued that the law was justified because it was designed to "protect against the victimization of a person or persons who are particularly vulnerable because of their membership in a group that historically has been discriminated against." The Court disagreed. Finally, the Court rejected the argument that the ordinance was "narrowly tailored to serve compelling state interests." The City of St. Paul had argued that "the ordinance helps to ensure the basic human rights of members of groups that have historically been subjected to discrimination, including the right of such group members to live in peace where they wish." While the Court agreed that these interests are "compelling," the Court held that "the 'danger of censorship' presented by a facially content-based statute requires that the weapon be employed only where it is '*necessary* to serve the asserted [compelling] interest.'" In this case, the Court found that the ordinance was not necessary to serve the interest: "An ordinance not limited to the favored topics, for example, would have precisely the same beneficial effect. In fact the only interest distinctively served by the content limitation is that of displaying the city council's special hostility towards the particular biases thus singled out. That is precisely what the First Amendment forbids. The politicians of St. Paul are entitled to express that hostility—but not through the means of imposing unique limitations upon speakers who (however benightedly) disagree."

Justice White, joined in whole or in part by three other justices, concurred, arguing that he would have decided the case on overbreadth grounds because the ordinance applied only to displays that one knows or should know will create "anger, alarm or resentment based on racial, ethnic, gender or religious bias." Justice Blackmun also concurred in the judgment. He would have upheld an ordinance that prohibited fighting words, but he believed that this ordinance went beyond "fighting words to speech protected by the First Amendment." Justice Stevens, joined by Justices White and Blackmun, also concurred, finding the law overbroad but rejecting the Court's discussion of content-based restrictions: "[O]ur entire First Amendment jurisprudence creates a regime based on the content of speech. . . . Whether a magazine is obscene, a gesture a fighting word, or a

Sidebar

R.A.V. AND CONTENT-BASED SPEECH RESTRICTIONS

Note that *R.A.V.* does not preclude the state from imposing content-based restrictions on speech. Indeed, as Justice Stevens noted in his concurrence, the Court's First Amendment jurisprudence is based on the notion that certain types of content may be treated differently from other types of context. For example, had the City of St. Paul sought to prohibit obscenity, the ordinance would have been upheld had it been carefully drafted. However, when content-based restrictions are upheld, the Court relies on the prohibitable nature of the content (for example, obscenity or child pornography). Political ideas are not prohibited based on their content.

photograph child pornography is determined, in part, by its content." Moreover, he argued that the ordinance was not content based or viewpoint based, but regulated based on "the *harm* the speech causes." "[T]he ordinance regulates only a subcategory of expression that causes *injuries based on* 'race, color, creed, religion or gender,' not a subcategory that involves *discussions* that concern those characteristics."

R.A.V. was followed by the holding in *Dawson v. Delaware.*[93] In that case, in a capital sentencing proceeding, the state introduced evidence showing that defendant was a member of an organization called the Aryan Brotherhood. The Court reversed Dawson's death sentence, finding a violation of defendant's right of association. The Court concluded that Dawson's racist beliefs "had no relevance to the sentencing proceeding in this case" because the murder victim was white and there was no linkage between racial hatred and the killing. The Court noted that this type of evidence might be relevant in terms of showing that defendant represents a future danger to society or in proving aggravating circumstances. But the Court expressed concern that the instruction allowed the jury to decide whether to impose the death penalty based on nothing more than Dawson's abstract beliefs. "[O]n the present record one is left with the feeling that the Aryan Brotherhood evidence was employed simply because the jury would find these beliefs morally reprehensible." Justice Thomas dissented, arguing that Delaware law allows a jury to consider "all relevant evidence in aggravation or mitigation" relating to either the crime or the "character and propensities" of the defendant. He found that the evidence made it clear "that the Aryan Brotherhood does not exist merely to facilitate formulation of abstract racist thoughts, but to "respon[d]" to gangs of racial minorities. The evidence thus tends to establish that Dawson has not been 'a well-behaved and well-adjusted prisoner' which itself is an indication of future dangerousness."

Dawson was qualified by *Wisconsin v. Mitchell,*[94] a case involving a statute that allowed sentence enhancement for a defendant who intentionally selected his victim based on race. Because Mitchell had intentionally selected his victim based on race, his sentence was increased to seven years. In an opinion by Chief Justice Rehnquist, the Court upheld the penalty enhancement, noting that sentencing judges have historically considered "a wide variety of factors in addition to evidence bearing on guilt in determining what sentence to impose on a convicted defendant" (for example, in murder cases, courts consider whether the murder was for pecuniary gain). Although the Court expressed concern about letting a sentencing judge consider a defendant's abstract beliefs, the Court held *R.A.V.* did not preclude penalty enhancement under these circumstances. The Court noted that the Wisconsin statute assumes that "bias-inspired conduct" is "thought to inflict greater individual and societal harm" because such conduct is "more likely to provoke retaliatory crimes, inflict distinct emotional harms on their victims, and incite community unrest." The Court found that Wisconsin's desire to redress these perceived harms provides an adequate explanation for its penalty enhancement provision over and above mere disagreement with offenders' beliefs or biases. The Court rejected allegations that Wisconsin statute was unconstitutionally overbroad: "The sort of chill envisioned here is far more attenuated and unlikely than that contemplated in traditional 'overbreadth' cases. We must conjure up a vision of a Wisconsin citizen suppressing his unpopular bigoted opinions for fear that if he later commits an offense covered by the statute, these opinions will be offered at trial to establish that he selected his victim on account of the victim's protected status, thus qualifying him for penalty enhancement." The Court also held that the "evidentiary use of speech" was permissible in a case like this to "establish the elements of a crime or to prove motive or intent."

F   A   Q

> **Q: Some universities and colleges have tried to regulate or limit hate speech. Are they free to impose restrictions on such speech?**
>
> A: In general, these codes have been struck down as unconstitutional. For example, in *Doe v. University of Michigan*, 721 F. Supp. 852 (E.D. Mich. 1989), the court struck down the University of Michigan's anti-harassment code as vague and overbroad. Likewise, in *UMW Post, Inc. v. Board of Regents of University of Wisconsin*, 774 F. Supp. 1162 (E.D. Wis. 1991), the court struck down the University of Wisconsin's prohibition against discriminatory epithets on similar grounds. These codes suffer from the same types of problems as the Minneapolis ordinance involved in *R.A.V.*, including vagueness and overbreadth. In addition, the codes can involve content-based or viewpoint-based restrictions on speech.

The Court distinguished *R.A.V.* in *Virginia v. Black*,[95] a case involving Virginia's cross-burning statute, which provided that "[i]t shall be unlawful for any person or persons, with the intent of intimidating any person or group of persons, to burn, or cause to be burned, a cross on the property of another, a highway or other public place. Any person who shall violate any provision of this section shall be guilty of a Class 6 felony." The statute included an evidentiary provision, which stated that "[a]ny such burning of a cross shall be prima facie evidence of an intent to intimidate a person or group of persons."

Black involved two cross-burning convictions. For the first, Barry Black, a Klu Klux Klan (KKK) member, led a KKK rally involving 25 to 30 people on private property near a state highway in the vicinity of eight to ten other houses. During the rally, KKK members "talked real bad about the blacks and the Mexicans," with one speaker suggesting that "he would love to take a .30/.30 and just random[ly] shoot the blacks." At the end of the rally, KKK members burned a 25- to 30-foot cross while playing the song "Amazing Grace" over loudspeakers. The second conviction involved Elliott, O'Mara, and a third person, who attempted to burn a cross in the front yard of an African American (Jubilee) who was Elliott's neighbor and who had spoken to Elliott's mother about gun shots fired from behind Elliott's home. Jubilee felt "very nervous" because he understood that "a cross burned in your yard . . . tells you that it's just the first round."

In upholding the convictions, the Court reviewed the history of cross burning, noting that the practice began in the fourteenth century when Scottish tribes used burning crosses to signal each other. In the United States, cross burning was linked to the KKK, which used cross burning as a "tool of intimidation and a threat of impending violence" against the targets of the cross burning. Because of this history of violence, the Court concluded that a burning cross can be used to convey a very serious threat: "When a cross burning is directed at a particular person not affiliated with the Klan, the burning cross often serves as a message of intimidation, designed to inspire in the victim a fear of bodily harm." Moreover, given the KKK's history, the Court found that this threat (of possible injury or death) should not be regarded as purely "hypothetical" because the cross involves "a serious threat, meant to coerce the victim to comply with the Klan's wishes unless the victim is willing to risk the wrath of the Klan." The Court concluded that "few if any messages are more powerful."

Although the Court recognized that the First Amendment right to freedom of speech protects "free trade in ideas," including ideas that most people find "distasteful or discomforting," the Court upheld the Virginia statute because it concluded that the right to free speech is not absolute and that the states may prohibit so-called true threats, which it defined as "those statements where the speaker means to communicate a serious expression of an intent to commit an act of unlawful violence to a particular individual or group of individuals." The Court held that such threats could be prohibited whether or not the speaker actually intends to carry out the threat because the doctrine is designed to protect individuals from the fear of violence as well as the "possibility that the threatened violence will occur." The Court readily concluded that cross burning can meet this definition of a true threat because it involves "intimidation" when "a speaker directs a threat to a person or group of persons with the intent of placing the victim in fear of bodily harm or death."

F A Q

Q: Can the holding in *Black* be distinguished from the holding in *R.A.V.*?

A: *Black* did distinguish *R.A.V.* Although the *Black* Court readily acknowledged that cross burning involves symbolic expression, the Court held that the First Amendment permits content discrimination "based on the very reasons why the particular class of speech at issue [is] proscribable." Indeed, the Court quoted *R.A.V.* for the proposition that some types of content discrimination do not violate the First Amendment: "When the basis for the content discrimination consists entirely of the very reason the entire class of speech at issue is proscribable, no significant danger of idea or viewpoint discrimination exists." The Court noted that the government may prohibit threats of violence directed against the president and may also prohibit that obscenity that is the most patently offensive in its prurience, even though it may not prohibit "only obscenity based on 'offensive *political* messages,' or 'only those threats against the President that mention his policy on aid to inner cities.'"

The Court concluded Virginia's statute was permissible under the First Amendment to the extent that it prohibited cross burning with intent to intimidate because it was not content based or viewpoint based and did not "single out for opprobrium only that speech directed toward one of the specified disfavored topics." In other words, under the statute, it did not matter whether an individual burns a cross with intent to intimidate based on the victim's race, gender, or religion, or based on the victim's "political affiliation, union membership, or homosexuality." In any event, the Court concluded that the First Amendment permits Virginia to outlaw cross burnings "done with the intent to intimidate because burning a cross is a particularly virulent form of intimidation," especially given "cross burning's long and pernicious history as a signal of impending violence."

Despite recognizing Virginia's right to prohibit cross burning, the Court concluded that the statute was unconstitutional because it contained a prima facie evidence provision, which stated that "[a]ny such burning of a cross shall be prima facie evidence of an intent to intimidate a person or group of persons." Although the true threats doctrine would allow a state to prohibit cross burning that involves an intent to intimidate, the prima facie evidence provision would permit conviction without a showing of intimidation. In other words, a conviction might be based solely "on the fact of cross burning itself, and therefore created an 'unacceptable risk of the suppression of ideas' without regard to whether there was intimidation." The Court noted that "[b]urning a cross at a political rally would almost certainly be protected expression" and might not involve an attempt at intimidation. Even if such burnings (at political rallies) may arouse a sense of anger or hatred, the Court concluded that this sense provided an insufficient basis for banning all cross burnings. There must be an intent to intimidate. Because of the prima facie evidence provision, the Court reversed the convictions of all three defendants. In regard to Barry Black (who burned a cross at a political rally), the Court concluded that his conviction could not stand and that the prosecution should be dismissed. In regard to Elliott and O'Mara, the Court reversed their convictions because of the prima facie evidence provision and remanded the case for further proceedings.

Justice Souter, joined by Justices Kennedy and Ginsburg, concurred in the judgment but dissented in part. They worried that even though the burning cross may have been selected because of its special power to threaten, "it may also have been singled out because of disapproval of its message of white supremacy, either because a legislature thought white supremacy was a pernicious doctrine or because it found that dramatic, public espousal of it was a civic embarrassment." Justice Thomas dissented, arguing that cross burning with intent to intimidate does not have an expressive component because it "has almost invariably meant lawlessness and understandably instills in its victims well-grounded fear of physical violence. Just as one cannot burn down someone's house to make a political point and then seek refuge in the First Amendment, those who hate cannot terrorize and intimidate to make their point. [Since the statute] addresses only conduct, there is no need to analyze it under any of our First Amendment tests."

In *Planned Parenthood of Columbia/Willamette, Inc. v. American Coalition of Life Activists*,[96] a federal appellate court applied the true threat doctrine to abortion protestors who sought to intimidate abortion providers. The case involved a civil suit by the physicians and abortion clinics against the American Coalition of Life Activists (ACLA), which produced posters depicting the "Deadly Dozen GUILTY" (which contained the names of various abortion providers), the "Crist" poster (which contained a provider's name, addresses, and photograph), and the "Nuremberg Files" (a list of abortion providers who the ACLA believed (or hoped) might be put on trial for crimes against humanity one day). The posters were regarded as true threats because they were circulated in the wake of other similar posters that identified abortion providers who were subsequently murdered. The suit was brought

Sidebar

BLACK'S SCOPE

Even though *Black* establishes an exception to *R.A.V.* for cross burnings undertaken with the intent to intimidate, the Court's holding may be limited in scope. It is unclear that any other symbol has quite the impact of a burning cross so that it can be regarded as a "true threat." Perhaps some gang symbols (for example, a coiled snake that a gang marks on the door of those whom it intends to hurt, maim, or kill) could be regarded as within this category of speech. But further decisions will be required to understand whether the Court will extend the true threats doctrine to such symbols.

under the Freedom of Access to Clinic Entrances Act (FACE) and the Racketeer Influenced and Corrupt Organizations Act (RICO). Plaintiffs were awarded both compensatory damages and punitive damages. However, the initial award of $108.5 million in punitive damages was remitted to $45,000 to $75,000 per defendant on due process grounds.[97]

(11) Commercial Speech

The term *commercial expression* includes speech that "propose[s] an economic transaction"[98] or that pertains "solely to the economic interests of the speaker and audience."[99] Commercial speech in its most common form consists of advertising. The most common example of commercial speech is advertising that was historically treated as constitutionally unprotected. In *Valentine v. Chrestensen*,[100] the Court upheld a local ordinance that prohibited the distribution of commercial leaflets on public streets. In that case, the distributor tried to evade the ordinance by including a political message on the back of a commercial handbill advertising public exhibition. In deciding the case, the Court focused on the advertiser's effort to attract viewers and held that the city's interest in controlling litter was sufficient to justify the ordinance. The Court observed simply that "purely commercial advertising" is not protected by the First Amendment in the same sense as other unprotected categories (for example, defamation, fighting words, and obscenity).

The Court's approach to commercial speech began to change in the 1960s. In *New York Times Co. v. Sullivan*,[101] the Court viewed a politically motivated advertisement as *political speech* rather than *commercial speech*. Then, in *Bigelow v. Virginia*,[102] the Court questioned *Valentine*'s premises, in a case involving advertising for abortion services, and suggested that it did not place all laws regulating commercial advertising beyond constitutional challenge. The Court concluded that a state could not prohibit an individual from advertising a lawful activity.

The groundwork laid in *Sullivan* and *Bigelow* bore fruit in the Court's landmark decision in *Virginia State Board of Pharmacy v. Virginia Citizens Consumer Council*,[103] a case that explicitly recognized the constitutional value of commercial speech. The case involved a Virginia law that banned the advertisement of prescription drugs on the basis that advertising might lead to price competition, which might force pharmacists to cut corners and engage in dangerous practices. The Court concluded that advertising had value because it provided increased information to the public, thereby facilitating competition. Rejecting Virginia's claim that it had the right to protect consumers against advertising, the Court concluded that the public interest is better served when consumers are able to make intelligent and informed decisions. Commercial speech helps consumers do that by providing them with "indispensable" information regarding the products they purchase and therefore is consistent with the "marketplace of ideas." However, the Court was unwilling to accord commercial speech as much protection as political speech and suggested that it could more readily be subjected to prior restraints, as well as disclaimers, disclosures, and warnings.

F A Q

Q: Is there a critical distinction between political speech, which receives a high level of protection under the First Amendment, and commercial speech?

A: Yes. For many years, the Court used this distinction as the basis for holding that commercial speech is not entitled to constitutional protection. In post-*Virginia State Board of Pharmacy* decisions, the Court has suggested that commercial speech (essentially advertisements) is of lesser value.

The Court's current approach to commercial speech was articulated in *Central Hudson Gas & Electric Co. v. Public Service Commission.*[104] In that case, the Court struck down a rule banning the promotion of electricity by public utilities that was adopted as an energy conservation measure and was based on the notion that advertising stimulates demand. While the Court agreed that commercial speech is protected under the First Amendment, the Court concluded that it is sufficiently different from political speech so that it is not entitled to the same level of protection, but nonetheless is entitled to something more than rational basis review. The Court then articulated a four-part test for evaluating commercial speech regulations. First, the focus must be on whether the regulated speech is misleading or related to an unlawful transaction, in which case regulation is permissible. Second, if the speech is not misleading or related to an unlawful activity, a reviewing court must decide whether the regulation is supported by a substantial government interest. Third, the Court must determine whether the regulation directly advances the interest. Fourth, the Court will inquire whether the governmental interest can be achieved by a more limited restriction on commercial speech.

The Court's approach to commercial speech has varied from case to case. For example, in *Posadas de Puerto Rico Associates v. Tourism Co. of Puerto Rico*,[105] the Court applied the *Central Hudson* test to a law that prohibited casino advertising aimed at tourists. In upholding the law, the Court determined that the commonwealth had a substantial health, safety, and welfare interest that would be advanced by restrictions on advertising. The Court held that the fit between regulatory means and ends was sufficiently tight, even though arguably less restrictive options were available (for example, education, counter advertising, vigorous law enforcement, and oversight of casino operations). By contrast, in *Rubin v. Coors Brewing Co.*,[106] the Court struck down a law prohibiting beer labels from displaying alcohol content. The goal of the law was to preclude competition on the basis of alcohol volume. Although rejecting the greater includes the lesser premise, the Court observed that states have more latitude to regulate speech promoting socially harmful activities than other types of expression.

In recent years, the justices have sometimes disagreed on the standard of review to be applied in commercial speech cases. For example, in *44 Liquormart, Inc. v. Rhode Island*,[107] the Court struck down a law that banned retail liquor advertising except at the point of sale, but a majority of the Court could not agree on the rationale. A plurality of four justices, led by Justice Stevens, applied a "rigorous" standard of review for total bans on "truthful nonmisleading commercial messages for reasons unrelated to the preservation of a fair bargaining process." The plurality expressed doubt regarding the validity of advertising bans that "keep people in the dark" and assumed that people will respond irrationally to the truth. Justice Thomas expressed a like concern for what he considered to be "impermissible" laws that keep consumers "in the dark." Justice O'Connor, joined by four other justices, applied the *Central Hudson* test and concluded that the liquor advertising ban could not pass this test because it imposed an undue burden. By contrast, the plurality opinion and the Thomas concurrence provided support for the proposition that total bans on truthful advertising should be subjected to strict scrutiny.

The Court applied the O'Connor approach in *Lorillard Tobacco Co. v. Reilly*[108] in striking down a comprehensive regulatory scheme that restricted outdoor advertising, point-of-sale advertising, retail and mail sales transactions, promotions, sampling, and labeling of tobacco products in an effort to curb cigarette smoking and the use of smokeless tobacco by underage consumers. The law also imposed cigar labeling requirements as a way of informing the public about the health risks of cigars, and prohibited self-service displays for tobacco products, or the shelving of such products in a way that was physically reachable by consumers, as a deceptive or unfair trade practice. The law also restricted outdoor and in-store advertising within 1,000 feet of a public playground or elementary or secondary school.

In applying the *Central Hudson* test, the Court especially emphasized the third and fourth prongs. Under the third prong, the Court held that the government was required to show that "the speech restriction directly and materially advanc[e] the asserted government interest," that this burden cannot be discharged by speculation or conjecture, but requires evidence that the harms are "real" and regulation will address them "to a material degree." The Court found ample evidence to support the state's premise that product advertising stimulates demand, and that suppression of advertising has the opposite effect. Applying the fourth *Central Hudson* prong, the Court concluded that the "broad sweep" of the regulations suggested that the state had not "carefully calculate[d] the costs and benefits" flowing from the restriction. In particular, the Court found that the 1,000 foot restriction would have functioned as a complete ban on communication of truthful information to adults in some areas, and therefore was too broad. In addition, the Court also found that the law restricted too broad of a spectrum of communications. For example, the law applied to both outdoor billboards and oral communications within 1,000 feet of a restricted use. In addition, the Court emphasized that the sale of tobacco products to and use by adults is legal, and that advertising restrictions unduly burdened the legitimate interests of sellers and consumers in receiving truthful information about a lawful product.

Lorillard produced an array of concurrences and dissents. Justice Thomas concurred, arguing that there is no basis for treating commercial speech as less valuable than other expression. Even though cigarette manufacturers may be selling harmful products, they should be allowed to advocate as much as suppliers of other dangerous items or proponents of other harmful ideas. As a result, he would have extended full First Amendment protections to commercial speech. Justice Stevens, joined by Justices Ginsburg and Breyer, dissented, arguing that the case should have been remanded for further proceedings.

The Court also applied the *Central Hudson* test in *Thompson v. Western States Medical Center*[109] to invalidate a federal law that prohibited manufacturers of compounded drugs (drugs tailored to the needs of a particular patient as opposed to mass-produced drugs) from advertising or promoting their drugs. In striking down the law, the Court held that the government failed to prove that the speech restrictions were no more burdensome than necessary to achieve the government's stated interests, and failed to adequately consider several potentially less burdensome options. Justice Thomas reiterated his opposition to the *Central Hudson* standard, as well as his position that commercial and noncommercial speech should be similarly treated. Justice Breyer, joined by four other justices, dissented, arguing that commercial speech regulation does not suppress free expression, is rarely related to the political process, and usually represents an effort by government to protect the consumer, public health, or the environment. He viewed that the Court's use of First Amendment theory to prevent the legislature from enacting necessary protections reflects a repetition of the Court's earlier (in his view, misguided) substantive due process precedent.

A number of commercial speech cases have focused on whether the First Amendment protects the advertising of professional services. Historically, states have tried to restrict the scope of professional advertising by various types of professionals (for example, doctors and lawyers) on the basis that such advertising undermines the dignity of the profession. In *Bates v. State Bar of Arizona*,[110] the Court struck down a disciplinary decision prohibiting a newspaper from carrying an advertisement listing a law clinic's fees, but not making any representations regarding the quality of the clinic's service or the results it could achieve. Relying on the logic of *Virginia State Board of Pharmacy*, the Court stressed the public's interest in receiving truthful information that might facilitate informed consumer decisions. It left open the possibility that a more narrowly tailored regulation (as opposed to a total ban) might survive constitutional scrutiny if it were directed at particularly objectionable perils (for example, predatory behavior) of lawyer advertising. In the Court's later decision in *Ohralik v. Ohio State Bar Association*,[111] the Court emphasized the potential for "fraud, undue influence, intimidation, overreaching, and other forms of 'vexatious conduct'" when lawyers solicit clients, as well as the state's interest in protecting the public against those harms. However, in *In re Primus*,[112] the Court distinguished ordinary lawyer solicitation for personal gain from solicitation by not-for-profit organizations that litigate to promote political or social agendas. Given the orientation of the latter type of groups, the Court found a diminished risk of abuse or overreaching. In *Edelman v. Fane*,[113] the Court struck down a state law banning personal solicitation of clients by accountants. However, in *Tennessee Secondary School Athletic Association v. Brentwood Academy*,[114] the Court held that a state athletic association could limit a high school football coach's recruitment of prospective athletes without infringing the First Amendment. The Court relied heavily on its prior decisions in *Ohralik* and *Bates*.

In a series of decisions, the Court has been forced to rule on whether lawyers can make claims regarding their competence. For example, in *In re R.M.J.*,[115] the Court held that a lawyer was improperly disciplined for advertising areas of practice and qualifications not permitted under state rules, noting that the advertisement was not deceptive and that the state had offered no substantial justification for limiting the content of the advertisement. Similarly, in *Peel v. Attorney Registration & Disciplinary Commission of Illinois*,[116] the Court

Sidebar

ATTORNEY DIRECT MAIL SOLICITATIONS

In *Shapero v. Kentucky Bar Association*, 486 U.S. 466 (1988), in a case arising out of Louisville, Kentucky, the Court struck down a ban on direct mail solicitations to potential clients involving truthful information relating to specific legal problems. The Court found that the risks of direct mail solicitation are less grave than those incurred with in-person solicitation and could be more easily monitored. However, in *Florida Bar v. Went for It, Inc.*, 515 U.S. 618 (1995), the Court upheld a 30-day ban on targeted direct mail by personal injury lawyers following an accident. The Court emphasized the vulnerability of accident victims and their families, as well as the potential intrusion on their privacy interests.

struck down a disciplinary rule that prohibited attorneys from representing them-selves as "certified" or "specialists" in particular areas notwithstanding a state supreme court's finding that such designations can be misleading. In *Zauderer v. Office of Disciplinary Counsel,*[117] the Court struck down a restriction that prohibited a newspaper advertisement, directed at women injured by a contraceptive device, that stated that legal services would be provided without charge unless damages were recovered. The Court noted that any restriction on advertising should be no greater than necessary to prevent consumer deception, and the advertisement was potentially deceptive because it did not mention the possibility of liability for court charges.

D. Overbreadth and Vagueness

In the First Amendment area, the Court frequently uses the overbreadth and vague-ness doctrines to limit governmental action and to protect free speech interests.

(1) The Overbreadth Doctrine

In overbreadth cases, plaintiffs claim that an overbroad law "chills" their expression by causing "persons whose expression is constitutionally protected [to] refrain from exercising their rights for fear of criminal sanctions by a statute susceptible of appli-cation to protected expression."[118] Because of this chilling effect, the Court has allowed individuals to attack overbroad laws, even though the conduct of those individuals is clearly unprotected by the First Amendment and even though their conduct could have been proscribed by a narrowly drawn law.

Illustrative of the overbreadth doctrine is the holding in *Board of Airport Commissioners v. Jews for Jesus, Inc.*[119] In that case, the Court invoked the over-breadth doctrine against a Los Angeles International Airport (LAX) regulation ban-ning all First Amendment activities in the main terminal of the airport as applied to representatives of Jews for Jesus, Inc., who were distributing religious literature. The Court concluded that the regulation was substantially overbroad because it prohib-ited all expressive activity, thereby creating what the Court referred to as a "First Amendment Free Zone." Indeed, the regulation was so broad that it seemed to pro-hibit even relatively minor acts such as talking, reading, or the wearing of campaign buttons or symbolic clothing. The Court doubted that any governmental interest could justify such an absolute prohibition of speech.

Both the vagueness and overbreadth doctrines can involve either a **"facial" challenge** to a law (a suit that alleges that a law is facially unconstitutional and should be struck down in its entirety) or an "as applied" challenge. Facial challenges are controversial because the party before the court may not be arguing that a particular law is "vague" or "overbroad" as to her (or her conduct), but may be asking the court to strike down a law because it is overbroad or vague as applied to others. In other words, the party may be seeking to raise the rights of others not before the court. In general, courts are hesitant to allow individuals to assert the rights of others and have generally required plaintiffs to establish standing. Nevertheless, in the First Amend-ment area, the courts have sometimes been willing to consider facial challenges because of the chilling effect of speech regulations.

Even when speech is involved, however, the Court tends to be restrictive in its application of the vagueness and overbreadth doctrines. For example, in *New York v.*

Ferber,[120] the child pornography case discussed earlier in the chapter, the Court referred to the "traditional rule," which prohibits litigants from raising the rights of others, and emphasized that (generally) "a person to whom a statute may constitutionally be applied may not challenge [a] statute on the ground that it may conceivably be applied unconstitutionally to others in situations not before the Court." Likewise, in *Gooding v. Wilson,*[121] the Court stated that facial challenges involve "strong medicine" because they allow "a defendant whose speech may be outside the scope of constitutional protection to escape punishment because the state failed to draft its law with sufficient precision."

F   A   Q

Q: Are there other reasons why a court might be disinclined to allow a facial challenge to a statute?

A: In *Broadrick v. Oklahoma*, 413 U.S. 601 (1973), the Court noted that it is better for a reviewing court to work from a developed record that provides the "facts needed for an informed judgment." By using this approach, the Court is better able to decide whether a law can be narrowly construed to avoid constitutional infirmities. Nevertheless, when a law is so vague or overbroad that it tends to "chill" free expression, the Court will sometimes allow a litigant to raise the rights of others.

As a result, the Court has tended to apply the overbreadth doctrine "only as a last resort," and has generally required that the overbreadth be "substantial" before a law will be invalidated on its face. *Broadrick v. Oklahoma*[122] illustrates the Court's attitude. That case involved restrictions on political campaign activity, and the Court noted that it had "never held that a statute should be held invalid on its face merely because it is possible to conceive of a single impermissible application." Likewise, in *Ferber*, the Court concluded that New York's child pornography law was not "substantially overbroad" because the law's legitimate applications far exceeded its impermissible applications. The Court held that the law was directed at "the hard core of child pornography," even though it might reach some "protected expression" ranging from medical textbooks to pictorials in the *National Geographic.*[123]

Sidebar

LIMITING CONSTRUCTIONS

Sometimes, in the face of an overbreadth claim, the Court will adopt a limiting construction that saves the law. For example, in *Board of Airport Commissioners*, the airport argued that the resolution was "intended to reach only expressive activity unrelated to airport-related purposes." The Court rejected this construction, noting that the construction was itself vague. The Court expressed concern that the limitation would give airport officials broad power to decide whether a given activity was "airport related" and therefore carried with it the potential for abuse.

(2) Vagueness

Closely related to overbreadth is the vagueness doctrine, which is grounded in the Due Process Clause. As the Court stated in *Connally v. General Construction Co.,*[124] "a statute which either forbids or requires the doing of an act in terms so vague that men of common intelligence must necessarily guess at its meaning and differ as to its application violates the first essential of due process of law."

There are various justifications underlying the vagueness doctrine. "First, [vague laws] may trap the innocent by not providing fair warning. Second, if arbitrary and discriminatory enforcement is to be prevented, laws must provide explicit standards for those who apply them. A vague law impermissibly delegates basic policy matters to policemen, judges, and juries for resolution on an ad hoc and subjective basis, with the attendant dangers of arbitrary and discriminatory application."[125] In addition, as the Court noted in *Grayned v. City of Rockford*,[126] "[u]ncertain meanings inevitably lead citizens to steer far wider of the unlawful zone than if the boundaries of the forbidden areas were clearly marked." This "chilling effect" is particularly objectionable when citizen's speech rights are implicated.

In *Coates v. Cincinnati*[127] the Court struck down an ordinance that prohibited three or more persons from congregating on a sidewalk and conducting "themselves in a manner annoying to persons passing by. . . ." The Court held that the ordinance was "impermissibly vague" because enforcement depended on the "completely subjective standard of 'annoyance.'"

Sidebar

VAGUENESS AND UNPOPULAR VIEWS

In *Cox v. Louisiana*, 379 U.S. 536 (1965), after construing a "breach of the peace ordinance" to mean that a person must act "to agitate, to arouse from a state of repose, to molest, to interrupt, to hinder, to disquiet," the Court struck the law down on vagueness grounds because it could be used to punish individuals merely for "expressing unpopular views."

E. Prior Restraints

In general, the First Amendment is viewed as imposing a very strong presumption against the validity of **prior restraints,** which involve restrictions on speech that are imposed prior to the dissemination of a communication. In common law England, the government imposed various types of prior restraints, including licensing requirements. In this country, prior restraints are presumptively invalid because they prevent ideas from reaching the public.[128]

(1) Licensing

The invention of the printing press revolutionized speech technology because it allowed people to communicate ideas more easily to a wider group of people. Prior to that invention, communication was more difficult because people were forced to communicate orally or through handwritten documents (which were laborious and time consuming to reproduce). The printing press revolutionized the communications process by allowing people to reproduce ideas quickly and to widely circulate them. Primarily because the printing press made it so easy for people to communicate with each other, governments regarded the invention as threatening and dangerous and took steps to limit and control its impact. For example, in England, the government sought to protect itself by imposing licensing schemes that required printers to submit manuscripts to government censors and to obtain a license prior to publication. A license could be denied, or it could be granted on condition that certain objectionable information be deleted or altered.

Under the First Amendment, the Court has consistently held that prior restraints are presumptively invalid. In its landmark decision in *Lovell v. City of Griffin*,[129] the

Court struck down a local ordinance that prohibited the distribution of circulars, handbooks, advertising, or literature within the city limits of Griffin, Georgia, without permission on pain of criminal sanction. The case arose when Lovell distributed a pamphlet and magazine setting forth the gospel of the "Kingdom of Jehovah" without first obtaining a permit. Lovell refused to apply for a permit because she believed that she had been sent "by Jehovah to do His work" and regarded the application as "an act of disobedience to His commandment." In invalidating the ordinance on its face, the Court flatly stated that licensing schemes are presumptively invalid because they strike "at the very foundation of the freedom of the press by subjecting it to license and censorship." The Court flatly stated that the "struggle for the freedom of the press was primarily directed against the power of the licensor" and "was a leading purpose in the adoption of the constitutional provision." Emphasizing that freedom of the press extends to pamphlet and leaflets, as well as to newspapers and periodicals, the Court noted that the former "have been historic weapons in the defense of liberty, as the pamphlets of Thomas Paine and others in our own history abundantly attest." Finally, the Court refused to distinguish between "distribution" and "publication," noting that the latter is as essential as the former. Since the ordinance was "void on its face," the Court held that Lovell was not required to seek a permit before distributing literature.

F A Q

Q: Why is the Court reluctant to review licensing decisions after the fact in an attempt to determine whether the licensor was motivated by improper considerations?

A: The Court's approach reflects the general aversion to prior restraints, as well as the fact that it will often be difficult to ascertain whether a licensor was motivated by proper considerations or improper considerations. Under *Lovell*, the Court simply presumes that licensing systems are invalid.

The Court has been a little more lax in applying the prohibition against prior restraints to motion picture licensing schemes. In *Kingsley International Pictures Corp. v. Regents*,[130] the Court dealt with a New York statute that allowed censors to refuse to license films containing material that was "obscene, indecent, immoral, inhuman, sacrilegious, or [was] of such a character that its exhibition would tend to corrupt morals or incite to [crime]." The Court concluded that the licensing authority acted improperly in refusing to issue a license for distribution of *Lady Chatterley's Lover* on the basis that the film was immoral since it presented "adultery as a desirable, acceptable and proper pattern of behavior." The Court held that the state could not simply ban the idea that adultery may be proper behavior under certain circumstances without running afoul of the "basic guarantee" of the "freedom to advocate ideas." Justice Douglas concurred, arguing that he could find no room in the First Amendment for a censor, "whether he is scanning an editorial, reading a news broadcast, editing a novel or a play, or previewing a movie."

Despite *Kingsley*'s holding, the Court has upheld some motion picture licensing schemes. In other words, the Court did not invalidate such schemes on their face as the Court did with the licensing scheme at issue in *Lovell*. For example, in *Times Film*

Corp. v. City of Chicago,[131] the City of Chicago required that all motion pictures be licensed (after submission and review) before they could be shown. An exhibitor of films challenged the law on the basis that "the requirement of submission without more amounted to a constitutionally prohibited prior restraint" and that the "constitutional protection includes complete and absolute freedom to exhibit, at least once, any and every kind of motion picture [even] if this film contains the basest type of pornography, or incitement to riot, or forceful overthrow of orderly [government]." The Court disagreed and upheld the licensing scheme against a facial challenge, concluding that "[t]he protection even as to previous restraint is not absolutely unlimited."

LICENSING AND SEXUALLY ORIENTED BUSINESSES

In *FW/PBS, Inc. v. Dallas*, 493 U.S. 215 (1990), the Court reaffirmed portions of the *Freedman* opinion in a case involving a municipal ordinance requiring a license for the operation of a sexually oriented business. Although there was no majority opinion, a majority agreed that the first two *Freedman* safeguards are essential even in this context. In other words, the licensing authority must decide whether to issue a license within a specified and reasonable time period (during which there is a right to distribute and exhibit), and there must be a prompt judicial review process if the license is denied. A different majority refused to apply the third *Freedman* requirement in this context.

Times Film Corp. was followed by *Freedman v. Maryland*,[132] which involved a Maryland statute that prohibited the exhibition of films that had not been submitted to the State Board of Censors. Although the State of Maryland admitted that the movie did not violate the statutory standards and that Freedman would have been granted a license to show the film had he applied for one, it charged Freedman with violating the statute for refusing to submit the movie. Although the Court struck down the law because of concerns about delays, as well as because of the lack of prompt judicial participation, the Court recognized that motion pictures are not "necessarily subject to the precise rules governing any other particular method of expression." Nevertheless, the Court reiterated the presumption against prior restraints and recognized that any "censorship system for motion pictures presents peculiar dangers to constitutionally protected speech." As a result, the Court concluded that a valid motion picture licensing scheme must contain a number of components:

> First, the burden of proving that the film is unprotected expression must rest on the censor. . . . Second, while the State may require advance submission of all films, [the] requirement cannot be administered in a manner which would lend an effect of finality to the censor's determination whether a film constitutes protected expression. [The] exhibitor must be assured, by statute or authoritative judicial construction, that the censor will, within a specified brief period, either issue a license or go to court to restrain showing the film. Any restraint imposed in advance of a final judicial determination on the merits must similarly be limited to preservation of the status quo for the shortest fixed period compatible with sound judicial resolution. [T]he procedure must also assure a prompt final judicial decision, to minimize the deterrent effect of an interim and possibly erroneous denial of a license.

The Court concluded that, without these safeguards, a distributor might find it too burdensome to seek judicial review of a censor's determination and might be deterred from engaging in the expression. "An exhibitor's stake in a given picture may be insufficient to justify expensive onerous course of litigation, particularly when the censor can freely distribute the film elsewhere."

Bantam Books, Inc. v. Sullivan[133] did not involve a licensing scheme, in the sense that a license was required for publication, but did involve a "notification" scheme. The Rhode Island legislature created a "Commission to Encourage Morality in Youth" and gave it "[the duty] to educate the public concerning any book, picture, pamphlet, ballad, printed paper or other thing containing obscene, indecent or impure language, or manifestly tending to the corruption of the [youth], and to investigate and recommend the prosecution of all violations of said [sections]." The Commission's practice was to notify distributors on official Commission stationery that certain designated books or magazines distributed by them had been reviewed by the Commission and that a majority of its members found the publication to be objectionable for sale, distribution, or display to youths under 18 years of age. The notice reminded distributors of the Commission's obligation to recommend obscenity prosecutions to the state attorney general. The Court struck the law down, construing the blacklists as involving not merely "legal advice" but a system of administrative restraint. Reiterating the presumption against prior restraints, the Court found that the Rhode Island law lacked adequate safeguards because it failed to provide for an immediate judicial determination regarding the validity of any determination. Justice Harlan dissented, arguing that the Commission could express its views on reading materials, enlist the cooperation of publishers and distributors, and issue notices to publishers, distributors, and members of the public so long as it refrained from "overbearing utterances."

Despite the presumption of invalidity that attaches to licensing schemes, courts have upheld content neutral time, place, and manner restrictions on parades and other public events.[134] Such restrictions are deemed essential to "prevent confusion by overlapping parades or processions, to secure convenient use of the streets by other travelers, and to minimize the risk of disorder." These permit requirements are discussed later in this chapter.

The Court has also struck down a municipal scheme requiring a license to erect racks for the sale of newspapers on public streets. In *City of Lakewood v. Plain Dealer Publishing Co.*,[135] the ordinance authorized the mayor to grant applications for newsrack permits, but required the mayor to state the reasons for a denial. If the mayor granted an application, the city would issue a permit provided that the city's Architectural Board of Review approved the newsrack design, the newsrack owner provided insurance, and the newsrack owner complied with any "other terms and conditions deemed necessary and reasonable by the Mayor." In striking down the ordinance, the Court expressed concern that the law vested "unbridled discretion" in a government official to deny expressive activity and might lead newspapers to censor themselves. Given the absence of standards, it was impossible to show that a denial was "unconstitutionally motivated" and therefore newspapers were at risk of being forced to conform their speech to the censor's preferences. The Court specifically rejected the dissent's suggestion that newspaper racks should be treated like machines selling soft drinks, noting that newspapers are engaged "in the business of expression."

Sidebar

LICENSING AND FUNDRAISING

In *Riley v. National Federation of the Blind,* 487 U.S. 781 (1988), the Court struck down a North Carolina statute that prohibited professional fundraisers from soliciting without a license. The Court concluded that fundraisers were "speakers," even though they were paid by others to speak, and that "speakers need not obtain a license to speak." However, the Court suggested that North Carolina might be free to impose reasonable time, place, and manner restrictions. Chief Justice Rehnquist, joined by Justice O'Connor, dissented, arguing that the law did not prohibit fundraisers from engaging in protected speech, but simply required them to obtain a license before engaging in solicitation.

(2) Injunctions

Just as the Court has been unwilling to sustain licensing schemes, it has also been reluctant to uphold injunctions against expression. The seminal decision is *Near v. State of Minnesota*,[136] in which the Court struck down a Minnesota statute that provided for abatement as a public nuisance of any "malicious, scandalous and defamatory newspaper, magazine or other periodical." Under this statute, the county attorney obtained an injunction against *The Saturday Press* for publishing articles that he regarded as "malicious, scandalous and defamatory." The articles alleged that a Jewish gangster controlled gambling, bootlegging, and racketeering in Minneapolis and that law enforcement officials were "not energetically performing their duties." The articles also charged that the chief of police had engaged in "gross neglect of duty, illicit relations with gangsters, and with participation in graft," that the county attorney was aware of "existing conditions and [failed] to take adequate measures to remedy them," and that a member of the grand jury was in sympathy with the gangsters.

Even though the Court acknowledged that the articles made serious accusations, the Court overturned the injunction based on the prohibition against prior restraints. The Court held that defamed individuals must resort to defamation actions to protect their reputations because of the potential for suppression and restraint. The Court emphasized that "for approximately one hundred and fifty years, there has been almost an entire absence of attempts to impose previous restraints upon publications relating to the malfeasance of public officers is significant of the deep-seated conviction that such restraints would violate constitutional right." The Court found that it made no difference that the press had charged the plaintiffs with "derelictions which constitute crimes." As we saw previously, *New York Times Co. v. Sullivan* held that even defamatory publications are entitled to First Amendment protections.

The Court applied the prohibition against prior restraints, notwithstanding the argument that the injunction was issued only after a hearing. In other words, under the law, a publisher could show, prior to issuance of an injunction, that the matter published was true and was published with good motives and for justifiable ends. The Court found that the freedom to publish does not depend on proof of truth. Justice Butler dissented, arguing that the articles revealed "malice" and concluded that it "is of the greatest importance that the states shall be untrammeled and free to employ all just and appropriate measures to prevent abuses of the liberty of the press." In addition, he rejected the idea that the Minnesota law operated as a prior restraint because it simply prevented the paper from printing allegations that had already been found to constitute a nuisance.

F   A   Q

Q: Why does the Court label the *Near* injunction as a "prior restraint" on speech?

A: The injunction functions as a prior restraint because, even though it is based on a finding that the previously published articles were malicious and defamatory, the injunction prohibits future publications. In other words, it shuts the paper down and prohibits the publication of similar articles. The injunction is a prior restraint as to those future publications.

In *New York Times Co. v. United States*,[137] also known as the *Pentagon Papers* case, the Court extended the prohibition against prior restraints to publications that implicate national security interests. In that case, the United States sought to prohibit newspapers from publishing classified documents (the "Pentagon Papers") entitled "History of U.S. Decision-Making Process on Viet Nam Policy" that had been stolen from the Pentagon. Although some lower courts refused to enjoin publication, the Second Circuit issued an injunction. In a per curiam opinion, the U.S. Supreme Court vacated the injunction reaffirming the prohibition against prior restraints, which it concluded come with a "heavy presumption" against "constitutional validity" and required "a heavy burden of showing justification for the imposition of such a restraint." The Court concluded that the government failed to meet the required burden and therefore vacated the injunction.

F   A   Q

Q: Since the *Pentagon Papers* case involved documents that had been stolen from a governmental agency, why was it not appropriate for the Court to issue an injunction?

A: There was considerable disagreement among the justices regarding the proper outcome in this case. Moreover, the newspapers did not steal the documents from the government, but instead received them from the thief. Moreover, given the speech value of the Pentagon Papers and their relationship to matters of public interest, the Court was inclined to overlook the fact that the documents were stolen. Some dissenters did focus on the fact that the documents were stolen in arguing that an injunction was appropriate.

Even though a majority of the Court agreed that the injunction should be vacated, the justices held widely divergent opinions. Those opinions are worth examining because they probe the meaning and application of the First Amendment in the national security context. Justice Black, taking a strong anti-prior restraint position, argued that the case should have been dismissed and the injunction vacated without oral argument: "Both the history and language of the First Amendment support the view that the press must be left free to publish news, whatever the source, without censorship, injunctions, or prior restraints." Justice Black's position was founded on his view of the press as a protector of the public and as an exposer of deception in government, and he argued that the *New York Times*, the *Washington Post*, and other newspapers "should be commended for serving the purpose that the Founding Fathers saw so clearly" for them. Justice Douglas concurred, arguing that the "First Amendment [leaves] no room for governmental restraint on the press," and noting that the history of the First Amendment suggests that courts should not assist government in suppressing embarrassing information.

Justice Brennan also concurred and also took a strong position in favor of disclosure. He viewed the First Amendment as imposing an "absolute bar" against prior restraints and as prohibiting all injunctive relief except in a "single, extremely narrow class of cases." "[S]uch cases may arise only when the Nation is at war," and the government is trying to "prevent actual obstruction to its recruiting service or the publication of the sailing dates of transports or the number and location of troops." He would have vacated the injunction because he found that the government had not shown that publication would precipitate problems of that magnitude.

Justice Stewart, concurring, also emphasized the importance of the press in a free society. He noted that the only "effective restraint upon executive policy and power in the areas of national defense and international affairs may lie in an enlightened citizenry — in an informed and critical public opinion which alone can here protect the values of democratic government. For this reason, it is perhaps here that a press that is alert, aware, and free most vitally serves the basic purpose of the First Amendment. For without an informed and free press there cannot be an enlightened people." But Justice Stewart was also concerned about the government's need for secrecy, and he believed that the government had ultimate power over these issues. He would have dismissed because the government failed to show "direct, immediate, and irreparable damage to our Nation or its people."

Justice White also concurred, emphasizing the presumption against prior restraints and the government's failure to meet the "very heavy burden" required for such a restraint. He also expressed concern that the injunction created a standardless restraint since "the material at issue here would not be available from the Court's opinion or from public records, nor would it be published by the press."

Chief Justice Burger dissented, arguing that the matter was rushed to decision, but that he generally agreed with the dissents of Justices Harlan and Blackmun. Justice Harlan, dissenting, would have preferred not to have reached the merits of the case. "Forced" to do so, he dissented, noting that the judiciary may not "redetermine for itself the probable impact of disclosure on the national security." He would have vacated and remanded for further proceedings. Justice Blackmun also dissented, noting that the First Amendment is only one part of the Constitution, that Article II gives the executive branch power over foreign affairs, and that the case required a weighing of the broad right of the press to publish against the government's right to suppress. As a result, he would have remanded the cases for further development.

Sidebar

THE FRENZIED TRAIN OF EVENTS

Justice Harlan complained about the "frenzied train of events" that brought the *Pentagon Papers* case to the Court. He noted that both circuit courts of appeal rendered judgment on June 23, but that the case was briefed and argued before the U.S. Supreme Court only three days later. He believed that the Court should have approached the case more deliberately.

The *Pentagon Papers* case was followed by *United States v. Progressive, Inc.,*[138] a district court decision that raised compelling issues. In that case, the federal government sought to enjoin Progressive, Inc., from publishing an article entitled "The H-Bomb Secret: How We Got It, Why We're Telling It." The article provided readers with information about how to build a hydrogen bomb. The government invoked a federal law that authorized relief against one who discloses restricted data "with reason to believe such data will be utilized to injure the United States or to secure an advantage to any foreign [nation]." The magazine responded that it wanted to publish the article to demonstrate laxness in the government's security system. The government argued that much of the article's information was not in the public domain and that some of the information had never before been published. The magazine claimed that the article was based entirely on publicly available information. While disagreeing, the government contended that, whether or not the information was publicly available, others could not replicate the author's feat (the preparation of an article on the technical processes of thermonuclear weapons). The government emphasized that the article was dangerous because it exposed concepts never heretofore disclosed in conjunction with one another and that it could help a medium-sized nation build the H-bomb. The trial court entered the injunction, but ultimately lifted it when it became clear that another magazine had published the information.

Even though *Near* made it difficult for public officials to obtain injunctions prohibiting defamatory statements, there is less certainty regarding the ability of private individuals and public figures to obtain injunctions. In *Tory v. Cochran,*[139] attorney Johnnie Cochran brought a state law defamation action against petitioner Ulysses Tory. The state trial court determined that Tory had engaged in unlawful defamatory activity because Tory's claim that Cochran owed him money was without foundation, he had engaged in a continuous pattern of libelous and slanderous activity, and he had used false and defamatory speech to "coerce" Cochran into paying "amounts of money to which Tory was not entitled" as a "tribute" or a "premium" for "desisting" from this libelous and slanderous activity. Since Tory indicated that he would continue to engage in this activity, the court granted a permanent injunction restraining him from "picketing," from "displaying signs, placards or other written or printed material," and from "orally uttering statements" about Johnnie L. Cochran Jr. and about Cochran's law firm in "any public forum." While the matter was on appeal, Cochran died and his widow was substituted as the plaintiff in the case. The Court concluded that the case was not moot, but held that it need not deal with the question of whether the First Amendment forbids the issuance of a permanent injunction in a defamation case by a plaintiff who is a public figure and whether the injunction was properly tailored. The latter issues were moot because Tory could not hope that further picketing would coerce Cochran into making a monetary payment. As a result, the Court concluded that the "injunction, as written, now amounts to an overly broad prior restraint upon speech, lacking plausible justification."

F A Q

Q: Does *Tory* suggest that the Court's approach to prior restraints is in a period of transition to a lower, less protective standard?

A: Perhaps, but not necessarily. After all, the language is dicta. Further decisions will be required to understand whether a change is in the offing. The holding in the case is consistent with prior precedent.

The Court did sustain a prior restraint in *Madsen v. Women's Health Center, Inc.*[140] In that case, petitioners (anti-abortion protestors) challenged the constitutionality of an injunction entered by a state court that imposed various restrictions on their protest activities. The injunction imposed various restrictions, including a 36-foot buffer zone around the clinic, prohibited the protestors from "singing, chanting, whistling, shouting, yelling, [using] bullhorns, auto horns, sound amplification equipment or other sounds or images observable to or within earshot of the patients inside the [c]linic" during the hours of 7:30 A.M. through noon on Mondays through Saturdays, a prohibition on "images observable" from within the clinic, a requirement that petitioners refrain from physically approaching any person seeking services of the clinic "unless such person indicates a desire to communicate" in an area within 300 feet of the clinic. The state court was attempting to prevent clinic patients and staff from being "stalked" or "shadowed" by the petitioners as they approached the clinic and to prohibit picketing, demonstrating, or using sound amplification equipment within 300 feet of the residences of clinic staff.

In deciding the case, the Court was forced to grapple with whether the injunction involved either content-based or viewpoint-based restrictions on speech. If the Court concluded that the injunction was content based, it would have applied strict scrutiny. If not, the Court would have applied a lesser standard of review. The Court concluded that an injunction should not necessarily be regarded as a content-based or viewpoint-based restriction on speech simply because it is directed at particular speech. "An injunction, by its very nature, applies only to a particular group (or individuals) and regulates the activities, and perhaps the speech, of that group." Moreover, it does so because of the "group's past actions in the context of a specific dispute between real parties" and the Court is "charged with fashioning a remedy for a specific deprivation, not with the drafting of a statute addressed to the general public."

Analyzing the facts, the Court rejected the argument that the injunction was viewpoint based because it restricted only abortion protestors and not those who protested in favor of abortion. Moreover, the Court found no basis for concluding that the Florida courts would "not equally restrain similar conduct directed at a target having nothing to do with abortion; none of the restrictions imposed by the court were directed at the contents of petitioner's message." The injunction was content neutral because the trial court imposed restrictions on petitioners' anti-abortion message as a result of repeated violations of the court's original order.

Despite finding that the injunction was not content based or viewpoint based, the Court decided that a simple rational basis standard was too low. The Court distinguished injunctions from ordinances, noting that had this case involved an ordinance imposing a time, place, and manner restriction on the use of a "traditional public forum," the Court would have scrutinized the ordinance to determine whether the regulations were "narrowly tailored to serve a significant governmental interest." The Court suggested that injunctions should still be subject to a "more stringent" standard of review that focuses on whether there is a "fit between the objectives of an injunction and the restrictions it imposes on speech" so that the relief is "no more burdensome to the defendants than necessary to provide complete relief to the plaintiffs."

In applying the "significant government interest" test, the Court upheld the 36-foot buffer zone around the clinic, noting a distinction between "the type of focused picketing banned from the buffer zone" and activities such as handbilling and solicitation. The Court viewed the buffer zone as designed to protect the entrances to the clinic and the parking lot and as ensuring that petitioners do not block traffic. In addition, the trial court had few other options to protect access given the narrow confines around the clinic. Although the Court questioned whether a complete buffer zone was really necessary, it deferred to the trial court on this issue, except for striking down the buffer zone as it applied to private property on the back and side of the clinic. The Court noted the purpose of the buffer zone (to protect access to the clinic and to facilitate the orderly flow of traffic) need not include private property.

Sidebar

CONTENT-BASED VERSUS NONCONTENT-BASED RESTRICTIONS

As *Madsen* suggests, the Court has been particularly concerned regarding statutes or other legislative acts that discriminate on the basis of content or viewpoint. *Madsen* holds that a lower standard of review applies to injunctions because, almost by definition, they arise in the context of a particular case and focus on one party and its views. Some justices argue for a higher standard of review in this context because an injunction is issued by a solitary individual (a judge), and there is a significant risk that disfavored views will be subject to persecution.

F   A   Q

Q: What's the difference between "strict scrutiny," which the Court has applied in a number of First Amendment cases, and a "significant government interest" test?

A: There are several differences. First, strict scrutiny requires that the governmental interest must be "compelling" or "overriding" rather than simply "significant." In addition, in terms of tailoring, strict scrutiny requires that government adopt the "least restrictive means" necessary to accomplish the compelling interest. The "significant governmental interest" test provides only that government must burden no more speech than necessary to achieve the objective.

The Court also upheld that part of the injunction that restrained petitioners from "singing, chanting, whistling, shouting, yelling, [using] bullhorns, auto horns, sound amplification equipment or other sounds or images observable to or within earshot of the patients inside the [c]linic" during the hours of 7:30 A.M. through noon on Mondays through Saturdays. The Court emphasized that "place" is important in determining whether restrictions burden more speech than necessary, and concluded that noise control is important in the areas surrounding hospitals and medical facilities during surgery and recovery periods.

The Court struck down the "images observable" provision. While the trial court had the power to prohibit "threats or veiled threats," the Court held that the "images observable" provision burdened more speech than necessary to achieve the purpose of limiting threats. The goal of that ban was "to reduce the level of anxiety and hypertension suffered by the patients inside the clinic." However, the Court concluded that if patients were distressed by the anti-abortion message, the clinic could deal with the problem by pulling the curtains.

The Court also struck down the prohibition on physically approaching any person seeking clinic services "unless such person indicates a desire to communicate" in an area within 300 feet of the clinic. The Court noted that these contacts could not be prohibited as fighting words. In addition, if the goal was to prevent clinic patients and staff from being "stalked" or "shadowed," the Court held that the restriction burdened more speech than necessary to ensure access to the clinic and prevent intimidation. Citizens must "tolerate insulting, and even outrageous, speech in order to provide adequate breathing space to the freedoms protected by the First Amendment."

The Court also struck down the prohibition against picketing, demonstrating, or using sound amplification equipment within 300 feet of the residences of clinic staff and the prohibition against impeding access to streets that provide the sole access to streets on which those residences were located. Petitioners could be required to turn down the volume on their amplification equipment if the protests were too loud. Moreover, while the Court was sympathetic to the need to ban targeted residential picketing, viewing the privacy of the home as an interest "of the highest order in a free and civilized society," the Court concluded that the 300-foot zone around the residences was too large because it would effectively ban marching through residential neighborhoods or walking in front of a block of houses. The Court held that such a broad ban was unwarranted because "a limitation on the time, duration of picketing, and number of pickets outside a smaller zone could have accomplished the desired result."

Justice Stevens concurred in part and dissented in part. He argued that injunctive relief should be evaluated under a more lenient standard than ordinances because the latter apply to a whole community while "injunctions apply solely to an individual or a limited group of individuals who, by engaging in illegal conduct, have been judicially deprived of some liberty—the normal consequence of illegal activity." As a result, he would have struck down a statute prohibiting demonstrations within 36 feet of an abortion clinic, but he suggested that a more limited injunction directed at a small group of persons who have engaged in unlawful conduct near the same clinic might be valid if it were no more burdensome than necessary. In addition, because of circumstances, he believed that an injunction might place appropriate restraints on future activities to prevent a reoccurrence and eliminate consequences.

Justice Scalia, joined by Justices Kennedy and Thomas, concurred in part and dissented in part, arguing that the Court should apply strict scrutiny to injunctions whether they are content based or content neutral. He expressed concerned that injunctions might be used to suppress expression and argued that the likelihood of suppression was higher with injunctions than with ordinances because they are sought by persons and organizations "with a business or social interest" in suppressing this particular view. He also argued that strict scrutiny should be applied because speech-restricting injunctions are issued by judges, individuals whose prior orders have been violated, and he questioned whether control over speech should "lightly be placed within the control of a single man or woman." Moreover, an injunction is more objectionable than an ordinance because in a contempt proceeding, only limited defenses can be raised, and a defendant cannot argue that an injunction is unconstitutional. Finally, he concluded that the injunction in this case was content and viewpoint based because all who espoused similar views would be deemed to be acting in concert or participation with them. He concluded that an "injunction against speech is the very prototype of the greatest threat to First Amendment values, the prior restraint" and "comes to this Court with a 'heavy presumption' against its constitutional validity."

F. Symbolic Speech

In many instances, individuals engage in "pure speech" such as when a newspaper publishes an article. In other instances, speech is intertwined with conduct, and the question is whether the speech should be handled differently on the theory that conduct is more dangerous than pure speech.

If a governmental regulation of expressive conduct focuses on the expression itself (in other words, it is content based), the Court tends to apply a strict level of scrutiny. On the other hand, if the government approaches the matter from a content-neutral perspective, the Court has tended to apply a more lenient standard of review. The controlling precedent is *United States v. O'Brien*,[141] which involved a criminal conviction for burning a draft card outside a courthouse and a challenge to the federal law (prohibiting the knowing destruction of a draft card) on which the conviction was based. While the Court recognized that defendant's action contained a communicative element (opposition to the war), it refused to hold that any conduct that expresses an idea should be evaluated as speech. On the contrary, the Court held that when speech and nonspeech elements coalesce, incidental restrictions on First Amendment freedoms can be justified by a governmental interest in regulating the nonspeech element. As a result, the Court fashioned a four-part test to be used in reviewing laws that incidentally burden speech. When such a law is challenged, the questions are whether (1) government has the power to regulate in the field, (2) the regulation advances a substantial or important government interest, (3) the interest is unrelated to suppressing freedom of expression, and (4) the incidental burden on speech is no more than necessary to achieve the interest. In applying these standards to the prohibition against destroying draft cards, the Court upheld the articulated governmental interests, concluding that the federal government has the power to raise and support armies, that the government has an important interest in the smooth and efficient operation of the military draft, that this interest is unrelated to the suppression of speech, and that the law was framed narrowly to account for operational smoothness and efficiency.

F   A   Q

Q: Could it have been argued that the law prohibiting the destruction of draft cards was enacted to eliminate, and therefore discriminate against, protestors who burned draft cards to symbolize their position?

A: Yes. In *O'Brien*, there was evidence suggesting that legislators were motivated by a desire to suppress this particular type of speech — that is, to engage in content-based discrimination. However, the Court concluded that the evidence was vague and insufficiently conclusive, and that the proffered justification for protecting draft cards was sufficiently important and valid.

The *O'Brien* standard was framed in the context of a case concerning symbolic expression. In other words, even though O'Brien could have made his point (opposition to the war) through a speech, he choose to do so symbolically by burning his draft card. Symbolic speech can arise in many different ways. Examples include sit-ins, prayer vigils, the wearing of armbands to symbolize a position, and a multitude of other symbols, actions, or images. When symbolic speech is at issue, it must first be determined whether the actor is intending to communicate a message. If so, and if the regulation is directed toward a governmental interest unrelated to the suppression of expression, the Court will apply the *O'Brien* test. On the other hand, if the government has targeted the symbolic speech because of its content, the Court will apply strict scrutiny (assuming that the speech is not low value, such as obscenity). Illustrative are the holdings in *United States v. Eichman*[142] and *Texas v. Johnson*,[143] in which the Court struck down flag desecration statutes. The regulations were deemed to be content based because the focus was on whether the flag destruction was respectful. The Court concluded that the government could not articulate a compelling governmental interest for the destruction.

Following the decision in *Texas v. Johnson*, there have been numerous attempts to amend the Constitution to allow the government to prohibit flag burning. Supporters of the amendment view the flag as an important national symbol that government has the right to protect. Some opponents, including some veterans of foreign wars, claim that the flag symbolizes free speech, including the right to dissent. As a result, they argue that the United States should not attempt to prohibit flag burning. The most recent attempt to amend the Constitution failed in June 2006. Although the proposed amendment again passed in the U.S. House of Representatives, it failed by one vote in the U.S. Senate.

G. Public Forum Doctrine

The Court has developed special rules that apply when individuals attempt to use public places for speech purposes. Initially, the courts must determine whether the public place is an appropriate place for expressive activity. **Traditional public fora** are those that have historically been dedicated to assembly and debate, including streets, sidewalks, parks, and in front of government buildings. (The term *traditional* is used advisedly in this context because the Court's recognition of these fora is relatively recent.) **Designated public forums** are places that, while not traditionally available for expressive activities, the government has chosen to open for those purposes. For example, a school may choose to make its auditorium available to public organizations, or a university activity fund may provide financial support for the publications of student groups, thereby creating designated public fora. Of course, some venues (for example, jails) are treated as "nonpublic" in the sense that they are closed to expressive activities.

F   A   Q

Q: How is it possible to argue that streets and sidewalks are appropriate for assembly and debate when their more obvious function is to allow for the safe and expeditious passage of vehicles and people?

A: There can be no doubt that the primary purpose of streets and sidewalks is to allow for the safe and expeditious passage of vehicles and individuals, and the Court has imposed restrictions on public forum doctrine designed to protect these functions. Nevertheless, for decades, if not centuries, people have used streets and sidewalks for expressive purposes. People who want to communicate with others typically go to those places where they can interact with the most people. Streets and sidewalks are one place where that can be done.

As in other areas of the law, one concern with governmental control of public fora is the risk that government will try to regulate or control the content of expression. Modern **public forum doctrine** recognizes that governments may have legitimate noncontent-based reasons for restricting access to fora based on the time, place, and manner of the expression. These reasons include the protection of governmental property, the management of competing uses, efficient traffic flow, public safety, and other considerations. As a result, the courts have generally upheld content-neutral restrictions on the time, place, or manner of expression. For example, government might justifiably require those who wish to hold a parade to obtain a permit so that government can anticipate and deal with traffic disruptions. Standards of review for time, place, or manner regulation accordingly reflect an appreciation that First Amendment interests are implicated in these circumstances. The scope of judicial review is determined largely by the nature of the forum.

Early judicial decisions were hostile to the notion of public forum doctrine. Indeed, in *Davis v. Massachusetts*,[144] the Court upheld state and city policies that prohibited public speaking in a park or on a highway. In doing so, the Court rejected the argument that parks "from time immemorial" had been open to public speaking and held that the legislature could limit use of parks to the extent that it deemed such restrictions advisable. The Court found that the foreclosure of public speaking in a highway or public park was no more of an infringement than for a homeowner to prohibit it in his or her house.

Modern public forum doctrine began to take shape in the late 1930s as the Court began to recognize the importance of parks and highways for speech and assembly purposes. In *Hague v. C.I.O.*,[145] a concurring Justice Roberts remarked that: "[w]herever the title of streets and parks may rest, they have been immemorially been held in trust for the use of the public and, time out of mind, have been used for purposes of assembly, communicating thoughts between citizens, and discussing public questions. Such use of the streets and public places has, from ancient time, been a part of the privileges, immunities, rights, and liberties of citizens." In a later opinion that same year, *Schneider v. State*,[146] the Court recognized that government has legitimate interests unrelated to speech that may provide the basis for regulation of speech activities in the streets (for example, the primary purpose of public streets is to carry traffic), and that the people's right to free expression did not necessarily entitle them to violate valid traffic laws. Nevertheless, in *Schneider*, which involved a regulation that prohibited distribution of handbills on public streets, the Court struck down the restriction as an overly burdensome imposition on freedom of speech. The Court was unconvinced that the stated justification for the prohibition ("litter control") provided adequate justification for the restriction on expression.

In the 1960s, as an outgrowth of the civil rights movement, the Court increasingly began to recognize the right of the people to use public places for speech and assembly purposes. For example, in *Edwards v. South Carolina*,[147] the Court held that the grounds of a state capitol should be treated as a traditional public forum, and the Court reversed a breach of peace conviction based on the refusal of civil rights protesters to cease their demonstration on police command. Likewise, in *Cox v. Louisiana*,[148] the Court reversed the conviction of civil rights protesters who picketed and demonstrated on public sidewalks. In *Brown v. Louisiana*,[149] the Court reversed the breach of peace conviction of several defendants who staged a silent civil rights protest in a public library. Even though a library had not been recognized since "time immemorial" as a place for expressive activity, the Court determined that the orderly nature of the demonstration was not incompatible with a library's primary purpose.

Because of the higher level of scrutiny, content-based restrictions on public forum use have generally been struck down. For example, in *Police Department of Chicago v. Mosley*,[150] the Court struck down an ordinance that prohibited all public picketing except by labor organizations within a designated distance from schools and during specific hours. The Court concluded that, unless the city could offer a compelling justification for distinguishing one type of picketing from another, the content-based nature of the rule made it presumptively invalid: "Once a forum is opened to assembly or speaking by some groups, government may not prohibit others from assembling or speaking on the basis of what they intend to say."

Likewise, in *Carey v. Brown*,[151] the Court struck down a law that prohibited picketing of dwellings but excepted places of employment implicated in a labor dispute. However, in *Frisby v. Schultz*,[152] the Court upheld a restriction on residential picketing directed toward a particular household finding that the stated interests in the "well-being, tranquility, and privacy of the home" were of the "highest order." Because the law did not ban all picketing in a neighborhood, but focused only on picketing aimed at a particular household, the Court concluded that the restriction was narrowly tailored. The Court left open the possibility that focused picketing might be permissible if it was directed at a house being used as a place of business or for a public meeting.

When individuals seek to hold a parade on a public street, government might require them to obtain a permit. However, the permit requirement must be a content-neutral time, place, and manner restriction. For example, in *Saia v. New York*,[153] the Court struck down a municipal ordinance that prohibited sound trucks unless authorized by the police chief on theory that the police chief's discretion was not sufficiently limited, as well as because the noise problem could be addressed by less restrictive regulatory methods.

Sidebar

PROHIBITING OVERNIGHT DEMONSTRATIONS

In *Clark v. Community for Creative Non-Violence*, 468 U.S. 288 (1984), demonstrators sought to establish a tent city in a Washington, D.C., park to draw public attention to homelessness. The Court concluded that the government had a substantial interest in maintaining the park for its intended public uses and upheld a limit on overnight usage of a public park as a valid content-neutral regulation. Because opportunities existed for protest during hours when the park was open, the Court was satisfied that the regulation left open sufficient alternative channels for communication.

F A Q

Q: With newspapers and books, the Court has generally struck down licensing schemes for fear of governmental attempts to regulate or control content. Why are permit schemes more palatable or permissible in this context?

A: The Court is concerned regarding the need for public safety. If the Klu Klux Klan is going to hold a march on a downtown street, the police want to be notified in advance so they can provide necessary protection and crowd control. In the public forum area, while the Court has upheld licensing schemes, it has generally insisted on rules designed to limit an administrator's discretion and prohibit content discrimination. In other words, the Court has upheld content-neutral time, place, and manner restrictions.

In a number of public forum cases, an important consideration is whether the governmental restriction is "narrowly tailored." For example, in *Ward v. Rock Against Racism*,[154] the Court upheld a noise control rule governing the use of a band shell in New York City's Central Park. The regulation required performers to use sound equipment and technicians provided by the city, and was designed to strike a balance between the desire of those using the band shell to use sound amplification equipment and the interests of other park users and adjacent residences. The Court rejected the argument that the rule was content based because it interfered with artistic judgment, and instead viewed the regulation as a means of furthering the substantial interest in protecting citizens from unwelcome noise. Although the Court requires that the restriction be narrowly tailored, it does not require proof that it is the least burdensome alternative. A law will not be struck down merely because a court can identify a less-restrictive alternative means. Likewise, in *Los Angeles City Council v. Taxpayers for Vincent*,[155] the Court upheld a city ordinance banning signs on public property, including political campaign signs. The Court held that the city has an important interest in maintaining community aesthetics and that the regulation was narrowly tailored toward this end. However, the Court emphasized that the regulation was not directed at speech, but at clutter, and emphasized that political candidates have other means for communicating their message to the public.

Although streets, sidewalks, and parks have long been recognized as venues for expressive activities, some recent cases have focused on whether other sites must be made available for expressive purposes. Historically, in answering that question, the Court has focused on the property's main use and whether expressive activity is compatible with that use. However, decisions sometimes focus on whether government intended to open the particular site as a forum for speech and thereby create a "designated public forum" for expressive activity.[156] While the government is not required to create a free speech forum or to maintain that forum indefinitely, it must comply with traditional forum analysis while it keeps a forum open. In other words, to engage in content-based discrimination in a designated forum, the discrimination must be supported by a compelling state interest and must be narrowly drawn to achieve the objective. Of course, the government can impose time, place, and manner restrictions if they are content-neutral, narrowly tailored to achieve a significant government interest, and leave open ample alternative channels of communication.

F   A   Q

Q: Does the focus on governmental intent make sense? After all, in regard to the traditional venues, they become public fora even though the government has not indicated an intention to open those venues up for expressive purposes.

A: Governmental intent is only one factor to be considered. At times, the Court will focus on the nature of the governmental property involved and whether freedom of expression is consistent with the nature and use of that property. For example, at a document facility that handles "top secret" documents, public access to the building for expressive purposes might be inconsistent with the function of the building. Moreover, the government may have no intent to open the building for expressive purposes. In other contexts, governmental intent may be important. For example, if a university sets aside a portion of the campus for expressive purposes, then that area is explicitly opened for expressive purposes. In a few instances (for example, parks and streets), governmental intent may be irrelevant.

Example: Illustrative of the modern approach is the holding in *Heffron v. International Society for Krishna Consciousness*,[157] although that decision predates the Court's development of clear distinctions among forum types. The case involved a state fair policy that restricted all sellers, vendors, and distributors to booths that could be rented on a first-come, first-served basis, and to fixed locations on the fairgrounds. The regulation was adopted as a crowd control measure. The Court found that the policy was content-neutral and that it advanced the state's significant interest in maintaining order and access. Because the Court was convinced that no other regulatory means would have advanced the state's interest as effectively, the narrowly tailored requirement was satisfied. The ability to communicate from a fixed position, and the ability to interact off-property, indicated the availability of adequate alternative channels of communication.

Despite the growth of public forum doctrine, it is important to recognize that not all government property is necessarily open for speech and assembly purposes. In other words, government ownership of property by itself does not establish a First Amendment right of access. Like private property owners, federal, state, and local governments have an interest in using the property under their control for the uses to which they are lawfully dedicated. Traditional public forums are well established in their identity and thus are readily discernible. Some reserved forums are relatively easy to identify, including jails[158] and military bases,[159] but it can sometimes be difficult to find the dividing line between a designated forum and a reserved forum. In *Perry Education Association v. Perry Local Educators Association*,[160] the Court held that a collective bargaining agreement that gave the teachers' elected bargaining agent a right of access to teacher mailboxes did not create a public forum. Although the school also allowed certain community groups to use the mail system, the contract denied a rival union access. The Court held that the mailboxes were not public forums by tradition or designation. The Court focused on the district's purpose and differentiated between a policy that creates general access and a provision for specific access consistent with the place's operational needs. If the district had intended to open the mailboxes for general access, then it would have created a designated forum. On the other hand, since the district provided for only selective access, the Court chose to characterize the property as a nonpublic forum.

Examples: The Court has found "reserved" uses in a number of instances. In *United States Postal Service v. Council of Greenburgh Civic Associations*,[161] the Court held that the U.S. Postal Service did not have to provide unlimited public access to mailboxes because such access would disrupt the postal service's ability to operate an efficient mail system. Likewise, in *Members of the City Council of Los Angeles v. Vincent*,[162] the Court refused to hold that utility poles could be characterized as either traditional or designated forums.

Airports have been a particular source of forum litigation in recent years. In *International Society for Krishna Consciousness, Inc. v. Lee*,[163] the Court refused to treat airports as traditional public fora. Unlike public streets and parks, airports have not been used since "time immemorial" for expressive purposes, and they are dedicated primarily to travel rather than speech and assembly. The Court rejected arguments that airports are variable use facilities that are adapted to speech and assembly.

F   A   Q

Q: Why aren't airports treated similarly to streets and sidewalks — that is, as public fora?

A: The Court focuses on the fact that airports have not been used since "time immemorial" for speech purposes — a strange idea given that airports have not been around as long as streets and sidewalks, and especially given that planes have not been around since time immemorial. Moreover, one can argue that our conception of public fora should evolve over time, and airport concourses are the modern equivalents of streets and sidewalks. Of course, even if the Court had treated airport concourses like streets and sidewalks, the Court might have held that they should be treated differently because of the security concerns.

Sidebar

PUBLIC TELEVISION AND CANDIDATE DEBATES

In *Arkansas Educational Television Commission v. Forbes*, 523 U.S. 666 (1998), the Court held that a public television station had created only a reserved forum when it established a debate for congressional candidates. In creating the debate, the station did not offer to provide general public access to the airwaves, but instead established eligibility requirements for candidates that required proof of a minimum level of public support. The Court rejected a third-party candidate's claim that his exclusion was a function of viewpoint discrimination.

In other contexts, as well, the courts have struggled to define the concept of public forum. For example, in *United States v. American Library Association*,[164] the Court held that Internet terminals in libraries should not be treated as forums for public speech. Libraries do not provide terminals to create speech fora, but instead do so to facilitate research, learning, and recreational activities. In other words, the Court analogized Internet access to providing readers with access to bookshelves, and noted that the Internet had not been historically used as a forum for speech purposes.

Public forum doctrine by definition ordinarily does not apply to private property. In general, the Court imposes a state action requirement for invocation of the First Amendment. However, under certain circumstances, there might be sufficient governmental involvement or attributes to justify treating private action as governmental action. For example, in *Marsh v. Alabama*,[165] the Court held that a company town functioned like a public city and therefore its actions should be treated as state action for purposes of the First Amendment. In *Marsh*, the Court held that First Amendment protections extended to a

Jehovah's Witness arrested for disseminating literature in a private town. Following *Marsh,* a series of cases addressed the question of whether shopping centers were state actors subject to First Amendment constraints. In *Amalgamated Food Employees Union Local 590 v. Logan Valley Plaza, Inc.,*[166] the Court treated a privately owned shopping center as the equivalent of public property for First Amendment purposes. The shopping center functioned like the municipal shopping district in *Marsh.* However, the Court overruled itself in *Hudgens v. National Labor Relations Board,*[167] in holding that a shopping center owner could exclude speech and assembly without First Amendment implications. In *PruneYard Shopping Center v. Robins,*[168] the Court held open the possibility that public access to private property could be reserved by state law.

H. Religious Speech: Establishment Clause — Free Speech Tension

In a number of recent cases, the Court has been asked to decide how the First Amendment applies to religious speech. Although the First Amendment's speech clause gives all citizens the right to free expression, that amendment also prohibits the government from "establishing" religion. These fundamental principles can collide when religious groups seek to use governmental facilities or seek governmental funding for their speech.

In this collision of principles, the Court has been reluctant to allow the government to discriminate against religious speech in public forums. Illustrative is *Widmar v. Vincent,*[169] which involved a university policy that allowed student groups access to campus facilities, but excluded groups that wished to use the facilities for religious purposes because of Establishment Clause concerns. The Court ultimately struck down the policy as a content-based restriction on speech. Although the Court found that the university had a compelling state interest in avoiding an Establishment Clause violation, the Court held that the regulatory means were improper. The Court concluded that an equal access policy would promote a secular purpose (equal access), rather than a religious purpose, and created no risk of entanglement between church and state. Moreover, with or without an equal access policy, the university was obligated to implement the provision on a nondiscriminatory basis, barring a compelling reason for excluding religious groups. Of course, the university could have opted to close the forum to all student groups.

A similar decision was rendered in *Lamb's Chapel v. Center Moriches Union Free School District.*[170] That case involved a public school's decision to allow outside groups to use school facilities after hours for "social, civic or recreational use," but to prohibit use "by any group for religious purposes." Under the policy, the school excluded a church that wanted to present films teaching family values from a Christian perspective. The Court overturned the exclusion, holding that because the films "dealt with a subject otherwise permissible" (the teaching of family values), the district's exclusion of the church constituted unconstitutional viewpoint discrimination. Under *Widmar,* the school's Establishment Clause concerns could not be regarded as rising to the level of a compelling government interest, and the exclusionary policy was viewed as representing an unconstitutional exercise in viewpoint discrimination.

Q: If *Lamb's Chapel* involved what was essentially a religious activity, why was the school precluded from excluding it?

A: The school could have excluded the group had it sought to use public facilities solely for religious services. However, the evidence showed that the group was trying to teach family values from a religious perspective. Since the group's activities fit within the scope of the stated purpose of the forum, the school could not exclude Lamb's Chapel, even though the teaching was undertaken from a religious perspective.

Perhaps the most fascinating recent decision is the holding in *Rosenberger v. Rector & Visitors of the University of Virginia.*[171] That case struck down a university policy that funded the publications of registered student organizations, but specifically excluded religious groups. In *Rosenberger*, the University of Virginia authorized payment to outside contractors from its Student Activities Fund (SAF) for the costs of printing a variety of student publications. To qualify for funding, a student organization was required to register as a Contracted Independent Organization (CIO). Any group could claim CIO status provided that a majority of its members were students, its managing officers were full-time students, and the organization complied with other stated requirements. University guidelines provided that funding was available for a variety of purposes, including "student news, information, opinion, entertainment, or academic communications media groups." Wide Awake Publications (WAP), a CIO, was denied funding because its student paper "primarily promotes or manifests a particular belief in or about a deity or an ultimate reality." The paper wrote about "philosophical and religious expression" offering "a Christian perspective on both personal and community issues, especially those relevant to college students at the University of Virginia."

In an opinion by Justice Kennedy, the Court concluded that WAP was entitled to funding on an equal basis with other student publications. The Court began by reaffirming the basic principle that once a government has opened a limited public forum, the government must abide by the rules it has established for the forum and may not discriminate against speech based on its viewpoint. Content discrimination is permitted only to the extent that it serves the purposes of the limited forum. The Court found that the SAF may be a forum "more in a metaphysical than in a spatial or geographic sense," but the same principles apply. The Court easily found viewpoint discrimination because, although the university did not exclude religion as an acceptable subject, it singled out for "disfavored treatment" journalistic efforts with religious editorial viewpoints. The Court found that such "viewpoint discrimination" is unconstitutional:

> Vital First Amendment speech principles are at stake here. The first danger to liberty lies in granting the State the power to examine publications to determine whether or not they are based on some ultimate idea and, if so, for the State to classify them. The second, and corollary, danger is to speech from the chilling of individual thought and expression. That danger is especially real in the University setting . . . . For the University, by regulation, to cast disapproval on particular viewpoints of its students risks the suppression of free

speech and creative inquiry in one of the vital centers for the Nation's intellectual life, its college and university campuses.

The Court rejected the university's argument that its actions were compelled by the Establishment Clause. Justice Souter, joined by Justices Stevens, Ginsburg, and Breyer, dissented, arguing that if the University of Virginia gave funding to the WAP, it would run afoul of the Establishment Clause. In addition, he argued that the university did not engage in viewpoint discrimination because the university's guidelines applied to other faiths as well as to agnostics, atheists, and theists. "[A] university's decision to fund a magazine about racism, and not to fund publications aimed at urging repentance before God does not skew the debate either about racism or the desirability of religious conversion."

F   A   Q

Q: How could the state be required to pay for what is essentially religious proselytization?

A: The parameters of the school's forum were broadly defined to include "student news, information, opinion, entertainment, or academic communications media groups." Under these circumstances, Wide Awake's speech fit within the parameters of the permissible discussion, and the SAF was not allowed to discriminate against it.

Rosenberger was followed by the holding in *Good News Club v. Milford Central School.*[172] That case involved a school board's "community use" policy, which allowed buildings to be used for a number of purposes including "instruction in any branch of education, learning or the arts," as well as for "social, civic and recreational meetings and entertainment events, and other uses pertaining to the welfare of the community, provided that such uses shall be nonexclusive and shall be opened to the general public." Under the policy, school officials denied the Good News Club's request to hold meetings in the school cafeteria for elementary age children. School officials concluded that, although the club would discuss subjects such as childrearing, development of character, and development of morals, it would do so from a religious standpoint involving "the equivalent of religious instruction itself." In an opinion by Justice Thomas, the Court held that the Good News Club was entitled to use school facilities, concluding that the school had created a limited public forum and that the state could place restrictions on the use of the forum provided that it does not engage in viewpoint discrimination, and provided that the restriction is "reasonable in light of the purpose served by the forum." Relying on *Lamb's Chapel* and *Rosenberger*, the Court found that the Milford School had engaged in viewpoint discrimination, noting that Milford had opened its facilities to a variety of purposes related to the welfare of the community including discussions of childrearing and the development of character and morals. Although the Good News Club also taught morals and character development to children, it was precluded from teaching it from a religious perspective. The Court rejected the district's claim that it would be violating the Establishment Clause if it allowed the club to use its facilities. Justice Stevens dissented, arguing that the school did not intend to exclude all speech from a religious point of view. Instead, it sought to exclude proselytizing religious speech. Justice Souter, joined by Justice Ginsburg, also dissented, noting that the Good News Club was engaged in evangelical worship. Justice Scalia disagreed with Justice Souter, noting that the Court had "previously rejected the attempt to distinguish worship from other religious speech" because "the distinction has [no] intelligible content" and no "relevance" to the constitutional issue.

I. Campaign Finance Laws

(1) Foundational Principles

There has been considerable litigation whether campaign financing (both political contributions and expenditures) involves constitutionally protected speech. One of the most famous campaign finance decisions is *Buckley v. Valeo*,[173] a per curiam opinion. That case involved a challenge to the Federal Election Campaign Act of 1971 (FECA) and related provisions of the Internal Revenue Code of 1954, all as amended in 1974. The act contained a number of provisions, including the following:

- a prohibition that prevented any person from giving more than $1,000 to any single candidate for an election campaign;
- a prohibition that prevented individuals from contributing more than $25,000 in a single year;
- a provision (§608(b)(2)) that allowed "political committees" to contribute no more than $5,000 to any candidate with respect to any election for federal office;
- a provision that excluded from the definition of contribution "the value of services provided without compensation by individuals who volunteer a portion or all of their time on behalf of a candidate or political committee" (certain expenses incurred by persons in providing volunteer services to a candidate are exempt from the $1,000 ceiling only to the extent that they do not exceed $500);
- an overall $25,000 limitation on total contributions by an individual during any calendar year;
- a provision (§608(e)(1)) that "[n]o person may make any expenditure . . . relative to a clearly identified candidate during a calendar year which, when added to all other expenditures made by such person during the year advocating the election or defeat of such candidate, exceeds $1,000";
- limits on expenditures by a candidate "from his personal funds, or the personal funds of his immediate family, in connection with his campaigns during any calendar year" (§608(a)(1)) (these ceilings varied from $50,000 for presidential or vice presidential candidates to $35,000 for senatorial candidates, and $25,000 for most candidates for the House of Representatives);
- a limitation (§608(c)) on overall campaign expenditures by candidates seeking nomination for election and election to federal office (presidential candidates could spend $10 million in seeking nomination for office and an additional $20 million in the general election campaign. The ceiling on senatorial campaigns was pegged to the size of the voting-age population of the state with

minimum dollar amounts applicable to campaigns in states with small populations. The Act imposed blanket $70,000 limitations on both primary campaigns and general election campaigns for the House of Representatives with the exception that the senatorial ceiling applied to campaigns in states entitled to only one representative.);

- §434(e) required "[e]very person (other than a political committee or candidate) who makes contributions or expenditures" aggregating over $100 in a calendar year "other than by contribution to a political committee or candidate" to file a statement with the Commission.

The Court quickly held that campaign finance laws implicate First Amendment interests because they involve discussions regarding public issues and the qualifications of candidates, and the Court held that such discussions are essential in a free society. The Court reiterated the fundamental idea that the "First Amendment protects political association as well as political expression."

F A Q

Q: Should the Court have treated FECA's contribution and expenditure limitations as regulations of "conduct" rather than "speech"?

A: The Court found that "the giving and spending of money" produces communication that sometimes involves speech alone, sometimes involves conduct, and sometimes involves a combination of the two. Moreover, the Court found that even if such activities involve conduct rather than speech, the *O'Brien* test would not be satisfied because campaign finance laws suppress communication (electoral communication).

In first focusing on the act's expenditure limitations, the Court found that expenditure limitations involve "substantial rather than merely theoretical restraints" on political speech. The Court noted that the act's $1,000 ceiling on spending "relative to a clearly identified candidate" would exclude virtually all citizens and groups (except candidates, political parties, and the institutional press) "from any significant use of the most effective modes of communication." The Court was concerned even about the limitations on expenditures by campaign organizations and political parties, noting that those limits would have restricted the scope of a number of congressional and presidential campaigns and would have constrained candidates who raised sums in excess of the spending ceiling.

The Court viewed the contribution limitations as having a more limited impact on free expression. Although a contribution "serves as a general expression of support for [a] candidate and his views," it "does

Sidebar

CAMPAIGN FINANCE AND TIME, PLACE, AND MANNER RESTRICTIONS

In *Buckley*, the Court also rejected the argument that act's contribution and expenditure limitations should be treated as time, place, and manner restrictions. The Court noted that modern communication methods require the expenditure of large amounts of money and that a restriction on expenditures "necessarily reduces the quantity of expression by restricting the number of issues discussed, the depth of their exploration, and the size of the audience reached."

Why contribution is less important

not communicate the underlying basis for the support." Moreover, the "quantity of communication by the contributor does not increase perceptibly with the size of his contribution, since the expression rests solely on the undifferentiated, symbolic act of contributing. At most, the size of the contribution provides a very rough index of the intensity of the contributor's support for the candidate." In addition, in order for contributions to become speech, they require communication by someone else (the candidate or the candidate's campaign). As a result, the Court concluded that a limitation on the amount of money a person may give to a candidate or campaign organization involves less direct restraint on political communication because it permits the symbolic expression of support and does not otherwise infringe the contributor's right to publicly discuss candidates and issues. Nevertheless, the Court recognized that contributions play an "important role" in financing political campaigns and that "contribution restrictions can have a severe impact on political dialogue if the limitations prevented candidates and political committees from amassing the resources necessary for effective advocacy." But the Court found that the act's contribution limitations would not have a "dramatic adverse effect on the funding of campaigns and political associations." If the size of contributions was restricted, candidates and political committees would simply be forced to raise funds from a greater number of persons. Those who wanted to exceed the limits could make direct expenditures on behalf of the candidate (as opposed to contributions).

Sidebar

REGULATING POLITICAL COMMITTEES

The *Buckley* Court upheld a provision of FECA that allowed "political committees" to contribute up to $5,000 to any candidate with respect to any election for federal office. The Court noted that rather than undermining freedom of association, the "provision enhances the opportunity of bona fide groups to participate in the election process, and the registration, contribution, and candidate conditions serve the permissible purpose of preventing individuals from evading the applicable contribution limitations by labeling themselves committees."

In analyzing the contribution limitations, the Court noted that both the right to associate and the right to participate in political activities are not absolute, and that interferences with those rights can be sustained "if the State demonstrates a sufficiently important interest and employs means closely drawn to avoid unnecessary abridgment of associational freedoms." The Court found a sufficient interest in the government's desire to limit the actuality and appearance of corruption. Of course, when large contributions are given to secure a "political quid pro quo from current and potential office holders, the integrity of our system of representative democracy is undermined." But the Court was equally concerned about the "appearance of corruption stemming from public awareness of the opportunities for abuse inherent in a regime of large individual financial contributions." The Court rejected the argument that bribery laws and narrowly drawn disclosure requirements constituted a less restrictive means of dealing with quid pro quo arrangements, finding that such laws deal with only the most blatant corruption.

In regard to the provision relating to volunteers' incidental expenses, the act excluded from the definition of contribution "the value of services provided without compensation by individuals who volunteer a portion or all of their time on behalf of a candidate or political committee." The Court upheld the restriction finding that if the general contributions are valid, then these provisions are valid as a "constitutionally acceptable accommodation of Congress' valid interest in encouraging citizen participation in political campaigns while continuing to guard against the corrupting potential of large financial contributions to candidates."

The Court also upheld the overall $25,000 limitation on total contributions by an individual during any calendar year. The Court found that the provision was "quite modest" and that it served "to prevent evasion of the $1,000 contribution limitation by a person who might otherwise contribute massive amounts of money to a particular candidate through the use of unearmarked contributions to political committees likely to contribute to that candidate, or huge contributions to the candidate's political party." The Court found that any imposition on associational freedoms was "limited" and "no more than a corollary of the basic individual contribution limitation that we have found to be constitutionally valid."

The Court then struck down §608(e)(1), which provided that "[n]o person may make any expenditure . . . relative to a clearly identified candidate during a calendar year which, when added to all other expenditures made by such person during the year advocating the election or defeat of such candidate, exceeds $1,000." Given the cost of advertising, the Court found that this section made it a federal crime "to place a single one-quarter page advertisement 'relative to a clearly identified candidate' in a major metropolitan newspaper." The Court held that the governmental interest in preventing corruption and the appearance of corruption was "inadequate" to justify this provision.

The Court specifically rejected the argument that the government had the right to equalize the resources of individuals and groups and "the relative ability of individuals and groups to influence the outcome of elections." The Court found that the "concept that government may restrict the speech of some elements of our society in order to enhance the relative voice of others is wholly foreign to the First Amendment. . . . The First Amendment's protection against governmental abridgment of free expression cannot properly be made to depend on a person's financial ability to engage in public discussion."

The Court also struck down the limitation on expenditures by candidates from personal or family resources. The Court concluded that this restriction imposed a substantial restraint on candidates and that a candidate has the right "vigorously and tirelessly to advocate his own election and the election of other candidates. Indeed, it is of particular importance that candidates have the unfettered opportunity to make their views known so that the electorate may intelligently evaluate the candidates' personal qualities and their positions on vital public issues before choosing among them on election day." The Court also held that the interest in actual and apparent corruption was also insufficient to justify this restriction. By relying on personal funds, candidates reduce their reliance on "outside contributions and thereby counteracts the coercive pressures and attendant risks of abuse to which the Act's contribution limitations are directed." In addition, the asserted interest of equalizing the relative financial resources of candidates competing for elective office could not justify the provision.

The Court also struck down the limitation on overall campaign expenditures by candidates seeking nomination for election and election to federal office. The Court found that the governmental interest in alleviating the corrupting influence of large contributions was insufficient. The Court noted that it had already sustained limitations on the amount of contributions and concluded that "the financial resources available to a candidate's campaign, like the number of volunteers recruited, will normally vary with the size and intensity of the candidate's support. There is nothing invidious, improper, or unhealthy in permitting such funds to be spent to carry the candidate's message to the electorate." The Court rejected the argument that the government had an interest in "reducing the allegedly skyrocketing costs of political campaigns." "The First Amendment denies government the power to determine that spending to promote one's political views is wasteful, excessive, or unwise."

The Court then upheld the reporting and disclosure requirements. Relying on *NAACP v. Alabama* (discussed in the next section), the Court found that the requirements must pass "exacting scrutiny" and that there must be a "substantial relation" between the governmental interest and the information required to be disclosed. But the Court expressed concern that disclosure requirements might have a "deterrent effect on the exercise of First Amendment rights." In addition, the Court expressed concern that "the invasion of privacy of belief" can be as significant when information regarding the giving and spending of money is disclosed as when it concerns the joining of organizations, for "[f]inancial transactions can reveal much about a person's activities, associations, and beliefs." The Court concluded that its past decisions had not drawn fine lines between contributors and members but had treated them interchangeably. Nevertheless, the Court found that the governmental interests were sufficient to outweigh the possibility of infringement:

> The governmental interests sought to be vindicated by the disclosure requirements are of this magnitude. They fall into three categories. First, disclosure provides the electorate with information "as to where political campaign money comes from and how it is spent by the candidate" in order to aid the voters in evaluating those who seek federal office. [The] sources of a candidate's financial support also alert the voter to the interests to which a candidate is most likely to be responsive and thus facilitate predictions of future performance in office. Second, disclosure requirements deter actual corruption and avoid the appearance of corruption by exposing large contributions and expenditures to the light of publicity. [A] public armed with information about a candidate's most generous supporters is better able to detect any post-election special favors that may be given in return. Third, and not least significant, record keeping, reporting, and disclosure requirements are an essential means of gathering the data necessary to detect violations of the contribution limitations described above.

Sidebar

CAMPAIGN FINANCE RESTRICTIONS AND OVERBREADTH

The *Buckley* Court expressed concern about whether FECA's disclosure provisions were overbroad since they swept in contributions as low as $10. The Court was also concerned that contributors of relatively small amounts may be "especially sensitive to recording or disclosure of their political preferences." Nevertheless, although the Court found that the "strict requirements may well discourage participation by some citizens in the political process," the Court held that it would not "require Congress to establish that it has chosen the highest reasonable threshold. The line is necessarily a judgmental decision, best left in the context of this complex legislation to congressional discretion."

Finding "substantial governmental interests" supporting the disclosure requirements, the Court then balanced those interests against the "burden" that disclosure requirements impose on individual rights. The Court recognized that by requiring public disclosure of contributions to candidates and political parties, the act would "deter some individuals who otherwise might contribute" for fear of harassment or retaliation. Nevertheless, the Court found that the disclosure provisions constituted "the least restrictive means of curbing the evils of campaign ignorance and corruption that Congress found to exist." The Court upheld the restrictions even as applied to minor parties and independent candidates. The Court found that the governmental interest in disclosure was lower because minor parties had little chance of winning elections, and they usually had "definite and publicized viewpoints" so that there was "less need to inform the voters of the interests that specific candidates represent." Nevertheless, the Court found that a minor party could "play a significant role in an election. Even when a minor-party candidate has little or no chance of winning, he may be encouraged by major-party interests in order to divert votes from other major-party contenders." In addition, the Court found that the disclosure provisions increase "the fund of information concerning those who support the candidates" and that "informational interest can be as strong as it is in coordinated spending, for disclosure helps voters to define more of the candidates' constituencies."

The Court also upheld the provisions providing for public financing of presidential election campaigns. Section 9006 established a Presidential Election Campaign Fund, financed from general revenues based on designations by individual taxpayers, to finance (1) party nominating conventions, (2) general election campaigns, and (3) primary campaigns. The law distinguished between "major," "minor," and "new" parties. A major party was defined as a party whose candidate for president in the most recent election received 25 percent or more of the popular vote. A minor party was defined as a party whose candidate received at least 5 percent but less than 25 percent of the vote at the most recent election. All other parties were new parties, including both newly created parties and those receiving less than 5 percent of the vote in the last election.

Major parties were entitled to $2 million to defray their national committee presidential nominating convention expenses, and the party must limit total expenditures to that amount and may not use any of this money to benefit a particular candidate or delegate. A minor party received a portion of the major-party entitlement determined by the ratio of the votes received by the party's candidate in the last election to the average of the votes received by the major parties' candidates. No financing was provided for new parties, nor is there any express provision for financing independent candidates or parties not holding a convention.

For general election campaign expenses, §9004(a)(1) gave each major-party candidate $20 million. Those receiving funds were required to promise not to incur additional expenses (beyond the $20 million) and not to accept private contributions except to the extent that the fund was insufficient to provide the full $20 million. Minor-party candidates were also entitled to funding, under the same conditions. Minor-party funding was again based on the ratio of the vote received by the party's candidate in the preceding election to the average of the major-party candidates. New-party candidates received no money prior to the general election, but any candidate who polled 5 percent or more of the popular vote in an election was entitled to post-election payments according to the formula applicable to minor-party candidates.

The law also established a third account, the Presidential Primary Matching Payment Account. This funding was intended to aid campaigns by candidates seeking presidential nomination by a political party in primary elections. The law required that the candidate raise at least $5,000 in each of 20 states, counting only the first $250 from each person contributing to the candidate. In addition, the candidate was required to abide by specified spending limits. Funding was provided according to a matching formula: Each qualified candidate was entitled to a sum equal to the total private contributions received, disregarding contributions exceeding $250 from any single person.

The Court upheld the public financing provisions, finding that public financing provides a "means of eliminating the improper influence of large private contributions" and furthers a "significant governmental interest." In addition, the Court found that Congress could permissibly choose to relieve "major-party Presidential candidates from the rigors of soliciting private contributions." In regard to the claim that the law discriminated against candidates nominated by "minor" parties, the Court found that "Congress' interest in not funding hopeless candidacies with large sums of public money, necessarily justifies the withholding of public assistance from candidates without significant public support. Thus, Congress may legitimately require 'some preliminary showing of a significant modicum of support,' as an eligibility requirement for public funds."

Both Chief Justice Burger and Justice White concurred in part and dissented in part. Chief Justice Burger disagreed with the Court's holding regarding the disclosure of small contributions. In general, he regarded "disclosure" as "the salutary and constitutional remedy" for the "ills" about which Congress was concerned. Disclosure of contributions by individuals and by entities, particularly corporations and labor unions, "is an effective means of revealing the type of political support that is sometimes coupled with expectations of special favors or rewards." But he expressed concern about the exceptionally low limits ($10) contained in the law. "Rank-and-file union members or rising junior executives may now think twice before making even modest contributions to a candidate who is disfavored by the union or management hierarchy. Similarly, potential contributors may well decline to take the obvious risks entailed in making a reportable contribution to the opponent of a well-entrenched incumbent." He concluded that the public's right to know was not "absolute when its exercise reveals private political convictions. [N]o legitimate public interest has been shown in forcing the disclosure of modest contributions that are the prime support of new, unpopular, or unfashionable political causes. There is no realistic possibility that such modest donations will have a corrupting influence especially on parties that enjoy only 'minor' status."

Chief Justice Burger also rejected the Court's distinction between the "communication inherent in political contributions from the speech aspects of political expenditures." He believed that candidates and contributors "spend money on political activity because they wish to communicate ideas, and their constitutional interest in doing so is precisely the same whether they or someone else utters the words." He argued that "freedom of association and freedom of expression were two peas from the same pod," and that the contribution restrictions were "hardly incidental" because they would "foreclose some candidacies" and "alter the nature of some electoral contests drastically." He argued that contribution limitations can be justified only by "the very strongest of state interests" and stated his belief that other alternatives should be adequate.

He also would have struck down the system of matching grants, arguing that it makes "a candidate's ability to amass private funds the sole criterion for eligibility for public funds." He believed that such an arrangement "can put at serious disadvantage a candidate with a potentially large, widely diffused but poor constituency. The ability of a candidate's supporters to help pay for his campaign cannot be equated with their willingness to cast a ballot for him."

Chief Justice Burger also expressed concern about the fact that the remaining (valid) provisions of the act caused inequity:

> A candidate with substantial personal resources is now given by the Court a clear advantage over his less affluent opponents, who are constrained by law in fundraising, because the Court holds that the "First Amendment cannot tolerate" any restrictions on spending. Minority parties, whose situation is difficult enough under an Act that excludes

them from public funding, are prevented from accepting large single-donor contributions. At the same time the Court sustains the provision aimed at broadening the base of political support by requiring candidates to seek a greater number of small contributors, it sustains the unrealistic disclosure thresholds of $10 and $100 that I believe will deter those hoped-for small contributions. Minor parties must now compete for votes against two major parties whose expenditures will be vast.

Justice White argued that he would have upheld the expenditure limitations because he viewed them as "reinforcing" the contribution limits and helping "eradicate the hazard of corruption." He went on to state that, without a limitation on total expenditures, "[p]ressure to raise funds will constantly build and with it the temptation to resort in 'emergencies' to those sources of large sums, who, history shows, are sufficiently confident of not being caught to risk flouting contribution limits. [S]uccessful candidates will also be saved from large, overhanging campaign debts which must be paid off with money raised while holding public office and at a time when they are already preparing or thinking about the next campaign. The danger to the public interest in such situations is self-evident. . . . [L]imiting the total that can be spent will ease the candidate's understandable obsession with fundraising, and so free him and his staff to communicate in more places and ways unconnected with the fundraising function."

Justice White also took issue with the Court's decision to invalidate §608(a), which limited the amount of money that a candidate or her family may spend on her campaign. "[By] limiting the importance of personal wealth, §608(a) helps to assure that only individuals with a modicum of support from others will be viable candidates. This in turn would tend to discourage any notion that the outcome of elections is primarily a function of money."

(2) Regulating Corporate Campaign Expenditures

In *Austin v. Michigan Chamber of Commerce*,[174] the Court held that the states were free to treat corporations differently from individuals for purposes of campaign finance. The Michigan Campaign Finance Act prohibited corporations from making contributions and "independent expenditures" in connection with state candidate elections. Under the law, an expenditure was regarded as "independent" if it was "not made at the direction of, or under the control of, another person and if the expenditure is not a contribution to a committee." The act exempted from this general prohibition against corporate political spending any expenditure made from a segregated fund, which includes funds separate from the corporate treasury (and, therefore, "segregated"). A corporation could solicit contributions for its political fund only from an enumerated list of persons associated with the corporation. The Court rejected a challenge brought by the Michigan State Chamber of Commerce, a nonprofit corporation that wanted to advertise on behalf of one candidate in a special election. The Chamber was established to promote economic conditions favorable to private enterprise. Since the prohibited expenditure was punishable as a felony, the Chamber sued to prevent enforcement of the act, arguing that the restriction on expenditures is unconstitutional under both the First and the Fourteenth Amendments.

In an opinion by Justice Marshall, the Court upheld the law. The Court began by referencing its prior decision in *FEC v. Massachusetts Citizens for Life, Inc.* (*MCFL*),[175] which held that a statute requiring corporations to make independent political expenditures only through "special segregated funds" burdened corporate freedom of expression. The Court reasoned that small nonprofit corporations would face "organizational and financial hurdles" in establishing and administering segregated political funds (for example, the corporation would be forced to appoint a treasurer, maintain records of all contributions, file a statement of organization, and submit updated financial statements periodically), and that these hurdles might remove incentives for them to engage in political speech. Corporations were allowed to solicit contributions to their segregated funds only from "members," which did not include persons who merely contributed to or indicated support for the organization.

In *Austin*, the Court found that Michigan's segregated fund requirement was similar to the Massachusetts requirement considered in *MCFL*, but nevertheless upheld the law finding a compelling state interest in the fact that state law granted corporations "special advantages" (for example, limited liability, perpetual life, and favorable treatment of the accumulation and distribution of assets) that help them attract capital and allow them to obtain "an unfair advantage in the political marketplace." Relying on *MCFL*, the Court noted that this political advantage can be unfair because "[t]he resources in the treasury of a business corporation [are] not an indication of popular support for the corporation's political ideas. They reflect instead the economically motivated decisions of investors and customers. The availability of these resources may make a corporation a formidable political presence, even though the power of the corporation may be no reflection of the power of its ideas." Whereas *Buckley* had focused on the danger of "financial quid pro quo" corruption, *Austin* relied on what it referred to as "a different type of corruption in the political arena: the corrosive and distorting effects of immense aggregations of wealth that are accumulated with the help of the corporate form and that have little or no correlation to the public's support for the corporation's political ideas." The Michigan law was not designed "to equalize the relative influence of speakers on elections," but to make sure that "expenditures reflect actual public support for the political ideas espoused by corporations." The Court held that this restriction was a sufficiently compelling rationale to support restrictions on independent expenditures by corporations. The Court also found that the restriction was "precisely targeted to eliminate the distortion caused by corporate spending while also allowing corporations to express their political views. . . . [P]ersons contributing to [segregated] funds understand that their money will be used solely for political purposes. . . ."

The Court rejected the Chamber's argument that the law was "substantially overinclusive" because it swept in "closely held corporations that do not possess vast reservoirs of capital." The Court held that, although "some closely held corporations, just as some publicly held ones, may not have accumulated significant amounts of wealth, they receive from the State the special benefits conferred by the corporate structure and present the potential for distorting the political process. This potential for distortion justifies §54(1)'s general applicability to all corporations. The section therefore is not substantially overbroad."

The Court also rejected the argument that the law could not be applied to nonprofit corporations like the Chamber. The Court noted that the Chamber engaged in a variety of nonpolitical purposes, including the fact that it "compiles and disseminates information relating to social, civic, and economic conditions, trains and educates its members, and promotes ethical business practices." The Court found that the Chamber's nonpolitical activities distinguished it from the ideological corporation involved in *MCFL*. The Court also rejected the idea that the Chamber should be exempt because there were no shareholders or other persons with a claim on its assets or earnings. Although the Chamber had no shareholders, its members might be reluctant to withhold their money from the Chamber's programs. In addition, the Court noted that the Chamber's political agenda was "sufficiently distinct from its educational and outreach programs that members who disagree with the former may continue to pay dues to participate in the latter." In addition, since the Chamber accepts money from for-profit corporations, it could serve as a conduit for corporate political spending.

The Court also held that Michigan's law was narrowly tailored to serve a compelling governmental interest: "[T]he State's decision to regulate only corporations is precisely tailored to serve the compelling state interest of eliminating from the political process the corrosive effect of political 'war chests' amassed with the aid of the legal advantages given to corporations." The exemption of media corporations was affirmed: "[M]edia corporations differ significantly from other corporations in that their resources are devoted to the collection of information and its dissemination to the public. We have consistently recognized the unique role that the press plays in 'informing and educating the public, offering criticism, and providing a forum for discussion and debate.'"

Justice Scalia dissented, arguing that the majority's position reflects the idea that "too much speech is an evil that the democratic majority can proscribe. I dissent because that principle is contrary to our case law and incompatible with the absolutely central truth of the First Amendment: that government cannot be trusted to assure, through censorship, the 'fairness' of political debate." Justice Kennedy, joined by Justices O'Connor and Scalia, made a similar argument. "[T]he Court adopts a rule that allows Michigan to stifle the voices of some of the most respected groups in public life on subjects central to the integrity of our democratic system. Each of these schemes is repugnant to the First Amendment and contradicts its central guarantee, the freedom to speak in the electoral process."

Despite *Austin*'s holding, in *First National Bank of Boston v. Bellotti*,[176] the Court struck down a criminal statute that prohibited expenditures by banks and business corporations for the purpose of influencing the vote on referendum proposals except for matters "materially affecting any of the property, business or assets of the corporation." A bank that wanted to spend money to publicize its views on a proposed constitutional amendment that would have permitted the legislature to impose a graduated tax on the income of individuals, sought to challenge the law. In invalidating the law, the Court concluded that it implicated speech "at the heart of the First Amendment" designed to inform and enlighten the public, and held that "the legislature is constitutionally disqualified from dictating the subjects about which persons may speak and the speakers who may address a public issue." The Court found that the "risk of corruption" so inherent in candidate elections was "not present in a popular vote on a public issue." Although corporate advertising could "influence the outcome of the vote," "the fact that advocacy may persuade the electorate is hardly a reason to suppress it." The Court placed faith in the people to judge and evaluate the relative merits of the conflicting arguments, and to consider and evaluate "the source and credibility of the advocate." The Court demanded proof of a compelling state interest and found that such interest was lacking.

(3) Independent Political Action Committee Expenditures

In post-*Buckley* decisions, the Court considered the constitutionality of independent expenditures by political action committees. In *FEC v. National Conservative*

Political Action Committee,[177] for example, the Court struck down portions of the Presidential Election Campaign Fund Act (PECFA), which gave presidential candidates of major political parties the option of receiving public financing for their general election campaigns, but made it a crime for independent "political committees" to spend more than $1,000 in support of a candidate who accepted the financing. The challenge was brought by the National Conservative Political Action Committee (NCPAC) and the Fund for a Conservative Majority (FCM), both of which were "political committees" within the meaning of the statute that were organized to attempt to influence directly or indirectly the election or defeat of candidates for federal, state, and local offices. NCPAC's board of directors made all decisions concerning which candidates to support or oppose, the strategy and methods to employ, and the amounts of money to spend. NCPAC contributors had no role in these decisions. NCPAC raised money by general and specific direct mail solicitations. FCM was in all material respects identical to NCPAC. Both NCPAC and FCM were ideological organizations with a conservative political philosophy, and both spent money on radio and television advertisements designed to encourage voters to elect Ronald Reagan as president. Their expenditures were "independent" of the official Reagan election campaign committee.

In striking down the PECFA, as applied to "political committees," the Court readily found that NCPAC and FCM were political committees, that Reagan was a qualified candidate, and that the PACs' expenditures included "qualified campaign expense" within the meaning of the act. But the Court also found that the expenditures involved "speech at the core of the First Amendment." Both organizations spent substantial monies to communicate their political ideas through media advertisements, and the act's $1,000 limitation was equivalent "to allowing a speaker in a public hall to express his views while denying him the use of an amplifying system." The Court also found that both NCPAC and FCM were entitled to First Amendment protection. Both organizations were "mechanisms by which large numbers of individuals of modest means can join together in organizations which serve to 'amplif[y] the voice of their adherents.'"

The Court rejected the notion that NCPAC and FCM were not engaged in "individual speech, but merely 'speech by proxy,' because the contributors do not control or decide upon the use of the funds by the PACs or the specific content of the PACs' advertisements and other speech." Moreover, the Court found that "contributors obviously like the message they are hearing from these organizations and want to add their voices to that message; otherwise they would not part with their money. To say that their collective action in pooling their resources to amplify their voices is not entitled to full First Amendment protection would subordinate the voices of those of modest means as opposed to those sufficiently wealthy to be able to buy expensive media ads with their own resources."

The Court emphasized that *Buckley* had held that preventing corruption or the appearance of corruption were the only legitimate and compelling government interests for restricting campaign finances. The Court found that the act's limitation on independent expenditures by political committees was unconstitutional because it was not designed to prevent corruption or the appearance of corruption. In addition, the amounts given to the PACs were "overwhelmingly small contributions, well under the $1,000 limit on contributions upheld in *Buckley*; and the contributions are by definition not coordinated with the campaign of the candidate." The Court found that "the absence of prearrangement and coordination undermines the value of the expenditure to the candidate, and thereby alleviates the danger that expenditures will be given as a quid pro quo for improper commitments from the candidate." In addition, the Court found that the law was overbroad. "It is not limited to multimillion dollar war chests; its terms apply equally to informal discussion groups that solicit neighborhood contributions to publicize their views about a particular Presidential candidate."

The Court then distinguished its decision in *FEC v. National Right to Work Committee*[178] (NRWC). The Court noted that NRWC "turned on the special treatment historically accorded corporations. In return for the special advantages that the State confers on the corporate form, individuals acting jointly through corporations forgo some of the rights they have as individuals." Although both NCPAC and FCM were incorporated, the Court found that §9012(f) applied "not just to corporations but to any 'committee, association, or organization (whether or not incorporated)' that accepts contributions or makes expenditures in connection with electoral campaigns. The terms of §9012(f)'s prohibition apply equally to an informal neighborhood group that solicits contributions and spends money on a Presidential election as to the wealthy and professionally managed PACs involved in these cases."

Justice White, joined by Justices Brennan and Marshall, dissented, arguing that the Court was concerned about protecting the right of association and the "effective political speech of those of modest means" through contributions, but argued that contributions are not speech. "[I]n the context of the public financing scheme, the apparent congressional desire that elections should be between equally well financed candidates and not turn on the amount of money spent for one or the other is all the more compelling, and the danger of funding disparities more serious."

On March 27, 2002, President Bush signed the Bipartisan Campaign Finance Reform Act of 2002 (BCRA), which contained a series of amendments to FECA, the Communications Act of 1934, and other portions of the United States Code. Notably, BCRA added rules concerning soft money contributions. (Under FECA, "hard money" was money raised in accordance with FECA's contribution limits. "Soft money" was money that was not raised in compliance with FECA's limits.) The law touched off a new round of campaign finance litigation. The most contentious issues focused on a soft money ban that applies to donations to national political party committees. The prior law allowed such committees to raise unlimited amounts of soft money, but allowed them to use that money only for limited purposes (for efforts designed to "get out the vote" and candidate recruitment). They could also use the money for candidate-specific broadcast advertising. The new law prohibits soft money. The law also increased the amount of permissible hard money contributions by an individual from $1,000 per candidate per election to $2,000.

The new law also prohibited corporations, trade associations, and labor organizations from making "electioneering communications" within 60 days of a general election and 30 days of a primary election using "treasury money." An "electioneering communication" is directed at a specific candidate and is run in that candidate's state or district. The new law does not apply to hard money expenditures by PACs established by a corporation, trade association, or union. This provision also included disclosure requirements.

BCRA was challenged in *McConnell v. Federal Election Commission*.[179] *McConnell* produced three majority opinions, as well as a variety of concurrences and dissents. In the first majority opinion, authored by Justices Stevens and O'Connor and joined by Justices Souter, Ginsburg, and Breyer, the Court upheld Section I and Section II of BCRA. The Court viewed BCRA as designed to deal with flaws in the prior campaign finance scheme. First, the prior scheme created a distinction between hard money and soft money contributions to federal campaigns. Although hard money was subject to FECA's disclosure requirements as well as to its source and amount limits, corporations, unions, and individuals could also contribute soft money in an effort to influence state and local elections, and political parties could use that money to fund various activities (for example, get-out-the-vote drives and generic party advertising), as well as the costs of "legislative advocacy media advertisements" (as long as the advertisements did not expressly advocate the candidate's election or defeat). The Court took notice of the fact that the amount of soft money had expanded dramatically since the decision in *Buckley* and that national parties were transferring ever larger amounts of soft money to state parties. Second, the Court expressed concern that *Buckley* had made what the Court regarded as an unjustified distinction between communications that "expressly advocate the election or defeat of a clearly identified candidate," which were subject to FECA's limitations and could be financed with only hard money, and "issue ads" (designed to state positions on issues and perhaps influence the legislative agenda on those issues), which could also be financed with soft money. The Court found that the distinction between the two types of ads was illusory because little practical difference existed between "an ad that urged viewers to 'vote against Jane Doe' and one that condemned Jane Doe's record on a particular issue before exhorting viewers to 'call Jane Doe and tell her what you think.'" In fact, if anything, the Court believed that issue ads were more effective than those that targeted a particular candidate. Third, the Court was concerned about what it perceived as a "meltdown of the campaign finance system." Relying on a congressional report, the Court noted that both political parties were promising special access to candidates and senior governmental officials in an effort to attract soft money donations. In addition, both political parties were using large amounts of soft money to pay for issue advertising in an effort to influence federal elections.

After discussing perceived flaws in the prior campaign system, the Court turned its attention to the specifics of BCRA. The Court began by upholding BCRA §323, which contained various restrictions including a prohibition on national party committees and their agents from soliciting, receiving, directing, or spending any soft money. The Court found that the provision was justified by the "important" governmental interests in preventing both actual corruption and the appearance of corruption. The Court emphasized evidence showing that national party committees were "peddling" access to federal candidates and officeholders in exchange for large soft money donations and were providing potential donors with "menus of opportunities for access." The Court rejected the argument that BCRA unduly infringed the right of political parties to associate, noting that the act simply subjected a greater percentage of contributions to parties and candidates to FECA's source and amount limitations, and did not prohibit an individual contributor from becoming a member of a political association or personally working for the association's candidates. In addition, the Court noted that BCRA did not prohibit a party's national officials from strategizing with local officials about how to raise and spend soft money so long as the national party officials did not personally involve themselves in spending, receiving, directing, or soliciting soft money. However, the law did prohibit state committees' ability to use large soft money contributions to influence federal elections in four distinct categories: (1) voter registration activity during the 120 days preceding a regularly scheduled federal election; (2) voter identification, get-out-the-vote, and generic campaign activity that is "conducted in connection with an election in which a candidate for Federal office appears on the ballot"; (3) any "public communication" that "refers to a clearly identified candidate for Federal office" and promotes, supports, attacks, or opposes a candidate for that office; and (4) the services provided by a state committee employee who dedicates more than 25 percent of his or her time to "activities in connection with a Federal election."

The Court rejected the argument that BCRA was impermissibly overbroad because it subjected *all* funds raised and spent by national parties to FECA's hard money source and amount limits including funds spent on purely state and local elections in which no federal office was at stake. The Court noted the close relationship between federal officeholders and the national parties, as well as the means by which parties have traded on that relationship, that have made all large soft money contributions to national parties suspect. The Court concluded that the government's interest in preventing corruption and the appearance of corruption justify subjecting all donations to national parties to the source, amount, and disclosure limitations of FECA.

The Court also rejected the argument that BCRA was overbroad because it impermissibly infringed the speech and associational rights of minor parties that, because of their lesser status and lesser chances for victory, did not pose a comparable corruption problem. The Court noted that the interest in preventing actual or apparent corruption applies to both minor parties and major parties alike. In any event, if a minor party could demonstrate that it is unduly affected by BCRA, it could bring an "as applied" challenge.

The Court also upheld BCRA §323(f), which prohibited candidates for state or local office, or state or local officeholders, from spending soft money to fund "public communications" — a communication that "refers to a clearly identified candidate for Federal office and that promotes or supports a candidate for that office, or attacks or opposes a candidate for that office." The Court concluded that this section only limited the source and amount of contributions that could be used for these activities and was permissible because it focused on "those soft-money donations with the greatest potential to corrupt or give rise to the appearance of corruption of federal candidates and officeholders."

Relying on *Buckley*, the Court also upheld the first section of Title II, §201, which required political committees to file detailed periodic financial reports with the FEC for "electioneering communications" referring to any "broadcast, cable, or satellite communication." The Court found that the "important state interests that prompted the *Buckley* Court to uphold FECA's disclosure requirements — providing the electorate with information, deterring actual corruption and avoiding any appearance thereof, and gathering the data necessary to enforce more substantive electioneering restrictions — apply in full to BCRA."

The Court also upheld §202 of BCRA, which amended FECA §315(a)(7)(c) to provide that disbursements for "electioneering communication[s]" that are coordinated with a candidate or party will be treated as contributions to, and expenditures by, that candidate or party. The Court held that there "is no reason why Congress may not treat coordinated disbursements for electioneering communications in the same way it treats all other coordinated expenditures."

Finally, the Court upheld a provision that prohibited corporations and unions from using funds in their treasuries to finance advertisements expressly advocating the election or defeat of candidates in federal elections. Under BCRA, corporations were required to form and administer separate segregated funds that the Court concluded "provided corporations and unions with a constitutionally sufficient opportunity to engage in express advocacy." Indeed, the Court found the state interest "compelling" because "the special characteristics of the corporate structure require particularly careful regulation." The Court also rejected the argument that the segregated fund provision unconstitutionally discriminates in favor of media companies by excluding from the definition of electioneering communications any "communication appearing in a news story, commentary, or editorial distributed through the facilities of any broadcasting station, unless such facilities are owned or controlled by any political party, political committee, or candidate." The Court concluded that the exception "is wholly consistent with First Amendment principles" and that a "valid distinction [exists] between corporations that are part of the media industry and other corporations that are not involved in the regular business of imparting news to the public."

The Court also rejected a challenge to §204 of BCRA, which applied the prohibition on the use of general treasury funds to pay for electioneering communications to not-for-profit corporations. The Court noted that its recent decision in *Federal Election Commission v. Beaumont*[180] confirmed that the requirement was valid except as it applied to a sub-category of corporations described as "*MCFL* organizations," as defined [by] *MCFL*.[181] The characteristics of these corporations include several criteria.[182] The Court assumed that the legislators who drafted this section were aware of existing law and intended for the section to be limited by it. As a result, the Court upheld the section.

In a second majority opinion, this one by Chief Justice Rehnquist, joined by Justices O'Connor, Scalia, Kennedy, and Souter (and joined as to BCRA §305 by Justices Stevens, Ginsburg, and Breyer, and as to particular sections by Justice Thomas), the Court upheld BCRA §311, which required that "electioneering communications" clearly identify the candidate or committee or, if not so authorized, identify the payor and announce the lack of authorization. The Court found the law bore "a sufficient relationship to the important governmental interest of 'shed[ding] the light of publicity' on campaign financing."

However, the Rehnquist majority opinion struck down BCRA §318, which added a provision prohibiting individuals "17 years old or younger" from making contributions to candidates and contributions or donations to political parties. The Court held that minors are protected by the First Amendment and that the asserted governmental interest (protecting against corruption, by preventing parents from circumventing contribution limitations by channeling money through their children) was too attenuated to "withstand heightened scrutiny." The Court found that Congress could have dealt with this potential problem through "a more tailored approach."

In a third majority opinion, Justice Breyer (joined by Justices Stevens, O'Connor, Souter, and Ginsburg) dealt with BCRA Title V. BCRA §504's "candidate request" provisions that required broadcast licensees to "keep" a publicly available file "of all requests for broadcast time made by or on behalf of a candidate for public office," along with a notation showing whether the request was granted, and (if granted) a history that includes "classes of time," "rates charged," and when the "spots actually aired." The Court concluded that all of these record-keeping requirements helped the FCC determine whether broadcasters were carrying out their statutory obligations. The Court doubted that the provision infringed the requestor's rights by requiring "premature disclosure of campaign strategy" because the information requested (for example, names, addresses, and the fact of a request) did not require disclosure of substantive campaign content.

McConnell produced an array of dissents. Justice Scalia noted that the Court had struck down restrictions on "such inconsequential forms of expression as virtual child pornography [and] sexually explicit cable programming," but upheld BCRA even though it goes to "the heart of what the First Amendment is meant to protect: the right to criticize the government." He went on to note that "effective public communication requires the speaker to [use] the services of others [and requires] money. [W]here the government singles out money used to fund speech as its legislative object, it is acting against speech [no] less than if it had targeted the paper on which a book was printed." He particularly objected to BCRA provisions restricting corporate speech because he believed that the "use of corporate wealth (like individual wealth) to speak to the electorate is unlikely to 'distort' elections — *especially* if disclosure requirements *tell* the people where the speech is coming from." He also objected to bans on attack ads. Finally, he noted that, although somewhere between $2.4 and $2.5 billion was spent on election advertising, "Americans spent [$7.8 billion on movie tickets and $18.8 billion on cosmetics and perfume.] If our democracy is drowning from this much spending, it cannot swim."

Justice Thomas concurred in part and dissented in part, arguing that the "fundamental principle that 'the best test of truth is the power of the thought to get itself accepted in the competition of the market' is cast aside in the purported service of preventing 'corruption,' or the mere 'appearance of corruption.'" Justice Kennedy also concurred in part and dissented in part, noting that the Court's prior decision in *Buckley* "held that only one interest justified the significant burden on the right of association involved there: eliminating, or preventing, actual corruption or the appearance of corruption stemming from contributions to candidates." He suggested that this standard had been watered down to include "any action that might gain the goodwill of a Member of Congress, and the Court assumes that 'access' without more is tantamount to corruption." He also objected to the segregated fund provision for corporations, noting that what "the law allows — permitting the corporation 'to serve as the founder and treasurer of a different association of individuals that can endorse or oppose political candidates — is not speech by the corporation.'" "[To] say [that corporations and unions] cannot alert the public to pending political issues that may threaten the country's economic interests is unprecedented."

Chief Justice Rehnquist, joined by Justices Scalia and Kennedy, dissented with respect to BCRA Titles I and V. He argued that a close association between individuals, "especially in the realm of political speech, is not a surrogate for corruption." He also noted that "BCRA extensively regulates state parties, primarily state elections, and state candidates [even though there] is scant evidence [that] federal candidates or officeholders are corrupted or would appear corrupted by donations for these activities." He also noted that "[n]ewspaper editorials and political talk shows *benefit* federal candidates and officeholders every bit as much as a generic voter registration drive conducted by a state party" and that "federal candidates and officeholders are surely 'grateful' for positive media coverage," so that Congress may now have the right to regulate the media. He concluded that "any circumvention rationale ultimately must rest on the circumvention itself leading to the corruption of federal candidates and officeholders."

Buckley was followed by the holding in *Randall v. Sorrell*,[183] which involved a Vermont campaign finance statute. In an opinion by Justice Breyer, the Court struck down the law that controlled the total amount a candidate for state office could spend during a two-year general election cycle that included the primary election and the general election. The expenditure limit varied by office according to the following formula: governor, $300,000; lieutenant governor, $100,000; other statewide offices, $45,000; state senator, $4,000 (plus an additional $2,500 for each additional seat in the district); state representative (two-member district), $3,000; and state representative (single member district), $2,000. These limits were adjusted for inflation in odd-numbered years based on the Consumer Price Index. However, incumbents seeking reelection to statewide office could spend no more than 85 percent of the limits, and incumbents seeking reelection to the state Senate or House could spend no more than 90 percent of the above amounts. With some exceptions, expenditures over $50 made on a candidate's behalf by others counted against the candidate's expenditure limit if those expenditures were "intentionally facilitated by, solicited by or approved by" the candidate's campaign. These provisions included within a campaign's expenditure limit any spending by political parties or committees that were coordinated with the campaign and benefited the candidate. And any party expenditure that "primarily benefits six or fewer candidates who are associated with the political party" is "presumed" to be coordinated with the campaign and therefore to count against the campaign's expenditure limit.

The act also imposed strict contribution limits that were also based on a two-year election cycle, and differed by the office: governor, lieutenant governor, and other statewide offices, $400; state senator, $300; and state representative, $200. Contribution limits were not indexed for inflation. "Political committees," defined broadly to include "any subsidiary, branch or local unit" of a party, as well as any "national or regional affiliates" of a party (taken separately or together), were subject to the same limits. Thus, for any national party (for example, Democrats or Republicans), the statute treated the local, state, and national affiliates of the party as a single entity and limited their total contribution to a single candidate's campaign for governor (during the primary and the general election together) to $400. The act also imposed a limit of $2,000 on the amount any individual could give to a political party during a two-year general election cycle. The act defined "contribution" broadly. Any expenditure made on a candidate's behalf counted as a contribution to the candidate if it was "intentionally facilitated by, solicited by or approved by" the candidate. And a party expenditure that "primarily benefits six or fewer candidates who are associated" with the party is "presumed" to count against the party's contribution limits. A candidate's own contributions to the campaign and those of the candidate's family fall outside the contribution limits. Volunteer services did not count as contributions; also excluded was the cost of a meet-the-candidate function, provided that the total cost for the function amounted to $100 or less.

Although the act also imposed disclosure and reporting requirements and created a voluntary public financing system for gubernatorial elections, those requirements and that system were not challenged. In addition, the act limited the amount of contributions a candidate, political committee, or political party could receive from out-of-state sources. However, the latter provision was struck down by the lower court, and that holding was not challenged.

Relying heavily on *Buckley v. Valeo*,[184] the Court struck down both the contribution limits and the expenditure limits. In doing so, the Court reaffirmed *Buckley*'s distinction between the two types of limits. In addition, the Court rejected the idea that expenditure limits should be sustained because they help protect candidates from spending too much time raising money rather than devoting that time to campaigning among ordinary voters. The Court concluded that the *Buckley* Court was aware of the connection between expenditure limits and a reduction in fundraising time, but found this connection insufficient to sustain expenditure limitations. In regard to the contribution limits, the Court reaffirmed *Buckley*'s holding that contribution limits, like expenditure limits, "implicate fundamental First Amendment interests," namely, the freedoms of political expression and political association. The Court concluded that contribution limitations are permissible as long as the government demonstrates that the limits are "closely drawn" to match a "sufficiently important interest." It found that the interest advanced in the case, preventing corruption and its appearance, was sufficiently important to justify the statute's contribution limits. Nevertheless, the Court struck down Vermont's limits, expressing concern that they were so low as to prevent candidates from "amassing the resources necessary for effective [campaign] advocacy" and could place challengers (who may need to raise and spend more money) at a significant disadvantage. Although the Court indicated that it would ordinarily defer to legislative judgments on such issues, the Court found "danger signs" in the Vermont law because its contribution limits were well below the limits sustained in *Buckley*, were the lowest contribution limits in the nation, and were lower than any previously upheld. As a result, the Court struck Vermont's limits for a variety of reasons: (1) they significantly restricted the funding available for challengers to run competitive campaigns; (2) they threatened to harm political parties' right to associate; (3) they severely limited political parties' ability to assist candidates' campaigns by coordinating spending on advertising, candidate events, voter lists, mass mailings, and yard signs; (4) they treated volunteers' expenses as "contributions," which impaired the ability of volunteers to "contribute" to campaigns because the contribution limits are so low; and (5) were not adjusted for inflation. The Court did not believe that Vermont had advanced a sufficient justification to justify such low limits given the serious associational and expressive problems.

Justice Kennedy concurred in the judgment but reiterated his rejection of major portions of the *McConnell* decision. He went on to suggest that the Court should reexamine its campaign finance precedent. Justice Thomas, joined by Justice Scalia, also concurred, arguing that "*Buckley* provides insufficient protection to political speech" and should be overruled. He would subject both contribution and expenditure restrictions to strict scrutiny. Justice Stevens, dissenting, was convinced that *Buckley* should be overruled, but he argued that the Court was wrong to "equate money and speech." In his view, the burden imposed by spending limitations is both "minimal and indirect." Moreover, since the limitations were viewpoint neutral and revealed no hostility toward speech or its effects, he would have treated them as "akin to time, place, and manner restrictions than to restrictions on the content of speech," and upheld them "so long as the purposes they serve are legitimate and sufficiently substantial." He went on to state that: "I am firmly persuaded that the Framers would have been appalled by the impact of modern fundraising practices on the ability of elected officials to perform their public responsibilities [and] would have viewed federal statutes limiting the amount of money that congressional candidates might spend in future elections as well within Congress' authority." Justice Souter, joined by Justices Ginsburg and Souter, also dissented. In his view, the "findings made by the Vermont Legislature on the pernicious effect of the nonstop pursuit of money [are] surely significant enough to justify the [remand to] decide whether Vermont's spending limits are the least restrictive means of accomplishing what the court unexceptionably found to be worthy objectives."

Portions of the *McConnell* decision were effectively overruled only three years later in *Federal Election Commission v. Wisconsin Right to Life, Inc.*[185] In that case, the

Court rejected *McConnell*'s notion of "sham" issue ads and struck down portions of BCRA as applied. Chief Justice Roberts announced the Court's judgment and authored an opinion joined by Justice Alito. While upholding BCRA to the extent that it prohibited express advocacy or its functional equivalent, the Chief Justice rejected *McConnell*'s notion of "sham" issue ads and the idea that such ads are the "'functional equivalent' of speech expressly advocating the election or defeat of a candidate for federal office." The Court noted that candidates, "especially incumbents, are intimately tied to public issues involving legislative proposals and governmental actions." As applied to Wisconsin Right to Life's advertisement (questioning the Senate filibusters designed to prevent confirmation votes on judicial nominees), the Chief Justice held that it was protected under the First Amendment. "[A] court should find that an ad is the functional equivalent of express advocacy only if the ad is susceptible of no reasonable interpretation other than as an appeal to vote for or against a specific candidate." In addition, he rejected the idea that any ad that includes "an appeal to citizens to contact their elected representative" is the "functional equivalent" of an ad saying defeat or elect that candidate. The Court found that, as applied to WRTL's ad, BCRA did not pass strict scrutiny because the issue advertisements could not be regarded as the functional equivalent of a campaign contribution. "[W]hen it comes to defining what speech qualifies as the functional equivalent of express advocacy subject to such a ban—the issue we do have to decide—we give the benefit of the doubt to speech, not censorship." Justice Scalia, joined by Justices Kennedy and Thomas, concurred, arguing that *McConnell* should be overruled on this issue.

J. The Right to Associate

Although the First Amendment does not explicitly mention the right to associate, it does contain a number of related rights, including the right to peacefully assemble. In addition, since the Constitution protects speech, it implicitly protects the right of association since people can speak more effectively when they join together to speak with a common voice.

(1) General Principles

The seminal decision on the right to associate is *NAACP v. Alabama*.[186] An Alabama statute required foreign corporations to file their corporate charters with the Alabama secretary of state and designate a place of business and an agent to receive service of process. In 1956, Alabama sought to enjoin the National Association for the Advancement of Colored People (NAACP) from conducting business because it failed to comply with the law. The state also sought to require the NAACP to produce records and papers showing the names and addresses of its Alabama members and agents. When the NAACP refused to produce the lists, the trial court held it in civil contempt and imposed a fine of $10,000. The U.S. Supreme Court reversed, recognizing the right to associate as a constitutional right, and holding that the right could be used to shield the NAACP's membership lists from disclosure. The Court based the right on the premise that "[e]ffective advocacy of both public and private points of view, particularly controversial ones, is undeniably enhanced by group association." Noting the "close nexus between the freedoms of speech and assembly," the Court held that the right to associate applied to the states by virtue of the Liberty Clause of the Fourteenth Amendment's Due Process Clause.

After recognizing the right, the Court found that the Alabama order imposed a "substantial restraint" on the NAACP's members' right of association. In the past, when the identity of NAACP members had been revealed, they had been subjected to various reprisals. As a result, the Court was concerned that disclosure of the membership lists might adversely affect the NAACP's ability to pursue their collective advocacy and dissuade prospective members from joining.

Even though the *NAACP* Court recognized that the interest in association was not absolute, it held that the state interest must be compelling to override that right. The Court found that Alabama's asserted interest (to determine whether petitioner was conducting intrastate business in violation of the Alabama foreign corporation registration statute) was not compelling. The NAACP had already admitted that it was conducting activities in the state, had offered to comply with the state's qualification statute, and had complied with the production order (except that part of the order that related to the membership lists) by furnishing the attorney general with various types of information (business records, the NAACP's charter and statement of purposes, the names of all of its directors and officers, and the total number of its Alabama members and the amount of their dues). Accordingly, the Court found that the state's interest in obtaining names of ordinary members was insufficient, and the Court vacated the civil contempt judgment including the $100,000 fine.

Despite the groundbreaking nature of the *NAACP* holding, the Court rejected an associational claim the following year in *Barenblatt v. United States*.[187] In that case, petitioner was convicted of refusing to answer certain questions put to him by a subcommittee of the House Committee on Un-American Activities during the course of an inquiry into alleged Communist infiltration into the field of education. The conviction was based on Barenblatt's refusal to answer five questions concerning past and present membership in the Communist Party, based on his privilege against self-incrimination. In rejecting Barenblatt's associational claims, the Court sought to balance the competing interests, but concluded that the balance favored the government. Congress was seeking information pursuant to its power to legislate, and the Court emphasized the "close nexus" between the Communist Party and violent overthrow of government. The Court was unwilling to treat the Communist Party as an "ordinary political party from the standpoint of national security." As a result, the Court was deferential to Congress. Justice Black dissented, expressing concern about the government's power to punish people for their political associations. He concluded that the Communist's Party's associational claims should be upheld:

> [O]nce we allow any group which has some political aims or ideas to be driven from the ballot and from the battle for men's minds because some of its members are bad and some of its tenets are illegal, no group is safe. . . . History should teach us [that] in times of high emotional excitement minority parties and groups which advocate extremely unpopular social or governmental innovations will always be typed as criminal gangs and attempts will always be made to drive them out.

With the passage of time, Justice Black's view has become the preferred interpretation of the First Amendment.

F   A   Q

Q: Based on the *NAACP* case, shouldn't *Barenblatt* have recognized the right of Communist Party members to conceal their identities?

A: *Barenblatt* treated the Communist Party differently because that group advocated the violent overthrow of the government. The Court therefore viewed the governmental interest as different and more important. Bear in mind that *Barenblatt* was decided at a time when the Court was more willing to permit suppression of the Communist Party. The case might be decided differently today.

The Court has applied the right to associate in a number of other cases. For example, *NAACP v. Claiborne Hardware Co.*[188] involved an NAACP boycott of white merchants in Mississippi that was accompanied by speeches and nonviolent picketing. When the merchants sued to recover losses caused by the boycott, as well as to enjoin future boycotts, a state court imposed joint and several liability on the defendants and found damages of $944,699. The Court reversed, holding that the boycotters were engaged in protected speech. Although the Court was unwilling to extend protections to violent activity, the Court did hold that the state could not impose liability on nonviolent protestors merely because of their association with violent protestors absent proof that "the group itself possessed unlawful goals and that the individual held a specific intent to further those illegal aims." The Court also rejected damage awards against Charles Evers, the NAACP's representative, despite the fact that Evers made several inflammatory speeches. The Court concluded that Evers "did not transcend the bounds of protected speech set forth in *Brandenburg*. . . . An advocate must be free to stimulate his audience with spontaneous and emotional appeals for unity and action in a common cause."

(2) Conflicts with Laws Prohibiting Discrimination

Many modern freedom of association cases focus not on whether the government can compel an organization to disclose the names of its members, as in *NAACP v. Alabama* and *Barenblatt*, but on whether government can force organizations to accept members that they do not want. The most important decision is *Roberts v. United States Jaycees*.[189] *Roberts* involved the United States Jaycees, which was established to provide young men "with opportunity for personal development and achievement and an avenue for intelligent participation by young men in the affairs of their community, state and nation, and to develop true friendship and understanding among young men of all nations." While the Jaycees allowed women to be associate members, regular membership was limited to men between the ages of 18 and 35. Associate members could not vote, hold office, or participate in certain leadership training and awards programs. Because of Minnesota law that prohibited gender-based discrimination, the Minneapolis and St. Paul chapters of the Jaycees began admitting women as regular members. When the president of the national organization indicated an intention to revoke the charters of both organizations, they filed discrimination charges with the Minnesota Department of Human Rights alleging a violation of the Minnesota Human Rights Act. A state hearing examiner concluded that the Jaycees had violated the act and ordered them to cease and desist from discriminating against any member or applicant on the basis of sex.

In upholding the Minnesota law, the Court concluded that there were two different prongs of the right to associate: the right to engage in "intimate human relationships" and the right to associate for expressive purposes. The Court quickly concluded that the Jaycees, a large business organization, was not engaged in association of an intimate nature. That prong protects "highly personal relationships" such as the "creation and sustenance of a family."

The second type of associational relationships is entered into to further speech and expression interests. The Court recognized that the right to speak, to worship, and to petition the government for the redress of grievances "could not be vigorously protected from interference by the State unless a correlative freedom to engage in group effort toward those ends were not also guaranteed." As a result, the Court reaffirmed the idea that "implicit in the right to engage in activities protected by the First Amendment a corresponding right to associate with others in pursuit of a wide variety of political, social, economic, educational, religious, and cultural ends."

In analyzing the Minnesota law, the Court expressed doubts about whether the state may control the membership of an organization, intruding into the organization's internal affairs and affecting the organization's ability to push its own views. "There can be no clearer example of an intrusion into the internal structure or affairs of an association than a regulation that forces the group to accept members it does not desire. Such a regulation may impair the ability of the original members to express only those views that brought them together. Freedom of association therefore plainly presupposes a freedom not to associate." Moreover, the Court held that infringements of this right should be subject to strict scrutiny in the sense that they must be supported by "compelling state interests, unrelated to the suppression of ideas, that cannot be achieved through means significantly less restrictive of associational freedoms." However, in applying this standard, the Court held that Minnesota's law was supported by a compelling interest in "eradicating discrimination against its female citizens" that justified the infringement of associational freedoms, and that this interest was unrelated to the suppression of expression. In addition, the Court found that the statute reflected "the State's strong historical commitment to eliminating discrimination and assuring its citizens equal access to publicly available goods and services." The Court viewed that goal as "compelling" and of the "highest order" and "unrelated to the suppression of expression."

After holding that the Minnesota law was justified by a compelling governmental interest, the Court concluded that it should apply to the Jaycees because they were involved in the equivalent of commercial or quasi-commercial conduct. Moreover, the Court concluded that Minnesota had advanced its interests through the least restrictive means. Although the Court agreed that the Jaycees engaged in expression, it found no basis for concluding that the admission of women as full voting members would "impede the organization's ability to engage in these protected activities or to disseminate its preferred views." The Jaycees were allowed to continue to adhere to their creed of promoting the interests of young men, and the organization was allowed to exclude any person (male or female) whose ideologies or philosophies were inconsistent with that objective. Moreover, the Court noted that the Jaycees already allowed women to share the group's views and philosophy and to participate in much of its training and community activities. The Court rejected the argument that women might hold different views regarding the necessity of promoting the young men and might seek to change that message. The Court concluded that these concerns were unsubstantiated. Moreover, even if the Act did cause "some incidental abridgment of the Jaycees' protected speech," the Court found that the effect was "no greater than . . . necessary to accomplish the State's legitimate purposes" of prohibiting invidious discrimination based on gender.

F   A   Q

Q: Would the Court have upheld the Minnesota act as applied to a political advocacy group?

A: Probably not. The Jaycees were treated differently because they were large, unselective, commercial in nature, and did not have much of a political message.

Justice O'Connor concurred, arguing that an association that is engaged exclusively in protected expression enjoys First Amendment protection of both the content of its message and the choice of its members. But she argued that only when an association is "predominantly engaged in protected expression . . . state regulation of its membership will necessarily affect, change, dilute, or silence one collective voice that would otherwise be heard." She distinguished the Jaycees, noting that once an association enters the marketplace of commerce in any substantial degree, it has a lesser right to control its membership. Although she found that the Jaycees were involved in expressive activities, she concluded that the organization "is, first and foremost, an organization that, at both the national and local levels, promotes and practices the art of solicitation and management," thereby providing its members an advantage in business. As a result, she believed that the State of Minnesota "has a legitimate interest in ensuring nondiscriminatory access to the commercial opportunity presented by membership in the Jaycees," and concluded that the First Amendment did not insulate the Jaycees against Minnesota's antidiscrimination law.

Roberts was followed and strengthened by the holding in *New York State Club Association, Inc. v. City of New York*.[190] That case involved a New York City law that prohibited discrimination by any "place of public accommodation, resort or amusement" in an effort to ensure that all people have the opportunity to "participate in the business and professional life of the city." The law expressed concern regarding "the discriminatory practices of certain membership organizations where business deals are often made and personal contacts valuable for business purposes, employment and professional advancement are formed." The Court upheld the law because it did not affect "in any significant way" the ability of individuals to associate to advocate their views. The Court noted that the law did not require the clubs to abandon expressive activities and did not preclude them from excluding those views that the clubs wish to promote, but instead simply prohibited them from "using race, sex, and the other specified characteristics as shorthand measures . . . for determining membership."

Roberts and *New York State Club Association* were followed and qualified by *Boy Scouts of America v. Dale.*[191] *Dale* involved the Boy Scouts, an organization dedicated to instilling values in young people, that regarded homosexual conduct as inconsistent with its message. The organization was sued under New Jersey's public accommodations law by an adult whose membership was revoked because of his sexual orientation. The Court concluded that the New Jersey law could not be applied to the Boy Scouts without significantly burdening their right of expressive association, which includes the right to express their views regarding homosexual conduct. The decision produced four dissents.

Sidebar

CLUBS ORGANIZED FOR EXPRESSIVE PURPOSES

New York State Club Association emphasized that if a club was organized to promote "specific expressive purposes" and could show that the law would affect its ability to express its desired positions, it might be constitutionally entitled to an exemption. However, the Court found that most large clubs subject to the law were "not of this kind."

Justice Stevens, dissenting, argued that "[Dale's] participation sends no cognizable message to the Scouts or to the world. . . . Dale did not carry a banner or a sign; [and] he expressed no intent to send any message."

(3) Regulating the Electoral Process

In some instances, government has tried to impose restrictions on the right to associate in the context of the electoral process. As a general rule, one might expect such restrictions to be constitutionally suspect. Such restrictions seem to directly implicate *Roberts*'s category of the right of association for expressive purposes.

Nevertheless, in *Timmons v. Twin Cities Area New Party,*[192] the Court upheld a Minnesota law that prohibited "fusion" candidates — candidates who appear on election ballots as the nominee of more than one party. A political party sued, claiming that it had an associational right to list the candidate of its choice regardless of whether that candidate was listed as the nominee of another party. The Court disagreed, noting that the law did not prevent any party from endorsing, supporting, or voting for the candidate of its choice and did not affect or control any party's internal structure, governance, or policymaking. Although the law might prevent a party from listing a particular candidate as its nominee, the Court found that this burden, while "not trivial," was not "severe" and was outweighed by the state's interest "in protecting the integrity, fairness, and efficiency of their ballots and election processes as means for electing public officials." The Court found that the states have a "strong interest in the stability of their political systems," which "permits them to enact reasonable election regulations that may, in practice, favor the traditional two-party system, and that temper the destabilizing effects of party-splintering and excessive factionalism." Justice Stevens dissented, arguing that a party's "choice of a candidate is the most effective way in which that party can communicate to the voters what the party represents and, thereby, attract voter interest and support." He argued that the state failed to show how the ban actually served the state's asserted interests.

Likewise, in *Clingman v. Beaver,*[193] the Court upheld a semi-closed primary system under which a political party could invite only its registered members and independents to vote in its primary. The Court held that the semi-closed system did not violate the right to political association because it imposed only a minor burden on associational rights of the state's citizenry and advanced important regulatory interests in preserving political parties as viable and identifiable interests groups (for example, it aided parties' electioneering and party-building efforts and prevented party raiding).

(4) The Right "Not to Speak"

One component of the right of association is the right not to be forced to be associated with ideas or principles with which one disagrees. Just as the First Amendment has been construed as containing a right to associate, it also includes a right to be left alone, or not to speak.

In a number of cases, the Court has held that the state may not compel individuals to endorse ideas with which they disagree. For example, in *West Virginia State Board of Education v. Barnette*,[194] the Court struck down a state law requiring students to salute the flag. The Court recognized that a flag salute is a "form of utterance" and that the First Amendment protects an individual from being forced to "utter what is not in his mind."

Likewise, in *Wooley v. Maynard*,[195] the Court struck down a state law requiring motor vehicle owners to display license plates with the motto "Live Free or Die." When the law was challenged by a Jehovah's Witness who found the motto morally and religiously objectionable, the state argued that it had a legitimate law enforcement interest in mandating uniform plates, which assisted police in identifying a particular state's plates and helped promote an appreciation of the state's history and (in this case) its pride in individualism. The Court applied strict scrutiny and concluded that neither of the stated interests was compelling. Not only could the license plates be readily identified without the motto, the interest in fostering state pride and appreciation of history could be fostered by less drastic means. Moreover, the asserted interest was outweighed by the individual interest because the right to freedom of thought includes not only the right to speak freely but "to refrain from speaking at all." As a result, a state simply cannot compel an individual, "as part of his daily life indeed constantly while his automobile is in public view to be an instrument for fostering public adherence to an ideological point of view he finds unacceptable."

Sidebar

UTILITIES AND FORCED MAILINGS OF CONSUMER PAMPHLETS

In *Pacific Gas & Electric Co. v. Public Utilities Commission*, 475 U.S. 1 (1986), the Court struck down a law requiring utility companies to include the publications of a consumers' group in its billing materials. The Court found that the measure violated the First Amendment because it forced utilities to associate with ideas with which they disagreed.

F A Q

Q: Is it clear that the *Wooley* plaintiffs were forced to "speak" against their will?

A: The justices did not agree on this point. The majority found that the plaintiffs were required to speak. However, Justice Rehnquist, joined by Justice Blackmun, dissented, noting that the state did not force "appellees to 'say' anything" and instead "simply required that all noncommercial automobiles bear license tags with the state motto." If an individual disagrees with that motto, she is free to express her disagreement with its statement through, say, a bumper sticker on the back of her vehicle.

The Court qualified *Barnette* and *Wooley* in *Rumsfeld v. Forum for Academic & Institutional Rights, Inc.*[196] *Rumsfeld* involved a federal statute (the Solomon Amendment) that required law schools to admit military recruiters on the same basis as other employers. Under President Clinton's "Don't Ask, Don't Tell" policy, the military discriminates on the basis of sexual orientation. However, some law schools have a policy (prompted by a national law school association) of excluding employers who discriminate on the basis of sexual orientation. The Solomon Amendment required these law schools to admit military recruiters on the same basis as other employers on pain of losing federal funding.

Rumsfeld rejected the law schools' argument that the statute forced them to engage in speech in violation of the compelled speech doctrine articulated in *Barnette* and *Wooley*. The Court held that the statute did not require law schools to express any ideas and instead forced them simply to post notices that military recruiters will be on campus at a particular place and time. The Court concluded that its compelled speech doctrine applied only when the speaker's message is "affected by the speech it was forced to accommodate," and that the Solomon Amendment does not affect the law schools' speech since the schools are not speaking when they host interviews and recruiting receptions. The Court noted that the "expressive component" of a law school's actions are not determined "by the conduct itself but by the speech that accompanies it," and the Court doubted that the compelled conduct in this case (allowing military recruiters to have equal access) was "so inherently expressive that it warrants protection."

The Court also rejected the argument that if law schools are required to give military recruiters equal access, the public might perceive that the law schools do not object to the military's policies. "We have held that high school students can appreciate the difference between speech a school sponsors and speech the school permits because legally required to do so, pursuant to an equal access policy. Surely students have not lost that ability by the time they get to law school."

F A Q

Q: Under the Solomon Amendment, are law schools and law students free to protest the presence of military recruiters on their campuses provided the schools provide access to the military?

A: Yes. The Solomon Amendment does not preclude law schools and law students from protesting the presence of the military, or expressing disagreement with its policies, so long as the schools provide access. Indeed, the amendment might run into constitutional difficulties if it did prohibit protests or disagreement.

The Court reached a different result in its prior decision in *Hurley v. Irish-American Gay, Lesbian and Bisexual Group of Boston.*[197] In that case, the Court held that parade organizers could not be forced to include a message that they did not want to convey in a joint St. Patrick's Day/Evacuation Day (which marked the date when royal troops and loyalists "evacuated" from the city) parade held on March 17 each year. The parade was sponsored by the South Boston Allied War Veterans Council, an unincorporated association of individuals elected from various South Boston veterans groups, which annually applied and received a permit for the parade. The city allowed the Council to use the city's official seal and provided printing services as well as direct funding. GLIB, a group of gay, lesbian, and bisexual descendants of the Irish immigrants, sought to march in the parade as a way of expressing "pride in their Irish heritage as openly gay, lesbian, and bisexual individuals, to demonstrate that there are such men and women among those so descended, and to express their solidarity with like individuals who sought to march in New York's St. Patrick's Day Parade." When the Council denied the request, GLIB sued claiming, inter alia, violations of the state and federal constitutions and of the state public accommodations law, which prohibited discrimination or restriction on account of sexual orientation in places of public accommodation, resort, or amusement.

In rejecting GLIB's challenge, the Court observed that parades are often organized for expressive purposes. In the case of the Boston parade, the Court noted that there were multiple messages (for example, "England get out of Ireland," "Say no to drugs"), and the Court found that the organizers did not forfeit the right to control their "message," even though they allowed "multifarious voices" to participate. More to the point, the organizers could exclude voices with which they do not wish to associate. Noting that GLIB's participation would be very expressive, the Court rejected GLIB's challenge, noting that the public accommodations law violated the "fundamental rule of protection under the First Amendment, that a speaker has the autonomy to choose the content of his own message." In this case, the parade organizers clearly decided to exclude GLIB's message as they had the right to do.

In recent years, there has been considerable litigation regarding whether government can compel individuals or groups to provide financial support for messages with which they disagree. The seminal decision is *Abood v. Detroit Board of Education*,[198] which involved nonunion public school teachers who challenged a collective bargaining agreement that required them to pay a "service fee" as a condition of their employment that was equivalent to union dues. The teachers complained that the union was using a portion of their dues to engage in political speech to which they objected, and they objected on freedom of association grounds to payment of those dues attributable to the speech. The Court held that any objecting teachers may prevent the union from using a portion of their required service fee to contribute to political candidates to which they object, and from expressing objectionable political views unrelated to the union's duties as exclusive bargaining representative.

Abood was followed and reinforced by the holding in *Keller v. State Bar of California*,[199] in which lawyers admitted to practice in California were required to join the state bar association and to fund activities "germane" to the association's mission of "regulating the legal profession and improving the quality of legal services." The Court held that while the state could require the lawyers to join the association as a condition of practicing law, it could not require them to fund the bar association's political expression.

However, the Court limited the scope of *Abood* and *Keller* in *Board of Regents of the University of Wisconsin System v. Southworth*,[200] in a case upholding the University of Wisconsin's student activity fee that went to a fund used to support student organizations (RSOs). Students could apply for funds, which were provided on a viewpoint neutral basis, or they could seek funding through a student referendum that could also be used to deny funding to RSOs. Relying on *Abood* and *Keller*, students challenged the activity fee, claiming that it required them to contribute to the speech activities of organizations with which they disagreed. In upholding the fee, with a nod to *Abood* and *Keller*, the Court noted that it would be "impractical" to allow each student to list those causes that he or she will or will not support without creating a system that was disruptive and expensive. Moreover, the university could choose to provide "the means to engage in dynamic discussions of philosophical, religious, scientific, social, and political subjects in their extracurricular campus life outside the lecture hall" and could impose a mandatory fee to finance the dialogue. However, the Court made clear that it would sustain only a viewpoint-neutral fee. The Court did express concern about the fact that the program provided for a referendum in which students could decide which speech to fund or to defund an organization. The Court remanded for further hearings on whether the referendum could result in discrimination against minority viewpoints.

The Court also distinguished its compelled speech doctrine in *Glickman v. Wileman Brothers & Elliott, Inc.*[201] In that case, which involved a Department of Agriculture rule that imposed generic advertising costs for a California tree fruit on the state's tree fruit growers, the Court found that the rule did not compel speech in a way that implicated the First Amendment. The Court emphasized that no fruit grower was forced to speak against his will or embrace any objectionable political or ideological message. However, in *United States v. United Foods, Inc.*,[202] the Court distinguished *Glickman* in a case involving mushroom growers. The Court noted that *Glickman* involved cooperative advertising as part of a broader collective enterprise in which freedom already was constrained by a general regulatory scheme. In *United Foods*, because the assessment for promotional advertising was not ancillary to a comprehensive regulatory scheme, but the principal object of it, the Court concluded that First Amendment interests against compelled speech and association should prevail. In a dissenting opinion joined by Justices O'Connor and Ginsburg, Justice Breyer found it difficult to understand why the factor of "heavy regulation" should be a determinative factor.

In *Davenport v. Washington Education Association*,[203] the Court upheld a Washington statute that prohibits public sector labor unions from using the agency shop fees of a nonmember for election-related purposes unless the nonmember affirmatively consents. In an opinion by Justice Scalia, the Court concluded that although prior decisions had simply prohibited unions from using the dues of objecting employees for political purposes, the Court found that the First Amendment was not violated by a law requiring explicit consent. "We do not believe that the voters of Washington impermissibly distorted the marketplace of ideas when they placed a reasonable, viewpoint-neutral limitation on the State's general authorization allowing public-sector unions to acquire and spend the money of government employees. . . . Quite obviously, no suppression of ideas is afoot, since the union remains as free as any other entity to participate in the electoral process with all available funds other than the state-coerced agency fees lacking affirmative permission." However, the Court limited its holding to public sector unions.

In *Johanns v. Livestock Marking Association*,[204] the Court upheld the Beef Promotion and Research Act of 1985 that was designed to promote the marketing and consumption of beef and beef products by using funds raised by an assessment on cattle sales and importation. The statute directed the secretary of agriculture to implement this policy by issuing a Beef Promotion and Research Order, which created an Operating Committee to administer the act and authorized the secretary to impose a $1-per-head assessment (or "checkoff") on all sales or importation of cattle and a comparable assessment on imported beef products. The assessment was used to fund beef-related projects, including promotional campaigns, designed by the operating committee and approved by the secretary. The secretary or his designee were required to approve each project and, in the case of promotional materials, the content of each communication. Under the program, more than $1 billion was collected, and much of the money was spent on advertising, some with the trademarked slogan "Beef. It's What's for Dinner." Some of the advertising included the notation "Funded by America's Beef Producers" or the Beef Board logo "BEEF." The act was challenged by two associations, both of which were required to pay the checkoff, that complained that the advertising promotes beef as a generic commodity in contravention of their efforts to promote the superiority of American beef, grain-fed beef, or certified Angus or Hereford beef.

In upholding the act, the Court distinguished the act's requirements from the Court's compelled speech decisions articulated in *Barnette* and *Wooley*. The Court found a distinction between "compelled support of government" and compelled speech. Although the Court had struck down laws requiring individuals to fund speech programs, the Court emphasized that all of these laws involved speech that "was, or was presumed to be, that of an entity other than the government itself." The Court concluded that individuals could not object to compelled support of government speech, even if the governmental program involved speech to which the individual objected. In *Johanns*, the Court found that the message was attributable to the government and that listeners would not attribute the government's message to the beef producers. The message was the government's because Department of Agriculture officials review all advertisements and the secretary exercises final approval authority. However, the Court remanded for consideration of whether the reference to "America's Beef Producers" would make a reasonable viewer conclude that the advertisements were being run by the industry rather than by the government.

Justice Thomas concurred. Although he recognized that government may not involuntarily associate individuals or organizations with an unwanted message, he concurred because he found that the "payment of taxes to the government for purposes of supporting government speech is not nearly as intrusive as being forced to 'utter what is not in [one's] mind,' or to carry an unwanted message on one's property." Justice Breyer also concurred on the basis that the act implicated economic regulation issues rather than speech. Justice Souter, joined by Justices Stevens and Kennedy, dissented, arguing that if the "government relies on the government-speech doctrine to compel specific groups to fund speech with targeted taxes, it must make itself politically accountable by indicating that the content actually is a government message, not just the statement of one self-interested group the government is currently willing to invest with power." He emphasized that the advertisements in question did not indicate that they were governmental speech, and in fact the ads concealed their origins by indicating that they were "[f]unded by America's Beef Producers."

K. Unconstitutional Conditions

Ordinarily, when government attempts to regulate or control speech, it does so directly. However, government can also try to regulate or control expressive liberty through encouragement or financial incentives, such as when it provides funding for speech. Government has the right to express itself and promote policies and programs in ways that are consistent with a particular ideology or agenda, and it can provide funds to convey a particular message while at the same time imposing requirements designed to ensure that the government's message is not undermined.

Nevertheless, while government may set policy, implement programs necessary to effectuate its goals, and establish conditions on distribution of resources, government must operate within constitutional limits, including those imposed by the First Amendment. Consistent with this premise, while government may distribute benefits, it may not condition their receipt on waiver of a basic right or liberty.

The **"unconstitutional conditions" doctrine** suggests that, in some instances, the nature or level of governmental encouragement or incentives transcends constitutional bounds. For example, in *Federal Communications Commission v. League of Women Voters*,[205] the Court struck down a federal law that denied federal funding to public broadcasting stations that editorialized on the air. Even though the law was designed to insulate public broadcasters from the possibility that their funding would be jeopardized by the airing of unpopular views, the Court was concerned because the restriction on expression implicated political speech. Even though political speech is ordinarily accorded high value under the First Amendment, and restrictions are generally subject to strict scrutiny, the Court has typically applied a mid-level standard of review to restrictions that affect broadcasting. The Court inquired whether the government regulation was supported by a substantial or important government interest that was narrowly tailored to achieve its purpose, and found such an interest in the government's goal of ensuring balanced coverage of public issues. Nevertheless, the Court found that an editorial ban underserved this interest.

League of Women Voters was distinguished in *Rust v. Sullivan*,[206] a case that upheld federal rules that denied federal funds to family planning clinics that counseled abortion or made abortion referrals. In upholding the condition on funding, the Court held that government is free to use private speakers — in this case, the doctors and other staff at the family planning clinic — to transmit information pertaining to its own program and may take reasonable steps to ensure that its message is clear and not distorted. If the private speakers disagree, they can refuse to participate in the program or can run an additional program that is separately funded. In the *League of Women Voters* case, freedom of expression was burdened without any government program or message that required protection.

On the other hand, the government's ability to impose restrictions on its speech funding is not unbounded. In *Rosenberger v. University of*

Virginia,[207] the Court struck down a government funding program because it involved viewpoint discrimination. The Court held that a university could not choose to fund student publications but exclude those of religious groups. In reaching its conclusion, the Court concluded that viewpoint discrimination is impermissible when, instead of conveying its own message, government has chosen to expend "to encourage a diversity of views from private speakers."

This premise was reaffirmed in *Legal Services Corp. v. Velazquez*,[208] in which the Court struck down a federal law that prohibited federally funded legal services offices from challenging the constitutional or statutory validity of welfare laws. The Court concluded that Congress was not obligated to fund legal services or to fund the entire range of legal claims. However, to the extent that Congress precluded legal services offices from pursuing theories that may be critical to effective litigation, the Court held that the law was invalid. In other words, Congress could not insulate the government's interpretation of the Constitution from challenge by legal services attorneys. Because only private speech is concerned in the context of developing and presenting legal theories, as opposed to government expression through an agent, the Court found the government's analogy to *Rust* inapt. The funding condition thus was declared invalid to the extent it was aimed to suppress ideas considered inimical to government's interests.

The Court's most recent unconstitutional conditions decision was rendered in *Rumsfeld v. Forum for Academic & Institutional Rights, Inc.*[209] That case, discussed earlier in connection with the right of association, involved a federal statute requiring law schools to admit military recruiters on the same basis as other recruiters on pain of losing federal funds. In an opinion by Chief Justice Roberts, the Court unanimously upheld the Solomon Amendment, noting that Congress has a constitutional right to provide for the common defense, which includes the power to require colleges and law schools to provide campus access to military recruiters. The Court rejected the notion that the unconstitutional conditions doctrine would limit Congress's authority to require law schools to provide access to military recruiters. The Court noted that the Solomon Amendment left colleges and law schools free to exercise their First Amendment rights because the Solomon Amendment "neither limits what law schools may say nor requires them to say anything." In addition, the Court viewed the Solomon Amendment as a regulation of conduct rather than a regulation of speech: "As a general matter, the Solomon Amendment regulates conduct, not speech. It affects what law schools must *do* — afford equal access to military recruiters — not what they may or may not *say*."

L. First Amendment Rights of Public Employees

A simmering debate has existed regarding whether, and to what extent, public employees may be treated differently from other citizens for First Amendment purposes. As we shall see, the questions raised by this issue arise in a variety of contexts.

(1) Political Activities

One context in which the Court has treated public employees differently is in regard to their ability to engage in partisan political practices. *United Public Workers of America v. Mitchell*[210] involved a challenge to §9(a) of the Hatch Act, which prohibited federal employees from taking "any active part in political management or in political campaigns." In upholding the Hatch Act, the Court applied a limited standard of review (whether Congress acted "within reasonable limits"), and the Court was deferential to Congress. In addition, the Court balanced the rights of employees to engage in free speech against the "evil of political partisanship by classified employees of government" and concluded that an "actively partisan governmental personnel threatens good administration" in that "political rather than official effort may earn advancement." The Court emphasized that Congress did not prohibit federal employees from voting in elections, and the law prohibited "only the partisan activity of federal personnel deemed offensive to efficiency." The Court emphasized that the Hatch Act did not prohibit employees for exercising their First Amendment rights in other ways (for example, by expressing their opinions on public affairs, personalities, or matters of public interest). Moreover, the Court concluded that the restrictions could be applied even if an individual employee's job was not connected to the public. For example, the Court held that the act could be applied to appellant Poole who worked as a "roller" at the Mint, performing essentially mechanical skills.

Justice Black argued that the Court would not have sustained a similar restriction on any other group (for example, farmers or businesspeople). As a result, he would have applied the law only if it were "narrowly drawn to meet the evil [and] affect only the minimum number of people [necessary] to prevent a grave and imminent danger to the public." He believed that the government could not satisfy this standard because it "[is hardly] imperative to muzzle millions of citizens because some of them [might] corrupt the political process." Justice Douglas, dissenting, recognized that government may have legitimate reasons for limiting the political activities of public employees, but argued that these interests should be balanced against the employees' free speech rights, which he regarded as "too basic and fundamental in our democratic political society to be sacrificed or qualified for anything short of a clear and present danger to the civil service system."

F   A   Q

Q: Does the holding in *United Public Workers* threaten the ability of public employees to participate in the political process?

A: The decision certainly threatens to limit or preclude public employees from full participation in the political process. Of course, the decision does not prevent them from voting. However, it does prevent them from participating fully in the political process in the same way that everyone else is allowed to participate (for example, working for campaigns, etc.).

In *United States Civil Service Commission v. National Association of Letter Carriers, AFL-CIO,*[211] the Court reaffirmed *Mitchell* and offered several justifications for the Hatch Act. In particular, the Court noted that a prohibition on partisan political activities reduces "the hazards to fair and effective government" by removing actual improprieties as well as the appearance of impropriety. In addition, the prohibition avoids the risk that the government workforce might be used "to build a powerful, invincible, and perhaps corrupt political machine." Finally, as the Court recognized in *Mitchell*, one's career in government service should not depend on political performance, and public employees "should be free from pressure and from express or tacit invitation to vote in a certain way or perform political chores in order to curry favor with their superiors rather than to act out their own beliefs."

(2) Honoraria

Despite the holding in *Mitchell*, not all restrictions on the expressive activities of public employees have been upheld. In *United States v. National Treasury Employees Union*,[212] the Court struck down a criminal statute that prohibited federal employees from accepting any compensation for making speeches or writing articles that applied whether or not the subject had any relationship to the employee's official duties. In striking down the law, the Court recognized that a number of "literary giants" had been public employees (Nathaniel Hawthorne and Herman Melville, for example) and noted that the law imposed a significant burden on expressive activity by taking away the financial incentive for more expression. Although the motivation for the law was rooted in problems related to a small group of law makers, the breadth of the law threatened to create a "large-scale disincentive to Government employees' expression" that would impose "a significant burden on the public's right to read and hear what the employees would otherwise have written and said." In addition, since the speech does not relate to the employees' jobs and takes place off the job, the law could not be justified as a means of preventing workplace disruption.

Sidebar

DISTINGUISHING A PUBLIC EMPLOYEE'S "PRIVATE SPEECH" FROM SPEECH RELATED TO MATTERS OF "PUBLIC CONCERN"

Modern cases concerning the First Amendment rights of public employees focus on a number of considerations, including whether the speech relates to matters of "public concern" or is "private speech." Determining the category in which a particular statement falls is not easy because it depends on context. If speech is more of private concern than public concern, the Court is likely to uphold the sanction. On the other hand, when the speech relates to matters of public concern, the Court will balance the employer's interest in regulating or controlling the speech against the speech's relationship to matters of public concern.

F   A   Q

Q: Might the Court have reached a different result in the *National Treasury Employees Union* case had the honoraria restriction been limited to situations when public employees were being paid to talk about matters related to their employment?

A: Perhaps. The Court suggested that the restriction might have been regarded differently had it been limited to speech related to the employee's job. In that situation, the government interest would be much stronger than with speech unrelated to the job, and the government might have a strong interest in preventing corruption and bribery.

(3) Other Free Speech Rights

May government impose other restrictions on the free speech rights of public employees? For many years, the conventional wisdom suggested that a public employee had no right to object to conditions on the terms of his employment, including restrictions on his constitutional rights. Beginning in the 1950s, the Court began to recognize that public employees had some right to free expression both on and off the job. For example, in *Wieman v. Updegraff,*[213] the Court held that public schoolteachers could not be required to swear an oath of loyalty to the state and to reveal the groups with which were they associated. Then, in *Pickering v. Board of Education,*[214] the Court held that public employees do not relinquish their right to comment on matters of public interest simple because of their status as public employees. In that case, the Court overturned the dismissal of a high school teacher who criticized a board of education's allocation of funds between athletics and education, as well as its methods of informing taxpayers about the need for additional revenue. While recognizing that the state has a greater interest in regulating the speech of its employees, the Court tried to strike a balance "between the interests of the [employee], as a citizen, in commenting upon matters of public concern and the interest of the State, as an employer, in promoting the efficiency of the public services it performs through its employees." This balance has subsequently been referred to as the *Pickering* balancing test. In overturning the dismissal, the Court concluded that Pickering's speech involved "a matter of legitimate public concern" on which "free and open debate is vital to informed decision-making by the electorate."

As a general rule, the *Pickering* balancing test has provided the basis for evaluating employee free speech claims. For example, in *Connick v. Myers,*[215] the Court sustained a district attorney's decision to dismiss an assistant district attorney for intra-office speech. The assistant, who was upset about a transfer, prepared a questionnaire on various office-related topics (transfer policy, morale, the need for a grievance committee, the level of confidence in supervisors, and whether employees felt pressured to work in political campaigns), and distributed the questionnaire to fellow assistants. When the district attorney learned about the questionnaire, he terminated Myers for refusing to accept the transfer and for insubordination in distributing the questionnaire. In upholding the dismissal, the Court held that it would be unnecessary "to scrutinize the reasons for her discharge" because "government officials should enjoy wide latitude in managing their offices, without intrusive oversight by the judiciary in the name of the First Amendment." While private speech is not beyond constitutional protection, the Court concluded that employee "speech on private matters falls into one of the narrow and well-defined classes of expression which carries so little social value, such as obscenity, that the state can prohibit and punish such expression by all persons in its jurisdiction." In this context, "a federal court is not the appropriate forum in which to review the wisdom of a personnel decision taken by a public agency allegedly in reaction to the employee's behavior."

In applying these principles to the assistant's speech, the Court concluded that the assistant's questionnaire did not relate to matters of "public concern." The Court viewed the questionnaire as focusing on questions relating to discipline and morale in the workplace, which of course relate to whether the agency is efficiently performing its duties, but the Court viewed the questionnaire as designed by Myers simply to "gather ammunition for another round of controversy with her superiors." The Court did hold that one of Myers's questions, which focused on whether employees had ever been pressured to work in political campaigns, touched on a matter of public concern. There is risk that such pressure involves "a coercion of belief in violation of fundamental constitutional rights," and the public has an interest in making sure that government employees should be evaluated based "upon meritorious performance rather than political service."

F   A   Q

Q: Doesn't the public have a legitimate interest in office morale and discipline in a government office?

A: Yes, it is quite possible that the information being gathered in the questionnaire would have been of great interest to the public, even if the employee's motive was largely to gather ammunition for a fight with her supervisor. However, since the information was not being published but was simply gathered for internal use, the Court was more inclined to regard the communication as private. Of course, it is difficult to gather information for public distribution without doing an investigation or sending out a questionnaire.

Despite the public importance of one of the questions, the Court upheld the dismissal. The Court held that not only was it required to evaluate the importance of the speech, but it was also required to consider the governmental interest in "the effective and efficient fulfillment of its responsibilities to the public." While the questionnaire did not impede Myers's ability to perform her own duties, it did cause a "mini-insurrection" in the office, interfered with working relationships, and undermined the district attorney's authority. The Court therefore deferred to the employer's conclusions regarding the need to fire Myers. In addition, although the survey involved matters of public concern in a limited sense, the Court held the questionnaire concerned "internal office policy," and the Court concluded that the First Amendment did not require the district attorney to "tolerate action which he reasonably believed would disrupt the office." In conclusion, the Court emphasized that it was seeking a balance between the "First Amendment's primary aim," which the Court regarded as "the full protection of speech upon issues of public concern," and the "practical realities involved in the administration of a government office."

Justice Brennan, joined by Justices Marshall, Blackmun, and Stevens, dissented. He argued that speech regarding the manner in which government "is operated or should be operated" is an essential part of the communications necessary for self-governance. He concluded that the Court's holding will "deter public employees from making critical statements about the manner in which government agencies are operated for fear that doing so will provoke their dismissal. As a result, the public will be deprived of valuable information with which to evaluate the performance of elected officials."

Even though the Court gave heavy deference to the employer in *Myers*, the same is not true of the holding in *Rankin v. McPherson*.[216] That case involved a deputy (McPherson) in a constable's office who was discharged during a probationary

Sidebar

NURSES IN GOVERNMENT JOBS

In *Waters v. Churchill*, 511 U.S. 661 (1994), the Court upheld a discharge for speech that involved a nurse in an obstetrics department who was terminated for talking about "how bad things are in [obstetrics] in general," as well as for criticizing a supervisor. The nurse denied making the statements, claiming that she actually supported the supervisor and did not complain about obstetrics, but admitting that she complained about the hospital's "cross-training" policy (under which nurses from one department could work in another department when their usual location was overstaffed). In upholding the discharge, the Court concluded that if the supervisors really believed the stories about the discharged employee's criticisms, based on their investigation, the discharge was reasonable.

period. Although the constable's office performed law enforcement functions, McPherson was not a commissioned peace officer, did not wear a uniform, was not authorized to make arrests or allowed to carry a gun, and performed only clerical duties. Her work station did not contain a phone and was located at a place to which the public did not have access. The case arose when McPherson and some fellow employees heard on the radio that there had been an attempt to assassinate President Reagan. McPherson then told a coworker, her boyfriend, "Shoot, if they go for him again, I hope they get him." McPherson was fired for the remark. In overturning the discharge, the Court again focused on the balance between the employee's interest in commenting on matters of public concern and the state's interest "in promoting the efficiency of the public services it performs through its employees." However, the Court found that McPherson's comment dealt with a matter of public concern because it dealt with the policies of the president's administration and was made in response to an attempt on the president's life. In balancing McPherson's interest in making the statement against the interest of the state, the Court concluded that the employer could not justify the discharge given that there was no evidence that McPherson's statement interfered with the efficient functioning of the office, that it disturbed or interrupted other employees, or even that anyone else heard the remark. In addition, the statement did not discredit the office (because it was made in a private conversation with another employee) or reflect "a character trait that made respondent unfit to perform her work." The Court also expressed concern that McPherson may have been discharged because of the content of her speech.

F   A   Q

Q: Would McPherson's comments have justified the discharge had she been overheard making an actual threat to assassinate the president?

A: Yes. A threat to kill the president is not constitutionally protected because of the criminal nature of the speech. However, the Court did not regard McPherson's comment as an actual threat to kill the president.

Justice Scalia, joined by Chief Justice Rehnquist and Justices White and O'Connor, dissented, arguing that a law enforcement agency is not "required by the First Amendment to permit one of its employees to 'ride with the cops and cheer for the robbers.'" He argued that McPherson's statement was not far removed from speech that receives no First Amendment protection, including threats to assassinate the president. Moreover, he believed that McPherson's statement might undermine confidence in the constable's office.

Ultimately, each employee speech case must be evaluated on its own facts weighing the public and private components. For example, in the Court's earlier decision in *Mt. Healthy City School District v. Doyle*,[217] after a principal issued a directive on teacher dress and appearance, one teacher provided a copy to a local disc jockey who announced it as a news item. A month later, the principal recommended that Doyle not be rehired for the following year because of "a notable lack of tact in handling professional matters which leaves much doubt as to your sincerity in establishing good school relationships." The principal's recommendation referred to the radio station incident and to an obscene gesture. The Court held that the dismissal was actionable if it was based on Doyle's communication with the radio station. Having shown that his speech was a "substantial factor" or a "motivating factor" in the Board's decision not to rehire, the Board was required to prove that it would have reached the same result even in the absence of Doyle's communication with the station.

However, there are a number of instances when the Court has concluded that the speech rights of public employees are trumped by the employer's needs. For example, in *City of San Diego v. Roe*,[218] a police officer was terminated for off-duty speech (selling videotapes depicting himself engaged in sexually explicit acts while wearing a police uniform and issuing a citation). The police department dismissed Roe, concluding that he had violated specific police department policies, including engaging in conduct unbecoming of an officer and immoral conduct. In reviewing the discharge, while the Court recognized that public employees do not "relinquish all First Amendment rights otherwise enjoyed by citizens just by reason of [their] employment," "a governmental employer may impose certain restraints on the speech of its employees, restraints that would be unconstitutional if applied to the general public." In evaluating an individual restraint, the Court indicated that it would use the *Pickering* balancing test, balancing the employee's interest in commenting on matters of public concern against the State's interest as an employer in promoting the efficiency of its services. However, balancing would not be required when the employee's speech could compromise the proper functioning of government offices. Applying these principles, the Court concluded that the police department had "demonstrated legitimate and substantial interests of its own that were compromised by [Roe's] speech." "[The] debased parody of an officer performing indecent acts while in the course of official duties brought the mission of the employer and the professionalism of its officers into serious disrepute." The Court also noted that Roe's expression had nothing to do with matters of public concern because Roe was not attempting to inform the public about any aspect of the police department's operation.

(4) Speech Pursuant to Duties

The Court's 2006 decision in *Garcetti v. Ceballos*[219] imposed an important new qualification on its precedents relating to the free speech rights of public employees. Ceballos was a deputy district attorney who was involved in a "heated exchange" regarding the handling of a case. He was subsequently subjected to a series of retaliatory employment actions. The Court refused to hold that the First Amendment protects a government employee from discipline based on speech made pursuant to the employee's official duties. Relying on its prior decision in *Pickering*, the Court indicated that two questions should be considered in cases involving public employee speech. "The first requires determining whether the employee spoke as a citizen on a matter of public concern. If the answer is no, the employee has no First Amendment cause of action based on his or her employer's reaction to the speech." "If the answer is yes, then the possibility of a First Amendment claim arises. The question becomes whether the relevant government entity had an adequate justification for treating the employee differently from any other member of the general public." The Court rejected Ceballos's First Amendment claim because his expressions were made "pursuant to his duties" as a prosecutor. "Restricting speech that owes its existence to a public employee's professional responsibilities does not infringe any liberties the employee might have enjoyed as a private citizen. It simply reflects the exercise of employer control over what the employer itself has commissioned or created." In addition, the Court noted that employers "have heightened interests in controlling speech made by an employee in his or her professional capacity." The Court recognized that "[o]fficial communications have official consequences, creating a need for substantive consistency and clarity. Supervisors must ensure that their employees' official communications are accurate, demonstrate sound judgment, and promote the employer's mission." The Court concluded that Ceballos's speech fit within this categorization: "It demanded the attention of his supervisors and led to a heated meeting with employees from the sheriff's department. If Ceballos' superiors thought his memo was inflammatory or misguided, they had the authority to take proper corrective action." The Court concluded that there were other means available for dealing with corruption. As a result, the Court rejected the notion "of a constitutional cause of action behind every statement a public employee makes in the course of doing his or her job."

Garcetti prompted much disagreement about the proper standard to be applied. Justice Stevens dissented, arguing that he doubted that it made sense "to fashion a new rule that provides employees with an incentive to voice their concerns publicly before talking frankly to their superiors." Justice Souter, joined by Justices Stevens and Ginsburg, also dissented, arguing that there is a distinction between "[o]pen speech by a private citizen on a matter of public importance," which he viewed as lying "at the heart of expression subject to protection by the First Amendment." By contrast, "a statement by a government employee complaining about nothing beyond treatment under personnel rules" raised "no greater claim to constitutional protection against retaliatory response than the remarks of a private employee." He regarded a public employee's speech on a significant public issue as lying between these two extremes because it "is protected from reprisal unless the statements are too damaging to the government's capacity to conduct public business to be justified by any individual or public benefit thought to flow from the statements." As a result, he felt that the *Pickering* balancing test was the proper approach because it recognized that a "public employee can wear a citizen's hat when speaking on subjects closely tied to the employee's own job." Justice Breyer, dissenting, also argued that the Court should apply the *Pickering* balancing test.

(5) Associational Rights

Even though a number of cases have suggested that public employees have limited expressive freedom, a number of cases suggest that public employees have associational rights. For example, in *Wieman v. Updegraff*,[220] the Court held that a state could not force its employees to recite a loyalty oath denying their past affiliation with Communists. Likewise, in *Keyishian v. Board of Regents*,[221] the Court invalidated New York statutes barring employment merely on the basis of membership in "subversive" organizations on the basis that political associations, by themselves, do not constitute an adequate ground for denying public employment.

In *United States v. Robel*,[222] the Court invalidated portions of the Subversive Activities Control Act of 1950, which provided that when a Communist-action organization is under a final order to register, it shall be unlawful for any member of the organization "to engage in any employment in any defense facility." The law was passed to protect security and prevent sabotage at defense facilities. Although the Court's prior decision in *Communist Party of the United States v. Subversive Activities Control Board*[223] sustained an order requiring the Communist Party of the United States to register as a Communist-action organization under the act, *Robel* held that the act violated the right to associate as applied to a member of the Communist Party who was employed as a machinist at a shipyard designated as a "defense facility." In striking down the act, the Court held that "the operative fact upon which the job disability depends is the exercise of an individual's right of association, which is protected by the provisions of the First Amendment."

The Court extended the public employee's right of association in *Elrod v. Burns*[224] to protect employees who were discharged because of their party affiliations. Although the discharged employees were not in merit system jobs, the Court held that they could not dismissed solely because of their political affiliations. In this case, non-Democrats could not be forced to compromise their political beliefs in order to keep their jobs. The Court rejected the argument that the law was supported by the need to make sure that the workforce supported the administration in power, noting that when large numbers of public employees are replaced each time the government changes hands, there is considerable inefficiency. In any event, the Court found that there were other means for ensuring employee effectiveness and efficiency, including dismissal for insubordination or poor job performance. The Court noted that it might be permissible to dismiss those in "policymaking" positions, but the Court noted that even individuals with substantial responsibilities such as supervisors may not have "policymaking" responsibilities. The Court remanded for a determination of whether the government could show an "overriding interest" in support of the dismissals. Chief Justice Burger dissented, arguing that the Court's decision "runs counter to longstanding practices that are part of the fabric of our democratic system." Justice Powell, joined by two other justices, also dissented, arguing that the discharged employees had accepted patronage jobs as a direct result of their political affiliation and "may not be heard to challenge it when it comes their turn to be replaced."

Elrod was followed by the decision in *Branti v. Finkel*,[225] which helped flesh out the definition of "policymaking." In *Branti*, the Court overturned the dismissal of an assistant public defender solely because he was a Republican, despite the argument he performed a "policymaking" function and therefore could be dismissed on the basis of his political beliefs. The Court emphasized that the "primary, if not the only, responsibility of an assistant public defender is to represent individual citizens in controversy with the State." Any "policymaking" that the defender exercises "must relate to the needs of individual clients and not to any partisan political interests."

Likewise, in *Rutan v. Republican Party of Illinois*,[226] the Court held that a state hiring freeze that did not permit exceptions without the governor's express permission was unconstitutional. The freeze was challenged by plaintiffs who claimed that they were denied promotions or transfers, denied employment, or not recalled from layoffs because they did not work for or support the Republican Party. In holding that the denials were unconstitutional, the Court concluded that employees "who do not compromise their beliefs stand to lose the considerable increases in pay and job satisfaction attendant to promotions, the hours and maintenance expenses that are consumed by long daily commutes, and even their jobs if they are not rehired after a 'temporary layoff.'" Justice Scalia dissented: "[T]he desirability of patronage is a policy question to be decided by the people's representatives."

In *Minnesota State Board for Community Colleges v. Knight*,[227] the Court upheld a Minnesota law that authorized public employees to select an exclusive representative to bargain collectively over the terms and conditions of their employment, but provided that a government employer could exchange views only on non-mandatory subjects with the exclusive representative. The law was challenged by faculty at one college who claimed a violation of their constitutional rights. In upholding the restriction, the Court concluded that members of the public do not generally have a right to be heard by public bodies engaged in policymaking, and concluded therefore that employees' speech and associational rights were not therefore infringed. "The state has in no way restrained appellees' freedom to speak on any education-related issue or their freedom to associate or not to associate with whom they please, including the exclusive representative. Nor has the state attempted to suppress any ideas." Justice Stevens, joined by two other justices, dissented: "[T]he First Amendment [guarantees] an open marketplace for ideas — where divergent points of view can freely compete for the attention of those in power and of those to whom the powerful must account. [T]he statute gives only one speaker a realistic opportunity to present its views to state officials."

M. The First Amendment in the Public Schools

There has been considerable litigation regarding the expressive rights of students in public schools. While the Court has recognized in a number of cases that students do not relinquish their First Amendment rights at the schoolhouse door, the Court has always been reluctant to hold that student speech rights are coextensive with those of adults.

An important early decision is the holding in *Tinker v. Des Moines Independent School District*.[228] In *Tinker*, the Court recognized that high school students have a First Amendment right of expression that permits them to wear armbands in school. The case involved two high school students and a junior high school student who wore black armbands to demonstrate their opposition to the Vietnam War in violation of a newly adopted policy providing for the suspension of any student who refused to remove an armband. The Court recognized that the wearing of armbands is "symbolic speech," is protected by the First Amendment, and is "closely akin to 'pure speech.'" While the Court also recognized that the free speech rights of teachers and students are tempered by the "special characteristics of the school environment" and the need to "prescribe and control conduct in the schools," the Court held that school officials could not discipline students "for a silent, passive expression of opinion, unaccompanied by any disorder or disturbance on the part of petitioners." In order to prevail, school officials were required to show that the students' conduct "materially and substantially interfere[s] with the requirements of appropriate discipline in the operation of the school." The Court found that school officials could not meet the required burden because there was no indication of a disruption attributable to the armbands, and the mere fact that schools officials feared the possibility of a disturbance was not an adequate basis for suppression.

An important aspect of the *Tinker* decision was the Court's concern that school officials had engaged in content-based discrimination against speech. Even though the school allowed students to wear a variety of emblems, including political campaign buttons and the Iron Cross (a symbol of Nazism), it had banned the black armbands. "In our system, students may not be regarded as closed-circuit recipients of only that which the State chooses to communicate. They may not be confined to the expression of those sentiments that are officially approved." Justice Stewart, concurred, arguing that a "State may permissibly determine that, at least in some precisely delineated areas, a child — like someone in a captive audience — is not possessed of that full capacity for individual choice which is the presupposition of First Amendment guarantees." Justice Harlan dissented, arguing that he would require the students to show that "a particular school measure was motivated by other than legitimate school concerns — for example, a desire to prohibit the expression of an unpopular point of view, while permitting expression of the dominant opinion."

F   A   Q

Q: If the primary purpose of schools is to teach children, then why shouldn't the school have the right to limit the scope of permissible speech?

A: As the Court has held in numerous cases, although school-age children do not have the same expressive rights as adults, they do not lose their First Amendment rights simply because they are in a school environment. As *Tinker* indicates, if student expression does not interfere with the functioning of the school, it may be constitutionally protected.

Nevertheless, because of the special characteristics of the school environment, the Court is more likely to uphold restrictions on student speech. For example, in *Bethel School District No. 403 v. Fraser*,[229] the Court upheld a disciplinary action against a high school student who delivered a "sexually explicit" speech at a school assembly during the nomination of a fellow student for student elective office. In upholding the disciplinary sanction, the Court distinguished *Tinker* on the basis that the sanctions were not viewpoint based, as well as on the basis that school officials might legitimately conclude that the student's "vulgar and lewd speech" might "undermine the school's basic educational mission."

Likewise, in *Morse v. Frederick*,[230] the Court upheld a principal's decision to suspend a student who displayed a banner with the words "Bong Hits for Jesus" at a school event (students had gone outside of the school, during the school day, to witness a runner bearing the Olympic torch go by). In upholding the suspension, in an opinion by Chief Justice Roberts, the Court held that "schools may take steps to safeguard those entrusted to their care from speech that can reasonably be regarded as encouraging illegal drug use." The Court emphasized that student free speech rights are not equivalent to those held by adults, and that *Tinker*'s requirement of a "substantial disruption" is not absolute. The Court emphasized the important governmental interest in deterring drug use by schoolchildren and the strong interest of schools in educating students regarding the dangers of drug use. Justice Stevens, joined by two other justices, dissented, arguing that Frederick's statement did not advocate illegal drug use.

In *Hazelwood School District v. Kuhlmeier*,[231] the Court upheld a high school principal's decision to require students to delete two pages from the school's newspaper. The pages dealt with students' experiences with pregnancy and the impact of divorce on students at the school. The principal ordered the deletion because there was no time to change the stories before the scheduled press, and he concluded that the subject matter of the stories was inappropriate for the student body. In rejecting the students' First Amendment claims, although the Court reaffirmed the notion that students do not "shed their constitutional rights to freedom of speech or expression at the schoolhouse gate," it recognized that a "school need not tolerate student speech that is inconsistent with its 'basic educational mission,'" and that school officials should be given deference in determining what speech is inappropriate. Moreover, the Court refused to hold that the newspaper was a forum for public expression, concluding instead that it was "a supervised learning experience for journalism students." As a result, the Court found that school officials were entitled to impose reasonable regulations on the contents of the newspaper and that educators retain a measure of discretion over school-sponsored publications and other expressive activities to ensure that "participants learn whatever lessons the activity is designed to teach, that readers or listeners are not exposed to material that may be inappropriate for their level of maturity, and that the views of the individual speaker are not erroneously attributed to the school." In addition, the school can disassociate itself from speech that is "ungrammatical, poorly written, inadequately researched, biased or prejudiced, vulgar or profane, or unsuitable for immature audiences." Focusing on whether the principal's actions were motivated by a "valid educational purpose," the Court upheld the principal's action, noting that student' identities were not adequately protected and that "the article was not sufficiently sensitive to the privacy interests of the students' boyfriends and parents."

F A Q

Q: Does the school's interference with the newspaper in *Hazelwood* involve content-based discrimination against speech?

A: It does. However, the *Hazelwood* Court did not treat the student newspaper as a public forum, which it did with the newspaper at issue in *Rosenberger v. Rector & Visitors of the University of Virginia,* 515 U.S. 919 (1995). The paper in *Hazelwood* was created as part of a class and therefore was a learning exercise. As a result, the school was allowed to retain a degree of content control.

Justice Brennan, joined by Justices Marshall and Blackmun, dissented, arguing that the principal should not be allowed to censor student expression that does not meet the *Tinker* standard (whether the student expression "materially disrupts classwork or involves substantial disorder or invasion of the rights of [others]"). He specifically rejected the argument that speech could be censored simply because of incompatability with the school's message. Otherwise, "school officials could [convert] our public schools into 'enclaves of totalitarianism,' that 'strangle the free mind at its source.'"

But there are limits to the ability of school officials to suppress expression in the school environment. For example, in *Board of Education v. Pico*,[232] a local school board ordered the removal of certain books from the libraries of a district high school and junior high school. The board characterized the books as "anti-American, anti-Christian, anti-Semitic, and just plain filthy," and asserted that "it is our duty, our moral obligation, to protect the children in our schools from this moral danger as surely as from physical and medical dangers." Five students sued the school district, alleging that the board's actions violated their rights under the First Amendment. A plurality concluded that "the Constitution protects the right to receive information and ideas" and that "students too are beneficiaries of this principle." They went on to observe that while school officials have "significant discretion to determine the content of their school libraries," they may not exercise their discretion "in a narrowly partisan or political manner." Moreover, the "Constitution does not permit the official suppression of *ideas*." As a result, if "petitioners *intended* by their removal decision to deny respondents access to ideas with which petitioners disagreed, and if this intent was the decisive factor in petitioners' decision, then petitioners have exercised their discretion in violation of the Constitution." The plurality found that the evidence did not foreclose the possibility that the school board's "decision to remove the books rested decisively upon disagreement with constitutionally protected ideas in those books, or upon a desire on petitioners' part to impose upon the students of the [junior and senior high schools] a political orthodoxy to which [the school board members] and their constituents adhered."

N. Government-Financed Speech

In some instances, the government provides financial support for speech, and questions have arisen regarding the government's right to dictate the message for which it pays. In some instances, these issues arise under the unconstitutional conditions doctrine (discussed above in section K) so that restrictions are challenged as direct violations of constitutional rights.

In general, when the government is financing speech the Court has been more willing to allow the government to impose restrictions. Illustrative is the holding in *Rust v. Sullivan*,[233] in which the Court upheld U.S. Department of Health and Human Services (HHS) regulations restricting the speech of those receiving federal funding for family planning services. In an effort to ensure that funds would be used only to support "preventive family planning services, population research, infertility services, and other related medical, informational, and educational activities," Title X of the Public Health Service Act specifically precluded the use of funds for "programs where abortion is a method of family planning." In addition, the secretary promulgated regulations imposing three additional restrictions: First, a "Title X project may not provide counseling concerning the use of abortion as a method of family planning or provide referral for abortion as a method of family planning." Second, the regulations broadly prohibit a Title X project from engaging in activities that "encourage, promote or advocate abortion as a method of family planning." Third, the regulations require that Title X projects be organized so that they are "physically and financially separate" from prohibited abortion activities.

The regulations were challenged by a group of Title X grantees and doctors who supervised Title X funds, who claimed that the regulations violated the rights of Title X clients and the First Amendment rights of Title X health providers. The Court rejected the argument that the regulations imposed viewpoint-based restrictions on speech by prohibiting discussion of abortion as a family planning option, and precluding counseling, referral, and the provision of neutral and accurate information about ending a pregnancy. The Court held that the government may "selectively fund a program to encourage certain activities it believes to be in the public interest, without at the same time funding an alternative program which seeks to deal with the problem in another way." "This is not a case of the Government 'suppressing a dangerous idea,' but of a prohibition on a project grantee or its employees from engaging in activities outside of the project's scope."

Sidebar

MORE ON UNCONSTITUTIONAL CONDITIONS

Rust also rejected the argument that the government had imposed an unconstitutional condition by conditioning Title X funding on the relinquishment of speech rights. The Court found that the regulations did not require Title X grantees to relinquish the right to engage in abortion-related speech or even to stop performing abortions or providing abortion-related services. They simply required that they "keep such activities separate and distinct from Title X activities." On the same theory, the Court rejected claims that the regulations violated the staff's free speech rights. The regulations prohibited only abortion counseling and referral while the staff was performing governmental duties. Otherwise, the employees were free to pursue abortion-related activities.

The Court also found that the regulations did not significantly impinge the doctor-patient relationship. The program did not require doctors to make statements that they did not believe to be true, and the program was not so "all encompassing" as to make patients believe that they were receiving comprehensive medical advice. Indeed, the program did not provide postconception medical care, and therefore a doctor's silence with regard to abortion cannot reasonably be thought to mislead a client into thinking that the doctor does not consider abortion an appropriate option for her. In any event, the doctor is free to state that abortion alternatives are beyond the program's scope.

Justice Blackmun, joined by Justice Marshall and partially joined by Justices Stevens and O'Connor, dissented. He argued that the government had engaged in viewpoint-based suppression of speech by "refusing to fund those family-planning projects that advocate abortion *because* they advocate abortion." "Under the majority's reasoning, the First Amendment could be read to tolerate *any* governmental restriction upon an employee's speech so long as that restriction is limited to the funded workplace." Indeed, the restriction could be used to support the suppression of truthful information. "One can imagine no legitimate governmental interest that might be served by suppressing such information."

One area of governmental funding that has produced considerable litigation is the funding of National Endowment for the Arts projects. Although most NEA grants are uncontroversial, there was considerable controversy over a grant that funded a retrospective on photographer Robert Mapplethorpe's work. The exhibit, entitled *The Perfect Moment*, included homoerotic photographs that some condemned as pornographic. Also controversial was Andres Serrano's work *Piss Christ*, which involved a photograph of a crucifix immersed in urine. Because of the controversy over these works, Congress amended the NEA to require the chairperson of the NEA to ensure that "artistic excellence and artistic merit are the criteria by which [grant] applications are judged, taking into consideration general standards of decency and respect for the diverse beliefs and values of the American public." Otherwise, Congress vested the NEA with substantial discretion to award grants and identified only the broadest funding priorities, such as "giving emphasis to American creativity and cultural diversity" and "professional excellence." The amendments also provided that "obscenity is without artistic merit, is not protected speech, and shall not be funded."

In *National Endowment for the Arts v. Finley*,[234] in an opinion by Justice O'Connor, the Court upheld the law, rejecting claims of viewpoint discrimination. The Court noted that the law imposed no categorical prohibition against any type of speech other than obscenity. On the contrary, the amendments simply admonished the NEA to take factors like "decency and respect" into consideration. As a result, the Court rejected the argument that the criteria were sufficiently "subjective" that they could be used to engage in viewpoint discrimination. "Any content-based considerations that may be taken into account in the grant-making process are a consequence of the nature of arts funding." Justice Souter dissented, arguing that the NEA amendments imposed viewpoint-based restrictions. He expressed concern that the government had adopted "a regulation of speech because of disagreement with the message it conveys."

Despite the holdings in *Rust* and *Finley*, the government does not have unfettered discretion when it decides to fund speech. In *Legal Services Corp. v. Velazquez*,[235] the Court struck down restrictions imposed on governmentally funded lawyers. The Legal Services Corporation Act established a nonprofit corporation (LSC) to fund the provision of legal assistance "in noncriminal proceedings or matters to persons financially unable to afford legal assistance," and the LSC hires and supervises lawyers to provide free legal assistance to indigent clients. In the Omnibus Consolidated Rescissions and Appropriations Act of 1996, and subsequent annual appropriations, Congress prohibited LSC grantees, including those paid for by non-LSC funds, from undertaking representation designed to amend or otherwise challenge existing welfare law. As interpreted by the LSC and by the government, the restriction prevented an attorney from arguing to a court that a state statute conflicts with a federal statute or that either a state or federal statute by its terms or in its application violates the U.S. Constitution. In an opinion by Justice Kennedy, the Court struck down the restriction. The Court held that "the LSC program was designed to facilitate private speech, not to promote a governmental message. Congress funded LSC grantees to provide attorneys to represent the interests of indigent clients." As a result, LSC attorneys speak for clients rather than on behalf of the government. Moreover, the Court expressed concern that the funding restrictions "distort[] the legal system by altering the traditional role of attorneys." Government "may not design a subsidy to effect this serious and fundamental restriction on advocacy of attorneys and the functioning of the judiciary." The Court found that the "restriction on speech is even more problematic because in cases where the attorney withdraws from a representation, the client is unlikely to find other counsel." Justice Scalia, joined by Chief Justice Rehnquist and Justices O'Connor and Thomas, dissented, arguing that the act created "a federal subsidy program, not a federal regulatory program." Moreover, he argued that the act did not create a public forum. "Nor does §504(a)(16) discriminate on the basis of viewpoint, since it funds neither challenges to nor defenses of existing welfare law. The provision simply declines to subsidize a certain class of litigation, and under *Rust* that decision 'does not infringe the right' to bring such litigation."

O. The Press Clause

Since the Press Clause specifically mentions the press, some have argued that the Framers intended to give the press a special status under the Constitution and to distinguish it from the Speech Clause. Justice Stewart referred to the Press Clause as a "*structural* provision [that] extends protection to an institution" and provides the "publishing business" with "explicit constitutional protection."[236] Under this view, the Press Clause is the basis for providing different and special protections to the media including, perhaps, protections against being forced to give grand jury testimony, protections against newsroom searches, access to prison facilities, and access to judicial proceedings. Chief Justice Burger disagreed, arguing that the Press Clause provides the press with no special rights. He perceived "no difference between the right of those who seek to disseminate ideas by way of a newspaper and those who give lectures or speeches and seek to enlarge the audience by publication and wide dissemination."[237] As a result, he did not view the press as some special preserve of a "definable category of persons or entities."

In general, as we shall see, the Court has rejected the notion that the press has a special status that provides it with special rights vis-à-vis the speech rights of other citizens. The case law suggests that the Court does not view the press as an institution, but simply as part of overall speech and the discussion that is critical to informed self-governance.

Even if the press is not accorded special privileges, it historically has performed a unique and important role in enlightening the public on the issues of the day. During the colonial period, newspapers and pamphleteers were very active in the revolutionary discourse. Since the founding, the press has continued to play a crucial role in informing the public.

F   A   Q

Q: If the Framers of the First Amendment did not intend to create a special status for the press, then why is the press mentioned separately in that amendment?

A: There is no clear answer. For one thing, as the debate between Justice Stewart and Chief Justice Burger illustrates, it is not clear that the Framers did *not* intend to create a special status for the press. But, if they did not, the presence of the word *press* in the First Amendment might still be explainable. In English history, the press had been subject to suppression, including licensing schemes and the crime of seditious libel. As a result, in deciding to give special constitutional protection to speech, the Framers might have decided to mention the press just to make clear that it, too, was protected.

By and large, in construing the Press Clause, the Court has focused on function rather than institutional structure. As a result, the Press Clause provides as much protection to the producers of pamphlets and circulars as it does to the "large metropolitan publisher."[238]

(1) The Reporter's Privilege

In the process of investigating and reporting, reporters sometimes acquire information that may interest governmental officials, especially criminal prosecutors. However, in some instances, reporters may obtain this information by promising that they will not disclose the identity of its source. In a number of high-profile cases, reporters have been ordered to disclose their sources on pain of a criminal contempt sanction. For example, in 2006, Judith Miller of the *New York Times* spent 85 days in jail for refusing to reveal the name of an informant.

In *Branzburg v. Hayes*,[239] the Court rejected the notion that reporters have a First Amendment privilege that shields them from being forced to testify before grand juries regarding their sources. The argument was made that reporters must be able to protect the confidentiality of their sources, or they will have less information available to them. Nevertheless, the Court held that the press has the same obligation as anyone else to provide testimony before a grand jury. In the process, the Court refused the argument that a reporter's privilege is essential to free speech, noting that the issue arises only when a source is implicated in a crime or possesses information relevant to the grand jury process, and the Court suggested that few cases involve that situation. Because the press flourished without a privilege in the past, the Court questioned whether the privilege was needed to prevent an adverse impact on the criminal justice process.

Sidebar

PROTECTING REPORTERS AGAINST SUBPOENAS

Branzburg does not suggest that reporters are never protected against orders to testify. Reporters, like any other individual, can move to quash a subpoena if there is proof of official harassment or bad faith. In addition, some states have legislatively provided reporters with a shield that protects their sources. The nature and scope of these legislated privileges vary, as do the level of protection. In some instances, courts have subordinated even seemingly absolute privileges to a defendant's right to a fair trial.

Modern case law generally supports an interpretation of *Branzburg* that is inconsistent with a journalistic privilege. This understanding was reflected in a federal appeals court decision in *In re Grand Jury Subpoena, Judith Miller*.[240] At issue was a special counsel investigation relating to leaks that identified a CIA operative. Grand jury subpoenas were issued requiring two reporters, Matthew Cooper and Judith Miller, to divulge their sources. Both refused to comply, and Miller was ultimately sent to jail for her refusal. Cooper escaped imprisonment when his source authorized disclosure of his identity at the last minute. After spending 85 days in jail, Miller was released when her informant also agreed to release her from her confidentiality obligation. That witness, Vice President Dick Cheney's chief of staff, Lewis "Scooter" Libby, was subsequently indicted and convicted. Interestingly, following her release, Miller left the *New York Times* over a controversy related to her reporting on the matter.

Given the holding in *Branzburg*, there is a risk that a reporter may breach a promise of confidentiality. In *Cohen v. Cowles Media Co.*,[241] the Court held that the First Amendment permitted a breach of contract claim against a reporter. In *Cohen*, the claimant was a political campaign aide who received a promise of confidentiality and agreed to leak embarrassing information about a rival candidate. In upholding the liability claim, the Court held that the First Amendment protects the right to publish lawfully acquired information, but held that the promise of confidentiality established an enforceable contractual obligation. The Court also rejected a newsworthiness defense premised on the idea that the breach provided the public (and, more particularly, voters) with relevant and important information.

(2) Newsroom Searches

Just as reporters can be subpoenaed to appear and testify before grand juries, prosecutors sometimes (albeit rarely) obtain warrants to search newsrooms. More commonly, because reporters and editors frequently seek information from the police and prosecutors, some news organizations voluntarily cooperate by providing information to the police. However, search warrants for newsrooms are not unknown and are more likely to be used in situations involving vanishing evidence.

In *Zurcher v. Stanford Daily*,[242] the Court held that a newsroom search did not violate the First Amendment. The case arose when police searched the editorial offices of a student newspaper pursuant to a warrant that was issued on the basis of probable cause. The police were searching for photographs of demonstrators who had assaulted police during a campus protest. In challenging the search, the newspaper claimed that the First Amendment prohibited newsroom searches on the theory that such searches disrupt and invade the editorial process, compromise the confidentiality of sources, and chill the editorial process. In rejecting these claims, the Court held that newsrooms are given no special immunity against search warrants and that the prosecutor is not required to proceed by a less invasive subpoena, provided that Fourth Amendment requirements are observed with "scrupulous exactitude" when First Amendment interests are implicated. Justice Stewart, dissenting, voiced concern that the decision would enable police to ransack newsrooms, chill sources, and impair the flow of information to the public.

> ## S i d e b a r
>
> **CONGRESS'S RESPONSE TO *ZURCHER***
>
> Congress responded to *Zurcher* by enacting the Privacy Protection Act of 1980, 42 U.S.C. §§2000aa-1 to 2000aa-12 (1980), which established a preference for subpoenas as a means for obtaining evidence from news organizations. The act established exceptions for situations when the information holder is suspected of a crime, as well as when there are exigent circumstances relating to life, serious injury, or loss of evidence.

F   A   Q

Q: Does *Zurcher* mean that the police, acting pursuant to a warrant, can ransack a newsroom, including reporters' notes that may contain references to confidential sources?

A: Yes, at least in theory, both can happen. The Court does give a slight concession to First Amendment values in holding that the warrant must be framed with "scrupulous exactitude."

(3) Access to Prisons

In a number of instances, the press has argued that it is entitled to special access to governmental institutions in order to gather information. In *Branzburg*, in dicta, the Court recognized that freedom of the press would be reduced to substantive insignificance if it did not afford "some protection for seeking out the news."[243] Nevertheless, in *Pell v. Procunier*[244] and *Saxbe v. Washington Post Co.*,[245] the Court upheld state and federal prison regulations prohibiting media interviews with inmates. The Court emphasized that the prisoners themselves have reduced First Amendment rights. In addition, the Court focused on security issues that arise with prisons and held that it would not second-guess prison administrators notwithstanding First Amendment concerns.

Similar issues were litigated in *Houchins v. KQED, Inc.*[246] That case involved a prison's decision to deny access to the part of a jail where a prisoner had committed suicide. In rejecting the press access claim, a plurality concluded that the First Amendment provides the press with no greater right of access than is available to the public. Justice Stewart concurred, but advocated for standards that would accommodate the practical distinctions between the press and public. Unlike the average citizen who might visit a prison, media often rely on sound and video recording equipment to capture information that is subsequently shared with the public.

Sidebar

PRISON OFFICIALS DETERMINE POLICY— EVEN WHEN IT ISN'T RELATED TO SECURITY

In *Beard v. Banks*, 542 U.S. 521 (2006), the Court upheld a prison policy that denied newspapers, magazines, and photographs to a group of specially dangerous and recalcitrant inmates. Relying on *Overton* v. *Bazzetta*, 539 U.S. 126 (2003), which held that the courts must show deference to prison officials, the Court upheld the restriction as applied to inmates who "exhibit behavior that is continually disruptive, violent, dangerous or a threat to the orderly operation of their assigned facility."

(4) Access to Judicial Proceedings

Generally, the courts have tended to hold that the public has a right to information regarding judicial proceedings, especially criminal proceedings, and that the press and the public have a right of access to such proceedings. The public's right of access was first recognized in *Richmond Newspapers, Inc. v. Virginia.*[247] In that case, the trial court attempted to close a trial to the press and the public. While the Court struck down the closure order, the case did not produce a majority opinion or rationale.

Sidebar

SPECIAL SEATING FOR THE PRESS

Even though many courts and legislatures provide special seating for the media on the theory that space is scarce, the Court has been unwilling to hold that such special seating is constitutionally mandated.

In the Court's following decision in *Globe Newspapers, Inc. v. Superior Court*,[248] the Court struck down a state law that required the closure of judicial proceedings in cases involving a juvenile victim of a sex offense. In addition to noting a tradition of open proceedings, the Court emphasized that public access and openness provide a safeguard against judicial abuse. The Court rejected the state's argument that closure was necessary to protect minors from further harm or embarrassment, as well as to encourage them to freely testify. The Court concluded that closure must be supported by a compelling governmental interest that is narrowly tailored to serve that interest. While the protection of minor sex offense victims was a compelling interest, the Court held that this interest did not justify mandatory closure.

F   A   Q

Q: Did *Globe Newspapers* hold that courts can never close judicial proceedings to the press and the public?

A: No. However, the Court applied strict scrutiny. So, in addition to demonstrating a compelling governmental interest that justifies closure, the government must be able to demonstrate that the restriction (closure) is a narrowly tailored approach to protecting the victim's interests while preserving the press's right of access as much as possible.

In subsequent cases, the Court has been protective of the right of access to judicial proceedings. For example, in *Press-Enterprise v. Superior Court*,[249] the Court held that a court could not close a voir dire proceeding absent an "overriding interest" and "findings that closure is necessary to ensure higher values and is narrowly tailored to serve that interest." Likewise, in *Waller v. Georgia*,[250] the Court held that a trial court could not close a preliminary hearing when the defendant objected to closure. Finally, in *Press-Enterprise Co. v. Superior Court*,[251] the Court held that the press and public have a right of access to some pretrial hearings. To decide whether a pretrial hearing may be closed, the trial court must first determine whether the particular process has a tradition of openness. In regard to pretrial hearings, the Court found that openness. The Court concluded that closure was permissible only if there is a substantial probability that fair trial rights will be compromised and there are no reasonable alternatives.

Sidebar

THE SCOPE OF PUBLIC ACCESS TO CRIMINAL PROCEEDINGS

Decisions like those rendered in *Waller* and the two *Press-Enterprise* cases demonstrate that the Sixth Amendment guarantee to a public trial and to public access to trials includes not only the trial itself, but also the pretrial process.

(5) The Media and Fair Trials

The right of press access to judicial proceedings creates the possibility for tension with a defendant's right to a fair trial free of prejudicial publicity, which is protected under the Fifth and Fourteenth Amendments' Due Process Clauses and the Sixth Amendment's guarantee of a "public trial, by an impartial jury."

The seminal decision on prejudicial publicity is *Sheppard v. Maxwell*.[252] In that case, the Court overturned Sheppard's murder conviction because it was influenced by massive and prejudicial pretrial publicity and disruptive media conduct during the trial. *Sheppard* involved a murder trial that received sensational and inflammatory media coverage. Not only did the press publish extrajudicial evidence (suggestive of defendant's guilt), it published the jurors' identities. In addition, the judge did not sequester the jury until deliberations began, and even then the jurors were given great freedom. During the trial itself, reporters were given broad access to the courtroom, and the judge took few steps to control pretrial publicity. While the Court recognized the importance of First Amendment interests, the Court held that the trial judge was required to take steps to ensure defendant's right to a fair trial and reversed defendant's conviction on the basis that he had been denied due process.

F A Q

Q: When a defendant faces the possibility of massive publicity, how does a trial court judge protect the defendant's right to a fair trial?

A: In general, the First Amendment favors the public's right to know. In *Sheppard*, however, the Court emphasized that a trial judge could take various steps designed to ensure the defendant a fair trial while remaining true to the First Amendment. While keeping the trial open to the public, the judge could limit the number of media representatives present and establish rules for press decorum. The judge could use the voir dire process to screen out jurors who have been unfairly influenced by prejudicial pretrial publicity or sequester jurors during the trial. Finally, the judge could order a change of venue, a continuance, or possibly a gag order. In other words, the trial judge should be active in terms of protecting the integrity of the trial process while maintaining an open proceeding.

Following *Sheppard*, aware of their obligation to protect defendants' due process rights, some judges imposed broad restrictions on pretrial publicity. For example, in *Nebraska Press Association v. Stuart*,[253] the Court struck down a pretrial order that prohibited the media from publishing confessions made to police, reporting information obtained during a preliminary hearing, or disseminating any information that strongly implicated the defendant. In striking down the order, the Court emphasized the fact that prior restraints are the "most serious and the least tolerable infringement on First Amendment rights" because they do not merely chill speech but prohibit it, and therefore are subject to a strong presumption of unconstitutionality and are subject to a heavy burden of justification. Although the case involved a substantial risk of prejudicial publicity, the Court concluded that the trial judge had less drastic means at his disposal.

While *Stuart* did not completely reject the possibility of a gag order, it did suggest that several requirements must be satisfied before one could be imposed. First, the trial court must determine that there is a clear and present danger (as opposed to a simple "possibility") that pretrial publicity will undermine defendant's right to a fair trial. Second, even if a clear and present danger exists, the trial judge must also conclude that alternatives to a gag order (for example, continuance or change of venue) are inadequate. Third, the trial court must determine that the gag order will actually be effective. Finally, the trial court may not restrain the media from accurately reporting information acquired in open court.

Sidebar

SPEECH RESTRICTIONS ON THE PARTIES TO A CRIMINAL PROCEEDING

The Court has been more willing to uphold speech restrictions imposed on parties to a proceeding and their attorneys. In *Gentile v. State Bar of Nevada*, 501 U.S. 1030 (1991), the Court held that restrictions could be imposed in this context provided that there is a "substantial likelihood of material prejudice."

(6) Cameras in the Courtroom

In recent years, there have been increasing demands to have cameras in the courtroom. The Court has never held that the press has a constitutional right to have cameras in the courtroom, and the issue usually arises in the context of a defendant's claim of prejudice based on the presence of cameras. In *Irvin v. Dowd*,[254] the Court found that defendant was denied due process when his trial was subject to such widespread television coverage that most of the jury had formed a belief as to his guilt prior to the trial itself. Likewise, in *Rideau v. Louisiana*,[255] the Court found a due process violation when there was a pretrial broadcast of defendant's confession and pervasive publicity. The Court did not require defendant to prove actual prejudice.

Because of due process concerns, early judicial decisions were less favorable to the presence of cameras in the courtroom. An earlier version of American Bar Association's Canons of Judicial Ethics required judges to ban cameras from the courtroom for fear that their presence would undermine the dignity of judicial proceedings. Consistently, in *Estes v. Texas*,[256] the Court found a due process violation based on the presence of radio and television cameras in the courtroom. The Court expressed fears that the presence of cameras might distract jurors, parties, witnesses, lawyers, and judges, as well as diminish the quality of legal representation. Justice Harlan concurred, expressing the hope that media technology might improve to the point that less intrusive equipment might become available.

Over time, the Court's attitude toward cameras in the courtroom began to change. In *Chandler v. Florida*,[257] the Court departed from *Estes* and held that the mere presence of cameras in the courtroom did not automatically violate due process, and that a defendant must prove actual prejudice to make out a violation of due process. To make this showing, defendant must show that the presence of cameras impaired the jurors' ability to decide the case based on the evidence presented or that their presence adversely affected the trial.

P. Media, Technology, and the First Amendment

Since the founding of the country, media technology has changed dramatically. When the First Amendment was ratified, the dominant technology was the print media. In addition to communicating orally, people could use the printing press to create newspapers, pamphlets, and letters to communicate with each other. Over the following centuries, media technology changed radically. The initial changes included broadcast communications (radio and television) and movies. More recent changes include cable, satellite radio and television, cell phone text messaging, and the Internet. Moreover, the nature of press ownership changed as large media corporations came into existence and began to alter the media landscape with mass-produced information. The nature of communication too has changed with the advent of such things as Web logs, or "blogs."

As technology has developed and morphed into different forms, the courts have expanded their definition of media entitled to First Amendment protection. In an early decision, the Court held in *Mutual Film Corp. v. Industrial Commission of Ohio*[258] that motion pictures do not come within the definition of the press and therefore are not entitled to First Amendment protections.

In later cases, the Court reversed itself and held that motion pictures fall within the definition of the "press" and are therefore protected under the First Amendment.[259]

F   A   Q

Q: How can movies be regarded as part of the press for purposes of the First Amendment?

A: We tend to think of the press as a daily or weekly newspaper. However, the press has always been conceived more broadly. For example, pamphlets and leaflets were a common method of communication at common law. Today, the press is more broadly conceived to include the Internet, which includes many traditional newspapers that publish their content in electronic as well as printed form. The press can also include movies, phones, and other communication devices because they communicate ideas.

Sidebar

THE ORIGINS OF MEDIUM-SPECIFIC ANALYSIS

The origins of medium-specific analysis are rooted in a concurring opinion by Justice Jackson. In *Kovacs v. Cooper*, 336 U.S. 77 (1949), a case that upheld a noise ordinance regulating sound trucks, Justice Jackson introduced a premise that eventually became a First Amendment fundamental. As he put it, "The moving picture screen, the radio, the newspaper, the handbill, the sound truck and the street orator have differing natures, values, abuses, and dangers. Each, in my view, is a law unto itself."

In general, the Court has developed medium specific standards for evaluating different types of technology. Historically, the Court has accorded the print media the highest level of First Amendment protection and has evaluated broadcast media restrictions under less protective standards. As the Court recognized in *Joseph Burstyn, Inc. v. Wilson*,[260] "each [medium] tends to present its own peculiar problems."

(1) The Print Media

The print media existed when the First Amendment was ratified and was clearly within the contemplation of the Framers. As a result, the courts historically have applied the highest level of scrutiny to governmental efforts to regulate printed press content. For example, in *Miami Herald Publishing Co. v. Tornillo*,[261] the Court struck down a state law that required newspapers to provide equal space for political candidates who they attacked editorially. The state sought to justify the requirement on the basis that it ensured fair and balanced coverage of candidates for public office, as well as because of the concentration of newspaper ownership in the hands of a small number of large corporations. In striking down the law, the Court emphasized that it unconstitutionally infringed the editorial discretion of newspaper editors. While editorial balance might be desirable, the law imposed impermissible costs because it might force a newspaper to publish one story rather than another. Such governmental regulation of editorial decisions is inconsistent with the requirements of the First Amendment.

F   A   Q

Q: How does the state law in *Tornillo* law intrude on the press when its effect was to increase the level of information available to the public?

A: The Court was concerned that a right of reply statute might make editors reluctant to publish attacks for fear that individuals would have a right to respond. The obligation to create space for the reply could have a chilling effect on freedom of expression.

(2) Broadcasting

Under its medium-specific approach to the First Amendment, the Court has generally provided less protection to the broadcast media. As the Court suggested in *Federal Communications Commission v. Pacifica Foundation,*[262] "of all forms of communication, it is broadcasting that has received the most limited First Amendment protection."

Reflective of the lesser status accorded to the broadcast media is the holding in *Red Lion Broadcasting Co. v. Federal Communications Commission.*[263] In that case, the Court upheld the FCC's "fairness doctrine," which required broadcasters to provide balanced coverage of controversial issues and imposed personal attack and political editorial rules that required broadcasters to provide reply time to those attacked. The Court treated the broadcast media differently from the print media because of the limited number of broadcasting bands available and the fact that those who are given bands are treated as trustees of the public airwaves (rather than owners of those waves). Interestingly, the Court refused to apply strict scrutiny and simply asserted the public's right "to receive suitable access to social, political, esthetic, moral, and other ideas."

Despite the *Red Lion* decision and the Court's use of medium-specific analysis, the Court has recognized that the broadcast media is entitled to exercise some control over broadcasting content. In *Columbia Broadcasting System, Inc. v. Democratic National Committee,*[264] despite broadcasting's diminished First Amendment status, the Court held that broadcasters retain editorial freedom regarding whether to accept political advertisements from the public. The case involved an anti-war message that was rejected based on the station's policy of rejecting controversial advertisements, as well as because the station believed that it already provided fair and balanced coverage of that (and other

Sidebar

RECONCILING *TORNILLO* AND *RED LION*

Commentators might legitimately question the different outcomes in *Tornillo* and *Red Lion*. While scarcity of bands is clearly an issue with regard to broadcasting, one might argue that there is a similar or greater scarcity problem with newspapers. In theory, anyone can start a newspaper. However, on both a national basis and a local basis, radio and television stations outnumber daily newspapers. Because of consolidations, many newspapers are owned by a small number of large media corporations, and economic considerations make it difficult for new newspapers to survive, much less to compete with existing ones. Of course, the possibility of becoming a broadcaster is limited by scarcity in the broadcast spectrum, as well as by the costs of establishing a new station, and the licensing of broadcasters is a direct outgrowth of this scarcity.

controversial) issues. In upholding the broadcaster's decision, the Court concluded that broadcasters were not required to function like common carriers. Although the fairness doctrine requires broadcasters to provide fair and balanced coverage of important public issues, the Court emphasized that broadcasters retained discretion to determine the method of coverage. The Court also was concerned that a system of public access would favor the wealthy. Justice Brennan was critical of the majority opinion, arguing that the Court undervalued the public interest in receiving views from advocates and partisans, and that some broadcasters shy away from controversy for fear of alienating viewers, listeners, and sponsors.

Sidebar

REVOKING THE FAIRNESS DOCTRINE

In dicta, the Court suggested in *League of Women Voters* that it might be prepared to abandon the scarcity rationale as applied to broadcasting. Not long afterwards, the FCC reconsidered and revoked the fairness doctrine. The FCC concluded that the doctrine had a chilling impact on expressive diversity because it discouraged broadcasters from presenting issues that would require more coverage to achieve balance. In addition, the FCC suggested that broadcasters should be treated more like the print media.

Also reflective of the editorial discretion accorded to broadcasters is the holding in *Federal Communications Commission v. League of Women Voters*,[265] striking down a law that prohibited public broadcasters from editorializing or endorsing political candidates. The Court articulated a new approach for evaluating broadcasting restrictions. Although the Court will not apply strict scrutiny, the government must nonetheless demonstrate the existence of an important government interest, and the restriction must be narrowly tailored to achieve that interest. In the *League of Women Voters* case, the Court identified an important governmental interest (shielding public broadcasters from funding cutbacks imposed as political retaliation for their expressed views), and the Court found that there were less speech-restrictive means of pursuing this interest (for example, by providing opportunities for competing viewpoints).

However, under its medium-specific analysis, the Court generally has provided less protection to sexually explicit but nonobscene expression in the broadcast format. For example, *Federal Communications Commission v. Pacifica Foundation*[266] dealt with a midafternoon broadcast of a famous comedian's monologue entitled "Filthy Words." The broadcast was aired as part of a program on contemporary attitudes toward speech and was preceded by warnings that it might offend some viewers. A motorist, who happened to be involved in an anti-indecency organization, came across the program while traveling with his son and filed a complaint. While the FCC did not impose formal sanctions, it did suggest that it might take regulatory action if there were future complaints. In upholding the FCC's determination, the Court concluded that the scarcity rationale was not implicated and identified two other aspects of broadcasting that warrant special restrictions: broadcasting's "uniquely pervasive presence in the lives of all Americans" and the fact that the broadcast medium is "uniquely accessible to children, even those too young to read." The Court's concerns regarding pervasiveness reflected a privacy concern insofar as individuals were exposed to unwanted expression in their homes or in public, and the Court seemed disinclined to suggest the remedy that it had suggested in other contexts ("avert[ing] one's eyes," or, in this case, their ears).[267] Even if a viewer or listener turns off a radio or television or switches stations, some exposure can occur. In regard to children, the Court was concerned about the fact that children could so easily access indecent material, and the Court emphasized the governmental interest in the well-being of youth. The Court suggested that a program of this nature might be permissible if it were confined to late-night hours when children were less likely to be listening.

F   A   Q

Q: Why wasn't the "Filthy Words" broadcast regarded as obscene under *Miller*?

A: For one thing, the "Filthy Words" was aired as part of a program on contemporary attitudes toward speech and therefore had significant social value. As a result, it could not be regarded as obscene.

Justice Brennan, dissenting, argued that the Court's decision revealed "a depressing inability to appreciate that in our land of cultural pluralism, there are many who think, act, and talk differently from the Members of this Court." Viewing the monologue as the work of a serious artist and social critic (George Carlin), he argued that the Court's reasoning might apply to a number of literary works including those of "Shakespeare, Joyce, Hemingway . . . and Chaucer" and could support suppression of much political speech. He contended that the asserted privacy interests were not significant in that listeners can simply switch programs.

In 2004, the FCC sought to crack down on offensive broadcasts. The FCC concluded that rock singer Bono's use of the "F" word during the Golden Globe awards was indecent (although the FCC did not impose fines against Bono because it concluded that Bono had not been given fair notice). In addition, the FCC proposed maximum fines against Howard Stern for a discussion of sexual practices with a couple who were allegedly having sex. Two years later in 2006, Congress passed the Broadcast Decency Enforcement Act to increase the fines for indecent broadcast communications to a range of $32,500 to $325,000.

S i d e b a r

POST-*PACIFICA* RESTRICTIONS ON INDECENT SPEECH

Following *Pacifica*, after a series of failed efforts to limit or ban indecent speech altogether, the FCC adopted rules that permit indecent broadcasts during late-night time slots (10:00 P.M. to 6:00 A.M.) when children are less likely to be listening.

F   A   Q

Q: Have decisions like *Pacifica* and the new FCC regulations severely limited the scope of expression available to adults?

A: Not really. Undoubtedly, the FCC's regulatory restrictions have limited the amount of content available to adults over the broadcast media. However, in recent decades, with the emergence of new media such as the Internet, satellite, and cable, adults have plenty of other options available to them. The relatively limited impact of FCC regulation, in fact, is highlighted by Howard Stern's decision to move from a commercial radio station to a satellite radio station. The move was prompted by the FCC's decision to crack down on indecent material.

(3) Cable Television

As expressive technology continued to evolve during the twentieth century, new methods of communication became available. The development of cable television was important because it permitted the retransmission of broadcast signals to more remote areas that could not easily receive broadcast signals. Broadcast signals are distinguishable from cable by the fact that they are transmitted by sound waves through the air whereas cable signals travel through coaxial cable or fiber optic lines. Broadcasters also differ by virtue of the fact that they are licensed by the FCC whereas cable operators receive franchises from local governments.

Unlike the broadcasting medium, scarcity of spectrum is not a problem with cable television. Most cable companies offer dozens, if not hundreds, of channels and programming options. Of course, most communities are served by a single cable operator that can control content. However, cable operators have competition from satellite companies.

Sidebar

CABLE TELEVISION AND THE FIRST AMENDMENT

In *City of Los Angeles v. Preferred Communications, Inc.*, 476 U.S. 488 (1984), although the Court held that the cable industry is entitled to First Amendment protection, the Court did not indicate whether cable should receive the lesser level of protection provided to broadcasters or the higher level of protection accorded to the print media. Although the Court stated that cable television "partakes of some of the aspects of speech and the communication of ideas as do the traditional enterprises of newspaper and book publishers, public speakers, and pamphleteers," it also stated that the cable industry appears to "implicate First Amendment interests as do the activities of wireless broadcasters."

In *Turner Broadcasting System, Inc. v. Federal Communications Commission*,[268] the Court upheld federal rules that required cable operators to carry the signals of local broadcasters (a/k/a "must carry rules") despite claims that the rules interfered with editorial discretion. The Court did not view the "must carry rules" as an invasion of editorial freedom because they were not content oriented or content based. As a result, the Court applied the content-neutral analysis and lower standard of review articulated in *United States v. O'Brien*.[269] In other words, in order to prevail, the government had to prove an important or a substantial governmental interest that is unrelated to suppression of expression and that restricts speech no more extensively than necessary to further its interest. The Court found substantial governmental interests (preservation of free local broadcasting, preservation of diverse information sources, and maintenance of fair competition in television programming).

In a later decision, the Court found that the rules directly advanced that interest because the cable industry had an interest in minimizing broadcasting's status as a competitor. The narrowly tailored requirement was satisfied because the number of broadcast signals being carried did not exceed the number of cable channels that were displaced. The Court concluded that the "must carry rules" did not implicate editorial freedom issues.

Problems with indecent programming have also arisen with regard to cable television. Congress responded to this problem in 1992 by enacting legislation requiring the FCC to implement indecency controls for leased access channels and public access channels. Under this law, cable television operators were (1) allowed to prohibit patently offensive programming from leased access channels; (2) required to segregate such programming on a single channel and block it or unblock it on the subscriber's written request; and (3) allowed to prohibit patently offensive programming from public, educational, and government access channels.

In *Denver Area Educational Telecommunications Consortium, Inc. v. Federal Communications Commission*,[270] the Court upheld the authority of cable operators to prohibit patently offensive programming on leased channels but struck down the block and segregate provisions and a prohibition on public, educational, and government access channels. A plurality of four justices applied strict scrutiny, found that the content restrictions for leased access channels were justified by a compelling state interest in protecting children, and was narrowly tailored. The plurality also suggested that cable operators had historically exercised editorial control over leased access channels. A majority of the Court struck down the segregate and block requirement on grounds it was not the least restrictive alternative. The blocking and unblocking requirement involved a 30-day notice from subscribers, and the Court concluded that this requirement imposed a planning burden on subscribers and exposed them to potential embarrassment if their names were disclosed. The Court suggested that blocking devices might serve the government's interest in protecting children without excessively burdening speech. In regard to the public access provision, the Court concluded that it did not represent the least restrictive alternative. A three-justice plurality concluded that public access channels typically are subject to more extensive self-policing controls. Unlike leased access channels that draw programming from a multiplicity of sources, public access channels typically are overseen by a government unit or entity that have mainstream orientations. The plurality also found that the public access provision, unlike the leased access provision, did not restore to cable operators any editorial rights they had possessed.

The *Denver Area Educational Telecommunications* decision reveals substantial disagreements between the justices regarding the standard of review for cable. Three justices (Thomas, Rehnquist, and Scalia) suggested that strict scrutiny should apply analogizing cable television to the print media. Four other justices (Breyer, O'Connor, Souter, and Stevens) resisted the analogy to the print media, and the application of strict scrutiny, and argued against applying a "a rigid single standard" that limits the Court's ability to address problems in "a new and changing environment."

At the same time that the Court has been unable to agree on the appropriate standard for evaluating content-based cable regulation, Congress has continued to enact laws containing content-based regulation, particularly with respect to indecency. For example, Congress has enacted legislation requiring cable and direct broadcast satellite operators to scramble audio and video signals carrying indecent programming on channels dedicated to sexually explicit programs. The law was designed to shield nonsubscribers from program bleed (where one channel is viewable on another) from sexually explicit channels, and prohibited broadcasters who refused to scramble from distributing their programming except between 10:00 P.M. and 6:00 A.M. In *United States v. Playboy Entertainment Group*,[271] the Court invalidated the law rejecting the government's argument that the law was needed to protect children. The Court applied strict scrutiny because the regulation was content based. Although the Court found a compelling state interest related to the protection of children, the Court found insufficient evidence that kids are likely to be exposed, and concluded that a less restrictive alternative existed in the ability of parents to block certain channels.

(4) Telecommunication

Telephones constitute one of the oldest electronic communication devices, and courts have recognized that this medium is entitled to First Amendment protection.

However, while telephone users are protected, the Court has refused to hold that providers of telephone service are protected. The latter have been treated as common carriers that are required to provide access to users on a nondiscriminatory basis. Since common carriers must provide access to anyone who can pay for the service, telephone providers were not historically regarded as having editorial discretion.

F   A   Q

Q: Does it make sense today to treat telecommunications as separate and distinct from cable, Internet services, or traditional media?

A: Probably not. After all, telephone companies no longer provide just telephone services, but commonly provide cable television and Internet services. As a result, it is increasingly difficult to separate telephone companies from other types of media companies.

As with other mediums, there has been litigation regarding the ability of government to regulate indecent or sexually explicit content of telephone services. In *Sable Broadcasting, Inc. v. Federal Communications Commission*,[272] the Court struck down a law that banned obscene communications and indecent dial-a-porn services. The Court distinguished broadcasting regulation from telephonic communications on the basis that they involved significantly different risks. Telephone communications are not as "uniquely pervasive" in that individuals must take affirmative steps to access the content. The Court applied strict scrutiny and concluded that the government's interest in protecting children was compelling, but concluded that the government had less restrictive alternatives available to it than a ban on indecent communications (for example, credit cards and access codes).

In recent years, even telephonic technology has been supplemented with the advent of text messaging. The Court has yet to rule on how this medium should be handled for First Amendment purposes.

(5) The Internet

Of course, the most dramatic technological advancement in recent decades is the Internet. The Internet's development has forced the Court to reassess its communications jurisprudence. Of course, the Internet did not develop in isolation but in conjunction with other forms of media already discussed, such as cable television and telecommunications. For example, most newspapers and magazines now offer most, if not all, of their content online. In addition, they use over-the-air signals, telephone lines, and satellite transmissions to transport content from editorial rooms to printing and distribution centers. These developments raise doubts regarding the continuing vitality of the medium-specific analysis that the Court has employed thus far.

Because of the pervasive nature and global impact of the Internet, Congress enacted the Communications Decency Act of 1996 (CDA) in an effort to protect children against the electronic media. The CDA prohibited the knowing dissemination of indecent messages to persons under the age of 18 and the knowing dissemination of "patently offensive" messages that would be available to persons under this age.

In *Reno v. American Civil Liberties Union*,[273] the Court was confronted by the question of whether the Internet should be treated like the print media (and therefore accorded a high level of protection), or like broadcasting (and therefore subject to greater regulatory restrictions), or whether some intermediate model of review should apply. The Court struck down portions of the CDA, concluding that the Internet should be treated more like the traditional print media. The Court found that the Internet was not analogous to broadcasting because a scarcity rationale did not apply. Unlike broadcasting, in which only a few broadcast spectrums are available, the Internet is almost universally accessible through personal computers. Individuals who cannot afford computers and Internet access can go online at libraries or cybercafes. Moreover, the Court noted a historical absence of governmental regulation, and lack of intrusiveness as with broadcasting (which is beamed into everyone's house and car over airwaves), and ultimately concluded that there was no justification for applying a diminished standard of review.

Applying strict scrutiny, the Court found a compelling governmental interest in the desire to protect children from exposure to indecent material. However, because the CDA could not be enforced against foreign sites and because age is difficult to verify, the Court concluded that the regulatory means were not designed to achieve that purpose. Moreover, the CDA imposed a significant burden on adult users by limiting their right to receive information unsuitable for children. The Court concluded that Congress could use less constitutionally restrictive means, including blocking or filtering software, to achieve its objectives. In addition, the Court held that the term *patently offensive* was unduly vague. Justice O'Connor would have upheld provisions of the legislation that prohibited knowing transmission, such as e-mails, of indecent materials to minors.

F   A   Q

Q: In *Pacifica*, the Court focused on the possibility that broadcasting could expose children to unsuitable content. Isn't there a similar problem with the Internet that might justify governmental regulation?

A: Absolutely. Indeed, in recent years, we have witnessed numerous examples of the potential impact of the Internet on children, particularly teenagers. However, unlike broadcasting, which can be "zoned" to particular hours of the day when children are less likely to be watching, the Internet is not as readily susceptible to time zoning. At any given moment of the day, it is "day" somewhere. Moreover, the Court was concerned that if Internet content could include only material that was suitable for children, adult content would be completely purged from the Internet.

Following the decision in *Reno*, Congress enacted the Child On Line Pornography Act (COPA), which was designed to limit children's exposure to indecent materials on the World Wide Web. COPA prohibited knowing communication for commercial purposes of any material that is harmful to minors. In *Ashcroft v.*

American Civil Liberties Union,[274] the Court addressed the question of whether COPA's use of the term *community standards* as the basis for determining whether material was harmful created a problem of substantial overbreadth. The Court concluded that because COPA applies to significantly less material than the CDA and defines harmful-to-minors by reference to well-established obscenity standards, the community standards provision was not overbroad. *Ashcroft v. American Civil Liberties Union* did not rule on whether COPA might be substantially overbroad or unconstitutionally vague, or whether it would survive strict scrutiny as the district court predicted once adjudication is complete.

In *Ashcroft v. Free Speech Coalition,*[275] the Court struck down the Child Pornography Prevention Act (CPPA), which prohibited the visual depiction, including computer or computer-generated images, of a minor engaged in sexually explicit conduct. In striking down the law, the Court emphasized that CPPA did not prohibit just images that appeal to a prurient interest or that are patently offensive, but also prohibited speech that had serious literary, artistic, political, or scientific value. The Court rejected the government's argument that the law was needed because pedophiles might use virtual child pornography to seduce children, noting that many innocent materials can be used for immoral purposes, including candy, video games, and cartoons, but those materials are not prohibited. In addition, the Court rejected the argument that virtual child pornography whets the appetites of pedophiles and encourages pedophilia, noting that speech cannot be banned merely for its bad tendency. Nor can speech within the rights of adults be silenced totally in an effort to protect children. The Court also rejected the argument that, because of production quality, allowing virtual child pornography makes it difficult to prosecute persons who use real children to produce pornography. The Court found that this argument "turned the First Amendment upside down" insofar as it would suppress lawful speech as a means of regulating unlawful speech.

SUMMARY

- Under the First Amendment, speech receives a high level of protection. However, courts do not treat First Amendment rights as absolute.

- Political speech receives the highest level of protection.

- Certain categories of speech (for example, obscenity, child pornography, and fighting words) are entitled to less protection, or no protection, under the First Amendment.

- Courts distinguish between governmental restrictions that target speech, and therefore are regarded as content based, and restrictions that only incidentally affect speech.

- Content-based restrictions on speech are regarded skeptically and subject to a higher standard of review. Courts are particularly inclined to strike down these types of restrictions.

- Noncontent-based restrictions on speech are subjected to a lower standard of review.

CONNECTIONS

Equal Protection Clause

A significant number of prominent free speech cases involve individuals who were protesting against segregation or racial oppression, and alleging violations of the Equal Protection Clause.

Establishment Clause

From time to time, government argues that it cannot accommodate religious speech without violating or transcending the First Amendment's prohibition against the establishment of religion.

Free Exercise of Religion

A number of free speech cases involve religious speech in which an individual is pursuing a First Amendment to freely exercise his or her religion.

Judicial Review

Courts frequently invoke judicial review to evaluate the constitutionality of laws or governmental actions that allegedly transcend the free speech provisions of the First Amendment.

Endnotes

1. John Milton, *Areopagitica* (1644).
2. Abrams v. United States, 250 U.S. 616, 630 (1919) (Holmes, J., dissenting).
3. United States v. Schwimmer, 279 U.S. 644, 654-655 (1929) (Holmes, J., dissenting).
4. U.S. Const., amend. I.
5. John Stuart Mill, *On Liberty* (1859).
6. Va. State Bd. of Pharmacy v. Va. Citizens Consumer Council, 425 U.S. 748, 763 (1976).
7. *E.g.*, Martin Redish, *Freedom of Expression: A Critical Analysis* (1984).
8. *E.g.*, Alexander Meiklejohn, *The First Amendment Is an Absolute*, 1961 Sup. Ct. Rev. 245.
9. *E.g.*, Vincent Blasi, *The Checking Value in First Amendment Theory*, 1977 A.B.A. Found. Res. J. 521.
10. *E.g.*, Whitney v. California, 274 U.S. 357 (1927) (Whitney, J., concurring).
11. Murdock v. Pennsylvania, 319 U.S. 105, 115 (1943).
12. Konigsberg v. State B. of Cal., 366 U.S. 36, 56 (1961) (Black, J., dissenting).
13. 376 U.S. 254 (1965).
14. 244 F. 535 (S.D.N.Y.), *rev'd*, 246 F.24 (2d Cir. 1917).
15. 249 U.S. 47 (1919).
16. 249 U.S. 204 (1919).
17. 249 U.S. 211 (1919).
18. 250 U.S. 616 (1919).
19. 268 U.S. 652 (1925).
20. 274 U.S. 357 (1927).
21. 299 U.S. 353 (1937).
22. 301 U.S. 242 (1937).
23. 304 U.S. 144 (1938).
24. 314 U.S. 252 (1941).
25. 341 U.S. 494 (1951) (plurality opinion).
26. 354 U.S. 298 (1957).
27. 367 U.S. 203 (1961).

28. 367 U.S. 290 (1961).
29. 385 U.S. 110 (1966).
30. 394 U.S. 705 (1969) (per curiam).
31. 395 U.S. 444 (1969).
32. 414 U.S. 105 (1973).
33. Police Dept. of Chicago v. Mosley, 408 U.S. 92, 95 (1972).
34. 315 U.S. 568 (1942).
35. R.A.V. v. City of St. Paul, 505 U.S. 377 (1992).
36. 343 U.S. 250 (1952).
37. 376 U.S. 254 (1964).
38. Barr v. Matteo, 360 U.S. 564 (1959).
39. Rosenblatt v. Baer, 383 U.S. 75, 85 (1966).
40. Monitor Patriot Co. v. Roy, 401 U.S. 265, 271 (1971).
41. Curtis Publishing Co. v. Butts, 388 U.S. 130, 164 (1967).
42. 388 U.S. 130 (1967).
43. 418 U.S. 323 (1974).
44. *Curtis Publishing*, 388 U.S. at 162.
45. 424 U.S. 448 (1976).
46. 443 U.S. 157 (1979).
47. 443 U.S. 111 (1979).
48. Gertz v. Robert Welch, Inc., 418 U.S. 323, 350 (1974).
49. 472 U.S. 749 (1985).
50. 485 U.S. 46 (1988).
51. 867 F.2d 1188 (9th Cir. 1988).
52. 277 U.S. 438 (1928).
53. 420 U.S. 469 (1975).
54. 435 U.S. 829 (1978).
55. 443 U.S. 97 (1979).
56. 491 U.S. 524 (1989).
57. 532 U.S. 514 (2002).
58. 385 U.S. 374 (1967).
59. 433 U.S. 562 (1977).
60. Chaplinsky v. New Hampshire, 315 U.S. 568, 572 (1942).
61. 354 U.S. 476 (1957).
62. 354 U.S. 476 (1957).
63. Jacobellis v. Ohio, 378 U.S. 184 (1964).
64. 383 U.S. 413 (1966).
65. 383 U.S. 463 (1966).
66. 413 U.S. 15 (1973).
67. Hamling v. United States, 418 U.S. 87 (1974).
68. Smith v. United States, 431 U.S. 291 (1977).
69. 418 U.S. 153 (1974).
70. 481 U.S. 497 (1987).
71. 394 U.S. 557 (1969).
72. 413 U.S. 49 (1973).
73. 475 U.S. 41 (1986).
74. 528 U.S. 962 (2000).
75. *City of Renton*, 475 U.S. at 51.
76. 529 U.S. 277 (2000).
77. 403 U.S. 15, 16-17 (1971).
78. 405 U.S. 518 (1974).
79. 415 U.S. 130 (1974).
80. 414 U.S. 105 (1973).
81. 438 U.S. 726 (1978).
82. 524 U.S. 569 (1998).
83. 422 U.S. 205 (1975).
84. 458 U.S. 747 (1982).
85. 495 U.S. 103 (1990).
86. 394 U.S. 557 (1969).
87. 535 U.S. 234 (2002).
88. *See* Andrea Dworkin, *Against the Male Flood: Censorship, Pornography and Equality*, 8 Harv. Women's L.J. 1 (1985); Catherine MacKinnon, *Pornography, Civil Rights and Speech*, 20 Harv. C.R.-C.L. L. Rev. 1 (1985).
89. Catharine A. MacKinnon, *Pornography, Civil Rights, and Speech*, 20 Harv. C.R.-C.L. L. Rev. 1, 21 (1985).
90. 771 F.2d 323 (7th Cir. 1985).

91. 343 U.S. 250 (1952).
92. 505 U.S. 377 (1992).
93. 503 U.S. 159 (1992).
94. 508 U.S. 476 (1993).
95. 538 U.S. 343 (2003).
96. 290 F.3d 1058 (9th Cir. 2002) (en banc).
97. *See* Planned Parenthood of Columbia/Willamette, Inc. v. Am. Coalition of Life Activists, 422 F.3d 949 (9th Cir. 2005).
98. Va. State Bd. of Pharmacy v. Va. Citizens Consumer Council, Inc., 425 U.S. 748 (1976).
99. Cent. Hudson Gas & Elec. Co. v. Pub. Serv. Commn., 447 U.S. 557 (1980).
100. 316 U.S. 52 (1942).
101. 376 U.S. 254 (1964).
102. 421 U.S. 809 (1975).
103. 425 U.S. 748 (1976).
104. 447 U.S. 557 (1980).
105. 478 U.S. 328 (1986).
106. 514 U.S. 476 (1995).
107. 517 U.S. 484 (1996).
108. 533 U.S. 525 (2002).
109. 535 U.S. 357 (2002).
110. 433 U.S. 350 (1977).
111. 436 U.S. 447 (1978).
112. 436 U.S. 412 (1978).
113. 507 U.S. 761 (1993).
114. 127 S. Ct. 2489 (2007).
115. 455 U.S. 191 (1982).
116. 496 U.S. 91 (1991).
117. 471 U.S. 626 (1981).
118. Gooding v. Wilson, 405 U.S. 518, 520-521 (1972).
119. 482 U.S. 569 (1987).
120. 458 U.S. 747 (1982).
121. 405 U.S. 518 (1972).
122. 413 U.S. 601, 610 (1973).
123. *Ferber*, 458 U.S. at 773.
124. 269 U.S. 385, 391 (1926).
125. Grayned v. City of Rockford, 408 U.S. 104, 108-109 (1972).
126. *Id.*
127. 402 U.S. 611 (1971).
128. Bantam Books, Inc. v. Sullivan, 372 U.S. 58, 70 (1962).
129. 303 U.S. 444 (1938).
130. 354 U.S. 436 (1957).
131. 365 U.S. 43 (1961).
132. 380 U.S. 51 (1965).
133. 372 U.S. 58 (1963).
134. *See* Cox v. New Hampshire, 312 U.S. 569 (1941).
135. 486 U.S. 750 (1988).
136. 283 U.S. 697 (1931).
137. 403 U.S. 713 (1971).
138. 467 F. Supp. 990 (W.D. Wis. 1979).
139. 544 U.S. 734 (2005).
140. 512 U.S. 753 (1994).
141. 391 U.S. 367 (1968).
142. 496 U.S. 310 (1990).
143. 491 U.S. 397 (1989).
144. 167 U.S. 43 (1897).
145. 307 U.S. 496 (1939).
146. 308 U.S. 147 (1939).
147. 372 U.S. 229 (1963).
148. 379 U.S. 559 (1965).
149. 383 U.S. 131 (1966).
150. 408 U.S. 92 (1972).
151. 447 U.S. 555 (1993).
152. 487 U.S. 474 (1988).
153. 334 U.S. 558 (1948).
154. 491 U.S. 781 (1989).
155. 466 U.S. 789 (1984).

156. Perry Educ. Assn. v. Perry Local Educators' Assn., 460 U.S. 37, 45 (1983).
157. 452 U.S. 640 (1981).
158. Adderley v. Florida, 385 U.S. 39 (1966).
159. 424 U.S. 828 (1976).
160. 460 U.S. 37 (1983).
161. 453 U.S. 114 (1981).
162. 466 U.S. 789 (1984).
163. 505 U.S. 672 (1992).
164. 539 U.S. 194 (2003).
165. 326 U.S. 501 (1946).
166. 391 U.S. 308 (1968).
167. 424 U.S. 507 (1976).
168. 447 U.S. 74 (1980).
169. 454 U.S. 263 (1981).
170. 508 U.S. 384 (1993).
171. 515 U.S. 919 (1995).
172. 533 U.S. 98 (2001).
173. 424 U.S. 1 (1976).
174. 494 U.S. 652 (1990).
175. 479 U.S. 238 (1986).
176. 435 U.S. 765 (1978).
177. 470 U.S. 480 (1985).
178. 459 U.S. 197 (1982).
179. 540 U.S. 93 (2003).
180. 539 U.S. 146 (2003).
181. 479 U.S. 238 (1986).
182. *McConnell*, 540 U.S. at 210. MFCL found that there were three characteristics of such corporations: "*First*, it was formed for the express purpose of promoting political ideas, and cannot
engage in business activities [so that] requests for contributions that will be used for political
purposes [reflect] political support. *Second*, it has no shareholders or other persons affiliated
[who] have a claim on its assets or earnings. . . . *Third*, [it] was not established by a business
corporation or a labor union, and it is its policy not to accept contributions from such entities
[so that the organization is not a conduit for] the type of direct spending that creates a threat to
the political marketplace."
183. 548 U.S. 230 (2006).
184. 424 U.S. 1 (1976) (per curiam).
185. 127 S. Ct. 2652 (2007).
186. 357 U.S. 449 (1958).
187. 360 U.S. 109 (1959).
188. 458 U.S. 886 (1982).
189. 468 U.S. 600 (1984).
190. 487 U.S. 1 (1988).
191. 530 U.S. 640 (2000).
192. 520 U.S. 351 (1997).
193. 544 U.S. 581 (2005).
194. 319 U.S. 624 (1943).
195. 430 U.S. 705 (1977).
196. 547 U.S. 47 (2006).
197. 515 U.S. 557 (1995).
198. 431 U.S. 209 (1977).
199. 496 U.S. 1 (1990).
200. 529 U.S. 217 (2000).
201. 521 U.S. 457 (1997).
202. 533 U.S. 405 (2001).
203. 127 S. Ct. 2372 (2007).
204. 544 U.S. 550 (2005).
205. 468 U.S. 364 (1984).
206. 500 U.S. 173 (1991).
207. 515 U.S. 819 (1995).
208. 531 U.S. 533 (2001).
209. 547 U.S. 47 (2006).
210. 330 U.S. 75 (1947).
211. 413 U.S. 548 (1973).
212. 513 U.S. 454 (1995).
213. 344 U.S. 183 (1952).
214. 391 U.S. 563 (1968).

215. 461 U.S. 138 (1983).
216. 483 U.S. 378 (1987).
217. 429 U.S. 274 (1977).
218. 543 U.S. 77 (2004).
219. 547 U.S. 410 (2006).
220. 344 U.S. 183 (1952).
221. 385 U.S. 589 (1967).
222. 389 U.S. 258 (1967).
223. 367 U.S. 1 (1961).
224. 427 U.S. 347 (1976).
225. 445 U.S. 507 (1980).
226. 497 U.S. 62 (1990).
227. 465 U.S. 271 (1984).
228. 393 U.S. 503 (1969).
229. 478 U.S. 675 (1986).
230. 127 S. Ct. 2618 (2007).
231. 484 U.S. 260 (1988).
232. 457 U.S. 853 (1982).
233. 500 U.S. 173 (1991).
234. 524 U.S. 569 (1998).
235. 531 U.S. 533 (2001).
236. Potter Stewart, *Of the Press*, 26 Hastings L.J. 631, 633-634 (1975).
237. First Natl. Bank of Boston v. Bellotti, 435 U.S. 765, 801-802 (1978) (Burger, C.J., concurring).
238. Branzburg v. Hayes, 408 U.S. 665, 704 (1972).
239. 408 U.S. 665 (1972).
240. 397 F.3d 964 (D.C. Cir. 2005).
241. 501 U.S. 663 (1991).
242. 436 U.S. 547 (1978).
243. Branzburg v. Hayes, 408 U.S. 665 (1972).
244. 417 U.S. 817 (1974).
245. 417 U.S. 843 (1974).
246. 438 U.S. 1 (1978).
247. 448 U.S. 555 (1980).
248. 457 U.S. 596 (1982).
249. 464 U.S. 501 (1984).
250. 467 U.S. 39 (1984).
251. 478 U.S. 1 (1986).
252. 384 U.S. 333 (1966).
253. 427 U.S. 539 (1976).
254. 366 U.S. 717 (1961).
255. 373 U.S. 723 (1963).
256. 381 U.S. 532 (1965).
257. 449 U.S. 560 (1981).
258. 236 U.S. 230 (1915).
259. Joseph Burstyn, Inc. v. Wilson, 343 U.S. 495 (1952); United States v. Paramount Pictures, Inc., 334 U.S. 131 (1948).
260. 343 U.S. 495 (1952).
261. 418 U.S. 241 (1974).
262. 438 U.S. 726 (1978).
263. 395 U.S. 367 (1969).
264. 412 U.S. 94 (1973).
265. 468 U.S. 364 (1984).
266. 438 U.S. 726 (1978).
267. *E.g.*, Cohen v. California, 403 U.S. 15 (1971).
268. 512 U.S. 622 (1994).
269. 391 U.S. 367 (1968).
270. 518 U.S. 727 (1996).
271. 529 U.S. 803 (2000).
272. 492 U.S. 115 (1989).
273. 521 U.S. 844 (1997).
274. 535 U.S. 234 (2002).
275. 535 U.S. 234 (2002).

The Establishment Clause 11

The meaning of the First Amendment's Establishment Clause — "Congress shall make no
law respecting an establishment of religion" —

has generated much debate and controversy. Most commentators agree that the
Framers sought to prohibit certain governmental activities that had been commonplace
in Europe: the establishment of a governmentally endorsed church, laws requiring
individuals to go to or remain away from church against their will, and laws forcing
individuals to believe or disbelieve a particular religion. Few, if any, Establishment
Clause cases, however, involve prohibitions of this nature since the federal government
has never attempted to declare a national religion, to require individuals to go to
church, or to prohibit them from possessing particular religious beliefs. As a result,
most Establishment Clause cases focus on whether certain other governmental activities, such as providing financial aid to religious schools or posting the Ten Comman-
ments in public places, constitute an establishment of religion. Because such
governmental activities do not fit squarely within the terms of the First Amendment,
courts have struggled to define the Establishment Clause's meaning on a case-by-case
basis.

A. FINANCIAL AID TO RELIGION

B. SCHOOL VOUCHERS

C. STATE-SPONSORED PRAYER

D. SCHOOL CURRICULA

E. OFFICIAL ACKNOWLEDGMENT OF RELIGION

   1. The Ten Commandments
   2. Church Vetoes
   3. Holiday Displays

F. ESTABLISHMENT-FREE EXERCISE AND FREE SPEECH TENSION

G. SPEECH AND RELIGION

A. Financial Aid to Religion

A number of Establishment Clause cases focus on whether the government may provide financial aid to religious organizations such as churches or schools. A common theme in these cases is the inherent tug and pull between the Establishment Clause and the Free Exercise Clause: While the government may wish to accommodate religion and religious beliefs in the sense of creating a situation that allows individuals to more freely observe their religious beliefs, it has generally sought to avoid financial arrangements that entangle the state with religion.

Illustrative of the tension is the holding in *Everson v. Board of Education*.[1] In that case, a New Jersey board of education decided to reimburse parents for money spent to transport their children to school on public buses. When the reimbursements were given to parents who sent their children to Catholic parochial schools, which provided both a secular education and religious instruction regarding the tenets of the Catholic faith, the disbursements were challenged as an establishment of religion. The Court recognized the tensions noted above. As a result, while the Court was concerned about allowing New Jersey to use tax-raised funds to support an institution that "teaches the tenets and faith of any church," the Court also recognized that the state should not hamper citizens in the free exercise of their religion and should not prohibit members of any faith, "*because of their faith, or lack of it*, from receiving the benefits of public welfare legislation."

After weighing these competing interests, the Court upheld the law, emphasizing that New Jersey had created a general program under which it paid the bus fares of pupils attending public and other schools. While the Court recognized that the subsidies might help some students attend parochial schools who might otherwise not be able to do so, the Court also pointed out that parents might not send their children to parochial schools if they were cut off from "such general government services as ordinary police and fire protection, connections for sewage disposal, public highways and sidewalks." The Court concluded that the Establishment Clause did not require the state to cut schools off from such benefits. On the contrary, the Establishment Clause "requires the state to be neutral in its relations with groups of religious believers and non-believers. . . . State power is no more to be used so as to handicap religions, than it is to favor them." Recognizing that parents could choose whether to send their children to religious schools or public schools, the Court upheld the subsidies, noting that the "State contributes no money to the schools. It does not support them. Its legislation [does] no more than provide a general program to help parents get their children, regardless of their religion, safely and expeditiously to and from accredited schools." Justice Black ended with a rhetorical flourish: "The First Amendment has erected a *wall between church and state*.

That wall must be kept high and impregnable. We could not approve the slightest breach. New Jersey has not breached it here."

F   A   Q

Q: Isn't a bus subsidy a long ways away from a governmentally mandated religion?

A: Perhaps. However, one of the concerns that underlay the Establishment Clause was the notion that individuals could be taxed (against their will) to support religions to which they do not belong and do not wish to support. Bus subsidies involve the use of tax money to support religious education and therefore fit within the larger concerns that motivated the colonists to demand protections against the establishment of religions. Moreover, there is a potential slippery slope problem. If government can pay for bus transportation, can it also pay for books, teachers, and buildings at parochial schools?

Justice Jackson dissented in *Everson*, noting that the law reimbursed students who rode buses to parochial schools, but not students who rode buses to other private schools. Justice Rutledge also dissented, stating his belief that the "First Amendment's purpose was not to strike merely at the official establishment of a single sect, creed or religion. [I]t was to uproot all such relationships. . . . It was to create a complete and permanent separation of the spheres of religious activity and civil authority by comprehensively forbidding every form of public aid or support for religion. . . ." He also expressed concern that such support would create divisiveness among religious groups as they competed for public funds.

As in *Everson*, other early decisions focused on whether financial aid was "neutrally" available. In other words, is the aid available equally to all individuals regardless of their religious beliefs? Although some commentators have expressed support for the idea of construing the religion clauses under a "neutrality" standard,[2] the breadth of such a standard is troubling. As a dissenting Justice Jackson recognized in *Everson*, a neutrality standard might justify providing broad-based public support for religious schools.[3] Professor Douglas Laycock notes that a neutrality standard might produce unacceptable results.[4] For example, during Prohibition, Congress created an exception for religious uses of alcohol that would be unacceptable under a neutrality standard because the use of alcohol

Sidebar

A "WALL" BETWEEN CHURCH AND STATE

Justice Black's metaphor regarding a wall between church and state has been widely discussed and restated. In *Everson*, for example, Justice Rutledge referred to it in his dissent: "Neither so high nor so impregnable today as yesterday is the wall raised between church and state by Virginia's great statute of religious freedom and the First Amendment." A number of other justices have questioned whether the Establishment Clause really was intended to create a "wall of separation."

would be prohibited during the Eucharist or the Seder. Professor Laycock argues that such a law, "enacted largely at the behest of Protestants that barred the sacred rites of Catholics and Jews, a law that changed the way these rites had been performed for millennia, could not be reconciled with any concept of religious liberty worthy of the name." He also argues that a neutrality standard could be used to justify providing large amounts of "unrestricted aid to religious schools, so long as the aid goes to all schools and not to religious schools alone." Indeed, any "aid to secular private schools *must* be given to religious schools, on exactly the same terms. To exclude religious schools from the aid program, or to impose restrictions on religious uses of the money, would be to classify on the basis of religion. That would violate *formal neutrality*." As we shall see, despite these criticisms, the neutrality test has been invoked by a plurality of the Court in at least one recent decision.

Since 1971, the Court has frequently analyzed Establishment Clause cases using the so-called *Lemon* test. That test, articulated in *Lemon v. Kurtzman*,[5] established a three-prong test for evaluating the validity of Establishment Clause issues:

> First, the statute must have a *secular legislative purpose* (in other words, the purpose must not be designed to enhance or promote religion); second, its principal or *primary effect* must be one that neither advances nor inhibits religion; finally, the statute must not foster "an *excessive government entanglement with religion*" (emphasis added).

Lemon itself involved a Rhode Island law that authorized state officials to supplement the salaries of teachers of secular subjects in private schools by paying the teachers an amount not exceeding 15 percent of their annual salaries. The act required that the assisted private schoolteachers teach only those subjects offered in the public schools and use only teaching materials used in the public schools. Also at issue in *Lemon* was Pennsylvania's Nonpublic Elementary and Secondary Education Act, which authorized direct payments to nonpublic schools for the actual cost of teachers' salaries, textbooks, and instructional materials. However, secular costs were required to be segregated from religious costs, and monies could be spent for courses only in mathematics, modern foreign languages, physical science, and physical education using state-provided textbooks and instructional materials. In addition, the courses had to be free of religious teaching, instruction in morals, or forms of worship.

The Court applied the three-part test and concluded that the Rhode Island and Pennsylvania laws failed the third prong of the test concerning entanglement. In considering the third prong, the Court reiterated Justice Black's metaphor regarding a wall between church and state. While Chief Justice Burger noted that a total separation between church and state is impossible, and that some links were inevitable (for example, fire inspections, building and zoning regulations, and state requirements under compulsory school-attendance laws), the "line of separation, far from being a 'wall,' is a blurred, indistinct, and variable barrier depending on all the circumstances of a particular relationship." In finding that both laws created excessive entanglement, the Court emphasized that teachers could choose to infuse religion into their courses and "that a dedicated religious person, teaching in a school affiliated with his or her faith and operated to inculcate its tenets, [will] experience great difficulty [remaining] religiously neutral." To ensure that the teacher acts properly, the state will need to engage in a "comprehensive, discriminating, and continuing state surveillance."

The Court also emphasized the tendency of both the Rhode Island and Pennsylvania programs to create "political divisiveness":

> Partisans of parochial schools, understandably concerned with rising costs and sincerely dedicated to both the religious and secular educational missions of their schools, will

inevitably [promote] political action to achieve their goals. Those who oppose state aid, whether for constitutional, religious, or fiscal reasons, will inevitably respond and employ all of the usual political campaign techniques to prevail. Candidates will be forced to declare and voters to choose. [M]any people confronted with issues of this kind will find their votes aligned with their faith.

While the opinion recognized that "political debate and division" are generally regarded as "normal and healthy manifestations of our democratic system of government," Chief Justice Burger believed that "political division along religious lines was one of the principal evils against which the First Amendment was intended to protect."

Justice Douglas, joined by Justice Black, concurred, expressing concern that governmental funding of parochial schools might lead to government meddling in parochial school affairs. He also argued that parochial schools are "organic whole[s] [living] on one budget" so that if taxpayers subsidize secular education, the schools are free to spend more on religious training. Justice Brennan also concurred, arguing that "direct subsidies of tax monies to the schools themselves and [the] secular education those schools provide goes hand in hand with the religious mission that is the only reason for the schools' existence." Justice White dissented: "[It] is enough for me that the States and the Federal Government are financing a separable secular function of overriding importance in order to sustain the legislation here challenged. [There] is no specific allegation [that] sectarian teaching does or would invade secular classes supported by state funds."

The *Lemon* test has been applied in an array of contexts involving financial aid to parochial schools, but the results have not always been consistent. For example, in *Board of Education v. Allen*,[6] the Court held that a state could loan textbooks to parochial schools, for the teaching of secular subjects, when the books were selected by (and were the same ones used in) the public schools. However, in *Meek v. Pittenger*[7] and *Wolman v. Walter*,[8] the Court held that a state could not loan "instructional material and equipment" (in this case, maps, charts, periodicals, photographs, sound recordings, films, and laboratory equipment) to parochial schools because such aid would have the impermissible effect of advancing religion by aiding "the sectarian school enterprise as a whole."

Other Examples: Likewise, although *Wolman* held that a state could pay for standardized testing in parochial schools, as well as for the scoring of those tests, provided the tests were the same ones used in the public schools and that nonpublic employees were not involved in the preparation or grading of the tests, *Levitt v. Committee for Public Education*[9] held that a state could not reimburse parochial schools for administering teacher-prepared tests because there were "no means to assure that the tests [were] free of religious instruction." In *Meek*, the Court struck down a law providing "auxiliary services" (remedial and accelerated instruction, guidance counseling and testing, speech and hearing services) directly to nonpublic school children with special needs, noting that excessive surveillance, entanglement, and political divisiveness would result. *Wolman* did hold that a state could provide speech and hearing diagnostic services and diagnostic psychological services to pupils attending nonpublic schools on the basis that such services have "little or no educational content and are not closely associated with the educational mission of the nonpublic school." In *Wolman*, the Court also upheld a statute that used state employees to provide therapeutic, guidance, and remedial services for students who had been identified as having a need for specialized attention. Finally, *Wolman* struck down a statute providing for state funding for student field trips "to governmental, industrial, cultural, and scientific centers designed to enrich the secular studies of students," finding "impermissible direct aid to sectarian education" and expressing concern about the need for "close supervision [and] excessive entanglement." In *Committee for Public Education & Religious Liberty v. Nyquist*,[10] the Court struck down a New York law that provided money grants to "qualifying" nonpublic schools for the "maintenance and repair [of] school facilities and equipment to ensure the health, welfare and safety of enrolled pupils" because those buildings were not reserved exclusively for secular purposes.

F A Q

Q: Can it be argued that the states should be allowed to provide books and teachers to parochial school students?

A: Unquestionably, the state has an interest in ensuring that individuals are educated so that they can be functioning and contributing members of society. At the same time, government may not be permitted to finance religious indoctrination. The concern with teachers and books is that parochial schools may use even secular subjects to indoctrinate religious beliefs. A teacher might begin a math class with a prayer, for example, or use a math book to teach counting through depictions of rosaries.

Some post-*Lemon* decisions dealt with governmental aid to higher education. For example, in *Tilton v. Richardson*,[11] the Court upheld a federal law that provided construction grants to religious colleges for buildings and facilities used for secular educational purposes. The Court concluded that college students "are less impressionable and less susceptible to religious indoctrination," and many "church-related colleges and universities are characterized by a high degree of academic freedom and seek to evoke free and critical responses" and not primarily concerned with religious indoctrination. In *Hunt v. McNair*,[12] the Court upheld a statute authorizing issuance of revenue bonds for the benefit of a Baptist college because the purpose was secular (education), and the Court found less chance of religious indoctrination. Likewise, in *Roemer v. Board of Public Works*,[13] the Court upheld a Maryland law that provided annual grants to private colleges subject to the restriction that the funds not be used for "sectarian purposes."

Not only has *Lemon* produced inconsistent results, but some justices have questioned whether the test is a sound one. In a dissenting opinion in *Wallace v. Jaffree*,[14] Justice Rehnquist argued that the *Lemon* test has not provided "adequate standards for deciding Establishment Clause cases" and has therefore produced inconsistent results. Likewise, in a concurring opinion in *Lamb's Chapel v. Center Moriches Union Free School District*,[15] Justice Scalia argued:

> Like some ghoul in a late-night horror movie that repeatedly sits up in its grave and shuffles abroad, after being repeatedly killed and buried, *Lemon* stalks our Establishment Clause jurisprudence once again. . . . [No] fewer than five of the currently sitting Justices have, in their own opinions, personally driven pencils through the creature's heart (the author of today's opinion repeatedly), and a sixth has joined an opinion doing so. The secret of the *Lemon* test's survival, I think, is that it is so easy to kill. It is there to scare us (and our audience) when we wish it to do so, but we can command it to return to the tomb at will. When we wish to strike down a practice it forbids, we invoke it, when we wish to uphold a practice it forbids, we ignore it entirely. Sometimes, we take a middle course, calling its three prongs "no more than helpful signposts." Such a docile and useful monster is worth keeping around, at least in a somnolent state; one never knows when one might need him.

In her concurring opinion in *Board of Education of Kiryas Joel Village School District v. Grumet*,[16] Justice O'Connor offered the following observations:

> It is always appealing to look for a single test, a Grand Unified Theory that would resolve all the cases that may arise under a particular Clause. There is, after all, only one Establishment Clause. [But this] may sometimes do more harm than good. . . . Shoehorning new problems into a test that does not reflect the special concerns raised by those problems tends to deform the language of the test. Relatively simple phrases like "primary effect [that] neither advances nor inhibits religion" and "'entanglement,'" acquire more and more complicated definitions which stray ever further from their literal meaning. . . . I think it is more useful to recognize the relevant concerns in each case on their own terms, rather than trying to squeeze them into language that does not really apply to them.

As more and more justices expressed discontent with *Lemon*'s three-part test, it became clear that the Court was searching for a new test. But the Court has struggled to reach consensus. For example, in *Agostini v. Felton*,[17] in an opinion by Justice O'Connor, the Court seemed to map out a new approach to Establishment Clause issues. The petitioners in that case sought relief from the Court's prior decision in *Aguilar v. Felton*[18] on the basis that *Aguilar* was not consistent with the Court's subsequent Establishment Clause jurisprudence and asked the Court to explicitly recognize that *Aguilar* was no longer good law. Petitioners relied on the statements of five justices in *Board of Education of Kiryas Joel Village School District v. Grumet*.[19] In *Agostini*, the Court agreed and seemed to chart a new direction for the Court's Establishment Clause jurisprudence.

Aguilar had held that the Establishment Clause barred the City of New York from sending public schoolteachers to parochial schools to provide remedial education to disadvantaged children. Board of Education rules provided that only public employees could serve as Title I instructors and counselors, and teachers were assigned to private schools on a voluntary basis and without regard to their religious affiliations or the wishes of the private school. In addition, the Board informed its Title I employees that (i) they were employees of the Board and accountable only to their public school supervisors; (ii) they had exclusive responsibility for selecting students for the Title I program and could teach only those children who met the eligibility criteria for Title I; (iii) their materials and equipment would be used only in the Title I program;

(iv) they could not engage in team-teaching or other cooperative instructional activities with private schoolteachers; and (v) they could not introduce any religious matter into their teaching or become involved in any way with the religious activities of the private schools. In striking down the program, the Court concluded that it created an "excessive entanglement" between church and state to the extent that it provided for teaching on the premises of sectarian schools. Following the decision, the Board modified its Title I program to revert to its prior practice of providing instruction at public school sites, at leased sites, and in mobile instructional units (essentially vans converted into classrooms) parked near the sectarian school. In the following ten years, the Board spent more than $100 million leasing sites and mobile instructional units and transporting students to those sites.

In *Agostini*, the Court also discussed its decision in *School District of Grand Rapids v. Ball*,[20] which was originally decided as a companion case to *Aguilar*. *Ball* involved two programs implemented by the school district of Grand Rapids, Michigan. The Shared Time program provided remedial and "enrichment" classes at public expense to students attending nonpublic schools. The classes were taught during regular school hours by publicly employed teachers, using materials purchased with public funds, on the premises of nonpublic schools. In *Ball*, the Court applied the *Lemon* test to the Shared Time program and concluded that it had the impermissible effect of advancing religion because

> (i) any public employee who works on the premises of a religious school is presumed to inculcate religion in her work; (ii) the presence of public employees on private school premises creates a symbolic union between church and state; and (iii) any and all public aid that directly aids the educational function of religious schools impermissibly finances religious indoctrination, even if the aid reaches such schools as a consequence of private decisionmaking.

Agostini overruled both *Aguilar* and *Ball* and held that the Court's "more recent cases" had in fact undermined the assumptions on which *Ball* and *Aguilar* had relied. The Court stated that it would continue to apply the first prong of the *Lemon* test (the purpose prong), but that its approach to the effect prong had changed because the Court abandoned its presumption that "the placement of public employees on parochial school grounds inevitably results in the impermissible effect of state-sponsored indoctrination or constitutes a symbolic union between government and religion." The Court was more willing to assume that program participants would dutifully discharge their responsibilities. In addition, the Court rejected the idea that any "government aid that directly aids the educational function of religious schools is invalid." Relying on its holding in *Witters v. Washington Department of Services for Blind*,[21] the Court held that the Establishment Clause did not prohibit a state from providing a tuition grant to a blind person who attended a Christian college to study to be a pastor, missionary, or youth director. The Court noted that the grants were made available on a nonsectarian basis and were paid to the recipients, who then chose to convey the money to the institution. As a result, the moneys were conveyed to the institutions as a result of private decision making and therefore could not be attributed to the state. Because of its shift in approach, the Court refused to assume that the Shared Time program (*Ball*) and New York City's Title I program (*Aguilar*) would have the effect of advancing religion through indoctrination. The Court found that there was "no reason to presume that, simply because she enters a parochial school classroom, a full-time public employee [will] depart from her assigned duties and instructions and embark on religious indoctrination." The Court also found that, simply because Title I teachers enter parochial school classrooms, there is no reason to assume that it will "create the impression of a 'symbolic union' between church and state."

The Court then altered its approach to the third *Lemon* prong, the "excessive entanglement" prong. In *Aguilar*, the Court based its finding of excessive entanglement on the need to monitor to ensure that Title I employees did not inculcate religion, the need for cooperation between public and religious officials to carry out the monitoring, and the concern that the program would create political divisiveness. *Agostini* held that the last two factors were "insufficient by themselves to create an 'excessive' entanglement." The Court rejected the excessive entanglement concern as well because it was unwilling to presume that "public employees will inculcate religion simply because they happen to be in a sectarian environment," and therefore it was unwilling to conclude that pervasive monitoring was required. The Court found that unannounced monthly visits of program supervisors would be sufficient to prevent Title I employees from engaging in inculcation of religion. As a result, the Court overruled both *Ball* and *Aguilar*. Justice Souter dissented in part, arguing that the New York program could be regarded as an "endorsement" of religion. He also expressed concern about the potentially broad nature of the Court's ruling. If the state could provide remedial education to parochial school students, then it might be able to "assume [the] entire cost of instruction [in any] secular subject in any religious school."

F   A   Q

Q: If the government can pay for remedial education to be conducted on-site at parochial schools, might it also pay for the teaching of secular subjects such as math on-site?

A: The ramifications of *Agostini's* holding are not entirely clear. However, it can be argued that the decision clears the way for greater aid to parochial schools. Much depends on the way the aid is structured. For example, if the government decides to send public schoolteachers to teach math in parochial schools, the Court might uphold the program. Unlike prior decisions, in which the Court assumed that pervasive monitoring was required, *Agostini* is unwilling to assume that monitoring and entanglement are necessary and inevitable. Moreover, *Agostini* was unwilling to assume that governmental aid for secular purposes would advance the overall religious mission.

Just as the Court seemed to be coalescing around *Agostini*'s modification of the *Lemon* test, the Court decided *Mitchell v. Helms*.[22] That plurality decision revived the concept of neutrality, and overruled one prior decision and part of another decision (*Meek* and *Wolman*). The case involved a law that provided federal funds "for the acquisition and use of instructional and educational materials, including library services and materials (including media materials), assessments, reference materials, computer software and hardware for instructional use, and other curricular materials." The funds could be used to "supplement," but could not supplant, funds from nonfederal sources. The "services, materials, and equipment" provided to private schools must be "secular, neutral, and nonideological," and private schools could not acquire control of them. In upholding the law, the plurality overruled *Meek* and *Wolman* and adopted the **neutrality principle**: "[I]f the government, seeking to further some legitimate secular purpose, offers aid on the same terms, without regard to religion, to all who adequately further that purpose, then it is fair to say that any aid going to a religious recipient only has the effect of furthering that secular purpose." The Court also noted that the program did not define "recipients by reference to religion." The plurality opinion also rejected any distinction between direct and indirect aid to religion.

In rendering its decision, the plurality abandoned several distinctions made in prior cases. First, the Court rejected the argument that any aid to religious schools must not be divertible to religious use: "[So] long as the governmental aid is not itself 'unsuitable [because] of religious content,' and eligibility for aid is determined in a constitutionally permissible manner, any use of that aid to indoctrinate cannot be attributed to the government and is thus not of constitutional concern." Second, the Court held that a school could receive aid even though the school was "pervasively sectarian": "[T]here was a period when this factor mattered. . . . But that period is one that the Court should regret. . . . The pervasively sectarian recipient has not received any special favor, and it [is] bizarre that the Court would [reserve] special hostility for those who take their religion seriously."

Mitchell produced several concurrences and dissents. Justice O'Connor concurred, arguing that the neutrality test involved a significant departure from precedent. She would have struck down any program in which aid "actually is, or has been, used for religious purposes." Justice Souter, joined by Justices Stevens and Ginsburg, dissented, arguing that the plurality had broken "fundamentally" with the Court's Establishment Clause jurisprudence. If the Court focused only on neutrality, or even-handedness, "religious schools could be blessed with government funding as massive as expenditures made for the benefit of their public school counterparts, and religious missions would thrive on public money." He also argued that this aid "was highly susceptible to unconstitutional use" because there were no safeguards to prevent diversion to religious uses.

THE POTENTIAL RAMIFICATIONS OF A NEUTRALITY TEST

Of course, one of the concerns with a neutrality test is that it might be used to justify broad-based support for religious institutions, provided that such aid is made available on a neutral basis. Indeed, as Professor Douglas Laycock has argued, such financial support might be constitutionally required. *See* Douglas Laycock, *Formal, Substantive and Disaggregated Neutrality Toward Religion*, 39 DePaul L. Rev. 993 (1990).

The decisions in *Agostini* and *Mitchell* have raised questions regarding the continuing vitality of a number of cases decided under the *Lemon* three-part test. Under *Mitchell*'s neutrality test, and even under *Agostini*'s modified three-part test, one can justify far more support to parochial schools. As a result, the following decisions have been drawn into question: *Levitt v. Committee for Public Education*, which struck down a law that provided reimbursement to church-sponsored schools for the expense of teacher-prepared testing; *Wolman*, which held that a state could not pay for student field trips without impermissibly providing direct aid to sectarian education and creating the potential for excessive entanglement; and *Committee for Public Education & Religious Liberty v. Nyquist*, which held that New York may not provide direct money grants to nonpublic schools for the maintenance and repair of parochial schools. Indeed, some commentators have argued that many of these types of support should be permitted under the Court's Establishment Clause jurisprudence. For example, Professor Jesse Choper once argued that "governmental financial aid may be extended directly or indirectly to support parochial schools without violation of the establishment clause so long as such aid does not exceed the value of the secular educational service rendered by the school."[23]

The Court's vacillation in terms of approach can have important consequences. For example, President George W. Bush implemented federal welfare amendments designed to permit "charitable choice," which would allow religious groups to receive government funds for antipoverty initiatives. The program allows religious organizations to retain their identities by displaying religious symbols and using religious criteria in selecting employees, but precludes them from proselytizing or from discriminating against recipients of other faiths. In addition, the proposal states that recipients who object to receiving services from a religious organization must be given the choice of receiving such services from secular providers. Under the *Lemon* test, as applied in earlier cases, this program is probably unconstitutional. However, under the newer approaches articulated in cases like *Agostini* and *Mitchell*, the proposal is arguably constitutional.

B. School Vouchers

A controversial form of aid to parochial schools are so-called school voucher programs. Under these programs, government provides vouchers to every parent that can be used to purchase an education at public or private schools (including parochial). The vouchers help parents send their children to the schools of their choice, be they private, public, or parochial. By introducing choice into the system, vouchers force schools to compete with each other and ideally lead to a better educational system.

A number of earlier cases dealt with tuition reimbursement schemes without definitively resolving questions relating to the validity of vouchers. For example, in *Committee for Public Education & Religious Liberty v. Nyquist*,[24] the Court struck down a law that provided for partial tuition reimbursements and tax benefits to the parents of elementary and secondary nonpublic school students. The Court concluded that the reimbursement plan violated the effects prong of the *Lemon* test because there was no mechanism to ensure that "the state aid derived from public funds will be used exclusively for secular, neutral, and nonideological purposes, [direct] aid in whatever form is invalid. . . . [T]he effect of the aid is unmistakably to provide [financial] support for nonpublic, sectarian institutions." Justice Rehnquist, joined by Chief Justice Burger and Justice White, dissented: "The reimbursement and tax benefit plans [are] consistent with the principle of neutrality. [T]he impact, if any, on religious education from the aid granted is significantly diminished by the fact that the benefits go to the parents rather than to the institutions." Likewise, in *Sloan v. Lemon*,[25] the Court struck down Pennsylvania's Parent Reimbursement Act for Nonpublic Education, which reimbursed parents for a portion of tuition expenses incurred at nonpublic schools. Although the law specifically precluded the administering authority from having any "direction, supervision or control over the policy determinations, personnel, curriculum, program of instruction [or] administration [of] any nonpublic school or schools," the Court struck the law down finding "no constitutionally significant distinctions between this law and the one declared invalid [in] *Nyquist*."

Notwithstanding the holdings in *Nyquist* and *Sloan*, in *Mueller v. Allen*,[26] the Court upheld a Minnesota law that allowed taxpayers, in computing their state income taxes, to deduct certain expenses incurred in providing for the education of their children. The deduction was limited to actual expenses incurred for the tuition, books, and transportation of dependents attending elementary or secondary schools, and could not exceed $500 per dependent in grades K through 6 and $700 per dependent in grades 7 through 12. In upholding the law, the Court applied *Lemon*'s three-part test and emphasized that the program was not invalid simply because it provided aid to a religious institution. The Court noted that the law had a "secular" purpose (defraying the cost of educational expenses incurred by parents, regardless of the types of schools their children attended, and helping to create an educated populace), and its "primary effect" did not advance religion. The deduction was only one of many deductions provided by the state, including deductions for such things as medical expenses and charitable contributions, and was allowed for all parents, including those with children in public schools. The law therefore "neutrally" provided state assistance to a broad spectrum of citizens. Finally, all aid to parochial schools came through individual parents, and as a result of their choice to send their children to private schools, rather than as direct payments to religious institutions. The Court noted that private schools provide alternatives to public schools, thereby promoting competition, and they relieve the tax burden on public schools by diverting students. As a result, the deduction could be "regarded as a rough return for the benefits [provided] to the state and all taxpayers by parents sending their children to parochial schools." The Court found that there was no excessive entanglement because financial aid came to religious institutions only as a result of individual decisions. Justice Marshall, joined by three other justices, dissented, arguing that the Establishment Clause prohibits the state from subsidizing religious education either directly or indirectly. "[Indirect] assistance in the form of financial aid to parents for tuition payments is similarly impermissible because [it does] not 'guarantee the separation between secular and religious educational functions [and] ensure that State financial aid supports only the former.'" Moreover, the deduction gives parents a financial "incentive to parents to send their children to sectarian schools."

The Court went a step further in *Zelman v. Simmons-Harris*[27] and upheld a voucher program (as opposed to the deduction provided in *Mueller*). *Zelman* involved a Cleveland, Ohio, school voucher program designed primarily for a low-income and minority school district that was in crisis. The program provided two kinds of assistance to parents in a covered district: a tuition aid program and tutorial aid for students who remained in public school. The tuition aid program was designed to provide educational choices to parents who could send their children to public schools or to participating schools, religious or nonreligious. Participating private schools were required to agree not to discriminate on the basis of race, religion, or ethnic background, or to "'advocate or foster unlawful behavior or teach hatred of any person or group on the basis of race, ethnicity, national origin, or religion.'" Public schools located in adjacent school districts could also participate in the program and receive a $2,250 tuition grant for each student accepted in addition to the full amount of per-pupil state funding attributable to each additional student. The tuition aid was distributed according to financial need with differential payments and co-payments based on need. However, religious institutions received funds only as a result of parental choice since parents endorsed the vouchers to schools. During the 1999-2000 school year, 56 private schools participated in the program, 46 (or 82 percent) of which had a religious affiliation. None of the public schools in districts adjacent to Cleveland elected to participate. Of the 3,700 students who participated in the program, 96 percent enrolled in religiously affiliated schools. Also included in the program were community schools that were funded by the state but were run by independent school boards with the authority to hire their own teachers and determine their own curriculum. There were 10 of these schools, which enrolled more than 1,900 students and received $4,518 per student under the tuition assistance program. Magnet schools were public schools that emphasized a particular subject area, teaching method, or service to students, and they received $7,746 per student and enrolled more than 13,000 students in 1999.

In an opinion by Chief Justice Rehnquist, the Court upheld the voucher program against an Establishment Clause challenge. The Court began by finding a valid secular purpose of providing educational assistance to poor children in a demonstrably failing public school system. The Court also found that the program did not have an impermissible effect because it did not provide direct aid to religious schools, but did so only as a result of parental choice. In addition, the program was neutral toward religion in that it "confers educational assistance directly to a broad class of individuals defined without reference to religion, i.e., any parent of a school-age child who resides in the Cleveland City School District" and "permits the participation of *all* schools within the district, religious or nonreligious. Adjacent public schools also may participate and have a financial incentive to do so." The only preference in the program is for low-income families, and the Court found no financial incentives that skewed the program in favor of religious schools because the program was administered based on "neutral, secular criteria that neither favor nor disfavor religion, and is made available to both religious and secular beneficiaries on a nondiscriminatory basis." If anything, the Court found a financial disincentive for private schools because they received less aid than community schools, magnet schools, and public schools in adjacent districts, as well as because they had to impose a copayment. The Court also rejected the argument that the Cleveland program created "a public perception that the State is endorsing religious practices and beliefs" because aid reached public schools only as a result of the independent decisions of private individuals, as well as because a "reasonable observer" would realize that the program is part of a broader plan "to assist poor children in failed schools, not as an endorsement of religious schooling in general," and provide them with educational choices.

The Court placed particular emphasis on the fact that the program provided a range of educational choices to Cleveland children. The Court did not find it determinative that 46 of the 56 private schools that participated in the program were religious schools because the "preponderance of religiously affiliated private schools certainly did not arise as a result of the program." The Court refused to find that a voucher program might be constitutional in places with a low number of parochial schools, but unconstitutional in places with a large number of such schools. The Court also refused to attach significance to the fact that 96 percent of the students enrolled in private schools attended religious schools because the "constitutionality of a neutral educational aid program simply does not turn on whether and why, in a particular area, at a particular time, most private schools are run by religious organizations, or most recipients choose to use the aid at a religious school." The Court went on to note that the program involved 1,900 Cleveland children in alternative community schools, 13,000 children in alternative magnet schools, and 1,400 children in traditional public schools with tutorial assistance. When the Court considered these children in the calculations, it found that "the percentage enrolled in religious schools [went] from 96% to under 20%."

F   A   Q

Q: Isn't a voucher program potentially troubling because the voucher might be used to pay for a child's entire parochial school education, including both secular and religious components?

A: Yes. As *Zelman* suggests, some of the Cleveland parochial schools charged tuition rates that were at or below the amount provided by the voucher. As a result, the voucher *is* paying for both the secular education and the religious education. Of course, this aspect of the voucher program might not be constitutionally objectionable. Some parochial schools charge lower tuition rates because the local parish or church helps subsidize the running of the schools. As a result, it might be argued that the religious institution is paying the cost of the religious education.

The case produced two major concurrences. Justice O'Connor argued that although the Cleveland program involved more than $8 million in public funds, "it pales in comparison to the amount of funds that federal, state, and local governments already provide religious institutions." She noted the various tax deductions for charitable groups, including property tax exemptions and monies given to religiously affiliated hospitals under Medicare and Medicaid. She emphasized that the "Cleveland voucher program is neutral as between religious schools and nonreligious schools" and that children arrive at religious schools because of private choice. Justice Thomas also concurred, arguing that "failing urban public schools disproportionately affect minority children most in need of educational opportunity. . . . If society cannot end racial discrimination, at least it can arm minorities with the education to defend themselves from some of discrimination's effects. . . ."

The case also produced important dissents, which reveal the current divide on the Court on this issue. Justice Stevens expressed concern for the impact of religious strife and argued that whenever "we remove a brick from the wall that was designed to separate religion and government, we increase the risk of religious strife and weaken the foundation of our democracy." Justice Souter also dissented and raised particular concerns about the concept of neutrality. He argued that neutrality has never been deemed sufficient, in and of itself, to justify a program under the Establishment Clause, and he viewed the Rehnquist opinion's approach to neutrality as improper because it considered both public school opportunities and private school opportunities. In addition, he expressed concern that the program was "influencing choices in a way that aims the money in a religious direction." He noted that 43 of the 46 private schools that accepted voucher students were religious schools, and that 96.6 percent of all voucher recipients go to religious schools. "Evidence shows [that] almost two out of three families using vouchers to send their children to religious schools did not embrace the religion of those schools. The families made it clear they had not chosen the schools because they wished their children to be proselytized in a religion not their own, or in any religion, but because of educational opportunity." In addition, he noted that the $2,500 cap that the program places on tuition for participating low-income pupils has the effect of curtailing the participation of nonreligious schools "that charged higher tuition and therefore could not afford to take more than a small number of voucher students." Justice Souter also expressed other concerns about the Cleveland program, arguing that it involved aid on a previously unprecedented scale. Further, he thought it created a risk of corruption because government might decide to impose restrictions on religious schools (for example, the Cleveland program imposed a prohibition against discrimination on the basis of religion in admissions or teacher hiring). Justice Breyer also dissented, noting that he feared that the program would lead to governmental meddling in religious schools and conflict over the governmentally imposed criteria for schools.

C. State-Sponsored Prayer

There has been considerable litigation regarding the permissibility of state-sponsored prayer. Beginning in the 1960s, litigation focused on the permissibility of prayer in public schools. In all these cases, the Court struck down school-initiated prayer. The seminal decision was *Engel v. Vitale*,[28] an opinion written by Justice Black. A local board of education, acting in its official capacity under state law, prescribed a prayer to be said aloud by each class in the presence of a teacher at the beginning of each school day: "Almighty God, we acknowledge our dependence upon Thee, and we beg Thy blessings upon us, our parents, our teachers and our Country." The Board adopted this procedure on the recommendation of the State Board of Regents, which exercised broad supervisory power over New York's public school system. The parents of ten students brought suit to challenge the prayer. In striking down the law, the Court applied a forerunner of the *Lemon* test and concluded: "[T]he constitutional prohibition against laws respecting an establishment of religion must at least mean that [it] is no part of the business of government to compose official prayers for any group [of] people to recite." In rendering its decision, the Court placed great emphasis on the history of the Establishment Clause and on the experience of many colonists who left Europe to escape state-imposed religions. The Court regarded the prayer as an establishment, even though it was denominationally neutral. "When the power, prestige and financial support of government is placed behind a particular religious belief, the indirect coercive pressure upon religious minorities to conform to the prevailing officially approved religion is plain." In addition, the Court expressed concern about governmental persecution of nonbelievers.

Justice Stewart dissented, arguing that the prayer did not constitute an establishment of religion. He gave numerous examples to support his argument, including that both chambers of Congress began their sessions with prayer, each of our presidents had asked for the protection and help of God, the Pledge of Allegiance refers to God, and that U.S. coins contain the words "In God We Trust." He concluded: "Countless similar examples could be listed, but there is no need to belabor the obvious. It was all summed up by this Court just ten years ago in a single sentence: 'We are a religious people whose institutions presuppose a Supreme Being.' *Zorach v. Clauson*, 343 U.S. 306, 313."

Following the decision in *Engel*, some tried to amend the Constitution to permit prayer in public schools. Later proposals would have authorized religious icons on government property and allowed government to provide financial aid directly to parochial schools. Supporters of these amendments claimed that the Court had "attacked and twisted and warped" the First Amendment, and stifled religious expression "right and left all over the country." None of these amendments have been adopted and ratified.

Following *Engel*, some states moved to adopt "moment of silence" laws. Under these laws, schools might impose a moment of silence during which children could choose to meditate, pray, or simply remain silent.

In *Wallace v. Jaffree*,[29] the Court confronted the validity of an Alabama law. In fact, Alabama passed three separate laws. The first authorized a one-minute period of silence in all public schools "for meditation." The second authorized a period of silence "for meditation or voluntary prayer." The third authorized teachers to lead "willing students" in a prescribed prayer to "Almighty God [the] Creator and Supreme Judge of the world." After the first and third moment of silence provisions were struck down in the lower courts, the Court held that the period of silence for "meditation or voluntary prayer" was also unconstitutional because it was premised on a religious purpose. The Court emphasized that the bill's sponsor stated in the legislative record as well as in testimony before the trial court that his motive in sponsoring the law was to return voluntary prayer to the public schools. The Court noted that one of the earlier laws referred only to "meditation" and allowed students to meditate or to pray during the meditation period: As a result, the Court found no secular purpose attributable to the addition of the words "or voluntary prayer" and concluded that the "addition of 'or voluntary prayer' indicated that the State intended to characterize prayer as a favored practice, and therefore violated the requirement of 'complete neutrality toward religion.'"

Wallace produced concurrences and dissents, which show the diverging views on the Court. Justice O'Connor concurred, but argued that moment of silence statutes can be valid and that children are free to pray during these moments. Indeed, in her view, a "moment of silence is not inherently religious" and a state does not necessarily encourage or "endorse any activity that might occur during the period." However, she agreed that the Alabama law had a religious purpose. Chief Justice Burger dissented, noting other instances in which the government recognized religion and arguing that the "statute does not remotely threaten religious liberty; it affirmatively furthers the values of religious freedom and tolerance that the Establishment Clause was designed to protect." Finally, the Chief Justice questioned whether the law was passed for religious reasons because all of the statements relied on were following passage of the law, and there was no evidence that the legislature was religiously motivated. "The sole relevance of the sponsor's statements, therefore, is that they reflect the personal, subjective motives of a single legislator." Justice

White also dissented, arguing that the Court would sustain "statutes that provide[d] for a moment of silence but did not mention prayer. But if a student asked whether he could pray during that moment, it is difficult to believe that the teacher could not answer in the affirmative. [I] would not invalidate a statute that at the outset provided the legislative answer to the question 'May I pray?'" Justice Rehnquist also dissented, arguing that the states are free to endorse prayer in the schools.

Engel was followed by the holding in Marsh v. Chambers,[30] which involved the Nebraska legislature's practice of beginning each day with a prayer by a chaplain. The chaplain was chosen by the Executive Board of the Legislative Council and paid out of public funds. The Court upheld the practice, pointing to the history of the Establishment Clause: "[From] colonial times through the founding of the Republic and ever since, the practice of legislative prayer has coexisted with the principles of disestablishment and religious freedom. [The] Continental Congress, beginning in 1774, adopted the traditional procedure of opening its sessions with a prayer offered by a paid chaplain." While the Court recognized that historical patterns and practices cannot justify an unconstitutional act, it viewed the historical evidence as shedding light on "what the draftsmen intended the Establishment Clause to mean" and "how they thought that Clause applied to the practice authorized by the First Congress." Mr. Justice Brennan dissented, applying the Lemon test and arguing that the "'purpose' of legislative prayer is preeminently religious" and the "'primary effect' of legislative prayer is also clearly religious." In addition, he would have found excessive entanglement between the State and religion: "[T]he process of choosing a 'suitable' chaplain, [and] insuring that the chaplain limits himself or herself to 'suitable' prayers, involves precisely the sort of supervision that agencies of government should if at all possible avoid." He was also concerned about the "divisive political potential."

Sidebar

DOES WALLACE DOOM ALL MOMENT OF SILENCE LAWS?

Wallace did not doom all moment of silence laws. A moment of silence law might be valid if it is enacted for a secular purpose (for example, to solemnize the opening of the school day). The difficulty with the Alabama law in Wallace was that there was evidence that the state adopted it with the intent of returning prayer to the public schools. Of course, some states (those that mandated prayer in public schools prior to Engel) might have more difficulty establishing a secular purpose for their laws. But even in these states, a moment of silence might be valid if it comes to the Court without the historical baggage that accompanied the Alabama law.

F   A   Q

Q: If the Establishment Clause does not preclude legislative prayer, then why does it preclude school prayer?

A: Part of the justification for upholding legislative prayer is historical: At the time the Constitution and the First Amendment were adopted, legislative prayer was constitutional. There were few public schools at the time of adoption. But a more fundamental concern is that schoolchildren are more impressionable, and it is considered improper for government to send a message that it adheres to a particular religious message.

After *Marsh*, it was clear that the Court would uphold prayer in some contexts, but unclear whether school prayer would ever be constitutional. While *Engel* made clear that state-mandated prayers were unconstitutional for younger, impressionable children, there was less certainty regarding the constitutionality of prayer for older children in other contexts. *Lee v. Weisman*[31] involved graduation prayers at middle schools and high schools. In Providence, Rhode Island, public school principals were allowed to invite clergy to offer invocation and benediction prayers at middle school and high school graduation ceremonies. The prayers were supposed to be nonsectarian, and the clergy were given instructions about what not to say. In an opinion by Justice Kennedy, the Court struck down the prayers on the basis that "government may not coerce anyone to support or participate in religion or its exercise, or otherwise act in a way which 'establishes a [state] religion or religious faith, or tends to do so.'" The opinion began by expressing concern about the potential for divisiveness and noted that this potential existed for a number of reasons, including the choice of the clergy member. The Court also expressed concern about the guidelines given to clergy. Relying on *Engel*, the Court noted that it is "'[no] part of the business of government to compose official prayers for any group [of] American people to recite as a part of a religious program carried on by government.'" While the Court recognized that the guidelines constituted an effort to avoid sectarian prayers, it questioned whether the government had any business intruding in this area — even if the instructions constituted a good-faith attempt to avoid sectarianism. The Court rejected the notion that a "practice of nonsectarian prayer" had developed. The Court also rejected the idea that the prayer could be regarded as an accommodation of religion: "[T]here are heightened concerns with protecting freedom of conscience from subtle coercive pressure in the elementary and secondary public schools. [Finding] no violation under these circumstances would place objectors in the dilemma of participating, with all that implies, or protesting. . . . [P]sychology supports the [assumption] that adolescents [are] susceptible to pressure from their peers towards conformity, and that the influence is strongest in matters of social convention. [T]he government may no more use social pressure to enforce orthodoxy than it may use more direct means. The Court was unpersuaded by the fact that attendance at graduation ceremonies was voluntary. The Court distinguished *Marsh*, noting that "[a]t a high school graduation, teachers and principals must and do retain a high degree of control over the precise contents of the program. . . . In this atmosphere the state-imposed character of an invocation and benediction by clergy selected by the school combine to make the prayer a state-sanctioned religious exercise in which the student was left with no alternative but to submit."

Weisman produced concurrences and dissents. Justice Blackmun concurred, noting that "when the government 'compose[s] official prayers,' selects the member of the clergy to deliver the prayer, has the prayer delivered at a public school event that is planned, supervised and given by school officials, and pressures students to attend and participate in the prayer, there can be no doubt that the government is advancing and promoting religion." Justice Souter also concurred, rejecting the argument that the Establishment Clause should be read to prohibit "nonpreferential" state promotion of religion. He also rejected a historical practices argument as a justification for school prayer. While granting that early presidents issued religious messages, Justice Souter rejected their significance: "[T]hose practices prove, at best, that the Framers simply did not share a common understanding of the Establishment Clause, and, at worst, that they, like other politicians, could raise constitutional ideals one day and turn their backs on them the next." Finally, Justice Souter rejected the argument that the omission of graduation prayer constituted a "burden" on the students' religious beliefs, noting that they could "express their religious feelings about it before and after the ceremony, or could organize a privately sponsored baccalaureate for religiously oriented students." Justice Scalia (joined by Justices Rehnquist, White, and Thomas), dissented. He began by pointing to history: "[The] history and tradition of our Nation are replete with public ceremonies featuring prayers of thanksgiving and petition." He also noted that Thanksgiving Proclamations, which included the "religious theme of prayerful gratitude to God," have been issued "by almost every President," as well as that both Congress and the U.S. Supreme Court have long-standing traditions of prayer. Finally, Scalia argued that students who do not wish to participate in a graduation prayer could simply sit in respectful silence. He noted that students are required to stand for the Pledge of Allegiance, which includes a reference to God. He also noted that graduating high school students should be treated differently than other students: "[G]raduation [is] significant [because] it [is] associated with transition from adolescence to young adulthood. Many graduating seniors [are] old enough to vote. Why, then, does the Court treat them as though they were first-graders?"

In *Santa Fe Independent School District v. Doe*,[32] the Court struck down a school district policy allowing nondenominational prayer at football games. Students were allowed to vote on whether to have the prayer and to select the student who would give it. The Court struck down the policy, applying the so-called endorsement test and concluding that an "objective Santa Fe High School student will unquestionably perceive the inevitable pregame prayer as stamped with her school's seal of approval." The Court went on to note that "Santa Fe's student election system ensures that only those messages deemed 'appropriate' under the District's policy may be delivered. . . . Because 'fundamental rights may not be submitted to vote; they depend on the outcome of no elections,' the District's elections are insufficient safeguards of diverse student speech." In addition the Court found that the policy "invites and encourages religious messages" at school-sponsored events. Chief Justice Rehnquist, joined by Justices Scalia and Thomas, dissented, arguing that the pregame prayer had "plausible secular purposes."

> **Sidebar**
>
> **GRADUATION PRAYER**
>
> Note that *Lee v. Weisman* invalidates graduation prayer, even though the children are not young and impressionable. The Court seems to be concerned about the bias toward the Christian religion and the messages sent to nonadherents.

D. School Curricula

A number of cases have dealt with the question of whether public schools can include Bible readings in their studies or ban views inconsistent with particular religious beliefs. For example, in *School District of Abington Township v. Schempp*,[33] the Court struck down a Baltimore, Maryland, law that required the reading of a chapter in the Holy Bible and/or the use of the Lord's Prayer in public school classes. Also at issue was a Pennsylvania law that required that "[a]t least ten verses from the Holy Bible be read, without comment, at the opening of each public school on each school day." In Abington, Pennsylvania, the verses were followed by recitation of the Lord's Prayer. The students reading the Bible verses were allowed to select passages and read from any version they chose, although the school furnished only the King James version. Students had actually used the King James, the Douay, and the Revised Standard versions of the Bible, as well as the Jewish Holy Scriptures. Students were allowed to absent themselves from the classroom or elect not to participate in the exercises. Again applying principles that would later be reflected in the *Lemon* test, the Court struck down both the Maryland and Pennsylvania practices. Even though the states tried to articulate secular purposes (the promotion of moral values, the contradiction to the materialistic trends of our times, the perpetuation of our institutions and the teaching of literature), the Court found that the purpose was primarily religious. "While the Free Exercise Clause [prohibits] the use of state action to deny the rights of free exercise to anyone, it has never meant that a majority could use the machinery of the State to practice its beliefs."

Sidebar

SECULAR HUMANISM

An interesting aspect of the *Schempp* decision was the Court's discussion of the "secular humanism" issue. Over the years, some have argued that because schools teach values and at the same time have banished prayer and religious teachings from the classrooms, that schools are essentially teaching a "religion of secular humanism." The Court did not believe that it was establishing "humanism," but agreed that the states "may not establish a 'religion of secularism' in the sense of affirmatively opposing or showing hostility to religion, thus 'preferring those who believe in no religion over those who do believe.'"

Justice Stewart dissented. He argued that the Court's holding created a religion of secular humanism:

[A] compulsory state educational system so structures a child's life that if religious exercises are held to be an impermissible activity in schools, religion is placed at an artificial and state-created disadvantage. [P]ermission of such exercises for those who want them is necessary if the schools are truly to be neutral in the matter of religion. And a refusal to permit religious exercises thus is seen, not as the realization of state neutrality, but rather as the establishment of a religion of secularism, or at the least, as government support of the beliefs of those who think that religious exercises should be conducted only in private.

He also argued that the "dangers" inherent in governmental support of religion were absent given that the Bible verses were read without comment. As a result, he viewed the Bible readings as an accommodation of religion.

F A Q

Q: After *Schempp*, is it possible for a school to offer a course on comparative religions?

A: Yes. A comparative religion course that objectively compares all religions but does not endorse any of them would be permissible. Indeed, the *Schempp* Court suggested that schools could have students study "comparative religion or the history of religion and its relationship to the advancement of civilization." It further noted that the "Bible is worthy of study for its literary and historic qualities." But the Court rejected the practice at issue in *Schempp* because it held that the state may not require a religious exercise.

There has also been considerable litigation regarding the teaching of evolution in public schools. Evolution is the idea that man evolved from lower human forms. The idea of evolution is inconsistent with the biblical notion of creationism, the idea that God created man in his present form.

"It's called monotheism, but it looks like downsizing to me."

The landmark evolution decision is *Epperson v. Arkansas*,[34] which struck down an Arkansas 1928 "anti-evolution" statute that made it illegal for teachers in state-supported schools or universities "to teach the theory or doctrine that mankind ascended or descended from a lower order of animals" or "to adopt or use in any such institution a textbook that teaches" this theory. The statute was modeled on the famous 1925 Tennessee "monkey law" that was upheld by the Supreme Court in the celebrated *Scopes* case in 1927.[35] A violation of the Arkansas law was punishable only as a misdemeanor but could lead to dismissal of the teacher. Until 1965, the official biology textbook at teacher Susan Epperson's school did not include a discussion of evolution theory. When the district adopted a textbook that discussed evolution, Epperson was faced with a choice between using the textbook and teaching evolution or following the Arkansas law. While the Court recognized that the State of Arkansas was free to stipulate the curriculum for its public schools, the Court concluded that the anti-evolution statute was religiously motivated: "[T]here can be no doubt that Arkansas has sought to prevent its teachers from discussing the theory of evolution because it is contrary to the belief of some that the Book of Genesis must be the exclusive source of doctrine as to the origin of man." The Court concluded that the law was not neutral. Justice Black concurred, questioning whether the law was religiously motivated and suggesting that Arkansas may have thought it "best to remove this controversial subject from its schools." He believed that a state could remove any subject from its curriculum that it found "too emotional and controversial."

Edwards v. Aguillard[36] dealt with the question of whether a state could pass a statute requiring a "Balanced Treatment for Creation-Science and Evolution-Science in Public School Instruction." A Louisiana act by that name did not require schools to teach either evolution or creation science, but did prohibit the teaching of evolution in public schools unless it was accompanied by instruction in creation science. In striking down the law, the Court applied the *Lemon* test and emphasized that it "has been particularly vigilant in monitoring compliance with the Establishment Clause in elementary and secondary schools" because of the impressionable nature of children, as well as because families "entrust public schools with the education of their children" and are entitled to assume that "the classroom will not purposely be used to advance religious views that may conflict with the private beliefs of the student and his or her family." In applying the *Lemon* test, the Court focused on the purpose prong. The Court noted that although it is normally deferential when a state articulates a secular purpose, the Louisiana act's stated purpose (academic freedom) was a sham. Indeed, the Court found that the purpose of act's sponsor was to "narrow the science curriculum." "Before the passage of the Act, there was no law that prohibited Louisiana public school teachers from teaching any scientific theory. Thus, the purpose was to restrict rather than to expand academic freedom." The Court also found a religious purpose in that the law discriminated in favor of creation science and against evolution by requiring that creation science be taught without requiring that evolution be taught. It also protected teachers of creation science without providing similar protections for teachers who taught evolution. The Court found, then, that the "preeminent purpose of the Louisiana Legislature was clearly to advance the religious viewpoint that a supernatural being created humankind." The Court noted that the sponsor of the bill had emphasized his "disdain" for the theory of evolution, which was contrary to his religious beliefs. While the Court did not rule out the possibility that a legislature could validly require "scientific critiques of prevailing scientific theories" if done "with the clear secular intent of enhancing the effectiveness of science instruction," this statute was invalid because it was motivated by religious purpose.

Justice Scalia, joined by Chief Justice Rehnquist, disputed the Court's conclusion that the act was religiously motivated, arguing that the "Balanced Treatment Act did not fly through the Louisiana Legislature on wings of fundamentalist religious fervor—which would be unlikely [since] only a small minority of the State's citizens belong to fundamentalist religious denominations." He argued that the bill was supported by Senator Keith himself, as well as scientists and educators with impressive academic credentials, who gave "lengthy [and] seemingly expert scientific expositions on the origin of life." In addition, there was legislative testimony showing that teachers "have been brainwashed by an entrenched scientific establishment composed almost exclusively of scientists to whom evolution is like a 'religion.'" The legislature found that the censorship deprived students of one of the "scientific" explanations for the origin of life and led them to accept evolution as a proven fact. Justice Scalia also quarreled with the majority's determination that the stated secular purpose was a

Sidebar

ARE SCHOOLS REQUIRED TO TEACH EVOLUTION?

Under *Epperson*, although schools may not prohibit the teaching of evolution, they are likewise not required to teach it.

sham: "Witness after witness urged the legislators to support the Act so that students would not be 'indoctrinated' but would instead be free to decide for themselves, based upon a fair presentation of the scientific evidence, about the origin of life."

One of the more interesting aspects of Justice Scalia's dissent is his argument that the Court's decision perpetuates secular humanism as a religion. He argued that evolution is a central tenet of that religion and that the censorship of creation science helps advance that religion. As one commentator argued, "[I]f we forbid the teaching of recognized religions in our public schools and forbid a prayer which simply acknowledges the existence of God and at the same time permit [the] teaching of some code of ethical conduct, some system of value norms, does not the system which the school then sponsors become the system of Secular Humanism or simply secular humanism? Do we not then prefer, in public education, one religion, Secular Humanism, over other religions which are founded upon a belief in the existence of God?"[37] Obviously, the Court has rejected these arguments.

F   A   Q

Q: Why shouldn't a legislature be allowed to require that both creationism and evolution be taught if one is going to be taught?

A: Arguably, if the schools are required to teach both doctrines and are prohibited from elevating one over the other, there is no establishment of religion. In *Edwards*, the Court was concerned that the balanced treatment law was religiously motivated and might be used to promote indoctrination.

Even though *Epperson* was decided over 40 years ago, litigation continues to arise regarding the teaching of the theory of evolution in the public schools. For example, in *Freiler v. Tangipahoa Parish Board of Education*,[38] the Fifth Circuit Court of Appeals struck down a school board rule mandating the reading of a disclaimer prior to the teaching of the theory of evolution.

E. Official Acknowledgment of Religion

There has been considerable disagreement about whether, and to what extent, the government may acknowledge the existence of religion. This issue has arisen in various contexts, including in cases on whether the government may display copies of the Ten Commandments.

(1) The Ten Commandments

Stone v. Graham[39] struck down a Kentucky statute that required the posting of a copy of the Ten Commandments on the wall of each public classroom in the state. Although the Commonwealth argued that the law was supported by a secular purpose — because the Ten Commandments represents the fundamental legal code of Western civilization and the common law of the United States — the Court found a religious purpose: "The Ten Commandments are [a] sacred text in the Jewish and Christian faiths, and . . . do not confine themselves to arguably secular matters, such as honoring one's parents, killing or murder. . . . Rather, the first part of the Commandments concerns the religious duties of believers: worshipping the Lord God alone, avoiding idolatry, not using the Lord's name in vain, and observing the Sabbath Day." In dicta, the Court indicated that the Ten Commandments need not be completely barred from the public schools. For example, they might be included in the school curriculum when the subject is history, comparative religion, or a related secular topic. However, the Court concluded that it was inappropriate to post the Ten Commandments in such a way as "to induce the schoolchildren to read, meditate upon, perhaps to venerate and obey, the Commandments" because there was no educational function. Four justices dissented, including Chief Justice Burger and Justices Blackmun and Stewart. Justice Rehnquist also dissented, arguing that the Court should have deferred to the state's articulated secular purpose given that "the Ten Commandments have had a significant impact on the development of secular legal codes of the Western World" and the state might justifiably have concluded that it "should be placed before its students, with an appropriate statement of the document's secular import." Since religion "has been closely identified with our history and government," he found it appropriate for Kentucky "to make students aware of this fact by demonstrating the secular impact of the Ten Commandments."

Stone was only the beginning of litigation regarding the constitutionality of Ten Commandments displays. Although the matter did not make it to the U.S. Supreme Court, Establishment Clause litigation arose when Alabama Supreme Court Chief Justice Moore decided to have a 5,280-pound Ten Commandments monument created and displayed at the Alabama Supreme Court. Justice Moore's actions were religiously motivated. When a federal court held that the display violated the First Amendment, Chief Justice Moore defiantly refused to remove it despite large contempt fines, arguing that the Establishment Clause does not apply to the states. Eventually, the other justices overruled Chief Justice Moore and ordered the monument removed, and Justice Moore was ultimately removed from the Alabama Supreme Court by an ethics panel.

F A Q

Q: Why would a judge argue that the Establishment Clause does not apply to the states?

A: Although such a position has historical legitimacy, it is no longer does. When the First Amendment was adopted and ratified, its Establishment Clause applied only to the federal government and not to the states. As a result, a state government was free to establish a religion assuming that its state constitution did not prohibit an establishment. During the twentieth century, the Establishment Clause (and the rest of the First Amendment) was incorporated into the Fourteenth Amendment's Due Process Clause and applied to the states. As a result, the federal Establishment Clause now applies to the Alabama Supreme Court.

In 2005, two more Commandment cases made their way to the U.S. Supreme Court. The first case, *Van Orden v. Perry*,[40] upheld the constitutionality of a display on the grounds of the Texas state capitol. The large display indicated that it was presented to the State of Texas by the Fraternal Order of Eagles. In upholding the display, a plurality of the Court concluded that the Court's precedent regarding the Establishment Clause points "Janus-like" in opposite directions. "One face recognizes and respects the strong role that religion and religious traditions have played in United States history. The other face recognizes that governmental intrusion into religious matters can endanger religious freedom." The plurality concluded that it was required to respect both faces of this tradition and that government must not "evince a hostility to religion by disabling the government from in some ways recognizing our religious heritage."

The plurality was also influenced by historical evidence suggesting all three branches of the federal government had recognized religion from the beginning. In 1789, both Houses of Congress passed resolutions urging President Washington to issue a Thanksgiving Day Proclamation to "recommend to the people of the United States a day of public thanksgiving and prayer, to be observed by acknowledging, with grateful hearts, the many and signal favors of Almighty God." The plurality also recognized that the Court's own decisions had allowed a state legislature to open its daily sessions with a prayer by a state-paid chaplain. In addition, the plurality noted that it had upheld laws prohibiting the sale of merchandise on Sunday.

The plurality also emphasized that religious displays were common throughout the United States, including at the U.S. Supreme Court, which contains a frieze of Moses holding two tablets that reveal portions of the Ten Commandments written in Hebrew, displayed along with other law givers. On the metal gates lining the courtroom, as well as on the doors, there is a representation of the decalogue. The plurality noted that there were similar depictions throughout Washington, D.C. In addition, the Chamber of the U.S. House of Representatives prominently features Moses, and God is reflected in various monuments and buildings including the Washington, Jefferson, and Lincoln Memorials.

While the plurality acknowledged that the Ten Commandments have religious significance, it found that they have dual meaning since Moses was both a law giver and a religious leader. While the Court concluded that it might be less inclined to sustain a display in an elementary or secondary school context where it might be viewed by impressionable children, the plurality indicated that it would be more likely to sustain religious displays in legislative chambers or capitol grounds. The Court also emphasized that the Texas display was only one of 17 monuments and 21 historical markers that "represented various strands in the State's political and legal history" and concluded that inclusion of the Ten Commandments monument in this group had a dual significance, partaking of both religion and government.

Van Orden produced an array of concurrences. Justice Scalia argued that he would prefer to reach the same result "by adopting an Establishment

> **Sidebar**
>
> **VAN ORDEN AND A POSSIBLE REEVALUATION OF PRIOR HOLDINGS**
>
> Note the greater tolerance toward religious displays evidenced by the *Van Orden* plurality. Although the plurality's approach has not been adopted by the Court, the increased level of tolerance might suggest that governmentally sponsored religious activities that were previously struck down (for example, prayers at school graduation ceremonies or football games) might be treated differently if this analysis were adopted.

Clause jurisprudence that is in accord with our Nation's past and present practices, and that can be consistently applied — the central relevant feature of which is that there is nothing unconstitutional in a State's favoring religion generally, honoring God through public prayer and acknowledgment, or, in a nonproselytizing manner, venerating the Ten Commandments." Justice Thomas also concurred, arguing that the Establishment Clause should not be regarded as incorporated and applied to the states. Even if it is incorporated, he argued that the concept of establishment included only coercive actions (for example, mandatory observance of religious practices or mandatory payment of taxes supporting ministers), and that the Texas monument did not compel Van Orden to do anything. Justice Breyer also concurred, arguing that the religion clauses seek to "assure the fullest possible scope of religious liberty and tolerance for all." However, he concluded that these goals mean that government must "neither engage in nor compel religious practices," must "effect no favoritism among sects or between religion and nonreligion," and must deter no religious belief. He argued that the Establishment Clause does not "compel the government to purge from the public sphere all that in any way partakes of the religious, especially one like the decalogue that also conveys a secular moral message about proper standards of social conduct, and a historical message about the relationship between those standards and the law."

The decision also produced a variety of dissents. Justice Stevens, joined by Justice Ginsburg, dissented, arguing that the Establishment Clause created a strong presumption against the display of religious symbols on public property because it risks offending nonmembers as well as adherents who find the display disrespectful. Justice O'Connor also dissented, arguing that an obviously religious display is inconsistent with the requirement of neutrality. She concluded that government may recognize the historical influence of the decalogue on our legal system "so long as there is a context and that context is historical." Hence, a display of the Commandments accompanied by an exposition of how they have influenced modern law would most likely be constitutionally unobjectionable. But she argued that "17 monuments with no common appearance, history, or esthetic role scattered over 22 acres is not a museum, and anyone strolling around the lawn would surely take each memorial on its own terms."

On the same day that the Court decided *Van Orden*, it struck down courthouse displays in *McCreary County v. American Civil Liberties Union of Kentucky*.[41] *McCreary County* involved Ten Commandments displays in two Kentucky courthouses, both of which included the King James version of the Ten Commandments with a citation to the Book of Exodus. In response to litigation, the counties posted several different displays that described the Ten Commandments as "the precedent legal code upon which the civil and criminal codes [of] Kentucky are founded" and stated that "the Ten Commandments are codified in Kentucky's civil and criminal laws." Although the initial display involved a large framed copy of the edited King James version of the Commandments, later displays included other documents in smaller frames with religious themes, including the "endowed by their Creator" passage from the Declaration of Independence; the Preamble to the Constitution of Kentucky; the national motto, "In God We Trust"; a page from the *Congressional Record* proclaiming the Year of the Bible and including a statement of the Ten Commandments; a proclamation by President Abraham Lincoln designating April 30, 1863, a National Day of Prayer and Humiliation; an excerpt from President Lincoln's "Reply to Loyal Colored People of Baltimore upon Presentation of a Bible," reading that "[t]he Bible is the best gift God has ever given to man"; a proclamation by President Reagan marking 1983 the Year of the Bible; and the Mayflower Compact. Assembled with the Commandments were framed copies of the Magna Carta, the Declaration of Independence, the Bill of Rights, the lyrics of the Star Spangled Banner, the Mayflower Compact, the National Motto, the Preamble to the Kentucky

Constitution, and a picture of Lady Justice. The collection, eventually entitled "The Foundations of American Law and Government Display," came with a statement of historical and legal significance. The comment on the Ten Commandments read: "The Ten Commandments have profoundly influenced the formation of Western legal thought and the formation of our country. That influence is clearly seen in the Declaration of Independence, which declared that 'We hold these truths to be self-evident, that all men are created equal, that they are endowed by their Creator with certain unalienable Rights, that among these are Life, Liberty, and the pursuit of Happiness.' The Ten Commandments provide the moral background of the Declaration of Independence and the foundation of our legal tradition." The counties offered various explanations for the new display, including a desire "to demonstrate that the Ten Commandments were part of the foundation of American Law and Government," and "to educate the citizens of the county regarding some of the documents that played a significant role in the foundation of our system of law and government."

Relying on its holding in *Stone,* in an opinion written by Justice Souter, the Court distinguished *Van Orden* and struck down the displays. The Court noted that the second McCreary County display was distinguishable from the *Van Orden* display because of its "predominantly religious purpose" and lack of neutrality between religions and between religion and nonreligion. The Court believed that the display "sends [the] message [to] nonadherents 'that they are outsiders, not full members of the political community, and an accompanying message to adherents that they are insiders, favored members.'" The Court emphasized that the second of the county's displays had an "unstinting focus" on religious passages and that the Ten Commandments were posted "precisely because of their sectarian content." The religious theme was reinforced by "serial religious references and the accompanying resolution's claim about the embodiment of ethics in Christ." The Court concluded that the third display was invalid, even though it included secular documents, focused on documents thought especially significant in the historical foundation of U.S. government, and expressed a desire "to educate the citizens of the county regarding some of the documents that played a significant role in the foundation of our system of law and government." Although the Court accepted the proposition that a sacred text can be integrated into a constitutionally permissible governmental display on the subject of law or U.S. history, the Court concluded that a "reasonable observer" would not believe that the counties "had cast off the [religious] objective so unmistakable in the earlier displays." The Court distinguished the frieze displayed in the U.S. Supreme Court (depicting Moses along with 17 other law givers, most of whom are secular figures) on the basis that "there is no risk that Moses would strike an observer as evidence that the National Government was violating neutrality in religion." Justice O'Connor concurred, arguing that "the purpose behind the counties' display conveys an unmistakable message of endorsement to the reasonable observer."

Justice Scalia, joined by Chief Justice Rehnquist and Justices Thomas and Kennedy, dissented, arguing that the Founding Fathers did not opt for a secular republic, but instead believed "that morality was essential to the well-being of society and that encouragement of religion was the best way to foster morality." Based on historical evidence suggesting that the Framers had publicly acknowledged religion in their governmental acts, Justice Scalia asked how the Court could "*possibly* assert that 'the First Amendment mandates governmental neutrality [between] religion and nonreligion.'" Justice Scalia also argued that the Constitution permits acknowledgment of monotheism. "[I]t is entirely clear from our Nation's historical practices that the Establishment Clause permits this disregard of polytheists and believers in unconcerned deities, just as it permits the disregard of devout atheists." Because of this historical evidence, Justice Scalia sought to draw a distinction between the "acknowledgment of a single Creator and the establishment of a religion." And he suggested that to "any person who happened to walk down the hallway of the McCreary or Pulaski County Courthouse[,] the displays must have seemed unremarkable — if indeed they were noticed at all." He noted that the courthouse walls are filled with historical documents and other assorted portraits, that the Ten Commandments display was not particularly distinguishable from these other displays, and that the explanation for the decalogue display was not sectarian. Indeed, the explanation for the third display simply asserted that the display "contains documents that played a significant role in the foundation of our system of law and government."

(2) Church Vetoes

In *Larkin v. Grendel's Den, Inc.*,[42] the Court struck down a Massachusetts law that vested in the governing bodies of churches and schools the power to veto applications for liquor licenses within a 500-foot radius of the church or school. Although the Court recognized that schools and churches have an interest in being insulated from businesses that serve liquor, the Court found that the state had impermissibly delegated zoning power to a religious institution in violation of the Establishment Clause. The Court was concerned that the law contained a "standardless" delegation "calling for no reasons, findings, or reasoned conclusions," and therefore might used "for explicitly religious goals, for example, favoring liquor licenses for members of that congregation or adherents of that faith." In addition, "the mere appearance of a joint exercise of legislative authority by Church and State provides a significant symbolic benefit to religion in the minds of some by reason of the power conferred." Justice Rehnquist dissented, arguing that the state does not "'advance' religion by making provision for those who wish to engage in religious activities [to] be unmolested by activities at a neighboring bar or tavern." He believed that should a church discriminate in favor of its own adherents, "it would then be time to decide the Establishment Clause issues."

Sidebar

LARKIN'S MEANING

Note that *Larkin* does not preclude a state from prohibiting all businesses that serve liquor from locating within so many feet of a church or school. The problem in that case was that the state gave a veto power to churches, and it was possible that the churches would use that power to favor their adherents.

(3) Holiday Displays

There has been considerable litigation regarding the constitutionality of holiday displays, particularly Christmas and Chanukah displays. Perhaps the most important recent decision was the holding in *Lynch v. Donnelly*,[43] which upheld a Christmas display in Pawtucket, Rhode Island. The display was erected by the city in a private park in a downtown shopping district, and included a Santa Claus house; reindeer pulling Santa's sleigh; candy-striped poles; a Christmas tree; carolers; cutout figures representing such characters as a clown, an elephant, and a teddy bear; hundreds of colored lights; a large banner that read "SEASONS GREETINGS"; and a creche. The Court found that the creche did not have the impermissible effect of advancing or promoting religion. In addition, the Court regarded any benefits the government's display gave religion as "no more than 'indirect, remote, and incidental.'"

Perhaps the most important part of *Lynch* was Justice O'Connor's concurrence. She argued that government is not allowed to "endorse" religion because it "sends a message to nonadherents that they are outsiders, not full members of the political community, and an accompanying message to adherents that they are insiders, favored members of the political community." In evaluating a "message" to see whether it constitutes an "endorsement," she argued that the focus should be on the message that the government's practice communicates based on the context in which it appears: "[A] typical museum setting, though not neutralizing the religious content of a religious painting, negates any message of endorsement of that content." In analyzing the Pawtucket display, Justice O'Connor believed that the overall display did not convey a message of endorsement. In addition to the creche, the display contained many other symbols, such as Santa Claus, carolers, and candy-striped poles. Justice O'Connor believed that because the creche is "a traditional symbol" of Christmas, a holiday with strong secular elements, and because the creche was "'displayed along with purely secular symbols,'" the creche's setting affected how the entire display was viewed. She found that the overall display would be understood to negate "any message of endorsement" of Christian beliefs.

Four justices (Justice Brennan, joined by Justices Marshall, Blackmun, and Stevens) dissented, arguing that the issue was "whether Pawtucket [had endorsed] religion through its display of the creche," and they agreed that the Court should focus on the context of the display. Thus, a majority of the Court agreed that the endorsement test should govern the Court's analysis. However, the dissenters disagreed with Justice O'Connor's application of that test, arguing that other elements of the Pawtucket display did not negate the message of endorsement. In the dissenter's view, the creche placed "the government's imprimatur of approval on the particular religious beliefs exemplified by the creche." As a result, in their view, the effect of the display on "minority religious groups [was] to convey the message that their views are not similarly worthy of public recognition nor entitled to public support."

F   A   Q

Q: How does the endorsement test dovetail with the *Lemon* test, or does it?

A: In fact, the endorsement test does not dovetail with the *Lemon* test. It is an alternate test that the Court sometimes uses to evaluate establishment claims, especially in the context of displays like the one involved in *Lynch*.

Lynch was followed by the holding in *County of Allegheny v. American Civil Liberties Union*,[44] which struck down a display. *County of Allegheny* involved two separate holiday displays. The first was a creche placed by a Roman Catholic group next to the grand staircase inside the county courthouse. The creche was surrounded by a wooden fence that bore a plaque stating: "[Donated] by the Holy Name Society." The county government placed poinsettia plants around the fence and a small evergreen tree, decorated with a red bow, behind each of the two endposts of the fence. At the apex of the creche display was an angel. Unlike the Pawtucket display upheld in *Lynch*, the *County of Allegheny* display did not include any secular Christmas symbols such as

Santa Claus. The county held its annual Christmas-carol program at the site of the creche and invited high school choirs and other musical groups to perform there during weekday lunch hours. The county dedicated these musical programs to world peace and to the families of prisoners of war and of persons missing in action in Southeast Asia. The second display was erected at the City-County Building about a block away from the county courthouse and involved a large Christmas tree under the middle arch outside the Grant Street entrance. At the foot of the tree was a sign bearing the mayor's name and the words "Salute to Liberty," and additional words that stated: "During this holiday season, the city of Pittsburgh salutes liberty. Let these festive lights remind us that we are the keepers of the flame of liberty and our legacy of freedom." The display also included an 18-foot Chanukah menorah of an abstract tree-and-branch design that was placed next to the Christmas tree. The menorah was owned by a Jewish group, but was stored, erected, and removed each year by the city.

A majority of the justices who participated in the *Lynch* case applied the endorsement test and held that the creche display violated the endorsement test because of its unmistakably religious message. However, the Court emphasized that the constitutionality of any display turns on the setting in which it is displayed, and concluded that "nothing in the context of the display detracts from the creche's religious message." As a result, the "county sends an unmistakable message that it supports and promotes the Christian praise to God that is the creche's religious message," notwithstanding the sign suggesting that the display is owned by a Roman Catholic organization. On the contrary, the "sign simply demonstrates that the government is endorsing the religious message of that organization, rather than communicating a message of its own." While the "government may celebrate Christmas in some manner and form," it may not do so in a way that endorses Christian doctrine.

The Court upheld the display at the City-County building. While the Court conceded that the Menorah is a religious symbol, the Court also recognized that the Menorah has both religious and secular dimensions. In addition, the Court emphasized that the Menorah was accompanied by a Christmas tree and a sign saluting liberty, which create an "overall holiday setting" that represents both Christmas and Chanukah. Because "government may celebrate Christmas as a secular holiday," it may also celebrate Chanukah in a similar manner. Indeed, it would involve "discrimination against Jews [to] celebrate Christmas as a cultural tradition while simultaneously disallowing the city's acknowledgment of Chanukah as [a] cultural tradition." The Court found that the combined displays did not endorse either religious faiths, but instead simply recognized that "both Christmas and Chanukah are part of the same winter-holiday season, which has attained a secular status in our society." Although Christmas trees once carried religious connotations, they now "typify the secular celebration of Christmas." Moreover, the tree was the predominant element in the display because of its 45-foot size, and the smaller Menorah was at its side. "[The] combination of the tree and the menorah communicates [a] secular celebration of Christmas coupled with an acknowledgment of Chanukah as a contemporaneous alternative tradition." Although the menorah is a religious symbol, it was "difficult to imagine a predominantly secular symbol of Chanukah that the city could place next to its Christmas tree." In addition, the Court concluded that the mayor's sign diminished the possibility that the tree and the menorah would be "interpreted as [an] endorsement of Christianity and Judaism." As a result, the Court concluded that it was not "sufficiently likely" that reasonable observers would "perceive the combined display of the tree, the sign, and the menorah as an 'endorsement' or 'disapproval [of] their individual religious choices.'" The Court remanded for consideration of whether the display might violate either the purpose or entanglement prongs of the *Lemon* analysis.

Justice O'Connor, joined in part by Justices Brennan and Stevens, concurred in part and concurred in the judgment. She argued that such things as legislative prayers or opening Court sessions with "God save the United States and this honorable Court" serve "secular purposes" in that they solemnize the occasion and should be regarded as nothing more than "ceremonial deism." In addition to the fact that such practices have historically been permitted, the "history and ubiquity" of these practices provides "the context in which a reasonable observer evaluates whether a challenged governmental practice conveys a message of endorsement of religion." She found no message of endorsement in these activities or in the Thanksgiving holiday, which, "despite its religious origins, is now generally understood as a celebration of patriotic values rather than particular religious beliefs." Justice Brennan, joined by Justices Marshall and Stevens, concurred in part and dissented in part, arguing that "[t]he menorah is indisputably a religious symbol, used ritually in a celebration that has deep religious significance. [That] is all that need be said." Justice Stevens, joined by Justices Brennan and Marshall, concurred in part and dissented in part, arguing that the Establishment Clause creates "a strong presumption against the display of religious symbols on public property." He felt that the Court should have held that even the Chanukah menorah and the Christmas tree were unconstitutional: "The presence of the Chanukah menorah, unquestionably a religious symbol, gives religious significance to the Christmas tree. The overall display thus manifests governmental approval of the Jewish and Christian religions."

Justice Kennedy (with Chief Justice Rehnquist and Justices White and Scalia) dissented, accusing the Court of hostility toward religion by prohibiting a display that did no more than "celebrate the season" and that involved nothing more than an accommodation of religion. He rejected the idea that the government had used its power "to further the interests of Christianity or Judaism in any way," viewing the creche and the menorah as "passive symbols of religious holidays" and noting that no one had been "compelled to observe or participate in any religious ceremony or activity." Those who disagreed with "the message conveyed by these displays are free to ignore them." In addition, Justice Kennedy rejected the endorsement test as a "most unwelcome" addition to the Court's "tangled Establishment Clause jurisprudence" because it "is flawed in its fundamentals and unworkable in practice." He viewed the test as one that would "trivialize constitutional adjudication [by embracing] a jurisprudence of minutiae": "A reviewing court must consider whether the city has included Santas, talking wishing wells, reindeer, or other secular symbols. . . . After determining whether these centers of attention are sufficiently 'separate' that each 'had their specific visual story to tell,' the court must then measure their proximity to the creche. [M]unicipal greenery must be used with care." He doubted that the Court's discussion of the menorah's history, both religious and secular, would be known by the average individual.

Numerous other cases have held that government may acknowledge religion in one respect or another. For example, in *Torcaso v. Watkins*,[45] the Court held that a state may not constitutionally require an applicant for the office of notary public to swear or affirm that he believes in God. In *McGowan v. Maryland*,[46] the Court held that state laws compelling a uniform day of rest from worldly labor do not violate the Establishment Clause, even though Sunday was chosen as the day of rest. The Court concluded that although the Sunday Laws were first enacted for religious ends, they were continued for reasons wholly secular — to provide a universal day of rest and ensure the health and tranquility of the community. Likewise, in *Estate of Thornton v. Caldor, Inc.*,[47] the Court upheld a law that granted employees the right not to work on their sabbaths.

Activity	Constitutionality
School prayer	Unconstitutional (unless part of a permissible moment of silence law)
Christmas displays	Depends on context
Bible readings in public schools	Unconstitutional (unless part of a secular discussion)
Prohibiting the teaching of evolution	Unconstitutional
Requiring the teaching of creationism	Unconstitutional
Ten Commandments displays	Depends on context

F. Establishment-Free Exercise and Free Speech Tension

As the previous discussion suggests, there is considerable tension between the Establishment Clause and the Free Exercise Clause. Under the Free Exercise Clause, the government may at times feel obligated to accommodate religion. On the other hand, in providing an accommodation, the government must be careful not to establish a religion.

Board of Education of Kiryas Joel Village School District v. Grumet[48] illustrates the conflict. In that case, the Court held that the State of New York could not establish a special school district coextensive with the boundaries of a village owned by members of a Satmar Hasidic Jewish sect. The Court described the Satmars as "vigorously religious people who make few concessions to the modern world and go to great lengths to avoid [assimilation]. They interpret the Torah strictly; segregate the sexes outside the home; speak Yiddish as their primary language; eschew television, radio, and English-language publications; and dress in distinctive ways that include head-coverings and special garments for boys and modest dresses for girls. Children are educated in private religious schools." Because the religious schools did not offer special services to handicapped children, the Monroe-Woodbury Central School District provided such services for the children of Kiryas Joel at an annex. This program was terminated following the decisions in *Aguilar v. Felton* and *School District of Grand Rapids v. Ball*. As a result, Kiryas Joel children who needed special education (including the deaf, the developmentally disabled, and others suffering from a range of physical, mental, or emotional disorders) were forced to attend public schools outside the village. Because the Satmars were so different, they encountered "the panic, fear and trauma [suffered] in [being] with people whose ways were so different." By 1989, only one Kiryas Joel child was attending Monroe-Woodbury's public schools. The village's other special education children received privately funded special services or received no education at all. The New York legislature then enacted a statute that provided for the village of Kiryas Joel to be a separate school district. New York Governor Mario Cuomo stated that he viewed the bill as "a good faith effort to solve th[e] unique problem" of providing special education services to those children in the village who needed them.

Although the statute gave the school district plenary legal authority over the elementary and secondary education of all school-aged children in the village, the district ran only a special education program for handicapped children. The village's other children attended parochial schools and received only transportation, remedial education, and health and welfare services from the public school district. If a non-handicapped student had sought a public education, the district would have sent the child to a nearby school district and paid tuition. In addition, several neighboring school districts sent their special needs Hasidic children to the Kiryas Joel school.

In an opinion written by Justice Souter, the Court struck down the law, finding that the state was required to "pursue a course of 'neutrality' toward religion." The Court believed that New York crossed the line because it delegated its "discretionary authority over public schools to a group defined by its character as a religious community, in [a] context that gives no assurance that governmental power has been or will be exercised neutrally." While the Court recognized that religious officials could not be denied the right to hold public office, the Court regarded the Kiryas Joel school district as unconstitutional because of the "government's purposeful delegation on the basis of religion and a delegation on principles neutral to religion, to individuals whose religious identities are incidental to their receipt of civic authority." Even though New York did not delegate power with express reference to the religious beliefs of the Satmars, the Court concluded that New York had effectively delegated power "by reference to doctrinal adherence." The Court emphasized that the district originated in a special act of the legislature, "the only district ever created that way," and noted that "[t]hose who negotiated the village boundaries [excluded] all but Satmars, [and] the New York Legislature was well aware that the village remained exclusively Satmar." The Court concluded that "[w]e therefore find the legislature's Act to be substantially equivalent to defining a political subdivision and hence the qualification for its franchise by a religious test, resulting in a purposeful and forbidden 'fusion of governmental and religious functions.'"

The opinion rejected the argument that the state's decision to create the special district constituted an accommodation of religion. Although the state can "accommodate religious needs by alleviating special burdens," the Court found this law invalid because the "proposed accommodation singles out a particular religious sect for special treatment." The Court suggested that it would be permissible for the district to provide bilingual and bicultural special education to Satmar children at a neutral site near one of the village's parochial schools. The Court concluded that it would "not disable a religiously homogeneous group from exercising political power conferred on it without regard to religion" (for example, Mormons in Utah), but it concluded that this school district was created "to separate Satmars from non-Satmars" and therefore failed the neutrality requirement. "It therefore crosses the line from permissible accommodation to impermissible establishment."

The decision produced a number of concurrences, which along with the dissent is an indication of the Court's efforts to establish a clear line between "establishment" and "accommodation" of religion. Justice Stevens (with Justices Blackmun and Ginsburg) argued that "[affirmative] state action in aid of segregation of this character [is] fairly characterized as establishing, rather than merely accommodating, religion." Justice O'Connor viewed accommodations of religion as permissible, "even praiseworthy," but "[b]ecause this benefit was given to this group based on its religion, it seems proper to treat it as a legislatively drawn religious classification." She wondered whether another group would be given the same preference and believed that it would be "dangerous to validate" what appears to be "a clear religious preference." Nevertheless, she believed that some accommodation of the Satmars might be permissible in that New York might decide to permit all villages to operate their own school districts, or it might set forth neutral criteria for the creation of village school districts. In addition, she believed that the state might provide the education on-site at sectarian schools in the village. Justice Kennedy also concurred, arguing that there "is more than a fine line [between] the voluntary association that leads to a political community comprised of people who share a common religious faith, and the forced separation that occurs when the government draws explicit political boundaries on the basis of peoples' faith." He concluded that New York had "crossed that line."

Justice Scalia, joined by Chief Justice Rehnquist and Justice Thomas, dissented, expressing surprise at the conclusion that the Satmars had become an "established religion." He noted that the "Grand Rebbe would be astounded to learn that after escaping brutal persecution and coming to America with the modest hope of religious toleration for their ascetic form of Judaism, the Satmar had become so powerful, so closely allied with Mammon, as to have become an 'establishment' of the Empire State." He was unwilling to find an establishment because the state provided "no public funding, however slight or indirect, to private religious schools." The education provided to special needs children was secular and did not involve "religious symbols or markings." "The only thing distinctive about the school is that all the students share the same religion." Ultimately, Justice Scalia viewed the district as a permissible accommodation of religion.

F   A   Q

Q: Where is the dividing line between an establishment of religion and an accommodation of religion?

A: In the Court's recent decisions, it has struggled to find the dividing line between an establishment and an accommodation. In *Kiryas Joel*, one sees that split as one reads the majority opinion and the dissents. The cases seem to suggest that government can, and indeed should, attempt to accommodate religious beliefs when possible. Difficulties arise when, in accommodating religion, government appears to be endorsing particular religious beliefs or the accommodation appears to be designed to promote religious beliefs.

The tension between the Establishment and Free Exercises Clauses is also revealed by the Court's recent holding in *Locke v. Davey*.[49] In that case, the Court upheld the State of Washington's Promise Scholarship Program (PSP), which provided renewable one-year scholarships for the payment of postsecondary education expenses. The scholarships were funded through the state's general fund. They were provided to students who graduated in the top 15 percent of their graduating classes or who attained on the first attempt a cumulative score of 1,200 or better on the Scholastic Assessment Test I or a score of 27 or better on the American College Test, and whose family income was below 135 percent of the state's median. While students could use PSP scholarships at either public or private institutions, including religious institutions, they could not be used to pursue a degree in theology, which the statute defined by reference to the state's constitutional prohibition against providing funds to students to pursue degrees that are "devotional in nature or designed to induce religious faith." The exclusion of theology degrees was challenged by Davey, who was otherwise entitled to funding under the PSP but who was disqualified because he chose to pursue a double major in pastoral ministries (which was regarded as devotional) and business management. Davey sued, raising free exercise, establishment, and free speech claims.

In upholding the exclusion, although the Court recognized that the Establishment Clause and the Free Exercise Clause can be in tension with each other, the Court rejected the argument that its prior decision in *Church of Lukumi Babalu Aye v. Hialeah*[50] required invalidation of the exclusion on the basis that the PSP was not facially neutral with respect to religion. The Court noted that the State of Washington did not impose criminal or civil sanctions on any type of religious service or rite, did not deny ministers the right to participate in political affairs, and did not require students to choose between their religious beliefs and receiving a government benefit. Instead, the state had merely chosen not to fund a distinct category of degree, and the Court recognized that "majoring in devotional theology is akin to a religious calling as well as an academic pursuit." Given that the First Amendment protects free exercise, as well as prohibits establishments, the Court concluded that it might be appropriate for a court to "deal differently with religious education for the ministry than with education for other callings," and that this differential in treatment simply reflects the tension between the religion clauses rather than "hostility toward religion." Moreover, the Court emphasized that most "States that sought to avoid an establishment of religion around the time of the founding placed in their constitutions formal prohibitions against using tax funds to support the ministry." Finally, the Court concluded that the PSP "goes a long way toward including religion in its benefits. The program permits students to attend pervasively religious schools, so long as they are accredited," and also allows students to take devotional theology courses (as long as they are not pursuing a devotional degree).

Justice Scalia, joined by Justice Thomas, dissented, viewing the PSP as involving discrimination against religion because the State of Washington "created a generally available public benefit" but excluded students who chose to study religion. He would have upheld the scholarships had they been "redeemable only at public universities, or only for select courses of study." In this view, either approach would have replaced "a program that facially discriminates against religion with one that just happens not to subsidize it. The State could also simply abandon the scholarship program altogether."

The Court has also dealt with Establishment Clause-Free Exercise tension in the context of Title VII of the Civil Rights Act of 1964. In *Corporation of Presiding Bishop v. Amos*,[51] the Court upheld the act, even though it exempted religious organizations from Title VII's prohibition against discrimination in employment on the basis of religion. Applying the *Lemon* test, the Court stated: "Where, as here, government acts with the proper purpose of lifting a regulation that burdens the exercise of religion, we see no reason to require that the exemption comes packaged with benefits to secular entities."

Katcoff v. Marsh[52] dealt with whether the employment of chaplains by the military was an establishment of religion. The Second Circuit Court of Appeals upheld the right of the armed forces to hire chaplains, which enabled soldiers to practice the religion of their choice, and to appoint the chaplains as commissioned officers with rank and uniform but without command. The court emphasized that the provision of chaplains began during the Revolutionary War and "has continued ever since then." The court also held that the provision of chaplains was justified by the unusual circumstances under which the armed forces work: "Unless there were chaplains ready to move simultaneously with the troops and to tend to their spiritual needs as they face possible death, the soldiers would be left in the lurch, religiously speaking." Finally, the court noted that chaplains are not authorized to proselytize soldiers or their families, and questioned whether chaplains were necessary in large urban areas where civilian religious personnel are available.

In *Illinois v. McCollum*,[53] the Court struck down an Illinois law that allowed religious teachers employed by private religious groups to enter public school buildings during the regular hours set apart for secular teaching, and substitute their religious teaching for the secular education provided under the compulsory education law. "This is [a] utilization of the tax-established and tax-supported public school system to aid religious groups to spread their faith [which] falls squarely under the ban of the First Amendment. . . ." However, in *Zorach v. Clauson*,[54] the Court upheld an arrangement whereby students are released from public school classes so that they may attend religious classes offsite.

In *Witters v. Washington Department of Services for the Blind*,[55] the Court was confronted by a Washington statute that authorized payments to "[p]rovide for special education and/or training in the professions, business or trades" to "assist visually handicapped persons to overcome vocational handicaps and to obtain the maximum degree of self-support and self-care." When the state denied assistance to a blind person who was studying at a Christian college to become a pastor, missionary, or youth director, the Court held that Witters was entitled to assistance, noting that the aid went to the student who choose to give it to the educational institution. As a result, any "aid [that] flows to religious institutions does so only as a result of [the] independent and private choices of aid recipients." In addition, the Court emphasized that the program is "made available generally without regard to the sectarian-nonsectarian, or public-nonpublic nature of the institution benefited, . . . and is in no way skewed towards religion."

In *Bowen v. Kendrick*,[56] the Court upheld a federal grant program, the Adolescent Family Life Act (AFLA), that provided funding to public or nonprofit private organizations addressing problems relating to pregnancy and childbirth among unmarried adolescents. The grants were intended to promote "self discipline and other prudent approaches to the problem of adolescent premarital sexual relations," the promotion of adoption as an alternative for adolescent parents, the establishment of new approaches to the delivery of care services for pregnant adolescents, and the support of research and demonstration projects "concerning the societal causes and consequences of adolescent premarital sexual relations, contraceptive use, pregnancy, and child rearing." An Establishment Clause challenge was asserted when Congress specifically amended the act to require grant applicants to describe how they will involve religious organizations in the programs funded by the AFLA. In rejecting the challenge, the Court emphasized that grantees need not be affiliated with any religious denomination. Moreover, the services provided were not religious in character, and there was nothing showing that religious participation had the effect of advancing religion. The Court noted that it was "Congress' considered judgment that religious organizations can help solve the problems" to which the act was addressed, and the Court held that nothing "prevents Congress from making such a judgment or from recognizing the important part that religion or religious organizations may play in resolving certain secular problems." Moreover, there was no indication that "a significant proportion of the federal funds will be disbursed to 'pervasively sectarian' institutions." The Court found that the program was not unconstitutional simply because of a potential overlap between the government's secular concerns and the religious groups' interest in the subject of the funding. The Court also rejected the argument that AFLA excessively entangled government with religion: "There is [no] reason to fear that the less intensive monitoring involved here will cause the Government to intrude unduly in the day-to-day operation of the religiously affiliated AFLA grantees." Justice Blackmun, joined by Justices Brennan, Marshall, and Stevens, dissented: "Whatever Congress had in mind, [it] enacted a statute [that gave] religious groups [a] pedagogical and counseling role without imposing any restraints on the sectarian quality of the participation."

G. Speech and Religion

In some instances, courts are forced to deal with the interplay between the speech and religion clauses. Illustrative is the holding in *Rosenberger v. Rector & Visitors of the University of Virginia.*[57] In that case, in an opinion written by Justice Kennedy, the Court held that the Free Speech Clause entitled a religious publication to state funding. The University of Virginia's Student Activities Fund (SAF) provided funding to an array of student publications, including programs focused on "student news, information, opinion, entertainment and academic communications media groups," but specifically excluded religious publications. Wide Awake Publications (WAP), a student publication, was denied funding because its student paper "primarily promotes or manifests a particular belief in or about a deity or an ultimate reality." The university was concerned that inclusion of religious organizations such as WAP would violate the Establishment Clause. The Court disagreed, noting that the university provided printing services to a "broad spectrum of student newspapers" so that any "benefit to religion is incidental to the government's provision of secular services for secular purposes on a religion-neutral basis." As a result, the Court concluded that the Establishment Clause did not require the university to deny funding to Wide Awake. On the contrary, the Court concluded that the university had discriminated against Wide Awake's religious speech by denying it funding.

A concurring Justice O'Connor found that Wide Awake could be funded without creating an endorsement of religion because the university would simply be "providing the same assistance to Wide Awake that it does to other publications." In addition, the student organizations were required to remain strictly independent of the university, and all student organizations were required to include disclaimers in their publications notifying readers of the publication's independence from the university. In addition, financial assistance was "distributed in a manner that ensure[d] its use only for [the] University's purpose [of] maintaining a free and robust marketplace of ideas, from whatever perspective." Finally, the university provided support to such a range of publications as to make "improbable any perception of government endorsement of the religious message." As a result, Justice O'Connor concluded that "[by] withholding from Wide Awake assistance that the University provides generally to all other student publications, the University has discriminated on the basis of the magazine's religious viewpoint in violation of the Free Speech Clause."

Justice Souter, joined by Justices Stevens, Ginsburg, and Breyer, dissented, noting that the Court "for the first time, approves direct funding of core religious activities by an arm of the State." He indicated that he would have held that the funding refusal was compelled by the Establishment Clause. "[WAP's] writing is no merely descriptive examination of religious doctrine or even of ideal Christian practice in confronting life's social and personal problems. [It] is straightforward exhortation to enter into a relationship with God as revealed in Jesus Christ, and to satisfy a series of moral obligations derived from the teachings of Jesus Christ." He would have held that the state was prohibited from subsidizing proselytizing, as well as from using public money and compelled student fees for that purpose.

F   A   Q

Q: Why does *Rosenberger* preclude the University of Virginia from refusing to fund this speech when it is highly religious and even involves an attempt to convert others?

A: The Court held that the state established a public forum by agreeing to fund the speech of private groups, and that the state cannot discriminate on the basis of viewpoint in this context.

Likewise, in *Widmar v. Vincent*,[58] the Court held that a state university that made its facilities generally available to registered student groups could not close those facilities to groups desiring to use them for religious worship and religious discussion. "Having created a forum generally open to student groups, the University seeks to enforce a content-based exclusion of religious speech. Its exclusionary policy violates the fundamental principle that a state regulation of speech should be content-neutral." Justice White dissented: "[This] case involves religious worship only; the fact that the worship is accomplished through speech does not add anything to respondents' argument."

In *Good News Club v. Milford Central School*,[59] the Court rendered a similar holding in the context of an elementary school that enacted a community use policy governing the use of its building after school hours, but denied the use of those facilities to a religious organization. When the Good News Club — a private Christian organization for children ages 6 to 12 — sought permission to meet in the

Sidebar

RECONCILING *GOOD NEWS CLUB* AND *ROSENBERGER*

Good News Club is consistent with *Rosenberger* in holding that once government creates a public forum, it cannot discriminate against religious speech in that forum.

cafeteria to recite Bible verses, pray, sing songs, and engage in games involving Bible verses, the school district rejected the club's request because it involved "conducting religious instruction and Bible study." The Court found that Milford was operating a "limited public forum"—a forum in which the state was permitted to reserve the forum for certain groups or for the discussion of certain topics—and concluded that it had improperly excluded the Good News Club based on viewpoint discrimination. "[T]he Club seeks to address a subject otherwise permitted under the rule, the teaching of morals and character, from a religious standpoint. . . . The only apparent difference [is] that the Club chooses to teach moral lessons from a Christian perspective through live storytelling and prayer." Justice Stevens dissented: "[A] school [need not open] its forum to religious proselytizing or worship." Justice Souter also dissented: "[Good News's] exercises blur the line between public classroom instruction and private religious indoctrination, leaving a reasonable elementary school pupil unable to appreciate that the former instruction is the business of the school while the latter evangelism is not."

SUMMARY

- At no time in the history of the United States has the government decreed one religion as the official or state-sanctioned religion. Most claimed establishments involve something far less dramatic: financial aid to parochial schools; Bible readings, prayer, and curricular issues in public schools; and questions regarding the validity of religious or holiday displays.

- Historically, the U.S. Supreme Court has analyzed Establishment Clause issues under the *Lemon* test, a three-prong test in which it inquires whether the action in question was motivated by a secular or a religious purpose, whether the action has a secular or religious effect, and whether the action promotes excessive entanglement between religion and governmental officials.

- While courts continue to apply the *Lemon* test, the Court also sometimes applies the endorsement test in which the Court asks whether the governmental action has the effect of endorsing religion in general or one religion in particular. If so, the action is invalid.

- The Court has reached variable results using these tests. As a general rule, governmental attempts to impose prayer in public schools have been invalidated, as have been governmental attempts to post the Ten Commandments in public schools or to impose religious curricula.

- It is important to recognize, however, that each case is individualistic and turns on the context in which the case arises.

CONNECTIONS

Judicial Review
In deciding whether a governmental action violates the Establishment Clause, the Court frequently invokes judicial review.

Freedom of Speech
There is a substantial relationship between the First Amendment right to free expression and the Establishment Clause: Once government creates a public forum, it cannot discriminate against religious speech in that forum.

Free Exercise Clause
Not uncommonly, there is a potential clash between the Free Exercise Clause and the Establishment Clause. When the government decides to grant an exemption for religion, some will claim that the government has impermissibly established religion.

Endnotes

1. 330 U.S. 1 (1947).
2. Philip Kurland, *Of Church and State and the Supreme Court*, 29 U. Chi. L. Rev. 1, 96 (1961).
3. *Everson*, 330 U.S. at 49.
4. Douglas Laycock, *Formal, Substantive and Disaggregated Neutrality Toward Religion*, 39 DePaul L. Rev. 993, 1000-1003 (1990).
5. 403 U.S. 602 (1971).
6. 392 U.S. 236 (1968).
7. 421 U.S. 349 (1975).
8. 443 U.S. 229 (1977).
9. 413 U.S. 472 (1973).
10. 413 U.S. 756 (1973).
11. 403 U.S. 672 (1971).
12. 413 U.S. 734 (1973).
13. 426 U.S. 736 (1976).
14. Wallace v. Jaffree, 472 U.S. 38, 111 (1985) (Rehnquist, J., dissenting).
15. Lamb's Chapel v. Center Moriches Union Free Sch. Dist., 508 U.S. 384 (1993) (Scalia, J., concurring).
16. Bd. of Educ. of Kiryas Joel Village Sch. Dist. v. Grumet, 512 U.S. 687, 720 (1994) (O'Connor, J., concurring).
17. 521 U.S. 203 (1997).
18. 473 U.S. 402 (1985).
19. 512 U.S. 687 (1994).
20. 473 U.S. 373 (1985).
21. 474 U.S. 481 (1986).
22. 530 U.S. 793 (2000).
23. Jesse H. Choper, *The Establishment Clause and Aid to Parochial Schools*, 56 Cal. L. Rev. 260, 265-266 (1968).
24. 413 U.S. 756 (1973).
25. 413 U.S. 825 (1973).
26. 463 U.S. 388 (1983).
27. 536 U.S. 639 (2002).
28. 370 U.S. 421 (1962).

29. 472 U.S. 38 (1985).
30. 463 U.S. 783 (1983).
31. 505 U.S. 577 (1992).
32. 530 U.S. 290 (2000).
33. 374 U.S. 203 (1963).
34. 393 U.S. 97 (1968).
35. Scopes v. State of Tennessee, 289 S.W. 363 (Tenn. 1927). The Tennessee court reversed Scopes's conviction on the ground that the jury and not the judge should have assessed the fine of $100.
36. 482 U.S. 578 (1987).
37. Leonard F. Manning, *The Douglas Concept of God in Government*, 39 Wash. L. Rev. 47, 63 (1964).
38. 185 F.3d 337 (5th Cir. 1999).
39. 449 U.S. 39 (1980).
40. 545 U.S. 677 (2005).
41. 545 U.S. 844 (2005).
42. 459 U.S. 116 (1982).
43. 465 U.S. 668 (1984).
44. 492 U.S. 573 (1989).
45. 367 U.S. 488 (1961).
46. 366 U.S. 420 (1961).
47. 472 U.S. 703, 709-710 (1985).
48. 512 U.S. 687 (1994).
49. 540 U.S. 712 (2004).
50. 508 U.S. 520 (1993).
51. 483 U.S. 327 (1987).
52. 755 F.2d 223 (2d Cir. 1985).
53. 333 U.S. 203 (1948).
54. 343 U.S. 306 (1952).
55. 474 U.S. 481 (1986).
56. 487 U.S. 589 (1988).
57. 515 U.S. 895 (1995).
58. 454 U.S. 263 (1981).
59. 121 U.S. 2093 (2001).

The Free Exercise Clause

12

In addition to demanding protections against an established religion, the American colonists also insisted on constitutional protections for

O V E R V I E W

religious freedom. These demands ultimately led the First Congress to include the Free Exercise Clause in the First Amendment — "Congress shall make no law respecting an establishment of religion, nor prohibiting the free exercise thereof." Although most commentators agree that the clause protects religious thought, there is less agreement regarding whether, and to what extent, it protects religious conduct. In struggling with this and other free exercise distinctions, the Court has made the standard of review a critical part of its analysis.

A. BURDENS ON RELIGION

1. Early Precedent
2. From *Sherbert* to *Smith*
3. The *Smith* Approach

B. DISCRIMINATION AGAINST RELIGION

A. Burdens on Religion

Most free exercise cases involve laws that "burden" religion either by prohibiting an individual from engaging in conduct required by religious beliefs (laws prohibiting polygamy) or by requiring conduct prohibited by religious beliefs (compulsory school attendance laws). No one doubts that government may prohibit certain types of conduct, even if it is engaged in for religious purposes (for example, the state can prohibit a religion that believes in human sacrifice from actually killing people). In most cases, these laws are not directed at religion per se, but deal with some societal problem that incidentally affects religious practices. Litigation usually focuses on whether the individual's interest in free exercise must give way in face of the societal interest or whether the state regulation must give way to accommodate the individual's free exercise interests.

(1) Early Precedent

There are a number of early cases on the subject, and some of these cases distinguished between "belief" and "conduct." For example, in *Reynolds v. United States*,[1] the Court upheld a federal law prohibiting polygamy as applied to a Mormon whose religion required him to engage in that practice. In doing so, the Court held that the government has broad authority to prohibit religious conduct: "Laws are made for the government of actions, and while they cannot interfere with mere religious beliefs and opinions, they may with practices." The Court rejected the argument that a religious exemption was required: "[Can] a man excuse his practices to the contrary because of his religious belief? To permit this would be to make the professed doctrines of religious belief superior to the law of the land, and in effect to permit every citizen to become a law unto himself. Government could exist only in name under such circumstances."[2]

F   A   Q

Q: How is it possible to reconcile *Reynolds*'s holding with the absolute language of the Free Exercise Clause?

A: As with the right to free speech, the Court has not construed the Free Exercise Clause as providing absolute protection for all religious practices. No one doubts, for example, that Congress and the states can prohibit human sacrifice. Likewise, in a number of cases, the Court has balanced the state interest against the religious interest.

Reynolds's distinction between belief and conduct was partially rejected in *Cantwell v. Connecticut*.[3] In that case, a Jehovah's Witness and his sons, ordained ministers, were convicted of attempting to sell religious magazines without a permit and of disorderly conduct. While the Court concluded that the statute prohibiting solicitation violated Cantwell's right to freely exercise his religion, the Court noted that the "First Amendment embraces two concepts — freedom to believe and freedom to act. The first is absolute but, in the nature of things, the second cannot be. Conduct remains subject to regulation for the protection of society." Nevertheless, the Court concluded that the state could not "unduly infringe" a protected freedom. On these facts, the Court held that a "state may not, by statute, wholly deny the right to preach or to disseminate religious views."

F   A   Q

Q: Why does the First Amendment apply to the states when it explicitly refers only to Congress?

A: As with other provisions of the Bill of Rights, the Court has held that the Free Exercise Clause is incorporated into the Fourteenth Amendment's Due Process Clause, and therefore applies to the states.

However, as *Cantwell* suggests, the right to engage in religious conduct is not absolute. For example, in *Prince v. Commonwealth of Massachusetts*,[4] the Court upheld a child labor law conviction against a woman who enlisted her nine-year-old daughter in her effort to sell religious magazines (*Watchtower* and *Consolation*). Prince claimed that she had a free exercise right to bring the child up in the tenets and practices of the faith, and that the girl's exercise rights entitled her to perform her religious duty to perform the

work and required her to do so on condemnation "to everlasting destruction at Armageddon." In upholding the conviction, the Court emphasized that the "power of the state to control the conduct of children reaches beyond the scope of its authority over adults, as is true in the case of other freedoms, and the rightful boundary of its power has not been crossed in this case." Justice Murphy dissented, arguing that "[r]eligious training and activity, whether performed by adult or child, are protected [except] insofar as they violate reasonable regulations adopted for the protection of the public health, morals and welfare. . . . The state [has] completely failed to sustain its burden of proving the existence of any grave or immediate danger to any interest which it may lawfully protect."

(2) From *Sherbert* to *Smith*

Despite holdings in cases like *Reynolds* and *Prince*, later cases struck down laws that infringed religious beliefs. For example, in *Torcaso v. Watkins*,[5] the Court struck down a state constitutional provision that required public officials to declare a belief in God as a prerequisite to assuming office. The Court held that the government may not compel anyone to affirm or deny a religious belief.

The critical question in free exercise cases is the standard of review. Is the Court inclined to apply the least stringent standard, **rational basis review** (which asks, essentially, whether the end pursued by government and the means used to pursue it are rational) or to apply the intermediate level, **heightened standard of review**? In a number of cases, the Court has applied the most stringent level of review, **strict**

scrutiny, to laws burdening religion. For example, in *Sherbert v. Verner*,[6] the Court held that a Seventh-day Adventist Church employee was entitled to unemployment benefits when she was discharged by her employer for refusing to work on Saturday, her Sabbath. *Sherbert* represented an arguable departure from the Court's prior holding in *Braunfeld v. Brown*,[7] in which the Court refused to hold that Sabbatarians were entitled to an exemption from Sunday closing laws. The *Braunfeld* Court found an important governmental interest (an interest in providing one uniform day of rest for all workers) that could be served only by declaring a single day (in this case, Sunday) of rest. The Court found that an exemption for Sabbatarians, while theoretically possible, presented an administrative problem of great magnitude and would give them a competitive advantage. *Sherbert* distinguished *Braunfeld* on the basis that the state interest provided less justification than in *Sherbert*. In *Sherbert*, when plaintiff was unable to obtain alternate employment that did not require Saturday work, she sought unemployment compensation benefits but was denied because she was found to have failed, without good cause, to accept "suitable work when offered [by] the employment office or the [employer]." In upholding her demand for benefits, the Court held that the law burdened the exercise of her religion because it forced her "to choose between following the precepts of her religion and forfeiting benefits, on the one hand, and abandoning one of the precepts of her religion in order to accept work, on the other hand." Moreover, the Court rejected the state's argument that unemployment compensation benefits constitute a privilege rather than a right. The Court applied heightened scrutiny, noting that "no showing merely of a rational relationship to some colorable state interest would suffice in this highly sensitive constitutional area." The Court struck down the law, concluding that the asserted state interest (fraudulent claims by unscrupulous claimants claiming religious objections to Saturday work) was insufficient and could be satisfied without denying Sabbatarians unemployment benefits.

In *Sherbert*, Justice Douglas concurred: "This case is resolvable not in terms of what an individual can demand of government, but solely in terms of what government may not do to an individual in violation of his religious scruples. [If] appellant is otherwise qualified for unemployment benefits, payments will be made to her not as a Seventh-day Adventist, but as an unemployed worker."

A common problem in cases like *Sherbert* is whether granting a religious exemption to a law that is applicable to everyone else fosters an "establishment" of religion. In *Sherbert*, the state argued that if it gave unemployment benefits to Sabbatarians but denied them to Sunday worshipers, it would establish religion. Justice Harlan, joined by Justice White, dissenting, made exactly this point: "[The] meaning of today's holding [is] that the State must . . . single out for financial assistance those whose behavior is religiously motivated, even though it denies such assistance to others whose identical behavior (in this case, inability to work on Saturdays) is not religiously motivated. . . . [Those] situations in which the Constitution may require special treatment on account of religion are, in my view, few and far between." The Court found no establishment because the exemption "reflects nothing more than the governmental obligation of neutrality in the face of religious differences, and does not represent that involvement of religious with secular institutions which it is the object of the Establishment Clause to forestall."

Disputes about unemployment compensation have generated a great deal of free exercise litigation. In general, these cases have reached the same result as *Sherbert*.[8] One of the more interesting cases is *Thomas v. Review Board*,[9] in which a Jehovah's Witness resigned his job because his religion forbade participation in the production of armaments. The Court held that he was entitled to unemployment compensation. The Court accepted his religious claim, even though another Jehovah's Witness found working on tank turrets "scripturally" acceptable.

F   A   Q

Q: When an individual seeks an exemption for a religious practice, how does the Court determine that the practice is a "genuine" or "valid" religious practice?

A: In general, the Court has been unwilling to delve into the sincerity of an individual's religious beliefs or to determine whether the belief is "genuine" or "valid." As the Court concluded in *Thomas*, the Court is "singularly ill equipped to resolve" differences of opinion regarding a particular religion's requirements or beliefs.

One of the more interesting free exercise cases is *Wisconsin v. Yoder*.[10] That case involved members of the Old Order Amish religion who refused to send their children to school after the eighth grade. Their violation of Wisconsin's compulsory school attendance law, which required them to send their children to school until age 16, resulted in convictions and fines of $5 each. The evidence showed that the Amish believed that salvation requires "life in a church community separate and apart from the world and worldly influences," and Amish communities were devoted to a life in harmony with nature and the soil, and to making their living by farming or closely related activities. The Amish did not object to formal schooling through the eighth grade because they believed that children needed to learn basic reading, writing, and elementary mathematics. However, they viewed formal education beyond the eighth grade as inconsistent with their central religious concepts, which required that those years be used to acquire Amish attitudes favoring manual work and self-reliance and the specific skills needed to perform the adult role of an Amish farmer or housewife. All of these traits, skills, and attitudes were best learned through example and "doing" rather than in a classroom. As the Court noted, the Amish have an excellent record as law-abiding and generally self-sufficient members of society. The Amish also objected to high school because they believed that the values taught conflicted with Amish values and the Amish way of life as well as because it exposed children to "worldly" influences in conflict with Amish beliefs. In particular, high schools emphasized

> intellectual and scientific accomplishments, self-distinction, competitiveness, worldly success, and social life with other students. By contrast, Amish society emphasized informal learning-through-doing; a life of "goodness," rather than a life of intellect; wisdom, rather than technical knowledge, community welfare, rather than competition; and separation from, rather than integration with, contemporary worldly society. In addition, high school teachers were not of the Amish faith and might even be hostile to it. As a result, high

school attendance could not only result in great psychological harm to Amish children, because of the conflicts it would produce, but would also ultimately result in the destruction of the Old Order Amish church community.

In an opinion by Chief Justice Burger, the Court recognized that the Free Exercise Clause applied and that it gave parents the right to control the upbringing of their children. Even though the states have the right to impose rules regarding the control and duration of basic education, the Court recognized that the state interest must "yield to the right of parents to provide an equivalent education in a privately operated system." As a result, a state's interest in universal education is subject to a "balancing process when it impinges on fundamental rights and interests, such as those specifically protected by the Free Exercise Clause of the First Amendment, and the traditional interest of parents with respect to the religious upbringing of their children."

An interesting aspect of the opinion was the Court's discussion of whether the "Amish way of life" qualified for protection under the Free Exercise Clause. The Court answered this question in the affirmative, noting that the "traditional way of life of the Amish is not merely a matter of personal preference, but one of deep religious conviction, shared by an organized group, and intimately related to daily living." In addition, the Amish "way of life" was based on their interpretation of the Bible and pervaded and determined their entire way of life.

Despite the fact that the Court concluded that Wisconsin's compulsory school attendance law was neutral toward religion, the Court concluded that the law was not supported by a governmental interest of the "highest order." The state asserted two interests in support of the law: "some degree of education is necessary to prepare citizens to participate effectively and intelligently in our open political system if we are to preserve freedom and independence" and "education prepares individuals to be self-reliant and self-sufficient participants in society." Although the Court accepted both of these interests as valid, the Court found that an exemption for the Amish would not prevent the state from achieving its objectives since the Amish are "highly successful," prepare children for adulthood in their own way, and rarely become a burden on society.

Justice Douglas dissented in part, arguing that the state may not override the parents' objection if a mature-thinking Amish child wanted to attend high school. "[T]he children themselves have constitutionally protectible interests." He also believed that the majority's emphasis on "the law and order record" of the Amish was irrelevant.

### F	A	Q

Q: What if *Yoder* instead concerned a 13-year-old who had rejected the Amish way of life and wanted to obtain a high school education?

A: As a general rule, the courts tend to defer to parents regarding the upbringing of their children. However, if the child has reached the age of 13 and truly desires to obtain a high school education, *Yoder* becomes a much more difficult case. It is not clear in that case that the Court would hold that the child is exempt from the state's mandatory education law.

Even during this three-decade period, the Court upheld some burdens on religion. For example, in *United States v. Lee*,[11] a member of the Old Order Amish refused to pay Social Security taxes because he had religious objections to the receipt of public insurance benefits and to the payment of taxes to support public insurance funds. The Court overruled the objections, noting that the Social Security system serves the public interest and depends on all employers and employees to share the costs of its comprehensive insurance and benefits system. Moreover, unlike *Yoder*, it would be difficult to accommodate the comprehensive Social Security system with myriad exceptions flowing from a wide variety of religious beliefs.

The Court upheld another burden on religion in *Jimmy Swaggart Ministries v. Board of Education*.[12] In that case, the Court held that a sales and use tax that applied to the sale of all goods and services could be applied to the sale of religious literature. And in *Goldman v. Weinberger*,[13] the Court held that a service person did not have a free exercise right to wear a yarmulke in conjunction with his military uniform in contravention of an Air Force regulation mandating uniform dress. The Court concluded that "the military is, by necessity, a specialized society separate from civilian society" and that "[t]he essence of military service is the subordination of the desires and interests of the individual to the needs of the service." The Court sustained the Air Force's distinction "between religious apparel that is visible and that which is not, and we hold [the] regulations challenged here reasonably and evenhandedly regulate dress in the interest of the military's perceived need for uniformity." Justice Brennan dissented: "It cannot be seriously contended that a serviceman in a yarmulke presents so extreme, so unusual, or so faddish an image that public confidence in his ability to perform his duties will be destroyed." Justice Blackmun also dissented: "[T]he Government has failed to make any meaningful showing that [the costs of an exemption are] significant."

The Court also rejected a free exercise challenge in *O'Lone v. Shabazz*.[14] Under a prison policy, prisoners being transferred from maximum security to minimum security prisons were first assigned to work gangs that labored outside the prison to allow them to adjust to the greater freedom allowed at minimum security facilities. While prisoners were away from the building, they were unable to attend Jumu'ah, a weekly Muslim congregational service that is commanded by the Koran and must be held every Friday after the sun reaches its zenith and before the Asr, or afternoon prayer. Prison officials refused to accommodate gang workers by allowing them to return to the prison because of security risks and administrative problems. In upholding the restriction, the Court emphasized that incarceration necessarily limits many of the prisoners' privileges and rights, judgments that are rightly left to prison administrators. The Court concluded that the prison had acted reasonably in this case because those returning from work details caused congestion and delays at the main gate, "a high risk area in any event," and placed additional pressure on the supervising guards. Justice Brennan, joined by three other justices, dissented: "Jumu'ah is the central religious ceremony of Muslims. ... Despite the plausibility of [alternatives,]

Sidebar

GOLDMAN AND EARLIER REVIEW STANDARDS

In *Goldman*, under the strict scrutiny standard applied in earlier decisions (e.g., *Yoder*), the military might have been required to make an exception for the wearing of yarmulkes if it could not demonstrate that it had a compelling interest in forbidding the conduct.

officials have essentially provided mere pronouncements that such alternatives are not workable."

(3) The *Smith* Approach

In *Employment Division v. Smith*,[15] the Court departed from the higher level of scrutiny applied in earlier cases and signaled a new approach to free exercise claims. *Smith* involved an Oregon law that provided criminal penalties for the knowing or intentional possession of a "controlled substance" unless the substance has been prescribed by a medical practitioner. Included on the list of controlled substances was the drug peyote, a hallucinogen. Respondents, who ingested peyote for sacramental purposes at a ceremony of the Native American Church, to which they belonged, were fired from their jobs with a private drug rehabilitation organization. When they applied for unemployment compensation, respondents were deemed ineligible because they had been discharged for work-related "miscon-duct." In an opinion written by Justice Scalia, the Court upheld the dismissal. The Court began by distinguishing *Sherbert, Thomas,* and *Hobbie v. Unemployment Appeals Commission of Florida*[16] as cases that conditioned the availability of unem-ployment insurance on an individual's willingness to forgo conduct required by his religion. The Court noted that none of the claimants in those cases had engaged in conduct prohibited by law.

In deciding the case, the Court marked out the parameters of the Free Exercise Clause as clearly protecting certain types of things, including "the right to believe and profess whatever religious doctrine one desires." In addition, it includes the right to perform or abstain from such acts as "assembling with others for a worship service, participating in sacramental use of bread and wine, proselytizing, abstaining from certain foods or certain modes of transportation." But the Court concluded that respondents sought to extend the meaning of the Free Exercise Clause by claiming that "their religious motivation for using peyote places them beyond the reach of a criminal law that is not specifically directed at their religious practice, and that is concededly constitutional as applied to those who use the drug for other reasons." The Court disagreed with their interpretation distinguishing laws that discriminate against religion or particular religious groups from otherwise valid laws that are not directed at religion but have the incidental effect of burdening religion. While the Court held that the former type of law should be subjected to strict scrutiny, the Court suggested that it had "never held that an individual's religious beliefs excuse him from compliance with an otherwise valid law prohibiting conduct that the State is free to regulate."

The *Smith* Court indicated that it would strike down a law that burdens religion in only two situations. The first, previously mentioned, is when a law is targeted at religions or religious groups. The second is when the law implicates other constitutional rights, particularly free speech rights. In *Smith*, the Court offered the example of *Wooley v. Maynard*[17] in which the Court held that a state could not compel an individual to display a license plate containing a slogan that offended his religious beliefs. But that case involved free speech and the concept that an individual could not be forced to associate with beliefs that he found repugnant (on religious grounds or otherwise). The Court also discussed *West Virginia Board of Education v. Barnette*[18] in which the Court struck down a state statute requiring a flag salute. Once again, the Court relied heavily on free speech principles. In *Smith,* the Court found that the Oregon law did not discriminate against religion and did not present a combination of constitutional claims.

The *Smith* Court specifically rejected *Sherbert*'s "compelling government interest" test, viewing *Sherbert* as applicable only in the unemployment compensation field, and only then when a "generally applicable criminal law" is absent. The Court feared that to create exemptions under such circumstances would be to allow a religious objector "to become a law unto himself." The Court believed that the "compelling government interest" standard promotes equality when speech and race are involved, but that in the free exercise area the standard produces "a private right to ignore generally applicable laws," something that the Court referred to as "a constitutional anomaly."

In *Smith*, respondents argued that even if the "compelling state interest" test is not applied to all free exercise claims, it should apply to religious conduct that is central to the individual's religion. The Court rejected this argument, noting that it is not the court's job to determine whether a particular belief is central to an individual's religious beliefs. In the Court's view, if the "compelling state interest" test is to be applied at all, it must be applied to "all actions thought to be religiously commanded." Moreover, the Court expressed concern that the "rule respondents favor would open the prospect of constitutionally required religious exemptions from civic obligations of almost every conceivable kind," including military service, tax payments, health and safety regulations, drug laws, child labor laws, and equal opportunity laws.

Justice O'Connor, joined by Justices Brennan, Marshall, and Blackmun, concurred in parts of the judgment. She began by stating that the Court had departed "dramatically" from "well-settled First Amendment jurisprudence" and argued that both religious conduct and religious beliefs are protected by the Free Exercise Clause. Moreover, she argued that a law should be scrutinized more carefully when "it unduly burdens the free exercise of religion." She also noted that the First Amendment does not distinguish between laws that target religious practices and laws that are generally applicable. As a result, she would have required the government to satisfy the "compelling state interest" test and to show that it has used "means narrowly tailored to achieve that interest." Despite her disagreement with the majority's approach, Justice O'Connor would have reached the same result under her analysis. Even though she found that Oregon's statute imposed a "severe burden" on respondents' ability to freely exercise their religion, she found that Oregon had compelling state interest in regulating peyote.

Justice Blackmun, joined by Justices Brennan and Marshall, dissented, arguing that Oregon had not shown "any concrete interest in enforcing its drug laws against religious users of peyote." He noted that the Native American Church placed restrictions on and supervised its members' use of peyote and forbid nonreligious use of peyote. Finally, he challenged the majority's claim that "granting an exception for religious peyote use would erode the state's interest in the uniform, fair, and certain enforcement of its drug laws" and create a "flood of other religious claims." He noted that nearly half the states, as well as the federal government, had exempted the

Sidebar

CRITICISM OF *SMITH*

Critics of the *Smith* decision argue that the decision is inconsistent with prior decisions, which seemed to impose a much higher standard of review, as well as inconsistent with the meaning and spirit of the Free Exercise Clause.

religious use of peyote for many years. He distinguished the Native American Church's limited use of peyote from the Ethiopian Zion Coptic Church's policy of smoking marijuana "continually all day." He also distinguished peyote from marijuana and heroin, "in which there is significant illegal traffic, with its attendant greed and violence, so that it would be difficult to grant a religious exemption without seriously compromising law enforcement efforts." As a result, he concluded that "the State might grant an exemption for religious peyote use, but deny other religious claims arising in different circumstances, would not violate the Establishment Clause."

In reaction to *Smith*, Congress passed the Religious Freedom Restoration Act (RFRA).[19] In enacting RFRA, Congress declared that the Framers of the Constitution viewed the free exercise of religion as an "unalienable right" and that *Smith* had "virtually eliminated the requirement that the government justify burdens on religious exercise imposed by laws neutral toward religion." Instead of the *Smith* test, RFRA provided that the government could not "substantially burden a person's exercise of religion even if the burden results from a rule of general applicability," unless it demonstrates that the burden to the person (1) is in furtherance of a compelling governmental interest and (2) is the least restrictive means of furthering that compelling governmental interest. RFRA further stated that its provisions should not be construed as affecting the Court's interpretation of the Establishment Clause. In *City of Boerne v. Flores*,[20] the Court struck down RFRA as applied to the states, concluding that, as broad "as the power of Congress is under the Enforcement Clause of the Fourteenth Amendment, RFRA contradicts vital principles necessary to maintain separation of powers and the federal balance."

However, it is important to realize that *City of Boerne* does not preclude all applications of RFRA or other congressional enactments mandating a higher level of review in free exercise cases. In the Court's later decision in *Gonzales v. O Centro Espirita Beneficente Uniao Do Vegetal*,[21] a unanimous Court used RFRA to strike down a federal ban on the use of sacramental tea by a religious organization. The Court applied RFRA to the federal law and concluded that the federal interest was insufficient to show that the government had adopted the least restrictive means of advancing a compelling interest.

In *Gonzales*, the government had offered three interests in support of the law: protecting the health and safety of church members, preventing the diversion of *hoasca* from the church to recreational users, and complying with the 1971 United Nations Convention on Psychotropic Substances (CSA) (a treaty signed by the United States and implemented by RFRA). Although both parties presented evidence regarding the health effects of *hoasca*, the trial court found that the evidence was in equilibrium. The government contended that the CSA establishes a "closed" system that prohibits all use of controlled substances except as authorized by the act itself, and "cannot function with its necessary rigor and comprehensiveness if subjected to judicial exemptions." In rejecting the United States' position, the Court noted that federal law has contained an exception for peyote use for the last 35 years and that Congress extended this exemption in 1994 to every recognized Indian tribe. Moreover, the Court noted that all of the government's arguments regarding *hoasca*—for example, its high potential for abuse, its lack of an accepted medical use, and its lack of accepted safety for use under medical supervision—applied as well to the use of peyote. Given the peyote exception, the Court was reluctant to conclude that the government had a compelling interest in prohibiting *hoasca*.

The Court also sustained heightened legislative protection in *Cutter v. Wilkinson*.[22] That case involved Section 3 of the Religious Land Use and Institutionalized Persons Act of 2000 (RLUIPA), which provided in part: "No government shall impose a substantial burden on the religious exercise of a person residing in or confined to an institution," unless the burden furthers "a compelling governmental interest," and does so by "the least restrictive means." Plaintiffs were current and former inmates of the Ohio Department of Rehabilitation and Correction who asserted that they were adherents of non-mainstream religions such as the Satanist, Wicca, and Asatru religions, and the Church of Jesus Christ Christian. Plaintiffs complained that prison officials violated RLUIPA by failing to accommodate their religious exercise in the following ways: "retaliating and discriminating against them for exercising their non-traditional faiths, denying them access to religious literature, denying them the same opportunities for group worship that are granted to adherents of mainstream religions, forbidding them to adhere to the dress and appearance mandates of their religions, withholding religious ceremonial items that are substantially identical to those that the adherents of mainstream religions are permitted, and failing to provide a chaplain trained in their faith."

The Court rejected plaintiffs' challenges against RLUIPA. First, it deflected the argument that Congress had exceeded its Commerce Clause power in enacting the law. The Court distinguished RFRA on the basis that the jurisdictional scope of RLUIPA was more limited. It applied only when a "substantial burden" on religious exercise is imposed by a program or activity that receives federal financial assistance or "the substantial burden affects, or removal of that substantial burden would affect, commerce with foreign nations, among the several States, or with Indian tribes." The Court also rejected the argument that RLUIPA improperly advanced religion in violation of the Establishment Clause, noting that RLUIPA involved a permissible legislative accommodation of religion "because it alleviates exceptional government-created burdens on private religious exercise." "RLUIPA thus protects institutionalized persons who are unable freely to attend to their religious needs and are therefore dependent on the government's permission and accommodation for exercise of their religion," and it makes religious accommodation subordinate to "an institution's need to maintain order and safety" in applying the compelling governmental interest standard.

Example: Although *Smith* is the most important recent decision, another significant pre-*Smith* decision is *Lyng v. Northwest Indian Cemetery Protective Association*,[23] in which the Court refused to stop the U.S. Forest Service from building a road through the Chimney Rock section of the Six Rivers National Forest. The road project was challenged by American Indians who claimed that the area was part of "an integral and indispensable part of Indian religious conceptualization and practice" and that "successful use of the [area] is dependent upon and facilitated by certain qualities of the physical environment, the most important of which are privacy, silence, and an undisturbed natural setting." Plaintiffs argued that the new road would seriously damage land that they considered sacred. The Forest Service rejected alternative sites as unfeasible. In an opinion by Justice O'Connor, the Court held that an accommodation was not required. While the Court acknowledged that respondents' beliefs were "sincere" and that the proposed road would severely affect the practice of their religion, the Court concluded that the "Free Exercise Clause claim simply cannot be understood to require the Government to conduct its own internal affairs in ways that comport with the religious beliefs of particular citizens." While the Free Exercise Clause might provide an individual some protection against "governmental compulsion[,] it does not afford an individual a right to dictate the conduct of the Government's internal procedures." The Court refused to consider the centrality or indispensability of the religious practice, noting that it had consistently refused to involve itself in determinations regarding the genuineness of religious beliefs or the centrality or indispensability of those beliefs. Justice Brennan, joined by Justices Marshall and Blackmun, dissented, arguing that respondents "have demonstrated that the Government's proposed activities will completely prevent them from practicing their religion, and such a showing [entitles] them to the protections of the Free Exercise Clause."

B. Discrimination Against Religion

In a number of cases, the Court has held that laws that discriminate against religion should be subjected to heightened scrutiny. For example, in *McDaniel v. Paty*,[24] the Court struck down a statute that prohibited ministers or members of religious orders from being members of state legislatures. Likewise, in *Fowler v. Rhode Island*,[25] the Court held that a municipal ordinance was unconstitutional when it was construed as prohibiting preaching in a public park by a Jehovah's Witness while allowing a Catholic mass or Protestant church service.

Smith reaffirmed the antidiscrimination principle, as did the Court's subsequent decision in *Church of the Lukumi Babalu Aye, Inc. v. City of Hialeah*.[26] *Church of the Lukumi Babalu Aye* struck down a local law prohibiting the religious sacrifice of animals. That case involved the Santeria religion, which believes in spirits called orishas that help people fulfill their destinies. The orishas exist on animal sacrifices, and the Santerias sacrifice animals such as chickens, doves, goats, and sheep at birth, marriage, and death rituals; to cure the sick; and at various initiation and annual celebration rituals. When the Santerias opened the Church of the Lukumi Babalu Aye in Hialeah, Florida, the city passed a series of ordinances prohibiting animal sacrifice. The ordinances, enacted on an emergency basis, provided that any person or organization practicing animal sacrifice "will be prosecuted."

The city council then passed three more ordinances. Ordinance 87-52 defined "sacrifice" as "to unnecessarily kill, torment, torture, or mutilate an animal in a public or private ritual or ceremony not for the primary purpose of food consumption," and prohibited owning or possessing an animal "intending to use such animal for food purposes." However, the ordinance also provided that the prohibition applied only to an individual or group that "kills, slaughters or sacrifices animals for any type of ritual, regardless of whether or not the flesh or blood of the animal is to be consumed." The ordinance contained an exemption for slaughtering by "licensed establishment[s]" of animals "specifically raised for food purposes." Then the city council declared "that the sacrificing of animals within the city limits is contrary to the public health, safety, welfare and morals of the community," and adopted Ordinance 87-71, which provided that "[i]t shall be unlawful for any person, persons, corporations or associations to sacrifice any animal within the corporate limits of the City of Hialeah, Florida." The final Ordinance, 87-72, defined "slaughter" as "the killing of animals for food" and prohibited slaughter outside of areas zoned for slaughterhouse use. The ordinance provided an exemption for the slaughter or processing for sale of "small numbers of hogs and/or cattle per week in accordance with an exemption provided by state law." The Church sought to challenge all of the ordinances as a violation of the Free Exercise Clause.

In an opinion by Justice Kennedy, the Court struck down the Hialeah ordinances. The Court recognized that animal sacrifice can constitute a religious practice, and the Court reaffirmed its holding in *Smith* — that the Court will not apply strict scrutiny to a law that is "neutral and of general applicability," even if that law incidentally burdens a particular religious practice. But the Court distinguished *Smith,* noting that the First Amendment "forbids an official purpose to disapprove of a particular religion or of religion in general" and that the Free Exercise Clause was included because of "historical instances of religious persecution and intolerance." The Court held that a law that discriminates on the basis of religion would be "invalid unless it is justified by a compelling interest and is narrowly tailored to advance that interest." In concluding that the Hialeah law discriminated against religion, the Court noted that its examination should begin with the text of the law. But facial neutrality would not, by itself, save a law, and the Court held that it was entitled to consider not only the wording and function of the ordinances, but also their background. In applying this test, the Court found that the Hialeah ordinances were facially neutral, but that the city's purpose was to discriminate against religion. The Court reached this conclusion because the only conduct reached by the ordinances was Santeria religious exercises. The ordinances prohibited "few if any killings of animals . . . other than Santeria sacrifice. . . . [K]illings that are no more necessary or humane [than the sacrifices] in almost all other circumstances are unpunished."

Of course, the mere fact that a law discriminates against religion does not require invalidation. It does necessitate proof of a compelling interest supporting the discrimination, and a showing that reasonable alternatives are unavailable. In *Church of the Lukumi,* the Court found that the "legitimate governmental interests in protecting the public health and preventing cruelty to animals could be addressed by restrictions stopping far short of a flat prohibition of all Santeria sacrificial practice." For example, if the city was concerned about the proper disposal of carcasses, it could have passed organic disposal regulations. The Court also found that a "narrower regulation would achieve the city's interest in preventing cruelty to animals." Of course, the narrower regulation would not prevent the sacrifice, but would ensure that animals were killed humanely by the simultaneous and instantaneous severance of the carotid arteries.

Although the Court found that one of the ordinances, Ordinance 87-72, applied to nonreligious conduct and was not overbroad, the Court struck it down because it operated "in tandem with the other ordinances to suppress Santeria religious worship." Not only did the Court find an intent to discriminate against religion, the Court held that the ordinances were not of general applicability. The Court reached this result after noting that the ordinances did not "prohibit nonreligious conduct that endangers these interests in a similar or greater degree than Santeria sacrifice does." Thus, even though the ordinance purported to prohibit cruelty to animals, the ordinances prohibited "few killings but those occasioned by religious sacrifice." Other types of animal deaths or killings for nonreligious reasons "are either not prohibited or approved by express provision." The Court also held that the city's interest in "public health" was not evenly applied either. "The city does [not] prohibit hunters from bringing their kill to their houses, nor does it regulate disposal after their activity. Despite substantial testimony at trial that the same public health hazards result from improper disposal of garbage by restaurants, restaurants are outside the scope of the ordinances."

In the final analysis, the Court concluded that "each of Hialeah's ordinances pursues the city's governmental interests only against conduct motivated by religious belief." The Court went on to find that the ordinances "'ha[ve] every appearance of a prohibition that society is prepared to impose upon [Santeria worshipers] but not upon itself.' This precise evil is what the requirement of general applicability is designed to prevent."

F A Q

Q: If the Free Exercise Clause does not protect Native Americans who wish to use peyote, why does it protect the Santerias in their sacrificial killing of animals?

A: *Church of the Lukumi* (animal sacrifice) arguably involves starkly different principles than *Smith* (peyote). Because *Smith* involved a neutral generally applicable law, which was not directed at religion, the Court was deferential and more inclined to sustain the statute. By contrast, *Church of the Lukumi* involved a law that was directed at, and involved discrimination against, religion. The Court tends to apply strict scrutiny to laws that discriminate against religion.

Type of Law	Scope of Review
Generally applicable criminal law	Rational basis
Law that discriminates against religion	Strict scrutiny
Law subject to RFRA	Strict scrutiny

SUMMARY

■ In early Free Exercise Clause cases, the U.S. Supreme Court applied heightened scrutiny to some laws that burdened an individual in the exercise of his or her religion.

■ In recent years, the Court has tended to apply a lower standard of review to generally applicable laws that burden or affect religion only incidentally.

■ By contrast, the Court applies strict scrutiny when it finds that government has tried to discriminate against religion or religious practices.

CONNECTIONS

Establishment Clause

The Establishment Clause and the Free Exercise Clause of the First Amendment are the religion clauses of the U.S. Constitution. In some respects, there is a tension between the two clauses in the sense that although the Free Exercise Clause seems to require government to accommodate religion, the Establishment Clause might preclude an accommodation that effects an establishment of religion.

Judicial Review

As in other constitutional areas, the Free Exercise Clause can be enforced through the medium of judicial review.

State Police Powers

In some instances, the Court has held that the Free Exercise Clause might require states to provide an accommodation that exempts a religious practice from the burdens of a law enacted under state police powers.

Commerce Clause

In some instances, the Court has held that the Free Exercise Clause might require states to provide an accommodation that exempts a religious practice from the burdens of a law enacted under the Commerce Clause.

Endnotes

1. 98 U.S. (8 Otto) 145 (1878).
2. *See also* Davis v. Beason, 133 U.S. 333 (1890).
3. 310 U.S. 296 (1940).
4. 321 U.S. 158 (1944).
5. 367 U.S. 488 (1961).
6. 374 U.S. 398 (1963).
7. 366 U.S. 599 (1961).
8. *See* Frazee v. Ill. Dept. of Employment Security, 489 U.S. 829 (1989) (Frazee, who refused employment because he would have been forced to work on his sabbath (Sunday), was held entitled to unemployment benefits); Hobbie v. Unemployment Appeals Commn., 480 U.S. 136 (1987) (Hobbie, who was discharged because she refused to work on a Friday evening or Saturday because she was a Seventh-day Adventist, was also entitled to unemployment compensation).
9. 450 U.S. 707 (1981).
10. 406 U.S. 205 (1972).
11. 455 U.S. 252 (1982).
12. 493 U.S. 378 (1990).
13. 475 U.S. 503 (1986).
14. 482 U.S. 342 (1987).
15. 494 U.S. 872 (1990).
16. 480 U.S. 136 (1987).
17. 430 U.S. 705 (1977).

18. 319 U.S. 624 (1943).
19. 42 U.S.C. §§2000bb et seq.
20. 521 U.S. 507 (1997).
21. 546 U.S. 418 (2006).
22. 544 U.S. 709 (2005).
23. 485 U.S. 439 (1988).
24. 435 U.S. 618 (1978).
25. 345 U.S. 67 (1953).
26. 508 U.S. 520 (1993).

The Second Amendment

13

One of the least litigated provisions of the Bill of Rights is the Second Amendment. This provision establishes that "[a] well-regulated Militia,

O V E R V I E W

being necessary to the security of a free State, the right of the people to keep and bear Arms, shall not be infringed." The initial challenge to understanding the Second Amendment is whether its scope is narrow and conditional or broad and unqualified. In this regard, there have been two primary competing interpretations. The first is that it prohibits the federal government from prohibiting state militias from arming their members. Exponents of this understanding note that the Second Amendment was framed and ratified at a time when militias were organized on an *ad hoc* basis. Pursuant to this model, citizens were called on to serve for a specific war or security purpose and were expected to bring their arms with them. The second understanding is that the provision protects individuals from those who would limit its scope to arms known to the framers to others who would brook no interference with the purported right.

A. HISTORICAL BACKGROUND

B. MODERN CASE LAW

A. Historical Background

Although the scope of "the right to own and bear arms" has been a prolonged and intense controversy, case law is scarce. In initially reviewing the Second Amendment, in *Presser v. Illinois*,[1] the Court determined that it was not incorporated into the Fourteenth Amendment. In this case, the Court upheld the state's power to regulate firearms in connection with public mock military activities.

Gun shows are a common and controversial source of firearms purchases. Approximately 5,000 of them are held annually in the United States.

© This file is licensed under Creative Commons Attribution 2.0. http://flickr.com/glasgows/.

The Court, in *United States v. Miller*,[2] determined that the federal government (pursuant to its commerce power) could prohibit interstate transportation of certain types of firearms. This case concerned the shipment of sawed-off shotguns. In its decision, the Court indicated that the right was conditioned upon the need to organize militias. It thus observed that such weapons had no "reasonable relationship to the preservation or efficiency of a well-regulated militia."

The next Supreme Court decision concerning the Second Amendment, *Lewis v. United States*,[3] addressed the relatively narrow issue of whether the federal government could prohibit felons from owning firearms. Like the cases that preceded it, the *Lewis* Court provided no indication of the scope of federal or state power to restrict gun ownership. Nor did it address the issue of whether common weaponry, such as handguns, could be regulated.

B. Modern Case Law

The Court, in *District of Columbia v. Heller*,[4] tacked away from its earlier indication that the Second Amendment is tethered by the need to organize a militia. In this case, the Court invalidated a District of Columbia law that prohibited handguns and required rifles to be disassembled or disabled by trigger locks in the home. Writing for the majority, Justice Scalia centered the decision on text and history. In this regard, he cited the origins of gun rights in seventeenth-century England and traced them through the American Revolution and Reconstruction. The Court determined that by the time of the nation's founding, "the right to have arms had become fundamental for English subjects." It further observed that "[t]he Second Amendment, like the Fourth Amendment, codified a pre-existing right."

Justice Stevens, in a dissenting opinion joined by Justices Souter, Ginsburg, and Breyer, acknowledged that the Second Amendment protects an individual right. The issue as he saw it was the scope of the right. From his perspective, the Second Amendment protected service in the militia and gave the legislature ample space to legislate.

The scope of the Second Amendment, pursuant to *Heller*, is uncertain. The Court, for instance, did not address whether a person has the right to carry guns outside the home. Nor did it decide whether firearms other than handguns can be restricted. Because the District of Columbia is a federal enclave, the issue of the Second Amendment's incorporation was not before the Court. Numerous cities throughout the nation have banned handguns and gun stores. To the extent these provisions are challenged, the threshold question will be whether the Second Amendment is incorporated into the Fourteenth Amendment Due Process Clause and thus applicable to the states.

Sidebar

AU TO ADD

The *Heller* case originated with a constitutional law scholar (Robert Levy) of the Cato Institute. He consciously modeled the litigation upon the NAACP's successful strategy for defeating segregation. Toward this end, he organized a team that researched the Second Amendment and developed the case. Levy, who never owned a gun, funded the litigation from his own pocket. The plaintiff was a security guard who carried a gun at work but, under the District of Columbia law, could not have it at home.

Problem

The City of Liberty, in response to increasing crimes of violence, wants to enact gun control legislation. As General Counsel for the city, you have been asked by the City Council to analyze relevant case law and draft a memorandum on the possibilities for an ordinance that does not run afoul of the Second Amendment. Among the factors you have been asked to consider are any differentiation that may be drawn between a federal and state enactment, the relevance of weapon type, and any distinguishing concerns may be pertinent to the outcome. Your practice in drafting memoranda of this nature is to develop an outline of key points. What would they be in this instance?

SUMMARY

- The Second Amendment for nearly two centuries had an uncertain meaning, due largely to sparse case law on it.

- Competing perspectives on the Second Amendment reflected understandings that it (1) was necessary to ensure an effective militia and (2) secured an individual right minus any such nexus.

- Modern case law reflects the former understanding of the Second Amendment.

- The boundaries of the Second Amendment to a large extent remain uncharted.

CONNECTIONS

Commerce Power

This power enables Congress to regulate commerce among the several states. Courts since the 1930s have tended to read it expansively, and thus it has emerged as a primary basis for federal regulation across a broad range of activities and interests.

Fourth Amendment

This guarantee protects the people against searches and seizures of "persons, houses, papers, and effects" that are unreasonable. The Fourth Amendment enumerates the prerequisites for a warrant, including probable cause.

Endnotes

1. 116 U.S. 252 (1886).
2. 307 U.S. 174 (1939).
3. 445 U.S. 55 (1980).
4. 128 S. Ct. 2783 (2008).

State Action

14

Most provisions of the Bill of Rights and the Fourteenth Amendment apply only if the state, either on its own or in conjunction with private

O V E R V I E W

parties, is sufficiently involved. Although private conduct may be actionable under tort or statutory law, it is not constitutionally prohibited. When plaintiffs assert a violation of the Bill of Rights or the Fourteenth Amendment, state involvement will be obvious in most instances. More difficult questions arise when the violation seems to be the result of private action. Since government is involved in virtually all private conduct in one way or another, the real question is whether the government is sufficiently involved so that the ostensibly private action effectively becomes state action. Questions about state action present difficult issues for the courts.

A. Government Function

One situation in which the Court has found state action is when a private entity performs a traditional **governmental function** (actions that are governmental in their function and nature). If a private entity is found to be performing a governmental function, then the protections of the Bill of Rights and the Fourteenth Amendment may apply to that governmental function. Determining what constitutes a traditional governmental function is the critical difficulty that lies at the center of governmental function cases.

(1) Company Towns

So-called company towns provide a classic example of state action. In such cases, a private town arguably is functioning like a public one, and therefore its actions should be treated like a public town for constitutional purposes. Illustrative is the holding in *Marsh v. Alabama*,[1] which involved a town (Chickasaw) owned by a private company. Like other towns, this one included residential buildings, streets, a sewer system, a sewage disposal plant, various businesses, a U.S. post office, a sheriff (paid by the company), and a business block with stores, paved sidewalks, and streets that connected to public highways. The Court treated the company town as a municipality for purposes of the First and Fourteenth Amendments, concluding that the "more an owner, for his advantage, opens up his property for use by the public[,] the more [his] rights become circumscribed by the statutory and constitutional rights of those who use it."

In reaching its decision, the *Marsh* Court emphasized that Chickasaw functioned like any other town, and the mere fact it was privately owned "is not sufficient to justify the State's permitting a corporation to govern a community of citizens so as to restrict their fundamental liberties and the enforcement of such restraint by the application of a State statute."

F   A   Q

Q: What is the logical consequence of concluding that a company town's actions should be treated as state action?

A: The logical consequence is that the company's actions will be treated as those of the state for constitutional purposes, and therefore the provisions of the Bill of Rights will apply. For example, in *Marsh*, the company sought to prevent a woman from engaging in expressive activity in the town on the grounds that it was private property. After concluding that the company town should be treated like any other town for purposes of state action, the Court held that the woman had a First Amendment right (as incorporated into, and applied to, the states by virtue of the Fourteenth Amendment) to engage in expressive activity in the town, even though she was on private property.

Towns like Chickasaw were constructs of the nineteenth century and have largely disappeared today. Nevertheless, there has been considerable litigation about whether the actions of private shopping malls should be treated as state action for purposes of the Constitution. As in *Marsh*, these issues often arise in the context of individuals who seek to use shopping malls for expressive purposes. For example, in *Amalgamated Food Employees Union v. Logan Valley Plaza, Inc.*,[2] union members peacefully picketed a business located in a private shopping center. When the owners of the center sought to enjoin the picketing as a trespass, the Court analogized to *Marsh*, saying, "The similarities between the business block in *Marsh* and the shopping center in the present case are striking." For that reason, the Court held that the shopping center's actions constituted state action, meaning that the First Amendment applied.

But *Logan Valley*'s holding did not survive. The Court's later decision in *Lloyd Corp., Ltd. v. Tanner*[3] distinguished *Marsh* and *Logan Valley* and held that the shopping center's conduct in *Lloyd Corp.* constituted private action. Like the company town in *Marsh*, the center in *Lloyd Corp.* was policed by private security guards hired by the center. When the center's security guards accosted individuals who were distributing handbills (expressing opposition to the Vietnam War) and ordered them to leave on pain of arrest, they sued. "[*Logan Valley*] was carefully phrased to limit its holding to the picketing involved, where the picketing was 'directly related in its purpose to the use to which the shopping center property was being put,' and where the store was located in the center of a large private enclave with the consequence that no other reasonable opportunities for the pickets to convey their message to their intended audience were available. . . . Neither of these elements is present in the case now before the Court."

In *Hudgens v. NLRB*,[4] the Court flatly overruled *Logan Valley* in a case that involved union members who were engaged in peaceful protesting inside a privately owned shopping center. When they were threatened with arrest by an agent of the owner, they sought declaratory and injunctive relief. The question was whether the threat constituted an unfair labor practice within the meaning of the National Labor Relations Act. The Court held that the picketers did not have a First Amendment right to picket inside the mall. As a result, the actions of the owners of private shopping malls are generally not regarded as state action today.

(2) Party Primaries

The other context in which governmental function issues have arisen is related to the conduct of electoral primaries. In a series of cases decided between 1927 and 1953, the Court was confronted by cases challenging the Democratic Party's efforts to preclude blacks from participating in its party primaries. Since political parties are generally regarded as voluntary associations of private individuals rather than as governmental entities, plaintiffs sought to use the governmental function doctrine to argue instead that the party's conduct should be treated as state action. In the party primary cases, the Court agreed.

The first case, *Nixon v. Herndon*,[5] involved a Texas statute that explicitly prohibited blacks from voting in the Democratic Party primary. The Court struck down the law, concluding that its mandated discrimination constituted state action. Following *Nixon*, the Texas legislature passed a new law giving the Democratic Party's Executive Committee the right to decide who could vote in its party primaries, and the party passed a resolution allowing only white Democrats to vote. In *Nixon v. Condon*,[6] the Court struck this law down too, finding state action on the basis that the "Committee operated as representative of the State in the discharge of the State's authority."

Condon left open the question of a party's inherent power to determine its own membership. That issue was presented in *Smith v. Allwright.*[7] After the prior laws were struck down, the Texas Democratic Party passed a resolution limiting membership to white citizens of the State of Texas. Since only party members could vote in the Democratic primary, this resolution effectively precluded blacks from participating. However, the resolution was adopted by the party on its own without statutory authorization. Although the Court initially upheld a similar restriction in *Grovey v. Townsend,*[8] the Court reversed in *Smith v. Allwright* and held that state action existed: The "statutory system for the selection of party nominees for inclusion on the general election ballot makes the party which is required to follow these legislative directions an agency of the state in so far as it determines the participants in a primary election." Although the Court was unwilling to hold that the "privilege of membership in a party" is a state concern, the Court held that state action existed since the privilege of membership "is also the essential qualification for voting in a primary to select nominees for a general election."

Following *Smith,* the Court decided *Terry v. Adams,*[9] involving a Texas county political organization called the Jaybird Democratic Association, or Jaybird Party, that excluded black voters from its pre-primary elections on racial grounds. The party's expenses were paid by assessing candidates for office for participating in its primaries. With few exceptions, those who won the Jaybird Party pre-primary subsequently won the general election. The Court recognized that a party may not prohibit voters from participating in a primary on the basis of race and found that the Jaybird Party was doing nothing more than using the primary to ratify the results of its discriminatory pre-primary. As a result, the pre-primary was the equivalent of a prohibited election: "The only election that has counted in this Texas county for more than fifty years has been that held by the Jaybirds from which Negroes were excluded." As a result, the effect "is to do precisely that which the Fifteenth Amendment forbids — strip Negroes of every vestige of influence in selecting the officials who control the local county matters that intimately touch the daily lives of citizens."

Sidebar

THE IMPORTANCE OF HISTORICAL CONTEXT

It is important to realize that decisions like *Condon* and *Smith* were probably a product of their times and the ongoing struggle for civil rights. As a result, they should not be read too broadly.

F   A   Q

Q: Why don't the Jaybirds' First Amendment rights allow them to hold a pre-primary that excluded blacks?

A: The First Amendment clearly protects the right of individuals to associate for expressive purposes. As a result, any group has the power to band together to promote those things in which it believes, and government does not have the right to prohibit individual or group beliefs, including racist beliefs. The Court probably struck down the Jaybird pre-primary because of the history of excluding blacks from the political process in the State of Texas and because the Jaybird pre-primary seemed to be just another attempt to end-run the Court's prior decisions.

It is difficult to know whether the *Smith* decision was simply a product of its times or whether it has broader application. A modern equivalent might exist if women's groups, anxious to elect more female candidates, banded together to vote on which candidates to endorse. Presumably, they prefer women or (perhaps) men with women-friendly agendas. It is difficult to believe that the Court would strike down such a pre-primary, even if the women were often successful.

(3) Other Modern Cases

Even though the company town and party primary cases were decided long ago, the governmental function approach to state action is hardly dead. In several more recent cases, the Court has applied governmental function principles. For example, in *Edmonson v. Leesville Concrete Co., Inc.*,[10] defendant used peremptory challenges to remove black persons from a prospective jury list. Relying on its prior holding in *Batson v. Kentucky*,[11] the Court focused on whether the defendant qualified as a state actor. In ruling that he did, the Court found that defendant had made extensive use of state procedures with "the overt, significant assistance of state officials," including Congress, which established the qualifications for jury service and the procedures for juror selection, and the judge. Justice O'Connor, joined by Chief Justice Burger and Justice Scalia, dissented, arguing that the peremptory challenge involves private action because it merely allows "*private* parties[] to exclude potential jurors [and] is left wholly within the discretion of the litigant." It therefore is "an enclave of private action in a government-managed proceeding."

The Court also found state action in *West v. Atkins*[12] in a case involving a private physician who contracted with a state prison to provide inmate medical care on a contract basis. The Court emphasized that the state had a legal obligation to provide adequate medical care to inmates, that inmates were allowed to use only the prison doctor, and that the state had essentially delegated its obligations by contracting out to a private doctor. In doing so, the Court distinguished its prior holding in *Polk County v. Dodson*,[13] which held that a public defender was not a state actor because he had a professional obligation "to be an adversary of the State." The Court found that a contract doctor was different because the state's decision to contract out prison medical care "does not relieve the State of its constitutional duty to provide adequate medical treatment to those in its custody." Even though a doctor has a "professional and ethical obligation to make independent medical judgments," that obligation does not place the doctor "in conflict with the State and other prison authorities."

B. State Involvement or Encouragement

Although the Court has decided a number of governmental function cases, far more cases involve allegations of **state involvement or encouragement**. In these cases, the question is whether government is sufficiently involved in private action, or has sufficiently encouraged private action, so that the actions of private individuals or corporations should be treated as state action. If a finding of state action is found, then the provisions of the Bill of Rights, as well as the Fourteenth Amendment, may apply to actions of the private individual or corporation.

The difficulty with the state involvement or encouragement cases is that government is almost always involved in private action in some way. For example, even if government does not explicitly encourage a particular action (for example, racial discrimination), government may have enacted laws that permit, or fail to prohibit, the individual acts of discrimination. The critical question in each case is whether there is enough involvement or encouragement in a given case to transform private discrimination into state action.

The seminal decision is *Burton v. Wilmington Parking Authority*.[14] That case involved a private coffee shop located in a public parking garage that refused to serve food or drinks to blacks, and the question was whether the coffee shop's discrimination should be treated as state action for purposes of the Fourteenth Amendment's Equal Protection Clause. Ordinarily, in the absence of proof of governmental involvement (or a statutory or other prohibition), private individuals are free to discriminate on the basis of race. However, in *Burton*, the Court concluded that the government was sufficiently involved in the discrimination so as to create state action. The Court noted that the parking garage was created by the city to provide adequate parking facilities for the public, that the land and the building were publicly owned, and that the commercial space was designed to generate revenue so that the facility would be economically viable and self-sustaining. In addition, the Court found a synergy between the parking garage and the shop in that the shop's customers could park in the garage and the shop helped create demand for the parking facilities. The net effect was that "profits earned by discrimination not only contribute to, but also are indispensable elements in, the financial success of a governmental agency." Finally, the Court emphasized that "the restaurant is operated as an integral part of a public building devoted to a public parking service," indicating a "degree of state participation and involvement in discriminatory action which it was the design of the Fourteenth Amendment to condemn." Noting that the city could have prohibited race discrimination in its lease, the Court emphasized that the "State has so far insinuated itself into a position of interdependence with Eagle that it must be recognized as a joint participant in the challenged activity, which, on that account, cannot be considered to have been so 'purely private' as to fall without the scope of the Fourteenth Amendment."

Each of the involvement or encouragement decisions must be evaluated on their own merits, and the outcomes might not always seem consistent. For example, in *Peterson v. City of Greenville*,[15] the Court found state action when petitioners were refused service at a lunch counter and ultimately convicted of trespass for their failure to leave. In reaching its conclusion, the Court emphasized that local law required businesses (like the lunch counter) to discriminate on the basis of race. "When a state agency passes a law compelling persons to discriminate against other persons because of race, and the State's criminal processes are employed in a way which enforces the discrimination mandated by that law, such a palpable violation of the Fourteenth Amendment cannot be saved by attempting to separate the mental urges of the discriminators."

F A Q

Q: Does *Peterson* suggest that the state cannot enforce trespass laws against those who refuse to leave a private business when asked to do so?

A: No. In general, private individuals have the right to discriminate on the basis of race unless some law or other enactment prevents them from doing so. The difficulty is that the law involved in *Peterson* required the proprietor to discriminate on the basis of race. This requirement transformed the private action into state action by creating a state mandate. By contrast, suppose that no state law requires discrimination. In that context, if a racist couple decided to discriminate on the basis of race in terms of whom they invite to dinner at their home, it is likely that the courts will not find state action, even if the couple used state trespass laws to help them exclude individuals of other races.

In some respects, decisions like *Burton* and *Peterson* are easy cases for finding state action. *Peterson* was especially easy because local law mandated the alleged discrimination so that the private actors were not free to choose to act in a nondiscriminatory manner. Other cases present facts that less obviously involve state action and that require more complex judgments by the courts. For example, *Norwood v. Harrison*[16] involved the question of whether the State of Mississippi's decision to loan textbooks to private schools (including schools that discriminated on the basis of race) implicated the state in that discrimination. In *Norwood*, the argument could have been made that the decision to discriminate was private because the textbook loans were made without regard to whether the school discriminated, and the decision to discriminate was made by the racially discriminatory schools themselves and by the parents who chose to send their children to those schools. Moreover, the state court assert a nondiscriminatory interest in support of the law (the state's desire to ensure that all of its citizens were well educated), and the textbook loan program predated desegregation.

Nevertheless, in *Norwood*, the Court found state action by virtue of the textbook loan program. The Court was undoubtedly influenced by the fact that the case arose in the context of the desegregation movement. Indeed, the Court emphasized that the number of private racially discriminatory schools had increased dramatically in the wake of desegregation efforts and noted that the existence of the private schools (and their racially discriminatory policies) was undercutting desegregation efforts. In addition, the Court focused on the fact that the cost of learning materials constituted an "inescapable educational cost" and provided support for discrimination. Finally, the Court emphasized that Mississippi's actions were constitutionally barred, noting that "[a] state may not induce, encourage or promote private persons to accomplish what it is constitutionally forbidden to accomplish."

Despite *Norwood*'s holding, not all governmental involvement in private discrimination is sufficient to create state action. For example, in *Moose Lodge v. Irvis*,[17] Irvis was refused service by Moose Lodge on the basis of his race. He sued, claiming a violation of 42 U.S.C. §1983 (which requires a demonstration that state officials denied federal rights under color of state law or, in essence, imposes the equivalent of a state action requirement). Although Irvis conceded that private clubs could discriminate in their choice of members, he alleged that state action existed because the club was licensed to sell alcoholic beverages. Given the importance of a liquor license to the survival of a private club, he argued that the record revealed sufficient state involvement and encouragement to constitute state action.

In *Moose Lodge*, the Court refused to find state action. Although the alcohol license gave Moose Lodge a benefit, the aid was insufficient to create state action. In reaching its decision, the Court emphasized that some state-furnished services qualify as necessities (for example, electricity, water, and police and fire protection) and that these services could not be treated as state action without utterly emasculating "the distinction between private as distinguished from state conduct." To constitute state action, the state must have "significantly involved itself with invidious discriminations." The Court found that Pennsylvania's liquor license did not "overtly or covertly encourage discrimination." Moreover, distinguishing *Burton*, the Court emphasized that Moose Lodge operated on private property and did not hold itself out as a place of public accommodation. Even though Moose Lodge held a liquor license, the only impact of the license was the fact that private licenses are counted in the total number of licenses that can be issued in a municipality. The Court concluded that the Lodge did not receive a monopoly because of the significant number of hotels, restaurants, and retail stores that also held liquor licenses. However, the Court did strike down a portion of the governing statute that affirmatively required licensees to adhere to their constitutions and bylaws— in this case, a discriminatory constitution and bylaws.

It is important to realize that the decision in *Moose Lodge* was not inevitable or clear-cut and that the Court could have reached the opposite result. Justice Douglas, joined by Justice Marshall, dissented in *Moose Lodge*, arguing that "the scarcity of liquor licenses makes its difficult for blacks to obtain liquor during parts of the week, and that the license is a necessity for the survival of an organization like the Moose Lodge." Justice Brennan, joined by Justice Marshall, also dissented: "When Moose Lodge obtained its liquor license, the State of Pennsylvania became an active participant in the operation of the Lodge bar. Liquor licensing laws [are] primarily pervasive regulatory schemes under which the State dictates and continually supervises virtually every detail of the operation of the licensee's business."

Although Moose Lodge involved a private club, the Court has been willing to find private action, even though a company holds a public license to operate and functions under a signification level of governmental regulation. For example, *CBS, Inc. v. Democratic National Committee*[18] involved a complaint filed with the Federal Communications Commission (FCC) against a radio station (WTOP) that refused to air a series of one-minute spot announcements expressing views on the Vietnam War. Because WTOP believed that it already provided "full and fair coverage of important public questions," it had a policy against selling time to individuals and groups who wished to expound their views on controversial issues. WTOP submitted evidence showing that it had aired views critical of the government's Vietnam policy on numerous occasions. In rejecting an allegation of state action, the Court emphasized that Congress opted for a system of private broadcasting. Although licensed and regulated by the government, license holders were treated as "public trustees" who were "charged with the duty of fairly and impartially informing the public audience." The government served simply as an "overseer" whose task was to ensure fairness, balance, and objectivity. In other words, broadcast licensees retained a measure of journalistic freedom so long as they discharged their duties as public trustees. The Court also emphasized that the FCC did not create or command the station's editorial policy, but simply left decisions on that issue to "journalistic discretion" so that the government was not a "partner" in the licensee's action.

Sidebar

EVALUATING THE EXTENT OF GOVERNMENTAL INVOLVEMENT

Moose Lodge illustrates the notion that even though the state may have some involvement in private action, the state's involvement may be insufficient to create state action. In *Moose Lodge*, the club's decision to discriminate was a private decision that was not encouraged or mandated by the state. As a result, the Court regarded the decision to discriminate as private. However, the fact that Moose Lodge was allowed to hold a liquor license could hardly be regarded as an insignificant governmental benefit. After all, most social clubs of this nature would find it difficult to survive without a liquor license. Nevertheless, the Court concluded that this benefit was insufficient to create state action.

Q: Is there a precise test by which the courts determine that sufficient governmental involvement or encouragement exists to justify a ruling of state action?

A: No. Each case must be analyzed on its own merits, and the decisions as a whole are not necessarily consistent. For example, if one compares *Moose Lodge* to *Gilmore*, one can argue that the governmental involvement or encouragement was greater in *Moose Lodge* than in *Gilmore*. After all, a liquor license is arguably more important to a private club than the right to use a public park is to a racially segregated school. Nevertheless, in *Gilmore* the Court found state action while in *Moose Lodge* the Court refused to do so.

As we saw in the prior cases, the mere fact that government fails to prohibit discrimination does not necessarily transform private action into state action. But suppose that state laws prohibiting discrimination are revoked. Does the revocation create state action? *Reitman v. Mulkey*[19] involved a challenge to a California constitutional amendment that removed the authority of state and local governments to "limit or abridge, directly or indirectly, the right of any person, who is willing or desires to sell, lease or rent any part or all of his real property, to decline to sell, lease or rent such property to such person or persons as he, in his absolute discretion, chooses." When individuals refused to rent property based on the lessee's race, in reliance on the amendment, the Court found that the private refusal was supported by state action. The Court viewed the statute as more than a repeal of existing statutes because it nullified local antidiscrimination policies and established "a purported constitutional right to privately discriminate on grounds which admittedly would be unavailable under the Fourteenth Amendment should state action be involved." Because of the amendment, the "right to discriminate, including the right to discriminate on racial grounds, was now embodied in the State's basic charter, immune from legislative, executive, or judicial regulation at any level of the state government." In other words, the "right to discriminate is now one of the basic policies of the State," and there is a risk that the amendment "will significantly encourage and involve the State in private discriminations."

Q: If in *Reitman* there had been no local laws banning discrimination and no constitutional amendment prohibiting the discrimination, would the discrimination by private landlords have been treated as state action?

A: Presumably not. In that case, the state would have done nothing more than fail to prohibit discrimination, and that failure by itself would not be enough to create state action.

C. Judicial Involvement

A recurring question in constitutional litigation is whether **judicial involvement** in private action, in the sense of enforcing a private right, transforms the private right into state action. The leading decision is *Shelley v. Kraemer*.[20] In that case, the Court held that judicial enforcement of private racially restrictive covenants involves state action. Although private parties had created the covenants without state support or encouragement, the Court noted that "but for the active intervention of the state courts, supported by the full panoply of state power, petitioners would have been free to occupy the properties in question without restraint." In other words, the states were making the "full coercive power of government" available to deny individuals "the enjoyment of property rights in premises which petitioners are willing and financially able to acquire and which the grantors are willing to sell." In the Court's view, this judicial involvement constituted state action.

It is doubtful that *Shelley* should be read broadly to suggest that judicial enforcement of private rights transforms those rights into state action. A more likely explanation of the decision is the fact that it arose out of the civil rights movement and an attempt to enforce a racially restrictive covenant. In some other contexts, it is unlikely that the court would find that judicial involvement constitutes state action. For example, suppose that a racist couple holds a dinner party once a month, but never includes anyone of a different race. Resentful about not being invited, someone of a different race repeatedly decides to crash the event by breaking down the front door and attempting to join the party. The racists decide to seek injunctive relief prohibiting the party crasher from interfering with their get-togethers.

It is difficult to believe that the Court would hold that a judicial decision to enter an injunction against the party crasher implicates the government in the private discrimination and therefore decide to invoke equal protection analysis. One would suspect that the Court would treat the racists' actions as private action. The trespass law is facially neutral, and enforcement of that law is not the same as enforcing a racially restrictive covenant. Moreover, even though the state has a strong interest in preventing individuals from enforcing racially restrictive covenants, it has less of an interest in preventing individuals from being racially neutral in whom they invite to dinner. Questions relating to whom one invites to dinner fit within private spheres and privacy interests.

Nevertheless, there are contexts in which *Shelley* retains validity. Indeed, *Shelley* was followed by the holding in *Barrows v. Jackson*,[21] in which the Court held that state action existed when a court awarded damages (rather than injunctive relief) for violation of a racially restrictive covenant. Although the Court recognized that private individuals could voluntarily adhere to such agreements, the Court concluded that if respondent were forced to pay damages, the consequence "of that sanction by the State would be to encourage the use of restrictive covenants." As a result, a judicial award of damages would constitute state action.

F   A   Q

Q: So, based on the holdings in *Shelley* and *Barrows*, restrictive covenants are illegal?

A: Not exactly. *Shelley* suggests that racially restrictive covenants are not judicially enforceable through an order overturning a willing conveyance. *Shelley* is reinforced by *Barrows*, which holds that such covenants cannot be enforced through an award of damages. Nevertheless, neither decision suggests that racially restrictive covenants are illegal, but they are effective only when individuals voluntarily comply.

Shelley and *Barrows* are reinforced by the decision in *Evans v. Newton*.[22] That case involved a U.S. senator who willed land to the City of Macon on condition that the land be reserved as a park for white people only. While the will stated that the senator had only the kindest feeling for blacks, he believed that the two races should be kept separate. The city kept the park segregated for years, but then began to integrate the park on the basis that it was constitutionally impermissible to maintain a segregated facility. At that point, the trustees of the will sued to remove the city as trustee and to appoint private trustees. The Court concluded that the park could not be segregated whether or not it was in private hands: "The predominant character and purpose of this park are municipal [and] requires that it be treated as a public institution subject to the command of the Fourteenth Amendment, regardless of who now has title under state law." Justice Harlan, joined by Justice Stewart, dissented: "The Equal Protection Clause reaches only discriminations that are the product of capricious state action; it does not touch discriminations whose origins and effectuation arise solely out of individual predilections, prejudices, and acts."

But the limits of *Shelley* and *Barrows* are revealed by the holding in *Evans v. Abney*,[23] a case that followed the decision in *Newton*. Following the decision in *Newton*, the senator's heirs sued to reclaim the park, claiming that the trust failed since the senator's intention to provide a park for whites only could not be fulfilled, and therefore the park reverted to the heirs by law. The Court could have relied on *Shelley* and held that judicial enforcement of the reverter provision constituted state action. However, the Court did not. Instead, the Court rejected a claim that the reversion would violate equal protection, noting that "there is not the slightest indication that any of the Georgia judges involved were motivated by racial animus or discriminatory intent of any sort in construing and enforcing Senator Bacon's will." Indeed, the "language of the Senator's will shows that the racial restrictions were solely the product of the testator's own full-blown social philosophy." The Court distinguished *Shelley*, noting that "the effect of the Georgia decision eliminated all discrimination against Negroes in the park by eliminating the park itself, and the termination of the park was a loss shared equally by the white and Negro citizens of Macon since both races would have enjoyed a constitutional right of equal access to the park's facilities had it continued." Justice Brennan dissented: "[U]nder the Equal Protection Clause a State may not close down a public facility solely to avoid its duty to desegregate that facility. [This] discriminatory closing is permeated with state action. [E]nforcement of the reverter is therefore unconstitutional."

However, it would be incorrect to suggest that *Shelley* is limited to its anti-racially restrictive covenant context. In later cases, the Court has held that judicial action enforcing creditors' rights involves state action within the meaning of the Fourteenth Amendment's Due Process Clause. The initial decision was *Sniadach v. Family Finance Corp.*,[24] in which the Court found state action when creditors invoked state-created garnishment procedures to enforce a debt. The Court's later decision in *Mitchell v. W. T. Grant Co.*[25] reached a similar result regarding a vendor's execution of a lien. In both *Sniadach* and *Mitchell*, the Court found state action because state agents aided the creditor in securing the disputed property, even though the litigation was between creditors and debtors and involved no state officials. The Court emphasized that the deprivation was "caused by the exercise of some right or privilege created by the State or by a rule of conduct imposed by the state or by a person for whom the State is responsible."

In recent years, however, the Court has refused to extend the due process decisions. In *Flagg Brothers, Inc. v. Brooks*,[26] the Court held that a warehouseman's proposed sale of goods entrusted to him for storage, as permitted by New York's Uniform Commercial Code, did not constitute state action. The challenge was brought by a woman, evicted from her apartment, to prevent the threatened sale as a violation of the Due Process and Equal Protection Clauses of the Fourteenth Amendment. The Court refused to find state action because no public officials were defendants in the suit, as well as because there was a "total absence of overt official involvement."

Of course, the *Flagg Brothers* Court could have found state action based on the fact that the warehouseman acted pursuant to statutory authorization. However, the Court rejected the idea that the state had delegated to the warehouseman a power "traditionally exclusively reserved to the State," concluding that few functions traditionally performed by governments have been "exclusively reserved to the State." Moreover, the Court emphasized that the state's "system of rights and remedies" seemed to recognize "the traditional place of private arrangements in ordering relationships in the commercial world" so that "the settlement of disputes between debtors and creditors is not traditionally an exclusive public function." The Court also rejected the idea that the state had "authorized and encouraged" the warehouseman's action, finding only "mere acquiescence." Justice Stevens, joined by Justices White and Marshall, dissented. "[W]hatever power of sale the warehouseman [has] derives solely from the State, and specifically from §7-210 of the New York Uniform Commercial Code," which authorizes the warehouseman "to resolve any disputes over storage charges finally and unilaterally."

Even though *Flagg Brothers* suggests that statutory authorization is insufficient by itself to create a finding of state action, the Court sometimes views the situation differently when governmental officials are involved in a creditor's action. For example, in *Lugar v. Edmondson Oil Co., Inc.*,[27] the Court held that a creditor's actions pursuant to a prejudgment attachment statute involved state action. The governing statute provided that a creditor could gain an attachment from a court only by alleging, ex parte, that the debtor was disposing of or might dispose of his property in an effort to defeat the creditor's rights. In *Lugar*, the Court held that the

Sidebar

SNIADACH'S IMPACT

Decisions like *Sniadach* have been an important source of rights for poor debtors. By finding state action, the Court was able to impose due process requirements on the debt enforcement process and thereby to protect debtors against possibly predatory creditors.

procedure involved state action within the meaning of the Due Process Clause, noting that the courts had consistently held that a private party's joint participation with state officials in the seizure of disputed property is sufficient to characterize that party as a state actor for purposes of the Fourteenth Amendment. The Court found "joint participation" because the state had created a system whereby state officials attached property on the ex parte application of one party to a private dispute. Chief Justice Burger dissented, arguing that the creditors did nothing "more than invoke a presumptively valid state prejudgment attachment procedure available to all," and that the invocation did not implicate the state or "transform essentially private conduct into actions of the State."

D. Mixed Cases

Most modern state action cases do not fit neatly into either the governmental function or the governmental involvement or encouragement category. In many cases, plaintiffs argue not only that defendant's conduct involves a governmental function, but that the government is implicated or involved in some way.

Marsh, Nixon, and *Herndon* were decided during the first half of the twentieth century. In cases since then, the Court has been somewhat less willing to find state action, even though it can be argued that there is governmental involvement or encouragement or that a party is performing a traditional governmental function.

(1) Private Corporations

In a number of modern cases, the Court has been forced to determine whether private corporations should be treated as state actors. Illustrative is the holding in *Jackson v. Metropolitan Edison Co.*[28] That case involved the question of whether a privately owned and operated utility company functioned as a state actor when it held a certificate of public convenience from a state utility commission that authorized it to deliver electricity in a defined area. As a condition of holding its certificate, the utility was subject to extensive regulation by the commission. In addition, under a provision of its general tariff filed with the commission, the utility had the right to discontinue service to any customer on reasonable notice of nonpayment of bills. When the company terminated a customer for failure to pay her bills, she sued under 42 U.S.C. §1983, seeking damages for the termination and an injunction requiring continued service to her residence. She argued that under state law she had an entitlement to reasonably continuous electrical service and that the termination constituted state action because it was authorized under a provision of the utility's general tariff filed with the state.

In finding that no state action existed, the Court concluded that the mere fact that a business is subject to state regulation did not, by itself, convert the company's actions into state action for purposes of the Fourteenth Amendment. In addition, the utility's monopoly status and the fact that it provided an essential public service were not enough, by themselves, to create state action. Indeed, the Court concluded that many businesses (for example, doctors, optometrists, lawyers, and milk distributors) are all affected with the "public interest." Moreover, the Court rejected the argument that Metropolitan's termination was not state action merely because the state had "specifically authorized and approved" the termination practice. The Court found that plaintiff could show nothing "more than that Metropolitan was a heavily regulated, privately owned utility, enjoying a partial monopoly in the provision of electrical service, and that it elected to terminate service in a manner permissible under state law." The Court concluded that the government's involvement was not sufficient to qualify as state action.

Characterization	Effect
Private action	Constitutional protections do not apply.
State action	Constitutional protections apply.
Private action (with governmental involvement or encouragement)	Constitutional protections may apply depending on circumstances.

F   A   Q

Q: Would *Jackson* have been decided differently if the utility had been municipally owned?

A: Absolutely. If the city had owned the utility, then the state would have been directly implicated in the action. The Court struggles with the state action issue only because the utility was privately owned.

As *Jackson* implies, the Court's attitude toward state action and the governmental function exception has changed over time. In cases like *Burton, Shelley, Marsh*, and *Terry*, the Court was more likely to have found state action. However, it is important to recognize that these cases may have been products of their times. Those cases arose during a period when there were substantial racial tensions and the Court may have been more inclined (perhaps, even stretching) to find state action because it felt the need to deal with pressing social issues such as racially restrictive covenants.

Despite the holding in *Jackson*, the Court has been willing to find that some private corporations are functioning as state actors. For example, in *Lebron v. National Railroad Passenger Corp.*,[29] the Court held that the National Railroad Passenger Corporation (a/k/a, Amtrak) was a state actor for purposes of the First Amendment when it rejected a billboard display. Like the utility in *Jackson*, the corporation was a private corporation. However, Amtrak was regarded as different because it was government created and controlled in the sense that it was created by a special statute and the federal government appointed six of the corporation's eight directors. Moreover, Amtrak was created to further federal governmental goals under the direction and control of federal governmental appointees. These facts suggested that Amtrak should be treated differently from the public utility at issue in *Jackson*. Justice O'Connor dissented. Although she recognized that the government had a "pervasive influence in Amtrak's management and operation," she emphasized that the government had no impact on Amtrak's decision to turn down this particular advertisement.

Each private corporation case must be evaluated on its own facts. For example, the Court refused to find state action in *San Francisco Arts & Athletics,*

Inc. v. U.S. Olympic Committee[30] in a case involving claims that the U.S. Olympic Committee (USOC) discriminated on the basis of sexual orientation. In that case, there was significant evidence of governmental involvement and encouragement, but the USOC was allowed to function independently of the government. Moreover, USOC was designated as the United States' representative to the International Olympic Committee, making it possible to argue that the USOC was performing a traditional governmental function.

Despite the evidence of governmental participation, the Court refused to find state action. The Court held that the USOC's federal charter did not, by itself, render the USOC a government agent because all "corporations act under charters granted by a government." Likewise, the fact that Congress granted the USOC exclusive use of the word *Olympic* was not dispositive because all "enforceable rights in trademarks are created by some governmental act, usually pursuant to a statute or the common law," even though the actions of the owners "nevertheless remain private." Governmental funding was also not regarded as creating state action because the "Government may subsidize private entities without assuming constitutional responsibility for their actions." Moreover, the Court found that the USOC was not performing a traditional governmental function since Congress simply authorized the USOC to "coordinate activities that always have been performed by private entities." In the final analysis, the Court concluded that the USOC's "choice of how to enforce its exclusive right to use the word 'Olympic' simply is not a governmental decision" because the federal government did not try to coerce or encourage the USOC in its decision making. At most, the government passively acquiesced.

The decision produced significant concurrences and dissents that illustrate the Court's division. Justice O'Connor, joined by Justice Blackmun, concurred in part and dissented in part, arguing that "the United States Olympic Committee and the United States are joint participants in the challenged activity and as such are subject to the equal protection provisions of the Fifth Amendment." Justice Brennan, joined by Justice Marshall, dissented, arguing that the USOC performs "important governmental functions" and arguing that there is a "sufficiently close nexus" between the government and the challenged action so that the USOC's actions should be treated as governmental action. Indeed, every "aspect of the Olympic pageant, from the procession of athletes costumed in national uniform, to the raising of national flags and the playing of national anthems at the medal ceremony, to the official tally of medals won by each national team, reinforces the national significance of Olympic participation." Moreover, "in the eye of the public," there is a strong connection between "decisions of the United States Government and those of the United States Olympic Committee." Finally, the federal government provides strong financial support for the USOC so that "profits earned by discrimination not only contribute to, but also are indispensable elements in, the financial success of a governmental agency."

(2) School Associations

The Court has been somewhat more inclined to find state action in cases involving school associations, especially when there is significant state involvement in the association. For example, in *Brentwood Academy v. Tennessee Secondary School Athletic Association*,[31] the Court held that a statewide association that regulated interscholastic athletic competition among public and private secondary schools in Tennessee (TSAA) qualified as a state actor. In reaching that conclusion, the

Court emphasized that almost all the state's public high schools belonged to the TSAA; that member schools could play or scrimmage only against other members (absent special dispensation); that voting rights were limited to high school principals, assistant principals, and superintendents; and that TSAA staff members were allowed to participate in the state's public retirement system (even though they were not state employees). In addition, Tennessee's State Board of Education acknowledged the TSAA provided "standards, rules and regulations for interscholastic competition in the public schools of Tennessee." For a while, the board adopted a rule designating the TSAA as "the organization" designated to supervise athletic activities, subject to the board's review, but the designation was later repealed.

The Court concluded that the TSAA was a state actor because of "the pervasive entwinement of public institutions and public officials in its composition and workings." The overwhelming majority of the TSAA's members were public schools, who were represented at the TSAA by public officials, and they elected the governing legislative council and board of control from eligible school officials. These public school officials were acting within the scope of their duties in representing their institutions before the TSAA. The Court concluded that the TSAA should be "charged with a public character and judged by constitutional standards." Justice Thomas, joined by Chief Justice Rehnquist and Justices Scalia and Kennedy, dissented, arguing that the Court had never "found state action based upon mere 'entwinement.'" He went on to note that the State of Tennessee did not create the TSAA, did not fund it, and did not pay its employees, and that the state had no involvement in the actions taken by the TSAA in this case. Moreover, he argued that the "organization of interscholastic sports is neither a traditional nor an exclusive public function of the States."

However, the Court took a different tack in evaluating the National Collegiate Athletic Association's involvement in intercollegiate athletics in *National Collegiate Athletic Association v. Tarkanian.*[32] In that case, the question was whether the NCAA functioned as a state actor when it suggested sanctions to the University of Nevada — Las Vegas (UNLV) against a coach. Like the TSAA, the NCAA is a private association that includes virtually all public and private universities that have major athletic programs. The NCAA's objective "is to maintain intercollegiate athletics as part of the educational program and to retain a clear line of demarcation between college athletics and professional sports," and it has adopted "legislation" governing issues such as academic standards for eligibility, admissions, financial aid, and the recruiting of student athletes. NCAA rules are administered by a Committee on Infractions, which has an investigative staff, makes factual determinations concerning alleged rule violations, and "impose[s] appropriate penalties" for violations that can include suspension or termination of membership. However, the NCAA may not sanction a member institution's employees directly, but its guidelines provide that member institutions "are expected to cooperate fully" with the administration of the enforcement program. Despite the fact that the UNLV's own investigation concluded that Coach Jerry Tarkanian was innocent of wrongdoing, the NCAA committee found that UNLV had violated various NCAA rules and that Tarkanian committed ten violations. The committee proposed various sanctions and threatened additional sanctions if UNLV failed to discipline Tarkanian. In response, the university fired Tarkanian, and he sued the NCAA under 42 U.S.C. §1983, claiming that the NCAA and the university deprived him of property and liberty without due process of law. In particular, he claimed that UNLV had delegated its own functions to the NCAA, clothing the association with authority both to adopt rules governing UNLV's athletic programs and to enforce those rules on behalf of UNLV.

UNLV was clearly a state actor, but the question was whether UNLV's compliance with the NCAA rules and recommendations turned the NCAA's conduct into state action. The Court held that neither "UNLV's decision to adopt the NCAA's standards nor its minor role in their formulation is a sufficient reason for concluding that the NCAA was acting under color of Nevada law when it promulgated standards governing athlete recruitment, eligibility, and academic performance." The Court also rejected the argument that UNLV delegated power to the NCAA. On the contrary, UNLV defended Tarkanian before the NCAA and functioned more like an adversary than a partner of the NCAA. In addition, the NCAA lacked the power to directly discipline Tarkanian, and it did not request that the university do so. It instead simply issued a "show cause" order against UNLV in case it decided not to suspend. In other words, UNLV had options other than suspension in that it could have risked additional sanctions or could have withdrawn from the NCAA. Finally, the Court rejected the argument that the NCAA's power is "so great that the UNLV had no practical alternative to compliance with its demands." Justice White, joined by Justices Brennan, Marshall, and O'Connor, dissented, arguing that the NCAA acted jointly with UNLV in suspending Tarkanian and thereby became a state actor.

(3) Other Modern Cases

Despite holdings like *TSAA*, there are a number of cases that suggest that the Court's more modern approach to standing is highly restrictive. Even though there is significant evidence of governmental involvement in a given case, the Court has refused to find state action. In part, this may reflect the Court's unwillingness to get involved in the merits of the case. Historically, doctrines like standing and ripeness (and other justiciability doctrines) have frequently been regarded as "disguised decisions on the merits." In other words, if the Court is disinclined to rule in favor of plaintiff on the merits, the Court rejects the case on threshold grounds such as standing or ripeness. Some have argued that the state action doctrine serves that same function.

Illustrative of the modern approach is the holding in *Rendell-Baker v. Kohn*.[33] In that case, the Court held that a private school did not function as a state actor in discharging employees, even though most of the school's income was derived from public sources and even though the school was regulated by public authorities. The school specialized in dealing with students who experienced difficulties in public schools (because of drug, alcohol, or behavioral problems, or other special needs) and received virtually all of its students and its funding from public schools or public agencies. The state imposed various regulations that applied to all schools on issues such as recordkeeping, student-teacher ratios, personnel policies, and requiring written job descriptions and written statements of personnel standards and procedures. However, the contracts under which the private school received employees provided that it was functioning as a "contractor" and that the school's employees were not city employees. The Court concluded that the private school was not functioning as a state actor notwithstanding the public funding: "Here the decisions to discharge the petitioners were not compelled or even influenced by any state regulation," and public officials "showed relatively little interest in the school's personnel matters." The Court also rejected the argument that the school was performing a public function. Even though the Court recognized that the "education of maladjusted high school students is a public function," the Court noted that the state had not until recently "undertaken to provide education for students who could not be served by traditional public schools." Finally, there was no "symbiotic relationship" between the school and the state arising from the fiscal relationship, which the Court viewed as "not different from that of many contractors performing services for the government." Justice Marshall, joined by Justice Brennan, dissented, arguing that a "symbiotic relationship" existed because "it is difficult to imagine a closer relationship between a government and a private enterprise" since the private school "receives virtually all of its funds from state sources," "is heavily regulated and closely supervised by the State," and "is providing a substitute for public education."

Also illustrative of the modern approach is the holding in *Blum v. Yaretsky*.[34] In that case, the Court refused to find state action in the transfer of Medicaid patients from nursing homes to other facilities without an opportunity for a hearing. New York directly reimbursed nursing homes for the reasonable cost of health care services provided that the patient satisfies income and resource standards and is seeking medically necessary services. However, federal regulations required nursing homes to establish utilization review committees (URC) of physicians that were required to periodically assess whether each patient was receiving the appropriate level of care and whether the patient's continued stay in the facility was justified. The case arose when a URC decided that respondents did not need the care they were receiving and should be transferred to a lower level of care.

The Court held that the actions of the URC did not constitute state action for purposes of the Due Process Clause of the Fourteenth Amendment. Even though the business was subject to state regulation, the Court concluded that there must be a "sufficiently close nexus between the State and the challenged action of the regulated entity." The Court failed to find that nexus, noting that a state is "responsible for a private decision only when it has exercised coercive power or has provided such significant encouragement, either overt or covert, that the choice must in law be deemed to be that of the State." "Mere approval of or acquiescence" is insufficient, even if the state responds to the actions by adjusting benefit levels. "The decisions [are] made by physicians and nursing home administrators, all of whom are concededly private parties." Even though the regulations required nursing home action for patients that were inappropriately placed, the decision to transfer ultimately turned "on medical judgments made by private parties according to professional standards that are not established by the State." Moreover, even though the state provided more than 90 percent of the funding for the facilities, the Court refused to find state action because privately owned enterprises were "providing services that the State would not necessarily provide, even though they are extensively regulated." Finally, the Court concluded that the nursing homes performed a function that has been "traditionally the exclusive prerogative of the State." Justice Brennan, joined by Justice Marshall, dissented, arguing that the states are responsible for decisions to transfer because the state and federal governments created and administered "the level system as a cost-saving tool of the Medicaid program." Moreover, state action existed because the state chose to direct, support, and encourage private parties to take specific action.

The Court's more restrictive modern approach to state action is also reflected in the Court's decision on state-mandated worker's compensation schemes. In *American Manufacturers Mutual Insurance Co. v. Sullivan*,[35] the Court dealt with a state's compulsory insurance system, which required employers to compensate employees for work-related injuries without regard to fault. The system used a utilization review procedure that required the reasonableness and necessity of an employee's past, ongoing, or prospective medical treatment to be reviewed before the employee's medical bill would be paid. The Court concluded that the actions of these utilization review boards did not constitute state action because their actions were not "fairly attributable to the State so as to subject insurers to the constraints of the Fourteenth Amendment." The Court failed to find a "sufficiently close nexus" between the state and the challenged action of the regulated entity because there was no state coercion and no evidence of "significant encouragement, either overt or covert," so as to make the insurer's choice that of the state. The mere fact that the private entities acted with the approval or acquiescence of the state was regarded as insufficient. While the Court found some encouragement in the fact that state gave insurers "the option of deferring payment for unnecessary and unreasonable treatment pending review," it concluded that "this kind of subtle encouragement is no more significant than that which inheres in the State's creation or modification of any legal remedy." The Court also rejected the argument that the state had delegated to insurers "powers traditionally exclusively reserved to the State." The Court concluded that "Pennsylvania 'has done nothing more than authorize (and indeed limit)—without participation by any public official—what [private insurers] would tend to do, even in the absence of such authorization,' i.e., withhold payment for disputed medical treatment pending a determination that the treatment is, in fact, reasonable and necessary."

Likewise, in *DeShaney v. Winnebago County*,[36] the Court held that the state did not deprive a boy of "liberty" without due process when he was severely beaten by his father and suffered permanent injuries, including mental deficiencies. Although the boy was removed from his father's custody by state social workers, they later returned him to the father's care. Petitioner sued the social workers and other local officials, claiming that their failure to remove the boy from a dangerous situation deprived him of his liberty in violation of the Due Process Clause of the Fourteenth Amendment. The Court concluded that the Due Process Clause does not protect individuals against the actions of private individuals or guarantee individuals the right to governmental aid. The Court rejected the idea that a "special relationship" existed between the boy and the state "because the State knew that Joshua faced a special danger of abuse at his father's hands, and specifically proclaimed, by word and by deed, its intention to protect him against that danger," thereby assuming an "affirmative duty" to protect him. The Court distinguished a state's obligation to prisoners, noting that the state has an affirmative obligation to protect prisoners because it restrains them and thereby prevents them from protecting themselves. The boy was not in state custody, but rather in the custody of his father. At most, the state had a tort duty to protect the boy, but the present claim could not survive because it was based on the Fourteenth Amendment, which required state action. Justice Blackmun dissented: "[T]he facts here involve not mere passivity, but active state intervention in the life of Joshua DeShaney—intervention that triggered a fundamental duty to aid the boy once the State learned of the severe danger to which he was exposed."

SUMMARY

■ Most provisions of the Bill of Rights, as well as the Fourteenth Amendment's Due Process Clause, apply only against actions of the government. To invoke those rights, an individual must show either that government has infringed his or her rights or that government was sufficiently involved in a private infringement of those rights.

- In a number of early cases, courts found that private action was effectively governmental action using various theories: governmental function doctrine, government involvement or encouragement, and, in a few cases, judicial involvement.

- In more recent cases, the Court has shown a greater reluctance to find that the government is sufficiently implicated in private action.

- In most modern cases, courts examine the degree of governmental involvement in an attempt to determine whether the level of governmental involvement is so great as to transform ostensibly private action into state action.

CONNECTIONS

Freedom of Speech and of the Press

In order for the First Amendment's guarantees of freedom of speech and freedom of the press to apply, the infringement must be attributable to state action.

Equal Protection

As with the First Amendment, the Fourteenth Amendment's guarantee of equal protection does not prohibit the actions of private individuals unless a sufficient connection to the state can be found through governmental involvement, encouragement, or mandate.

Due Process

Neither the Fifth Amendment's nor the Fourteenth Amendment's Due Process Clause applies unless state action is found.

Free Exercise of Religion

Before the Court will find a deprivation of the First Amendment right to freely exercise one's religion, the Court must conclude that the deprivation was caused by the state or with its involvement or encouragement.

Endnotes

1. 326 U.S. 501 (1946).
2. 391 U.S. 308 (1968).
3. 407 U.S. 551 (1972).
4. 424 U.S. 507 (1976).
5. 273 U.S. 536 (1927).
6. 286 U.S. 73 (1932).
7. 321 U.S. 649 (1944).
8. 295 U.S. 45 (1935).
9. 345 U.S. 461 (1953).
10. 500 U.S. 614 (1991).

11. 476 U.S. 79 (1986).
12. 487 U.S. 42 (1988).
13. 454 U.S. 312 (1981).
14. 365 U.S. 715 (1961).
15. 373 U.S. 244 (1963).
16. 413 U.S. 455 (1973).
17. 407 U.S. 163 (1972).
18. 412 U.S. 94 (1973).
19. 387 U.S. 369 (1967).
20. 334 U.S. 1 (1948).
21. 346 U.S. 249 (1953).
22. 382 U.S. 296 (1966).
23. 396 U.S. 435 (1970).
24. 395 U.S. 337 (1969).
25. 416 U.S. 600 (1974).
26. 436 U.S. 149 (1978).
27. 457 U.S. 922 (1982).
28. 419 U.S. 345 (1974).
29. 513 U.S. 374 (1995).
30. 483 U.S. 522 (1987).
31. 531 U.S. 288 (2001).
32. 488 U.S. 179 (1988).
33. 457 U.S. 830 (1982).
34. 457 U.S. 991 (1982).
35. 526 U.S. 40 (1999).
36. 489 U.S. 189 (1989).

TABLE OF CASES

INDEX